THE PAPERS OF
WOODROW WILSON

VOLUME 25

1912

SPONSORED BY THE WOODROW WILSON
FOUNDATION
AND PRINCETON UNIVERSITY

THE PAPERS OF

WOODROW WILSON

ARTHUR S. LINK, *EDITOR*

DAVID W. HIRST AND JOHN E. LITTLE

ASSOCIATE EDITORS

EDITH JAMES, *ASSISTANT EDITOR*

SYLVIA ELVIN, *CONTRIBUTING EDITOR*

Volume 25 · 1912

PRINCETON, NEW JERSEY

PRINCETON UNIVERSITY PRESS

1978

Note to scholars: Princeton University Press subscribes to the Resolution on Permissions of the Association of American University Presses, defining what we regard as "fair use" of copyrighted works. This Resolution, intended to encourage scholarly use of university press publications and to avoid unnecessary applications for permission, is obtainable from the Press or from the A.A.U.P. central office. Note, however, that the scholarly apparatus, transcripts of shorthand, and the texts of Wilson documents as they appear in this volume are copyrighted, and the usual rules about the use of copyrighted materials apply.

Publication of this book has been aided by a grant from the National Historical Publications and Records Commission.

Printed in the United States of America
by Princeton University Press
Princeton, New Jersey

INTRODUCTION

A S this volume opens, a huge crowd is gathered on the lawn
of the Governor's Cottage in Sea Girt, New Jersey, on August 7, 1912, to hear Wilson's speech accepting the Democratic
presidential nomination. It is largely a running commentary on
the Baltimore platform. After several outings, Wilson begins his
campaign in earnest in Buffalo on Labor Day, September 2, in
two speeches in which he focuses on the issues which he will
highlight until election day: the development, since the McKinley
administration, of a nexus between big business and Wall Street
and the Republican leadership, which has resulted in government
in favor of the few and wealthy; the Payne-Aldrich Tariff Act,
the most obvious piece of special-interest legislation in recent
American history; the spread of industrial monopoly since the
1890s, with a portentous lessening of opportunity for the small
businessman; the concentration of control of credit in Wall
Street; and Theodore Roosevelt's proposal to accept a large degree
of concentration in industry and to attempt to encourage and
protect competition through regulation by a powerful federal
trade commission.

Wilson calls for restoration of governmental power to the
people by the election of a Congress and President who truly represent all classes, the poor as well as the rich; tariff reform that
will remove all special privileges and encourage American manufacturers to compete in foreign markets; a merchant marine to
develop overseas trade; a new banking and currency system to
break Wall Street's control and open the channels of credit to
newcomers; and destruction of monopoly and protection of competition by clarifying the Sherman Antitrust Act through explicit
prohibitions of all forms of restraint of trade. At the same time,
while praising the humanitarian reform planks of the Progressive
platform, Wilson warns that Roosevelt's plan for a powerful trade
commission, if put into effect by the very men who had created
the political-industrial-banking alliance, would legalize the control of big business and end economic and political freedom in
the United States.

Wilson reiterates these themes on a midwestern tour; after a
brief rest, he hits the trail again in Pennsylvania and New England, appealing this time particularly for the votes of industrial
workers by saying that their right to unionize and bargain collectively should be as much protected by law as the right of
capital to combine.

By early October, the campaign is obviously a verbal duel between Wilson and Roosevelt, for President Taft is taking no part. Increasing the intensity and feeling of urgency in his speeches, Wilson returns to the Middle West and goes on to the Plains states and Colorado. He calls for a "New Freedom" for an emancipation of the American people from the forces that have virtually enslaved them, warns that the country is at "the parting of the ways," and declares that the fundamental issue is the life or death of liberty in the United States. After a final brief tour through Delaware, West Virginia, and Pennsylvania, he spends the last days of the contest in New Jersey campaigning for state and local candidates. And all the while during the final weeks, his speeches throb increasingly with a passion for social justice.

Wilson wins a plurality of the popular vote and a huge majority of the Electoral College on November 5. Soon afterward, he and his family flee to Wilson's beloved Bermuda for refuge from crowds and reporters. Returning home on December 16, Wilson plunges into conferences with party leaders about cabinet members and a legislative program. He also delivers three major speeches which indicate the intensity of his convictions and dedication as he looks ahead to the day when he will assume the presidential power.

EDITING WILSON'S CAMPAIGN SPEECHES

From August 7 to November 4, 1912, Wilson delivered sixty-five major campaign speeches, or perhaps more, depending on how one defines the word "major." He also delivered about one hundred shorter speeches—remarks to a group of foreign-language newspaper editors, a talk to the students of the University of Minnesota, remarks from the rear platform of his special car, and so on.

We have printed complete texts or substantial portions of forty major addresses and many short speeches and remarks. Inevitably, there is some repetition, although we have tried to excise as much repetitive text as possible without mangling the documents. In a few cases, particularly when he gave two speeches during the same evening, Wilson did repeat himself, and we have of course printed only one version of the speech.

Whatever repetition remains does not bother us, and we hope that it will not offend the reader. We think that it is important to show that there was a high degree of unity in Wilson's entire campaign, and that it is significant that he hammered on certain themes and issues. Moreover, his speeches during the campaign of 1912 were Wilson's greatest forensic achievement (indeed, we think that they are among the greatest speeches of modern history), and it would be unthinkable not to print them appropriately. Also, while Wilson usually highlighted the same themes, he rarely ever developed them in the same way, and each speech contains unique passages that shed new light. Most important, these speeches vividly illuminate Wilson's political philosophy in 1912 and reflect the political thinking of a large body of people at a critical juncture in American history. Indeed, they might be regarded as the climactic statement of Anglo-American Liberalism.

During the entire campaign, Wilson wrote only his acceptance speech. All the others he delivered extemporaneously, using only one-page outlines to remind himself of the points that he wanted to develop.

The adjective "extemporaneous" is, however, not properly descriptive. Webster's first definition of extemporaneous is "unpremeditated." Wilson's speeches were certainly not unpremeditated. It was his usual practice to retire to his Pullman compartment or hotel room for an hour or two before delivering a major address. It would perhaps be going too far to stay that he, to use modern jargon, programmed the full speech into his brain. However, he must have substantially composed it in his mind. There simply is no other explanation for the grammatical soundness of his many long and complex sentences, his perfect transitions, and the majestic beauty of his verbal prose.

We have no tapes or recordings of a single speech. We are still, as before, dependent upon imperfect shorthand reporters for all but the acceptance speech. In the task of reconstruction we used the following materials:

1. Charles L. Swem's transcripts. Swem, Wilson's personal stenographer, followed him throughout the entire campaign. We have not only Swem's transcripts but all of his shorthand notes as well.

2. Newspaper texts. We have found independent (that is, not prepared by Swem) transcripts of about 85 per cent of Wilson's major speeches. Sometimes two or three independent texts of the same speech exist.

3. A few printed texts distributed by the Democratic National Committee.

4. Transcripts of about one third of the speeches made by

Inez C. Fuller from Swem's notes for Ray Stannard Baker before Swem's own transcripts were available.

5. A selected edition of the speeches—John Wells Davidson, *A Crossroads of Freedom* (New Haven, Conn., 1956). The texts in this volume were based upon the Fuller transcripts, newspaper texts, and independent reading of the Swem shorthand notebooks.

Our method was to use the Swem transcripts as the basic texts, even though they are extremely corrupt for reasons which we will detail below. We then read Swem's transcripts against his shorthand notes, correcting his numerous typographical errors and anomalies (words that Wilson, or anyone else, could not possibly have said) according to the method described in the Introduction to Volume 24. We also supplied our own punctuation, used modern forms of spelling, and reparagraphed and resentenced when it seemed to us appropriate to do so. We then compared our corrected Swem transcripts with Mrs. Fuller's independent reading and Dr. Davidson's partially independent readings, and followed this with a complete second reading of our transcripts against the Swem shorthand notes. In a few cases, we worked through Swem's notes so many times that we felt justified in ascribing the transcriptions to ourselves.

At this point, we were reasonably sure that we had in hand Swem texts, pure and undefiled. However, we could not accept Swem's texts as being definitive or reliable, again for reasons which we will explain later. Thus in every possible case, we read the purified Swem transcripts against independent texts in newspapers. In many cases it was obvious that Swem was wrong on particular words and even entire sentences. In other cases, we chose between Swem and another reporter on a basis of our knowledge of Wilson's vocabulary and style. All told, we must have made at least 2,000 changes during this process that, we believe, clarified and corrected the Swem versions.

We print our texts without cluttering up the pages with brackets and other indications of variant readings. We are sure that imperfections remain. We only hope that they are few in number, and we think that we have done everything humanly possible to produce canonical texts of one of the greatest bodies of speeches in American history.

We would welcome to our offices any person desiring to examine the Swem notebooks and transcripts, our newspaper texts, and our manuscript copy of this volume, which shows the changes that we made.

SWEM AND HIS SHORTHAND

Charles Lee Swem was born on March 11, 1893, in Groveville, New Jersey. Nothing is known about his boyhood or early schooling, except that his family was poor and he did not go to high school.[1] In 1908, at the age of fifteen, he studied Gregg shorthand briefly at Rider Business School in Trenton. The following year, he became private secretary to John Robert Gregg, for whom his shorthand system was named, at the Gregg Publishing Company in New York. Swem's skill grew rapidly under the master's tutelage; he also continued his general education by taking night courses.

Swem's first encounter with Wilson came on October 1, 1911, when he reported Wilson's address to a Sunday School rally for the Trenton *True American*.[2] After reading the transcript, Wilson allegedly told his staff that it was the first time in his life that a reporter had "an absolutely accurate" transcript of one of his speeches.[3] It seems likely that the Wilson campaign headquarters used Swem to report some of Wilson's major speeches during the last months of the preconvention campaign. For example, the text of Wilson's speech to the Economic Club of New York on May 23, 1912, is almost certainly a Swem transcript.

In any event, Wilson employed Swem as his personal stenographer immediately after the Baltimore Convention. From this time on, except for a brief interruption during the war, Swem was almost daily at Wilson's side until 1921. After Wilson left the White House, Swem rejoined Gregg and collaborated with him. His reputation as a master of his craft grew; his *The Technique of Shorthand Reporting* (1941) is regarded as a classic work; and subsequently, as official reporter for the New York Supreme Court, he was regarded as one of the greatest practitioners of the Gregg reporting system. He died on December 27, 1956, in New York, from injuries suffered in a fall. Before he died, he had given all his notebooks and papers from the Wilson era (except for six notebooks in the Baker Collection in the Library of Congress) to the Princeton University Library. This invaluable collection will be described in the Introduction to Volume 27, along with other major sources for the Wilson era.

As we have said, the Swem transcripts were usually our basic

[1] Joseph Netlich and Nathan Behrin in *The Transcript*, xv (Feb. 1957), 2, 20.
[2] John Wells Davidson, "The Career of Charles Lee Swem," in Davidson (ed.), *A Crossroads of Freedom: The 1912 Campaign Speeches of Woodrow Wilson* (New Haven, Conn., 1956), p. 546.
[3] Louis A. Leslie, "Charles Lee Swem: Personal Reminiscences," National Shorthand Reporter, xxxvii (June 1977), 27.

texts of Wilson's speeches during the presidential campaign of 1912. As we have moved deeper into the presidential period we have gone back time and again to the Swem notebooks to check his transcripts of letters, speeches, diplomatic notes, and press conferences. We also found shorthand notes of 109 press conferences that Swem never transcribed and others that he transcribed only in part. Jack Romagna of Silver Spring, Maryland, who uses the Gregg reporting style and who served as a reporter for Presidents F. D. Roosevelt, Truman, Eisenhower, and Kennedy, has transcribed these press conferences and many other Swem shorthand notes for us. He did this with enthusiasm and consummate skill, and historians of the Wilson period will be eternally indebted to him for his accomplishment.

It is said that Swem in his prime was so perfect a practitioner of the reporting style that he could turn his notes of courtroom proceedings over to an assistant for transcription. However, his shorthand was far from mature when he went to work for Wilson and remained so at least to the period (June 1915) at which we are now working intensively in the documents. Gregg reporting style is compact and abbreviated for obvious reasons. Swem used additional shortcuts. He often left off beginnings and endings, used incomplete outlines (perhaps they were brief forms with which we are not now acquainted), wrote similar outlines alike, without making the essential differentiation, and omitted words. He also rarely wrote names in longhand and did not punctuate or capitalize. Above all, he relied heavily upon his memory in transcribing.

These defects would seem to account for many of the numerous errors in Swem's transcripts of Wilson's speeches during the campaign of 1912. To be sure, Swem often took down Wilson's speeches in crowded or noisy halls or out-of-doors, and some of his mistakes came from mishearing. Again, he had to type the transcripts under great pressure in order to get them to the newspapers for publication the next day. Even so, there are so many anomalies in these transcripts that it is obvious that there were many times when Swem could not read his own shorthand.

Swem's shorthand improved during 1913 and 1914, but problems remain, particularly in dealing with his transcripts of press conferences, in which anomalies still often occur. Moreover, a reading of his notes against his transcripts reveals frequent sentences in the latter which are missing from the former. Swem obviously reconstructed these from memory, perhaps after conferring with Tumulty, who usually attended the press conferences.

We of course worked with Mr. Romagna and our own secretary, Mrs. Robert Godbout, in going through the former's transcripts of the untranscribed notes of press conferences. In most cases, we were able to produce what we think is an accurate transcript. However, in some cases, the shorthand is so crude that we were able to make only a paraphrase; in other cases, the shorthand was simply unreadable.

None of the above is said in derogation of a man who was devoted to Wilson and became one of the great shorthand reporters of the twentieth century. It is only to explain why we have had to resort to every technique known to historical editors in our effort to reproduce Wilsonian texts free from error and anomalies. And perhaps it would be well to remind scholars working with shorthand transcripts that all shorthand reporters, however good, make mistakes; and that it is dangerous to rely upon a single text when parallel texts are available.

THE EDITORS

Princeton, New Jersey
May 5, 1977

CONTENTS

ILLUSTRATIONS

Following page 326

Oil painting of Wilson by Seymour Thomas

Wilson accepting the nomination, Sea Girt
Pach Bros.

Wilson and family on the porch at Sea Girt
Princeton University Library

Reception at Sea Girt
Library of Congress

Talking to school children in Minneapolis
Library of Congress

New Jersey Day at Sea Girt
Library of Congress

William Howard Taft
Library of Congress

Theodore Roosevelt
Library of Congress

With Mrs. Wilson and Eleanor in Bermuda
Library of Congress

ABBREVIATIONS

ALS	autograph letter signed
CC MS	carbon copy of manuscript
CCL	carbon copy of letter
CCLI	carbon copy of letter initialed
CLSsh	Charles Lee Swem shorthand
EAW	Ellen Axson Wilson
hw	handwriting, handwritten
HwCL	handwritten copy of letter
HwLS	handwritten letter signed
ICF	Inez C. Fuller
ICFT	Inez C. Fuller typed
LPC	letterpress copy
MS	manuscript
sh	shorthand
T	typed
TC	typed copy
TCL	typed copy of letter
TCLS	typed copy of letter signed
TLS	typed letter signed
T MS	typed manuscript
WW	Woodrow Wilson
WWhw	Woodrow Wilson handwriting, handwritten
WWhw MS	Woodrow Wilson handwritten manuscript
WWsh	Woodrow Wilson shorthand

ABBREVIATIONS FOR COLLECTIONS AND LIBRARIES

Following the National Union Catalog
of the Library of Congress

A-Ar	Alabama Department of Archives and History, Montgomery
CtY	Yale University
DLC	Library of Congress
DeU	University of Delaware
KyBB	Berea College
KyLoU	University of Louisville
MH	Harvard University
MH-Ar	Harvard University Archives
MH-BA	Harvard University, Graduate School of Business Administration
MHi	Massachusetts Historical Society, Boston
MdBJ-Ar	Johns Hopkins University Archives
MiU-C	University of Michigan, William L. Clements Library
NN	New York Public Library
NRU	University of Rochester
Nj	New Jersey State Library, Trenton
NjP	Princeton University
OCAJ	American Jewish Periodical Center, Cincinnati
RSB Coll., DLC	Ray Stannard Baker Collection of Wilsoniana, Library of Congress

ScU	University of South Carolina
UA, NjP	Princeton University Archives
ViU	University of Virginia
WHi	State Historical Society of Wisconsin, Madison
WC, NjP	Woodrow Wilson Collection, Princeton University
WP, DLC	Woodrow Wilson Papers, Library of Congress

SYMBOLS

[Aug. 7, 1912]	publication date of a published writing; also date of document when date is not part of text
[*Aug. 17, 1912*]	composition date when publication date differs
[[Sept. 8, 1912]]	delivery date of a speech if publication date differs
	⟨because he was not thought to be entirely above suspicion. . .⟩ matter deleted by author of document and restored by editors

THE PAPERS OF

WOODROW WILSON

VOLUME 25

1912

THE PAPERS OF
WOODROW WILSON

A Speech Accepting the Democratic Nomination in
Sea Girt, New Jersey

[Aug. 7, 1912]

Mr. James[1] and Gentlemen of the Notification Committee:

Speaking for the National Democratic Convention, recently assembled at Baltimore, you have notified me of my nomination by the Democratic party for the high office of President of the United States: Allow me to thank you very warmly for the generous terms in which you have, through your distinguished Chairman, conveyed the notification, and for the thoughtful personal courtesy with which you have performed your interesting and important errand.

I accept the nomination with a deep sense of its unusual significance and of the great honor done me, and also with a very profound sense of my responsibility to the party and to the Nation. You will expect me in accepting the honor to speak very plainly the faith that is in me. You will expect me, in brief, to talk politics and open the campaign in words whose meaning no one need doubt. You will expect me to speak to the country as well as to yourselves.

We cannot intelligently talk politics unless we know to whom we are talking and in what circumstances. The present circumstances are clearly unusual. No previous political campaign in our time has disclosed anything like them. The audience we address is in no ordinary temper. It is no audience of partisans. Citizens of every class and party and prepossession sit together, a single people, to learn whether we understand their life and know how to afford them the counsel and guidance they are now keenly aware that they stand in need of. We must speak, not to catch votes, but to satisfy the thought and conscience of a people deeply stirred by the conviction that they have come to a critical turning point in their moral and political development.

We stand in the presence of an awakened nation, impatient of

---

[1] Ollie Murray James' speech of notification is printed along with Wilson's in the pamphlet listed in the description-location line.

partisan make-believe. The public man who does not realize the fact and feel its stimulation must be singularly unsusceptible to the influences that stir in every quarter about him. The nation has awakened to a sense of neglected ideals and neglected duties; to a consciousness that the rank and file of her people find life very hard to sustain, that her young men find opportunity embarrassed, and that her older men find business difficult to renew and maintain because of circumstances of privilege and private advantage which have interlaced their subtle threads throughout almost every part of the framework of our present law. She has awakened to the knowledge that she has lost certain cherished liberties and wasted priceless resources which she had solemnly undertaken to hold in trust for posterity and for all mankind; and to the conviction that she stands confronted with an occasion for constructive statesmanship such as has not arisen since the great days in which her government was set up.

Plainly, it is a new age. The tonic of such a time is very exhilarating. It requires self-restraint not to attempt too much, and yet it would be cowardly to attempt too little. The path of duty soberly and bravely trod is the way to service and distinction, and many adventurous feet seek to set out upon it.

There never was a time when impatience and suspicion were more keenly aroused by private power selfishly employed; when jealousy of everything concealed or touched with any purpose not linked with general good, or inconsistent with it, more sharply or immediately displayed itself.

Nor was the country ever more susceptible to unselfish appeals or to the high arguments of sincere justice. These are the unmistakable symptoms of an awakening. There is the more need for wise counsel because the people are so ready to heed counsel if it be given honestly and in their interest.

It is in the broad light of this new day that we stand face to face,—with what? Plainly, not with questions of party, not with a contest for office, not with a petty struggle for advantage, Democrat against Republican, liberal against conservative, progressive against reactionary. With great questions of right and of justice, rather,—questions of national development, of the development of character and of standards of action no less than of a better business system, more free, more equitable, more open to ordinary men, practicable to live under, tolerable to work under, or a better fiscal system whose taxes shall not come out of the pockets of the many to go into the pockets of the few, and within whose intricacies special privilege may not so easily find covert. The forces of the nation are asserting themselves against every form of special privilege and private control, and are seeking bigger things than they have ever heretofore achieved. They are sweeping away what is unrighteous in order to vindicate once more the essential rights of human life; and, what is very serious for us, they are looking to us for guidance, disinterested guidance, at once honest and fearless.

At such a time, and in the presence of such circumstances, what is the meaning of our platform, and what is our responsibility under it? What are our duty and our purpose? The platform is meant to show that we know what the nation is thinking about, what it is most concerned about, what it wishes corrected, and what it desires to see attempted that is new and constructive and intended for its long future. But for us it is a very practical document. We are not about to ask the people of the United States to adopt our platform; we are about to ask them to entrust us with office and power and the guidance of their affairs. They will wish to know what sort of men we are and of what definite purpose; what translation of action and of policy we intend to give to the general terms of the platform which the Convention at Baltimore put forth, should we be elected.

The platform is not a program. A program must consist of measures, administrative acts, and acts of legislation. The proof of the pudding is the eating thereof. How do we intend to make it edible and digestible? From this time on we shall be under interrogation. How do we expect to handle each of the great matters that must be taken up by the next Congress and the next administration?

What is there to do? It is hard to sum the great task up, but apparently this is the sum of the matter: There are two great things to do. One is to set up the rule of justice and of right in such matters as the tariff, the regulation of the trusts and the prevention of monopoly, the adaptation of our banking and currency laws to the varied uses to which our people must put them, the treatment of those who do the daily labor in our factories and mines and throughout all our great industrial and commercial undertakings, and the political life of the people of the Philippines, for whom we hold governmental power in trust, for their service not our own. The other, the additional duty, is the great task of protecting our people and our resources and of keeping open to the whole people the doors of opportunity through which they must, generation by generation, pass if they are to make conquest of their fortunes in health, in freedom, in peace, and in contentment. In the performance of this second great duty we are face to face with questions of conservation and of development, questions of forests and water powers and mines and waterways, of the building of an adequate merchant marine, and the opening of every highway and facility and the setting up of every safeguard needed by a great industrious, expanding nation.

These are all great matters upon which everybody should be heard. We have got into trouble in recent years chiefly because these large things, which ought to have been handled by taking counsel with as large a number of persons as possible, because they touched every interest and the life of every class and region, have in fact been too often handled in private conference. They have been settled by very small, and often deliberately exclusive, groups of men who undertook to speak for the whole nation, or, rather, for themselves in the terms of the whole nation,—very honestly it may be, but very ignorantly sometimes, and very short-sightedly, too,—a poor substitute for genuine common counsel. No group of directors, economic or political, can speak for a people. They have neither the point of view nor the knowledge. Our difficulty is not that wicked and designing men have plotted against us, but that our common affairs have been determined upon too narrow a view, and by too private an initiative. Our task now is to effect a great readjustment and get the forces of the whole people once more into play. We need no revolution; we need no excited change; we need only a new point of view and a new method and spirit of counsel.

We are servants of the people, the whole people. The nation has been unnecessarily, unreasonably at war within itself. Interest has clashed with interest when there were common principles of right and of fair dealing which might and should have bound them all together, not as rivals, but as partners. As the servants of all, we are bound to undertake the great duty of accommodation and adjustment.

We cannot undertake it except in a spirit which some find it hard to understand. Some people only smile when you speak of yourself as a servant of the people; it seems to them like affectation or mere demagoguery. They ask what the unthinking crowd knows or comprehends of great complicated matters of government. They shrug their shoulders and lift their eyebrows when you speak as if you really believed in presidential primaries, in the direct election of United States senators, and in an utter publicity about everything that concerns government, from the sources of campaign funds to the intimate debate of the highest affairs of state.

They do not, or will not, comprehend the solemn thing that is in your thought. You know as well as they do that there are all sorts and conditions of men,—the unthinking mixed with the wise, the reckless with the prudent, the unscrupulous with the fair and honest,—and you know what they sometimes forget, that every class, without exception, affords a sample of the mixture, the learned and the fortunate no less than the uneducated and the struggling mass. But you see more than they do. You see that these multitudes of men, mixed of every kind and quality, constitute somehow an organic and noble whole, a single people, and that they have interests which no man can privately determine without their knowledge and counsel. That is the meaning of representative government itself. Representative government is nothing more or less than an effort to give voice to this great body through spokesmen chosen out of every grade and class.

You may think that I am wandering off into a general disquisition that has little to do with the business in hand; but I am not. This is business,—business of the deepest sort. It will solve our difficulties if you will but take it as business.

See how it makes business out of the tariff question. The tariff question, as dealt with in our time at any rate, has not been business. It has been politics. Tariff schedules have been made up for the purpose of keeping as large a number as possible of the rich and influential manufacturers of the country in a good humor with the Republican party, which desired their constant financial support. The tariff has become a system of favors, which the phraseology of the schedule was often deliberately contrived to conceal. It becomes a matter of business, of legitimate business, only when the partnership and understanding it represents is between the leaders of Congress and the whole people of the United States, instead of between the leaders of Congress and small groups of manufacturers demanding special recognition and consideration. That is why the general idea of representative government becomes a necessary part of the tariff question. Who, when you come down to the hard facts of the matter, have been represented in recent years when our tariff schedules were being discussed and determined, not on the floor of Congress, for that is not where they have been determined, but in the committee rooms and conferences? That is the heart of the whole affair. Will you, can you, bring the whole people into the partnership or not? No one is discontented with representative government; it falls under question only when it ceases to be representative. It is at bottom a question of good faith and morals.

How does the present tariff look in the light of it? I say nothing for the moment about the policy of protection, conceived and carried out as a disinterested statesman might conceive it. Our own clear conviction as Democrats is, that in the last analysis the only safe and legitimate object of tariff duties, as of taxes of every other kind, is to raise revenue for the support of the government; but that is not my present point. We denounce the Payne-Aldrich tariff act as the most conspicuous example ever afforded the country of the special favors and monopolistic advantages which the leaders of the Republican Party have so often shown themselves willing to extend to those to whom they looked for campaign contributions. Tariff duties, as they have employed them, have not been a means of setting up an equitable system of protection. They have been, on the contrary, a method of fostering special privilege. They have made it easy to establish monopoly in our domestic markets. Trusts have owed their origin and their secure power to them. The economic freedom of our people, our prosperity in trade, our untrammeled energy in manufacture depend upon their reconsideration from top to bottom in an entirely different spirit.

We do not ignore the fact that the business of a country like ours is exceedingly sensitive to changes in legislation of this kind. It has been built up, however ill-advisedly, upon tariff schedules written in the way I have indicated, and its foundations must not be too radically or too suddenly disturbed. When we act we should act with caution and prudence, like men who know what they are about, and not like those in love with a theory. It is obvious that the changes we make should be made only at such a rate and in such a way as will least interfere with the normal and healthful course of commerce and manufacture. But we shall not on that account act with timidity, as if we did not know our own minds, for we are certain of our ground and of our object. There should be an immediate revision, and it should be downward, unhesitatingly and steadily downward.

It should begin with the schedules which have been most obviously used to kill competition and to raise prices in the United States, arbitrarily and without regard to the prices pertaining elsewhere in the markets of the world; and it should, before it is finished or intermitted, be extended to every item in every schedule which affords any opportunity for monopoly, for special advantage to limited groups of beneficiaries, or for subsidized control of any kind in the markets or the enterprises of the country; until special favors of every sort shall have been absolutely withdrawn and every part of our laws of taxation shall have been transformed from a system of governmental patronage into a system of just and reasonable charges which shall fall where they will create the least burden. When we shall have done that, we can fix questions of revenue and of business adjustment in a new spirit and with clear minds. We shall then be partners with all the business men of the country, and a day of freer, more stable prosperity shall have dawned.

There has been no more demoralizing influence in our politics in our time than the influence of tariff legislation, the influence of the idea that the government was the grand dispenser of favors, the maker and unmaker of fortunes, and of opportunities such as certain men have sought in order to control the movement of trade and industry throughout the continent. It has made the government a prize to be captured and parties the means of effecting the capture. It has made the business men of one of the most virile and enterprising nations in the world timid, fretful, full of alarms; has robbed them of self-confidence and manly force, until they have cried out that they could do nothing without the assistance of the government at Washington. It has made them feel that their lives depended upon the Ways and Means Committee of the House and the Finance Committee of the Senate (in these later years particularly the Finance Committee of the Senate). They have insisted very anxiously that these committees should be made up only of their "friends"; until the country in its turn grew suspicious and wondered how those committees were being guided and controlled, by what influences and plans of personal advantage. Government cannot be wholesomely conducted in such an atmosphere. Its very honesty is in jeopardy. Favors are never conceived in the general interest; they are always for the benefit of the few, and the few who seek and obtain them have only themselves to blame if presently they seem to be contemned and distrusted.

For what has the result been? Prosperity? Yes, if by prosperity you mean vast wealth no matter how distributed, or whether distributed at all, or not; if you mean vast enterprises built up to be presently concentrated under the control of comparatively small bodies of men, who can determine almost at pleasure whether there shall be competition or not. The nation as a nation has grown immensely rich. She is justly proud of her industries and of the genius of her men of affairs. They can master anything they set their minds to, and we have been greatly stimulated under their leadership and command. Their laurels are many and very green. We must accord them the great honors that are their due and we must preserve what they have built up for us. But what of the other side of the picture? It is not as easy for us to live as it used to be. Our money will not buy as much.

High wages, even when we can get them, yield us no great comfort. We used to be better off with less, because a dollar could buy so much more. The majority of us have been disturbed to find ourselves growing poorer, even though our earnings were slowly increasing. Prices climb faster than we can push our earnings up.

Moreover, we begin to perceive some things about the movement of prices that concern us very deeply, and fix our attention upon the tariff schedules with a more definite determination than ever to get to the bottom of this matter. We have been looking into it, at trials held under the Sherman Act and in investigations in the committee rooms of Congress, where men who wanted to know the real facts have been busy with inquiry; and we begin to see very clearly what at least some of the methods are by which prices are fixed. We know that they are not fixed by the competitions of the market, or by the ancient law of supply and demand which is to be found stated in all the primers of economics, but by private arrangements with regard to what the supply should be and agreements among the producers themselves. Those who buy are not even represented by counsel. The high cost of living is arranged by private understanding.

We naturally ask ourselves, how did these gentlemen get control of these things? Who handed our economic laws over to them for legislative and contractual alteration? We have in these disclosures still another view of the tariff, still another proof that not the people of the United States but only a very small number of them have been partners in that legislation. Those few have learned how to control tariff legislation, and as they have perfected their control they have consolidated their interests. Men of the same interest have drawn together, have united their enterprises and have formed trusts; and trusts can control prices. Up to a certain point (and only up to a certain point) great combinations effect great economies in administration, and increase efficiency by simplifying and perfecting organization; but, whether they effect economies or not, they can very easily determine prices by intimate agreement so soon as they come to control a sufficient percentage of the product in any great line of business; and we now know that they do.

I am not drawing up an indictment against anybody. This is the natural history of such tariffs as are now contrived, as it is the natural history of all other governmental favors and of all licenses to use the government to help certain groups of individuals along in life. Nobody in particular, I suppose, is to blame, and I am not interested just now in blaming anybody. I am simply trying to point out what the situation is, in order to suggest what there is for us to do, if we would serve the country as a whole. The fact is that the trusts have been formed, have gained all but complete control of the larger enterprises of the country, have fixed prices and fixed them high so that profits might be rolled up that were thoroughly worth while, and that the tariff, with its artificial protections and stimulations, gave them the opportunity to do these things and has safeguarded them in that opportunity.

The trusts do not belong to the period of infant industries. They are not the products of the time, that old, laborious time, when the great continent we live on was undeveloped, the young nation struggling to find itself and get upon its feet amidst older and more experienced competitors. They belong to a very recent and very sophisticated age, when men knew what they wanted and knew how to get it by the favor of the government. It is another chapter in the natural history of power and of "governing classes." The next chapter will set us free again. There will be no flavor of tragedy in it. It will be a chapter of readjustment, not of pain and rough disturbance. It will witness a turning back from what is abnormal to what is normal. It will see a restoration of the laws of trade, which are the laws of competition and of unhampered opportunity, under which men of every sort are set free and encouraged to enrich the nation.

I am not one of those who think that competition can be established by law against the drift of a world-wide economic tendency; neither am I one of those who believe that business done upon a great scale by a single organization,—call it corporation, or what you will,—is necessarily dangerous to the liberties, even the economic liberties, of a great people like our own, full of intelligence and of indomitable energy. I am not afraid of anything that is normal. I dare say we shall never return to the old order of individual competition, and that the organization of business upon a great scale of coöperation is, up to a certain point, itself normal and inevitable.

Power in the hands of great business men does not make me apprehensive, unless it springs out of advantages which they have not created for themselves. Big business is not dangerous because it is big, but because its bigness is an unwholesome inflation created by privileges and exemptions which it ought not to enjoy. While competition cannot be created by statutory enactment, it can in large measure be revived by changing the laws and forbidding the practices that killed it, and by exacting laws that will give it heart and occasion again. We can arrest and prevent monopoly. It has assumed new shapes and adopted new processes in our time, but these are now being disclosed and can be dealt with.

The general terms of the present federal antitrust law, forbidding "combinations in restraint of trade," have apparently proved ineffectual. Trusts have grown up under its ban very luxuriantly and have pursued the methods by which so many of them have established virtual monopolies without serious let or hindrance. It has roared against them like any sucking dove. I am not assessing the responsibility, I am merely stating the fact. But the means and methods by which trusts have established monopolies have now become known. It will be necessary to supplement the present law with such laws, both civil and criminal, as will effectually punish and prevent those methods, adding such other laws as may be necessary to provide suitable and adequate judicial processes, whether civil or criminal, to disclose them and follow them to final verdict and judgment. They must be specifically and directly met by law as they develop.

But the problem and the difficulty are much greater than that. There are not merely great trusts and combinations which are to be controlled and deprived of their power to create monopolies and destroy rivals; there is something bigger still than they are and more subtle, more evasive, more difficult to deal with. There are vast confederacies (as I may perhaps call them for the sake of convenience) of banks, railways, express companies, insurance companies, manufacturing corporations, mining corporations, power and development companies, and all the rest of the circle, bound together by the fact that the ownership of their stock and the members of their boards of directors are controlled and determined by comparatively small and closely interrelated groups of persons who, by their informal confederacy, may control, if they please and when they will, both credit and enterprise. There is nothing illegal about these confederacies, so far as I can perceive. They have come about very naturally, generally without plan or deliberation, rather because there was so much money to be invested and it was in the hands, at great financial centers, of men acquainted with one another and intimately associated in business, than because anyone had conceived and was carrying out a plan of general control; but they are none the less potent a force in our economic and financial system on that account. They are part of our problem. Their very existence gives rise to the suspicion of a "money trust," a concentration of the control of credit which may at any time become infinitely dangerous to free enterprise. If such a concentration and control does not actually exist, it is evident that it can easily be set up and used at will. Laws must be devised which will prevent this, if laws can be worked out by fair and free counsel that will accomplish that result without destroying or seriously embarrassing any sound or legitimate business undertaking or necessary and wholesome arrangement.

Let me say again that what we are seeking is not destruction of any kind, nor the disruption of any sound or honest thing, but merely the rule of right and of the common advantage. I am happy to say that a new spirit has begun to show itself in the last year or two among influential men of business, and, what is perhaps even more significant, among the lawyers who are their expert advisers; and that this spirit has displayed itself very notably in the last few months in an effort to return, in some degree at any rate, to the practices of genuine competition. Only a very little while ago our men of business were united in resisting every proposal of change and reform as an attack on business, an embarrassment to all large enterprise, an intimation that settled ideas of property were to be set aside and a new and strange order of things created out of hand. While they thought in that way, progress seemed impossible without hot contest and a bitter clash between interests, almost a war of classes. Common counsel seemed all but hopeless, because some of the chief parties in interest would not take part,—seemed even to resent discussion as a manifestation of hostility towards themselves. They talked constantly about vested interests and were very hot.

It is a happy omen that their attitude has changed. They see that what is right can hurt no man; that a new adjustment of interests is inevitable and desirable, is in the interest of everybody; that their own honor, their own intelligence, their own practical comprehension of affairs is involved. They are beginning to adjust their business to the new standards. Their hand is no longer against the nation; they are part of it, their interests are bound up with its interests. This is not true of all of them, but it is true of enough of them to show what the new age is to be, and how the anxieties of statesmen are to be eased if the light that is dawning broadens into day.

If I am right about this, it is going to be easier to act in accordance with the rule of right and justice in dealing with the labor question. The so-called labor question is a question only because we have not yet found the rule of right in adjusting the interests of labor and capital. The welfare, the happiness, the energy and spirit of the men and women who do the daily work in our mines and factories, on our railroads, in our offices and marts of trade, on our farms and on the sea, are of the essence of our national life. There can be nothing wholesome unless their life is wholesome; there can be no contentment unless they are contented. Their physical welfare affects the soundness of the whole nation. We shall never get very far in the settlement of these vital matters so long as we regard everything done for the workingman, by law or by private agreement, as a concession yielded to keep him from agitation and a disturbance of our peace. Here, again, the sense of universal partnership must come into play if we are to act like statesmen, as those who serve, not a class, but a nation.

The working people of America,—if they must be distinguished from the minority that constitutes the rest of it,—are, of course, the backbone of the nation. No law that safeguards their life, that improve[s] the physical and moral conditions under which they live, that makes their hours of labor rational and tolerable, that gives them freedom to act in their own interest, and that protects them where they cannot protect themselves, can properly be regarded as class legislation or as anything but as a measure taken in the interest of the whole people, whose partnership in right action we are trying to establish and make real and practical. It is in this spirit that we shall act if we are genuine spokesmen of the whole country.

As our program is disclosed,—for no man can forecast it ready-made and before counsel is taken of every one concerned,—this must be its measure and standard, the interest of all concerned. For example, in dealing with the complicated and difficult question of the reform of our banking and currency laws, it is plain that we ought to consult very many persons besides the bankers, not because we distrust the bankers, but because they do not necessarily comprehend the business of the country, notwithstanding they are indispensable servants of it and may do a vast deal to make it hard or easy. No mere bankers' plan will meet the requirements, no matter how honestly conceived. It should be a merchants' and farmers' plan as well, elastic in the hands of those who use it as an indispensable part of their daily business. I do not know enough about this subject to be dogmatic about it; I know only enough to be sure what the partnerships in it should be, and that the control exercised over any system we may set up should be, so far as possible, a control emanating, not from a single special class, but from the general body and authority of the nation itself.

In dealing with the Philippines, we should not allow ourselves to stand upon any mere point of pride, as if, in order to keep our countenance in the families of nations, it were necessary for us to make the same blunders of selfishness that other nations have made. We are not the owners of the Philippine Islands. We hold them in trust for the people who live in them. They are theirs, for the uses of their life. We are not even their partners. It is our duty, as trustees, to make whatever arrangement of government will be most serviceable to their freedom and development. Here, again, we are to set up the rule of justice and of right.

The rule of the people is no idle phrase. Those who believe in it,—as who does not that has caught the real spirit of America?— believe that there can be no rule of right without it; that right in politics is made up of the interests of everybody, and everybody should take part in the action that is to determine it. We have been keen for presidential primaries and the direct election of United States Senators, because we wanted the action of the government to be determined by persons whom the people had actually designated as men whom they were ready to trust and follow. We have been anxious that all campaign contributions and expenditures should be disclosed to the public in fullest detail, because we regarded the influences which govern campaigns to be as much a part of the people's business as anything else connected with their government. We are working towards a very definite object, the universal partnership in public affairs upon which the purity of politics and its aim and spirit depend.

For there is much for the partners to undertake. In the affairs of a great nation we plan and labor, not for the present only, but for the long future as well. There are great tasks of protection and conservation and development to which we have to address ourselves. Government has much more to do than merely to right wrongs and set the house in order.

I do not know any greater question than that of conservation. We have been a spendthrift nation and must now husband what we have left. We must do more than that. We must develop, as well as preserve, our water powers and must add great waterways to the transportation facilities of the nation, to supplement the railways within our borders as well as upon the Isthmus. We must revive our merchant marine, too, and fill the seas again with our own fleets. We must add to our present post-office service a parcels post as complete as that of any other nation. We must look to the health of our people upon every hand, as well as hearten them with justice and opportunity. This is the constructive work of government. This is the policy that has a vision and a hope and that looks to serve mankind.

There are many sides to these great matters. Conservation is easy to generalize about, but hard to particularize about wisely. Reservation is not the whole of conservation. The development of great states must not be stayed indefinitely to await a policy by which our forests and water powers can prudently be made use of. Use and development must go hand in hand. The policy we adopt must be progressive, not negative, merely, as if we did not know what to do.

With regard to the development of greater and more numerous waterways and the building up of a merchant marine, we must follow great constructive lines and not fall back upon the cheap device of bounties and subsidies. In the case of the Mississippi River, that great central artery of our trade, it is plain that the federal government must build and maintain the levees and keep the great waters in harness for the general use. It is plain, too, that vast sums of money must be spent to develop new waterways where trade will be most served and transportation most readily cheapened by them. Such expenditures are no largess on the part of the government; they are national investments.

The question of a merchant marine turns back to the tariff again, to which all roads seem to lead, and to our registry laws, which, if coupled with the tariff, might also be supposed to have been intended to take the American flag off the seas. Bounties are not necessary, if you will but undo some of the things that have been done. Without a great merchant marine we cannot take our rightful place in the commerce of the world. Merchants who must depend upon the carriers of rival mercantile nations to carry their goods to market are at a disadvantage in international trade too manifest to need to be pointed out; and our merchants will not long suffer themselves,—ought not to suffer themselves,— to be placed at such a disadvantage. Our industries have expanded to such a point that they will burst their jackets, if they cannot find a free outlet to the markets of the world; and they cannot find such an outlet unless they be given ships of their own to carry their goods,—ships that will go the routes they want them to go,—and prefer the interests of America in their sailing orders and their equipment. Our domestic markets no longer suffice. We need foreign markets. That is another force that is going to break the tariff down. The tariff was once a bulwark; now it is a dam. For trade is reciprocal; we cannot sell unless we also buy.

The very fact that we have at last taken the Panama Canal seriously in hand and are vigorously pushing it towards completion is eloquent of our re-awakened interest in international trade. We are not building the canal and pouring out million upon million of money upon its construction merely to establish a water connection between the two coasts of the continent, important and desirable as that may be, particularly from the point of view of naval defense. It is meant to be a great international highway. It would be a little ridiculous if we should build it and then have no ships to send through it. There have been years when not a single ton of freight passed through the great Suez Canal in an American bottom, so empty are the seas of our ships and seamen. We must mean to put an end to that kind of thing or we would not be cutting a new canal at our very doors merely for the use of our men-of-war. We shall not manage the revival by the mere paltry device of tolls. We must build and buy ships in competition with the world. We can do it if we will but give ourselves leave.

There is another duty which the Democratic party has shown itself great enough and close enough to the people to perceive— the duty of government to share in promoting agricultural, industrial, vocational education in every way possible within its constitutional powers. No other platform has given this intimate vision of a party's duty. The nation cannot enjoy its deserved supremacy in the markets and enterprises of the world unless its people are given the ease and effectiveness that come only with knowledge and training. Education is part of the great task of conservation, part of the task of renewal and of perfected power.

We have set ourselves a great program, and it will be a great party that carries it out. It must be a party without entangling alliances with any special interest whatever. It must have the spirit and the point of view of the new age. Men are turning away from the Republican party, as organized under its old leaders, because they found that it was not free, that it was entangled; and they are turning to us because they deem us free to serve them. They are immensely interested, as we are, as every man who reads the signs of the time and feels the spirit of the new age is, in the new program. It is solidly based on the facts of our national life; its items are items of present business; it is what every man should wish to see done who wishes to see our present distempers made an end of and our old free, coöperative life restored.

We should go into this campaign confident of only one thing,— confident of what we want to do if entrusted with the government. It is not a partisan fight we are entering upon. We are happily excused from personal attacks upon opponents and from all general indictments against the men opposed to us. The facts are patent to everybody; we do not have to prove them; the more frank among our opponents admit them. Our thinking must be constructive from start to finish. We must show that we understand the problems that confront us, and that we are soberly minded to deal with them, applying to them, not nostrums and notions, but hard sense and good courage.

A presidential campaign may easily degenerate into a mere personal contest and so lose its real dignity and significance. There is no indispensable man. The government will not collapse and go to pieces if any one of the gentlemen who are seeking to be entrusted with its guidance should be left at home. But men are instruments. We are as important as the cause we represent, and in order to be important must really represent a cause. What is our cause? The people's cause. That is easy to say, but what does it mean? The common as against any particular interest whatever? Yes, but that, too, needs translation into acts and policies. We represent the desire to set up an unentangled government, a government that cannot be used for private purposes, either in the field of business or in the field of politics; a government that will not tolerate the use of the organization of a great party to serve the personal aims and ambitions of any individual, and that will not permit legislation to be employed to further any private interest. It is a great conception, but I am free to serve it, as you also are. I could not have accepted a nomination which left me bound to any man or any group of men. No man can be just who is not free; and no man who has to show favors ought to undertake the solemn responsibility of government in any rank or post whatever, least of all in the supreme post of President of the United States.

To be free is not necessarily to be wise. But wisdom comes with counsel, with the frank and free conference of untrammeled men united in the common interest. Should I be entrusted with the great office of President, I would seek counsel wherever it could be had upon free terms. I know the temper of the great convention which nominated me; I know the temper of the country that lay back of that convention and spoke through it. I heed with deep thankfulness the message you bring me from it. I feel that I am surrounded by men whose principles and ambitions are those of true servants of the people. I thank God, and will take courage.[2]

Printed reading copy (WC, NjP); *Speech of Governor Wilson Accepting the Democratic Nomination for President of the United States* . . . (Washington, 1912).
    [2] There is a WWsh draft of this speech in WP, DLC.

From Edwin Doak Mead[1]

Dear Mr. Wilson: Boston August 10, 1912.

I was profoundly disappointed that there was no single word in the Baltimore platform touching the great matters of world peace and order, which to so many of us seem incomparably the most imperative issues of the present time. I was disappointed that you did not recur to this subject in your admirable address the other day, although, of course, I recognize clearly that no man in your position can deliver his whole gospel at one time, and I am sure that you will duly come to this subject. It is, however, a subject so critical, with me so much more commanding than any other, that I feel the most anxious interest to know your exact point of view. The meeting of the Third Hague Conference will fall within your administration—I say your administration because it seems to me that your election is almost certain; and we who are working along international lines feel it to be of the highest moment that the United States should take a position on that critical occasion which shall be most advanced and possibly mark a new epoch in the struggle for international coöperation, and against the monstrous armaments which are sapping the resources of all peoples. I wish that you felt like personally holding up the hands of those Democrats in Congress who are at this moment struggling so nobly to make our government call a halt in its perfectly unnecessary and, I think, most mischievous naval appropriations. I wish to call your attention to the enclosed two speeches by Mr. Bryan[2] at the Mohonk Arbitration Conferences last year and the year before. I was greatly disappointed that he did not secure the expression in the Baltimore platform of the doctrines which he there expounded. It is of no use for any of us to talk these things unless we are prepared to put them resolutely into action when the opportunity and occasion come. The Baltimore platform began with an appeal to Thomas Jefferson, and we are talking about keeping the Republic true to the principles of the Founders. I do not need to remind you what Jefferson and the Fathers said on this subject and what the ideals were which they held for the Republic in this matter; but I am taking the liberty, for the economy of your time, to send you a recent Fourth of July oration of mine here in Boston,[3] in which (pages 23-28) I have summed up the positions of Jefferson, Franklin, and Washington.

I have a more practical and immediate reason for thus writing you. I am writing much for our Boston Herald, editorially and otherwise. It gives me great latitude and seems desirous to print whatever I send them. Your friends may have noticed that it is more or less critical about you, although, knowing that I support you, it does not suppress anything that I say, and I feel that under certain circumstances I might be able to swing it essentially to your side. This last I say, of course, confidentially. Before I feel free, however, to go too far I must have more distinct assurance as to your international program. It is here that we peace people feel under such tremendous obligation to President Taft, and that we are almost to a man against Roosevelt. We do not, however, want to support you simply for the sake of saving the country from Roosevelt. We are anxious to be able to support you because of assurance that you have the great international vision, and that you are bound to make your administration an epoch-making one in the service of Jefferson's Republic for the great ideals of peace for which Jefferson stood. I would willingly come to see you sometime for a personal conference upon this subject, which lies so closely to my heart, if in these crowded days you should have time for such a conference or should desire it; or if I can be of any other service to you in the field, I will gladly render it. The matter is of such momentous importance that I know you will pardon me for writing you thus freely and plainly; and I am, with high regard,   Yours truly,   Edwin D. Mead.[4]

TLS (WP, DLC).
[1] Reformer, editor, and publicist of Boston; director of the World Peace Foundation.
[2] They are missing, but they were William J. Bryan, "The Forces that Make for Peace," *Report of the Sixteenth Annual Meeting of the Lake Mohonk Conference on International Arbitration . . . 1910* (n.p., 1910), pp. 164-73, and "The Hopeful Outlook for Peace," *Report of the Seventeenth Annual Meeting of the Lake Mohonk Conference on International Arbitration . . . 1911* (n.p., 1911), pp. 44-49.
[3] It is also missing, but it was E. D. Mead, *The Principles of the Founders . . . Oration before the City Government and Citizens of Boston at Faneuil Hall, July 4, 1903* (Boston, 1903).
[4] Wilson's reply is missing in all Wilson collections and in the Mead and World Peace Foundation papers in the Swarthmore College Peace Collection.

To Mary Allen Hulbert

Dearest Friend,   Sea Girt, New Jersey 11 Aug., 1912.,

When am I to get a real letter from you? I am very hungry for one. I think you do not,—cannot,—know what letters from dear friends mean to me just now, amidst the pouring flood of letters from persons I do not know. They are like the sweet, familiar voice of loved ones amidst the continual deafening chatter of a mixed crowd, who mean nothing to you. This morning I seized very eagerly upon an envelope addressed to me in your handwriting,—but, alas! it held nothing but a schedule,—a schedule that suggested something very delightful, a visit to Sandanwede, but which was only a memorandum, after all. You know *all* that I am doing, if you take in one of the New York papers, and more than all (for much is invented or inferred or imagined) and there is nothing else for me to write of, these crowded and distracting days; but I know *nothing* of what you are doing, can form no image of your life from day to day; and that makes a great deal of difference to me! It is such a relief, such an escape, such a deep and subtle pleasure to have the means of sending my thoughts on errands to my friends. One can do it when the day drags most heavily or the pressure becomes too nearly intolerable. Will you not open *that* road of delight to my weary feet? There are many things nowadays that are almost intolerable to me. There is one circumstance, for example to which I *cannot* reconcile myself. The reporters (there are sixteen of them by me all the time) are required by their papers, upon pain of dismissal, to know where I am, who is with me, and what I am doing *at all times*. They must move as I move, go where I go. If there is anything they are not told, they will spy, *must* spy, it out. I must be under observation without intermission. All eyes are watchful of my slightest action. I have lost all freedom and all privacy. It is all but intolerable. It requires all the powers of self-control I possess to endure it. Shall I take the six o'clock boat some evening and bring all my sixteen keepers to Nantucket? How shall a poor nominee ever visit his friends without bringing the whole of the United States to camp at their door? I never imagined anything like it!

I am perfectly well. All join me in messages of affection to you all.   Your devoted friend,   Woodrow Wilson

ALS (WP, DLC).

To Thomas Mador Gilmore[1]

My Dear Mr. Gilmore: Sea Girt, N. J. August 12, 1912.

I am sorry to say that I cannot add anything to my letter to Mr. Shannon,[2] because it seems to me a matter[3] which must be judged of in each case by what the local unit should be. The particular thing which I cannot do and will not attempt, is to suggest a universal solution of this difficult question.

Sincerely yours,   [Woodrow Wilson]

CCL (WP, DLC).
 1 Of Louisville, Ky.; editor and co-publisher of *Bonfort's Wine and Spirit*

Circular, a trade publication; anti-prohibitionist writer and speaker on the reform of saloons.

² WW to T. B. Shannon, May 1, 1911, Vol. 22. This letter had been widely circulated.

³ That is, control of the liquor traffic.

From John Worth Kern, with Enclosure

Dear Governor,   Indianapolis August 12, 1912

I enclose copy of letter which I addressed to Mr Gompers[1] last Saturday. I hope it may accomplish something.

I returned here from Washington last Saturday and found the Roosevelt and Beveridge[2] (for Governor) movement booming, and it will prove to be dangerous, unless our local leaders and candidates make a strong stand for progressive principles.

The sentiment of this middle western country is overwhelmingly progressive. The people are firmly resolved to have what they want. Some of our leaders here do not seem to know, nor want to know of this sentiment. Governor Marshall seems to have conceived a great dislike to the word "Progressive." I hope he will not make that dislike manifest in his speech of acceptance, for it would be well nigh fatal.

Yours Very Truly   Jno. W. Kern

I shall presume to speak to the Governor on the subject

ALS (WP, DLC).

¹ Samuel Gompers, president of the American Federation of Labor.

² Former Senator Albert J. Beveridge, Progressive candidate for Governor of Indiana.

ENCLOSURE

John Worth Kern to Samuel Gompers

Dear Mr. Gomper: Indianapolis, Ind. August 10, 1912.

I write to remind you of the action of the Democratic National Convention, at Baltimore in adopting a platform, which, in so far as its declarations on the labor questions were concerned, was written by yourself and adopted by the Committee on Resolutions without the dotting of an "i" or the crossing of a "t."

I also remind you of the action of the Democratic House of Representatives in Washington in redeeming the pledges of the Denver Platform.[1]

In view of the above facts, is it not in fairness due to the Democratic party from your Federation, that its Executive Council which meets in Atlantic City next week should by resolution or otherwise, show its appreciation of the party's action in National Convention and in the branch of Congress controlled by that Party?

As Chairman of the Platform Committee at the Baltimore Convention, I am especially cognizant of the treatment of organized labor by that body, and respectfully urge that your Council should take action in respect thereto similar to that taken by it with reference to the Denver platform.[2]

With kind personal regards to you and your associates, I am,

Yours very truly,   Jno. W. Kern

TCLS (WP, DLC).

[1] The Democratic platform of 1908.

[2] The council took no formal action on any of the candidates. However, as the campaign progressed Gompers and the A. F. of L.'s journal, *The American Federationist*, became increasingly explicit in their support of Wilson. See Arthur S. Link, *Wilson: The Road to the White House* (Princeton, N. J., 1947), p. 500.

From William Frank McCombs

My dear Governor: New York, Aug 13, 1912

I have your letter of August 12th. Since Friday I have been in bed with a severe attack of Toxemia, the same trouble that sent me to Carlsbad two years ago. I sincerely trust I will be able to get out of it soon, as much must be done.

I have carefully noted the letter of Breckenridge.[1] Of course, I had nothing to do with the selection of Mr. Camden[2] who managed the Kentucky State Campaign. That is a state affair. It came about without any designation from these headquarters. It is a matter with which we could have nothing to do. No designation of committeemen whatever has been made in Kentucky by me or by the Committee.

The reference to Senator Watson's[3] proposed bargain is entire news to me.

With kind regards, I am

Yours Sincerely,   W F McCombs

Since writing the above my physical conditon has become decidedly worse and I am doubtful whether I can continue in the work.

HwLS (WP, DLC).

[1] Henry S. Breckinridge.

[2] Johnson Newlon Camden, Jr., of Versailles, Ky., horse and cattle farmer with extensive interests in coal mines.

[3] Senator Clarence Wayland Watson of Fairmont, West Va.

From the Diary of Oswald Garrison Villard

August 14, 1912

I had a long and interesting interview with Woodrow Wilson yesterday. I went out on the eleven o'clock train and found him at his office in the Capitol democratically wandering about and talking to the people in the outer office who were waiting to see him. There are never any fuss and feathers where he is. As usual he was very cordial and he took me, his brother, who is a nice simple Southerner, city editor of the Nashville Banner, and his fine young secretary, Joseph Tumulty, to the pretty Country Club just outside of Trenton. There we sat on a wide verandah surrounded by superb trees and the beautiful golf links all around us and talked until three o'clock when he hurried back to his office and I caught the train back to New York.

I went down prepared to speak to him on four subjects,—the New York situation, the navy, the negro and woman's suffrage. He listened, as always, with the utmost courtesy and attention and was as friendly and cordial as one could ask. I pointed out to him the situation in this State which is outlined in my editorial of this date,[1] and told him our fear that this might really be a doubtful State with more than a possibility that T.R. will carry it if Tammany should nominate a "yellow dog" ticket. He was entirely sympathetic, thinks that the up-State men are pursuing the proper course in threatening to bolt, and made no plea that there should be party harmony because this was a Presidential year. He said that that sort of argument would be used every year, and the thing to do was to go ahead, that the responsibility lay not with us but with those who were driving us from the party. He has pledged himself not to interfere in local fights, doing so because he believed that this would be the best way to prevent any boss from using him oe [or] misleading him, but he told me that he would exercise all the influence he could legitimately and honorably use through the national committee, and I am just going to lunch with McAdoo and put the case before him. McAdoo, by the way, is our most promising candidate for Governor, so we may vote for a Southerner for President and a Southerner for Governor of our Empire State,—a striking sign of the conquest of the North by the South.

To my great regret I found that the Governor favors a large navy, and that he has been quite deluded by all that silly jingo talk about Germany making a raid on South America. He also alarmed me by saying that this was a period when the big nations of the earth were not going to put up with misbehavior by the small ones. I argued with him as best I could and found that he was in ignorance of many things, and, in fact, I think his whole position is largely due to a failure to know much about international affairs; they have never appealed to him, naturally. But he is open to reason and weighs every argument candidly and on its merits, and I think he was impressed. I am writing him today and stirring up others to write to him begging him not to commit himself. I am repeating to him what I said yesterday, that when he gets to Washington and realizes what a dangerous militaristic clique we are raising and how powerful a national guard, army and navy lobby we are creating, he will feel differently. That impressed him, and he expressed his disapproval of the bill to pay the militia eight millions of dollars annually.

On the negro question, on the other hand, I was quite delighted with his attitude. He said that, of course, he should be President of all the people, that he would appoint no man to office because he was colored, any more than he would appoint one because he was a Jew or a Catholic, but that he would appoint him on his merits. "The only place," he said, "where you and I will differ is as to where the entering wedge should be driven." He stated that he would not make an appointment like that of Crum at Charleston[2] because he felt that it resulted in very great injury to the colored people and increased race antipathy, which, he said, we must try to avoid. I told him of many cases of injustice and notably two cases I cited in my recent article on the Deserted Negro,[3] and he urged that they be prosecuted, saying that they were all wrong and contrary to the spirit and letter of the Constitution and must be defeated. (These are the attempts to prevent negroes from building on land they have purchased in certain sections of Southern towns.) Again, I told him of the conditions of the colored people which prevented their being able to lift a voice in their own government, and of the 5000 colored children walking the streets of Atlanta without hope of an education, predestined to vice and crime and ignorance. I told him the Virginia Christian story,[4] which also moved him not a little, and how they were killing that girl this week because being a child of a child race and compelled to live in the horrible slums, more or less of an outcast, she had had no chance to be anything else than what she was. This made quite an impression upon him, and he told me with a great deal of feeling of the "worst phase" of his governorship; that the poor and victims of injustice find their way to him all the time and that he cannot help them because the Governor of New Jersey has no power in such matters. He said of course he would speak out against lynching, "every honest man must do so," but that he did not wish the colored people to get the impression that he could help them in that matter as President, as the President had no power. He has promised me a statement probably for the Crisis and the Evening Post, or if not, one to be spread broadcast to help me in writing a letter to the negro newspapers and otherwise helping his candidacy.

I then presented a letter to him from Mrs. Fitzgerald,[5] written to me, begging a statement from him on the woman suffrage question saying that he was losing thousands of votes in Massachusetts because of Roosevelt's advocacy of suffrage. He said,— "I have no doubt it is true," and said that Roosevelt would gain an enormous advantage in the woman suffrage States, but that he was not like Roosevelt and could not change his opinion in order to get votes. He said, "I cannot do anything"; I said "You certainly cannot change now unless you are converted, without putting yourself in Roosevelt's class." He said that was it exactly.

T diary (O. G. Villard Papers, MH).

[1] "The Democracy in This State," New York *Evening Post*, Aug. 14, 1912. About the New York Democratic situation, see Link, *Road to the White House*, pp. 494-95.

[2] About this episode, see n. 2 to the extract from the diary of Mary Yates printed at July 31, 1908, Vol. 18.

[3] A lengthy editorial in the New York *Evening Post*, Aug. 8, 1912.

[4] Virginia Christian, a black girl about seventeen, was executed in Richmond, Va., on August 16, 1912. She had been convicted of robbing and murdering her white female employer in Hampton, Va., on March 18, 1912. The Governor of Virginia had refused to yield to numerous pleas for clemency made by persons from many parts of the country. An account of the case appears in *The Crisis*, IV (Sept. 1912), 237-39.

[5] See O. G. Villard to Susan W. Fitz Gerald, Aug. 14, 1912.

A Fragment of a Letter from Oswald Garrison Villard

My dear Governor: [New York] August 14, 1912.

I send you herewith the promised statement of Dr. Waldron of his interview with you.[1] As to the statement which you are going to give me, I can only add that you will see from this what the colored people want and that you will go as far as you consistently can in giving them assurances that they will have equal treatment before the law and that you will not discriminate against them either in the matter of appointments to office or in other ways. I should like to have this statement for publication in the Crisis, the excellent monthly devoted to the colored people of which I am one of the editors, and in which Miss Jane Addams among others is interested, and also in the Evening Post. We shall transfer it to the Associated Press, of course. I trust this will be satisfactory.

Mr. Lowry[2] asks me to say that he awaits word from Mr. Tumulty as to when he shall come to tell you about the Chicago Convention.[3]

In regard to the navy matter which we discussed, may I not most earnestly suggest that you defer, if possible, a definite committment of yourself on this issue? It is not pressing and cannot really be called an important question of this campaign. I feel so strongly that you might modify your opinion on getting to Washington and seeing the side of this big navy mania which is visible in Washington.

CCL (O. G. Villard Papers, MH).
　[1] It is printed at Sept. 1, 1912.
　[2] Edward George Lowry, managing editor of the New York *Evening Post*.
　[3] That is, the national convention of the new Progressive party.

From Edwin Bird Wilson, with Enclosure

Dear Governor Wilson:　　　　New York City August 14th [1912]

In accord with our recent conversation, I take pleasure in enclosing a list of names. All of these people are recognized leaders. Also, they are persons favorably disposed toward you and would almost certainly accept an invitation to a conference on the subject we have in mind. If I may be permitted to make a suggestion, would advise you to invite them to *confer* with you on the subjects touching the wide interests of their people, e.g. naturalized citizenship, immigration, distribution of immigrants, etc. I think it would be wise to refer to them as recognized leaders of their respective people, but unwise to refer to the misunderstanding in regard to your attitude—in the invitation I mean. The situation is serious, but not hopeless and I believe that you can win back a large percentage of these people, by careful action along the lines suggested. Your speech and news of the gathering at Sea Girt will be given the fullest publicity in the papers which will do you the most good for this purpose.[1] I have the positive promise of my influential friend on this point.

Am sending you some clippings[2] which I have not read, for obvious reasons! Perhaps your interpreter may be of assistance.
　　　　　　　　Sincerely yours,　Edwin B. Wilson

P.S. If you think I could be of service in offering further suggestions as to the points advisable to touch upon in your address, please command me.　　　　　　　　　　　　EBW

ALS (WP, DLC).
　[1] There is no evidence that any of these editors came to Sea Girt. Probably

they were among the larger group with whom Wilson conferred and to whom he talked in New York on September 4.
² They are missing.

E N C L O S U R E

Mr. Leon F. Wazeter, 52 Avenue A, New York City.
    Publisher "Tygodnik Polski" (Polish Weekly)
Mr. S. J. Tyburski, 179 South Pennsylvania Avenue,
    Wilkesbarre, Pa.
    Publisher of a Polish paper.
Mr. Charles Barsotti, 42 Duane Street, N. Y. City.
    Publisher "Il Progresso" (Italian Daily)
Mr. John Vicario, 243 Canal Street, N. Y. City.
    Publisher three Italian papers, "Il Telegrafo"
                                    "Il Corriere D'Italia"
                                    "L'Araldo Italiano"
Mr. G. D. Berko, 178 Second Ave., N. Y. City,
    Publisher "Amerikai Magyar Nepszava" (Hungarian Daily)
The Hon. John Kosek, Wilkesbarre, Pa.
    Mayor of Wilkesbarre.
Mr. Jos. A. Di Silvestro, 906 Carpenter St., Philadelphia, Pa.
    Publisher "Voce del Popolo," (Italian Daily)
Rev. J. Pitass, 389 Peckham St., Buffalo, N. Y.
    Polish High Priest for the Diocese of N. Y. State.
Mr. Roman B. Mirr, 618 Mitchell St., Milwaukee, Wis.
    Publisher of an important Polish paper.
Rev. Father Gordon, 1455 West Division Street, Chicago, Ill.
    Polish High Priest for the United States and owner of a large
    Polish paper.
Mr. A. F. Lakowka, 1455 West Division St., Chicago, Ill.
    Publisher Father Gordon's paper.
Mr. Sol. Sulzburger, 77 East 89th St., N. Y. City.
    Mr. Sulzburger is National Treasurer of the independent
    order of B'nai B'rith, an important Jewish organization of
    35,000 members.
Mr. A. Mastro-Valerio, 307 New Era Bldg., Chicago, Ill.
    Publisher "Tribuna Italiana."
Mr. L. E. Miller, 153 E. Broadway, N. Y. City.
    Publisher "Warheit" (Jewish Daily.)
Mr. F. A. Fiore, 139 Eighth Ave., Newark, N. J.
    Italian Publisher.
Mr. Luigi Solari, 21 State St., N. Y. City.
    President Italian Chamber of Commerce.

Mr. Cab. Frank Cuneo, 1608 Masonic Temple, Chicago, Ill.
President Italian Chamber of Commerce.
Mr. Samuel S. Dorf, 601 West 144th St., New York City.
Grand Master of the Order Brith Abraham which has 62,000 members, and 340 Lodges.
Mr. S. J. Vlasto,
Publisher "Atlantis" New York City and
Archbishop of Greek Catholic Church for America.

T MS (WP, DLC).

Oswald Garrison Villard to Susan Walker Fitz Gerald[1]

Dear Mrs. Fitzgerald: [New York] August 14, 1912.

Within five hours after receiving your letter yesterday I laid it before Governor Wilson. He was, of course, impressed by it and he realized perfectly that Roosevelt has got the jump on him and Taft, to use a football expression. But he simply says that he is not in Mr. Roosevelt's class.[2] In other words, he cannot change his opinions on this subject because he is a candidate for office. He did not say very much, but I gathered from what he did say that he would prefer defeat to stultifying himself by coming out for a measure in which he does not believe. I am awfully sorry it is so and told him so frankly, because I think there is no doubt that Roosevelt will carry the five suffrage States. I labored with him a year ago, but it was of no avail. I respect him for his consistency and honesty however sorry I am to differ from him,
With kind regards,
Sincerely yours,   [Oswald Garrison Villard]

CCL (O. G. Villard Papers, MH).
1 Mrs. Richard Y. Fitz Gerald, social worker and woman suffrage leader of Boston, recording secretary of the National American Woman Suffrage Association.
2 The platform of the Progressive party stated: "The Progressive party, believing that no people can justly claim to be a true democracy which denies political rights on account of sex, pledges itself to the task of securing equal suffrage to men and women alike."

A Public Letter

Sea Girt, N. J. [c. Aug. 15, 1912]

The Democratic party has chosen its candidates this year in manifest response to the spirit and circumstances of the day. It has chosen men who represent, both in character and in the record they have made as governors of their respective states, the determination to use parties and all governmental machinery for the benefit of the people at large. Character and purpose have spoken in their official acts and are manifest in their character and splendid reputation.

In supporting them, you are given an opportunity to restore our government to your own real representatives. In order to be your real representatives, they must be elected without incurring any obligations that will bind them to any special interest whatever. They, therefore, depend upon you for support. It is you who maintain our government. It is you for whom it is being administered. If you will assume some part of the burden of making proper selections, you can make absolutely certain that you will live under a free government.

We, therefore, frankly solicit your contributions to the fund which is necessary to pay the legitimate expenses of the campaign carried on for the scale of the whole nation. We take the liberty of urging you to send us your subscriptions as liberally as possible and would be obliged if you would transmit them to the Headquarters of the National Democratic Committee, No. 200 Fifth Avenue, New York City.

CCL (WP, DLC).

To Alexander Jeffrey McKelway

My dear Mr. McKelway: Sea Girt, N. J. August 15, 1912.

I was not able to adopt the suggestions contained in your interesting letter of July twenty-third when making my speech of acceptance because it did not seem to me right at that time. It seemed to be adding planks and programmes to the platform adopted at Baltimore, but I think you know me well enough that I am not likely to lose my interest in the great subject of child labor laws. I hope that many opportunities will be afforded me to discuss them seriously and with the feeling that I am part responsibile for the solution of the matter.

With warmest regard,
          Cordially and sincerely yours,   Woodrow Wilson

TLS (A. J. McKelway Papers, DLC).

An Address at a Farmers' Picnic
at Washington Park, New Jersey

[Aug. 15, 1912]

Mr. Chairman,[1] Ladies and Gentlemen: I remember very distinctly, and with a great deal of pleasure, being here just a year ago. As I was coming down on the train I was asking myself the difference between this occasion and that. At that time we were on the eve of a state political campaign, as we are now. This time the view has widened to the nation itself, and we are now about to combine with the choice of state officers the choice also of a President and Vice-President of the United States.

Have I come therefore on a different errand? It seems to me that although I was not a candidate last time, and am a candidate this time, that so far as my thought is concerned that has very little to do with it. I am interested in politics not as a search for office but as a great contest devoted to something very definite and practical indeed. Politics ought not to be considered as a mere occasion for oratory. Politics ought to be considered as a branch of the national business, and a man who talks politics ought to tell his fellow citizens very distinctly what he thinks about their affairs and what his own attitude towards them is.

There was another thought that was prominent in my mind as I came down today. Here we are at a farmers' picnic, and on this day I suppose that here at Washington Park we might say that the farmers occupy the center of the stage. When did the farmers ever occupy the center of the stage in our politics? I don't remember any time. I do remember a time written of with great enthusiasm by historians in the far year 1775 when the farmers around about Lexington in Massachusetts gathered along the roadside to prevent the retreat of a little handful of British troops who had been bent upon an illicit errand. I have read a great deal of poetry about the embattled farmers at Lexington, and I know that every war that we have fought has seen the farmers of this country along with the other patriotic men embattled in the nation's defense. But when it comes down to the voting, when it comes to the making of laws, where are the embattled farmers? When have the farmers ever occupied the center of the stage in politics?

Do you ask me whether I want the farmers to organize themselves in such a way that they shall thrust others aside and usurp the center of the stage? I reply, no. There is not a single class of the nation that ought to demand that it should be occupying con-

[1] Congressman William Hughes.

stantly the center of the stage, but there is also not a single class in the nation that ought not to demand constantly that it be regarded as a member of the firm in the great partnership.

I have seen the interests of a great many classes especially regarded in legislation, but I must frankly say that I have never seen the interests of the farmer very often regarded in legislation. And one of the greatest impositions upon the farmer of this country that has ever been devised is the present tariff legislation of the United States. I have not heard of farmers waiting for a hearing before the committee of Ways and Means of the House and the Finance Committee of the Senate in order to take part in determining what the tariff schedule should be. I have not heard anybody but orators on the stump say that the tariff was intended for the benefit of the farmer, because you have to be on the stump to keep a straight face when you make a statement like that. When the United States was the granary of the world and was supplying the world far and near with the foodstuffs that it subsisted upon, the farmers were not looking for protection; and while they were not looking everything else had duties imposed upon it, and the cost of everything that they had to use was raised upon them and raised upon them, until now it is almost impossible for them to make a legitimate profit.

While you were feeding the world, Congress was feeding the trusts. Nobody doubts what the process of tariff legislation has been, because everybody who has been curious enough to inquire knows what the process of tariff legislation has been. We could give you a list of the gentlemen who have been most prominent in securing tariff legislation. We know the kind that secured it and the purpose they secured it for; and they weren't thinking about the general prosperity of the United States. They were thinking about the balance sheets in particular investments. And those investments were not investments which were easily within the reach and work of the farmer himself.

I would be ashamed of myself, ladies and gentlemen, if I tried to stir up any feeling on the part of any class against any other class. I wish to disavow all intention of suggesting to the farmer that he go in and do somebody up. That isn't the point. All that I am modestly suggesting to you is that you break into your own house and live there. And I want you to examine very critically the character of the tenants who have been occupying it. It is a very big house and very few people have been living in it; and the rent has been demanded of you, and not of them. You have paid the money which enabled them to live in your own house and dominate your own premises.

I regard this campaign as I regarded the last one, and the one before the last, and every campaign in which people have taken part since the world began, as simply a continued struggle to see to it that the people were taken care of by their own government. And my indictment against the tariff is that it represents special partnerships and does not represent the general interest. It is a long time since tariffs were made by men who even supposed that they were seeking to serve the general interest, because—as I think my friend, Congressman Hughes, will bear me out in saying—tariffs are not made by the general body of the members of either house of Congress. They have in the past been made by very small groups of individuals in certain committees of those houses, who even refused information to their fellow members as to the basis upon which they had acted in framing the schedules. One of the gentlemen who have been most conspicuously connected with this thing has in recent years prudently withdrawn from public life. I mean the one-time senior Senator from Rhode Island, Mr. Aldrich. I, at least, give Mr. Aldrich the credit of having had a large weather eye. He saw that the weather was changing in Rhode Island—even in Rhode Island as well as in the rest of the Union; that men who had long known that he was imposing upon them felt that the limit had been reached and they were not going to be imposed upon any longer. They saw that he wasn't even doing what he pretended to do, namely, to serve the special interests of Rhode Island, because he was serving only some of the special interests of Rhode Island and not all of them. You cannot go into a game like that without narrowing and narrowing and narrowing the circle of interest, until presently you will not think about anything but one particular individual interest. The only way you can conduct politics is in widening circles, not in narrowing circles, and these gentlemen have been trying to conduct it in ever narrowing circles which centered about particular interests, whose maneuvers in politics we are painfully familiar with. Every time we get on the platform, therefore, we put on our war paint and say we are in this thing to see that everybody is considered a member of the great firm of the United States of America when we transact business.

Now, there are various questions which you gentlemen ought to realize are pending, questions that directly concern the farmer of this country. The tariff intimately concerns the farmer of this country. It makes a great deal of difference to you that Mr. Taft the other day vetoed the steel bill. It makes a difference to you in the cost of practically every tool that you use upon the farm; and it is very significant, or ought to be very significant, to you that a Democratic House of Representatives has just passed the steel tariff reduction bill over the President's veto—a thing I am informed is unprecedented in the history of the country; that a house should have passed two tariff measures, the wool measure and the steel measure, over the veto of the President. Why? Because those gentlemen know that they are pushing this thing forward against some of the most powerful combined interests of this country and that they are under bonds to represent the people of the United States and not the special parties in it.

Tariff measures are not measures for the merchant merely, and the manufacturer. The farmer pays just as big a proportion of the tariff duties as anybody else. Indeed, sometimes when we are challenged to say who the consumer is as contrasted with the producer, so far as the tariff is concerned, I am tempted to answer, "the farmer," because he does not produce any of the things that get any material benefit from the tariff, and he consumes all of the things which are taxed under the tariff system.

Now, there is another matter. You know we are digging a tremendous ditch across the Isthmus of Panama. It is predicted by the engineers in charge of that colossal enterprise that we shall be able to open it to the ships of the world by the year 1915. What interest have you in opening it to the ships of the world? We don't own the ships of the world. By a very ingenious process, which I would not keep you standing in the hot sun long enough to outline, the legislation of the United States has destroyed the merchant marine of the United States. The chief road by which your crops travel to the Orient is through the Suez Canal. They don't go around by the Pacific. Most of your maps do not show you the short road to the Orient, because they are spread out flat. If you will get a globe and draw a circle around the globe you will see that your short road is through the Suez Canal, not across the Pacific, and that the western farmer therefore has to ship his crops across the continent in order to reach the ships that are to take that road. And when his crops reach the port, do they find American ships waiting for them? Not at all. In most years not a single ship carrying the American flag goes through that canal carrying freight. Some ships carry the American flag through that canal, but they are mostly private yachts. A friend of mine who has just traveled around the world told me that he did not see the American flag once between New York and Hong Kong—going by way of the canal—until he reached the Island of Ceylon, and then he saw the flag of Mr. James Gordon Bennett's yacht. And if the shipowners of other nations carry your grain and cargoes, they are going to carry them by routes and to markets which suit them, not the routes and the markets which are chosen by you. One of the great objects in cutting that great ditch across the Isthmus of Panama is to allow farmers who are near the Atlantic to ship to the Pacific coast by way of the Atlantic ports, to allow all the farmers on what I may standing here call this half of the continent to find their outlet at the ports of the Gulf or the ports of the Atlantic seaboard, and then to have coastwise steamers carry their products down around through the canal and up the Pacific coast, or down the coast of South America.

Now at present there are no ships to do that. And one of the bills pending, just passed by Congress—passed I believe yesterday by the Senate as it had passed the House—provides for free tolls for American ships[2] through that canal and prohibits any ship from passing through that canal which is owned by any American railroad company. You see the object of that, don't you? We don't want the railroads to compete with themselves because we understand that kind of competition. We want water carriage to compete with land carriage, so as to be perfectly sure that you are going to get better rates around by the canal than you would across the continent.

The farmers of this country are in my judgment just as much concerned in the policy of the United States with regard to that canal as any other class of citizens in the United States. Probably they are more concerned than any other one class of citizens. And what I am most desirous to see is the farmers of the United States coming forward as partners in the great national undertakings and take a wide national, nay, international, view of these great matters, feeling all the pulses of the world that beat in the great arteries of commerce and are part of the pulse of their own life and prosperity. Everything that is done in the interest of cheap transportation is done directly for the farmer as well as for other men. So that you ought not to grudge the millions poured out for the deepening and opening of old and new waterways.

Then there is another thing you ought to be deeply interested in that is in the program of the great party I belong to. That is the parcels post. This is the only civilized country in the world whose government does not see to it that every man has an express agency at his own door. It is the only government in the world that does not see to it that rates established by the government and facilities established by the government enable men to ship their goods, large and small, as they please from one end

[2] Actually, free tolls only for American ships in the coastwise trade.

of the continent to the other. We have no parcels post until you reach the ports, and from the ports to the other side of the Atlantic you can have parcels post rates, but you can't have them inside the United States. Because—may I conjecture the reason?—because there are certain express companies which object.

Now, I move that the objections of all private enterprises be overruled. I move that we establish a parliamentary procedure by which they will not even be considered; not in order that men who have made legitimate investments of capital may not have their proper return, but in order that they may not look to the government for their proper return. The trouble with the business of the United States under the tariff is that men think they can't make money without the assistance of the government. And as long as you allow them to think that, they keep every mother's son of us tied to the apron strings of the old grandmother sitting in the Capitol at Washington. Now, for my part, I am free and twenty-one, and I don't want any assistance of the government to enable me to make a living. You will say that I am not in a protected industry. I suppose that public office and public oratory are not protected industries, but they are a great drain on the capital of the people investing in them, and especially when you speak outdoors, a great drain on the physical constitution. But I want at every turn of every argument that I make of this nature to say that the legitimate business enterprises of this country have absolutely nothing to fear provided they will stand on their own bottoms; but that they have everything to fear if all they have under them is the prop of a tax which everybody is obliged to pay in order that they may be able to conduct their business—and I believe that that is the just principle of government.

There is another matter in which I am deeply interested. There are only three lines devoted to it in the Democratic platform, but there are no lines devoted to it in the Republican platform; and there are so many lines in the Bull Moose platform[3] that I haven't found it yet. It is a Sabbath day's journey through that program. If there are such lines I have not reached that station yet. But in the Democratic platform there are three lines in which the party declares it to be its duty to devote such funds of the national government as it may constitutionally devote to such purposes to the promotion of industrial, agricultural, and vocational education.

The specific meaning of that part of the platform is this: You know that in our universities there is stored up no end of infor-

[3] The Progressive platform.

mation which would be extremely useful to the farmer, if the farmer could only get at it. We can't let the farmer leave the fields and come to the university to get the information because we would starve in the meantime. But we can organize matters in such a fashion that the university will carry the information to the farmer; and it is our business to see that the chemistry of soils, all the investigation that has been going on in the world of science for a generation and more, in the proper rotation of crops, all the information which has been gathered with regard to the proper time and method of planting certain crops and the adaptation of certain crops to certain soils—all questions which have been exhaustively studied in the universities—should be carried to the farms and the men on the farms given free use of these accumulations of knowledge.

There is a bill pending in the House now for the purpose of beginning this system of what may properly be called university extension to the farm. Congressman Hughes tells me that it is pending and under consideration this very day in the House of Representatives—showing that the men in the House are not waiting until you elect national officers on their platform. They are going ahead with their duty now because our platform is not molasses to catch flies. It means business. It means what it says. It is the utterance of earnest and honest men who intend to do business along those lines and who are not waiting to see whether they can catch votes with those promises before they determine whether they are going to act upon them or not. Because the American people are now taking notice in a way in which they never took notice before, and gentlemen who talk one way and vote another are going to be retired to a very quiet and private retreat. So that when we speak of vocational education, when we speak of assistance to those lads who want to learn how to do scientifically and carefully the things that they are attempting to do, we are speaking of that whereof we know and that which we intend to do, for let me say—in this American audience it can be said without embarrassment—that America is very much behind some of her chief competitors in the commercial world in the manner in which she prepares her people to earn their living by skilled work.

There is one label that I often see on goods sold in our shops that makes me blush a little bit. That label is "Made in Germany." Why should that be a commendation? Why should you prefer to buy something made in Germany rather than something made in the United States? The only conceivable reason is that you believe that the hands that made that in Germany were better trained than the hands that made the similar article in the United States. And what I don't like to admit, but must admit, is that in some instances that is true. We don't give our lads a chance to learn how to do the work as well as it is done in Germany, because the German government long ago saw the signs of the times, saw that we must live by science, by knowledge, by skill, by the infinite dexterity of our hands, and that if they were to be masters in the world of commerce they must also have supremacy in the world of knowledge.

Now America has been trusting to her native capacity, to her native wits, and she has had so much of them that she has been able to trust to them for a long time, but the world is getting a little more difficult. Competition is becoming a little more strenuous. You can't do things now with the flat hand. You must do it with the skillful touch of the finger, and America like Germany must see to it that her young men are skilled workmen. She must see to it that when they go into a vocation they go into it with the knowledge of its tasks and the skill to address themselves to its tasks. And that affects the farmer just as it affects anybody else. We must carry the university to the farm.

Not only that, but there is something else. The farmer is interested in the size and variety of the markets into which the merchants of the United States enter. You know that we have not established ourselves in foreign markets very successfully as yet, as compared with competitors, because we have been so complacently content with the domestic market. We have been complacently content with the domestic market because by ingenious legislation we were making the prices of the domestic market most inviting. And if we could get all the money we wanted out of the pockets of our neighbors there was no particular interest in stirring our brains to find what pockets we could get it out of on the other side of the world. But America has so prospered! She is now so productive of almost everything that the human race uses that she has got too much to sell to herself. If prosperity is not to be checked in this country we must broaden our borders and make conquest of the markets of the world. That is the reason why America is so deeply interested in the question of which I have already spoken—the merchant marine, and that is also the reason why America is so much interested in breaking down, wherever it is possible without danger to break it down, that dam against which all the tides of our prosperity have banked up, that great dam which runs around all our coasts and which we call the protective tariff. I would prefer to call it the restrictive tariff. I would prefer to call it the tariff that holds us back. I should prefer to call it the tariff that hems us in, the tariff that chokes us, the tariff that smothers us, because the great unmatched energy of America is now waiting for a field greater than America itself in which to prove that Americans can take care of themselves.

I don't want to belong to a crowd that can't take care of themselves. After a while if you keep on with this tariff business we will have to have a special board of guardians to look after the United States. Now, we have tried one board of guardians in Jersey. I speak this with bated breath, because a distinguished member of that board[4] lives not so very far from here and used to have a great deal to do with the thoughtful protection of this public resort, but nevertheless I am frank to profess my belief that New Jersey not so very long ago used to be looked after by a very particular board of guardians, and they saw to it that their friends were taken care of, as guardians always do. Guardians have not a large imagination. Guardians have not a large liberality. Guardians attend to business, and I don't want to see the United States any longer in the hands of guardians.

There was a time, ladies and gentlemen, not many years ago, when I would have uttered sentiments like these with a certain degree of heat; because I would have known—I would have felt, at any rate—that I was against an almost irresistible force. But I don't feel the least heat now. We have got them on the run now, and the resistance is very little. The friction is going to come when they try to put on brakes and try to stop. There is no heat in the business now; there is hopeful confidence that the people of the United States at last realize their opportunity, know what it is they want, and are out to get it. I have never known anything like the awakening that has occurred in the United States in recent years. It is just as if we had all been taking a long and comfortable sleep, with sometimes very disturbing dreams. We would wake up once in a while in a nightmare and say, "Who is this sitting on my chest?" And then we would turn over and go to sleep again, and at last we waked up and found there was somebody sitting on our chests. And now we have come entirely to the consciousness of the new day. There are not going to be any more nightmares. It is going to be daytime all the time, and somebody is going to be on the lookout all the time to see that this thing does not happen again. And what we are trying for in this campaign is merely this: Who of you, how many of you, which of you, have enlisted for the fight? I believe that it is going to be one of those general recruitments when you won't need to

4 David Baird.

have recruiting officers. I was talking to a friend the other day who said, "We must go round and form clubs." I said, "My dear boy, they are forming themselves." They don't have to have presidents and secretaries and constitutions. Every group you meet on the street corner is a club, and somewhere about their clothes they have got a club, and the men that need to watch the weather are the men for whom that club is reserved.

I believe that there is going to be a great, handsome, peaceful, hopeful revolution on the fifth day of November 1912,[5] and that after that revolution has been accomplished men will go about their business saying, "What was it that we feared? We feared chains and we have won liberty. We feared to touch anything for fear we should mar it, and now everything wears the bright face of prosperity. And we know that the right is also the profitable thing, and that nobody can serve a nation without also serving himself."[6]

T MS (C. L. Swem Coll., NjP), with corrections from the complete text in the *Trenton Evening Times*, Aug. 16, 1912.
[5] The date of the general election.
[6] There is a WWhw outline of this speech, with the composition date of Aug. 11, 1912, in WP, DLC.

To Anthony Geronimo[1]

My dear Mr. Geronimo: [Sea Girt, N. J.] August 16, 1912.

I am very much obliged to you for your frank letter of July 20th,[2] in which you say that some of your fellow Italian citizens have misgivings as to my attitude upon the immigration of Italians and other Southern Europeans, and I take the greatest pleasure in answering it. I am glad that your investigation has satisfied you that my view is one of friendliness and welcome to America of the many thousands of worthy Italians who are among our most useful and most respected citizens.

The Democratic party would not, without forgetting its very origin, advocate an illiberal policy in the matter of immigration. The party may almost be said to have originated in opposition to the Alien and Sedition Laws, by which the Federalist party sought to all but shut the doors against naturalization and at the same time silence the criticism of our own people against their government. America has always been proud to open her gates to everyone who loved liberty and sought opportunity, and she will never seek another course under the guidance of the Democratic party. I am in hearty accord with the ancient faith and practice of the party that has honored me by nominating me for President.

There must be regulation of immigration. Criminals must not be admitted. Those who are diseased or defective must be excluded, in order to safeguard the physical integrity of our people. Neither can we receive those who are unable to support themselves. And we should see to it that those who come are not unfitted to enter into the life of the country.

The necessary limits have been recognized again and again in such legislation. There was a time when, through the efforts of steamship companies of men who wished to bring over those whom they could at once use and impose upon, there were brought into the country by the thousands men who it was demoralizing to receive. But timely legislation stopped that. Sound and honest men and women out of every one of the great European stocks, who come of their own volition and make permanent homes for themselves, are welcome amongst us; no one can justly criticise our laws if only those who are sound and honest are admitted. Debased men and men of an unserviceable kind may come out of any race or stock; but America has enriched her genius, has made it various and universal, as she has renewed herself out of the ancient peoples from Norway to Italy and the rich lands of the Mediterranean who have made the literature and history of the world.

Cordially and sincerely yours,   Woodrow Wilson.[3]

TCL (WP, DLC).

[1] Of Stamford, Conn., president of the Italian American Association of Connecticut and operator of a chain of theaters in that state.

[2] A. Geronimo to WW, Aug. 12, 1912, TLS (WP, DLC).

[3] Wilson used most of this letter for a statement circulated in the foreign-language press. A WWsh copy of the statement is in WP, DLC.

To Oswald Garrison Villard

Personal.

My dear Mr. Villard: Sea Girt, N. J. August 17, 1912.

I thank you for your letter of August fourteenth and shall prepare the statement for the colored people just as soon as possible. Today I am overwhelmed for it is Jersey Day.

There will be no trouble about delaying committing myself in the matter of the Navy. You made a great impression on me the other day about it.

In haste,

Cordially and sincerely yours, Woodrow Wilson

TLS (O. G. Villard Papers, MH).

To Eugene Noble Foss

My dear Governor Foss: Sea Girt, N. J. August 17, 1912.

I am very much obliged to you for your considerate and candid letter of yesterday.[1] I may say to you very frankly that I do not think that it would be best to bring the woman suffrage question into the national campaign, so far as we are concerned. It is not a national question but a state question.

So far as it is a state question, I am heartily in favor of its thorough discussion and shall never be jealous of its submission to the popular vote. My own judgment in the matter is in an uncertain balance, I mean my judgment as a voting citizen.

With warm regard,

Cordially and sincerely yours,   [Woodrow Wilson]

CCL (WP, DLC).

[1] E. N. Foss to WW, Aug. 15, 1912, TLS (WP, DLC). Foss wrote that "a great deal of pressure" was being placed on him by representatives of the woman suffrage movement in Massachusetts to learn Wilson's position on that question. He was writing privately to ask Wilson whether he expected to speak out on woman suffrage and what reply he wished him, Foss, to make to inquiries. Foss himself believed that the question should be submitted to popular vote in Massachusetts.

To Charles Sumner Hamlin

My dear Mr. Hamlin: Sea Girt, N. J. August 17, 1912.

I hope that you will never apologize for taking up my "valuable time" on any subject of importance. I am sincerely obliged to you for your letter of August first and shall turn to it again from time to time because I feel that I need instruction upon the all-important question of banking and currency.

Cordially and sincerely yours,   Woodrow Wilson

TLS (C. S. Hamlin Papers, DLC).

To Edwin Bird Wilson

My dear Mr. Wilson: Sea Girt, N. J. August 17, 1912.

I thank you sincerely for your letter of the fourteenth with the valuable list enclosed and I shall take pleasure in acting upon the matter at the earliest possible time.

In haste,

Cordially and faithfully yours,   Woodrow Wilson

TLS (received from Ethel Wilson Fruland).

A News Report of a Jersey Day Address at Sea Girt

[*Aug. 17, 1912*]

WILSON HAILED BY JERSEYMEN

Sea Girt, N. J., Aug. 17.—Governor Woodrow Wilson was acclaimed by his home folks today—by the men and women of New Jersey whom he has so signally served, and who are now earnestly engaged in the struggle to raise him to new honors and to share with the whole Union the blessings that he has helped to bestow upon the people of his own State. Hailed by thousands of his friends and neighbors as the next President of the United States, the Governor repaid the compliment with the most earnest address of his campaign.

He talked of New Jersey and of the transformation that had come over its affairs in two short years through the power of the aroused conscience of the people, but to the history his hearers listened, as they sincerely believed, as to a prophecy of the larger work that their leader would soon be called upon to perform in the wider arena of the nation.

Solemnly and soberly he warned them that the invidious influences of bossism and corporation control which had held revel in their Capitol so short a time ago, were plotting diligently to return there so soon as the vigilance of the people and their public officers should be relaxed. Militantly the Governor described the old fight, and as if yearning for the fray at Washington, laid down the simple rules by which the foe in the jungle had been routed.

For the first time Governor Wilson dealt seriously for a moment with the new Progressive party, and it was in a way to make the hearers gasp at his candor and courage. Speaking of the old order of things in New Jersey, before the Democratic party had shown itself an unbossed progressive, militant party of the people, he had referred to the hopelessness that had seized upon the citizens of the State, their despair of achieving reform.

"You know the force that is underneath this new party, the so-called Progressive party," he continued. "It is the discontent with the regular parties of the United States. The people have tired of going up blind alleys; they want to find an open way out."

Lest his words might be misconstrued as an indorsement of the belief that the new party was justified or necessary, the Governor later amplified the statement and pointed out that the Democratic party now held greater hope for genuine progressives than the new party, or any other.

"What has happened is this," he said, "the independent and

progressive forces of the country have utterly failed to get control of the Republican party, but have absolutely proved their ascendancy and their entire control within the Democratic party, and the people have found that they could make use of the Democratic party as a proper medium of their purposes."

The whole tone of the Governor's address was aggressive. He assailed the stupidity of short-sighted men of affairs who opposed the progress of the times; he mercilessly attacked the "arch-conservatives who fervidly praise the Constitution of the United States and of the State while distorting those documents to serve their selfish aims and who play hide and seek behind them while betraying the people whom they are supposed to serve." He predicted that the so-called radicalism of our day would sweep such men from the stage, for which they had only themselves and their crooked games to thank.

Printed in the *Philadelphia Record*, Aug. 18, 1912.

Remarks to Democratic Women[1] at Sea Girt

[[Aug. 17, 1912]]

I am unaffectedly embarrassed in my present position, because no man can claim to speak with the charm with which a woman speaks, and, after all, I fired my shot to-day, and I had only one cartridge.

When the women, who are in so many respects at the heart of life, begin to take an interest in politics, then you know that all the lines of sympathy and intelligence and comprehension are going to be interlaced in a way which they have never been interlaced before, so that our politics will be of the same pattern with our life. This, it seems to me, is devoutly to be wished.

Now, if I were to make a political speech to the ladies I would perhaps appeal to them, as my distinguished friend, Senator Martine, is accustomed to do, on the cost of living. They are in contact with some parts of the cost of living men know nothing about, because the men, thank God, don't have to determine their own fashions. We are dressed by our tailors, and sometimes very grotesquely dressed, whereas the ladies have to exercise their taste, and they sometimes exercise a great deal of it. Women do the purchasing; they do the skimping; they do the fearful planning which is necessary in these days of tremendous cost to adjust our incomes to our lives.

We talk a great deal about the cost of meat and the cost of potatoes, &c., but we don't buy a pound of meat or a peck of potatoes once in a month, we men don't.

And so, when the women come into politics they come in to show us all those little contacts between life and politics on account of which I, for myself, rejoice that they have come to our assistance.

Printed in the *New York Times*, Aug. 18, 1912.
    [1] A delegation led by Florence Jaffray (Mrs. J. Borden) Harriman of New York.

To Mary Allen Hulbert

Dearest Friend,   University Club [New York] 17 Aug., 1912

That was a *real* letter,[1]—and how glad I was to get it! It was like old times,—like a talk as we threaded the steep path to the South Shore. It had your old play and variety and irresponsibility in it. Perhaps Nantucket can't work the old *poetic* charm upon you that Bermuda used to work, but it is working a charm of its own, and is bringing you back to yourself again! I am grieved, deeply grieved to know that Mrs. Allen is failing. You know, of course, with how much genuine affection and admiration I regard her. I was pleasing myself with thoughts of the haven into which she had at last run, the dear gentle, brave soul, and of how she could now *enjoy* her beloved daughter, in whom she lives, whose days of bondage are over, and whom she must so rejoice to see renewing her vigour, her charm, her vivid contact with everything about her! To see the daughter for whom all these years she has agonized and whom in her gentle way she has shielded now at last *free*, the old light returning to her eyes, must give her deep peace and joy. Ah, how I hope she may linger and enjoy it all! As for what you write of yourself (please always write of yourself,—nothing is too trivial, as you tell it, with unconscious self-revelation) you are as true a Democrat (I've got in the habit of writing it with a capital, though I very well know that you belong to no party, but were *born* so) as God ever made! *I'd* like to shake hands with the little Irishman in the ship, too, and with the cheery expressman, and all your other friends among the plain folk; and tell them how intensely I share their admiration of you and their instinctive impulse to be your champion. What will you take for more letters of the same kind? They are a perfect delight to me, and strike into the confusion and meaningless bustle of these distracting days like music across noise and empty chatter. They remind me of quiet talks—quiet and yet full of laughter and gay comradeship—and the give and take that makes us so *sympatica* when we are together. Send them to me as often as you can (it is delightful to hear that it is a pleasure to you to write them,—I had begun to fear it was not)—Heaven bring you to the mood every week of your life! They may save my life, by taking the strain off and letting sheer pleasure in! I have come in to the club here to be alone. My sixteen keepers sent one of their number in with me this evening, the representative of the Associated Press, an old pupil of mine at Princeton,[2] to keep an eye on me, but promised not to tell anyone *else*, provided they themselves did not lose sight of me, where I had run to cover. I shall sleep 'no end' to-morrow, and return to Sea Girt to-morrow evening. I am very well,—astonishingly well, and shall easily keep my elasticity if my *real* friends will keep in constant touch with me and not abandon me to the public. Most affectionate messages to Allen and Mrs. A.   Your devoted friend   Woodrow Wilson

ALS (WP, DLC).
  [1] It is missing, as are all of her letters during the months covered by this volume.
  [2] David Lawrence, Princeton 1910.

From William Jennings Bryan

My Dear Gov,   En route Aug [1]8 [1912]
    You have probably seen my article[1] on your letter. While I would have preferred to have you more specific in your treatment of issues still most of the Democrats are not as exacting as I am and I think it is quite favorably rec'd. But my object in trespassing again upon your time is to say that I hope you will not construe our platform to endorse a large navy. It was not so construed in the committee. I notice that some of the members have tried to construe it to mean two batt[l]eships—that is a forced construction. I think the less said about the navy the better[.] I dont think the average man pays much attention to it.
    Dont count on holding the *reactionaries*—they are going to Taft; our only hope is in *holding our* progressives and in winning progressive Republicans. There is where I can render you the largest service—that is why I think I can do most good in the Middle West. You know my personal friend T. H. Birch of Burlington. I may send you some personal messages through him. Am glad to report a very friendly sentiment toward you out here. With regards to the family I am
                                          Yours truly   W. J. Bryan

P. S. I see *continued signs* of defection along the line I mentioned

ALS (WP, DLC).
  [1] "Gov. Wilson's Speech of Acceptance," *The Commoner*, XII (Aug. 16, 1912), 1.

From William Frank McCombs

My dear Governor: New York, Aug 19, 1912

I enjoyed your visit yesterday more than I can tell you. I am in about the same condition to-day as the past few days.

I was disappointed in not seeing Colonel House today. The presence of a guest at his house, who had arrived from a long distance, prevented him from coming. I shall not be able to see him before I go away.

Believe me, with highest regards,
                    Yours Sincerely,   Wm F. McCombs.

HwLS (WP, DLC).

A News Report of a Riotous Affair

[Aug. 20, 1912]

BULL MOOSE PARTY USELESS, SAYS WILSON

Whatever Need There Was for It Was Met, He Says, by the Baltimore Convention.

TALKS TO 10,000 GERMANS

Supplementing his declaration of Saturday[1] that the Bull Moose Party was born of a feeling that the people had gone into blind alleys often enough in following the old political leadership and were determined to open a new road for themselves, Gov. Woodrow Wilson declared yesterday before 5,000 German picnickers at Schuetzen Park, near Hoboken, that a battle was fought at Baltimore which left the Democratic Party free from the bosses and made it an organized force capable of carrying out every just demand of the people.

Gov. Wilson held that the Bull Moose Party, while it might have been considered to be necessary before the Baltimore Convention, was rendered useless and unnecessary by that convention, and was not likely, for that very reason, to menace his own party's success at the polls in November.

"Nobody owns me and the men on the ticket with me," said Gov. Wilson. "I not only have not made a promise to any man, but no man has dared to ask me to make a promise. My ears are free, therefore, to hear the counsels of my fellow-citizens. I am entering upon this campaign not only with hope of victory, but with an absolute confidence. I know that the people of this country have determined to take possession of their own affairs, in order that their own thoughts may be translated into the affairs of government."

Gov. Wilson had a chat yesterday morning with Charles F. Grasty, publisher of The Baltimore Sun, who brought him enthusiastic assurances of a clean sweep in Maryland. In the afternoon he went to Schuetzen Park, at Union Hill, as the guest of the Plattdeutsch Volksfest Vereen [Verein], a charitable organization of 10,000 members, which was holding its thirty-eighth annual outing, and in the evening he came to New York to look over for the first time since he became a candidate the headquarters of the Democratic National Committee and the Campaign Committee. . . .

Gov. Wilson's appearance at Union Hill before the German picnickers was the signal for an outburst of applause that lasted half an hour and afterward broke loose at such frequent intervals that the Governor was unable to go ahead with the speech he had intended to make. Four German bands intervened so often that the Governor was finally driven in defeat from the platform. He arrived at Schu[e]tzen Park at 4:30 P.M. . . .

"I have sometimes protested against speaking of German-Americans and Irish-Americans," commenced Gov. Wilson, "because"—but at that point a German band in a far distant corner of the grounds began its blare, and the Governor simply had to wait.

"It seems to me we might as well have no hyphenated Americans," the Governor explained between cheers and interruptions, "because after you have gone through the catalogue those of us who are left constitute a comparatively small number, and if you are going to give special labels to the majority of Americans, how are you going to label the minority?

"It is merely a question of a comparative length of time when any of us came from the older countries to this side of the water, and I want to say that it seems to me America has been peculiarly enriched by the admixture of blood, which constituted her the country that she is.

"America has never grown old. America is for the world in 1912 just exactly what she was in the days of her settlement. I have great admiration for your distinguished German Emperor, and yet at the same time I know why you came to these shores. You came to seek a free field for your energies that you realized could be obtained nowhere where government is bound by the restrictions of classes. It is that America stands for in the view of the world just as she did at her beginning.

"Our responsibility is to see that America is the country she is supposed to be by those who have not yet come to it. We have to ask ourselves, is this a country where every man may become anything his gifts and energies make possible? If this is a free field are we keeping it free? If this is the home of political liberty are we seeing to it that political liberty is unspoiled? If we are not we are not true Americans.

"It is just about two years since I began my campaign for Governor in New Jersey, and I remember that my first audiences looked at me with a very critical eye and seemed to say: 'Does this academic person know what he is talking about?' By degrees, I am proud to say, it began to dawn upon them that perhaps he did know what he was talking about and that perhaps if he were given a chance he had just so little experience in politics that he would actually undertake to do what he said he would undertake to do.

"These men who knew the inside of politics said 'it is not possible.' It seemed to me that time, and it seems to me now, that the inside of politics is so much smaller than the outside that all that is required is for the people outside to storm the inside and they will get what they want.

"I am not use[d] to competing with a band," Gov. Wilson said when the music became intolerably loud, "but the band quite fully expresses my own feeling of affairs. A band is not intellectual, but it is very spiriting. It affects the emotions, and I am ready to follow a band—after the fifth of November."

Printed in the *New York Times*, Aug. 20, 1912.
  1 In his Jersey Day speech at Sea Girt.

To Raymond Blaine Fosdick

My dear Fosdick: Sea Girt, N. J. August 21, 1912.

I learned with deep pleasure, the other evening, that it was possible you might be generous enough to take some part in the management of my campaign at Headquarters. If you could find it possible, in your generosity, to act as secretary of the Finance Committee and auditor, I know how greatly it would aid Mr. Wells, the Treasurer, and how safe he would feel in his reliance on you. I should myself feel greatly honored that a former pupil, who has so distinguished himself in a position of trust, should turn to me at this time.

        Cordially and sincerely yours,   Woodrow Wilson

TLS (WP, DLC).

From Maurice F. Lyons

Dear Governor Wilson: New York, Aug. 21, 1912.

Mr. McCombs has had two or three very bad spells since he wrote you. He is still in bed and is weak. His doctors do not give him any definite assurances as to when he will be able to return; one says three weeks, one says at least four, and the other makes no definite statement.

To-day he dictated to me this statement for you:

"I am doing the very best I can, but the rapidity of my recovery has thus far been disappointing. I think it may be prejudicial to the cause if the public get the idea that I am to return within a certain time, inasmuch as many people might defer taking up pressing matters with headquarters until that time. I am under the best of treatment, but in my condition will not dare to predict when I can get back—I sincerely trust soon enough to be of service to you." Yours sincerely, Maurice Lyons,
Secy.

ALS (WP, DLC).

From Garrett Droppers

Personal

Dear Governor Wilson: Williamstown, Mass. Aug. 21, 1912

I have delayed replying to your letter largely because I was in doubt what to say. One man, however, who had just returned from a meeting with you said to me: "Governor Wilson asked me what I thought of his speech of acceptance and my courage failed me. I told him I liked it. It is the first lie I ever told." He added that if the Hearst papers did not support you it was your fault as he had warned you three weeks ago. Governor Foss said "I know that Gov. Wilson's managers are frightened to death for fear they will lose the Hearst support."

Now all this (and more) struck me the wrong way. If you want the support of the Hearst papers do what you can honorably to get it. If the terms cannot stand the test of honor and publicity then do not let the managers of the campaign tell anybody that they are frightened for fear of losing that support.

About three years ago you spoke at Delmonico's before a Williams' alumni gathering (you will remember the occasion)[1] on the subject of a college education. You then compared your feelings with those of Pres. Garfield by saying you felt like Vesuvius looking down (at him) on the smiling plains below. Well that described my feelings precisely. If I were in your place I should let Vesuvius smoke a little. It looks now (though I know nothing definitely about it) as though Hearst was going to support Roosevelt. I have not seen a Hearst paper for two weeks. Gov. Foss fears their power. In your place I should clearly make up my mind. I think you can win in spite of Hear[s]t's opposition. I do not like his methods. But I should be clear about it.

I know that you cannot entirely trust Hearst. To me he is an enigma. He is capable of fine things—but almost sinister in others. Perhaps the whole business had better be managed by one of the Committee.

This is strictly *personal*

In haste Yours very sincerely Garrett Droppers

ALS (Governors' Files, Nj).
[1] On February 5, 1909. See the news report printed at Feb. 6, 1909, Vol. 19.

From Edward Mandell House

Dear Governor Wilson: Beverly, Mass. August 21st, 1912.

I want to congratulate you and felicitate with you over your letter of acceptance.

It is altogether the best paper of the kind that has been issued within my memory and seems to me to be a campaign document sufficient for all purposes.

I also want to congratulate you upon your decision not to go into Maine before the state elections. If you made a personal effort there and the democrats failed to win it would have a disquieting effect throughout the country.

I have not been to New York yet for the reason that the weather has been too warm for me to be of any service to the cause there, but within ten days or two weeks I think it will be possible for me to go down and remain practically all the time until the end.

My daughter is to be married here on the fourteenth of September[1] and outside of that I shall make no commitments that will interfere in any way with my endeavors in your behalf.

I would suggest that I might be of some value during the next ten days in Vermont and Maine and I am ready and willing to take hold of those two situations in any way which may seem best. I am already in touch with Vermont and have been urging our friends to make as good a showing there as is possible.

In my opinion, the greatest asset that we have is the scare that Roosevelt is giving the conservative Republicans and I have found that my efforts proselyting prominent Taft adherents have been successful whenever I have been able to show that a vote for Taft is a half vote for Roosevelt.

With kind regards and best wishes, I am

Your very sincere,   [E. M. House]

CCL (E. M. House Papers, CtY).
¹ Janet House married Gordon Auchincloss.

To Edward Mandell House

My dear Friend: Sea Girt, N. J. August 22, 1912.

It is delightful to have you on this side of the water again, and so full of generous enthusiasm about the campaign. I wish Beverly were nearer. I would run up to see you. I shall look forward with eagerness to the time when you can come down to be with us, with your hand beside ours on the steering gear.

I have no doubt that you can be of the greatest help in Vermont and Maine, and they ought to post you from Headquarters as to just what the threads of the pattern are in the present arrangement.

It is delightful that you should have liked and approved the speech of acceptance entirely.

In haste,   Faithfully yours,   Woodrow Wilson

TLS (E. M. House Papers, CtY).

To Willard Saulsbury

My dear Mr. Saulsbury: Sea Girt, N. J. August 22, 1912.

I was late in hearing of the sad thing that happened to you.¹ I know what it must mean to you, and I grieve that you should have received so desperate a blow. My heart goes out to you in deepest sympathy.

Cordially and faithfully yours,   Woodrow Wilson

TCL (W. Saulsbury Papers, DeU).
¹ His mother, Annie Milby Ponder Saulsbury, died in Dover, Del., on August 16.

To Oswald Garrison Villard

Personal.

My dear Mr. Villard: Sea Girt, N. J. August 23, 1912

I have read with amazement Dr. Waldron's version of our conversation.¹ He has certainly given his own translation to it.

I, of course, assured my visitors, as he says, that if elected, I would seek to be President of the whole Nation and would know no differences of race or creed or section, but to act in good conscience and in a Christian spirit through it all. And I also assured him of my confidence, as he says, that even if the President and both Houses of Congress should be Democratic, the negroes had nothing to fear in the way of inimical legislation.

I did not tell him that this was my understanding with the Party leaders, for I have not discussed the matter with them nor did I assure him that if by any accident such legislation should be passed, I would veto it. I would, of course, make no such general promise to anybody about my executive action.

Neither did I give them an assurance about patronage, except that they need not fear unfair discrimination. It distresses me that men cannot quote me correctly.

If you can advise me as to any way in which I could put out a general statement along the line of what I have just written, I would be very glad to act upon your advice, for I want these people to be reassured, though I have never said that I needed their political support or was giving the assurances I have mentioned for the sake of obtaining it. I think that would be an unworthy position to take.

In haste,
   Cordially and sincerely yours, Woodrow Wilson

TLS (O. G. Villard Papers, MH).
 [1] It is printed at Sept. 1, 1912. A news report of this meeting is printed at July 17, 1912, Vol. 24.

To Louis E. Miller

My dear Mr. Miller: Sea Girt, N. J. August 23, 1912.

Confirming our conversation of the other day, I want you to know very definitely what my views are with regard to immigration.

The Democratic party may almost be said to have originated in a defense of the "open door" to immigrants, for one of the things which brought it into life was opposition to the Alien and Sedition laws, forced through Congress by the Federalists in the first years of the government,—and the last years of Federalist power. By the Alien laws they sought so to restrict naturalization as almost to forbid it. I, like other Democrats, have always held liberal views with regard to immigration. I feel that it would be inconsistent with our historical character as a Nation if we did not offer a very hearty welcome to every honest man and woman who comes to this country to seek a permanent home and a new opportunity.

At times, this privilege of settlement and naturalization has been abused. The steamship companies have taken advantage of it of various kinds for their own profit, and men have been brought over who did not come of their own initiative. Conditions arose which made it necessary for Congress to pass laws regulating the matter somewhat strictly and I think that every American, whether born in this country or not, must feel that there may arise from time to time conditions with regard to labor in this country and with regard to the safeguarding of the various interests, both temporary and permanent, when regulation of one kind or another may become necessary. But these things are not inconsistent with the general policy of liberal welcome with which I myself heartily sympathize.

The attitude of the party and the strength of public opinion in this matter was shown in the most interesting way in the matter of the recent abrogation of our treaty with Russia,[1]—the whole country resenting any action on the part of a foreign government which would discriminate against any American on any ground.

Cordially and sincerely yours,   [Woodrow Wilson]

CCL (WP, DLC).
    [1] About this, see WW to H. Bernstein, July 6, 1911, n. 2, Vol. 23.

To Henry Beach Needham

My dear Mr. Needham: Sea Girt, N. J. August 24, 1912.

I have felt obliged recently, because of my absolute preoccupation and because of my desire to center all I have to say upon my speeches, to decline interviews. One or two interviews have been put together by using extracts from my utterances on various occasions, but I have declined to be interviewed.

I remember our journey together with a great deal of interest and pleasure, and it would be very pleasant to see you again, but I feel tied by these circumstances which seem to demand that I should be impartial all around.

Cordially and sincerely yours,   Woodrow Wilson

TLS (U. S. Presidents Papers, MiU-C).

From Josephus Daniels

Dear Governor: New York Aug. 24, '12.

Thirty editors of papers printed in languages other than the English desire to call to see you this day week, Saturday, August 31, at such an hour as would best suit you. They are New York men. Our friend Dr. Herman Bernstein will be with the delegation, and all here feel that it is a matter of importance.

Please write me whether you can see them on Saturday, and if not when. Saturday is the day they much prefer, and I hope you can arrange it.   Sincerely yours,   Josephus Daniels

TLS (WP, DLC).

To Mary Allen Hulbert

University Club [New York]

Dearest Friend,   25 August, 1912

Here I am again in covert at the University Club, and a real covert it is. If I give orders to that effect, no one, not a member of the Club, will be allowed to get at me. Once inside the door, I can hold the world at arm's length,—and what a comfort and respite it is! It's odd to have to run away from home for privacy,—not only to obtain privacy for myself but to obtain it for the dear ones I leave behind me at Sea Girt,—for they are let alone if I am not there. I got to town last evening about 7:30 (accompanied by my keepers) and, after a bite at the station, went to the theatre with [Charles Raymond] Macauley, the *World's* cartoonist, an interesting fellow. The play was "The Merry Countess,"[1] beautiful music and brilliant dancing, but a vulgar plot. It was after midnight when I got to bed; but I made up for lost time and repaired much of the damage of the week by sleeping till two this afternoon. I have just come down from lunch (the dining room is at the top of the house). I shall stay in town till to-morrow about noon,—in covert all to-day, for I have an important speech to study, and to-morrow a conference with the campaign committee to block out my speech-making engagements for the next two months. Of what significance is it, I wonder, that the election is to take place on the fifth of November, Guy Fawkes' Day? Does it mean that some nefarious plot against the government will be thwarted then, as before? There is no doubt *some*thing in precedents! Do not be too confident of the result. I feel that Roosevelt's strength is altogether incalculable. The contest is between him and me, not between Taft and me. I think Taft will run third,—at any rate in the popular, if not in the electoral, vote. The country will have none of him. But just what will happen, as between Roosevelt and me, with party lines utterly confused and broken, is all guess work. It depends upon what the people are thinking and purposing whose opinions do not get into the newspapers,—and I am by no means confident. He appeals to their imagination; I do not. He is a real, vivid person, whom they have seen and shouted themselves hoarse over and voted for, millions strong; I am a vague, conjectural personality, more made up of opinions and academic prepossessions than of human traits and red corpuscles. We shall see what will happen! I am not eager. You remember what I said to you once when we had walked to the South Shore and were sitting together on the sand,—that I would go in for this thing, if I were called on, but that the next President of the United States would have a task so difficult as to be heartbreaking and that I w'd probably sacrifice my life to it if I were elected? That is still the way I feel. Roosevelt never works the heart out of himself—I doubt if he *has* a heart for anybody but himself—but I do, and there are some strains (of responsibility *plus* stupid and corrupt resistance and fight) my heart cannot bear for long together. The business at Princeton nearly did for me. But none of this daunts me or makes me hesitate; and certainly there were never more fine elements or powerful elements of public opinion to use and save one's heart by. It would be a splendid adventure and it would make me solemnly glad to undertake it.

I am perfectly well, still elastic and strong, and happy, *so* happy, in my friends! All join in affectionate messages.

Your devoted friend,   Woodrow Wilson

ALS (WP, DLC).
1 An adaptation by Gladys Unger of Johann Strauss's *Die Fledermaus*, with English lyrics by Arthur Anderson, playing at the Casino Theatre in New York.

Two News Reports

[*Aug. 28, 1912*]

GOV. WILSON AGREES WITH MR. BRANDEIS
Lunch at Sea Girt Together and Discuss Means
of "Accomplishing Industrial Freedom."

SEA GIRT, N. J., Aug. 28.—Louis D. Brandeis came to Sea Girt to-day to talk over with Gov. Wilson some of the things in the Democratic platform and in bills before Congress that are making, as he put it, "toward industrial freedom." He refused to call the new party the Third Party. His parting declaration was one of emphatic opposition to the fundamental ideas of the Bull Moosers.

"I found Gov. Wilson a man capable of broad, constructive statesmanship," he said, "and I found him to be entirely in accord with my own views of what we need to do to accomplish industrial freedom."

Mr. Brandeis came for luncheon and departed three hours later. He stood alongside Gov. Wilson while the Governor declared to a delegation of Italians from Essex County that the immigration conditions he criticised in his history of the American people had been remedied by restrictive legislation immediately after the book was written, so that his much exploited criticisms in no way applied to problems of to-day. . . .

Mr. Brandeis was obviously impressed by Gov. Wilson, and he did not hesitate to say so when he was catching a train back to New York.

"Why did I leave Taft to go to La Follette and then join with the Wilson movement?" he repeated.

"Well, I prefer to express the situation in the terms of parties rather than persons. One would like naturally to be with the party that promises the most progress in the direction of industrial freedom."

"And what did you discuss with Gov. Wilson?"

"Oh, a number of bills. They all had to do with our industries. I am for Wilson because I found him in complete sympathy with my fundamental convictions, which are opposed to the convictions of Mr. Perkins and others of the new party."

"And did you get down to the tariff?"

"No, we had no time to reach that."

"And the Bull Moosers?"

"The new party," said he, "must fail in all of the important things which it seeks to accomplish because it rests upon a fundamental basis of regulated monopoly. Our whole people have revolted at the idea of monopoly and have made monopoly illegal, yet the third party proposes to make legal what is illegal.[1] The important thing to-day, so far as the preservation of our liberty goes, is the industrial relation of man to man. The third party stands out and says that that relation shall be one of absolutism. The party is trying to make evil good, and that is a thing that cannot be done. The only practicable thing is to eliminate the evil and introduce good as a substitute.

"We must undertake to regulate competition instead of monopoly, for our industrial freedom and our civic freedom go hand in hand and there is no such thing as civic freedom in a state of industrial absolutism. Thus the new party in its programme becomes a house divided against itself. There can be no progress for the workingman under an absolutism, and those who are working for the upbuilding of the common man regardless of creed or race or occupation have got to build on the solid foundation of liberty, on which all our Government rests.

"I am extremely sorry to see that so many good men who are seeking only the best things have been misled into following the new party when in Gov. Wilson's candidacy they are confronted with an opportunity such as they have never had before in this country. They can follow a candidate who is absolutely free, who stands for the things that mean industrial liberty, who has no obligations and has made no promises except the promise he has made all his life to do the best he can for the community. We have a wonderful opportunity before us to put Gov. Wilson in office and give him the opportunity of using his fine character and great attainments for the advantage of all."

"Would you favor jail sentences for our trust heads?" Mr. Brandeis was asked.

"Much more important," he answered, "would be some laws that would define what business can do and how it can go ahead. The present laws suppress advance and throttle progress, and Gov. Wilson would go ahead in the right direction."

Mr. Brandeis said he hoped to visit Sea Girt several times more before election.

"Both of us," said Gov. Wilson, discussing his conference with Mr. Brandeis, "have as an object the prevention of monopoly. Monopoly is created by unregulated competition, by competition that overwhelms all other competitions, and the only way to enjoy industrial freedom is to destroy that condition."

With reference to the Sherman anti-trust law, the Governor was asked whether Mr. Brandeis had proposed means of strengthening that law.

"Not so much to strengthen it," replied the Governor, "as to supplement it. We want a law that will assist people in their business instead of tying them up."

The Governor declared that Mr. Brandeis more than any other man he knew had studied "corporate business from the efficiency to the political side."

"I drew him out for my own benefit," remarked Gov. Wilson.

Printed in the *New York Times*, Aug. 29, 1912.

[1] The plank of the Progressive platform on "Business," representing largely a distillation of the thought of Theodore Roosevelt and George W. Perkins, read in part as follows:

"We . . . demand a strong National regulation of inter-State corporations. The corporation is an essential part of modern business. The concentration of modern business, in some degree, is both inevitable and necessary for national and international business efficiency. But the existing concentration of vast wealth under a corporate system, unguarded and uncontrolled by the Nation, has placed in the hands of a few men enormous, secret, irresponsible power over the daily life of the citizen—a power insufferable in a free Government and certain of abuse.

"This power has been abused, in monopoly of National resources, in stock watering, in unfair competition and unfair privileges, and finally in sinister influences on the public agencies of State and Nation. We do not fear commercial power, but we insist that it shall be exercised openly, under publicity, supervision and regulation of the most efficient sort, which will preserve its good while eradicating and preventing its ill.

"To that end we urge the establishment of a strong Federal administrative commission of high standing, which shall maintain permanent active supervision over industrial corporations engaged in inter-State commerce, or such of them as are of public importance, doing for them what the Government now does for the National banks, and what is now done for the railroads by the Inter-State Commerce Commission.

"Such a commission must enforce the complete publicity of those corporation transactions which are of public interest; must attack unfair competition, false capitalization and special privilege, and by continuous trained watchfulness guard and keep open equally all the highways of American commerce.

"Thus the business man will have certain knowledge of the law, and will be able to conduct his business easily in conformity therewith; the investor will find security for his capital; dividends will be rendered more certain, and the savings of the people will be drawn naturally and safely into the channels of trade." Printed in Arthur M. Schlesinger, Jr., and Fred L. Israel (eds.) *History of American Presidential Elections, 1789-1968* (4 vols., New York, 1971), III, 2190-2191.

❖

[*Aug. 28, 1912*]

WILSON TALKS WITH BRANDEIS ON TRUSTS AND IMMIGRATION
GREETS FOREIGNERS

Sea Girt, August 28.—Trust legislation, constructive rather than destructive, and immigration, were among subjects to which Governor Woodrow Wilson gave his attention today. He talked about trusts with Louis D. Brandeis, of Boston, and expressed himself on immigration before a delegation of Italians from Essex County. . . .

The delegation of Italians through their spokesman, Antonio Petroni,[1] told the Governor that those who had seen fit to criticize his views on immigration "had made a mountain out of a mole hill."

"Intelligent Italians," said Mr. Petroni, "prefer to have their own opinion in the matter, and are willing to allow the historian the latitude that writing of impartial history requires."

The Governor, in his response, said:

"In my history, I referred to conditions which did exist when I wrote, and which afterward were corrected by legislation. These abuses were brought about mainly by steamship companies attempting to force immigration, and I believe in legislation that will correct all abuses."

Printed in the Trenton *True American*, Aug. 29, 1912.

[1] Listed as a newspaper correspondent in the Newark city directories of this time. He spelled his name Petrone.

From Oswald Garrison Villard, with Enclosure

My dear Governor: [New York] August 28, 1912.

I thank you for your letter and am much surprised to find that your recollection of the conversation with Mr. Waldron and others differs from their account. May I respectfully suggest that this points to the desirability of having a stenographer present at such interviews as the average man's mind is so fallible that he often inadvertently misquotes, and we all know how difficult it is for three or four persons to have heard a conversation and repeat it a day or two later with anything like accord.

So far as your proposed statement is concerned, I feel very strongly that nothing important can be accomplished among the colored people until we have an utterance from you which we can quote. They not unnaturally mistrust you because they have been told that Princeton University closed its doors to the colored man (and was about the only Northern Institution to do so) during your presidency.[1] They know that besides yourself, both Mr. McAdoo and Mr. McCombs are of Southern birth, and they fear that the policy of injustice and disfranchisement which prevails not only in the Southern States, but in many of the Northern as well, will receive a great impetus by your presence in the White House. Again, as I explained to you, they want some assurance that they will not wholly be excluded from office, office meaning so much to them because the bulk of their race are absolutely deprived of any self-government, even in the smallest matters such as schools and the making of the town ordinances in which they live. I enclose a suggestion which is chiefly the work of Dr. DuBois with certain emendations by me. As much more as you can say in the line of definite statements will, of course, help.

May I add, also, that I find as I go about that the only criticism of your addresses since nomination which seems to be widely held, is that your speeches lack definite proposals. I trust you will forgive my frankness, but I want to be helpful, and lay the situation before you precisely as I see it.

With kind regards,

Sincerely yours,   [Oswald Garrison Villard]

CCL (O. G. Villard Papers, MH).
 1 Actually, he simply kept the door shut. See WW to J. R. Williams, Sept. 2, 1904, Vol. 15.

ENCLOSURE

The time has come when the attitude of the Democratic Party toward Americans of Negro descent may be easily and clearly defined. The Democratic Party as a political organization working for the best governing of men recognizes no distinctions of race or caste among citizens. It asks the votes of citizens not because they are Italian, German or Negro, but because they are Americans. It offers no bribe of office or special class legislation but only the legitimate bribe of good government. If American Negroes desire more equitable tariff taxes, a wider participation of the people in government, a curbing of the sinister political power of accumulated wealth, then they should vote for the Democratic Party and the Party will welcome their support.

On the other hand, no class of rich or poor, black or white, has anything to fear from the triumph of this party. We are not in favor of unfair discriminating laws against any class or race, and we believe that the qualifications for voting should be the same for all men. If ignorance and crime be a bar to the suffrage, it should be just as much a bar to white men as to black.

On this broad platform, without special promises or discrimination of any kind, the Democracy appeals to the Voters of all races represented in our cosmopolitan citizenship. I shall be, if elected, President of the whole nation and treat every citizen according to the spirit of our institutions. I am glad of this opportunity to deny the published reports of many negro newspapers that I am hostile to the colored people, and that if I am elected no colored man will be appointed to office. It would seem as if my record as Governor of New Jersey would forbid anyone misrepresenting me by saying that I will connive at any form of civic wrong or injustice.

CC MS (O. G. Villard Papers, MH).

From Walter Hines Page

My dear Wilson: Garden City, N. Y. August 28, 1912.

As I telegraphed you this morning, I kept Captain White and Dr. Wallace[1] from calling on you today, in spite of your kindness in telegraphing me that you would see them this afternoon. I didn't know until Arthur[2] told me that they had written to you; and, since you have had a full correspondence with them, they have no right to take your time.

But I do heartily hope that you will be able to go to this Conservation Congress, and I am putting the matter now before Mr. McAdoo. It is an important gathering of people, and they have an important following. It is a real occasion, and in no sense a manufactured one, and these are very serious men that have it in hand. The meeting will be in Indianapolis October 1 to 4, and if it be practicable for you to go, I think it would be a good thing to do.[3]

But I say this all on one condition. From something I heard yesterday, I infer that they are inviting Mr. Roosevelt, also. I am not quite sure of the wisdom of your going if he is to be there. Yet this first impression may be wrong. Perhaps his presence may be the best of all reasons why you should go. Of course, the whole meeting is non-partisan and non-political, but he never forgets his brass band. I shall find out today whether he is going, and put all the facts into Mr. McAdoo's hands.

You have to thank me for relieving you of one call. It is a great joy to hear that you are keeping up well under the pressure of the never-ending procession of human beings, great and small.

Very heartily yours,   Walter H. Page

P.S. My impression an hour after dictating this is that T.R's presence, if he go, is all the greater reason why you should *go too*!

TLS (WP, DLC).
    [1] John Barber White, president of the Missouri Lumber and Mining Company and active in many other business enterprises in Kansas City, and Henry Wallace, publisher and editor of *Wallace's Farmer*, Des Moines, Ia. White was president of the National Conservation Congress for 1911-12. Wallace had been president of the organization the preceding year, and both he and Page were members of the executive committee for 1911-12.
    [2] His son, Arthur Wilson Page, associated with him in the publishing business.
    [3] Wilson's speech to the National Conservation Congress is printed at Oct. 3, 1912.

From James Charles Monaghan[1]

My dear Mr. Wilson: Bayonne, N. J. August 30, 1912.

I see no reason to do anything to change my opinion about the campaign. You will have heard, by this time, from Mr. Malone, and Mr. Larkin,[2] about the meeting in Louisville.[3] It was well worth our while to send Mr. Larkin to Louisville. I feel safe in saying that very few Catholics will be found against you when the votes are counted. Some seem to think it a matter of duty to stand by Mr. Taft because of his kindness, so-called kindness, to Catholics in the Philippine Islands. The Catholic papers of the country are with you. The papers influence thousands of votes, while the clergy influence few, if any votes. I am writing to all the Catholic editors to keep their eyes on this so-called Catholic movement. Thus far the papers that I deem strongest, are with you, heart and soul. From the Pacific coast, from St. Paul, Minneapolis in Minnesota, from Milwaukee, Omaha and Kansas City, from Chicago as well as from all parts of the country comes the assurance "we are for Wilson, first, last and *all* the time." To be anything else would be unwise, would be worse than a mistake, would be a blunder. I know these men personally and I know whereof I speak when I say we, you and your friends, have nothing to fear.

I believe I am serving you best when I suggest work for those having your campaign in charge. I believe it will be worth your while, well worth your while, to get Mr. McAdoo or some man who can be counted on to get busy with the Germans. They are a good people, they are a sincere people, they are honest and they can be relied upon on *Election Day*. I believe your campaign committee can do little or better work than to go out among the Germans. I see that the Jews are at work and can be counted on in the cause. . . .

I am trying to get information for you, either directly or through Mr. Malone, about Mr. Smith and his work in this State. It seems to me wise and best for you to take stand not against anybody, but for somebody. I understand that a Mr. Hughes, member of Congress, from Paterson, wants to be Senator. I hear that we are to have several candidates. If Mr. Hughes and Mr. Smith are candidates let them appear at the primaries. It will be wisest and best to let Mr. Smith alone. If we begin to make a martyr of him, he will be helped rather than hindered in his canvass. Mr. Smith is posing as martyr already. His friends are trying to place him as a victim of your hostility. So high have you and your friends held the banner that you can afford to pass on leaving to Mr. Smith and to his friends the words of unkindness unmerited by you and *your* friends. I believe we are to have the greatest campaign since Lincoln's time, and our candidate is far more like what Lincoln was than any man who has appeared in public life in fifty years. Dudley Malone said "our candidate is Lincoln with a college education." I agree with him. We will work away, with the will and the purpose of putting our people in the way *you* want them, *we* want them, to walk. Of the millions of new voters we will get by far the largest share.

Sincerely yours,   J. C. Monaghan

TLS (WP, DLC).

[1] Publicist of Bayonne, N. J., national lecturer for the Knights of Columbus, author of *Is Woodrow Wilson A Bigot?*, published by the Democratic National Committee, 1912.

[2] William P. Larkin, chairman of the New York chapter of the Knights of Columbus and operator of a taxi service in New York City.

[3] The eleventh annual convention of the American Federation of Catholic Societies, held in Louisville August 18-21, 1912.

From Raymond Blaine Fosdick

My dear Dr. Wilson: New York August 30, 1912.

I cannot tell you how much I appreciate your letter of August 21st in regard to the possibility of my serving as Secretary of the Finance Division of the National Democratic Committee. I have already taken the matter up with the directors of my company[1] and I hope shortly to complete arrangements so as to be able to serve in the capacity that has been suggested. I cannot but feel honored by the invitation to participate in a campaign such as yours.

Very cordially yours,   Raymond B. Fosdick

TLS (WP, DLC).

[1] An attempt at humor. He was still commissioner of accounts of the City of New York.

To Moses Edwin Clapp

My dear Senator Clapp: Sea Girt, N. J. August 31, 1912.

You are quite right in assuming that we shall be most happy to cooperate with you in the investigation of the pre-convention campaign funds, and I know that Mr. McCombs will be most willing.

Unhappily, Mr. McCombs is very far from well and is at present in the Adirondacks seeking recuperation. I hope and believe that he will be in fit shape again by the thirtieth of September, and I shall take pleasure in apprising him of your desires just so soon as business can wisely be laid before him. He, and he alone, handled the campaign funds for me prior to the nomination.

Sincerely yours,   [Woodrow Wilson]

CCL (WP, DLC).

A Report by John Milton Waldron

[Sept. 1, 1912]

Several delegations of colored men have waited on Governor Wilson, the Democratic nominee for President. The first delegation reports the result of their interview as follows:

"Mr. Wilson assured us, first of all, that if elected he intended to be a President of the whole nation—to know no white or black, no North, South, East or West, and no home-born or foreign-born, but that he would treat every citizen according to the law—not only the letter, but according to the spirit of the law—and that he would discharge his obligations, his duties of office, in the spirit of Christ, and with justice and fairness to all. In the second place, even if the President and both houses of Congress should be Democratic, he did not believe that any measures inimical to colored people would be passed. He said that it was the understanding with the party leaders that this should be the case, but if by any accident such a measure or measures should be passed he would veto them. In the third place, he gave us to understand that so far as patronage was concerned he could assure us that the colored people would fare as well under his administration as President as they had fared under Republican administrations. In the fourth place, he promised as soon after his formal notification as possible he would get out a statement over his own name to the entire country refuting the falsehoods which are being so indiscriminately circulated against him by most of the colored newspapers and by many of the white papers and magazines of the country relative to his enmity to and hatred of the colored man. We called the governor's attention to the fact that it had already been repeatedly stated that if he became President he would use his power to spread 'Jim Crow' and disfranchisement acts against the colored man and to abolish the Fourteenth and Fifteenth Amendments. He said that these were false statements; that he had no intention of doing any such thing and would frown upon the efforts of any who undertook to promote such acts. In short, he expressed himself as feeling the need of and desiring the colored vote and stated that he was willing to do anything that was right and legal to secure that vote, and that if elected President of the United States the colored people would have no occasion to regret having voted for him."

Printed in *The Crisis*, IV (Sept. 1912), 216-17.

To Mary Allen Hulbert

Century Club [New York]

Dearest Friend,   1 September, 1912

I wonder if the journey from Nantucket to Sea Girt is so round-about and difficult as to puzzle the letters that start from your end, and they lose their way and fail to find me? Or does the post-master who presides over your correspondence know how spirited and spontaneous and interesting they are and impound them, for his own delectation. If he does, there will be vengeance after the fourth of March next, in the event of a certain thing happening! For I am *very* impatient for a letter and have not had one this half-moon. I hope with all my heart that none of you is ill, and that nothing has gone wrong,—which is equivalent to hoping that you have just plain ignored and neglected me! Somehow I feel *more* neglected when all the world, whose letters I do not desire, is writing than I would if no one *else* were paying any attention to me. The exception seems so singular,—becomes day by day more noticeable! Do you refuse to do so common a thing as to write to me,—is *that* the trouble,—does it lack distinction? Don't be so stuck up and exclusive! Come on and join the little procession to Sea Girt. It will not hurt you, and it will delight the poor gentleman who feels so lonely when *every*body is calling *except* his friends.

I have had very sad feelings to-day. Archie Alexander,[1] my personal aide and a very fine fellow, only thirty-two,—a one-time pupil of mine at Princeton and long my personal friend, died, of a most malignant attack of typhoid, last Friday, and was buried to-day. I have just returned from the funeral and am low in my mind. What would I not give for a chat with you, to put me in spirits again,—nothing does it so quickly (another argument for a letter, since I can do no better!). Ellen came up with me, to the ceremony, but has gone back to Sea Girt. I must stay here till evening, when I am to take a train to Buffalo, for two speeches to-morrow (Labour Day). With these speeches the campaign really begins. From this on I shall be almost constantly on the go. There are twenty-five or thirty speeches ahead of me which must be delivered here, there, and yonder over all the great space between us and the tier of States beyond the Mississippi, during the next eight weeks. "Gee whiz, what a pity that is"! I don't mind talking, but I do mind being dragged over half a continent. Would it were smaller! I've had a wretched sick headache for the last two days, due to an ill-behaved digestion, and this afternoon feel dull and stupid; but this is exceptional,—not the dullness and stupidity, but the headache and the indigestion; for I keep singularly well. I've gained seven pounds and a half since I was nominated. I weigh 177½ pounds. I am obviously becoming a person of some weight,—at any rate on the scales. If my days are trying and so full of—everything that fatigues and distracts—as to make them quite overwhelming, they at least fly past with satisfactory rapidity, and it will not be long before I am either elected or bidden to stay quietly at home. I would not dare say which I preferred—when I have a sick headache! All join me in affectionate messages for you all, and I am your waiting and

Devoted friend,   Woodrow Wilson

ALS (WP, DLC).
¹ Archibald Stevens Alexander.

A Luncheon Talk in Buffalo¹

[Sept. 2, 1912]

Gentlemen: There has been one peculiarity of America which perhaps it would be advantageous to change. She has always insisted upon hearing her public men talk and she has not often insisted upon having them act. I am very much more interested in what may follow the fifth of November than I am in what precedes the fifth of November. Because in talking about great national affairs one always feels that the only weight the words bear are the weight that is given to the man who utters them by those who believe in his character, and that words ought to be more thoroughly tested than that.

I have noticed this most interesting circumstance, that no matter how badly a man talks, for example an old soldier, if you feel that he has been through the brunt of battle, if you feel that he has carried his country's cause forward on the field, he is listened to as if he was speaking with the deepest and the most elevated eloquence. It is because you then feel that this is a man who has acted, and the validity of life lies in the action, not in the words. The thing that hampers a candidate for office, if he be conscientious, is that he cannot put up the bluff of making people suppose that he knows the whole thing. The only qualification for office to which I can lay claim for myself is this, that all my life long

I have taken pains to train my mind to understand. I know things when they are stated to me. I am suited to be the center of counsel if men will frankly counsel me, and I have lived long enough to distinguish between those who are frankly counseling me and those who are not. I don't want to put up any bluff, and I can generally distinguish a bluff when I see it. That, I suppose, would be the sort of qualification for office that the soil has to produce crops, that if the right seed is planted the right crop will be produced. So that the period of embarrassment for me when I was running for Governor was when I was asking people to vote for me. I was not in the least embarrassed after I became Governor and was able to tackle some of the gentlemen who didn't trust me.

I have noticed this thing, that as compared with the college politician, some of the gentlemen I have more recently dealt with are amateurs. Because this may be said of the politicians in the field of politics, that they play their hand rather openly. I don't mean all the time, but they are always up to the same job. Now the college politician does it carefully. He plays it very shrewdly, and he has such a gift of speech that he could make black sound as if it were white at any time that he chooses. Because the literary gift is a very dangerous gift to possess if you are not telling the truth, and I would a great deal rather for my part to have a man stumble in his speech than to feel that he was so exceedingly smooth that he had better be watched both day and night.

I am very much complimented that you should have come here to meet me today, and the advantage, I want to say, is wholly mine, because, as I have just intimated, I try to learn by contact with men who know and by intercourse with men who really purpose the best things for the country. Politics in my mind is not a game of seeing particular classes get justice so much as a means of letting all classes realize that justice is the same for all of them. There isn't a particular justice for one class of society and another brand of justice for another class; and the only thing that has retarded, or rather the chief thing that has retarded progressive measures in this country is that some men, and I am afraid some of the most intelligent men, in the country have refused to see that their interest was linked with those policies just as much as the interest of the humblest man in the community. So soon as we see that vision of a common interest, so soon as we can all see that we are all serving a single thing, then the whole path will be open, and we can work together for the betterment of America, as we never have worked in the future. I thank you.

T MS (C. L. Swem Coll., NjP), with minor corrections from the complete text in the *Buffalo Express*, Sept. 3, 1912.
[1] Informal remarks to a group entertained at luncheon in the Hotel Lafayette by Norman E. Mack.

A Labor Day Address in Buffalo[1]

[Sept. 2, 1912]

Mr. Chairman[2] and Fellow Citizens: I feel that it is an honor and a privilege to address an audience like this, and yet I feel, more than the honor of the occasion, the responsibility of it, because I have learned from occupying a responsible executive position that the thing that grips a man most is what he promised the people that he would attempt to do before he was elected.

When I was engaged in the campaign before my election as Governor of New Jersey, I made a good many promises, and I think that a great many people who heard me supposed that it was the usual thing that these promises were made in order to get votes, and that the man who made them would not feel the full responsibility of keeping them after he was elected. I don't know what the reason is—perhaps because I went into politics rather late in life—but I felt that every promise that I made in that campaign I was bound to try to fulfill. No man can promise more than that he will do his best. I had not tried my hand at politics. I did not know, and I told my friends in New Jersey that I did not know, whether I could bring those things to pass or not, but I did tell them that there was one thing I did know: that I would make everybody very uncomfortable if these things were not done. And I did not except the members of my own party. I promised to make the men of the Democratic party, as well as the men of the Republican party, very uncomfortable if the promises of the campaign were not fulfilled; and it was more the dread of discomfort than anything else that brought about the passage of the bills which constituted one of the most extraordinary programs of reform that we have seen in modern times in a single state.

I don't claim any credit for that. I speak of it in order to point a moral which seems to me the most important moral in politics. The only strength I had was that I was known to be, in the circumstances, the spokesman of the people of New Jersey, and the only reason I was dreaded was not that I had offices to give away —for I would not condescend to give an office in order to accom-

[1] Delivered in the afternoon to the United Trades and Labor Council of Buffalo in Braun's Park.
[2] John Clark, president of the United Trades and Labor Council of Buffalo.

plish a political end—but because it was known that all I had to do was to ask the people of New Jersey what they thought, and they would say what they thought. . . .

Why is it that the people of this country are in danger of being discontented with the parties that have pretended to serve them? It is because in too many instances their promises were not matched by their performance, and men began to say to themselves, "What is the use of going to the polls and voting? Nothing happens after the election." Is there any man within the hearing of my voice who can challenge the statement that any party that has forfeited the public confidence has forfeited it by its own non-performance? Very well, then, when I speak to you today I want you to regard me as a man who is talking business. I want in the first place to say that I shall be scrupulous to be fair to those with whom I am in opposition, because there is a great deal to be said for the programs of hopeful men who intend to do things even if they haven't struck upon the right way to do them, and we ought not to divorce ourselves from sympathy with men who want the right things simply because we don't think they have found the way to do them.

I want to speak upon this occasion of course on the interests of the workingman, of the wage earner, not because I regard the wage earners of this country as a special class, for they are not. After you have made a catalogue of the wage earners of this country, how many of us are left? The wage earners of this country, in a broad sense, constitute the country, and the most fatal thing that we can do in politics is to imagine that we belong to a special class and that we have an interest which isn't the interest of the whole community. Half of the difficulties, half of the injustices of our politics, have been due to the fact that men regarded themselves as having separate interests which they must serve even though other men were done a great disservice by their promoting them. We are not afraid of those who pursue legitimate pursuits, provided they link those pursuits in at every turn with the interest of the community as a whole; and no man can conduct a legitimate business if he conducts it in the interest of a single class. I want, therefore, to look at the nation as a whole today. I would like always to look at it as a whole, not divided up into sections and classes. But I want particularly to discuss with you today the things which interest the wage earner. That is merely looking at the country as a whole from one angle, from one point of view, to which for the time being we will confine ourselves.

I want, as a means of illustration, not as a means of contest, to use the platform of the third party as the means of expounding what I have to say today. I want you to read that platform very carefully, and I want to call your attention to the fact that it really consists of two parts. In one part of it, it declares the sympathy of the party with a certain great program of social reform and promises that all the influence of that party, of the members of that party, will be used for the promotion of that program of social reform. In the other part, it itself lays down a method of procedure, and what I want you to soberly consider is whether the method of procedure is a suitable way of laying the foundation for the realization of that social program. With regard to the social program—the betterment of the condition of men in this occupation and the other, the protection of women, the shielding of children, the bringing about of social justice here, there, and elsewhere—with that program, who can differ in his heart, who can divorce himself in sympathy from the great project of advancing the interests of human beings wherever it is possible to advance them?

But there is a central method, a central purpose, in that platform from which I very seriously dissent. I am a Democrat as distinguished from a Republican because I believe, and I think that it is generally believed, that the leaders of the Republican party—for I always distinguished them from the great body of Republican voters who have been misled by them—I say not the Republican party, but the leaders of the Republican party, have allowed themselves to become so tied up in alliances with special interests that they are not free to serve us all. And that the immediate business, if you are to have any kind of reform at all, is to set your government free, is to break it away from the partnerships and alliances and understandings and privileges which have made it impossible for it to look at the country as a whole and made it necessary for it to serve special interests one at a time. Until that has been done, no program of social reform is possible, because a program of social reform depends upon universal sympathy, universal justice, universal cooperation. It depends upon our understanding one another and serving one another.

What is this program? What is the program of the third party with regard to the disentanglement of the government? Mr. Roosevelt has said—and up to a certain point I sympathize with him—that he does not object, for example, to the system of protection, except in this circumstance, that it has not inured to the benefit of the workingmen of this country. It is very interesting to have him admit this, because the leaders of the Republican party have been time out of mind putting this bluff upon you men that the protective policy was for your sake. I would like to know what you ever got out of it that you didn't get out of it by the better effort of organized labor. I have yet to learn of any instance where you got anything without going and taking it. The process of our society, instead of being a process of peace, has sometimes too much resembled a process of war, because men felt obliged to go and insist in organized masses upon getting the justice which they couldn't get any other way. It is interesting, therefore, to have Mr. Roosevelt admit that not enough of the "prize" money, as he frankly calls it, has gone into the pay envelope. I admit that not enough of the money has gone into the envelope. I wish it were not "prize" money, because dividing up "prize" money and dividing up earnings are two very different things. And it is very much simpler to divide up earnings than to divide up "prize" money, because the money is "prize" money for the reason that a limited number of men got together and obtained it from the Ways and Means Committee of the House and the Finance Committee of the Senate, and we paid the bills.

But Mr. Roosevelt says that his object will be to see that a larger proportion gets into the pay envelope. How does he propose to do it? I am here, not to make a speech, I am here to argue this thing with you gentlemen. How does he propose to do it? I don't find any suggestion anywhere in that platform of the way in which he is going to do it, except in one plank. One plank says that the party will favor a minimum wage for women and then it goes on to say that by a "minimum wage" it means a living wage, enough to live on. I am going to assume, for the sake of argument, that it proposes more than that, that it proposes to get a minimum wage for everybody, men as well as women, and I want to call your attention to the fact that just as soon as a minimum wage is established by law, the temptation of every employer in the United States will be to bring his wages down as close to that minimum as he dare, because you can't strike against the Government of the United States, you can't strike against what is in the law. You can strike against what is in your agreement with your employer, but if underneath that agreement there is the steel and the adamant of federal law, you cannot tamper with that foundation. And who is going to pay these wages? Do you know that one of the great difficulties about wages now is that the control of industry is getting into fewer and fewer hands, and that therefore a smaller and smaller number of men are able to determine what wages shall be? In other words, one of the entanglements of our government is that we are dealing not with a community in which men may take their own choice in what they shall do, but with a community whose industry is very largely governed by great combinations of capital in the hands of a comparatively small number of men; in other words, we are in the hands in many industries of monopoly itself. And the only way in which the workingman can get more wages is by getting it from the monopoly.

Very well, then. What does this platform propose to do? Break up the monopolies? Not at all. It proposes to legalize them. It says in effect, "You can't break them up. The only thing you can do is to put them in charge of the federal government." It proposes that they shall be adopted and regulated, and that looks to me like a consummation of the partnership between monopoly and government, because when once the government regulates the monopoly, then monopoly will have to see to it that it regulates the government. This is a beautiful circle of change.

We now complain that the men who control these monopolies control the government, and it is in turn proposed that the government should control them. I am perfectly willing to be controlled if it is I myself who controls me. If this partnership can be continued, then this control can be manipulated and adjusted to its own pleasure. Therefore I want to call your attention to this fact, that these great combined industries have been more inimical to organized labor than any other class of employers in the United States. Is not that so? These monopolists that the government, it is proposed, should adopt are the men who have made your independent action most difficult. They have made it most difficult that you should take care of yourselves, and let me tell you that the old adage that God takes care of those who take care of themselves is not gone out of date. No federal legislation can change that thing. The minute you are taken care of by the government, you are wards, not independent men. And the minute they are legalized by the government, they are protégés and not monopolists. They are the guardians and you are the wards. Do you want to be taken care of by a combination of the government and the monopolies? Because the workingmen of this country are perfectly aware that they sell their commodity, that is to say labor, in a perfectly open market. There is free trade in labor in the United States. The workingmen of all the world are free to come and offer their labor here, and you are similarly free to go and offer your labor in most parts of the world; and the world demand is what establishes for the most part the rate of wages. At the same time, these gentlemen who are paying wages in a free-trade market are protected by an unfree market against competition that would make them bid higher because bid in competition and not bid under protection. If I am obliged to refrain from going into a particular industry by reason of the combination that already exists in it, I can't become an employer of labor and I can't compete with these gentlemen for the employment of labor, and the whole business of the level of wages is artificially and arbitrarily determined.

Now I say, gentlemen, that a party that proposes that program cannot, if it carries out that program, put forward these other handsome purposes of social regeneration, because they have crystallized, they have hardened, they have narrowed the government which is to be the source of this thing. After all this is done, who is to guarantee to us that the government is to be pitiful, that the government is to be righteous, that the government is to be just? Nothing will then control the powers of the government except open revolt, and God forbid that we should bring about a state of politics in which open revolt should be substituted for the ballot box! I believe that the greatest force for peace, the greatest force for righteousness, the greatest force for the elevation of mankind, is organized opinion, is the thinking of men, is the great force which is in the soul of men, and I want men to breathe a free and pure air. And I know that these monopolies are so many cars of Juggernaut which are in our very sight being driven over men in such ways as to crush their life out of them. And I don't look forward with pleasure to the time when the Juggernauts are licensed. I don't look forward with pleasure to the time when the Juggernauts are driven by commissioners of the United States. I am willing to license automobiles, but not Juggernauts, because if any man ever dares take a joy ride in one of them, I would like to know what is to become of the rest of us, because the road isn't wide enough for us to get out of the way. We would have to take to the woods and then set the woods on fire.

I am speaking partly in pleasantry, but underneath, gentlemen, there is a very solemn sense in my mind that we are standing at a critical turning point in our choice.

Now you say, on the other hand, what do the Democrats propose to do? I want to call your attention to the fact that those who wish to support these monopolies by adopting them under the regulation of the Government of the United States are the very men who cry out that competition is destructive. And they ought to know, because it is competition as they conducted it that destroyed our economic freedom. They are certainly experts in destructive competition, and the purpose of the Democratic leaders is this, not to legislate competition into existence again, because statutes can't make men do things, but to regulate competition. What has created these monopolies? Unregulated competition. It has permitted these men to do anything that they chose to do to squeeze their rivals out and to crush their rivals to the earth. We know the processes by which they have done these things. We can prevent those processes by remedial legislation, and that remedial legislation will so restrict the wrong use of competition that the right use of competition will destroy monopoly. In other words, ours is a program of liberty and theirs is a program of regulation. Ours is a program by which we say we know the wrongs that have been committed and we can stop those wrongs, and we are not going to adopt into the governmental family the men who have done the wrongs and license them to do the whole business of the country.

I want you men to grasp the point because I want to say to you right now the program that I propose doesn't look quite as much like acting as a Providence for you as the other program looks. But I want to frankly say to you that I am not big enough to play Providence, and my objection to the other program is that I don't believe there is any other man that is big enough to play Providence. I have never known any body of men, any small body of men, that understood the United States. And the only way the United States is ever going to be taken care of is by having the voices of all the men in it constantly clamorous for the recognition of what is justice as they see the light. A little group of men sitting every day in Washington City is not going to have a vision of your lives as a whole. You alone know what your lives are. I say, therefore, take the shackles off of American industry, the shackles of monopoly, and see it grow into manhood, see it grow out of enshackled childishness into robust manliness, men being able to take care of themselves and reassert the great power of American citizenship. These are the ancient principles of government the world over. For when in the history of labor here in this country, or in any other, did the government present its citizens with freedom and with justice? When has there been any fight for liberty that wasn't a fight against this very thing—the accumulation of regulative power in the hands of a few persons?

I in my time have read a good deal of history and, if I were to sum up the whole history of liberty, I should say that it consisted at every turn in human life in resisting just such projects as are now proposed to us. If you don't believe it, try it. If you want a great struggle for liberty that will cost you blood, adopt this program, put yourselves at the disposal of a Providence resident in

Washington and then see what will come of it. Ah, gentlemen, we are debating very serious things, and we are debating this: Are we going to put ourselves in a position to enter upon a great program of understanding one another and helping one another? I can't understand you unless you talk to me. I can't understand you by looking at you. I can't understand you by reading books. With apologies to the gentlemen in front of me, I couldn't even understand you by reading the newspapers. I can understand you only by what you know of your own lives and make evident in your own actions. I understand you only in proportion as you hump yourselves and take care of yourselves, and make your force evident in the course of politics. And, therefore, I believe in government as a great process of getting together, a great process of debate.

There are gentlemen on this platform with me who have seen a great vision. They have seen this, for example. You know that there are a great many foreigners coming to America and qualifying as American citizens. And if you are widely acquainted among them you will know that this is true, that the grownup people who come to America take a long time in feeling at home in America. They don't speak the language, and there is no place in which they can get together with the general body of American citizens and feel that they are part of them. But their children feel welcome. Where? In the schoolhouse. The schoolhouse is the great melting pot of democracy, and, after the children of these men who have joined us in their desire for freedom have grown up and come through the processes of the schools, they have imbibed the full feeling of American life.

Now somebody has said, somebody repeated to me the other day, the saying of one of these immigrants, that when he went to a meeting or to a series of meetings in the evening in a schoolhouse, where all the neighborhood joined together to discuss the interests of the neighborhood, he for the first time saw America as he had expected to see it. This had been America as he had imagined it—this frank coming together of all the people in the neighborhood, of all sorts and conditions, to discuss their common interests. These gentlemen to whom I have referred have devoted their lives to this, to making the schoolhouses of this country the vital centers of opinion, to opening them out of school hours for everybody who wants to discuss anything, and for making them, among other things, the clearinghouses where men who are out of jobs can find jobs, and where jobs who are out of men can find men. Why shouldn't our whole life center in this place where we learn the fundamentals of our life? Why shouldn't the schoolhouses be the constant, year in and year out, places of assembly where things are said which nobody dares ignore? Because if we haven't had our way in this country it has been because we haven't been able to get at the ear of those who were conducting our government. And if there is any man in Buffalo, or anywhere else in the United States, who objects to your using the schoolhouses that way, you may be sure that there is something that he doesn't want to have discussed.

You know, I have been considered as disqualified for politics because I was a schoolteacher. But there is one thing a school-teacher learns that he never forgets, namely, that it is his business to learn all he can and then to communicate it to others. Now I consider this to be my function. I have tried to find out how to learn things and learn them fast, and I have made up my mind that for the rest of my life I am going to put all I know at the disposal of my fellow citizens. And I know a good many things that I haven't yet mentioned in public which I am ready to mention at the psychological moment. There is no use firing them off when there is nobody to shoot at, but when they are present then it is sport to say it. And I have undertaken the duty of constituting myself one of the attorneys for the people in any court to which I can get entrance. I don't mean as a lawyer, for, while I was a lawyer, I have repented. But I mean in the courts of public opinion, wherever I am allowed, as I am indulgently allowed today, to stand on a platform and talk to attentive audiences,—for you are most graciously attentive,—I want to consti-tute myself the spokesman, so far as I have the proper table of contents, for the people whom I wish to serve; for the whole strength of politics is not in the leader but in the followers. By leading I do not mean telling other people what they have got to do. I mean finding out what the interests of the community are agreed to be, and then trying my level best to find the methods of solution by common counsel. That is the only feasible program of social uplift that I can imagine. And, therefore, I am bound in conscience to fight everything that crystallizes things so at the center that you can't break in.

It is amazing to me that public-spirited, devoted men in this country have not seen that the program of the third party pro-claims purposes and in the same breath provides an organization of government which makes the carrying out of those purposes impossible.

I would rather postpone my sympathy for social reform until I had got in a position to make things happen. And I am not in a position to make things happen until I am part of a free organization which can say to every interest in the United States: "You come into this conference room on an equality with every other interest in the United States, and you are going to speak here with open doors; there is to be no whispering behind the hand; there is to be no private communication; what you can't afford to let the country hear had better be left unsaid."

What I fear, therefore, is a government of experts. God forbid that in a democratic country we should resign the task and give the government over to experts. What are we for if we are to be scientifically taken care of by a small number of gentlemen who are the only men who understand the job? Because if we don't understand the job, then we are not a free people. We ought to resign our free institutions and go to school to somebody and find out what it is we are about.

I want to say that I have never heard more penetrating debate of public questions than I have sometimes been privileged to hear in clubs of workingmen, because the man who is down against the daily problem of life doesn't talk about it in rhetoric, he talks about it in facts. And the only thing I am interested in is facts, and I do not know anything else that is solid to stand on.

I beg, therefore, that in the election that is approaching you will serve your own interests by discriminatingly serving the whole country and holding it as your ultimate aim to see to it that liberty, the initiative of the individual, the initiative of the group, the freedom of enterprise, the multiplicity of American undertakings, is the foundation of your judgment. Do not let America get tied up into little coteries; see to it that every door is open to the youngster as well as to the older man who has made his way. See to it that those who are swimming against the stream have some little glimpse of the shore. See to it that those who are sweating blood know that they must not sweat blood all their lives but that if they devote their energy, they will devote it in hope and not in despair, as their own masters and not as men's servants, as men who can look their fellows in the face and say, "We also are of the free breed of American citizens." Why, gentlemen, we are at this juncture recovering the ideals of American politics, nothing else. By forgetfulness, by negligence, by criminal discrimination against one another, we have allowed our government to come to such a pass that it does not serve us all without discrimination, and we are about to recover it.

I am not here to commend one party above another. I am here to commend one purpose rather than another and to challenge every man to vote, not as he has been in the habit of voting merely because that has been his habit, but as he deems the interests of the community, as he believes will be most effective in the long run. In other words, choose measures, choose paths, choose men, and, if you please, forget that there are parties.

I am a party man. I believe in party organization except where party organization goes to seed and becomes a machine, and then I think that part ought to be cut off. But I am for something that will dominate party organization. That is the reason I am interested in this schoolhouse business. I am for the organization of public opinion which at every election will say: "You can't label us. You can't drive us into a pen. You can't tell us how we are going to vote by the caption at the top of the ticket. We are going to read the ticket; we are going to find who are on it; we are going to find who made the ticket; we are going to find out what the program is behind the ticket; and we are going to choose accordingly." For only in that way can America be governed as she ought to be governed.

It is very embarrassing to me, I will tell you frankly, to appear as one who solicits your votes. I would a great deal rather get elected first and then come back to you and say, "Now, what are we going to do?" Because before election a man is in this unpleasant position: he is as much as saying "Elect me, and you just see what I will do." Now, no man is big enough to say that truthfully. He can say it, but he oughtn't to say it. But after the election the point is not what will he do, but what will you back him up in doing?—what will *we* do? I had rather argue politics in the plural than in the singular. It is a lonely business arguing it in the singular. All that you can promise in the singular is that there'll be a good deal doing, that you won't allow yourself to be fooled, even by your own party, and that the pledges you take upon yourself individually you will do your best to carry out, whether anybody else goes with you or not. But I am not afraid of that. If the American people elect a man President and say, "You go on and do those things," nobody is going to head him off, because there is a force behind him which nobody dares resist,—that great impulse of just opinion without which there is no pure government at all.

I don't know any other appeal, therefore, than this appeal to you as Americans, as men who constitute the bone and sinew of American citizenship and who, when you address yourselves to the discussion of public affairs, know what the realities are, and are not deceived by the appearances. Let us get together and serve the Government of the United States.

T MS (C. L. Swem Coll., NjP); with corrections and one addition from the ICFT transcript of CLSsh notes in RSB Coll., DLC, and with corrections from the nearly full text in the *Buffalo Express*, Sept. 3, 1912.

An Evening Address in Buffalo[1]

[Sept. 2, 1912]

Mr. Chairman,[2] ladies and gentlemen: I must say in the circumstances that I am very glad they put me off in Buffalo, for
certainly your greeting makes my heart very warm indeed. I have
come here tonight for the purpose of discussing just as candidly
as possible the political situation in which we find this country
which we love, because I am not one of those who believes that
politics is a process of depreciating the men you are opposed to
or of belittling the forces with which you have to contend, or
as anything else than a frank determination of what it is we are
to get together and do and how we are to do it. Because, while the
very generous speaker[3] who has just taken his seat has told you
of some of the things accomplished in New Jersey, he has given
me personally undue credit for that achievement, because I want
you to know that those things were done by the people of New
Jersey and that I was merely their spokesman. If I can't be your
spokesman, I don't want you to vote for me. If you don't believe
the things that I believe, I don't want you to vote for me. Because
the thing I do not wish to do is to speak in national affairs with
only my own voice. I want to feel, if I am elected to the office of
President, that I am speaking the purposes and impulses and
judgments of the people of the United States.

We must be very candid with one another, therefore. We must
very diligently inquire whether we are of the same mind or not
and whether we do understand in the same terms the things
which we are attempting to do. What is it that we wish to do now
in the year 1912? I am not going to review the history of parties.
I am not going to review conditions in a day that is gone because
the exigency of our politics consists in this, ladies and gentlemen,
that the year 1912 does not present political problems in the
same light in which they were ever presented before. We have
got to look at them, therefore, in the new air which has been
bred in a new day, and I want to say to you that in my opinion
the people of this country wish two things. If you wish them, then
we are together. They wish two things. They wish, first, to clear
their government for action by making it free and then, when it
is free, they wish to use it, not to serve any class or any party, but
to serve civilization and the human race.

We are men; we are not politicians. We do not live our lives

[1] Delivered to a Democratic mass meeting in the Broadway Arsenal.
[2] George Brinton McClellan Burd, lawyer and New York state senator from
Buffalo.
[3] George H. Kennedy, lawyer of Buffalo, active in Democratic politics.

in the polls; we live them in our homes, in the factories, in the mines, in the forests, in the rolling mills, in all the myriad work-shops of a great nation. And the thing that we are interested in is the character of our life and the conditions of our life in those places. We are interested in politics only as a means of getting the law to serve our life as it should serve it. Therefore, when you ask which party you are going to support and which candi-date you are going to support, you are not asking the paltry ques-tion, "Do you prefer the record of the Democratic party or the record of the Republican party?" You are asking this funda-mental question: "By which means and by which choice can we best serve ourselves and those whom we love and who are dependent upon us?" That is what I understand politics to be.

Politics differs from philanthropy only in this, that in philan-thropy we sometimes do things through pity merely, while in pol-itics we merely do it, if we are righteous men, on the grounds of justice. Sometimes in our pitiful sympathy with our fellow men we must do things that are more than just. We must forgive men. We must help men that have gone wrong. We must help men that have gone criminally wrong. But the law says we are merely go-ing to equalize conditions, see that every man has a fair chance, see that injustice and wrong are not wrought in the name of gov-ernment. And yet philanthropy and government are linked in this, that they are both meant for the service of humanity. Why, government was set up in America because men of all classes were not served anywhere else in the world. Under every other government in the world, when the American government was set up, the government served only some of the classes of the com-munity, and we boasted, we hoped, we were confident that we had set up a government in this country which would serve every class without discrimination—the most humble along with the most powerful. Only so long as we keep the American government up to that ideal and standard will it be worthy of the name Ameri-can. And, therefore, the critical circumstance of the year 1912 is this, that we fear that we have found that our government is not serving all classes, that our government is serving only a portion and that the most powerful portion of the community which could take care of itself. I am very much more interested in seeing government take care of the people who are not power-ful than I am in seeing it take care of the people who are power-ful. And when I say the powerful control the government, then I say this is not American government, this is not the government of the people.

Our task this year is to place the government back into the

hands of all classes of American citizens. That is what we mean by putting it in the hands of the people. But it is one thing to talk that way, and it is another thing to accomplish the object. How are you going to accomplish the object? I dare say that every orator in every campaign in the history of the United States, where there is more politics to the square mile than anywhere else in the world, has said that his object was to serve the people. So I am not telling you anything new. What you have to find is whether in my case it is a bluff or not. And you can't find it out by looking at me. You have got to exercise your minds. You have got to discriminate. You have got to set the chess board fully up and see how the game is going to be played. And you have got only one of three choices to make.

I am going to try to be very candid about all three of them. I want to set the stage for you. I want to discuss the three parties now seeking your support. I know there are more than three parties in the United States, and it is not out of any disrespect to the parties that have commanded a smaller number of votes than these three in the past that I leave them out of the reckoning for the present. I have a great respect for the Socialist party because I know how many honest and serious men are in it. I have a great respect for the Populist party because I know that it is seeking to serve the people. I have a great respect for all the minor parties in proportion as they have this object in view, but it is not disrespectful to them to say that one of three parties is going to win this time and, therefore, I am going to confine my discussion to those three.

Let me go back to where I started. We want to disentangle our government, clear its decks, and set it free—to do what? To serve civilization and mankind. By that standard let us judge the parties which are candidates for our suffrages—for I would rather express it in terms of parties than in terms of individuals. There is one sense in which I am not interested in individuals. I am interested in any one individual in politics only in proportion as I can see in him the candidate serving more other individuals, only in proportion as I consider him the representative, the great representative, of a great body of my fellow citizens who have a cause at their hearts. The more we can turn away from the individual and his personal qualifications and discuss the parties, the better it will be.

Now I am going to stand up here before you as the first candidate for your suffrages, the Republican party, I mean the old-line, stay-where-it-is Republican party. A great many of you, perhaps a great proportion of you, have been in the habit of voting for that party. I am perfectly ready to forgive you because I think I know, I think I can imagine by putting myself in your place, exactly why you did it. I never did it, but I can imaginatively conceive myself doing it. I am like the man they found somewhere in the remote parts of the country who they said could tell the truth. He wasn't found telling it, but he could tell it when he heard it. Now I have never been found voting the Republican ticket but I understand how it is done. And I want to have you realize that there is a great deal of difference between the Republican party and certain groups of gentlemen who have been in the habit of leading and directing the Republican party.

When I speak of the Republican party that is a candidate for your suffrages tonight, therefore, I mean that party as represented by the men who are leading it. That is the only way I know how to test its political capacity. That party is the very party which has got us into the difficulties we are now trying to get out of. I don't have to prove that, because we have got into those difficulties in the last fifteen years, and during the last fifteen years that party has been in power. If it didn't get us into these difficulties, who did? It's had a free field. It's had possession of the government. It could at any time guide the legislation of the United States and, if it has not been able to keep those things from happening which have wrought a deep evil upon us, it has proved its impotence, whereas if it deliberately did these things, it has proved its untrustworthiness.

Mark you, I am not saying that the leaders of this party knew that they were doing us an evil or that they intended to do us an evil. For my part, I am very much more afraid of the man who does a bad thing and doesn't know it is bad than of a man who does a bad thing and knows it is bad, simply because I think that in public affairs stupidity is more dangerous than knavery. If you don't know enough to know what the consequences are going to be to the country, then you can't govern the country in a way that is for its benefit. And, therefore, I am perfectly ready to admit that these gentlemen may have been guided by nothing but the most patriotic intentions, for I am not indicting anybody, I am simply trying to state the circumstances of our day. These gentlemen, whatever may have been their intentions, linked the Government of the United States up with the men who control the big finances of the United States. They may have done it innocently or they may have done it corruptly without affecting my argument at all. Provided you admit that they tied the Government of the United States to the big financial interests of the United States, you have admitted my point, and they, themselves, cannot escape from that alliance.

If you have once constructed your policy upon that basis, how are you going to face the men who have hitherto supported you, if you desert them in the midst of affairs? This, ladies and gentlemen, is the old question of campaign funds. If I take a hundred thousand dollars from a group of men representing a particular interest that has a big stake in a certain schedule of the tariff, I take it with the knowledge that those gentlemen will expect me not to forget their interest in that schedule, and that they will take it as a point of implicit honor that I should see to it that they are not damaged by too great a change in that schedule. Therefore, if I take their money I am bound to them by a sort of tacit pledge of honor and, if I desert them, I change the whole character of the government. The regular Republican leaders have got us into the very thing that we must get out of if we would set our government free, and they themselves cannot get out of it without reversing the whole character of their administrations.

I want to point out to you again that I am not indicting their character. They hold a theory of government which has been held for a great many thousand years. I don't know whether they have ever admitted it to themselves. The first man, the first great man, who avowed that theory in the United States was Alexander Hamilton. He said that he believed that only that government was stable that was based upon the support of the men who had the biggest material stake in it. Now I can argue that way, if I choose, and any man can make a very plausible argument to show that the men with the biggest stake in the life of a country are the very men to look to to see that that country prospers and that its government is stable. But the trouble is, and the trouble has been since the beginning of time, that these men do not understand the interests of common men, that these men do not understand the circumstances which are making the workingmen of our country sweat blood every day of their lives in their struggle to make a living. Government is a matter of insight and of sympathy, and if you don't know what the great body of men are up against, how are you going to help them? And if you don't help them, if you don't consider government the business of helping them, how are you going to serve a great voiceless nation?

I tell you, ladies and gentlemen, the men I am interested in are the men who never have their voices heard, who never get a line in the newspapers, who never get a moment on the platform, who never have access to the ears of governors or of anybody who is responsible for the conduct of government, but who go silently and patiently to their work every day, carrying the burden of the world. How are they to be understood by the masters of finance, if only the masters of finance are consulted? The masters of finance ought to be consulted because they are a part of the people of the United States, but they ought to be consulted only in proportion as they are part of the people of the United States.

I have heard many orators who represent the point of view I am now criticising speak of the people and of what should be done for the people, and it was always perfectly obvious that they did not include themselves. They spoke of the people as a great body of persons whom it was their business to take care of. Now, I am perfectly willing in speaking of the people to include them, but they are not willing to include the people. I am perfectly willing to include the great financial interests of this country, provided they will include themselves when they speak of the people. Now, the confirmed point of view of certain Republican leaders whom I might name is that the business of the government is to take care of the people, that it ought to be conducted for the people but not by the people, because a sort of shudder seems to run through them when you suggest that ordinary men ought to have a voice in the counsels of government. They say, "What do they know about it?" I always feel like saying, "What do you know about it? You know your interests, but who has told you their interests, and what do you know about them?" For the business of every leader of government is to hear what the nation is saying and to know what the nation is enduring. It is not his business to judge for the nation but to judge through the nation as its spokesman and voice. I do not believe, ladies and gentlemen, that this country can safely allow a continuation of the policy of men who have faced affairs in that light.

Now if not the regular Republicans, whom are you going to trust? There is a large body of Republicans now in open rebellion, and what interests me about them and draws me to them is that they are in revolt because their consciences couldn't stand what was going on. I think I understand the moral point of view of the insurgent Republican because I know what he is in revolt against, and he is dead right. And a great body of Republicans in revolt have now formed a third party, and that third party deserves your careful consideration when you are debating the question which party you are going to support. I would be ashamed of myself if I did not realize and admit that some of the sober forces of this country are now devoted to the promotion of that new movement and party, but these insurgent Republicans, who have formed the new party, are not all of that new party. That party has two other elements in it that interests me even more than the insurgent Republicans, because I have known the insurgent Republicans a long time. They first began to crop up in that supposedly backward State of New Jersey a great many years ago. There we called them the New Idea Republicans, when the idea of what the Republicans were doing at Washington was wrong was a new idea— a new idea among Republicans. It was a rather old idea among Democrats. And I have been closely associated, it has been my privilege to be closely associated, with some New Idea Republicans, and I think their new ideas were so remarkably like my old ideas that I was perfectly willing to admit their validity.

But there are other elements in the new party which we ought very candidly to consider also. I have not heard of many Democrats who have joined that party—to tell you the truth, I haven't heard of any Democrats who joined it. I have heard reports that there were some, but I haven't found them, I haven't personally encountered them or heard their names. And, therefore, in looking around for the other elements, I find that they are two. All the other members of that party have joined it for their own special purposes. (Wait a minute. Some of those purposes are very noble. Some of them are not.) There is a noble group of men and women who have joined that party because the program, or rather the platform of that party, embodies most of the ideas and most of the purposes for which they have fought more or less hopelessly for a long generation. And they are ready to tie to a party which professes to believe in those things. And those purposes are elevated, disinterested, noble purposes and belong to part of the program that I have been talking of—that if we can get a free government, we want it to serve civilization and humanity. I don't believe that through that party you can get a free government. But if they could get a free government through that party, then mention what program of that party is conceived in the service of civilization and humanity.

Then there are other persons who have their own aims to serve who joined that party, and the less said about them the better. Because it would only be interesting to discuss them if I could mention their names, and I have forbidden myself that indulgence. I dare say that the leaders of that party are just as much embarrassed by their presence as we are critical of their presence in it. The difficulty with any party, ladies and gentlemen, is to invite people not to join or is to suggest to people having joined they had better get out. You can't do it. That is against the eti- quette of politics, because what they are working for is votes and, if you can, without smirching your own hand, get men to vote for you who don't really intend to let you have your way, you may nevertheless have your way after they have voted for you.

I have known that to happen. Just between you and me, there were gentlemen in New Jersey who voted for me who had no intention of allowing me to have my way, and they thought that being an innocent, academic person, I wouldn't know how to get my way when I got in. Now, I do not hold myself responsible for having fooled them because I told them beforehand exactly what I was going to try to do so that the game was perfectly even and on the level. But I would advise gentlemen who don't want me to do what I say I am going to do, if I am elected President, not to vote for me this time. Because now they know what is going to happen.

But I say all these things merely because I want you to understand that my analysis of the new party is not a hostile analysis, is not an unreasonable criticism. I simply ask you this, "If the new party is preferred on the fifth of November next, will it be in a position to clear the decks and carry out the policy which many noble gentlemen have conceived that it was sincerely bent upon?" That is the only question because politics, particularly now, is intensely practical. We can't afford to vote on the fifth of November and then wait another four years. The processes of reform in this country must take place within the next four years. If the leader of the third party is made President of the United States, what will be his situation? Does anybody within the sound of my voice suppose that he will have a third-party Congress behind him? Doesn't everybody know that there will be in Congress such a mixture of elements and groups and parties that it is almost a certain prediction that the next President in such circumstances can't get anything consistent done?

We have had samples of it already. We have got a very queerly assorted Senate of the United States. There are some Democrats in it, some near-Democrats, some Republicans, and some ex-Republicans, and it has been a gambler's chance whether they will get together on anything or not. Nobody has ever known after a bill passed the House of Representatives exactly what was going to happen to it when it got into the Senate, and the roll call in the votes has seldom shown the same list of names. Now suppose you had a House of Representatives mixed like the present Senate. I think we could all go fishing for the next two years! And if at the same time you had a leader insistent upon certain policies, I think the air would be full of clamorous voices, but the statute book would be very empty of fulfilled promises, not because, it may be, nobody was trying to fulfill the promises, but because everybody was trying to fulfill a different promise.

It seems to me that that way lies the way of confusion, that that way lies the way by which to establish an interval in our politics instead of the way along which we can press for the accomplishment of those things which the mind of the country has been made up with regard to.

Well, there is one circumstance upon which I must dwell for a moment. The new party doesn't even propose to clear the decks because the central proposal in the whole program is to legalize monopoly. The central proposal is, instead of defeating, instead of breaking up, the evil things that have been done under the mistaken leadership of regular Republican leaders, the result of their mistakes shall be legalized and made regular by being taken under the direct supervision of the Government of the United States. And whatever may be the philanthropic purpose of that program, the inevitable result will be to confirm by law the partnership between great trusts and the Government of the United States. I do not say that this is what the leaders of that party expect or purpose, but there has been a history of the human race and a history of government, and the kind of thing they propose has always led to the result which I have predicted.

You must see to it that your law prevents monopoly. You must see to it that the processes by which monopoly is established are made impossible under the statutes of the land. You must see to it that the freedom of enterprise is restored, not the limitation of enterprise confirmed. You must see to it in order that our youngsters, as they come along, may at least find that it is possible to organize business independently for themselves, in order that they may not find that in order to do business they must come under the regulations and the categories and the determinations of a federal commission—that federal commission already having regularized, already having legitimized, the very undertakings which in size and power are now limiting the field of enterprise throughout the United States.

Therefore, it is impossible that a program of civilization and humanity should be carried out by a government that isn't free. Ah, what a prize the government at Washington would be to capture! It is prize enough now, but how overwhelming the temptation would be then to see this thing regulate us. Therefore, let us get on the inside and regulate it. And remember that they would not have to get on the inside, they are on the inside. They are tenants of the house at this moment, and we are outside. Our project is to get into our own premises and administer our own affairs, not to draw a perpetual lease by which, under conditions imposed from the outside, they were to enjoy life on the inside. And, therefore, seeing no prospect in that direction of a free government, I see no prospect of a humane program.

Then you have got only the Democratic party left. And you will ask me how I can set up a claim for the Democratic party. Well, it is rather a fine discipline, ladies and gentlemen, to have been on the outside for sixteen years. Put it at its worst, we haven't entered into any arrangements because we haven't had a chance. That is the worst. That is the minimum you will have to admit for the Democratic party. We haven't formed any partnership because we didn't have any capital to offer. We can't form a co-partnership just on our looks. You have got to be able to do business. Well, we were not in a position to do business. And, therefore, I am now stating it in the terms in which perhaps the most confirmed Republican present would state it, and, therefore, we are innocent. But, gentlemen, if you will let me speak my own deep conviction, there is something a great deal better than that in it. You haven't entrusted the Government of the United States to the Democratic party because the Democratic party has been opposed all these years to the things that the Republican leaders were doing. Isn't that the mere statement of fact?

Haven't we been attacking it and opposing it and supporting programs that once looked radical and now look reasonable for all these years? We haven't just begun being progressive. We have been progressive for sixteen years, and we saw the year 1912 half a generation before it came. Are you going to give us no credit for vision? Don't you think it counts for something to stay out in the cold on a conviction for sixteen years? We could have made our bargains, we could have traded, we could have compromised, we could have surrendered, but we did not because we stood upon an eternal conviction that that wasn't the way to serve the people of the United States. Through all these years, therefore, of self-chosen exile, while we have been purged and purified —I won't say all of us, but most of us—the great rank and file of the Democratic party never accepted an office, never wanted an office, voted persistently in the minority, knowing that they were going to be in the minority, taunted in some regions because they didn't have sense enough to come over to the majority, made fun of as if they were following an idiosyncracy, as if they were queer, because it was rooted and grounded in them, whether they could prove it or not, Thomas Jefferson had been right. Most of them didn't know what Thomas Jefferson had said, but they knew that he had said something that would knock those fellows out if the people of the United States only believed it. And, therefore, they swore by the name and conjured with the name, Thomas Jefferson. I tell you, you talk about literary fellows, but if by the grace of God you can say something that will inspire your fellow men for several generations, it is worthwhile having been a literary fellow.

Now the Democratic party is perhaps for the first time in a generation united, solid, and enthusiastic. Why, I don't know how many old Democrats I have met coming out of the woods. They say, "Is it possible that in the Providence of God we have lived to see the day when the people of the United States are about to admit that we were right after all?" They are going to come out and vote. They are going to come out and vote in triumphant numbers because the spirit of triumph, of triumphant principles, has risen up in their hearts. And I feel that the only justification for any degree of pride that I may have is that at this particular time I am accorded the privilege of speaking for them, speaking convictions that were bred in me, that I learned in the school of experience, that I have learned from books and from men, the things that lie at the heart of the whole history of living since government was organized among men. I tell you, it is no small privilege to be allowed to stand up before great bodies of my fellow citizens and express my deep conviction that these things are true, and that these things will make us free. But, ladies and gentlemen, the Democratic party is the only organized force by which you can set your government free.

I was bred in a football college, and I know that what wins is team work, and I want to tell you that we have now got a Democratic team schooled in years of adversity that can hold together against any team that can be put in the field, and as compared with which some teams recently organized are only scrub teams. What I have tried to show to you is that you have a Democratic object, namely, to set your government free, to enter upon a program of service, and that you are working for a team that can do it, and I say without fear of contradiction that there is only one team ready. I am not predicting when any other team will get ready. I am saying that in the year 1912 there is only one team that is ready for the job and that that team is better organized, more wholesomely constituted, more enthusiastically united than it has been in my recollection.

What, therefore, is the dictate of common sense? There is a very interesting passage in a very great English writer on politics, a writer in whose heart beat the pulse of sympathy for the rights of men as strongly as it ever beat in any breast, who said, "What are you to say of a man with the best intentions in the world, with the most patriotic purposes, who nevertheless acts in a way that will make his convictions ineffectual?"[4] What are you to say of men in this year making this party choice, who deliberately choose the instrumentality which will not now work to accomplish their purpose? One instrumentality which I discussed is not ready because it doesn't know how. The other instrumentality has not yet been made ready for anything in particular. And there is an old, indomitable organization that can't be frightened or discouraged that now offers itself for the service of the nation.

I believe that I can predict the choice that my fellow countrymen will make because America is practical and hardheaded, and votes are not meant to be sentimentally used. You don't vote for the satisfaction of voting, I take it for granted—for it is not, so far as my experience would show, a pleasurable sensation to vote —but because you believe that vote to be the contribution to a particular vital force working through the minds and hearts of the people of the United States. And, therefore, I am very much more interested in this part of the campaign than I am even in the eventual act on the fifth of November. It is a great deal more interesting and a great deal more vital to stand face to face and frankly discuss the public interests than it is for each of us to go in a particular booth and, where nobody looks on, cast his secret ballot.

And the real business of politics is transacted in rooms like this. It ought to be transacted in a great many more rooms. Big, numerously attended meetings are very fine for the sharing of great impulses and common sympathies, but the real business of politics is in little groups of people who come together and match their minds in little groups collecting at night in the school-houses, little neighborhood conferences in which men really lay their minds bare to one another. For if you would look at what makes the great river as it nears the sea, you must travel up the stream, you must go up into the hills and back into the forests and see the little rivulets, the weltered streams all gathering in hidden places to swell the great body of water in the channel. And so with the making of public opinion back in the country on the farms, in the shops, in the hamlets, in the homes of citizens, where men get together and are frank and true with one another, there come trickling down the streams which are to make the mighty force of the river. And the river is going to drive all the handsome enterprises of human life, and subsequently it is going to emerge into the great common sea of humanity. And so I

4 The Editors have been unable to find this quotation.

am more interested in exploring the streams than I am in traversing the ocean. I want to see where all the force comes from, and I shall consider it my privilege to challenge my fellow citizens to get together and think these things out and, if they will think them out, I pledge myself to accept with satisfaction the result which they register on the fifth day of November.[5]

Transcript of sh notes (C. L. Swem Coll., NjP); ICFT transcript of CLSsh notes (RSB Coll., DLC); with corrections from the complete text in the *Buffalo Evening Times*, Sept. 3, 1912, and the nearly complete text in the *Buffalo Express*, Sept. 3, 1912.

[5] There is a WWhw outline of this address, with the composition date of Sept. 1, 1912, in WP, DLC.

From Edward Mandell House

Dear Governor: Beverly, Mass. September 2nd [1912].

Mr. McCombs is seriously thinking of resigning and may do so tomorrow.

There are reasons why his resignation at this time would be a serious blow to the cause. I cannot go into an explanation here, but you would readily understand the reason if all the facts were before you.

You may or may not take any action in the premises but I thought you should be informed.

Mr. McAdoo has asked me to go to Maine which I shall do tomorrow night or Wednesday morning and when I return I should be glad to come to New York if you will let me know when you will be there.   Your very sincere,   [E. M. House]

P.S. I think it important that what I have written should be known only to you and me.

TCL (E. M. House Papers, CtY).

From Thomas Davies Jones

My dear Governor   Lake Forest, Illinois Sept 2, 1912

I have just read in the evening papers the Associated Press report of your Buffalo speech to the United Trades and Labor Council, and I am delighted with it. You have marked out admirably what should be the real fighting ground of the campaign. Excellent in substance and in tone

Faithfully Yours   Thomas D Jones

ALS (WP, DLC).

From Herbert Spencer Hadley

My dear Governor Wilson: Jefferson [Mo.] September 2, 1912.

Ever since the Baltimore convention I have had in mind writing you to convey my sincere congratulations upon your nomination. This feeling of congratulation is not only due to the fact that I think you deserved to win and were the strongest candidate the Democratic party could have selected, but also on account of the fact that your nomination was, in my judgment, the best nomination that could have been made for the Republican party and the future of American politics.

Any other nomination would have unquestionably brought about the result of three national parties with neither of sufficient strength to control and be responsible for the conduct of our national government. Such a condition, in my opinion, would be unfortunate. Though this may come about in spite of your nomination, the probability of it has been materially lessened thereby.

It may be [of] interest, and, I assume, satisfaction, to you to know that from information coming to me from all parts of Missouri, I am satisfied you will have the united support of the Democrats of this State and a great many Republicans.

Mrs. Hadley[1] joins me in personal regards to Mrs. Wilson and you.   Very truly yours,   Herbert S. Hadley

TLS (WP, DLC).
  [1] Agnes Lee Hadley.

To James Charles Monaghan

                                                  Sea Girt, N. J.
My dear Professor Monaghan: September 4, 1912.

Your letters have given me the greatest gratification. It is fine to have so influential, so loyal and so helpful a friend. Your letter of August thirtieth is particularly full of important suggestions and you may be sure that I will heed them if it is possible. I wish that I had time to send a letter in return worthy of your own.

         Cordially and sincerely yours,   Woodrow Wilson

P.S. I fear open opposition to Mr. Smith is unavoidable. The whole country expects and demands it.   W.W.

TLS (Berg Coll., NN).

A Talk in New York to Editors
of Foreign-Language Newspapers[1]

[Sept. 4, 1912]

Mr. Chairman and Ladies and Gentlemen: Your very cordial and gracious greeting confirms the impression with which I came to this place. It confirms the impression that we are not separated in ideas or in opinions, that I am not the American and you the foreigners. That is exactly the impression which has never been in my mind, and your greeting of me shows me it is not in yours. Because there is a certain sense in which we do America an injustice by classifying ourselves as native born and foreign born. And I have always pleased myself with the idea that America in some degree exists in spirit all over the world, and that there are men coming to these shores, men who have displayed their force in our affairs, who bring to America a more vivid conception of what it means than those of us who were born and bred here ourselves entertain.

I remember being told this story which cuts very close to the heart of the subject I am talking about: You know there has sprung up in various parts of this country, notably in the northern part of this state, a movement called the Social Center Movement, centering in the schoolhouses. I suppose that every one of you has realized that where the immigrant gets his real introduction to the life of this country is through his children who go to the public schools, and that the children feel that they are introduced into American life sooner than their parents do. And when you imagine a movement which makes the schoolhouse the center of the community life of a neighborhood, when you imagine the neighbors gathering there in the evening and going to school to one another in the discussion of public affairs and of those matters which concern all equally, you are imagining the thing which is likely to be more potent than any other to restore the original character of America. Because I have always held, with Jefferson, that the breeding ground of America used to lie in the town meeting, of which everybody was a member and where all public officers, local officers, without distinction, had to come and render account of themselves. It is a great deal easier to render an account of yourselves through writing than to appear before a body of your fellow citizens and answer questions in person, and before the town meetings the town officers used to be obliged to

[1] At the National Arts Club in Gramercy Park. Herman Bernstein presided at this gathering of approximately one hundred editors of foreign-language newspapers of the United States.

appear in person and render an account of themselves and their stewardship. And they were rendered acutely aware of the fact that it was a stewardship, because they had to render this account to the men whom they were serving. You get a sort of a vague idea that you are serving the people of a state, for example, if you sit in a governor's office, but I dare say that if the people of the state could conveniently assemble in any one place and speak their mind to the governor, he would have a very much more vivid conception of it than his imagination conveys to him.

And I see in this turning back to the original practice of American life, by meetings for the discussion of every legitimate public interest in the schoolhouse, something like a return to our original practices.

Now, I have gone a long way around to set the stage for my story. My story is simply this: I was told that an immigrant who had been in this country several years was drawn into one of these schoolhouse meetings, and after it was over he said, "At last I have seen the America of which I dreamed, the America where everybody, where men of all conditions, meet together and discuss the same things as neighbors, and where that discussion renders the public officer heedful of public opinion." Very well, then, the thought that is in my mind is this: that man brought to America a more vivid conception of America than some of our school officials have had who have refused to allow the schoolhouses to be used for such purposes. If I go to a country reputed to be a country of equality and of liberty, I must expect to find constant, visible, and open signs of liberty and equality; and therefore I carry to that country a demand which that country must satisfy. But I carry it only on one condition, namely, that I have gone to that country with that idea. I carry it only as I have gone to America because I was really, without knowing it, born an American. I wanted that thing that I thought I could get in America, and therefore I broke the tender connections of old associations, the intimate connections of a birthplace, and went to a far country looking for an ideal. And that is the distinction between voluntary immigration and involuntary immigration. That is the distinction between voluntary immigration and assisted immigration, is it not? And that, it seems to me, furnishes one of the clues to the only basis that we can have when we discuss the limitations that must be put upon immigration.

If we can hit upon a standard which admits every voluntary immigrant and excludes those who have not come of their own motion, with their own purpose of making a home and a career for themselves, but have been induced by steamship companies or others to come in order to pay the passage money, then we will have what we will all agree upon as Americans. For I am not speaking to you in a foreign country. I am speaking to you as also Americans with myself, and just as much Americans as myself, and if we all take the American point of view, namely, that we want American life kept to its standards, and that only the standards of American life shall be the standards of restriction, then we are all upon a common ground, not of those who criticize immigration, but of those who declare themselves Americans.

I am not saying that I am wise enough out of hand to frame the legislation that will meet this ideal. I am only saying that that is the ideal and that is what we ought to hold ourselves to.

Now, strange as it may seem to some gentlemen who have criticized me, the only blunder I have made, the only practical blunder I have made in my interest in a liberal policy with regard to immigration, is that I got into the wrong society[2] to encourage it. So that it was an indiscretion of judgment and not an indiscretion of purpose, for my interest in immigration is to see that the immigrant is properly informed, is properly safeguarded against imposition of every kind, whether by the government or anybody else, and is directed to the place where he can attain the objects he has come for with the greatest advantage to himself. That to my mind is the solution of the immigration question.

Of course, if the immigrants are to be allowed to come in uninstructed hosts and to stop at the ports where they enter, and there to compete in an over-supplied labor market, there is going to be unhappiness, there is going to be deterioration, there is going to be everything that will be detrimental to the community as well as detrimental to the immigrant. And, therefore, it is to the interest of the government that the government itself should supply, or at any rate encourage, the instrumentalities which will prevent that very thing, will multiply the ports of entry for that purpose, for example, will ease and facilitate and guide the process of distribution, and will above all things else supply the sympathetic information which is the only welcome that is acceptable to those who come.

And, therefore, I close as I began, by a very respectful protest against calling yourselves foreign editors or anything with the word foreign in it. Your newspapers and magazines are published in languages which are not the general language of America, which is modified English, but at this stage of the melting-pot process every language in which you print a paper is largely used

---

2 The National Liberal Immigration League of New York. Wilson had joined in 1906 as a director. See Link, *Road to the White House*, p. 387.

in the United States, and is used for the conveyance of American ideas. Now, I would just as leave Americanize a language as Americanize an individual, and I welcome the process by which you are Americanizing other foreign languages as the rest of us have Americanized English, or, speaking as someone wittily said, the English Slanguage. All my interest is that you shouldn't regard the language in which you print your periodicals as a foreign language when printed in America for the conveyance of American thinking. Then we will have taken another step towards that combination of elements which is in the long run going to make America more various, I dare say, in its natural gifts, more variegated in its genius than any other country in the world.

You know a quaint old writer of New England in the time of the early settlement of the country said, speaking complacently of himself and those who had come over with him, that God had winnowed a whole nation to select this seed which had been brought over and planted in America,[3] having no doubt the same gratification in saying it that I once enjoyed when I addressed a Scotch-Irish society,[4] that being the peculiar mixture which renders me disagreeable or agreeable, as the case may be. I had the great satisfaction, in eulogizing the Scottish-Americans, of feeling that I was really eulogizing myself. So this gentlemen felt that God had winnowed a whole nation to pick out him in particular and others in general.

And yet, putting pleasantry aside, there is a sense in which voluntary immigration is the winnowing of a nation, of bringing over the men of initiative, the men who have chosen their own career, and chosen it with difficulty, and chosen to begin it at a great distance, in making up a new home for themselves, and adding to the richness and variety of America.

I didn't know, gentlemen, when I came here that I was going to make you a speech, else I would have had a speech as happily phrased, I hope, as Mr. Bernstein's, but I did hope that that would happen which I now hope will happen, that I might meet you individually.

T MS (C. L. Swem Coll., NjP); minor corrections from the text in *Gov. Wilson a Friend of Immigration* (n.p., n.d.).
    [3] See n. 2 to the Thanksgiving Day address printed at Nov. 24, 1910, Vol. 22.
    [4] See n. 2 to the announcement printed at Jan. 5, 1901, Vol. 12.

An Address at a Workingmen's Dinner in New York[1]

[Sept. 4, 1912]

Mr. Announcer,[2] Ladies and Gentlemen: I wanted to get the explosive part of my speech over first.[3] It is a real privilege to me to stand in the presence of an audience like this, not only because there are a great many workingmen present, and I always esteem it a privilege to address them, but also because there are others present not technically classified as workingmen and working women. I always like to feel that the company in which I am speaking represents no class and no class feeling, but represents the united interests of a people which can be divided, if divided at all, only artificially. Because it seems to me that in this campaign we are discussing not so much the merits of parties as what we ought always to discuss when we are discussing politics if we be men of reason and men of patriotism—we are discussing the interest of the country. We ought not to determine the issues of this campaign upon any other basis whatever. And the interest of this country is founded in the last analysis upon its material prosperity and its social justice. I put material prosperity first, because, after all, you can't attend to your spiritual interests unless you are at least physically sustained. After a man's appetite for the means of sustaining himself passes a certain point it becomes abnormal and perhaps misleads him into many mistaken courses, but undoubtedly our first instinct is to live, and is to live in such fashion that our minds and our spirits may act normally.

Therefore, the material prosperity of the nation, in other words its wealth, is of the first consequence, and the makers of wealth in this country are, of course, chiefly the men who do the daily work, chiefly but not exclusively. Manifestly, none of us would work to advantage unless we were captained and directed. Men waste their energies if they do not cooperate in the proper way, and, therefore, the way in which large bodies of laboring men are guided and directed and united is of capital consequence in the creation of wealth. If every man acted on his own initiative and absolutely for himself, we should not be half so well off as we are under a system of careful co-ordination, each to the other. And, therefore, captains of industry and those who actually perform the industry of the day with their hands are united in a

---

1 Delivered to a "dollar dinner" of the Woodrow Wilson Working Men's League, held at the Yorkville Casino, 210 East 86th Street, New York.

2 John N. Bogart, the president of the league.

3 Wilson here probably referred to the enthusiastic reception he had been given when introduced. According to the New York *World*, Sept. 5, 1912, "men and women stood upon their chairs and shouted themselves hoarse."

single body, and just so soon as they regard themselves as separated and antagonistic, one or the other of them is mistaken.
Sometimes it is the one, and sometimes it is the other. I won't
say with whom the mistake most often lies.

Prosperity, therefore, is necessarily the first theme of a political
campaign. We want the country to prosper economically. It is,
therefore, of the first consequence that we should understand
what prosperity consists in. I am not going to moralize about it.
I am not going to remind you that we can't have genuine prosperity unless the wealth that we get leads to a very widely diffused
happiness. All that I want to illustrate now is the material side
of it: You can't have prosperity unless you have freedom of
achievement. I am not devoted to the idea of freedom merely as
a political idea. I am devoted to the idea of freedom as an economic idea, because it is demonstrable by the most superficial
study of history that only those nations have been rich as nations
in which there was absolute industrial freedom. Therefore, it
seems to me that we should look at the interests of all classes from
the point of view of freedom. When we find the control of industry, or even of important branches of industry, concentrated in
too small a number of hands, we know that a condition exists
which is just as inimical to the true interests of the men in whose
hands it is concentrated as it is to the interests of the general
body of citizenship of the country. Men who wish to concentrate
the control of industry are wishing themselves harm for the very
reason that the whole vigor of the race, the whole vigor of civilization, consists, at any rate originates, in the consciousness on
the part of every man that he is not shut out from independent
action and from achieving the highest possible power himself by
independent initiative on his own part. I believe in democracy
because it releases the energies of every human being. If I were
not free, I would feel suppressed. If I did not feel that there was
a field in which I could let my energies have their way, they
would be stunted because restrained, they would lack nourish-
ment because there was no kindly earth into which they could
strike their roots. And, therefore, individual freedom is for every
society the source of life, of every kind of life.

You know that literature has always languished in countries
where it was known that some authority, whether it was the authority of the church or the authority of the state, forbade men to
say what they really thought. You can't have a great literature if
men are to speak like parrots and say what they are taught to
say. You can't have great spirits if men dare not express their
spirits. You can't have free men if you go upon the assumption

that God is afraid to hear the truth. You must go on the theory that the Maker of truth is willing to hear it or else you will have a puny race, a restrained energy, a contemptible polity. When I resist, therefore, when I as a Democrat resist the concentration of power, I am resisting the processes of death, because the concentration of power is what always precedes the destruction of human initiative, and, therefore, of human energy.

Now, in the second place, prosperity almost by inevitable consequence from what I have said consists in the growth of enterprise and the growth of commerce. One of the reasons why I am opposed to an exaggerated protective policy is that it is a choosing beforehand to be provincial and to have as little to do with the rest of the world as possible. I hear a great deal said nowadays about the danger of free trade. There are circumstances in this country which render it absolutely impossible in our time, I dare say, that we should have free trade. We have so divided the sphere of taxation, both by principle and by practice, between the federal and the state governments that direct taxation is almost exclusively reserved for the state governments and indirect taxation is the chief resource of the federal government. And the indirect taxes which we would not pay if we knew we were paying them are chiefly paid at the customhouses. If you want to be certain that we wouldn't pay them if we knew we were paying them, watch the people who come back from Europe and go through the customs. They are the most indignant, and from the point of view of some of my compatriots, the most unpatriotic, Americans imaginable, because they kick like steers against the payment of the duties, because they are then and there consciously and visibly paying them out of their own pockets. And there would be a very different customs policy on the part of this country if everybody consciously and visibly paid the customs duties out of his own pocket directly into the hands of an officer of the government. We ought periodically, all of us, to go outside and then come in again to realize what is happening. So that when people talk to you about the danger of free trade and the folly of the free trader, don't be afraid that you will meet a free trader in the dark anywhere, because there isn't any free trader who can get abroad in America at present.

All that we are considering, therefore, in considering the policy of protection, is relative freedom in trade. And what I want to point out to the workingmen here tonight, and along with the workingmen everybody else, is that America has got to such a pass that her provincialism is now in danger of working her a cruel and permanent injustice, because America is as a matter of fact producing a great deal more than there is a domestic market for, and, as I have several times said before, if she doesn't get bigger foreign markets she will burst her jacket. There will be a congestion in this country which will be more fatal economically than any widest opening of the ports could be. The workingmen of this country allowed themselves to be deceived for a long time by being told that the protective policy was for their sakes. But I notice that it is admitted now that they do not get their share, and they never did get their share, except by united effort they went and got it. And, therefore, the workingman is now waking up to the fact that the bigger the market for American goods the more work there will be, and the bigger the market for American goods the greater the triumph of American industry will be; and that American workingmen, if they get their due share of the earnings of production, will begin to put the money of the world in their pockets as well as the money of America. When we are fighting for a more extended and a freer commerce, we are fighting to increase the production of American goods, to increase the sale of American goods, to increase the variety of the prosperity of the American people, and it is now too late to consider any other policy because our domestic market is too small. If you want to see more and more men thrown out of employment, therefore, if you want to narrow the market for labor, keep the door shut tight, and you will see this whole process working in upon us in such fashion that presently things will be altered too rapidly to be suitable to the political and economic stability of the United States.

We have reached, in short, a critical point in the process of our prosperity. It has now become a question with us whether it shall continue or shall not continue, and that question should be settled largely by the settlement of the tariff question. Therefore, the prosperity of the nation and the prosperity of the workingman are one and the same thing, and the interests of the workingman and the interests of the nation are one and the same thing, partly for a very interesting reason, partly because the men who work constitute the greater part of the nation; and I dare say that the prosperity of a nation consists of the prosperity of most of the people that live in it. We have been too apt in recent years to suppose that it consisted of the inordinate prosperity of a very small portion of the people who lived in it. I don't envy them. I mean I don't grudge them any of their prosperity, provided they earned it through the means of the general prosperity. But I grudge them every dollar they earn which isn't earned by way of contributing to the general welfare. I always think of business as a social service rendered for private profit, and the profit is legitimate only in proportion as it is a service rendered.

Very well, then, how are we going to benefit the nation, and by benefiting the nation benefit ourselves? In the first place, we are going to remove—I say this with perfect confidence, whether one set of men does it or another is beside the mark, for it is going to be done—we are going to remove the artificial advantages which some men have enjoyed and substitute for them general advantages. It is amazing to me, nothing less than amazing, that any political party should propose to fix the present condition of things upon the people of the United States, and to propose to let things stand where they are. And merely to have the government be a commission to take charge of them is to remedy nothing, is to create no freedom, is to perpetuate and license the concentration of control. To remedy an evil thing by making it permanent is something that I cannot understand. I shall make war upon that to the utmost of my power. To remedy a thing by connecting it with the very processes of the government, to say that the government will merely do this, say to the people, "We can't change what has taken place, but we can ease it off for you, we can mollify it, we can remove frictions, we can stand in your stead and manage it," is merely to proclaim a helplessness which goes to the length of despairing of individual initiative and freedom. It is the very opposite of the whole process of civilization which has produced political and economic liberty. For whether these gentlemen know it or not, these same things have been tried before in other forms and have uniformly led to unsatisfactory, and at length to disastrous, results. They sound new simply because the form is new.

They remind me of a friend of mine who thought he had discovered a way to express in a single set of terms all the development of art, all the way from music to architecture, and showed his scheme to a friend of his and asked him what he thought of it. "Well," he said, "my dear fellow, that is all right, except that that same notion has been exploded ever since the time of Aristotle. You can try it over again if you wish; you can dress it up in new clothing and make a new verbiage for it, but I can guarantee beforehand that it won't work." And so we can guarantee with regard to the beneficence of government that it won't be beneficent. No government ever has been beneficent when the attitude of government was that it could take care of the people. Let me tell you that the only freedom exists where the people take care of the government. We are grown up and twenty-one, and we don't have to have anybody tell us what is good for us. We live our own lives; we know our own lives; it is our own lives that concern us, and we will tell the government what we want.

Moreover, there is nothing occult, nothing hidden, about the methods in which monopoly has been set up. We know the exact processes. Gentlemen have told us who did it. They have told us under oath before our courts and congressional committees. And do you mean to say that we can't stop a thing when we know what it is? Do you mean to say that when we know what our criminal and civil law ought to be we can't make it that and then administer it?

This is not an age of unrestricted competition, and it can't be, because there was an age of unrestricted competition and certain gentlemen got together and hogged the competition. They killed the competition of people less strong than themselves. And competition ate itself up. That is what happened! Now, we must care for the digestion of competition and not allow it to eat itself up. We know the kind of competition which has produced monopoly, and we must stop that kind of competition. We mustn't license monopoly, but we must regulate competition, a very much more feasible thing to do, and a thing in the doing of which it will be very much more possible to get suggestions from the country, instead of knowing the whole job ourselves and doing it in a little esoteric circle. For monopoly is the control of industry. The control of industry is the control of labor, and the government that controls controlled industry controls labor, and when government controls industry and labor, then what are to be your processes of independence? What are to be your processes of resistance, except processes by which to resist the government? Resist the government in America? Resist the creature of our own hands? Resist the thing that we made and can unmake? I tell you, there are some sentences which we wrote, and understood when we wrote them, and have forgotten the meaning of, and continue to repeat without understanding. We once wrote in all our declarations of right that the people had the right to create a government, and, when it no longer served their purposes, the right to alter it to the uttermost and to abolish it. And we say it every Fourth of July and forget it in betweentimes.

This government that we made, shall we not own it? Shall we be its wards? Shall we be told by it what the processes of our industry shall be? There isn't any body of men who knows enough to do it. I have heard men speak of experts on the tariff. Well, I have lived among so-called economic experts all my life, and I know that anybody who pretends to be an expert on the tariff is a fake. Because to claim to be an expert on the tariff is to claim to have digested in your own comprehension the whole business of the United States, and I know that nobody knows enough to know that. I have met men who thought they knew it, but then I have met men who thought they knew a great many things that weren't so! That is the malady that most of us grow into sooner or later! The trouble, by the way, with some parts of our community, the standpat part, is that they still think that they know things that were once so but are no longer so. They are living under the hallucination that the conditions of the year 1912 are just about the conditions of the year 1860. They won't all admit that they go back that far, but they are really still thinking the facts that their fathers supplied them with. Because most of us live on borrowed information, and much of our information has been borrowed from the last generation. The business of politics right now is to bring things up to the year 1912, to require that every alleged fact shall have the 1912 stamp on it, and to see that nobody faked and put the stamp on it last year.

Now, there are other positive ways of securing freedom of achievement and, through freedom of achievement, the growth of enterprise and of prosperity. There is not only the negative way of seeing that nobody has a chance to monopolize it, that the kind of competition that kills is absolutely prevented. And then there is the positive way. The positive way will make a very different country of the United States. We have been thinking in terms of our own enterprise and of our own life so long that it is costing some gentlemen apparently a physical effort to think about the rest of the world. In order to make America prosperous, she must supply the world with the example and the substance of American enterprise and American ingenuity and industry.

I do not like to say it but, upon my word, I have been impressed sometimes with a very marked difference between American businessmen whom I have talked with and foreign businessmen. I am not speaking merely of the rank and file of businessmen here; I am speaking of some of the businessmen who stand highest in the management of American business. As compared with many a foreign businessman, they seem to be veritable provincials, ignorant of the markets of the world, ignorant of the courses and routes of commerce, ignorant of the banking processes even by which goods are exchanged. Why, do you know, I haven't looked this up recently, but when I last looked it up practically the whole business of buying foreign bills of exchange was in the hands of Canadian bankers, who had had to come down to New York and San Francisco and our other great ports in order to do that part of banking which is absolutely indispensable to the international exchanges of the world; because the Canadian banks were equipped for commerce with the world, and the American banks were not. And it was doubtful, I was told, whether the federal banking act made it possible for national banks to engage in that. I don't know whether that is any longer true or not, but the idea of a great commercial nation turning all its processes in on itself and not taking advantage of the enormous energy which it has not yet released!

I was saying today to a body of foreign-born fellow citizens of ours that what interested me about immigration, when it was not assisted by the steamship companies, was that the man who started from some distant country to come to America started with a vision of America in his mind. You know, I was reminded by one of these very gentlemen whom I was addressing that Mr. Israel Zangwill[4] conceived this very beautiful idea. He said that Judea was not now a place but a spiritual conception, and that every Jew everywhere who had the true Jewish spirit in him was a spiritual part of Judea.[5] And it seems to me that men who long for the kind of liberty which they believe they can get in America, and come to America to get it, bring spiritual America along with them. Then when they get here they find that the reverse is more true, that America has not itself a touch with the great outlying world, that she has confined her own industries to her own borders. That was no doubt inevitable. We had a pretty big continent to get possession of and develop, and we had a lot of things to do before we would have a lot more goods than we could consume; but we have passed that now, and it is absolutely indispensable that we should, among other things, develop a merchant marine.

When it is again my privilege, and I hope I shall live to see the day, to see the stars and stripes upon many and many a ship upon every sea, however distant, I shall know that the pulse of American labor beats in every quarter of the globe, that you have only to go on deck in order to see presently sweep above the horizon that emblem of our liberty which means that America is abroad. How we have confined her! How we have cheated ourselves by not letting our valor in industry and our valor in thought and our valor in enterprise of every sort exhibit itself before the whole face of the world! Liberty is its own reward. I had a thou-

---

[4] English novelist and playwright, specializing in stories of Jewish life and the ghetto.

[5] Formerly a leader in the Zionist movement, Zangwill broke with the Zionists in 1905 over the question of whether Palestine was indispensable as the location of the projected Jewish state. Zangwill then devoted himself to the Jewish Territorialist Organization, which had as its objective an autonomous Jewish homeland anywhere in the world. See Maurice Wohlgelernter, *Israel Zangwill* (New York, 1964), pp. 158-74.

sand times rather be free than be taken care of. Don't you remember how long it seemed to take to get to be twenty-one, so you could strike out for yourselves? Now, how long is it going to take the United States to be twenty-one? How long is it going to take it to reach its majority? How long is it going to take businessmen in America to find out that they have got brains enough not to depend upon the Ways and Means Committee of the House and the Finance Committee of the Senate, not to go to their dear grandmother down at Washington to ask her not to let anybody hurt them, not to let anybody use brains against them that would beat their brains? Think of the admission that is in that! If I want my brains protected, you may make sure that I suspect I haven't got many. And if I want my skill kept out of competition with others, you may be sure that I know I haven't developed my skill. And yet we boast, and boast with truth, that we have the most skillfull workmen in the world.

Afraid of our own prowess! Afraid to venture out! Afraid to go beyond the road! It seems to me, therefore, that we are preaching a very inspiriting thing in this campaign. For if you will let me, I will bring the campaign into the room for a minute. We are preaching nothing less than the original evangel of labor and achievement, and I, for my part, would not think myself fit to live under that flag if I did not believe in those things. That flag was flung to the breeze originally to proclaim that this little nation, with only three million people in it, was ready to show the rest of the round globe how to be free. And now, with between ninety million and a hundred millions in it, we have even suppressed the flag, so far as displaying it in foreign waters is concerned, except occasionally upon a yacht. We send certain well-dressed and extremely well-mannered gentlemen around the world to take care of the flag and to display it at their mastheads, and I am very well satisfied to be represented by their manners and their courtesy and all that belongs to them. But I don't like to feel that we can't trust our flag also to the men who are doing the work in the very act of carrying the flag.

Freedom is, in the modern world, at any rate, an American enterprise, and, as an American, I would be ashamed to stand for anything but freedom. And as an American, I should be particularly ashamed to invite my fellow countrymen to let me take care of them.[6]

T MS (C. L. Swem Coll., NjP); with minor corrections from the ICF transcript in RSB Coll., DLC, and from the partial texts in the New York *Evening Post* and *New York Times*, Sept. 5, 1912.

[6] There is a brief WWhw outline of this speech dated Sept. 4, 1912, in WP, DLC.

To Louis Wiley

Confidential

My dear Mr. Wiley,   Sea Girt, New Jersey 5 Sept., 1912

When you were at Sea Girt one day, you were generous enough to say to me that I might call on you for anything that you could do in my behalf. I am going to take advantage of your kindness and speak of a matter which I approach with genuine reluctance.

The Mr. [Isaac K.] Russell who represents *The Times* in the little group of reporters down here is a *very* honorable, likeable, ingenuous fellow, of whom we are all very fond, and I would not for the world do him a disservice, but he is singularly unable to see anything *simply* and just as it is. Everything he touches takes colour from his own (disinterested but whimsical) fancy, and once or twice he has embarrassed me very much by the squint he has, quite innocently, given things. He is entirely lacking in the political sense,—does not see where implications lead,—gives his stories a "human value" which puts the humans of whom he is writing in a very false light. If he *could* be withdrawn without humiliation or detriment to himself, it would relieve me of an anxiety that is growing burdensome to me. It would be a great comfort to have some fellow of a less complex mind, who looks at things more directly and simply and sees them as they *are*!

Forgive me if I have gone too far in response to your kindness; and pray, if you heed my wish, give poor Russell something quite as good. He would understand many things, but he does not comprehend a political candidate or a political campaign.

With warm regard,
          Cordially and sincerely Yours,   Woodrow Wilson

ALS (L. Wiley Papers, NRU).

Remarks to an Italian-American Delegation at Sea Girt[1]

[Sept. 5, 1912]

Gentlemen: I am very much complimented by this visit. There is no sort of visit more welcome to me now, because I fear that things I have written have been most grossly misinterpreted. I have had frequent occasions recently to meet delegations similar to this, and it has been a great gratification to me that they all speak not only in generous language of appreciation towards myself, but also with an extremely broadminded apprehension of what my real position is and of what my real feelings are.

The fact of the matter is that America has been enriched by

having the aspirations of some of the finest races in the world brought to her shores. I don't know whether we ought to rejoice that other countries are in the same degree impoverished, but for myself, as an American along with yourselves, I rejoice most heartily in the circumstances that men of every European blood have brought to this country their highest aspirations, because they can't bring those aspirations without adding to the aspirations of the country and making the country greater and freer than it would be without them.

For myself, I have never felt the slightest jealousy of the right kind of immigration, and by the right kind of immigration I mean the voluntary kind. When men of their own initiative come with a preliminary love for, or desire for, America, to establish homes for themselves here and to identify themselves with the country, the result cannot be anything but good for the country itself. I have been jealous, as we have all been jealous—I am sure I am including all of you—in assisted immigration, of the immigration which is got up by the steamship companies, by contractors who wish to bring over men who will be at their beck and call rather than men of independence who elect for themselves. But while we all agree there must be certain restrictions to guard the health of the country, for example, we shall all agree, I am sure, if we have the true democratic spirit that that is the only sort of limitation which is legitimate.

I have reminded my friends several times that the Democratic party originated in one sense in a very warm protest against the action of the Federalist party, which first had control of the government of the United States, to limit the process of naturalization so sharply as to make it almost impossible. You will remember that the famous Alien and Sedition laws aimed first of all to limit naturalization, and second to limit any criticism that American citizens might level at their own government. In other words, they struck at one and the same time against immigration and against freedom of speech in America. And the flame of protest which sprang up at that time may be said to have been the flame in which the Democratic party was born. It would be inconsistent with those old traditions, therefore, if it adopted any other policy. But the generous spirit in which you yourselves have spoken shows that you don't have to have these things explained to you.

And I particularly liked the phraseology in which you spoke of yourselves as Americans of foreign birth. I don't like to hear people speak of Italian Americans and German Americans and Swedish Americans, and the rest of them, because that seems to cut us up into sections. I was saying yesterday at a meeting of publishers and editors of American papers published in European languages that I didn't feel that a language was foreign after it had been Americanized. The English language has been Americanized, as we all know. Some Englishmen are very insistent that it has been injured in being Americanized. And whenever a foreign language is used to express American ideas, I think that it has become a naturalized language. And so when we live American ideas, we are Americans, and at no other time. And when we live American ideas, we can forget our diversity of race and birth.

I am sincerely obliged to you for the compliment you have paid me in this visit.

T MS (C. L. Swem Coll., NjP); with two minor corrections from the ICF transcript in the RSB Coll., DLC.

[1] Wilson received and spoke briefly to several delegations of Italian Americans at Sea Girt on September 5, 1912. One of them was from Brooklyn. The newspaper accounts differ as to whether there were one or two other groups and whether they were from New York City or New Jersey, or both.

From Cleveland Hoadley Dodge

Upper Saranac P. O. Franklin Co. N. Y.

My dear Woodrow,   Sept. 5th, 1912

For the past two years, I have tried to keep in the background, & avoid "butting in," & to do what I could for you quietly, but I am now forced to bother you with a matter of importance.

McCombs will be obliged very soon to make a full report of his pre-nomination receipts and expenditures,[1] and the situation is a little embarrassing owing to the fact, that, the publication of the names of some of the contributors will excite comment, & be used by your opponents. I am not worried, however, so much on that account, as I am by the fear that McCombs may possibly try to evade the issue, & not be perfectly frank & open. That would not only not be right but it would do infinitely more harm than good.

A large share (about one half) of what McCombs spent was received from me, and although he did not *know exactly* where & in what amounts it came from, he did know that I represented a small group of your warm Princeton friends, most of whose names he knew.[2] If he does not testify fully as to the sources, I would be called & if I declined to give the names, say, on the ground that I was pledged to secrecy the result would be unfortunate. David Jones spent last Tuesday with me & we fully agreed that the only right and wise thing for McCombs to do, is to get from me the exact list, and frankly tell the whole truth and nothing but the truth, with the kind of explanation which he could well give. I would gladly give my testimony if necessary, but I cannot help having a sneaking fear that, if I should appear before the Committee, they might bring up the matter of that newspaper,[3] which would be unpleasant.

I feel sorry for Cyrus, who is worried on account of the Harvester suit, but as Perkins said to me the other day "Why doesn't Cyrus come out in the open as I have done." (He knew of course that Cyrus is for you). The Jones's gifts & mine would excite no comment, and if McCombs reported the gifts of Cyrus & his brother & mother[4] the murder would at least be out, & in ample time before election. Probably there would be little harm done, but even if there were, none of us could possibly favor any other course. An additional advantage would accrue from the fact, that if the names of your pre-convention friends were known, everyone would expect them to contribute to the present campaign expenses, and they could then come out in the open, and give the liberal financial aid, which they are ready and anxious to give, if it is needed and can be wisely accepted.[5] David Jones will see Cyrus in a few days, and I trust that he will look at the matter in the same light that we do. It seems absurd for me to write as I have, for I know how you must feel about it, and I remember what you said about Cyrus, that night on the yacht. I am probably wrong in worrying about McCombs, whom I highly respect, but I am compelled to unburden my mind, and, if I have erred, I trust that you will forgive me, and in any event I know that you will do what is right & best.[6]

I am sending this through Mr. McAdoo's hands, so as to be sure of having it reach you, and you will likely wish to discuss the matter with him. Do not bother to make a long reply, but if you will simply write me three or four lines, addressed as above, & reassure my mind, it will be a great comfort to me.

I expect to be back in New York, about the 25th of the month, in ample time to see McCombs if he desires to see me, or if necessary, I could run down for a day or two, at an earlier date.

Congratulating you heartily on your capital speeches & the fine prospects, believe me, with warm regards to you & yours.

Most cordially & affectionately   Cleveland H Dodge

ALS (WP, DLC).

[1] Before the subcommittee of the United States Senate, Senator Moses E. Clapp, chairman, which held hearings on campaign contributions from June 14, 1912, to February 25, 1913. McCombs and McAdoo both testified on October 14.

[2] Dodge himself contributed $51,300. In addition, he received $1,000 from Edward W. Sheldon, $10,500 from David B. Jones, $10,500 from Thomas D. Jones, and $12,500 from Cyrus H. McCormick. As Dodge indicates, this total

of $85,800 represented almost one half of the reported total sum of $193,565.81 spent on Wilson's prenomination campaign. See *Campaign Contributions: Testimony before a Subcommittee of the Committee on Privileges and Elections*, U.S. Senate, 62nd Cong., 3d sess. (2 vols., Washington, 1913), I, 868-69; II, 946.

3 The Trenton *True American*. About this matter, see WW to C. H. Dodge, June 20, 1911, n. 2, Vol. 23. Dodge did testify before the Clapp committee on October 15 on this as well as other matters. Henry Jones Ford and Edward Howe also testified about the *True American* on that date. See *Campaign Contributions*, II, 948, 950, 952-60.

4 The contribution of $12,500 from Cyrus H. McCormick included donations from his mother, Nettie Fowler McCormick, and his brother, Harold Fowler McCormick.

5 Dodge and the others mentioned in n. 2 above did give generously to the Democratic presidential campaign of 1912. Sheldon gave $1,000; Thomas D. Jones, $10,000; David B. Jones, $10,000; and Dodge, himself, $35,000. See *Report of the Treasurer, Democratic National Committee, Receipts and Disbursements Prior to November 30, 1912* (St. Louis, 1913), pp. 5, 14, 33.

6 As it turned out, shortly after McCombs' testimony before the Clapp committee, Dodge decided that McCormick's contribution to the prenomination campaign should be refunded. After obtaining McCormick's consent, he returned the money. See the draft of a statement printed at Oct. 25, 1912.

From William Gibbs McAdoo

PERSONAL.

Dear Governor: New York September 5, 1912.

I enclose the tentative itinerary which we discussed yesterday. If I were you I would not announce any definite dates beyond September 21st. It is possible that we may want to revise the others somewhat.

Please let me urge upon you strongly the necessity for preparing your speeches for this trip so that they may be given to the Associated Press at least a week in advance of their delivery. Even though you do not stick to your text, it is of great importance that this be done, if possible. We are not getting the degree of publicity for your speeches that we ought to have, and it is due solely to the fact that you do not give out advance copies. It is much better to repeat to a large degree former speeches you have made, and to give out advance copies, than to make extemporary speeches and suffer their emasculation in print.[1]

I think you will make a great hit in your forthcoming speeches if you drive hard at Mr. Roosevelt for many of the things he is saying in his speeches. If you have your Secretaries look out for some of Mr. Roosevelt's speeches you will find that he is beginning to make the bold charge that your nomination was arranged by Taggart, Sullivan and Murphy at the Baltimore Convention. This, of course, is an absolute falsehood, and you may have to notice it. I enclose an article which I had in mind.[2]

I submit these things merely for your consideration. I have given out no statement about your itinerary, leaving this entirely to you.   Very sincerely yours,   W G McAdoo

TLS (WP, DLC). Enc.: typed itinerary.
    [1] Wilson continued to give only extemporaneous speeches. His aides supplied the wire services with advance texts by giving them copies of Wilson's recent speeches.
    [2] "Says Bosses Named Wilson," New York *Evening Post*, Sept. 5, 1912, reported on a speech by Theodore Roosevelt in St. Paul. McAdoo circled a paragraph in which Roosevelt was quoted as saying: "The nomination of Mr. Wilson was arranged by Mr. Taggart of Indiana and Mr. Sullivan of Illinois, with Mr. Murphy of New York finally joining in."

To Chester Childs Platt[1]

My dear Mr. Platt: Sea Girt, N. J. September 6, 1912.

Allow me to acknowledge the receipt of your letter of August thirtieth[2] and to express my sincere interest in it. The information and judgment it conveys impressed me very much, indeed. I feel as deeply as you do the gravity of the New York State situation and hope with all my heart that the forces that are working for a wise choice in the matter of the governorship will prevail.[3]

I have the highest respect and regard for Mr. Sulzer and can fully understand your feeling with regard to his possible candidacy.

I am going to take the liberty of sending your letter on to National Headquarters where I am sure that it will be read with the greatest interest.

              Cordially and sincerely yours,   Woodrow Wilson

TCL (WP, DLC).
    [1] Editor of the *Batavia*, N. Y., *Times*.
    [2] It is missing.
    [3] Essentially, it was a question of whether Charles F. Murphy would permit the nomination for governor of an anti-Tammany candidate by the forthcoming Democratic state convention.

To Richard Heath Dabney

My dear Heath: Sea Girt, N. J. September 6, 1912.

I congratulate you with all my heart. It is perfectly delightful that the little daughter[1] should have come so promptly to greet you and cheer you, and I share your happiness. I must rush this message off to you at once because my heart was made very full by your letter.[2]

              Always affectionately yours,   Woodrow Wilson

TLS (Wilson-Dabney Corr., ViU).
  1 Alice Saunders Dabney, born September 4, 1912.
  2 It is missing.

To Franklin Potts Glass

Personal.

My dear Glass: Sea Girt, N. J. September 6, 1912

Thank you warmly for your letter of September second.[1] I am very much distressed to learn of your daughter's[2] illness and relieved that you think it is not going to be severe.

Alas! it seems a physical impossibility for me to get into the South during the campaign. I haven't a Bull Moose's strength, as Roosevelt seems to have, and it seems imperative, both to the Committee and myself, that I should devote the few remaining weeks of the campaign to the debatable parts of the country. I regret this very keenly because I realize to the full the force of all you say.

Mrs. Wilson joins me in warm regards to you all. I wish I had time to write real letters. I have to write in a sort of shorthand of phrasing.

Cordially and faithfully yours,   Woodrow Wilson

TCL (RSB Coll., DLC).
  1 F. P. Glass to WW, Sept. 2, 1912, TLS (WP, DLC).
  2 Louise. She was recovering from typhoid fever.

To Daniel T. O'Regan[1]

My Dear Mr. O'Regan: Sea Girt, N. J. September 6, 1912.

I have read your letter of yesterday with great interest. The questions it contains call for the frankest answer.

Since the passage of the Geran act, I have come to realize that the provision of that act which permits the bracketing of candidates[2] does operate, as you suggest, against independent candidacy. I cannot say that the bracketing of candidates is, in my opinion, against the spirit of the law because the law explicitly permits it; but I will frankly say that I regret that that provision was put into the law and I have the warmest and strongest sympathy with what is, of course, the general purpose of the act to open wide the doors to nomination.

I, of course, did not help to select candidates in Hudson County; I have felt at liberty, when consulted, to express my opinion about individuals whether they deserved to be supported or did not, and

I have been equally frank in both particulars, but I have felt it my duty not to attempt to control such matters in any way but to leave the action taken entirely to the judgment of those who consulted me. I have in no case departed from this rule.

Cordially and sincerely yours,   [Woodrow Wilson]

CCL (WP, DLC).

1 Lawyer of Union, N. J. He was a non-organization candidate for Democratic nomination for the Assembly from Hudson County. He was not nominated.

2 Under the provisions of the Geran election law, the names of all primary candidates for the same office were ordinarily printed in alphabetical order under the several designations of the office to be voted for. However, candidates might by their own request be grouped together by means of a bracket under certain designations.

To Thomas Davies Jones

My dear Friend: Sea Girt, N. J. September 6, 1912.

Thank you heartily for your little note of encouragement. It did me a lot of good. I am extremely glad that you liked the Buffalo speech.

In haste,   Faithfully yours,   Woodrow Wilson

TLS (Mineral Point, Wisc., Public Library).

From Louis Wiley

Personal.

My dear Governor: Times Square. September 6, 1912.

Acknowledging your note of yesterday: I have taken up the suggestion you courteously make, with our Managing Editor Mr. [Carl V.] Van Anda, who will carry it out. It may not be acted upon promptly, as it may take a little time to make the change without humiliation to the young man affected. I am sorry the service he has performed has not been in all respects satisfactory. I sincerely hope his successor will meet your approbation.

I look forward to the pleasure of seeing you soon. I told Mr. Tumulty over the telephone the other day that if there comes a time on one of your visits to New York when you do not wish to go to the University Club or the hotel, my bachelor abode at the Wyoming, West 55th Street and Seventh Avenue, is at your disposal,—and if you would come I shall be honored and delighted.

With best regards,

Always sincerely yours,   Louis Wiley

ALS (WP, DLC).

To Louis Wiley

Personal.

My dear Mr. Wiley: Sea Girt, N. J. September 7, 1912.

Thank you warmly for your courtesy and kindness. I am sure you know how much I appreciate it.

It is very thoughtful of you to offer me the use of your bachelor quarters, and I wish with all my heart I could look forward to the chance to avail myself of your kindness. Apparently, escape to covert is the hardest thing in the world for me now.

Cordially and sincerely yours,   Woodrow Wilson

TLS (L. Wiley Papers, NRU).

To Thomas Davies Jones

My dear Friend: Sea Girt, N. J. September 7, 1912.

I had discovered my mistake before your letter of September fifth[1] came and I am heartily ashamed of having made it. I was misled, as the compilers of the textbook[2] evidently have been, by statements purporting to be official which ought to have been carefully scrutinized before they were used. I am permitted not an half hour a day for my own use and take things often at second hand which I ought to verify for myself. I took the statement about harvester machines from what was said to be a report from one of our consuls in Great Britain. This is an explanation, not an excuse. For such blunders are not excusable. I am sincerely sorry and I am warmly obliged to you for your letter.

Just as a matter of detail, I did not explicitly say that reapers and mowers were among the agricultural implements which were sold more cheaply abroad than in the United States. But, nevertheless, the statement, as I made it, did clearly imply that I included them.

I am going to send your letter at once to the Campaign Committee. I fear that the mischief is already done by the printing of the whole edition of the campaign book, but I shall do what I can to correct it.

Of course, I need not tell you that I have made no "attack" on anybody. I was trying to state what I supposed to be the facts, under the operation of the tariff and it would not have occured to me to impute moral blame to any manufacturer who showed what seems to be a common practice.

With warmest regard and appreciation,

Faithfully yours,   Woodrow Wilson

TLS (Mineral Point, Wisc., Public Library).
    ¹ T. D. Jones to WW, Sept. 5, 1912, TCL (Mineral Point, Wisc., Public Library).
    ² *The Democratic Text-Book 1912 . . . Issued by the Democratic National Committee . . .* (New York, 1912), pp. 189, 206-207, 237-40.

To Mary Allen Hulbert

Dearest Friend,   Sea Girt, New Jersey 8 Sept., 1912

I find myself not a little disturbed about you. I have heard not a line from you for more than three weeks. I fear that you or some one dear to you is ill. The feeling has so taken hold upon me that my mind will not let itself *go* for a free chat with you till I hear and know. We are all well,—as well as one can be amidst strenuous days,—and all unite in the prayer that you will let us see your handwriting again!

                    Your devoted friend,   Woodrow Wilson

ALS (WP, DLC).

To the Democrats of New Jersey

[[Sept. 8, 1912]]

Mr. Smith has, of course, a perfect right to offer himself at the primaries as a candidate for the Democratic nomination for Senator of the United States. He is acting frankly and in the spirit of the new law, and if he is preferred at the primaries it will be the duty of every Democratic member of the next Legislature to vote for him when a Senator is chosen. But I feel that I ought to speak very frankly about the significance of his candidacy.

It is not only my privilege as a citizen but my duty as the leader of my party to point out just what is involved in this matter for the Democratic party in this state and for the party in the nation. When I was elected Governor I put myself under the most solemn and explicit pledges to the people of New Jersey. I had told them during the campaign in which I sought their support that I would understand my election to mean that they commissioned me to act as the leader of my party and as the spokesman of all the people of the state; that I would deem it my duty to keep them advised concerning every important matter that affected their political welfare and safety, and that I would give them the best and frankest counsel I could with regard to every public matter in which my advice might be of service to them. These are promises which I cannot in conscience ignore.

It is very distasteful to me to be obliged to make public comment upon Mr. Smith's candidacy, but it is an obligation which I cannot honorably escape. Interests of the greatest consequence both to the party and to the nation are involved, and I cannot be silent. The fact that I am at present the responsible leader of my party in the nation, as well as in the state, makes my duty all the more clear and imperative.

Mr. Smith's selection as the Democratic candidate for the Senate would be the most fatal step backward that the Democrats of the state could possibly take. It would mean his restoration to political leadership in New Jersey the moment my service as Governor ended, and with his restoration, a return to the machine rule which so long kept every active Democrat in the state in subordination to him and prevented every progressive program conceived in the interest of the people from being put into effect.

I speak with knowledge in this matter because at every turn of my administration since I became Governor I have found his hand against the new plans of the party—his influence working steadily but covertly against everything that has substituted hope and pride for discouragement and shame in the politics of New Jersey during the twenty months during which I have been permitted to serve the people of the state.

It is of particularly sinister import that Mr. Smith should seek to return to the Senate of the United States at this time. He was sent to the Senate once before, when the tariff had been the chief issue of the national campaign and when the Democrats had, for once in a generation, an opportunity to relieve the people of intolerable burdens and the industry of the country of the trammels which bound it like a straitjacket. If the tariff could have been wisely revised then, we might have been spared some part, at least, of the crop of trusts and combinations which now rule and circumscribe our markets.

Mr. Smith was one of a small group of Senators, calling themselves Democrats, who, at that critical and hopeful juncture in our politics, utterly defeated the program of the party.[1] His election now might bring the party face to face with a similar disaster and disgrace, and would unquestionably render the satisfactory administration of the federal functions in New Jersey all but impossible for a Democratic President.

These are plain words, my fellow citizens, but I cannot permit any reluctance on my part to speak in criticism of a fellow citizen to stand even for a moment in the way of my duty as the leader of a party pledged to the people's interest and now under peculiar obligation to fulfill that pledge. If the Democratic party does not keep its promises now it will never have another opportunity to do so. Mr. Smith could not and would not lend himself to any program of genuinely progressive legislation.

My first allegiance is to the progressive policies to which I have openly and solemnly dedicated every power I possess. Everything else must stand aside in the interest of the country and of the great state of which I am Governor. I have pointed out to you facts and forces toward which you may, perhaps, have grown indulgently indifferent in this brighter day of New Jersey's regeneration. I know how you will act when you are reminded of them. We can indulge nothing when the stake is our country's welfare and prosperity and the honor of our party.[2]

Printed in the *Trenton Evening Times*, Sept. 9, 1912, with one correction from the text in the *New York Times*, Sept. 9, 1912.

[1] About this matter, see E. A. Stevens to WW, Nov. 29, 1910, n. 2, Vol. 22.

[2] There is a WWsh draft of this statement, with the composition date of Sept. 5, 1912, in WP, DLC.

An Address to the New York Press Club

[Sept. 9, 1912]

Mr. Toastmaster:[1] I count it very handsome of a kid brother not to have given me away.[2] When he got to his feet, I trembled in the anticipation of what might be revealed. But the Wilsons are discreet.

It is customary to say, particularly on interesting occasions like this, that it is very gratifying to be present. But I can say it with more than the customary zest because, without thinking too highly of newspapermen, I do realize that they are men who, when you get close to them, can understand more things in five minutes than most other men can understand in half an hour. I am not promising that I will be through in five minutes. And to speak seriously, whether the very gracious predictions as to what I am to be that have been made this evening[3] are verified or not, I shall at least for a few weeks enjoy a very much coveted privilege. For I have long coveted the privilege of discussing with my fellow citizens the affairs of the country as if I were not a candidate but a citizen of the country.

It seems to me that it is high time that even those who have parties themselves to commend to the approval of the country should speak of our public affairs with absolute candor and with-

[1] Charles Raymond Macauley, president of the New York Press Club.

[2] Macauley had called on Joseph R. Wilson, Jr., who was working in the Democratic campaign headquarters, to introduce his brother.

[3] By Ralph Pulitzer, among others.

out attempting to overstate even the claims of the parties which they themselves try to represent. Because my dream of politics all my life has been that it is the common business, that it is something we owe it to each other to understand, and owe it to each other to discuss with absolute frankness; for when we discuss the questions pending in a political campaign, we are not only determining in whose hands the government shall be placed, but for what purposes the government is to be used when placed in those hands. And it makes a great deal of difference whether we have a candid understanding beforehand with one another or not. I should be ashamed of myself if I tried to obscure or misstate the pending problems, and I promised myself as I came here tonight the privilege, if I might, of setting the scene of the present contest and trying to point out as clearly as I could what seemed to me to be involved.

Whatever we may say about the particular character in detail of the problems that we are now facing, the fundamental problem of all is to set our government free to deal with them. Because if there be any tithe of truth in the things which we have said are now entangling our politics and making just action impossible, it is true that in past decades the Government of the United States has not been free to act in the interest of all of us. It has had special rather than general connections. And it is the problem of the present campaign to set it free for action. When it is set free, what is it to do? Why, it seems to me that it is to do a very great thing. It is to serve civilization and humanity.

When we set up this government, we deliberately set ourselves at the front of the enterprises of civilization and of humanity. We said, "Governments hitherto have not been suited to the general interest. We are going to set up a government that is. Governments hitherto have not been interested in the general advancement of the welfare of men of all classes and conditions. This government shall be." We are not at liberty as Americans, if we maintain the standards which we professed at the outset, to treat our government as if it were merely the instrument for party control, and as if parties were merely the instruments for putting first the interests of this class and then the interests of the other at the front.

Now, if we are to free our government to serve civilization and humanity, what are we going to do in the present campaign? I am not going to pretend that we shall find a perfect means of doing either of these things. I simply want to put before us a comparative study of the means that are at our disposal to accomplish this thing. I am going to discuss the claims of three parties as the condition to undertake this task. I am leaving out the other parties, of which there are a number, not out of any disrespect to them, for some of them profess very noble purposes, but merely because of the more than likelihood, the certainty, that they will not be able to get control of the government of the country. Let's confine ourselves then to three parties.

If you want to set the government free, can you employ the party that entangled it? My implication in asking that question is not that any set of Republicans deliberately made partnerships which rendered it impossible for them to serve the people. Moreover, I want in every such discussion to discriminate between the great body of my fellow citizens who have usually voted the Republican ticket and that small body of my fellow citizens who have usually misled them into voting it. For the leaders of the Republican party are one thing; and the Republican party rank and file is a very different thing, constituting some half of the American nation. And I am quite ready to admit that the leaders who have led these voters to do things which would not inure to the interests of the country would not intend to pursue any impolitic or deleterious course. I am not uttering an indictment. I am simply pointing out what I believe most of you will admit to be the facts.

The Republican party, by reason of the tariff policy in particular, has tied the administration of this government to certain great interests, chiefly by the means of campaign contributions, so thoroughly and in such complicated fashion that it is unreasonable to suppose that the very next administration should seek to do what even this administration has not even attempted to do. If there were symptoms that the present administration had attempted to do this, if there were symptoms that the present administration had pursued any consistent course whatever by which we would be able to calculate the orbit of another administration of the same sort, then perhaps the case would seem to need argument. But it does not seem to me to need argument. It speaks for itself.

I am not going to detain you to further analyze the answer to the question, "Can you set the government free and serve civilization and humanity through the regular Republican party?"

I am one of those who entertain a very great respect for the history of the Republican party. I do not see how any man, though like myself bred a Democrat from the beginning, can fail to realize with how great a purpose it came into existence and how high a destiny for the time it pursued. The entanglements of modern economic development set a very different scene for the Republican party from that which was set forth when it came upon the field of action. I am discussing only the year 1912 and trying to forecast the years which will follow the year 1912.

Well, if not the regular Republican party, to whom shall we turn? There is a new party which it is difficult to characterize because it is made up of several elements. As I see it, it is made up of three elements in particular. The first consists of those Republicans whose consciences and whose stomachs couldn't stand what the regular Republicans were doing. They were called at first in New Jersey New Idea Republicans, when it was a new idea that a Republican could do wrong. Later, in other states, they came to be called insurgent Republicans—Republicans, that is to say, were setting up an insurrection against the control of their own party. And now the insurrectors are outside and have set up for themselves and constitute a very important element, perhaps the largest element in the new party.

But added to this element is a second one that interests me very deeply. A great many men and women of noble character, of the most elevated purpose, have joined themselves to the new party because in the platform adopted by that party most of the reforms, which ought a long time ago to have been undertaken but most of which have been absolutely ignored by political parties, have been embodied. Irrespective of the present, I venture to conjecture, these high-spirited men and women believe that this combination of forces may in the future bring them out on a plane where they can accomplish these things which their hearts have so long desired. I take off my hat to these people. I sympathize with their impulses. I haven't a word of criticism of them for allying themselves with any force, any honorable force, which they think can accomplish these things.

Then there is a third element in the new party of which the less said the better. To discuss it would be interesting only if I could mention names, and I have forbidden myself that indulgence.

It is not a homogeneous party, therefore. You see it is made up of elements old and new, made up of some elements that are only absolutely new in politics because they have never before distinctly aligned themselves with a political party.

And the question that arises when we ask ourselves, "Shall we put the government in the hands of that party?" is this: Can it carry out this program of social betterment and reform? I don't know how to test that matter, how to answer that question, except by examining the portion of the program which seems to be distinctly political rather than social. Because, let me remind you, the problem we start out with is: We want a free political instrument by which we can do these things. If we can't get it, it can't be done by that instrument.

You have in this new party two things—a political party and a body of social reformers. Will the political party contained in it be serviceable to the social reformers? I do not think that I am mistaken in picking out as the political part of that platform the part which determines how the government is going to stand related to the central problems upon which its freedom depends. The freedom of the Government of the United States depends upon getting separated from, disentangled from, those interests which have enjoyed, chiefly enjoyed, the patronage of that government. Because the trouble with the tariff is not that it has been protective, for in recent years it has been much more than protective. It has been one of the most colossal systems of deliberate patronage that has ever been conceived. And the main trouble with it is that the protection stops where the patronage begins, and that if you could lop off the patronage, you would have taken away most of the objectionable features of the so-called protection.

This patronage, this special privilege, these favors doled out to some persons and not to all, have been the basis of the control which has been set up over the industries and over the enterprises of this country by great combinations. Because we forgot, in permitting a regime of free competition to last so long, that the competitors had ceased to be individuals or small groups of individuals, and it had come to be a competition between individuals or small groups on the one hand and enormous aggregations of individuals and capital on the other; and that, after that contrast in strength had been created in fact, competition, free competition, was out of the question, that it was then possible for the powerful to crush the weak.

That isn't competition; that is warfare. And because we did not check the free competition soon enough, because we did not check it at the point where pigmies entered the field against giants, we have created a condition of affairs in which the control of industry, and to a large extent the control of credit in this country, upon which industry feeds and in which all new enterprises must be rooted, is in the hands of a comparatively small and very compact body of men. These are the gentlemen who have in some instances, perhaps in more than have been exhibited by legal proof, engaged in what we are now expected to call "unreasonable combinations in restraint of trade." They have indulged themselves beyond reason in the exercise of that power which makes competition practically impossible.

Very well then, the test of our freedom for the next generation lies here. Are we going to take that power away from them, or are we going to leave it with them? You can take it away from them if you regulate competition and make it impossible for them to do some of the things which they have been doing. You leave it with them if you legitimatize and regulate monopoly. And what the platform of the new party proposes to do is exactly that.

It proposes to start where we are, and, without altering the established conditions of competition, which are conditions which affect it. We shall say what these giants shall do and to what the pigmies shall submit, and we shall do that not by law, for if you will read the plank in its candid statement—for it is perfectly candid—you will find that it rejects regulation by law and proposes a commission which shall have the discretion itself to undertake what the plank calls "constructive regulation." It shall make its rules as it goes along. As it handles these giants, so shall it shape its course. That, gentlemen, is nothing more than a legitimatized continuation of the present order of things, with the alliance between the great interests and the government open instead of covert.

There will then be nothing wrong in the alliance. The alliance will be grafted into the policy of the nation, and we shall simply say to one another, "Big as these men are, the federal government is bigger than they are. And we will depend upon the federal government to take care of them." But, gentlemen, that depends on who takes care of the federal government. And if you make it necessary, in order that they may have a comparatively free hand in the conduct of their colossal business, that they control the government, what is to prevent their controlling a government which for a generation they have already controlled? In other words, instead of setting your government free, you have consented to a continuation and perpetuation of the existing alliance between the government and big business.

This alliance may be perfectly unimpeachable on the ground of honesty, and I am not intimating that there will be colossal corruption. I am merely pointing out that there will be a union of power between them, an inevitable union of power. And I say to these noble men and women who have allied themselves with that party because of the social program: Who will guarantee to us that this master will be just and pitiful? Do we conceive social betterment to lie in the pitiful use of irresistible power?

Or do we conceive it to arise out of the irresistible might of a body of free men? Has justice ever grown in the soil of absolute power? Has not justice always come from the press of the heart and the spirit of men who resist power?

Liberty has never come from the government. Liberty has always come from the subjects of the government. The history of liberty is a history of resistance. The history of liberty is a history of the limitation of governmental power, not the increase of it. Do these gentlemen dream that in the year 1912 we have discovered a unique exception to the movement of human history? Do they dream that the whole character of those who exercise power has changed, that it is no longer a temptation? Above all things else, do they dream that men are bred great enough now to be a Providence over the people over whom they preside?

Great kings have been born into the world, gentlemen, men with big enough hearts to include their kingdoms, men with big enough brains to comprehend anything that can come within the scope of their understanding. But there are only twenty-four hours in the day of a king, as there are only twenty-four hours in the day of the humblest workman. And no brain in its twenty-four-hour day can comprehend the complex business of a nation.

Representative government, representative assemblies, are necessary, not because their individual units are wise, but because their individual units are various; because, picked out of every class and condition, they speak what no ordinary man can speak —the voice of all classes and conditions.

The voice of a nation never came from any single lips except occasionally in a lyric in some burst of inspiration on the part of a truly great poet from whose imperishable words there seemed to come a song that did embody the impulse of a great people. But you can't translate poetry into polity. You can't translate even the song of a people into the measures which will safeguard its life. And no poet had ever vision enough to conceive a body of measures which would suffice for that purpose.

A very interesting thing happened—I don't know whether it was an editorial accident or not. Mr. Roosevelt spoke, as I remember, before the constitutional convention in Ohio last spring. I happened to be on a railway journey when he delivered the speech, and the paper I picked up in the morning after he had delivered it was the St. Louis *Post-Dispatch*. On the front page, in large headlines, were words that indicated that Mr. Roosevelt had adopted the whole program of radicalism. The story ran with the quotation of the speech for two or three columns—I have forgotten how much—and then said "continued on page four."

Let's see, I have forgotten what page it was. But on that page four, when I turned to it, were these words: "Mr. Roosevelt Outlines Conservative Program." Walter Measday here was with me; he can corroborate this circumstance. And the point of the story is this: that that was the correct caption on the fourth page; that the sentiment of the speech, the sympathy of the speech in the first part, was with radical ideas; but the program of the speech was conceived for the purpose of showing that big business and the government could live on amicable terms with one another. It was in substance a very interesting article which Mr. Roosevelt previous to that time had written for and published in *The Outlook*,[4] a very interesting article, indeed, which is the progenitor of the corresponding planks in the present platform.

Now, I say that in that way lies no thoroughfare for social reform, and that those who are hopeful of social reform through the instrumentality of that party ought to realize that in the very platform itself is supplied the demonstration that it is not a serviceable instrument. They do propose to serve civilization and humanity, but they can't serve civilization and humanity with that kind of government.

If I am right about that, you know what you have got to do— you have got to choose the Democratic party. There are several things that I want to take leave to say about the Democratic party. The Democratic party has no entangling alliances. And the most grudging Republican will admit that, even though he adds that that is for the very good reason that they haven't had a chance to have them, that not having any political assets to offer in the partnership, they have not found acceptable partners. Having nothing to trade with, there was no trade. The most grudging of you will have to admit that, whether from virtue or necessity, the Democratic party has no entangling alliances.

But I, as a Democrat, will add that it is very strange to me if a party was inclined to trade that it refrained from trading for sixteen years. A voluntary exile of sixteen years is very unusual. And when you remember that all those sixteen years this party has had the same provisions and the same program that it has in the year 1912, what does it mean? Doesn't it mean that the Democratic party foresaw the year 1912 before any other party did and had prepared its mind and its heart for the present year a half generation ago?

Now, a very large proportion of the people of the United States all those years have persistently belonged to the minority though

[4] "The Trusts, the People, and the Square Deal," *The Outlook*, xcix (Nov. 18, 1911), 649-56.

most of them, for example, in such states as Vermont, knew that it was always going to be a minority, though some of them were laughed at, were scoffed at, though some of them to my certain knowledge were called fools for their pains because they wouldn't get on to the winning side and get the profits and preferences that might come from being on the winning side. Notwithstanding contempt and temptation, these people have voted in a minority for half a generation because they believed that Thomas Jefferson was right. They didn't know what Thomas Jefferson had said, but they knew that he had said something which, if the people of the United States would only believe in in sufficient numbers, they would set their government free. They couldn't have expounded to you any doctrine of Thomas Jefferson, but they knew there was some virtue in the conception and imagination of that great man which had shown and illuminated the path of liberty. And so they called themselves "Jeffersonian Democrats." They set their theme and called themselves "Jeffersonian Democrats" and said they would see other people in warmer regions before they gave him up. So that they have gone through a long series of years of purification, because you don't stay in a minority sixteen years without growing thoughtful.

You can be in a majority without knowing why—just by the common instinct of the crowd. You can be in a majority just by the instinct that has been in you, ever since a boy, to climb on the band wagon. And you can be in the majority. The majority can go out and whoop without thinking anything about it, but the minority stands on the side lines and sees the game played and thinks how it might be better played if there were better umpires and better rules to the games and better all sorts of things. So that not because—if I may be permitted to say so—not because they didn't have anything to sell, but because they had what they wouldn't sell, Democrats have been in a minority. Now, when the year has come in which the whole country turns to them and says, "Why, after all it may be that you were right," they stand up and say: "Yes, we were right. Now will you set your government free, or won't you? Will you trust it? Will you trust it to men who are willing to stay out in the cold rather than get warm on terms that they won't pay for? Here is a free party which can set up a free government."

I can say without even a touch of personal reference, almost, that the Democratic party at least has a candidate who by circumstance, or whatever way you may explain it, is not attached to any interest whatever. The alchemy that accomplished that was practiced at Baltimore, not merely practiced at my birth, because I was born a very pugnacious person.

Now in these circumstances, gentlemen, for I have tried to be, so far as my lights served me, absolutely frank about this analysis, in the face of all of these circumstances, isn't it rational in this situation that the voters of this country should try the Democratic party again? And isn't the Democratic party in a better position than it was ever in before? And isn't the Democratic party the very party which is old-fashioned enough to believe that the processes of liberty have not been reversed; that liberty is not to be got from the government, but that liberty is to be got from the self-assertion of the people?

The fortunate circumstance of our time is that the people of this country are wide-awake and know what they are looking at. Because after you look back to a period which I do not remember, almost for the first time in our lifetime, the people of this country are looking to see things as they are, and are going to choose upon the basis of reality and not upon the basis of fancied party loyalty or of any imaginative thing whatever. Therefore, if we are not frank, we must make a virtue of necessity and submit to defeat. Because the people are not going to trust those who do not trust them, are not going to trust those who do not believe that they, the people, are trustworthy.

Nothing has disturbed me more in recent months than the evident circumstance that some distinguished regular Republican orators, when they spoke of the people, evidently didn't include themselves. I don't think I can have been deceived about that. They are constantly speaking of what should be done for the people. Now, who am I to do something for the people unless I conceive myself to be one of the people? I'm generous enough to include them when I speak of the people. I want them to be intelligent enough to include me, and until we can include one another, there is no basis for conference whatever. We can't get together on the theory that some of us have to take care of the rest of us.

We are not going to vote sentimentally. We have made a mess of voting sentimentally. We have made a mess of being disinclined to vote tickets which our fathers wouldn't vote. The number of men who are tied to the tradition of their fathers, when their fathers lived in an absolutely different age, in circumstances which have now absolutely disappeared, who are yet voting precisely as their fathers voted, shows how long we remain children and how long it takes us to grow up and reach years of discretion and majority. There are men who have told me within the day that they were for the first time in their lives going to vote the Democratic ticket, with an evident expression on their faces which meant this: "It seems incredible. It is a violation of the whole moral creed of my family. I am not sure that I can die comfortably and encounter the old man again, but some extravagant impulse of insurrection has got the better of me, and I am actually going to vote the Democratic ticket." One would think that it was a violation of the law of nature, that they were expecting to do something unnatural. And so I say that they are still tied up to sentiment and that no vote should be cast upon sentiment, except, upon rare occasions, upon the sentiment of patriotic devotion.

There are some things occasionally, I dare say—but I can't think of another just on the spur of the moment—but I dare say there are moments when we must sink our own opinion because there is some danger threatening the country, and we must all act from some unified patriotism. I suppose if a war were threatening us, which endangered the independence of the nation, we wouldn't stop to remember whether we voted Republican or Democratic. We would vote to sustain the government. But those are very rare occasions. A vote for business. A vote for an intellectual judgment. A vote for the conclusion of a man who loves those who are dependent upon him, loves his city, loves his state, has some reasoned conviction with regard to what is best for them and what is bad for them. And who deposits his vote has a choice. If it isn't a choice, it doesn't mean anything at all. Therefore, we must be absolutely candid with ourselves. Accept my conclusions or reject them, but make this comparison of the three parties for yourselves and make a choice on this basis: Shall we, can we, set our government free? Can we get a government that will serve civilization and humanity?

Transcript of shorthand notes (C. L. Swem Coll., NjP), with corrections from the partial texts in the *New York Tribune*, Sept. 10, 1912, and the New York *World*, Sept. 10, 1912.

From Charles Henry Grasty

My dear Governor: Baltimore, Md. September 9th, 1912.

From our point of view in THE SUN Office the Democratic cause has grown by leaps and bounds in the past two or three weeks. We are very much pleased and gratified with the conditions. I think your speeches have been bulls-eye hitters. It seems to me that your treatment of the action of the Moose Convention was most happy. They can't make things too good, and the present Democratic leadership puts the seal of its approval on righteousness whenever and wherever found! Incidentally, I think Brother Murphy will have to toe the mark. Your frank and fair, but straight-from-the shoulder attack on Jim Smith, and his kind, will inspire enthusiasm where enthusiasm most counts, among the young, the optimistic and the open-minded.

In The Sun territory—the close states of Maryland and West Virginia—and Delaware, Virginia and the Carolinas—we can report conditions that are as good as they possibly could be.

I am of opinion that the dangers we touched upon in our conversation at Sea Girt have now entirely passed.

With heartiest good wishes,

Sincerely yours,   Charles H Grasty

TLS (WP, DLC).

An Address to Spanish War Veterans in Atlantic City

[Sept. 10, 1912]

Mr. Mayor,[1] Mr. Commander in Chief,[2] Ladies and Gentlemen: It is my privilege to be here tonight to extend the greetings of the state to this body of Spanish War veterans who have gathered for the interesting meeting at which they are engaged in welding again those links of comradeship which bound them together while their country was at war. One cannot greet this particular body without thinking that it is a privilege to one state to welcome a body of men whose past history has the significance that attaches to the Spanish-American War, because not until the Spanish-American War did sectional feeling disappear in America. And to welcome the veterans of that war is to experience the satisfaction of thinking that the pulse of the nation for the moment beats in New Jersey, because I believe that future historians will more and more look upon the Spanish War as one of the most important turning points in the development of America as a nation.

America has only slowly found her way towards that unity which would naturally have characterized her had she not spread her population over a great continent and experienced the variety of life which came with the variety of conditions on that great continent. But not until we were bound together in a com-

[1] William Riddle.
[2] Maurice Simmons, lawyer of New York and commander in chief of the United Spanish War Veterans.

mon impulse of service did we feel that the nation was completed, that now at last we felt as a single people.

I am an advocate of peace, and yet I must say that there are some splendid things that come to a nation by the discipline of war. An interesting friend of mine, who is a very ardent and a very efficient friend of peace, wrote a very interesting essay a few years ago entitled, "Christmas, Its Unfinished Business,"[3] and the theme of the essay was this, that peace would supplant war just so soon as peace became as handsome as war. He called attention to the significant circumstance that you never go into a household and see a yardstick or a spade or any symbol or implement of peace hung up over the mantelpiece to symbolize the service of some son of the household; but that very often you see hanging there a sword or a musket, and the reason is that the sword and the musket were used for somebody else and not for the men who wielded them. There are many selfish purposes served by war, there are many ugly ambitions that bring on war, there have been wars that have disgraced humanity because the blood spilled was not spilled in any righteous cause, but the rank and file of the soldiery did not share in the disgrace because they bore arms as those who served a command which they dared not question and who had absolutely nothing to gain and everything to lose. If a man offer his life for a thing that does not bring him profit, shall we not say that he is distinguished among his fellows? Now, when men spend their lives in peace, not merely for their own private profit, but as the conscious servants of a great nation, there will be no more war and peace will be as distinguished as war. Then we will hang up the symbols of peace in our households and say, "Our son served humanity."

The reason the Spanish War bound the nation together was that men were banded together in an unselfish thing, which drew all sections of the country together in a common service. And so it is with peculiar pleasure that I think of this comparatively bloodless war, this war which drew us into singleness of purpose without shedding too much of the precious blood of our sons and our brothers and our fathers. I suppose that in coming together the members of this association are chiefly drawn by the impulse of comradeship. They want to see men who were comrades in arms, even though they did not personally know them while the armies were in camp and in the field. But it seems to me that there is something very much greater than comradeship in it.

[3] Samuel McChord Crothers, "Christmas: Its Unfinished Business," *Atlantic Monthly*, xciv (Dec. 1904), 721-27.

There is the fellowship in patriotism which goes a great deal deeper and which is the only thing that constitutes the true spirit of a nation.

I belong to a political party. For the time being I represent a political party; but I respect a political party merely as the means of banding men together for a service [after] which, when they have done to the uttermost, they have forgotten parties in a common service. Not all men think alike, and therefore men must group themselves according to their convictions and their thoughts, but the impulse back of every one of them must be the same, if it is indeed the impulse of patriotic conviction. And so I congratulate you upon having gone to school in at least one of of the schools of patriotism. Not the only school, but the school where you have learned that a man must lay down, if it need be, his life for those with whom he lives. For you have had that only thing that makes a nation great. You have had a vision of the common interest.

I wish that party battles could be fought with less personal passion and more passion for the common good. I am not interested in fighting persons, but I am interested in fighting things. I am interested in fighting bad tendencies, bad systems, things that lower all the levels of our political and economic morality. And I could wish that these things were visible and tangible so that we wouldn't have to fight them through persons. I wish that they were of such a sort that you had only to hold them up to let the whole nation see how ugly they are and how undesirable. For we must get this vision before we are true with our politics, the same vision that the soldier gets—that it doesn't make any difference what part of the country he comes from, it doesn't make any difference what he has; the point is that there is something that binds him to his fellows which he cannot break without committing treason. The thing he cannot break is the bond of common sympathy and of common understanding, that he is engaged in a cause, and that only the cause can make him great.

I wonder that men sometimes miss the whole lesson of greatness. A man borrows greatness, doesn't possess it. A man borrows greatness from the trust of his fellow citizens. He borrows greatness from his comprehension of and identification with a great cause and principle. He is as big as the thoughts and the impulses that he has received from the common life of the people about him, and all his greatness is thus borrowed from the great capital stock of the human race. He is not worthy of confidence unless he puts that great borrowed greatness out at usury and sees to it that it brings something in not only to himself but to those who have trusted him with the sacred thing which he has borrowed.

The trouble with this country is that it has been blindly at war within itself by a competition of interests, when there should have been a union of interests. The way not to cure it is to set one class against another. The way to cure it is to see the classes understand one another, that they all know that there is such a thing as a common interest which touches them all alike.

Now, will you men, in having seen the vision, assist to communicate it to the great body of people around us who are inevitably, because of the necessities of life, burdened all day long with the mere necessity of earning what they must eat and what they must wear and what they must put above their heads by way of shelter? They haven't time, many of them, to see the vision. We have camped on the field, some of us, we have been in the battle, we have heard the rattle of small arms and the dull thunder of the cannon, and all the while we have been thrilled through with this impression—that we were on a mission for the American people and that the arms we bore were typical of a great duty. No man who has slept on the tented field and failed to see the vision is a true soldier. And no man is a true patriot who, once having seen the vision, does not lift it high for the contemplation of his fellow men.

I welcome you to Atlantic City—to which all sorts and conditions of men come, on legitimate and illegitimate errands—as a body of men who may among the multitude catch in some degree the imagination of those who have seen them sit together; because people come to Atlantic City from all over the United States. And after you have gone to your several homes—perhaps some evening sitting in the family circle—you will be reminded of this gathering and of the thing that I have feebly tried to remind you of. And there will go around the little circle the thrill of the consciousness that there is a great American people whose destiny is to show the way to freedom and to peace, and that you have drunk at some of the fountains of their inspiration.[4]

T MS (C. L. Swem Coll., NjP).
[4] There is a WWhw outline of these remarks, with the composition date of Sept. 8, 1912, in WP, DLC.

From Thomas Davies Jones

My dear Governor: [Chicago] September 10, 1912.

I thank you very cordially for your letter of the 7th instant. Your attitude is just what I was sure it would be; nevertheless, it is a pleasure to have it so generously stated.

It is true, as you suggest, that the practice of "dumping" has not, in the past, been regarded as morally indefensible. The practice is one that tariff laws invite; and the average business man might well be excused for asking why should anyone be blamed for accepting such an invitation. But business morals are in the making. Therein lies the hope of the future. The charge of "dumping" made persistently against the International Harvester Company, and without a particle of justification, has done more than anything else, to embitter the farmers against it. It may be a trust, and as such it may be dissolved. That issue is presented by the suit of the Government, and it is an entirely respectable issue. But it has never dumped.

I rejoice to see that you are following up very effectively your attack upon the adoption of monopoly as a settled policy of this country. That, and the tariff, are the vital issues of this campaign.

Faithfully yours,   [Thomas D. Jones]

CCL (Mineral Point, Wisc., Public Library).

From Thomas Mott Osborne

My dear Governor: [New York, c. Sept. 10, 1912]

Having come down to New York in a rather depressed frame of mind & preparing to return in a still more depressed frame of mind, I am going to ask you to grant me the privilege of writing to you once more,—& this the last time,—about the situation here in New York.

I have talked today with a number of Democrats, including Senator O'Gorman, & I am greatly disturbed over the situation; for I fear that some of your friends entirely fail to grasp the situation. While Governor Dix is so unpopular that he would certainly be defeated if renominated, the trouble lies deeper than Dix. It is the *Murphy Cancer* that is bringing death to the party in New York State.

Any candidate who is named at Syracuse by Murphy will be beaten; & many of these Democrats who most ardently desired your nomination & are most anxious for your election will be forced to bolt the party ticket. I am not speaking of myself; as one man I am a negligible quantity; I mean leaders of influence & thousands of the rank & file of the party. Their resentment at the record of the last two years goes way beyond Dix; & the nomination of Straus[1] has provided a refuge for those who will refuse to support Murphy's ticket; & many thousands are already preparing to avail themselves of that refuge.

Now in the face of such a situation what folly to talk of naming for Governor an obediant Tammany henchman (however charming socially) like Dowling or Gerard,[2] or a Tammany demogogue like Sulzer! I heard today no less than five men, among the most influential independent Democrats of New York City say that [they] would openly oppose both these men.

Senator O'Gorman can not understand, I fear, what the Tammany brand would mean in this campaign.

Why do I bother you with this? Because Mr. McAdoo does not comprehend the situation. He has not himself fought with the beasts at Ephesus—as you have. Only last week he said with an air of surprise: "Why wouldn't you support Dowling?"

Because if you can not come to our aid, (& Heaven knows we dont deserve your aid even if it is possible for you to give it), I hope that at least you will say or do nothing which will express approval of a Murphy ticket or some dastardly compromise.

Don't let them fool you with a Bensel or a Treman![3] Dont let them fool you with the candidate of a rotton & boss-ridden convention!

Senator O'Gorman expresses the hope of securing a strong ticket. How is he going to get it? From Murphy? The Senator could, if he would, wrest the control of the Convention from Murphy & thus get it. Will he?

Excuse my trespassing upon you; but my intense interest compels me. Excuse hasty writing—

Sincerely yours   Thomas M. Osborne

ALS (WP, DLC).

[1] That is, the nomination of Oscar Solomon Straus for governor on the Progressive ticket on September 6.

[2] Victor James Dowling and James Watson Gerard, justices of the Supreme Court of New York and long-time Tammany stalwarts.

[3] John Anderson Bensel of New York City, state engineer and surveyor of New York, was an active candidate for the Democratic gubernatorial nomination; Charles Edward Treman, president of a wholesale hardware company in Ithaca and former New York State superintendent of public works, had been mentioned as a possible candidate but had thrown his support to John A. Dix.

To Cleveland Hoadley Dodge

My dear Cleve., Century Club New York 11 Sept., 1912

Your letter, handed me by Mr. McAdoo, was yourself in every line of it, and did my heart good to read. Since I received it I have seen McCombs, and he is entirely of our mind about the matter,—showed not a moment's hesitation. If you can, will you not send him a full memorandum of the contributers and sums. He is really very unwell, poor heroic chap, and his mind will not rest easy (which is very important to him) until he has the details in hand. I do not wish, unless it becomes absolutely necessary, to ask you to come down for the purpose,—though that is what McCombs asked me to do.

It is going to be embarrassing, but that should not stand in the way of utter candour, and I shall welcome the opportunity to avow the friendship of those who have so honourably and disinterestedly stood by me as the McCormicks have.

In haste, with love and increased admiration.

Faithfully Yours,   Woodrow Wilson

ALS (WC, NjP).

To Edward Mandell House

Dear Friend, Century Club New York 11 Sept., 1912

Never fear. I shall not be so foolish as to accept McCombs' resignation. But do not take anything for granted. Your advice is as necessary as it is acceptible

Here's hoping to have you soon at my elbow

In haste,   Faithfully Yours,   Woodrow Wilson

ALS (E. M. House Papers, CtY).

To the Editor of the *Brooklyn Daily Eagle*

My dear Sir: [Jersey City, N. J. Sept. 11, 1912]

My attention has been called to an article which appeared in your paper yesterday afternoon,[1] in which it is stated that efforts are being made by uncertain [certain] persons to oust Mr. McCombs from the chairmanship of the Democratic National Committee. These reports distress me very much. They are utterly without foundation. I can not but believe that the false and cruel rumors upon which they are founded proceed from some malicious source. They are so entirely untrue that their only object must be to embarrass the action of the Democratic Committee. I feel sure that in the circumstances you will not give them further countenance.

Mr. McCombs will not only remain chairman, but his counsel is of constant service to the committee even while he is confined to his room. We are looking forward with the greatest pleasure to his active resumption of his duties.

Very truly yours,   Woodrow Wilson

Printed in the *Brooklyn Daily Eagle*, Sept. 11, 1912.
1 The main part of the story in the *Brooklyn Daily Eagle*, Sept. 10, 1912, follows:
"Numerous rumors to the effect that William F. McCoombs, chairman of the Democratic National Committee, would resign because of ill health or in deference to certain opposition to his conduct of Governor Wilson's campaign, culminated today in the flat declaration of some of McCoombs' friends that a determined fight was being waged against his continuance as the Democratic National Chairman.
"In addition it is known that many of the old-time leaders have never become reconciled to the idea of the newcomer being put in the position of supreme authority. The youthful Princeton man has not taken the old wheel horses into his confidence and they feel the slight. It is generally believed that Murphy, Taggart, Sullivan and the rest would welcome the permanent sidetracking of McCombs.
"Although no one in authority at the Democratic National Headquarters in Manhattan would discuss the matter for publication, it was asserted in other reliable quarters that 'strong financial influences' were being brought to bear to force Mr. McCoombs out of the chairmanship. So marked has this situation become during the last few days that Democratic National Headquarters has taken on almost the aspect of an organization composed of two camps, in one of which Mr. McCoombs' friends are rallying to his support and the other marking those opposed to him.
"This analysis of conditions comes from personal friends of Mr. McCoombs, who have marked the manner in which William G. McAdoo, vice chairman of the National Committee and acting chairman during the absence of Mr. McCoombs, has been thrust forward as the head and forefront of the Democratic campaign."

Remarks to Democrats in Jersey City[1]

[Sept. 11, 1912]

Gentlemen: I did not expect to make a speech today, but I am always willing to make a speech in Hudson County, because I have so many splendid friends here that I feel almost like coming home when I come to Hudson. And there is so much to create enthusiasm now that it is very easy to make a speech. There was a time, I dare say, when we had to pump pretty hard to get enthusiasm in the expectation of victory, but now we don't have to pump at all, because we are on the right side. We are all absolutely united. We are all working together in the right direction, and when the voting comes I expect to see Hudson County roll up another 26,000 majority. Because Hudson County is looked to now by the whole state to sustain the regime that has been established in New Jersey. I don't think she will be without company. I think that even in Essex they will sustain it. And I don't say even in Essex because I think that they are poor Democrats in Essex, but because I think we are all united now in a common cause. And I expect this vote on the fifth of November to be a record-breaking vote, which will bring old New Jersey back into the column in which she belongs. Then, when we have got her going, we will carry her still further along the road that leads to real popular rights and to the kind of government we can all think that we belong to, or know that we belong to, or rather, that we shall all know that belongs to us. Because the real difficulty in the government has been not always that it has been deliberately doing wrong, but that it hasn't known what was right, because it wasn't in real contact with public opinion. It didn't hear the people because it didn't listen to the people. If you listen to a very small group you may sooner or later conclude that all wisdom resides with that group, but just as soon as you get outside you find that there are other people who know a thing or two, and that the only men who understand the interests of everybody are those who are connected with everybody. So that the kind of government we want is the kind of government that was intended to be established in America, and, God helping us, we will get it again.

T MS (C. L. Swem Coll., NjP).
1 Delivered from a stand in front of city hall following a review of some 4,000 marching members of the Hudson County Democratic Association.

An Address on the Tariff in Syracuse, New York[1]

[Sept. 12, 1912]

Your Excellency,[2] Ladies and Gentlemen: There are all sorts of occasions upon which I am told that it is not proper to talk politics; but there are two kinds of politics, explicit and implicit. Today I am going to talk implicit politics. If I occasionally yield to the habit of the moment and talk explicit politics, it will only be between the lines.

I am very much embarrassed nowadays at being introduced in terms which describe, and always exaggerate, my intellectual gifts, because I find that my intellectual gifts are very offensive to my opponents, and I would not do them an intentional dis-

1 Delivered at the State Fair grounds late in the morning.
2 Governor John A. Dix.

courtesy. Because, whenever argument touches the raw and goes to the quick, whenever you show that you know what the facts are and what they mean, then it is hurled back at you that you are academic. The only way not to be academic apparently is not to know what you are talking about and not to understand the significance of the facts you are discussing. Argument is academic, assertion is manly. Therefore, I will indulge in as little argument as possible, or rather, I will conceal the arguments that I use as carefully as possible. I will use them in the guise of assertions rather than in the guise of close reasoning. And, after all, it doesn't require very much close reasoning to see what is going on in our day. After all, it is open to anybody who has eyes to see what the situation of the country is and what it is necessary to do. It requires only a very little amateur analysis to see how much of it is likely to be done under some of the proposals that are submitted to us.

Because we have grown up. We are no longer children. We cannot be imposed upon. When I look abroad upon a company like this I always make up my mind that I am not going to talk about a special topic. There are various reasons why I should not discuss agriculture. The best reason is that I don't know anything about it; and one of my intellectual gifts is to keep off of subjects that I do not understand. I suppose that discretion is an intellectual gift. At any rate, it is an intellectual gift to know when you don't know anything. After all, it is a great deal more profitable upon some occasions to discuss those things which concern all of us alike.

Now, the people gathered here are not interested in politics as a means of preferring one party to another party. They are interested in politics as part of their lives, and they know that politics touches their lives. They know that there are some things that the government might do that would make living easier, and that there are things that government does not do that make living very hard to bear, indeed. You may say what you will about the analysis of public questions, but whether it is possible for us to live or not is the fundamental question. Whether we go to our work in the morning full of hope and elasticity or not; whether we come home at night overdone and discouraged or not; whether we feel that if we but expend our energy we shall have our reward, or that no matter how much we expend our energy we will get not enough reward to make it possible to pay the bills—that after all is what concerns us, and we have the right to look to the government, not to support us, but to remove the obstacles to our individual self-support.

When the question of high prices is pressed home upon the men in this, that, and the other manufacturing industries, they reply, "Prices have risen all over the world." Yes, they have; but nowhere have they risen so fast or so high as in the United States. That is the answer to that. They say they have risen all over the world. Yes, they have, and they have risen faster and higher in high tariff countries than in low tariff countries. There again intellectual gifts stand in the way of the assertion, because we don't have to have very much brains to read statistics—and statistics are open to every man—which show that the United States is burdened with the cost of living as no other country in the world is, and there must be something special in the United States which makes that true.

In order to get at what is the special thing, let us take a particular example. Take the price of meat; and the price of meat is at the heart of the business because it is meat that makes the blood red. It's meat that builds the muscle. It's meat that makes the work easier. And if a man can't afford to buy meat, he can't afford to exert his energy as he might afford to exert it if he could eat meat. Very well, then, the price of meat has gone up in the United States 30 and 40 per cent within ten years, and the price of American meat has not gone up a fraction of a cent per pound in the London markets. American meat is selling cheaper in England by 30 or 40 per cent than it is selling in the United States. And when gentlemen who are engaged in this monopoly tell me that it is because of the circumstance of local supply and demand, I ask them how it is that local supply and demand, how is it that economic laws, change when you put the product on salt water and send it across. What is the effect of salt water on economic processes? There are a great many chemists here. I would like them to take that question up. Why, if meat can't be sold cheaply in this country, can the same meat be sold cheaper three thousand miles away from this country after paying the ocean freights and after paying all the other expenses that are incident to the killing and preparation of meat that is sold in our own market?

Why, you know the reason perfectly well, gentlemen. The reason is this: Gentlemen who are afraid of intellectual processes tell you that high prices are not due to the tariff. And it is true that the tariff did not at one time make prices very much higher in the United States, and I'll tell you why. Because the United States is an immense area within which there are no tariff duties as between one part and another, and while there was active, energetic domestic competition, prices were kept down. And the argument for protection when there is domestic competition is a very different argument from the argument for protection when there is not domestic competition. This wall of the tariff enabled certain gentlemen to get behind it and to say, "Now, we are all of us together secure against foreign competition. Why cut one another's throats? Why not get together?" And, alas, they did get together and then determined the price of meat even without running the danger of coming into collision with some of the provisions of the law. For I can say to you,[3] "Now, we are in the same business. It would be a little dangerous if we made a legal combination of our two businesses—a lawyer's combination, it wouldn't be legal—therefore we won't combine, but we will appoint a third person who will write us a polite note about every two weeks suggesting that the price of our product should be thus and so, and we will agree as gentlemen to go without any writing in the matter, then we will take the suggestions."

That is what the meat men did. I am not imagining this. It came out in the trial of the meat packers. There was a circular letter which in the politest terms suggested the appropriate prices for the various kinds of meat, and with a gentility quite unsurpassed in the history of business etiquette the suggestion was always accepted. What law can prevent your accepting a suggestion? But suppose that if you do accept the suggestion to buy meat from the Argentine—meat from South America—the same meat with which you are competing in the London markets and in the other English markets will come in and undersell you. Then you will see, after all, it would be a little awkward to accept that suggestion.

Tell me that high prices are not due to the tariff! The tariff gave these men the chance to do the thing which has produced the high prices. But I beg your pardon; I am indulging in an intellectual process.

(Crowd on the other side clamoring to "look their way.") I feel rather dubious about my good looks. By the way, just between you and me, I received a high compliment the other day. I was told that I looked like the American eagle, a family that any man might be pleased to belong to.

Now, the cost of meat is not a case by itself. It is just a sample taken out of a list so long that it includes practically all the necessaries of life, particularly something that it is very common to allude to—I mean that famous Schedule K, which includes the woolen tariff. I met a man the other day who took my breath

[3] Swem garbled these words. Wilson undoubtedly said, "For I can tell you that they said to each other . . ."

away. He said, "Governor, you are dead right and I am going to support you; and I have got something to tell you: I am a woolen manufacturer, and I am interested in Schedule K." "Well," I said, "I have found a man, then." I said, "You know that it is wrong, don't you?" He said, "I do know that it is wrong, and it should be changed." And one of the bright signs of our times, gentlemen, is the number of businessmen of high integrity and intelligence who are beginning to recognize that they themselves have been profiting by things that are wrong and who no longer desire to profit by them. This is not a nation of dishonest businessmen. This is a nation of honest people, and the businessmen of this country have, half of them, been doing things that they did not realize the effect of. And after they realize them, they are just as ready to correct them as you and I are. Otherwise, I should fear that there was no bright prospect of reform ahead of us.

Very well, then, why have these high duties been maintained and these opportunities for high prices created? For that is the fair way to state it. They have been maintained because of the "prize money", as Mr. Roosevelt has called it. The government, or rather the gentlemen who are running the government, got a very considerable slice by way of campaign contributions. Why should you kill the goose that lays the golden egg, particularly when she is a very ancient and a wise goose, who knows her own interests and her own business? And these gentlemen felt that if they did kill the goose they would kill a system which had sustained a party in power for over a generation, or, rather, had sustained the leaders of that party in power. For I never want to allude to the Republican party without separating the men who have voted the Republican ticket from the men who have induced them to vote the Republican ticket. The men who have induced them to vote the Republican ticket have been very astute persons. They have known their own business.

But I forgot, I was going to indulge only in implicit politics. We will eliminate that passage and go on from where we started. What I want to point out to you is that a government which depends upon the patronage of men who profit by a system which results in high prices isn't the kind of government that can give you low prices. If you are interested, therefore, in the conditions of your lives, you are above all things interested in the kind of government which can deal impartially and justly and efficiently with those conditions. What are the ways in which the government can deal with your lives? There isn't merely this question of high prices. There is also the question of what the government can do to equalize conditions in every other matter. There is also the question of what the government can do to safeguard health, to put men in a position to get their full strength and use their full hope in their daily work.

There is an immense program of social and economic reform which ought to be undertaken right away, and what I want to point out to you is that the men who propose to leave the tariff and the trusts standing are the men who cannot carry out their program. I find myself the subject of largess and generosity on the part of some of the gentlemen whom I am opposing. They have given over to me the issue of the tariff and the issue of the trusts. They have all of them said, "We believe in the tariff," and they have said, "We are not going to disturb the trusts; we are simply going to help them administer themselves through government agency." I am very much obliged to them for having handed over to me these central things, because if you will give me the citadel you can have the country that lies round about—my guns will command it.

Any man who says that his only objection to the tariff is that the spoils are not properly divided, and any man who says that he intends to let the trusts stay as they are, but act under the control of the government, is a man who has declined to attack the very center of our political and economic difficulties, and he is utterly unable afterwards to solve any of the questions of our life. If he hasn't nerve enough to cut to the center he cannot save the life. My figure suggests a surgical operation. Very well, let us take the surgical operation as an instance. Suppose that there is some foreign growth, some virulent thing, in your system. What am I going to do if I am a competent surgeon? Am I simply going to put you in the government hospital and make you comfortable? Am I simply going to see that you get the right things to eat and the kindest nurses I can find for you, as they are trying to get for the trusts? Am I merely going to say, "I will see that your declining years are happy?" No, I'll say, "My dear friend, I am going to perform an operation; but I am not going to touch a single living tissue that is wholesome and is connected with the sustaining of your life. I am going to employ the most dexterous methods that are known to science; but I am going to cut the deadly thing out and save your life." The man who does not propose to cut the deadly thing out is a quack, and not a surgeon. And don't let the quackings of the quack deceive you. We have got to go to the heart of this business justly, like men who know and not like rash men. But we have got to go to the heart of it, and we have got to go fearing no man, fearing only God and justice and righteousness.

And so I can't refrain from politics when I see a body of people like this. You have got to live. You can't live happily except under a free and just government, and therefore the only thing I can think of to talk to you about is a free and just government.

I'll tell you this, I am sorry for the man who will have the responsibility. A man would be a rash fool to covet it for his own aggrandizement. It will be the most solemn responsibility that any man has undertaken in our generation, and nothing but the counsel of wise men throughout the country and the grace of God will suffice to sustain the function. Let us think of our lives, therefore, not as partisans, my fellow citizens, but as men bound together in a common interest. Let us think of politics as we would think of a deep fundamental business of life. Let us see to it that America has the kind of government that matches her ancient ideals; that every time we look at the flag that symbolizes our unity and our nationality, we shall have a fresh thrill with the thought that we have not deceived mankind, that we have set up liberty and justice, that we have shown the way to the emancipation of mankind from that which is evil and wrong and of bad repute.

T MS (C. L. Swem Coll., NjP); with a few corrections from the partial text in the *New York Times*, Sept. 13, 1912.

A Talk to New York State Democratic Leaders in Syracuse[1]

[Sept. 12, 1912]

Mr. Chairman[2] and Gentlemen: You are certainly most gracious in your reception of me, and I take it as an indication that you have the same sort of feeling that I have in this meeting. We are certainly face to face with a great, perhaps I might say an unprecedented, opportunity for the Democratic party. You are the workers and captains in this great Empire State. You are, if you choose to be, in touch with the people throughout the length and breadth of it. And while the great State of New York, because of her strength and her population and all that makes her great, occupies a very conspicuous place in the nation, the people of New York are not different from the people of the rest of the country, and the people of New York feel, as we feel, the thrill of a new day. The thrill of that new day is the thrill of a new

[1] Delivered in the Onondaga Hotel. About the unusual circumstances of this occasion, see Link, *Road to the White House*, pp. 494-96.
[2] George M. Palmer, chairman of the State Democratic Committee.

conception and a new purpose. We are aware that we have been running after shadows in some things, that we haven't seen realities often enough, and that the fundamental reality is the life of the people, and that they will have absolutely nothing to do with us whatever if we don't serve that life with absolute singleness of purpose. That is the message from the American people to political leaders throughout the length and breadth of the United States in the year 1912. That is the lesson to which I am seeking to listen as a man would who goes to school to his neighbors, to the men of his state, to the men of his nation. And I feel that I am of consequence only in proportion as I am the spokesman and voice of these impulses, which are deeply serious impulses.

I'll tell you frankly, the people of the United States are tired of politics. They are sick of politics. They know down to the bottom of their natures that they are tired of everything except that which makes the public service look like public duty, and legislation look like the translation of the public need into public acts.

I feel that I am facing a body of men who have an extraordinary opportunity and an extraordinary duty. For the example of New York State is marked as perhaps the example of no other state is marked, and the people are waiting to see—I mean the people of the nation are waiting to see—if we all have our eyes open and all see the lesson and the duty, or, as I should prefer to say, the privilege of the time. I am not saying this because I doubt you see it. I believe you see it. I rejoice to believe you see it. And I am confident that the Democracy of New York will show the nation that they know what the nation is waiting for. For the nation is waiting.

The only chance for a new party is that both the old parties should be discredited. One of the old parties is discredited. Ours *shall* not be. The only hope of those who would administer the government in a way that we do not believe in is that we should verify their predictions, verify their hopes, for their predictions are born of their hopes. I say these words to you by way of cheer, because I believe that the action of the Democracy throughout this country will prevent that catastrophe. And I believe that nothing will be more inspiring, nothing will be more inspiriting, than to see the Democracy of New York lead the way. For as I think of my own position I realize that there is no virtue in me as an individual to do the things which the nation expects; that the only strength I can have will be the transmutation through me of the strength of the Democracy of the country; that the greatness of a leader—of a political leader—consists in the trust and in the agreement of those who are associated with him and who follow him; that he is buoyed up, that he is carried by the common sentiment; and that that common sentiment is the only thing that constitutes vitality and reality and permanency in politics. For we build not for a day. I would a great deal rather lose in a cause that I know some day will triumph than triumph in a cause that I know some day will lose. Liberty is not mocked. She knows her children, and she can wait for them to recognize their kinship.

Old Dr. Oliver Wendell Holmes one day said, "You needn't be afraid of truth. The truth is no invalid. You can treat her roughly and she'll survive it." You needn't be afraid of liberty. We may retard her by our blunders and mistakes and blindnesses, but we can't defeat her, because she lives and breathes in the human spirit, and you can't crush the human spirit. And, therefore, I would rather tie my wagon to a star knowing its orbit than trust to any forces that I myself had created.

The strength of a party, the fighting strength of a party, lies in its organization, but the strength of the organization lies in the purpose which it has in view. Without the right purpose, organization can't succeed in the long run. With the best of purposes you can't succeed without organization. And that is the whole quandary of politics. That is the whole thing that we are constantly fighting with—to keep down, to ride down, to suppress our own ambitions and our own selfishness. In order to do what? In order to ride higher. In order to see more of the empyrean. In order to make a longer flight. Because the man who sinks his own personal judgments and ambitions in the common good will in the long run ride the furthest and ride the highest. If he doesn't ride into office he will at any rate be borne up by the love of his fellow citizens, and his single example will sometimes benefit a party.

You know, we are an interesting people, we human folks. We are afraid of men who have power and use it wickedly, but we are never proud of them. And the only people we rear statues to are the men who forgot themselves and served others. And that statue will stand there as an example as long as the bronze will last, to fire young hearts forever; while the grave of the other man is trodden under foot and forgotten and some day is a plowed field again, its quiet crops feeding the human race, and he is dead. And so it is a day, it is a year, it is an age of inspiration, and the party that absorbs the most of the inspiration is the permanent party and the triumphant party, and there is plenty of inspiration abroad to intoxicate the best of us. I am afraid it has gone to the heads of some people already.

I didn't know I was going to make a speech to you, gentlemen; I don't know that I have made a speech. I only know that I consider it a great privilege to stand up among the crowd of men who are bearing the heat and burden of the hard work, of the detailed work of politics, and just lay my mind bare to them for the moment. Because there is no use being the representative of the party for the time being unless you understand it, unless you know the man you are dealing with. I must in candor, I must in faithfulness to you, try to show you the inside of my mind, and if I have found the words to do so, I am very happy.

T MS (C. L. Swem Coll., NjP); with corrections from the texts in the *New York Times*, Sept. 13, 1912, and the Syracuse *Post-Standard*, Sept. 13, 1912.

Remarks to Newspapermen[1]

[Sept. 12, 1912]

You boys evidently want to ask me if I allowed myself to be made use of in any way. I will answer your question without your asking it. Nobody can make use of me by merely meeting me. I merely met the New York leaders, met them in public, and came away as absolutely free as when I went. My speech to the committeemen will enable anybody who can read to understand what I stand for and what I shall always stand for.

T MS (C. L. Swem Coll., NjP).
[1] On the train on his return to New Jersey.

From John Wesley Wescott

My dear Governor: Camden, N. J. Sept. 13th, 1912.

The deplorable situation concerning the U. S. Senatorship[1] does not worry you one-half so much as it does me. I must respect myself, as well as the law and the opinion of the people who invoked the law, but I would make any sacrifice, short of dishonor, to be out of this senatorial controversy. I was put into it by men whose words I relied on implicitly, only to find that political exigency seemed to be more potent with them than veracity. My chief concern is your relation to the whole wretched business. Pretty much all I have said and written has suffered misinterpretation. Your success, past, present and future, rests entirely upon the belief that the people generally have in mind unqualified sincerity and truthfulness. Any progress and any achievement of a permanent character can rest only on that basis. I have endeavored, on every occasion, to make it appear that your relation to the senatorial matter is based entirely on that principle. Some of the New Jersey papers, and the Philadelphia Times, through a correspondent in Trenton, have published, in a variety of forms, the statement that Mr. Hughes is your candidate, that I would be forced to take the same action as Mr. Gebhardt[2] and that Judge Hughes had resigned his judgeship in order to be entirely free to devote himself to the campaign.[3] I regret very much to say that such statements, despite every effort I can make to neutralize or destroy their force, are doing you marked injury, and, if not stopped, may make that injury much more pronounced and wide-reaching. It will not do to have the people of New Jersey, and, per-consequence, the people of the nation, to think that you are undertaking to control, by direct or indirect means, this unfortunate controversy. I say these things with the hope that you may in some way, find means to stop further currency of wrong statements. Of course they are made, by those who make them, without giving thought to the possible consequences.

Very cordially yours,   John W. Wescott

TLS (WP, DLC).

[1] Wescott, William Hughes, and William C. Gebhardt had all entered the Democratic primary contest for United States senator. The problem was that they would split the progressive vote and enable Smith to win.

[2] Gebhardt withdrew from the race on September 11.

[3] Wilson had appointed Hughes judge of the Court of Common Pleas of Passaic County on April 1, 1912. Hughes had not resigned his judgeship. He resigned from Congress on September 27 following the senatorial primary three days earlier.

To John Wesley Wescott

My dear Judge:　　　　　Sea Girt, N. J. September 14, 1912.

I have read with real distress your letter of yesterday. It cuts me to the quick that I should be deliberately misrepresented in the newspapers and elsewhere when I have, with a degree of punctiliousness that I never observed, kept absolutely out of the matter so far as taking sides was concerned. I have found by experience that it is impossible to catch up with these misrepresentations and a statement by me would only be a breach of the rule I have set for myself. I could not make a candid statement without showing my deep anxiety. I begin to believe that the upshot is going to be the utter breakdown of the new regime in New Jersey by a minority choice which will put us back just where we started, when I undertook the guidance of affairs. I am sick at heart.　　Faithfully yours,　Woodrow Wilson

TLS (J. W. Wescott Coll., NjP).

Remarks from the Rear Platform in Union City, Indiana

[Sept. 16, 1912]

My friends: I am very much obliged to you for this greeting, which I did not expect. I have a rather strong objection to talking from the back platform of a train. I believe that the back platform just now belongs to the Republicans, and not to the Democrats. We belong on the front platform. Not only that, but this is the kind of platform that I don't like to stand on. It changes too often. It moves around and shifts its ground too often. I like a platform that stays put. I would rather, therefore, stand on the platform that has been framed at Baltimore than the platform that is carried around the country.

And yet to speak seriously, gentlemen, it is a great pleasure for me to be able to greet little groups of my fellow countrymen in this way, because I know they want to see what I look like, at least; not for the sake of my beauty, but for the sake of forming their own opinion as to what sort of chap I seem to be. But I would a great deal rather they would see the inside of my head than the outside of it.

T MS (C. L. Swem Coll., NjP).

A Campaign Address in Sioux City, Iowa[1]

[Sept. 17, 1912]

Mr. President,[2] ladies and gentlemen, I feel as if the arrangements of this race track were singularly reversed today. I am one of the entries and this is the judges' stand. I will not ask what odds are offered. This is one of those races where it is impossible in the preliminary canter, really, to show one's paces. You won't know what kind of a President I am going to be until I become President. All I can do today is to show you some part of my table of contents. For the feeling that comes over me most strongly, whenever I face a body of my fellow citizens, is the feeling of responsibility with regard to comprehending what it is that this campaign is about. Some people have commended me for not entering into personalities. I have not done so, not because of any virtue, but because persons seem so insignificant as compared with the interests of this great country.

We are discussing great questions of the deepest moment, and

[1] Delivered at the Interstate Livestock Fairgrounds in the afternoon. For events earlier in the day, see the news report printed at Sept. 18, 1912.

[2] Fred Laurine Eaton, president of the Interstate Livestock Fair Association and of the Sioux City Stock Yards Co.

it would almost be impertinent to bring in questions of individual idiosyncrasy and peculiarity.

(By a listener: The other fellows are doing it.)

The other fellows are welcome, because, when they are not inventing, they are showing themselves capital humorists, because I think that humor generally consists in the things that are obviously not true, and they don't need to have any note appended to explain that they are not true.

As I have thought today of this hour, as it approached, it seemed to me that the proper thing to do was to take, as an illustration of the matter that is constantly in my thought, some subjects with which perhaps you would be particularly familiar and in which you would be particularly interested.

The subject that is in my thought all the time, is this: Not what it is desirable that the Government of the United States should do for the people of the United States, but how we are going to make the Government of the United States free and ready to do those things. Because I am as much enlisted as any man in the great enterprises of good service which remain to be rendered in this country, but I have been interested in these things for half a generation, and you have been interested in them for half a generation, and nothing has happened. . . .

Very well then, there is something to do before we subscribe to the great public programs of social betterment. I want to say here, as I have said elsewhere, that when it comes to a great part of the program of the third party, for example, represented by Mr. Roosevelt, I subscribe, as all public-spirited men subscribe, to the greater part of that program. And some very noble and public-spirited people all over the United States have been drawn to that banner because those enterprises of public justice were inscribed on that banner. But I am bound in judging of that party to say whether the rest of the program of that party permits it to carry out that program.

Now, the illustration I want to draw with you, gentlemen and ladies, today is this: I am profoundly interested in the question of pure food. You know that a great deal of the food that these teeming and abundant acres in this wonderful state of Iowa produce does not come to us straight from you. It goes through a lot of intermediate processes. For example, there are all the breakfast foods. Some man said during the coal famine[3] that if the coal gave out, there was at least the breakfast foods. There are so many of them and they would make very decent fuel, some of

[3] During the anthracite strike of 1902.

them, because they contain a great deal beside food, occasionally. The Government of the United States has undertaken, in recent years, with the support of every man in the United States who wished the protection of the lives and energies of the people, to see to it that the people of this country get what they suppose they are getting when they buy these foods. That what these foods consist of shall be on the label, that the meats which are killed in great stockyards, or at any rate sold in great stockyards, shall, after they have been shipped to great distances, be subject to the kind of inspections which will make it certain that they are still pure, still in such a condition as to furnish us with wholesome and nutritious food. But everybody now suspects—and the suspicion is based upon a great many facts that can be established by proof—that these pure food laws are not lived up to; that the inspection is not always what it ought to be, and that a great many things are permitted to be done which nullify the pure food laws.

Let me give you an illustration. I am not a chemist, but I have lived very close to chemists a good deal of my life—quite close enough to perceive some of the odors from their laboratories; and the question of benzoate of soda has interested me very much. I suppose that most of you know that a great controversy arose because Dr. Wiley,[4] who was in charge of the Pure Food administration, objected to the use of benzoate of soda in certain things that were sold to us, particularly in cans, for food. Now, a very nice thing occurred. The gentlemen who wanted to use benzoate of soda persuaded the President, Mr. Roosevelt, that this was a scientific question, and therefore he ought to have a board of chemists to determine it.

And Mr. Roosevelt picked out some of the most eminent and honest chemists in this country, headed by a personal friend of mine, the President of Johns Hopkins University,[5] and he submitted to them this question: "Is benzoate of soda hurtful to the human stomach or to the human digestion when taken inter-

---

[4] Harvey Washington Wiley, chief of the Bureau of Chemistry, United States Department of Agriculture, 1883-1912. A long-time crusader for pure food and drugs, he was largely responsible for the passage of the Pure Food and Drug Act of 1906. His zeal in attempting to enforce this law against heavy business opposition resulted in some six years of well-publicized bureaucratic warfare in the Department of Agriculture, which culminated in his resignation on March 15, 1912. Previously a lifelong Republican, Wiley campaigned for Wilson in 1912 and contributed an article to the *Democratic Text-Book, 1912* (pp. 326-31), recounting his experiences in the Roosevelt and Taft administrations. See Oscar E. Anderson, Jr., "The Pure-Food Issue: A Republican Dilemma, 1906-1912," *American Historical Review,* LXI (April 1956), 550-573.

[5] Ira Remsen.

nally?" Observe that that was the only question submitted to them, and that was exactly what the people who wanted to use benzoate of soda for wrong purposes wanted to limit the inquiry to; because these gentlemen had to say that benzoate of soda in itself was not hurtful to the human system, as I believe it is not. But they were not asked this question, "Can benzoate of soda be used to conceal putrefaction? Can it be used in things that have gone bad to conceal the fact that they have gone bad, and to induce people to put them in their stomachs after they have gone bad?" They weren't asked that question, because if they had been, they would have said, "Yes, it can be used in that way." And Dr. Wiley knew that it was used in that way.[6]

I want to warn the people of this country to beware of commissions of experts. I have lived with experts all my life, and I know that experts don't see anything except what is under their microscope, under their eye. They don't even perceive what is under their nose. And an expert feels in honor bound to confine himself to the particular question which you have asked him.

I was approached once by a very public-spirited person who asked me if I didn't think that alcohol was poison. I said, "I don't think anything about it; I have no right to judge. I have understood that in some circumstances it is and in some circumstances it isn't, and I generally am on the safe side and don't risk it." But suppose you wanted to settle the liquor question by asking a body of experts whether alcohol was poison or not. I believe they would have to tell you that it isn't poison. But does that settle the liquor question? There are a great many things that you can take into your stomach that are not poison that will make you crazy. There are a great many things that you can take into your system which will make you very disagreeable to your family. And yet your expert would have to give them a clean bill.

And the expert tariff board is very much of that character. It knows what it knows, but it doesn't know what we want to know. It knows what it inquires into, but it does not answer this question, "Are the present tariff duties in the United States suitable to the present business conditions in the United States?" And when the third party proposes a permanent body of experts, it proposes a permanent postponement of tariff legislation.

Now, who wanted this expert board of chemists? The men who wanted to sell us things that weren't fit to eat. And who were they? They were representatives of some of these very special

6 Wilson's summary of the controversy over benzoate of soda was essentially accurate. See Anderson, pp. 556-560, and I. Remsen to WW, Sept. 28, 1912, n. 1.

interests with which the government has been allied. . . . If
you want pure food laws, therefore, make sure you have first
got an independent and courageous government.

Now, I want to point out to you how the third party proposes
to get an independent and courageous government. You know we
have trusts in this country. You may have heard of them. Now a
trust is not merely a business that has grown big. I am not afraid
of a business that has grown big. I don't care how big it grows
by the intelligence and skill and even by the audacity in business
of the men who are in charge of it. But I'll tell you the difference;
I'll illustrate for you the difference between a business that has
grown big and a business that is made big. The men who were
manufacturing steel in this country a few years ago found that
there was one man amongst them whom they couldn't beat. His
name was Andrew Carnegie. He had so much more brains in
finding out the best processes; he had so much more skill in sur-
rounding himself with the most successful assistants; he knew so
well when a young man that came into his employ was fit for
promotion and was ripe to put at the head of some branch of his
business and was sure to make good, that he could undersell
every mother's son of them in the market for steel rails. And they
bought him out at a price that amounted to three or four times the
known value of his properties and of his business, because they
couldn't beat him in competition. And then in what they charged
afterwards for the product—the product of his mill included—they
made us pay the interest on the four or five times the amount of
the value of his property that they had paid him. Now, that is the
difference. That is the difference between a big business and a
trust. A trust is an arrangement to get rid of competition, and a
big business is a business that has survived competition by conquering in the field of intelligence and economy. I am for big
business, and I am against trusts. Any man that can survive by
his brains, any man that can put the others out of the business
by making the thing cheaper to the consumer at the same time
that he is increasing its intrinsic value and quality, I take off my
hat to, and I say, "You are the man who can build up the United
States, and I wish there were more of you!" But the third party
says that trusts have come and that they are inevitable; that is
the only way of efficiency. I would say parenthetically that they
don't know what they are talking about, because the trusts are
not efficient. If I had time for another speech I could prove that
to you. They have passed the point of efficiency. Their object is
not efficiency, though when they sell you their stock they say it
is. Their object is monopoly, is the control of the market, is the

shutting out by any means, fair or foul, of competition in order that they may control the product.

Now, the third party says these things have come to stay. Mind you, these artificially built up things, these things that can't maintain themselves in the market without monopoly, have come to stay, and the only thing that the government can do—the only thing that the third party proposes should be done—is to set up a commission which is to regulate them! It accepts them! It says, "We will not undertake, it were futile to undertake, to prevent monopoly in this country, but we will go into an arrangement by which we will make these monopolies kind to you. We will guarantee that they shall be pitiful. We guarantee that they shall pay the right wages. We guarantee that they shall do everything kind and public-spirited and which they have never heretofore shown the least inclination to do. And everything that we do for pure food, everything that we do for the rectification of things that have been done wrong, hereafter shall be done through the trusts, which we ourselves regulate."

Don't you realize that that is a blind alley? You can't find your way to liberty that way. You can't find your way to pure food or anything else. I am merely using pure food as an illustration. You can't find your way to social reform through the forces which have made social reform necessary. Let them first set the government free, and then we will follow them or any other honest men in setting up a schedule of social reform.

Now, there are things that have to be regulated, but they are not to be regulated through the trusts. They are to be regulated by those processes, now perfectly discoverable, by which monopoly can be prevented and broken up. Because these monopolies that are to be made permanent, if this program goes through, are the very things that are limiting the field of enterprise, limiting the market for labor, determining the wages of labor, determining the distribution of products throughout the country. Because, take one instance: The twenty-four gentlemen who constitute the directors of the United States Steel Corporation act either as presidents or vice-presidents or members of the boards of directors of more than half the railways of the United States. Now, if you want to sell steel and ship steel and are on the board of directors of a railway that is carrying steel, what do you think is going to happen? Are you going to play into your own hand, or aren't you? And since you are on the inside, do you think you are going to find out how to play into your own hand, or are you not?

I tell you, the tentacles of these things spread in every direction. And until we have broken their inside control the government is helpless to assist the people to a righteous process of judgment and of law. There are two instruments that the people use in government, two voices, for, after all, it is what is known, what is spoken, what is believed that moves great bodies of opinion in a free country like ours. What heartens me in recent years is to see how our political audiences have grown more and more serious, how they really want to hear something said, how they really want to get some argument that they can get their teeth into and not hear buncombe, not hear rhetoric. I dare say I could build up structures of rhetoric myself, but they are too thin. I don't want to climb on them. They are too insubstantial, and the American people isn't going to be fed any longer with words. . . .

Now, I don't want a smug lot of experts to sit down behind closed doors in Washington and play providence to me. I want to have a voice in this mundane providence that concerns my own affairs. There is a Providence to which I am perfectly willing to submit, because He settles questions that I don't understand. But as for setting other men up as providence over myself, I seriously object. I have never met a political savior in the flesh, and I never expect to meet one. I am reminded of Gelett Burgess'[7] verse:

> I never saw a purple cow, I never hope to see one,
> But this I'll tell you anyhow, I'd rather see than be one.

And that is the way I feel about this saving of my fellow countrymen. I'd rather see a savior of the United States than set out to be one; because I have found out, I have actually found out, that the men I consult with know more than I do, particularly if I consult with enough of them. I never came out of a committee meeting or a conference without seeing more of the question that was under discussion than I saw when I went in. And that to my mind is the image of government. I am not willing to be under the patronage of the trusts, no matter how providential a government presides over the process of their control of my life. I am not questioning the motives of these gentlemen. They may think that thing will work, but unless they are going to make an exception to all the history of mankind, I can tell them confidentially that it won't. They may not have read history. I haven't read as much of it as I would like to have read, but it is written so plain upon the pages of all human experience that I almost feel like apologizing to them for teaching them the ABC's of government.

Now, these are the questions. This is a cross section of the question of the day: What are we going to do with our govern-

---

[7] Frank Gelett Burgess, prolific popular author and illustrator, whose fame, however, ultimately rests on the brief verse which Wilson quotes.

ment? First, of all, determine what our government is. What are you going to do with a particular instrument? What is that instrument suited to do? You've first got to make sure of your instrument, then you can do what you wish to do with it. For my part, I believe that we are upon the eve of recovering some of the most important prerogatives of the American people. You know that only a few years ago, for example, we were not interested in questions of the initiative and the referendum. I met a man the other day who thought the referendum was some kind of an animal, because it had a Latin name, and there are people in this country yet who have to have it explained to them what the initiative and the referendum are. But we are interested in them now. Why? Because we have felt that in too many instances our government didn't represent us, and we said, "We have got to have a key to the door of our own house; and the initiative and the referendum are keys to our own premises." That is what they are. Now, if the people inside will run the business as we want it run, we will keep those latchkeys in our pockets. But if they don't, we will get them out and re-enter upon possession. And the government trying to act through the trusts will need to have the latchkey used on it very often, so that the whole impulse of American life is now an impulse of seeing things as they are. That is the reason that party lines are breaking—some party lines. I don't notice any serious breaks in the Democratic line. But parties are getting a good deal mixed, not because we are getting mixed in our minds, but because we are getting independent in our action, not because we are losing any reverence whatever for the great history of the parties which have served the nation in moments of emergency and of crisis, but because we have come upon a new kind of emergency and a new sort of crisis, and are determined that we are going to have an instrument suitable to serve us now in the year 1912.

The preliminary contest is over. There remains now nothing but that the judges should confer and on the fifth of November come to a conclusion. I want, if you will permit me, to be very candid with you. I want to say that my interest in this contest is not a personal interest. I do not know of any responsibility that will compare to the responsibility to be borne by the next President of the United States. I would be ashamed of myself if I bragged that I was confident that I was fit for the emergency. I only know this, a man can't know his abilities, but he can know his heart, and every beat of my heart is for my country. And I tell you that the only thing I know about myself is that I have had this vision of a people acting in common for itself along the old lines of American independence, and that image will always be found at the center of my heart.[8]

T MS (C. L. Swem Coll., NjP); with a few corrections from the partial texts in the *Sioux City, Ia., Journal,* Sept. 18, 1912, and in the New York *Evening Post,* Sept. 18, 1912.
    [8] There is a WWhw and WWsh outline of this speech, with the composition date of Sept. 11, 1912, in WP, DLC.

A Speech from a Rear Platform in Elk Point, South Dakota

[Sept. 17, 1912]

Friends and fellow citizens, it is a real pleasure for me to find myself again in South Dakota. For some reason there is room to think out in this big western country, and the inspiring thing about the present situation is that the American people are doing a lot of serious thinking. It is very delightful to see how impossible it is now to impose upon them. It is very delightful to see how they make a wry face over having to swallow mere rhetoric, but want substantial things to think about. I was not merely paying you a compliment just now when I said there seemed to be room to think in out here, because in this region where great big cities do not abound, where men live in comparatively quiet towns, where, as they follow the plough as they go to their daily work, there are spaces in which they can think, not hurried by the heated life of some other parts of the country. One realizes that a great deal of sober, serious reflection goes on here. Now that is the best thing that could happen for the country. As you think from day to day, are you satisfied with the circumstances? Are you satisfied with the markets, for example? Are you satisfied with the way you can get at your market? Are you satisfied that nobody stands between you and your market?

Many of the men who are listening to me here are old enough to remember the older conditions of this country. You remember how the people in this great middle western region used to agitate the things that would liberate them from the domination of the railways, how they used to agitate for their own grain elevators, for equal chances for shipment. They felt that somebody was hindering them and that there was not a free movement in every direction for the things that they wanted to do.

Now there is another thing I want to ask you: Are you satisfied that the gates of opportunity are just as wide open to the youngsters, to your sons, as they used to be? Do you think that the channels for independent action in this country are as wide open as they used to be? Do you feel easy about the way in which your governments are controlled? I will tell you one proof that you don't feel easy. There is one thing that political parties dare not do now. They do not dare to put corporation lawyers up for office, particularly lawyers who have been the advisers of railway corporations. Now I used to be a lawyer myself before I repented, and I don't see anything dishonest in giving legal advice to a railway company. I do not see anything dishonorable in being the adviser of any great corporation. They have a right to know what the law is. They have a right, if they pay for it, to get the best legal advice obtainable. Then why is it you don't want to elect corporation lawyers to office? Why is it that the distinguished gentleman,[1] who the other day was running for the office of governor in the distant state of Vermont, had it as a part of his record that he had never taken any fees from corportaions? What is the matter with corporations if lawyers don't dare advise them? You must be under the impression, if these circumstances are true, and you know they are, that the corporations are having a bigger voice in the government of this country than you are, and that you don't want to put their particular advisers in control of the government. Just another way of saying that you don't like the way in which your governments are controlled by special interests. Don't you feel that somebody is holding you off at arm's length and saying: "Yes, at election time we have to come around and consult you. We have got to let you vote. But after you have voted, we have arranged it. We will see to it that the things are done which the big interests bring about, but you are not classified as one of the big interests."

The government of this country, therefore, is not as accessible to the people of this country as it ought to be, and what I want to ask you men, particularly who are going to vote on the fifth of November, is this: How are you going to get next to your own government, and who is going to deliver you from these situations? Now there are two programs: The Democratic program is this, to see to it that competition is so regulated that the big fellow cannot put the little fellow out of business, for he has been putting the little fellow out of business for the last half generation. Whereas the program of the third party is to take these big fellows that have been putting the little fellow out of business and regulate them, saying, "That is all right, you have put the other fellows out of business, but we are not going to put the little fellows back where you destroyed them, but we are going to adopt you and say, you run the business of the country, but run it the way we tell you to run it."

Now you may like that program, and that is the choice you have got to make between a program which will prevent the little fellow from being crushed, and a program which will take the big fellow and have the business of the country run through him, under government regulations; notwithstanding the fact that he has built up his business by watered stock, on which you have got to pay interest, just as long as he does business and is permitted to do business.

The only thing you have to choose between, therefore, is this: Are you going to have fresh brains injected into the business of this country, and the best man win, or are you going to make the present combinations permanent? You have got to make that choice, and the more you think of it, the more you will see how you are shut in to that choice.

If the government is to tell big businessmen how to run their business, then don't you see the big businessmen have to get closer to the government than they are now? Don't you see they have to capture the government in order not to be restrained too much by it? Got to capture the government—they have already captured it. Are you going to invite the fellows inside to stay inside? They don't have to get there. They are there. Are you going to own your own premises, or are you not? That is your choice. Are you going to say you didn't get into the house the right way, but you are in there, God bless you, and we will stand out here in the cold and tell you how to do it?

T MS (C. L. Swem Coll., NjP).
1 Harland Bradley Howe, lawyer of St. Johnsbury, Vt., Democratic candidate for governor in 1912.

Extracts from a Speech in Sioux Falls, South Dakota

[Sept. 17, 1912]

Now, here is the parting of the way. You say, "Well, if we are not going to legalize the trusts and control them, what are we going to do?" Well, haven't you observed how the trusts were built up? You say, "Are you going to return by law to the old-fashioned competition?" I say, "No." It is the old-fashioned competition that enabled these men to build up these combinations, because the old-fashioned competition used in the new way was this: Here is a man with his own personal capital or with his own personal credit at the local bank, and he tries to set out in a little business; and here in another city is a great combination of men with millions of money at their back, who come there and say, "No, my dear little fellow, you can't come into this thing. We don't want any interlopers here. You have got only your little local market. Very well, we will come into your little local market and sell at a loss, sell at a figure that you can't possibly sell at, because everywhere else in the United States we will sell at a profitable figure and meet our loss in your locality. And we will put you out of business."

That is not a fictitious, hypothetical case. That thing has happened by scores and hundreds of instances all over the United States.

Now, that is competition. But what sort of competition is it? And the alternative to regulating monopoly is to regulate competition, to say that to go into a community and sell below cost for no other purpose—for it can't be the purpose of profit—than to squeeze out a competitor shall be an offense against the criminal law of the United States, and anybody who attempts it will have to answer at the bar of a criminal tribunal. It won't make any difference whether he is big or little, he will have to answer at that tribunal.

For we have been having trials and investigations by Congress, and we know the processes of unrestricted competition by which these men have accomplished the setting up of their monopolies. And if we don't know how to stop them, then the lawyers of this country have lost their ingenuity and their intelligence. I was saying at one of the way stations where they permitted me to make a short speech this afternoon that it was a very serious thing that if a man became a candidate for office and it was discovered that at any time he had been counsel for a great corporation, he had to spend the rest of the campaign explaining that away; and that after the campaign ended he wouldn't have had time enough to explain it sufficiently to get elected.

Now, there is nothing dishonorable in advising a corporation, is there? Any body of men in this country doing their business legitimately is entitled to the advice of counsel, and it is not dishonorable to advise them. Why are corporation lawyers, therefore, excluded from running for office? Because it is thought, sometimes unjustly but universally thought, that what they have been advising their clients to do is something that has been to the detriment of the business of this country. Can you imagine any other explanation? I know scores of lawyers who have been the intimate counsel of great corporations and have never advised them to do anything illegal; but there are a great many legal things that you can do now that will put the little man out of business. And that is the reason that I want to change the law, not the lawyer. I was a lawyer myself once, and you can't change a lawyer. But you can change the law, and then the whole atmosphere will clear. The lawyer will be obliged to say, "Yes, my dear sirs, that is a very fine scheme, but if you follow it, you will get into the penitentiary; because you have been found out." . . .

Where was this method of regulating the trusts suggested? It was suggested in the inquiry by the House of Representatives into the steel trust, and it was suggested by Mr. Gary and Mr. George W. Perkins.[1] They have thought this thing out. I am not interested to question their motives. It may be, for all I know, that they think—and honestly think—that that is the way to safeguard the business of this country. But whatever they think, this they know, that it will save the United States Steel Corporation from the necessity of doing its business better than its competitors. For if you will look into the statistics of the business of the United States Steel Corporation, you will find that wherever they have competitors, the amount of the product which they control is decreasing, not increasing; in other words, that they are less efficient than their competitors, and their control of the product is increasing only in those branches of the business where by purchase and otherwise they have a practical monopoly.

Now, if you will give me a monopoly, I can beat anybody. But if you don't give me a monopoly, I'll have to yield to the man who can do the business better than I can. And surely that is for the advantage of the United States. Moreover, I have this to say to the workingmen: Carry out the plan of Mr. Gary and Mr. Perkins and you will have given over a control of the market for labor which will suit these gentlemen perfectly. They don't want competitors to come into the market for labor, because new competitors for labor will mean new wages and new wage scales, and these are the very men, and almost the only men, who have successfully opposed union labor in the United States and shut it out of their shops and bribed it to be content to be shut out by all sorts of benevolent schemes of profit sharing, and otherwise, benefits which a man would forfeit if he left the shops or joined a union.

I am not imagining these things. As a friend of mine said, I am not arguing with you, I am telling you. These are the actual facts of our existing industrial system. I, if I chose, could build you up a splendid excuse for all these things. They happened very naturally. I have never been one of those who thought that a number of gifted gentlemen got together into a room and said to one another, "Here, let's put it over the people of the United States." These things were not malignly invented, but they were very happily discovered. And I can show you a report written, I believe, for the benefit of the managers of the United States Steel Corporation, in which a scheme was set forth which explicitly stated that if that scheme was carried out the corporation could make $50,000,000 for nothing. That was stated in the scheme. Now, it is a beautiful arrangement for getting money out of our pockets if by shifting the pieces on the board—making a new combination which doesn't cost you anything, and doesn't produce a dollar's worth of goods—you can pocket $50,000,000. And after the game was discovered I dare say it became very fascinating. I might be fascinated by it myself, for all I know, as a game, but I do not believe that men who once realize that by a game, and not by service, they are getting millions of dollars out of the pockets of their fellow men can rest with very easy consciences thereafter.

T MS (C. L. Swem Coll., NjP); a few typographical corrections from the text in the New York *Evening Post*, Sept. 18, 1912.
    1 For Gary's remarks, see n. 8 to the interview printed at Aug. 26, 1911, Vol. 23; for Perkins' opinions, see n. 2 to the two news reports of campaign speeches in Georgia printed at April 18, 1912, Vol. 24.

Remarks from a Rear Platform in Hawarden, South Dakota

[Sept. 17, 1912]

I want to say very sincerely that it is very delightful to be greeted in this most unexpected way. I was eating my dinner, but this is very much more enjoyable and very much more refreshing, for such greetings as I have got in Iowa and South Dakota go straight to the heart. This is a part of the country that I have visited more than once. Of course, on my previous visits I didn't attract any particular attention. So that I know the country well enough to feel at home in it, not only, but to feel that there is something in these big wholesome spaces out here and in these fertile fields that is truly representative of America, of America's power to renew herself and take care of herself. And the satisfaction in talking to people out in this part of the country is to know that they do their own thinking and that nobody is going to impose on them by mere formation of words. There are very serious choices to be made in this campaign, ladies and gentlemen.

T MS (C. L. Swem Coll., NjP); one correction from the text in the New York *Evening Post*, Sept. 18, 1912.

A News Report of a Day in Sioux City, Iowa

[Sept. 18, 1912]

THOUSANDS FETE WILSON
DEMOCRATIC CANDIDATE PUTS IN BUSY DAY HERE.

Gov. Woodrow Wilson, democratic candidate for president of the United States, yesterday was in Sioux City seven hours, from 9 o'clock in the morning to 4 o'clock in the afternoon as the guest of the Interstate Live Stock Fair association, the city of Sioux City and democrats gathered here from Iowa, Nebraska, South Dakota and Minnesota. The governor and his party departed at 4 o'clock for Sioux Falls, S. D., in charge of a reception committee composed of 100 business and professional men of all parties of Sioux Falls.

Gov. Wilson appeared to enjoy every minute of his stay in Sioux City and, a short time before he departed, he said to the committee which had remained with him during the day, that the day had been one of the most pleasurable of the campaign.

Rain was falling when Gov. Wilson awoke yesterday morning in his private car. The train at that time was leaving Missouri Valley. Nevertheless, the great fields of corn, stretching away for miles on either side of the railway tracks, were not without their charm, and the governor said:

"Iowa looks beautiful, even if she must smile through her veil."

Upon arriving in Sioux City Gov. Wilson was taken to Morning Side college, where he addressed the students of the institution. He then was rushed back to the city and escorted to the Tribe of the Sioux Wigwam in the Auditorium, where he was made a warrior. At 12:30 o'clock the governor was the guest at a private luncheon of democrats at the West hotel. At 2 o'clock he spoke to an immense throng at the Interstate Fair grounds. . . .

Gov. Woodrow Wilson is a full feathered warrior of the Tribe of the Sioux. He took the oath yesterday morning at a special ceremonial held at the tribal wigwam in the Auditorium, the pledge being administered by Will H. Beck, who is an officer of the order, also of the Fair association, a leading democrat and a booster preeminent. Being all of these things in one, Mr. Beck was chosen as the proper representative to administer this friendly obligation to the city's distinguished visitor and present him with a diamond studded badge, emblematic of the tribe.

The oath was administered in private, but the presentation of the badge was made in public before an audience which filled every available seat in the Auditorium, while hundreds were standing in the pit in front of the stage.

George R. Whitmer, democratic county chairman, had introduced Gov. Wilson to the audience in a little speech in which he had said that when the governor shall be president he will not be found looking for Armageddon or any other mythical place in the clouds, but will be found right on earth dealing with everyday questions in a pratical way. Mr. Beck then was introduced by Mr. Whitmer, and he advanced to the center of the stage and shook hands with the governor. Mr. Beck explained it had been the hope of the Tribe of the Sioux to have had Gov. Wilson as their honored guest at the great powwow held last night, but the engagements of the governor had decreed otherwise and, if the governor was to be made a warrior at all at this time, it was necessary for him to assume the obligation by special dispensation, which had been granted.

Mr. Beck read the obligation which provoked much laughter and cheering. It was as follows:

On the sacred tomahawk and pipe I solemnly and sincerely promise and vow that henceforth and forever I shall endeavor to be a "good Indian," whether successful or unsuccessful in the quest of moose or any other game, and that no matter how exalted my station in life I shall neglect no opportunity to contribute to the welfare of the Tribe of the Sioux, never forgetting that here in Sioux City, War Eagle, patriarch and warrior, friend of the white man, camped with his braves, whose indomitable spirit is typified in the people of Sioux City and of the reservation of Min-neb-ia-dak.

Mr. Beck then spoke the pleasure and honor he felt in presenting to the newest member of the Tribe, the distinguished governor of New Jersey, the emblem of the order. As Mr. Beck said he sincerely hoped the governor would accept the little token in the spirit in which it was given, and that for many years to come he may look back with pleasure upon his few short hours in Sioux City, the great crowd burst into a storm of cheering. The governor bowed and smiled his pleasure and thanks.

"Mr. Chairman, ladies and fellow braves," he began, and the applause was renewed.

"I am a little embarrassed in my new relation of good Indian, for my understanding always has been that the only good Indians are dead ones," and the crowd roared its appreciation.

"There is a certain symbolism, interesting to my mind, in this ceremonial," the governor continued, "for the Indian never boosts anything without first knowing that the one boosted can boost some himself. Now, I don't understand that Sioux City wants to put every other city out of business, but in boosting itself, it is showing the proper spirit. Rivalry, if it be honorable, if it be conducted in the true spirit of knighthood, will result in community of spirit and in unity of purpose. A city does not have to be big to be great.

"The little cities of America are the vital spots rather than the big ones. In a big city you are just as like as not to know your next door neighbor. The hardest thing in the world is to create a community of interest in a large city. I believe the commission form of government helps this along in our cities, and I understand you have that form in Sioux City. Patriotism always is greatest when it has a local footing. First of all, love your home, then your state, then your nation. The vitality is in the tap root, namely, the home. Be proud of Sioux City and presently you will be proud of Iowa and then see that the United States matches Iowa, so that you may be proud of your country."

Prolonged cheering followed the speech, after which the governor shook hands with thousands of persons who passed him in front of the stage.

Printed in the *Sioux City, Ia., Journal*, Sept. 18, 1912.

An After-Breakfast Talk to the Commercial Club of Minneapolis

[Sept. 18, 1912]

Mr. Chairman,[1] your Honor,[2] Gentlemen: I am not in the habit of interfering with my fellow citizens' digestion so early in the morning, and I hope that nothing I may say will be so serious as to incommode you for the day. And yet I must admit that my thoughts are constantly very serious in this campaign, because it is no light matter to attempt to counsel a great nation with regard to its complicated affairs. I feel, however, particularly at ease in a company like this, because I believe that the programs chiefly to be considered in this campaign touch the commercial interests of the country very nearly indeed. I am one of those who believe that we have put such restrictions upon the prosperity of this country that we have not yet come into our own, and that by removing those restrictions we shall set free an energy which, in our generation, has not been released. It is for that reason that I feel free to criticize with the utmost frankness those restrictions themselves and the means by which they have been

[1] Robert Jamison, prominent lawyer, businessman, and Republican leader of Minneapolis.
[2] James C. Haynes, mayor of Minneapolis.

brought about. And I believe that this is a time when there should be absolutely unqualified frankness. One of the distressing circumstances of our day, gentlemen, is this: I cannot tell you how many men of business, how many important men of business, have communicated their real opinions about the situation in the United States to me privately and confidentially. They are afraid of somebody. They are afraid to make their real opinions known publicly; and they tell them to me behind their hands. That is very distressing. That means that we are not masters of our own opinion, except when we vote, and then we are careful to vote very privately indeed.

It is alarming that that should be the case. Why should any man in free America be afraid of any other man in free America? And when we have cleared the air and are free, then I believe that the collisions of classes will cease and that there will begin to rise upon our horizon that sun which has not illuminated us for a long time—the sun of our common interest, the thing that unites us, the thing that vivifies, the thing that produces growth and fertility in our minds and in our spirits. That is the reason that it is necessary in public speech to strike out straight and strike out hard from the shoulder, not in order to damage anybody, but in order to do good to those who refuse to be benefited. The mystery of American economic life is why men who are the leaders in our economic development don't see that they are in a straitjacket. I don't wonder that they are sometimes mad. Madness generally goes with a straitjacket. And the encouraging side of it is that they are beginning to perceive that, after all, there are a great many things that ought to be changed.

Now, the difficulty of a popular campaign is that the most successful thing is assertion, and the most difficult thing is argument, and that argument is considered academic, that every intellectual process is under suspicion, that if you happen to know the facts and happen to know how to reason from them you are supposed to have gotten all you know from books. Now, the men of books in our day don't live between the covers of the volumes they read. The university man has been thrust out into the open. Long before I nominally entered public life, I was constantly called upon to discuss public questions because I had considered them. I must admit that I always had the greatest freedom in discussing those that I had not carefully considered, because the less you know about a subject, the more liberty you have in public speech. With regard to those matters that you have merely studied, you are a-sicklied o'er with a pale cast of thought, and the thing sounds very mild and very much qualified and limited as you utter it. I remember once being called upon by a body of bankers to talk upon the elasticity of the currency, and I said that, being a man living on a salary, I supposed I had been called as an impartial witness. As I had never had any personal experience in its elasticity, so I might have been eloquent on its rigidity.[3] And so, long before I made an adventure of public life, I had made a study of public life. And now it has become an adventure. I hope not an adventure undertaken in the spirit of the freebooter.

A very distinguished gentleman has recently spoken of the profits that come from the protective tariff as "prize money". And that has interested me very much, because the implications of the phrase are so many. They do not imply piracy, because what the pirate gets is not prize money; but they do imply capture, and they do not imply any process of earning whatever. But I beg your pardon; that is a process of intellectual deduction and is academic.

It is true, nevertheless, that we are getting to the point where we see that we have been living in an imaginary world. We have been saying that our economic policy was for the sake of the workingman of America, for example, and most of us have known all along that he didn't get the benefit that was intended for him, that somebody intercepted it, and were too shy to inquire who it was that intercepted it. Now, shyness has gone out of our public life. We are now actually audacious enough to point out the men who have intercepted the benefit and upon occasion, when necessary, to name them by their personal names, so that you can find them in the city directory. For definiteness in politics is the only thing that clarifies. Definiteness sometimes sends a chill down your back, because you know your own personal relations to the gentlemen mentioned, but at the same time it is a wholesome chill. It is like the chill that you get when you get under the shower bath. It makes your blood circulate, and you are a better man and have a better digestion for having cleared your mind for the rest of the day.

It seems to me that it ought to be in this spirit of good nature and of frankness that we ought to deal with the questions of 1912. And all that I have to suggest to you gentlemen is that there is this explicit choice to be made in 1912. I was saying last night that, when you state it, it sounds a little bit abstract, but it is the parting of the ways. And two ways parting at a very slight angle may seem almost to run parallel with one another, but,

3 About this talk, see the news report printed at Dec. 19, 1902, Vol. 14.

if you notice, they are diverging, and the goal at the end of one of them is very distant from the goal at the end of the other one. Your direction is what you have got to choose in 1912.

Now, here is the choice: on the one hand accepted and regulated monopoly; on the other hand, regulated competition which will prevent monopoly. I have studied history, and I daren't take the road that leads to regulated monopoly; because by regulating monopoly you adopt it, you render it permanent, you accept all the things by which it has been established. Even simply adopting it as inevitable means you can make the best of it and see that it does as little damage as possible in the circumstances. Whereas, in the other direction, instead of leaving yourself tied up with this established domination, you take a road that by slow degrees only diverges from the other, but nevertheless presently radically diverges, a road in which men can walk with greater and greater freedom, in which they can determine their own lives with the knowledge that while they are little they can't be crushed by the fellow that is big.

Any man who can get by the place where he is little and get big, as you know, can either survive separately or get bought up at a profitable figure, but in order even to get bought out he has got to pass the stage where he is little. Because as long as his market is local he may be crushed, and when his market becomes general then he may be taken into partnership or bought out. That has been the process of our development, has it not? Which means that the independent man can't remain independent, and by the nice arrangement—largely accidental, I don't think they are malignant or intentional—but by the nice arrangement of our modern fiscal system, or rather our banking system, it is very difficult, indeed, for the new adventurer in the economic world to get the necessary credit as against the men who don't want his competition to interfere with their enterprises. Because sometimes he needs big credit and he can't get it, because to get credit makes him big, and there are big fellows who don't want any more big ones.

We have got to see that the little fellows are protected, and that means that we have got to meet the criticism of the old, unrestricted competitive system which has been justly leveled against it. Men who have built up these great monopolistic enterprises, for they virtually are such, have been right in saying that the whole system was of a character to be destructive. They ought to know, because they have done the destroying. They know how the destroying is done. And I admit that it can be done, and the only way to stop that is not by legalizing the enterprises that have done the destroying but by seeing that no more destroying is done. And that is what I call regulated competition. Because I know, and every man in his heart knows, that the only way to enrich America is to make it possible for any man that has the brains to get into the game. I am not jealous of the size of any business that has grown to that size. I am not jealous of any process of growth, no matter how huge the result, provided the result was obtained by the processes of growth which are the processes of efficiency, of economy, of intelligence, and of invention.

I am constantly using this illustration, and you gentlemen know that it is a true one: The United States Steel Corporation had to buy Mr. Carnegie out because Mr. Carnegie organized his business, economized his processes, ordered his plants in such a fashion that he could beat every mother's son of them in manufacturing steel rails. He had the market because he could legitimately undersell them, and they had to pay him I don't know how many times, three or four times, the value of his property and of his business in order to get rid of him, in order not to be beaten by him in open competition.

Now, do you want that sort of thing to go on? Do you want the efficiency of your business lowered by creating the necessity and temptation to put those men out who are the most efficient? Hasn't America profited by the growth of just such enterprises, and isn't it about time that we put every undertaking in the United States on its mettle? That we said to it, "If you are now conducting a business upon which you have to pay interest on securities that vastly exceed the value of your business and of your properties, then that is your lookout, not ours. You got into that. This country isn't going to continue to pay the price of things out of which it gets nothing."

I am not inveighing against watered stock. I know all the statistical arguments, and they are many, for capitalizing earning capacity. It is a very attractive and interesting argument, and in many instances it is legitimately used. But there is a line where you cross, and where you are not capitalizing your earning capacity, but capitalizing your control of the market, capitalizing the profits which you get by your control of the market and didn't get by efficiency and economy.

These things are not hidden even from the laymen. They are not even hidden from college men! The days of innocence have passed, and the days of sophistication have come. And we know what is going on because we live in a talkative world, full of statistics, full of congressional inquiries, full of trials of all sorts, of persons who have attempted to live independently of the statutes of the United States. And so a great many things have come to light under oath which we must believe upon the credibility of the witnesses, who are in many instances very eminent and respectable witnesses.

Now, I have wandered abroad in this little talk of mine, but I simply wanted to show you the inside of my mind, so that there need be no misunderstanding between us, so that you wouldn't think I was one of those wild fellows running amuck because I knew something was the matter and didn't know exactly what. This is no Donnybrook Fair. I have got my shillelagh, but I am not hitting every head I see. I have selected the heads, and if they'll only engage in a little hard thinking underneath the endangered craniums they needn't be hit at all. Because the whole thing is as much in their interest as in the interest of the rest of us. If I didn't believe that, I wouldn't touch it; I wouldn't go out. I was inducted the other day into an association in Sioux City in which I became a good Indian, but that has not bred in me the desire for scalps. I am not out after any man's topknot; I am not aware of entertaining the least feeling that we ought to get even with someone. I am only possessed with the passion to create a condition that will be even for everybody.

T MS (C. L. Swem Coll., NjP); with corrections from the complete text in the New York *Evening Post*, Sept. 18, 1912.

A Talk at the University of Minnesota

[Sept. 18, 1912]

Mr. President,[1] ladies and gentlemen: This is a very familiar scene. I was just telling President Vincent that I was trying to recall that distant time, two years ago, when I was a university man. And yet, to speak seriously, there is no time when a man can forget or ought to forget that he is a university man, because the only serious thing that needs remedying in American universities is that the American undergraduate does not consider himself part of the life of the nation. He is an inveterate boy. He won't consent to grow up. I am not saying anything about the young ladies in the university because I don't want them to grow up. But it is a little tiresome, year after year in university work, to find how many men there are who take what is told

[1] George Edgar Vincent.

them without questioning it, who sit like good little birds with their mouths open to have predigested food inserted into their systems.

This is the only country in the world that does not take its university students seriously. Any kind of political demonstration in the European university is taken as an indication of the flame that is about to spread to the people in general. But when did any political flame ever have its first ignition among American undergraduates? They are as old as European undergraduates; they are certainly as gifted as European undergraduates. Why do they wait to enter upon life? Why do they spend a third of their life without accomplishing their initiation into it? When a man is twenty-one, he ought to have made a running start that will put every other man on his mettle to keep up with him, but he has not got any start until he is straining at the leash. He says, "Give me my diploma and let me start." In heaven's name, who is stopping you? Why don't you start? What are you waiting for? Why are you consenting to be a subordinate to the burden of a past generation when you belong to your own?

There is one objection, only one danger in education, and that is the real danger to undergraduates who have the point of view I am alluding to. That is the danger that each new generation will be made according to the pattern of the last generation and that every mother's son of you will be standpatters to begin with. Because there is a great deal, figuratively speaking, of the mother's milk in the standpat attitude. It is what you imbibe from a day that is passing away, for whose standards, for whose moral standards, for whose ideals, you ought to have a great veneration, and for whose ideals you ought to seek a new translation into action. I don't find the young men of this country concerting action. What a force they could be, what a tremendous breath of fresh impulse would come into the affairs of this country, if they would only go into it as a business and not as a mere lesson which they had learned! Nothing vital ever comes in learning lessons except the vitality that comes from learning the lessons of experience. Experience is your real schoolmaster, and you must not wait until you are old and stiff before you submit to its discipline.

I have uttered this homily, not only because I am in the habit of lecturing university people, but also because I know, and every man must know who is thoughtful, the very difficult tasks that confront this nation. They are not tasks which can be undertaken and carried through by prescription. Nobody has written the prescription which will fit them. They are not tasks which can be performed in a spirit of passion. They are not tasks which can be performed in haste. They are not tasks which any man ought to try to undertake in ignorance. They are tasks which can be accomplished only by knowledge guided by intelligence and backed by absolutely indomitable courage. Only if you are afraid of nothing except not being right, only if you are afraid of nothing except not knowing what you are about, can you lead in the generations that lie ahead of us. America has spent her youth, her reckless youth, her spendthrift youth, in which she has used her resources as though they had no limit and no end. She has passed those periods when it was not necessary to take careful reckoning of economy and efficiency.

There is no task in America now in which the men who are learned do not have to employ men who are learned. The brains of the universities are called upon for all the difficult technical tasks of the variegated industries of this country. And while men of natural genius may still preside over many of these processes, because given by nature a singular insight into the situation as a whole, they cannot be served unless there is sound learning, and presently this sound learning will be the basis of all our life. There is one sentence of Burke's that I used to quote to all my classes in politics, for I didn't teach political science in my day, I taught politics. "Politics," said Burke, "ought to be adjusted to human nature, of which the mind constitutes a part, but by no means the principal part."[2]

The thing that governs a nation is its passions, but there are two kinds of passion. There is the reckless, ignorant passion, and there is the constructive and handsome passion. Love is a passion, as well as hate. Patriotism is a passion as well as that impulse which makes us fling out against law. And what a nation ought constantly to be schooling itself in is the supremacy of the handsome passions, of those things which will lead us to forget particular interests in the serving of the general interest and will enlighten our hearts to perceive that the general interest includes the individual interest, and that no man can long serve himself without first serving mankind to which he belongs.

What is a university for? It is for a great many particular tasks, but it is for this general task—to take young men for a little while out of the circles in which they have been bred and carry them up into the high places from which they may see the

2 For the source, see n.1 to the notes for lectures on politics printed at March 5, 1898, Vol. 10.

kingdoms of the world, the kingdoms of the mind, and the king-doms of the spirit, in which they may be shown the map of life and be told, "Now, you will be presently down in the thick and dusty strife on the plains below, but never, we adjure you, forget where the roads lead. You have seen them; here is their map, yonder are the hills to which some of them lead, yonder are the sloughs in which some of them descend. Don't be fools and forget that you have seen these things and seen their direction."

Not only that, but I once said in partial playfulness, but more than half in earnest, that the business of the university was to make young men as much unlike their fathers as possible, by which, of course, I did not mean any criticism of their fathers, but merely this—that by the time a man was old enough to have a son in college he had become so immersed in a particular undertaking of some kind that in nine cases out of ten his per-ceptions were narrowed, and in some instances necessarily nar-rowed, to the thing he was putting his hand to every day, and it was necessary to take each generation out of this atmosphere of specialization and to put it into another atmosphere. Then when the youngster joins his father again, he could contribute to his father what that father had contributed to *his*—the breath of a new day, the support of a detached observer, the counsel of one who, though young, and because his mind was without pre-possession, had seen the new world with a new scope and a new vision.

That, it seems to me, is the business of universities, and once we do that we shall not pile one generation on another. What we are trying to do in politics just now, ladies and gentlemen, is to build, but to build with new stuff not incompatible with the world, not removed from the foundations of the world, but rising with a greater and a greater beauty of discovery in respect of the revealed article, displaying heaven-aspiring lines and lifting men constantly nearer those places of revelation from which they can see life and see it wholly.

T MS (C. L. Swem Coll., NjP).

An Afternoon Address at the Parade Grounds in Minneapolis

[Sept. 18, 1912]

Mr. Chairman[1] and fellow citizens: I feel that it is a particu-lar privilege to stand in this place—I mean in this open space to

[1] Thomas Dillon O'Brien, lawyer of St. Paul; associate justice of the Supreme Court of Minnesota, 1909-11; active in Democratic politics for many years.

which all men may come without distinction of class or origin—not only because it is under the open heavens, but because a congregation like this seems to me to mean something in particular. It is a very gratifying circumstance to me that a great city like Minneapolis should have this place to which every man is free to come and speak his mind. It is sometimes inconvenient for crowds to gather on street corners, but it is never inconvenient for the people of a great country to have anybody who has anything to say speak his mind. It is absolutely indispensable that in every great municipality in the United States there should be some great public forum, like Hyde Park in London, where everybody may come, where everybody may speak his grievance, if he have one, and where, reasoning together, men may understand one another and know what it is that they have in common and what it is that they differ about. Because ony in this way will genuine public opinion be put together, and no kind of law, no kind of authority, ought ever to act against the absolutely full expression of private opinion.

I was saying only this morning to a group of gentlemen prominent in commercial and manufacturing business that one of the disturbing circumstances of the day to my mind was this, that so many men of business, men in a large way of business, who agreed with me regarding the things that ought to be done to rectify existing conditions, did not feel at liberty to speak their opinions publicly but conveyed them to me in confidence, as if they were afraid of somebody, as if there were somebody who could bring some sort of pressure that would damage them in their business. Have we come to a time, my fellow countrymen, when opinions must be privately expressed with regard to public matters in the United States? Is truth such an invalid that we must treat her tenderly?

There isn't anything quite so good for the explosion of foolish ideas as their exposure in public, and there isn't anything that is as comparable to that same kind of exposure as giving sound ideas currency among the whole body of the people. And in this day, if I may use a somewhat vulgar expression with regard to all opinions, it is a case of "put up or shut up." It is a case of saying what you really think and then making good on your opinions. I have often thought that the only strength of a public man consisted in the number of persons who agreed with him, and that the only strength that any man can boast of and be proud of is that great bodies of his fellow citizens trust him and are ready to follow him. It is not only a belief in his character, but it is an agreement with his opinions. That is the reason that gentlemen have to go around, as I am going around, and expose themselves to the public gaze, not because it is a particular indulgence of taste to look at them, because personal beauty is not necessarily their strong point. Perhaps I may be permitted to repeat to you a limerick that I am very fond of:

> For beauty I am not a star
> There are others more handsome by far.
>   But my face I don't mind it,
>   Because I'm behind it.
> It's the people in front that I jar.

But what you are interested in and what you ought to be interested in is not the binding of the book but the table of contents —what is inside of it, what kind of purpose, what kind of understanding of your interests. Because the trouble with the Government of the United States has been that it did not understand the interests of the whole people of the United States. I am not one of those who can draw up an indictment against a great body of my fellow citizens because I don't agree with them. But I am here to assert that the men who have recently been leading the great Republican party have gone upon a false theory in the leadership which we have followed. That theory I am going to try to expound, if I can, with perfect candor, and yet at the same time with perfect fairness.

In the first place, I want you to understand that when I speak of the Republican party I am not speaking of that great body of my fellow citizens who have been in the habit of voting the Republican ticket. I am speaking of that comparatively small body of my fellow citizens who have been in the habit of misleading them, and whom they have allowed to "put it over" them. The theory that they have been themselves guided by is a perfectly tenable theory. It isn't sound, but you can make a very good argument for it, and you can make all the better argument for it because men have presented the argument time out of mind. It is an argument as old as the history of political systems. It is this, that it is only those men having the biggest material stake in the community who understand what is good for that community. That is rather a plausible theory. If my business covers the United States, not only, but covers the world, it is to be presumed that I have a pretty wide scope in my vision of business. But the flaw is that it is my business that I have a vision of, and not the business of the men who lie outside of the scope of those plans which I have made to make a profit out of the transactions I am connected with. And you can't, by putting together a large number of men who understand their own business, no matter how large it is, make up a body of men who will understand the business of the nation, that is to say, who will see the interest of the nation as contrasted with their own interest. In other words, the leaders of politics in this country in recent years have thought that we were safe only in the hands of trustees; and the trustees have become so conspicuous that we could write out a list of them. They have become so conspicuous that their names are mentioned upon almost every political platform. We know who the men are who have undertaken the interesting job of taking care of us.

I am one of those who absolutely reject that theory. I have never found a man who knew how to take care of me, and, reasoning from that point out, I conjecture that there isn't any man who knows how to take care of all the people of the United States. And I suspect that the people of the United States understand their own interests better than any group of men in the confines of the country. I don't have to prove that. You all know that that is so. Not only that, but I know this, that the men who are on the make, the men who are swimming against the stream, the men who are sweating blood to get their foothold in the world of endeavor, understand the conditions of business in the United States very much better than the men who have arrived and are at the top. They know what the thing is they are struggling against. They know how many blind walls they come up against. They know how difficult it is to start a new enterprise. They know how far they have to search for any kind of big credit that will put them upon an even start and footing with the men who have already built up industry in this country. They know that somewhere, by somebody, the development of industry in this country is being controlled, and they want to know how they are going to get into the enterprise themselves.

The trustees have charge of it, and the gentlemen who are running politics are the trustees. And the gentlemen who are running politics are generally known as bosses. I have met bosses in my time, and I know exactly what they are. And I know that you only have to state in public in their presence what they are to put them out of business. They are the agents of special interests, to see that nobody gets into office who won't serve those special interests and that no law gets on the statute book that is inimical to the men who are at the head of those interests. That is what a boss is. A boss isn't a leader of a party. Parties don't meet in back rooms; parties don't have private understandings; parties don't make arrangements which never get into the newspapers. Parties, if you reckon them by voting strength, are great masses of men who, because they can't vote any other ticket or can't find any other ticket to vote, vote the ticket that was prepared for them by the aforesaid arrangement in the aforesaid back room in accordance with the aforesaid understanding. Now, the thing that you have to do is to turn those back rooms wrong side out. I have said, and I want to repeat it, that the cure for bad politics is the same as the cure for tuberculosis—it is living in the open. So there can't be any germs of bad politics around here today. Our lungs have God's air in them, and we are able to see things in the light of God's sun.

Now, what I want particularly to talk to you about today— because I know from past delightful experiences that the audiences to be met here are audiences that like to hear serious discussions of great public questions; they are very much more interested in the fortunes of the nation than they are in the fortunes of individuals—the great question that I want you to consider with me for a few minutes today is the question of conservation.

Don't think that I am going to carry you to Alaska. Don't think that I am going to leave this great State of Minnesota and go out where the forests are in danger of being destroyed, upon the slopes of the Rockies. Don't think that I am going to discuss with you merely the question of whether our rivers are running dry or not, or whether we are giving away the water franchises which we ought to preserve for the public benefit. We are doing all those things, but you don't see those things with your own eyes here in Minneapolis. The question of conservation is a very much bigger question than the conservation of our natural resources, because in summing up our natural resources there is one great natural resource which underlies them all, and seems to underlie them so deeply that we sometimes overlook it. I mean the people themselves.

The strength of America is proportionate to the health, the buoyancy, the elasticity, the hope, the energy, of the American people. What would our forests be worth without these intelligent bodies of ambitious men to make use of them? Why should we conserve our natural resources if we could by a sort of magic of industry transmute them into the wealth of the world? And who transmutes them into that wealth if not the skill and the touch of the great bodies of men who go daily to their toil and who constitute the great body of the American people? What I am interested in is having the Government of the United States more concerned about human rights than about property rights. Property is an instrument of humanity; humanity isn't an instrument of property. And yet, when you see some men engaged in some

kinds of industries, riding their great industries as if they were
driving a car of Juggernaut, not looking to see what multitudes
prostrate themselves before the car and lose their lives in the
crushing effect of their industry, you wonder how long men are
going to be permitted to think more of their machinery than they
think of their men. Did you never think of it, men are cheap and
machinery is dear, and many a superintendent will be dismissed
for overdriving a delicate machine that wouldn't be dismissed for
overdriving an overtaxed man? Because you can discard your
man and replace him—there are others ready to come into his
place—but you can't without great cost discard your machine and
put a new one in its place. And you are not looking upon your
men as the essential, vital foundation part of your whole business. I say, therefore, that property as compared with humanity,
as compared with the vital red blood in the American people,
must take second place, not first place, and that we must see
to it that there is no overcrowding, that there is no bad sanitation, that there is no unnecessary spread of avoidable diseases,
that there is every safeguard against accident, that women are
not driven to impossible tasks and children not permitted to spend
their energy before it is fit to be spent, that all the hope of the
race must be preserved, and that men must be preserved according to their individual needs and not according to the programs
of industry merely. Because what is the use having industry if
we die in producing it? If we die in trying to feed ourselves, why
should we feed ourselves? If we die trying to get a foothold in the
crowd, why not let the crowd trample us sooner and be done
with it? I tell you, gentlemen, that there is beginning to beat in
this nation a great pulse of irresistible sympathy which is going
to transform the process of government amongst us.

(Slight commotion in audience below) I am sorry, a gentleman seems to have fainted, I am afraid, with the heat. What I
was about to say has been driven out of my head by another kind
of sympathy.

There is more than the safety of the people to be considered.
There are the opportunities of the people; there are the things
that we must do for the people in order to facilitate their lives.
And what I want to call your attention to is that every time we
discuss any one of these questions we come up against some
economic objection. This is not theoretical with me, because I
have handled these matters in the State of New Jersey, and I
know that men say, "We can't be more pitiful, we can't be more
considerate to our men in this shop, because if we were, the men
who are less considerate in the next shop, not spending as much

money for the safety of their men as we would spend, could underbid us in the market and beat us in the competition." There is only one thing to do, therefore, and that is for the government itself to step in and say that in all shops these safeguards must be observed—these arrangements for the public and the general health.

But, gentlemen, these things are not going to be done until you change the point of view of the government. So long as the point of view of the government is the point of view of successful big business merely, it will not yield to the counsel of the rest of us, which says that before the interests of big business must come the interests of humanity. In other words, it's perfectly useless to talk about great programs of reform unless you first get a government that is going to institute the reform. Therefore, it is absolutely necessary that I should remind you of the fundamental question of the present campaign.

I want to say here, as I have said on so many other occasions, that there is a great deal in the program of the new third party which attracts all public-spirited and hopeful men, that there is a great program of human uplift included in the platform of that party. A man would be niggardly and untrue to himself who would not say that. But when I ask myself who is going to carry out this program, then the thing wears another aspect.

Voice: Shoot it at him.

You think that I am referring to an individual. I am not. I am referring to the method by which that individual and the others associated with him propose to deal with the central economic difficulty. The reason the government has not heretofore done these things is that it has been controlled from the point of view of special interests. These special interests are lodged in what we call the trusts. Don't deceive yourselves into supposing that the trusts naturally grew big by being efficient. They didn't. They grew big by crushing little fellows that would have been big if they hadn't crushed them, and by buying up those who had already got big and couldn't be crushed. And they spent so much money buying up those whom they couldn't beat in the competition that they have to charge us high prices in order to pay the interest on their investment. In other words, they bought efficiency out of the market instead of creating efficiency by their combinations.

Now, the third party program is this, not to retrace a single step, not to prevent a single preventable thing in the processes by which these monopolies have been built up, but to take charge of the monopolies and regulate them. The government, in other words, is going to enter into a closer partnership than ever with the trustees who have been running this government. I am trying to state this thing perfectly fairly. I believe that that is the inevitable result of that program. And these same trustees are the men who have consistently fought the interests of organized labor as well as every other interest that resisted the processes by which they have built up their monopolistic power.

The government under this program would promise us that they would see to it that these men were kind to us. But suppose that these men who ought to be kind to us are themselves more influential than anybody else in choosing the very men who are going to regulate them, what will happen then? If the government is going to be the stakeholder, who is going to hold the stakeholder? If you deposit all your capital of independence and of free enterprise with the government, then you will have to sit up nights with the government to see that somebody doesn't get to it while you are asleep. And you know that the very men whom they are going to regulate are the men who now have the ear of the government and have long had the ear of the very gentlemen who are proposing this program. Therefore, in this year when you come to vote you have got to make this choice: Are you going to vote for a government which will regulate your masters, or are you going to be your own masters and regulate the government and through the government these men who have tried to regulate you?

Everybody who has even read the newspapers knows the means by which these men built up their power and created these monopolies. Any decently equipped lawyer can suggest to you statutes by which the whole business can be stopped, and after you have stopped the business you won't have to regulate it. The fundamental point of my creed is that I absolutely deny that monopoly is inevitable. I absolutely deny that we have lost the power to set ourselves free. I absolutely deny that the American people don't know enough to run their own enterprise without the suggestion of the government. Just let some of the youngsters I know have a chance and they'll give these gentlemen points. Lend them a little money; they can't get any now. See to it that when they have got a local market they can't be squeezed out of that local market by some giant who has the markets of the world coming in and underselling them in that local market. Give them a chance to capture that market and then see them capture another one and another one and another one, until these men who are carrying an intolerable load of artificial securities find that they have got to get down to business to keep their foothold at all.

All that I ask—and if they are men they can't decline the challenge—all I ask is let us put them on their mettle and see whether they know how to run their business or not—see whether they can stand up against intelligent, economical, efficient competition, not the old-fashioned competition where it was let the strongest survive, but where the weak are protected, competition regulated, the processes safeguarded, and every man made as strong by the arm of the government as the strongest man with whom he can come into contest. Because the arm of the government is not intended for the strong. It is intended for the weak. The iron structure of the law is meant to uphold those parts of the economic-social structure that can't stand for themselves. And those men who have established their supremacy could do without law. They have their own police force. They have their own detectives. They have their own processes, as it were, of government. They don't have to be taken care of. All they are praying for is to be let alone. And the worst of it is that they are drawing together singly and are no match for the government; but, ladies and gentlemen, if they ever got all together, the government would be no match for them.

You have got your choice. If you make the wrong choice in the year 1912, you may not have a chance to change it in our generation.

I am not here, therefore, to exhibit myself as an attractive person. I am not here to exhibit myself as somebody who knows exactly how the thing ought to be done. I am not here to assert that the schemes are worked out by which mankind can be saved. But I am here to challenge you to make a very deliberate and intelligent choice when you vote on November fifth with regard to the fundamental parts of the program involved. Don't let any man fool you. Don't let any platform fool you. Do your own thinking. And when the American people have done their own thinking, I for one am sport enough to take the consequences. If you don't elect me you won't find me saying you have made a mistake, whatever may be my private opinion. It would be very bad taste for me to express my private opinion after the public expression has taken place.

And so I do not feel—I would be abashed if I did feel—that I was discussing a question of personal choice between candidates. I have a great respect for the individuals, for many of the individuals, whom I am opposing. They are a very mixed lot, you will have to admit, and you can't include them all in any one statement. The third party, for example, is a very variegated aggregation. It consists, in the first place, of old-line Republicans whose consciences couldn't stand the game any longer, and, in the second place, of a very noble lot of social reformers who think they have found the party to serve them at last; and, in the third place, of gentlemen about whom the less said the better—what one might call the discards of other parties. Not a large element, I want to say in fairness to the new party, but it is very noticeable, the kind of element that makes itself very noticeable. Just as when I used to be president of a university I noticed that the very small minority who were in the habit of getting on "tears" were the sort that were always in the public eye and gave the reputation to the university. So these discards are apt to be very much in the public eye and they give a character which they perhaps do not deserve to those with whom they are associated.

And, therefore, I can't speak with respect concerning all my opponents, but I can with regard to most of them. I want to pay my tribute of personal respect to the President of the United States. I do not believe that any man in the United States who knows the facts can question the patriotism, or the integrity, or the public purpose of the man who now presides at the Executive Office in Washington. If he has got into bad company, that is no fault of his, because he didn't choose the company; it was made beforehand. And if he has taken their advice, it was because they were nearest to him and he didn't hear anybody else.

That is the reason why I would rather have the advice of a crowd like this than the advice of a cabinet. I would at least hear more, I would at least learn more. I would feel what I always pray I shall feel in vital connections with those over whose destinies—and not over mine—I should in public office be presiding. For I have for two years occupied a responsible public office, and I have had a good deal of enjoyment in it. I have had a good deal of enjoyment in seeing certain men disappear, because I had got tired looking at them. I have had a great deal of deeper enjoyment than that—in finding men come to the front who had hitherto not had heart to come to the front, men who had lost heart in the effort to reform their own communities and had sat down with a sort of dull despair in their hearts, as those who say, "Well, there is some blind force against us with which we can't cope." There isn't any such force. I used to think before I went into politics that these fortresses of greed were real fortresses, but I found they were made of cardboard. You had only to throw the weight of honest men against them to see them collapse. The guns that frowned at their embrasures wouldn't go off. They were rusty. They were loaded with buncombe. When they exploded, it was the sound of words and not of shot. And all you had to do was to walk up to them without any words and take possession of what had all along belonged to you.

This thing of politics is getting to be a very serious matter of business in the United States. The people of the United States are not going to be fooled any longer. They are going to think for themselves. They are going to make their own choices. I dare say they are going to make their own mistakes. But they are all bound in one direction, and the man who doesn't join the procession will have to fall out of the lines entirely.

That is my only objection to the standpatter; he doesn't know there is a procession. He is asleep in the back part of his house. He doesn't know that the road is resounding with the tramp of men going to the front. And when he wakes up, the country will be empty. He will be deserted, and he will wonder what has happened. Nothing has happened. The world has been going on. The world has a habit of going on. The world has a habit of leaving those behind who won't go on with it. The world has always neglected standpatters.

And therefore the standpatter does not excite my indignation. He excites my sympathy. He is going to be so lonely before it is all over. And we are good fellows; we are good company; why doesn't he come along? We are not going to do him any harm. We are going to show him a good time. We are going to climb the slow road until it reaches some upland where the air is fresher, where the whole talk of politicians is still, where men can look in each other's faces and see there is nothing to conceal, that all they have to talk about they are willing to talk about in the open and talk about with each other; and then, looking back over the road, they will say at least we have fulfilled our promise to mankind. We said to all the world, "America was created to break every kind of monopoly and to set men free upon a footing of equality, upon a footing of opportunity that matches their brains and their energies." And now we have proved that we meant it. Now we are free men and can say to all the world, "Here under this emblem of liberty we have redeemed our pledges to mankind." And the influence of America has spread even to China. How all the old crusts are breaking, all the whole impulses are being renewed in the rejuvenated earth!

Just a while ago, as I came through the streets of this great city, the children of three schools had turned out to pay us the compliment of seeing us go by, and I saw in their faces how they were mixed of all the different national stocks that have made up the variety and the strength of America. And I remembered what a comparatively recent immigrant to this country had told me. He said that when he came to America he expected everything, he expected to feel a new air, and the only place he had found what he really had looked for was in the public schools, that there was the genuine melting pot of equality into which when children entered they came out Americans, adjusted to the conditions of our life, acquainted with each other, having a common impulse, a common training, a common point of view. And then I thought of what so many noble men and women in this country are now interested in—letting the whole country go to school in those same schoolhouses, letting the grown-up people in the evening, when the pupils are not there, use them as the forums in which they will discuss the interests of the neighborhood, use them as the place where they will acknowledge no difference of race or of creed or of conditions, and where those things can be displayed which are nowhere else to be found.

One of the valuable lessons of my life was that at a comparatively early age in my experience as a public speaker I had the privilege of speaking in Cooper Union in New York.[2] The audience in Cooper Union is made up of every kind of man and woman, from the poor devil who simply comes in to keep warm up to the man who has come in there to take a serious part in the discussion of the evening. I want to tell you this, that in the questions that were asked after the speech was over, the most penetrating questions that I have ever had addressed to me came from some of the men who were the least well dressed in the audience—came from the plain fellows, came from the fellows whose muscle was up against the whole struggle of life. And they asked questions which went to the heart of the business and put me to my mettle to answer them. I felt as if their voices were a voice out of life itself, not a voice out of any school less than the severe school of experience. And what I like about this social-center idea of the school is that there is the place where the ordinary fellow is going to get his innings, going to ask his questions, going to express his opinions, going to convince those who do not realize the vigor of America, that the vigor of America runs through the blood of every American, and that the only place he can become a true American is in this clearinghouse of absolutely democratic opinion.

When we have gone to school, then we will have no masters. When we have graduated from these conferences of neighbors,

<hr>

[2] An outline of his lecture at Cooper Union is printed at Nov. 19, 1898, Vol. 11.

we will not need to be afraid of any men. The only people I have ever heard object seriously to that use of the schoolhouse were gentlemen who had packed the school boards and controlled them and knew that in the schoolhouses their own performances would be discussed, and the last thing that they want is to have these things discussed. When we are done discussing, when the noise is over, when the American people has sat down to the consideration of its own affairs, then parties will begin to fall into definite line again, then men will take sides with patriotic conviction, then men will stop seeking their own selfish interests and get together in that comradeship which is the spirit of America.[3]

T MS (C. L. Swem Coll., NjP); with corrections from the partial text in the *St. Paul Pioneer Press*, Sept. 19, 1912.
[3] There is a WWhw outline of this address, with the composition date of Sept. 11, 1912, in WP, DLC.

To John Wesley Wescott

Chicago Ills Sept. 19 [19]12

Admire you more than ever[1]   My affectionate congratulations on your patriotic action   All democrats here join in the message
Woodrow Wilson

T telegram (J. W. Wescott Coll., NjP).
[1] Wescott had just withdrawn from the senatorial race. He and Hughes had submitted their claims to an arbitration committee composed of William G. McAdoo, Senator O'Gorman, and Josephus Daniels. They recommended that one of the contestants withdraw.

Remarks in Michigan City, Indiana, from a Rear Platform

[Sept. 19, 1912]

I have tried discussing the big questions of this campaign from the rear end of a train. It can't be done. They are too big— that is the long and short of the matter. By the time you get started and begin to explain yourself the train moves off. I would a great deal rather make your acquaintance than leave a compound fracture of an idea behind me.

T MS (C. L. Swem Coll., NjP).

A Rear Platform Talk in Kalamazoo, Michigan

[Sept. 19, 1912]

(A voice: Kalamazoo is for you.)

That is fine, then I don't have to say anything. We don't need any speeches this time. Everything is going Democratic anyhow.

(College cheer) That sounds very familiar. I am very much obliged to you boys. I would a great deal rather make your acquaintance individually than make you a speech. I have found that the subjects to be discussed in this campaign are so tremendous that they can hardly be handled in speeches from the rear end of the train. Moreover, the rear platform is not the Democratic platform this time. We are at the front, and not at the back. But I must say that since I have got into Michigan I have felt a singular stimulation because we have stopped at several other cities, and everywhere there is the same spirit of hope and confidence. I can explain it only this way, that we are genuinely interested in the one subject that lies nearest my own heart, namely, setting the government free. Because, ladies and gentlemen, whether it was done intentionally or not, there is no doubt about it that our government in recent years has been seriously entangled with special interests of various kinds, and the men who got it entangled cannot get it disentangled. That is the whole point of the matter, because their whole political habit has been formed upon the basis of the practices which their judgments approve and which nevertheless have got us into most of the difficulties that now have to be cured. There is no time to discuss here how we got into it or how we are to get out of it. But the point is that the people of the United States have made up their minds to get out of it, and there is only one team ready to do the business, and that is the Democratic team. I am speaking in the terms of a man who has been bred in a football college. I know the third team is not organized, it doesn't even know the signals, and the regular Republican team is very much weakened. It has lost some of its principal players. But there have been no losses on the Democratic side. On the contrary, there have been a great many gains, and the game is familiar to the Democrats that we have to play now.

I call you to witness that while it took some gentlemen half a generation to discover what progressive platform was necessary for this country, the Democratic party has known it for sixteen years.

It didn't wait until 1912 to find it out, and it didn't compromise with anybody in the meantime in order to get into office. And now that the country is recognizing the readiness of the Democratic party to serve it, the Democratic party, thank God, is ready for the task.

T MS (C. L. Swem Coll., NjP).

A Campaign Address in Detroit[1]

[Sept. 19, 1912]

Mr. Chairman,[2] your Honor,[3] Ladies and Gentlemen: I esteem it a rare privilege to face an audience like this. I must say that I have never felt the exhilaration of contest as I feel it in the year 1912, because there seems to have come into our politics again some of the original spirit which created the great government under which we live. Our Fourth of July celebrations had grown perfunctory. We had begun to repeat certain great phrases that had illuminated our history as if we had forgotten their meaning —the phrases of the Declaration of Independence and of the Virginia Bill of Rights, in which it is written, though men repeated it as if they didn't understand it, that whenever a great free people comes to the conclusion that its government is not suitable to its present needs, it has the right, the indefeasible right, to change that government as it will. We had begun to repeat that like an empty phrase and to forget that it was the foundation stone of everything that we had builded. Because in these latter years we have become aware that our governments, our state governments and our federal government, were not responsive to our needs, didn't lend themselves to the use of the common life in this country.

There are a great many symptoms that this is true. How long is it, will you tell me, that this country has been interested in the question of the initiative and the referendum? Why is it interested in these questions now? Do we want to change the fundamental character of our government? No, we do not. But we want to get at our government, and we know that something has been standing between us and it. The initiative means this, that if a representative assembly does not represent us, then we will undertake to legislate for ourselves; that if a legislative assembly does not represent us and passes bills of which we disapprove, then we shall insist that those bills be submitted to us for our judgment, for fear they should put upon the statute books things

---

[1] Delivered in the National Guard Armory.
[2] James Phelan, judge of the Detroit police court.
[3] William Barlum Thompson, Mayor of Detroit, 1907-1908, 1911-12.

that do not act for the general benefit of the community. That is the meaning of the initiative and referendum. Nobody has proposed to substitute popular legislation for representative legislation as a practice, as a rule. This is something which we have occasionally in some parts of this country demanded in order that we should again recover the control of our own affairs. And we will recover it unless we lose the spirit of 1776 and forget what all our declarations of right mean. And so it seems to me in this year of 1912 we are changing the rhetoric of the Fourth of July into the reality of political action.

Now, I say these things for this reason, that the fundamental question we are debating in 1912 is this: Shall the Government of the United States be serviceable to the whole people of the United States? That is the question. And underlying that question is this: What kind of government can be serviceable to the people of the United States? There is only one kind that can be, and that is a free government, a government which is not dominated by some of us, but is responsive to all of us. And our study in the present campaign is a study of the best method of regaining control of the instrumentalities by which we govern ourselves. I do not need to expound to you—it is so familiar that passion has passed out of the question—that the Government of the United States has been responsive to special interests, and in our time has seemed not to be responsive to the general interest of the people of the United States. I have seen this upon a small scale myself in the State of New Jersey. I dare say there have been times when you have seen it in this great state. I have just gathered from the intimation of your Mayor that you have seen it in this city. There is hardly a part of the United States where men are not aware that some secret private purposes and interests have been spending their money and controlling their actions, and they have determined that they are going to break through these barriers and govern themselves.

Well, what has been governing them? Why, the special interests have been governing them, and they have been governing them through those interesting persons whom we call political bosses. A boss is not so much a politican as he is the business agent in politics of the special interests, at least that is the kind of boss I have known. And the kind of boss that I have known is not a partisan. He is quite above politics because he has an arrangement with the boss of the other party so that whether it is heads or tails, he wins. They receive contributions from the same sources—the two bosses. They spend these contributions for the same purposes. They undertake to carry out the same program, and the amazing thing to me is that I have recently met some bosses who didn't realize that time had been called on the game. What I am amazed at in the political boss is not his subtlety, but his stupidity. He is a perfect Bourbon. He never changes his mind. He never learns anything. He never forgets anything. And some of them don't know that the people are now on to them, and that the way that is certain to spoil every purpose that they have is to dare to show their hand in it. I say I am amazed that they don't see it. But they will see it.

It isn't more than five weeks before they will see it, because as I travel from one part of this country to the other I don't see any difference among the people in the different parts of this great country of ours. The same thing is written in their eyes, and it isn't a gleam of fierceness. It is the light of confidence. They know what they want, and they know they are going to get it. And anybody who supposes that economic questions and political questions are two different things is very much mistaken, because these things have been so closely married with one another that it is impossible to discriminate between them. For the man engaged in the interests of big business to see that nothing is done by way of reform, politics is business, and for the politician whom he uses, politics is business. And I am not going to waste my time or my brains discriminating between politics and business when we are in this part of the discussion.

And this gives me an opportunity to allude to something that I read about half an hour ago. The *Journal* of today has an editorial in which I must say that it does me personally much more than justice.[4] But it sees in me an unintentional Machiavelli. It says: "This is an honest man. He honestly believes that a protective tariff is unconstitutional; and if he gets a chance, being an honest man, he will upset this unconstitutional arrangement." That is good reasoning, but it is entirely inconsistent with another part of the editorial which very kindly ascribes brains to me, for it concedes that I am not only an honest man but an intelligent and a well-informed man. I would not have claimed that for myself, but we will assume that in the argument. One of the things that I know is that about half the people in the United States are Democrats. I know that they are engaged in every kind of industry, and that they couldn't unite to accomplish economic destruction without also deliberately accomplishing economic suicide. And I do not believe that half the people of the United States are going to combine to ruin the industries of the United States. I

4 *Detroit Journal*, Sept. 19, 1912.

am too intelligent to think that's likely. Moreover, so far as I am myself concerned, I would with the greatest respect call the editor's attention to a little utterance which I ventured to make upon accepting the nomination for the presidency, in which I explicitly laid down the program which I thought we ought to pursue with regard to the protective duties. I said that they ought not to be changed except in such a way and at such a rate as would not in any way interfere with the course of sound business in the United States.

I also said, and that is what makes this parenthesis applicable to my discourse tonight, that we were going to begin with those particular items where we found special privilege entrenched. We know what those items are. These gentlemen have been kind enough to point them out themselves, and what we are interested in first of all with regard to the tariff is getting the grip of special interests off the throat of Congress. We do not propose that special interests shall any longer camp in the committee rooms of the Committee of Ways and Means at the House and of the Finance Committee of the Senate. We mean that those shall be places where the people of the United States shall come and be represented in order that these things may be done in the general interest and not in the interest of particular groups of persons who already dominate the industries and the industrial development of this country. Because, no matter how wise these gentlemen may be, no matter how patriotic, no matter how singularly they may be gifted with the power to divine the right courses of business, there isn't any group of men in the United States or any other country that is wise enough to have the destinies of a great people put in their hands as trustees.

And we know, those of us who handle the machinery of politics, that the great difficulty in breaking up the control of the political boss is that he is backed by the money and the influence of these very people who are entrenched in these very schedules. To quote a phrase of which I am very fond, I will say I am not arguing with you, I am telling you. These things are things of actual tangible experience. I have dealt with bosses myself. I could write you out a list, if you were interested in it, of the number of gentlemen, not exceeding half a dozen, who used to own the legislature of New Jersey. All that you had to do was to stand them up in front, metaphorically, of audiences all over the State of New Jersey and call the roll, and you broke their power by the mere exposure of them. Because everybody knew that the people of New Jersey had found it impossible before the election of 1910 to get anything done that they voted should be done. You are not to suppose that the people of New Jersey didn't vote programs of reform before 1910. They had been voting them for half a generation, but they didn't get them. Every platform was put out with a huge wink. Every platform was just a concession, a bluff on the part of the men who put them forth, serviceable for the election, but not to serve as a guide after the election. And I can name in series the particular corporations in the State of New Jersey which made it impossible to carry out that program. If I were in New Jersey I would name them, but I am not going to be impolite enough to name them outside of New Jersey. I have named them in New Jersey, and therefore it isn't necessary that I should name them tonight. Besides, some of them have retired from that business.

Very well then, how are you going to get a free government? That is the point. You are not intelligent if you are interested in a party program that doesn't begin by some suggestion that will show you that you can get a government that can carry out that program. Isn't that a plain proposition? What is the use having ambitious programs of social uplift if there isn't anything to lift up with? If you can't get a new partnership, you can't improve the business. If you can't get a new atmosphere for government, you can't change the action of it. The absolutely necessary first step is to disentangle it from the things with which it has been entangled. What we want is free enterprise, for one thing, but we haven't got it. What we want is free markets for our commodities and free markets for our labor, and we haven't got them. What we want is free competing water routes, for example, that will enable us to handle the heavier kinds of our goods in transportation without depending too much upon railway rates, and we haven't got them and can't get them as things stand now. What we want is genuine conservation of our natural resources, and we can't get it as things stand now.

Have you noticed that the trouble about conservation is that the Government of the United States hasn't any policy at present? It is simply marking time; it is simply standing still. Reservation is not conservation. Simply to say "We are not going to do anything about the forests" when the country needs to use the forests is not a practicable program at all. To say that the people of the great State of Washington can't buy coal out of the Alaskan coal fields doesn't settle the question. They have got to have that coal sooner or later. And if you are so afraid of the Guggenheims and all the rest of them that you can't make up your mind what your policy is going to be about those coal fields,[5] how long are we going to wait for the government to make up its mind? We know perfectly well that there can't be a workable program until there is a free government.

And what I want to point out to you, ladies and gentlemen, is this: The center of all our economic difficulties is that there is not freedom of enterprise in the United States. It would be a long journey to give you the particulars of what I mean, but I mean, for instance, this: If you make an invention in a particular field and require, let us say, a million dollars to build a plant in order to manufacture that thing and get it on the market, and advertise it, and try to get the money, you will apply for it in vain unless you will go in with the gentlemen who are already controlling the industries which that invention will affect. This is not a hypothetical question. I can cite you instances. If it is a large sum of money you need, you can't get it, and you might as well whistle for it. Make up your mind now that the inventive genius and initiative of the American people is being held back by the fact that our industrial field is so controlled that new entries, newcomers, new adventurers, independent men, are feared, and if they will not go partners in the game with those already in the control of it, they will be excluded.

What does that mean? What does that mean with regard to your sons? What does that mean with regard to the next generation? What does it mean with regard to the present generation? You have got to get into this complicated nexus of monopolistic control in order to make your way along the routes of big business in the United States. I see men here and there in this audience nodding their heads when I say that: I know they have been up against it. And unless we can break that up, there is going to be stagnation, for I want you to remember how this control was built up. It was built up by competition, by free competition, by absolutely unrestricted competition. So that when a man got big and had a market larger than the local market, and money enough to back himself with to be independent of local credit, he could squeeze the little man who had only the local market out of business by underselling him at unprofitable rates which he recouped himself by his sales in other parts of the country, and so making it impossible for him to do business. Or if he found him too little to squeeze, he seldom found him too big to buy, because he was ready to pay him two or three times the

[5] Identified in n. 3 to the address printed at Nov. 4, 1910, Vol. 21.

price of his business to get rid of his competition. And after he had paid him two or three times the price of his business, he had to pay interest either upon his bonds or dividends upon his stock in order to carry on the business which he had thus overcapitalized in order to control it. And every time you add to the interest account, you add to the necessity of getting high prices from the consumer. I think that is plain to every man who knows anything about business in this audience. These are the processes which, because we didn't safeguard the little fellow, the big fellow has brought into existence. The pigmy hasn't any chance in America; only the giant has. And the laws give the giant free leave to trample down the pigmy. What I am interested in is laws that will give the little man a start, that will give him a chance to show these fellows that he has brains enough to compete with them and can presently make his local market a national market and his national market a world market, and put them to their mettle to do the business more intelligently and economically and systematically than he can.

But those are not the conditions existing now. That brings me to my point. Any party that can give you a free government and will give it to you can give you all the rest. How does the new third party propose to give you a free government? So far as I can discover, it doesn't propose to do it at all. For it proposes, not to protect the little fellow, but to adopt the big fellow. I understand that the leader of the third party has recently said that he didn't suggest this just the other day, that he had suggested it while he was President in one of his messages to Congress, during that same term of the presidency in which trusts grew faster and more numerously than in any other administration we have had; and that his conclusion was—he doesn't say, but this must be the inference—his conclusion was that the trusts had come to stay, that it wasn't possible to put them out of business, it wasn't possible to check their supremacy, that all you could do was to accept them as necessary evils and appoint an industrial commission which would tell them how they were to do their business. Not an industrial commission which should tell you how other men should be admitted into the field of competition, but an industrial commission which should take care of the people of the United States by saying to these trusts: "Now, go easy, don't hurt anybody. We believe that when you are reminded of your moral duties you are not malevolent, you are beneficent. You are big, but you are not cruel, and when you show an inclination to be cruel, here is a governmental agency that will remind you what are the laws of Christianity and of good conscience."

Now, who is going to be the keeper of the public conscience in respect of the reformation of our affairs through the trusts? If that is the program, why, this same government which has adopted the trusts, this same government is perpetuating the partnership which is now at the very root of the evil which we are fighting. Because the moment you legalize the trusts, the moment you say that the evil they have done cannot be undone, you have crystalized the very conditions which now hold American industry as if in a straitjacket. For the means that I would propose to deal with the trusts is simply to see if they can carry their overcapitalization without toppling down. Because if the business is worth a hundred million and it is capitalized at five hundred million, and somebody else can come in with a hundred million and do that business in competition with the five-hundred-million concern, he can do it at an advantage that is five times greater than the other fellow. And then we will see to it whether by genius and invention and economy and administration they can make a five hundred million watered institution pay. All that I want is that these gentlemen should prove their case that the trusts are organized for the sake of efficiency, for that is the only legal ground they have to stand on. The whole process by which they have built up the trusts show that they depend not upon efficiency but upon monopoly; when they can't beat a man they buy him out invariably.

The notable example is the way in which Mr. Carnegie was bought out of the steel business. Mr. Carnegie could build better mills and make better steel rails and make them cheaper than anybody else connected with what afterwards became the United States Steel Corporation. They didn't dare leave him outside, because no matter what their capital might be, he would beat them. And so they paid him four or five times what his business was worth in order to get rid of him. The most complimented man that I know of in the industrial history of America is Andrew Carnegie. These men, whose business genius is boasted of, knew they were no match for him, and the only thing they could do to beat him was to make his bank account so big that it wasn't worthwhile for him to work any more.

Now, if we can have men encouraged to come into the field with natural genius and put everybody else in that business on their mettle, then there will begin to be an industrial revival and a buoyancy of business in this country such as we have never known before. Limit the field of competition and you limit the field of development. There is not now free enterprise in the United States.

Ah, how the laboring men of this country have been deceived! How they have permitted themselves to be deceived! Don't you know that these very men who have been most successful in building up these trusts are also the very men who have been most successful in preventing the organization of labor? Don't you know that one of the objects of their combination is to control the labor market? And do you imagine that they have ever set deliberate plans for giving the workingman anything comparable in the way of wages to his proportion of the profits which they themselves pocket? Why, they don't have to give the laboring man any more than he can get in the competition of the market. And they don't give him any more. And, as a matter of fact, some of the most highly protected industries in this country pay very much lower wages than the unprotected industries in this country. And some of the most highly protected pay wages that are below the living scale, and at the same time that these enterprises are making earnings so great that they can build new factories out of their surplus every second year. It is one of the grandest pieces of bluff and humbug that has ever been known in the history of human deception.

I want to widen the market for American labor. I want to see conditions exist in which men will compete for American labor. I want men to come to a time again when they will realize that the highest priced labor in the world is the cheapest labor in the world, that what is produced by brains and intelligence and skillful touch is a great deal cheaper than what is produced by stupidity and dullness and the whip of the master. I tell you this, that American labor up to date is the cheapest in the world. I can prove it. American manufacturers compete in foreign markets in the sale of goods manufactured in those markets, near those markets, by labor that receives only one third the remuneration of American labor. Now, what does that mean? It means that they can afford to pay American workingmen three times as much and still undersell their competitors in the foreign market. And yet the American workingman is told that the amount of his wages depends upon the protective tariff. It doesn't. It depends upon him. It depends upon what is inside his thinking box. And when you once get to a system of regulated monopoly, then you get to a system of controlled labor. Don't forget that. Narrow the lines of competition and you stiffen the lines of labor control. You haven't a free market for your labor any more than you have a free market for your commodities, for under this system of monopoly, regulated or unregulated, the monopolists can determine the amount of goods to be produced and therefore determine the prices that those goods are to bring. There isn't a free market for the goods, and these same gentlemen who will be regulated under this precious system are so interlaced in their personal relationships with the great shipping interests of this country, with the great railroads, that they can determine the rates of shipment.

The people of this country are being very subtly dealt with. Do you know that you can get rebates without calling them such at all? The most complicated study I know of is the classification of freight by the railway companies. If I want to make a special rate on a special thing, all I have got to do is to put it in a special class in the freight classification and the trick is done. And when you reflect that the men who control the United States Steel Corporation, for example, the twenty-four men who control it, are either presidents or vice-presidents or directors in 55 per cent of the railways of the United States—reckoning by the valuation of those railroads and the amount of their stocks and bonds—you know just how close the whole thing is knitted together in our industrial system. And these twenty-four gentlemen administer that corporation as if it belonged to them. The amazing thing to me is that the people of the United States have not seen that the administration of a great business like that is not a private affair; it is a public affair.

Why, I and half a dozen other gentlemen start a corporation, a joint stock corporation, and we advertise in the newspapers, send out a dragnet for everybody's savings or surplus deposits, and people all over the United States buy our securities. And then we sit down to administer the millions which they have poured into our enterprise and talk about it as our private business. We do it by asking for and getting their unquestioning proxies, and any time that the stockholders, counted sometimes by the hundreds of thousands in this country, should choose to assert themselves, it would be discovered whose business this was. I have myself sat for a short time—in a representative, not an owning capacity—in the board of directors of a great corporation,[6] and it has been amazing to me how little anybody was considered except those who were sitting around that board. The idea that it is a trust relationship dawned so slowly upon their comprehension! And yet it is a trust relationship, and until that has

[6] The Mutual Life Insurance Co. of New York.

soaked into the consciousness of the people of this country they won't know how to get control of their own investments and of their own business. So that all I am after all along the line is breaking up the smug control of these self-constituted trustees and masters of our economic fortunes, letting them know that the government has ears for other people than themselves. Not in order to do them any injury whatever, but merely in order to bring them to their senses and make them conduct their business upon the basis of fair dealing and equality all along the line.

There again I fall back upon the editorial in the afternoon paper and take leave to ascribe to myself a certain degree of intelligence. I am not interested in disturbing the great course of business in this country. But I am interested in enriching it. I am interested in varying it. And I know that the only way to do it is by the methods that I have suggested, of regulated competition instead of legitimatized monopoly. After you have made the partnership between monopoly and your government permanent, then I invite all the philanthropists in the United States to come and sit on the stage and go through the motions of finding out how they are going to get philanthropy out of their masters. I don't want any assistance from the government which is given in condescension and pity. I want only that consideration that is given in justice and righteousness and good faith. We are not children to be taken care of. We live in a free government and can't breathe anything but free air, and we want leave to take care of ourselves. This business of setting up individuals or parties as special Providences is one of the things that is played out. So far as my pride is concerned, I would just as leave have a malevolent boss as a beneficent boss. I don't want any boss at all.

Now, ladies and gentlemen, this is a year of critical choice. After the year 1912 it may be too late to turn back. Don't deceive yourselves for a moment as to the pervasive power of the great interests which now dominate our development. They are so great that it is almost an open question whether the Government of the United States can dominate them or not. Go one step further, make their organized power permanent, and it may be too late to turn back. The roads diverge at the point where we stand very little, but they stretch their vistas out to a region where they are very far separated from one another. And at the end of one is the old tiresome story of a government tied up with the special interests of the nation, and at the other shines that light which we have followed all our lives—the light of individual initiative, of individual liberty, of individual freedom, the light of untrammeled enterprise.

I, for my part, do not consent to regard that light as an *ignus fatuus* which we have been following as if we were pursuing a mirage. I believe that light to shine out of the heavens that God himself has created. I believe in human liberty as I believe in the wine of life. There is no salvation for me in the mere power of government. Law was brought in not to guard the strong but to protect the weak. Law was made more for the infant in the cradle than for the man who has achieved middle life and found his standing in the world. Law is made more for the boys than for the men. Law is made more for the beginners in every enterprise than for those who have achieved. Law is beckoning on to future generations, heartening them, cheering them, saying: "Be afraid of no man; come on, the field is open; spend your power, and know that in the spending you shall get legitimate usury. Let your hearts be afraid of nothing except slavery; be afraid of nothing except being deceived by the sophistry of men who would master you. Open your eyes, look into their eyes, question their character, search their programs, and then choose whom you will follow."

I pity the man who in the year 1912 promises the people of the United States anything that he cannot give them. I used to say sometimes, when I was attempting to write history, that I could sit on the side lines and look on with a certain degree of complacency upon the men who were performing in the arena of politics. Because, I said, after the game is over some quiet fellow like myself will sit down in a remote room somewhere and tell the next generation what to think of you fellows, and they will think what he tells them to think. He assesses, he sums up. You may talk yourself tired, and your own estimate of yourselves will be discounted. And now that I am myself exposed, I think of that quiet jury sitting in those rooms surrounded by nothing but shelves and books and documents. I think of the anticipated verdict of another generation. And I know that the only measure and standard by which a man can rise or fall is the standard of absolute integrity, that he can deceive nobody but himself and his own generation for a little space.

There is no immortality in politics except the immortality of honesty. There is no immortality for a nation except the immortality of freedom. America has promised herself and promised the world this great heritage. Shall she break the promise? Shall she deceive herself and deceive mankind? Shall she not recover the spirit in which she made constitutions and with that same spirit revive them, rejuvenate them, shoot them through and through with a spirit and an air of indomitable courage? And shall she not at every choice at the ballot box silently vindicate her claim to wisdom and to liberty itself?

T MS (C. L. Swem Coll., NjP), with corrections from the complete texts in the *Detroit News*, Sept. 20, 1912, and the *Detroit Free Press*, Sept. 20, 1912.

From Edward Mandell House

Dear Governor Wilson:　　New York City. September 19th, 1912.

I was with Mr. McCombs yesterday and he very much desires to have a conference with us at the earliest moment that is convenient to you.

I think, myself, that it is of more or less importance to discuss the matters he has in mind, therefore I hope you may find it possible to do as he desires.

He has moved to Larchmont on the outer edge of New York and if you can go to him I will motor you out in a few minutes at any time you indicate.

We have taken a furnished apartment here until January 1st and our telephone number is 5997 Madison Square.

　　　　　　　Your very sincere,　[E. M. House]

CCL (E. M. House Papers, CtY).

A Speech to Businessmen in Columbus, Ohio[1]

[Sept. 20, 1912]

Mr. Chairman,[2] ladies and gentlemen: I am very much complimented that the busy men of a particularly busy city should take an hour in the middle of the afternoon to come out and give me the pleasure and the privilege of saying a word or two to them. I would very much prefer that you should, for the time being, forget that I am a candidate for the presidency because, if I may say to you very frankly, the consciousness that I am a candidate and am supposed to be soliciting the suffrages of my fellow citizens sometimes embarrasses me. Because I do not wish the thought of an occasion like this, or of any other occasion, for that matter, to be centered upon myself as an individual. I would a great deal rather, if it were possible—if you were not so numerous —for you to talk than talk myself, because I regard a meeting like this as a sort of conference in which we can become aware of one another's points of view, and of one another's opinions about matters which concern all of us.

1 Delivered in the Hartman Theater.
2 James Kilbourne, leading businessman of Columbus.

One of the most amazing fictions of our politics is that the Democratic party is not interested in the business welfare of the United States. When you reflect that the Democrats of the United States comprise about half of the population, it is very interesting that half of the population should be suspected of the desire to commit commercial hari-kari. There are Democrats in every walk of life. There is not an important undertaking in this country with which some Democrat is not connected, upon whose success some Democrat's achievements do not depend. And therefore it is amazing that any body of the citizens should have long entertained the delusion that the Democratic party, as such, has any designs upon the material prosperity of our country.

What we are privileged to say to one another upon this matter, we should say very frankly indeed. Are you satisfied with the business conditions of the United States? Do you feel the same freedom in enterprise that obtained in this country when those of you who are middle aged were youngsters? Do you feel that your sons have as open a field for the exercise of their gifts in business as they would have had if they had been born a generation ago? Do you feel no concentration of the control of our industrial development in certain quarters? Do you feel no increased difficulty about obtaining the larger kinds of credit in order to start the larger kinds of undertakings? Are there inventors among you? Do you see nothing taking place in the market for inventions? Is this company of businessmen satisfied that they are now as free in business as they need to be, and that America has as untrammeled a future in her material development as she once seemed to have? Are you conscious there is any such thing as monopoly? Are you ignorant of the processes by which monopoly has been created? And are you content to continue to live under conditions which will perpetuate monopoly?

The questions answer themselves. You are not satisfied with the present conditions of business. If you accept them, it is because of a certain kind of despair. You know these things ought not to have happened. You know that the processes ought not to have been permitted by which they were brought about. But you feel that big business has come to stay, and you don't see how to break up the present processes of big business and substitute better ones. And therefore, with a spirit quite uncharacteristic of America, you shrug your shoulders and say, "Well, perhaps the best we can do is to submit and to regulate the thing if we can find men of genius enough to regulate it." . . .

Now what we have got to ask ourselves is this question: What are we going to do about the present unsatisfactory conditions of American business enterprises? I am not going to argue that they are unsatisfactory. I am going to take that for granted, for I know you will agree with me in thinking that they are. They became unsatisfactory through unregulated competition, because competition being left unregulated and certain circumstances—which it would take me too long in this connection to explain—having made it possible for men to get together in great combinations in the same kind of business, there has been pitted competitors who have a market as big as America against competitors who have markets only as big as Columbus. And the competitor with a market as big as America can afford to sell at a loss in Columbus so as to kill the Columbus competitor so long as he can maintain profitable prices throughout the rest of the United States. And one of the processes by which unrestricted competition established monopoly has been this process of killing out the beginner —seeing to it that there were no entries in the race for commercial supremacy or manufacturing supremacy in the United States, seeing to it that there were no apprentices sworn in, seeing to it that everything was kept tight, and nobody allowed to come in who wouldn't come in on the basis of cooperation and agreement. And then when a competitor was found whose competition had become too widespread and whose capital was too great to be dealt with in the way in which a local competitor could be dealt with, they would buy him out.

Take the shoe industry. The men who combined to control the shoe industry combined to control all the machinery that was used in the manufacture of shoes. And then arose a man[3]—just at this moment I have forgotten his name—who proceeded to build up from the bottom and invent new shoe machinery that was better than the machinery that this combination controlled. He succeeded, and presently it was absolutely necessary that the shoe combination should kill this competitor by buying him out, or else, without buying him out, he would have gotten rid of them. And therefore the usual thing happened: they bought him out at probably two or three times, I don't know how many times, the value of his plant and of his business, and then proceeded to put upon the shoes which we wear the burden of the extra load of capital which they had to carry in order to buy him out.[4]

I am not describing anything to you that you are not perfectly

3 Thomas G. Plant of Boston, owner of the Thomas G. Plant Co., shoe manufacturers.

4 About this matter, see Alpheus T. Mason, *Brandeis: A Free Man's Life* (New York, 1946), pp. 214-29.

familiar with. I am merely reminding you of what has been going on in this country. In other words, the law enforcers of this country have stood on one side and let the giants kill the pigmies. They have absolutely kept their hands off where the law was needed for the protection of the weak and have given leave to the strong, given supremacy to the strongest. That doesn't mean the ablest, that doesn't mean the men who study economy, who have mastered efficiency. Necessarily in some instances they have, but it doesn't necessarily mean that. By pigmy I mean the man who hasn't grown up to his full stature, who, if you will give him time enough and see to it that he is not swept off his feet, will build up a business more economical, more efficient, harder to compete with than the business which now, simply because it is big, can crush him while he is little. And so we have been suppressing the independent initiative of the American inventor and the American manufacturer and the American merchant, and we have got to release these forces in order to make America prosper at all.

How are you going to release them? Are you going to run amuck with your law among the big things that have been built up? Not at all. That isn't necessary. I am perfectly willing that they should remain big if they can beat everybody else by economy and efficiency, but I am not willing they should thrive on any other terms. Therefore, I am for the regulation, not of monopoly, for to regulate it is to adopt it into the family and accept it, but the regulation of competition, so as to see to it that the man who has brains enough and initiative enough to come into the field and put these men on their mettle; to see to it that there is no such control of large credit in this country that the beginner can't get the means to begin with; to see that there is no such control of manufacturing processes that the inventor cannot make an independent use of his invention; to see to it that the merchant has absolutely free choice as to whom he should buy his goods from, and absolutely free choice as to his competition in the market with regard to price, so that he isn't obliged to buy at a particular price, and isn't put under promise to sell at a particular price.

These are the processes by which America is cheating herself of her greatness, and I say that we have got to devise laws which will so regulate competition that we shall encourage beginners. Gentlemen, do you realize why we prefer democracy to monarchy? It is because we can't afford to be anxious as to what kind of sons a man has. If you have a monarchy or an aristocracy, your leaders have to come from the loins of those men. Suppose they don't come? Then you are cheated of the energy of the nation unless you can say it doesn't make any difference what kind of sons they have, there are plenty of sons to take their places from other ranks. And the whole structure of liberty has been built up out of the circumstance that the unknown men, regardless of the humbleness of their origin or the obscurity of their beginnings, have had an absolutely free channel in which to enter with their energy and establish their lordship over those less competent than themselves.

That is the reason that I am a Democrat, that is the reason that every man in America who is thoughtful is at least a democrat with a little d. And the interesting circumstance about the present campaign is that men are beginning to see there is no use in being a democrat with a little d unless you are a democrat with a big D, because the channels opened by those who are not democrats with a big D do not lead to the real processes of democracy with a little d. They lead to exclusiveness. They lead to the regulation of monopoly. They simply offer to guarantee to us that monopoly will be good to us. Now, there isn't any living man that can guarantee that unless he will see to it that men all over the country are challenged to come out and beat these fellows at their own business. That is the only law of freedom. And our trammels just now, our political difficulties, arise out of the fact that those who control our government have taken counsel, not with the men who are about to make beginnings, but with the men who have achieved, who are at the top of industry, who have already earned their mastery, and who can see nothing except the desirability of maintaining the conditions under which their mastery has been obtained.

A very subtle and perhaps a cynical English writer[5] has made a very interesting remark. He says it is not true altogether to say of a man who has established himself abundantly in business that you can't bribe a man like that. Because he says the point is that he has been bribed, not in any gross sense, not in any corrupt sense, but he has got his mastery under existing conditions. And existing conditions have put him under bonds to see to it that they are not changed. He has learned one game and he isn't going to risk another. He has learned how to get to the top by the ladder that is under him now, and he doesn't propose to let anybody change the process by which men have to climb. He is going to see to it that things are held where he has them and where he wants them to stay. I am not criticizing it; it is per-

---

[5] G. K. Chesterton, whose comment has been cited several times in this series.

fectly natural. And they have to be changed without his consent. I am very sorry; I would apologize to him if I knew him, but these things will have to be changed without his consent.

The men that I am listening to, as well as I can, in politics are the men of the next generation, the men knocking at the door of opportunity, thundering at these closed gates and crying to us: "Yes, you have built up a great structure of wealth, but what of us? Where is our hope? Where is our opening? Where is our opportunity of achievement? Are you going to shut the gates upon us and keep them shut? Are you going to open just such little wickets as you care to keep the key to and let us slip in and join your organization? Or are you going to open the main portal and say, 'Come in, the future is yours as much as it is ours, and no man shall contest it with you except by brains and honesty of character?'" Every artificial obstacle to free opportunity in this country must be battered down, and nobody will profit more, nobody will feel the buoyancy and spring more, than the men already in business in the United States.

One of the things that makes the currency question most pressing and significant at this moment is that we are certain now, in my judgment, to remove some of the artificial obstacles to our prosperity in business. And the minute you do that there is to be such an increase in the economic activity of America that this stubborn, stiff, antiquated currency system of ours can't stand the strain. You've got to make it elastic, you've got to change it, or else you can't stand your own prosperity; there won't be any means of carrying it. America is now straining at the leash, and I could name some of the gentlemen who hold the leather thong that is attached to the leash. I don't know whether they know they are holding it or not—it doesn't make any difference to me whether they do or not. The leash is there and America is straining to be free. And, God willing, she shall be free.

T MS (C. L. Swem Coll., NjP); with a few corrections from the nearly complete text in the Columbus *Ohio State Journal*, Sept. 21, 1912.

A Campaign Address in Columbus[1]

[Sept. 20, 1912]

Governor Harmon, Chairman Finley,[2] Ladies and Gentlemen: I consider it a real privilege to take part in the opening of this great campaign in the noble State of Ohio; and I want to thank

1 Delivered in Memorial Hall.
2 William L. Finley of Columbus, chairman of the Democratic State Executive Committee.

Governor Harmon for the very generous and gracious words with which he has introduced me. I feel just the responsibility which he has indicated. The people of this country are tired of assertion. They are now waiting to consider their own affairs and decide them upon the evidence—upon the proof—of intention, upon the offering of a program which they can see from the outset will work them the permanent advantage they now wait for.

Before I started west and was considering what would be worth presenting to this great audience, it occurred to me that this singular thing had happened: that the Republican party and the third party had already handed over to the Democratic speakers the two chief issues of the campaign. They are not even professing to know how, or upon what principle, the tariff ought to be revised, and neither of them is proposing to meet the question of monopoly by way of remedy. The only thing proposed is to mollify it, to make it as mild, as governable, as bearable, as possible. So that the very heart of our difficulties is avoided and declined by the orators of both the regular Republican party and of the very irregular Republican party.

I do not know how it would be possible to characterize the third party, because it is made up of so many elements that no characterization would fit all of its elements. In the first place, it is made up of a great many Republicans who feel simply this, that their consciences couldn't any longer stand what the regular Republican party was doing. And, in the second place, it is made up of a great many public-spirited people who have been looking for somebody who would profess their program, but have not stopped to consider sufficiently whether they have found somebody that can carry out that program. And, in the third place, it consists of a certain number of persons about whom the less said the better. It would be very interesting if I could mention some of their names, but I have laid upon myself certain restrictions of etiquette in this campaign which I do not care to overstep.

For I am not interested in individuals. I am not interested in candidates. I am interested in the feasibility of reform and the validity and reality of it; and I know that reform cannot begin with such a government as either Mr. Taft or Mr. Roosevelt will supply us with, for the simple reason that neither of these gentlemen proposes to supply us with a government which is free to act in the interests of the people. The first thing we must get is a free government—we haven't a free government now. And we know why we haven't a free government. The Government of the United States is not free because it takes its counsel with regard to the economic policy of the people of the United States from a very limited group of persons. And so long as it takes its counsel from that limited group of persons it cannot serve the interests of the nation as a whole.

My chief indictment against the program of both the other parties is that they do not propose to cure the causes. They merely propose to treat and try to remedy the results. For the causes are plain enough. Take the tariff: I am not going to discuss the tariff here tonight in any analytic fashion, but I want to point out to you that they haven't even realized that the tariff question is an absolutely new question. The most that either of the other platforms says is that some of the schedules are too high, and the most that one of the candidates says is that they are too high, chiefly because there isn't enough of the "prize money" that goes into the pay envelope of the employee. He doesn't object to the high prices when he speaks of the tariff. He doesn't admit that the high prices are due to the tariff. He simply says that there isn't an equitable division of the spoils. And he doesn't realize that there wouldn't be any spoils under the tariff system if it weren't an absolutely new question.

I say that it is an absolutely new question for this reason: When Mr. McKinley used to argue for high protective duties, when Mr. Blaine used so brilliantly to defend them, when the older apostles who built up the system, like Henry Clay, laid the foundations of their argument, what was it? It was that while it was true that we had excluded foreign competition, it was also true that we had established in the United States such a splendid arrangement of domestic free trade and free competition that prices would be kept at their normal level by reason of the clashing genius of men inside America who would compete with one another for the markets of the great continent. And for a long time prices were kept at a reasonable and normal level by that very competition, and if that competition had continued, I dare say it would have been very difficult to make the people of the United States as uneasy as they now are about the tariff. For why are they uneasy about it? They used to be told that it was for the benefit of the American workingman; and now they know that the American workingman hasn't got the benefit that was intended for him. They used to be told that it was for the stimulation of American industry, and now they see some power closing in on American industry which has deprived it of its elasticity and of its power to expand. And they see what has laid its hand on us.

Under what spell are we? There is fear in the air. Of what are we afraid? There is paralysis. What withholds our hands? Why, chiefly that this domestic competition has largely disappeared and that in all the greater fields of industry men have banded themselves together to see that no fresh competitors come into the field of contest. There isn't a businessman in the United States who doesn't realize that this is true, not only, but that there is more than the machinery of combination. There is the machinery of the clearinghouse association, for example, where the leading bankers of whole regions of country exchange information as to how much particular firms and business concerns are borrowing and suggest upon occasion that so and so, and so and so, and so and so, ought not to be extended any further credit. So that there is getting to be a black list with respect of credit, and a preferred list, by the cooperation of a force that is drawing more and more together and that is interlocked with the very men who do not desire competitors. Because, when you take the directors of any one of the great monopolistic organizations like the Standard Oil Company, or the United States Steel Corporation, and then find that these same gentlemen are on the boards of directors of railways and banks and mining companies and manufacturing institutions of every sort and degree, until one man will be found upon the lists of as many as sixty boards of directors, and that these gentlemen who control transportation also control credit, you will know how likely it is that if you start an enterprise that will interfere with theirs you will get money enough to get very far beyond your first beginning.

And so, held in the hand of monopoly, we look about us and see what gave those men a chance to grapple us thus. And just as soon as you ask the question, you will see that the laws of this country have failed to do what laws were originally and only intended to do. Laws are not intended for the assistance of the strong. They are intended for the protection of the weak. And the thing that has done this is the thing which before the era of combinations was the very thing that stimulated us. Just as it may turn out that while protection once stimulated us, it is now choking us and enthralling us. The thing that once stimulated us was individual competition, but when you set against the individual or a little group of individuals a vast combination of capital, against which it is impossible for him to do anything but break his strength, then you know that what you are suffering from is unrestricted and unregulated competition, and that just as soon as we learn how, as we can easily learn how, to regulate competition, then we will defend the newcomers into the lists. Then we will see to it that the man with only a local market is allowed to live long enough until he gets a market as wide as his state, as wide as his reputation, as wide as his genius will carry him with wings of commerce from one end of the globe to the other. We will see to it that we establish this rule that the entries to the race are absolutely open and free, and nobody shall be excluded. We are not going to regulate the strength of the competitors. We are going to say to the newcomers, "It depends upon your genius, upon your initiative, upon your power to originate and use inventions, upon your knowledge of how to organize business and economize processes, upon your art of getting customers and widening your market. But what we are going to see to is that no man uses any means except brains and a better business capacity than yours to beat you." That is what we have got to see to. Then what will happen? I'll tell you what will happen. You know that you are all the time hearing about watered stock, which simply means stock that has been issued without any valuation, any real valuation, over against it to sustain it, to justify it. And you know how these monopolies have been built up. Not only has the little fellow been squeezed out—that doesn't cost much money, because they can afford to undersell him for a little while in the market where alone he can trade, until he is put out of business—but it costs them a great deal of money to do the other thing, namely, to buy out the bigger competitor of whom they are afraid. Because these combinations have been made by a process which I can illustrate by an illustration which I used to some of you this afternoon. I use it again, because when I used it this afternoon I was guilty of a certain inaccuracy, and I want to get it straight. I said that the shoe manufacturers of this country had formed a combination whereby they controlled all the shoe-making machinery of the United States. I was wrong in that statement. It is not the shoe manufacturers, it is the manufacturers of shoe machinery that have formed a trust. And the manufacturers of shoes are suffering just as much from the exactions of that trust as anybody else, because they can't get their machinery from anybody else, and they either have to buy it or lease it upon such terms as the monopoly requires of them. A man arose—I think his name was Plant—who began to develop a new set of machines for the manufacture of shoes. He succeeded in building up plants that were not only as good as those which were equipped with the machinery of the shoe machinery trust, but which were better; and it became absolutely necessary for them to buy him out, since they didn't have brains enough to beat him. And they bought him out, as usually happens, at two or three times the value of his plants and his business. What was the result? If we can equalize the terms of competition in such a fashion that some other man of some other name will come in and still further improve the processes of manufacture in that business, and can get the money to float him until he is on his feet, then this top-heavy concern that has in order to carry its business to pay dividends on two or three times what its business is worth will be at a very great disadvantage, and will either have to economize and build up upon processes which only their brains can originate or be beaten by the more economical and effective competitor.

I want to put every industry in this country on its mettle and let it live or die according to the capacity of those who are conducting it, not according to any artificial advantage whatever. The Democratic party is the only party that is proposing this new era of equality and opportunity. The third party leaders propose to you merely that we should adopt monopoly as it stands and regulate it. And I reply that that is adopting under the aegis of the government itself, among other things, the very organizations which are the only organizations in the United States which have been able to defeat organized labor and exclude it from their employ. And when I state that, inasmuch as they cannot deny it, they come back with this suggestion, "Then why is it that the railroads, though their almost inevitable monopoly is adopted by the government and regulated by the Interstate Commerce Commission, do not crush out organized labor?" If they knew the rudiments of our economic conditions, they wouldn't ask the question.

In the first place, the railroads before they were regulated did not fight organized labor. And one of the finest, one of the noblest, labor organizations in the United States lies at the center of that great industry—the Association of Locomotive Engineers, an association distinguished among American labor organizations by the sanity, not to say the statesmanship, with which its affairs have been governed. And, in the second place, these gentlemen ought to know, if they do not, that the railways of this country are of necessity a single unit. You can't stop the operation of one of them, for every one of them is interlaced with all the others. The mails of the United States, for one thing, must be carried. If the roads are not run in one way, they must be run in another. And at the same time these gentlemen ought to know that the way the Steel Corporation, for example, has been able to successfully fight organized labor is this—that every factory is a unit by itself, every mine is a unit by itself, and if the men in this region of the country, or in this factory, strike, they can shut up that factory or that mine and wait until those men are starved out and conquered, while the factories and the mines in all the rest of the country go on producing the raw material and the manufactured steel. By using half a dozen units to crush a single unit, they can always crush the efforts of organized labor.

These things are fundamental. These are the A B C's of our experience. The railways can't do that, and that is the fundamental difference between the two cases. Therefore, no conclusion with regard to the effect upon organized labor can be drawn from the successful regulation of the railways of the country by the Interstate Commerce Commission. Moreover, these gentlemen, if they knew the rudiments of political economy, would know that a railway, inasmuch as it must use certain advantageous lines linking the cities of a great district, is of necessity a monopoly. You waste capital by building a parallel line. You make it necessary for cooperative administration to unite those railroads sooner or later. That is not true in the rest of the industrial field, and every student of the matter knows that it is not true, so that what these gentlemen propose to do is to continue to let the giants crush the pigmies, is to continue to let these gentlemen suggest to the Government of the United States that it is not advantageous to have any new competitors come into the field, suggest that if inventions are made by the prolific American mind they must of necessity go into the mill of the existing organization and in it be absorbed in a kind of business where efficiency does not have to be studied, because efficiency is not the basis of its success, but the control of the market.

So that the tariff has created the opportunity of monopoly. And monopoly is going to be adopted by this irregular Republican host as the only means of directing the economic development of this country and the life of the working people of this country. They throw their hands up in impotence and say, "We have created a thing which has become our master, and the most that we can do is to see that it does not absolutely crush us. We must see that these proud men who ride this car of Juggernaut are not disturbed as they go crashing through the opportunities of men in every community, mastering credit and controlling production." What a monstrous program! What an inconceivable program for men who call themselves statesmen and friends of liberty! And so it is amazing to me, it is nothing less than the confession of failure that neither of these parties even attempts to face the two central issues of the campaign, this monopoly-breeding tariff and this absolute control of American industry and American development by the monopolies which the tariff has created.

Ah, gentlemen, I wish that every man here had been for a little while on the inside of the administration of government. I wish that you knew some of the heartrending details of how men are made to do the bidding of these great powers. I wish you knew how many businessmen in this great country of ours, businessmen of high standing, have come to me and told me that they were utterly in agreement with me and then begged me never to mention their names or to say that they had told me. They were afraid, and they were justly afraid, for there are powers in this country that could crush them. You criticize your legislators. You say that they do not represent you, that is to say, the great body of the people. You say that they do the bidding of special interests. Well, do you know what sometimes happens? You don't pay these legislators enough to make them independent upon their legislative salary. Most of them are lawyers, businessmen, men whose support of themselves and of those whom they love depends upon somebody else's employment and never upon opportunities made in the great field of business itself. And when you remember that there are places—I could name them—where if they didn't obey orders their notes would be untimely called and they would be sent into bankruptcy, when you know, as I know, instances where within the region that they are known there isn't a bank that would give them further credit if their notes were once called by one member of the confederacy, and then put yourself in their position and remember that they are ordered to vote for this, that, or the other or take the consequences, you would feel gladder than ever that you had at least given yourselves the opportunity in Ohio to pass laws for yourselves. Because they can't call everyone's note. They can't call the notes of a whole community. They can't put everybody out of business. They can't penetrate the secrets of the voting booth and find out how their employees and dependents voted. They will indubitably know that this is a free people which by hook or by crook is going to have the laws which will maintain its liberty. For the degree of tyranny which is possible under the existing circumstances is beyond belief. I never would have ventured to become a governor of a state if I had had a note in the bank. Because, although I dare say they couldn't have overawed me, they might have made an end of me.

I tell you, frankly, it is hard to withhold one's mind from passion when these things are dissected in the raw, as they are. And, yet, if we are just, and with our knowledge of how these things have come about, we will withhold ourselves from passion. These things have grown up within twenty years, gentlemen. The men concerned have not realized what they were doing. They really believe that they know more how to conduct the business of this nation than anybody else does. They really think that it is for our benefit that they should be our trustees and masters. They are honest men, many of them, and very few of them are malevolent men. Some of them don't care how much blood trickles through their fingers, but most of them don't dream that there is any blood in the business. Most of them repeat that old heartless pagan maxim that "business is business," which means that business has no touch of humanity in it, that business need have no touch of justice in it, that business is power, and the man that gets crushed by power merely gets crushed by the natural processes of nature herself. I say that that is pagan, not Christian, heartless, inconceivable. If men will but realize how many have their backs to the wall, how many find that life is a hopeless struggle, how many carry the burden of the day and see no outlet whatever!

And here at the turning of the ways, when we are at last asking ourselves, "Can we get a free government that will serve us, and when we get it, will it set us free?" they say, "No, you can't have a free government, and you ought not to desire to be set free. We know your interests. We will obtain everything that you need by beneficent regulation. It isn't necessary to set you free. It is only necessary to take care of you." Ah, that way lies the path of tyranny; that way lies the destruction of independent, free institutions. Because all through the highways of history stand those permanent indestructible signs which say, "This is the way to the destruction of human liberty and of human life." And no man who has any imagination, or in thought traveled those desolate ways, can do anything but tremble to see America standing and questioning as to whether she shall start out upon that path or not. And then these gentlemen who say that they are going to take care of you promise to be beneficent, offer in their largess of generosity to be a Providence to you, declare that they know what your interest is and that you need not fear if they take charge of your interest. Whereas all the processes of liberty are turned about.

The processes of liberty are that if I am your leader, you should talk to me, not that if I am your leader I should talk to you. I must listen, if I be true to the pledges of leadership, to the voices out of every hamlet, out of every sort and condition of men. I must listen to the cry of those who are just coming into the lists. I must even be very still and hear the cry of the next approaching generation saying, "Is America to be free for us? Are we to have a heritage? Are we to be children taken care of and directed, or are we to be men and give America another lusty generation of achievement?" I must listen to the voices that the politician does not hear. I must listen to the voices which the self-appointed savior cannot hear, the voices that seem to pulse with the movement of the blood, the voices that are accompanied by those shining eyes of hope and of confidence which are the distinguishing characteristics of America.

Did you ever take a trip to the other side of the Atlantic and note the difference between the people in the steerage on the outward-bound voyage and the people in the steerage on the incoming voyage? Did you never notice the difference between the eyes of men who have been in America and the eyes and countenances of men who have never been in America? If you have noticed it, would you ever thereafter wish us to close the doors of America against these people who will have the fires of hope lighted in their countenances if they can but touch our altars? Would you wish America to be less than she is, the fertilizing ground of the world, where men coming add richness to richness, energy to energy, hope to hope, knowing that they are building up a great composite people, whose unity shall be their love of freedom, whose energy shall come from those indestructible instincts, those universal powers of mankind, which are excited to action only when men lift their heads in proud independence, where there is no man to make them afraid?

The only thing to be afraid of is the thing that isn't true. The only thing to quail before is iniquity. If you are right, why should you quail? Men have to die anyhow. Isn't it better to die with your face to the light than to fall like a craven with the light shining on your back? Shall the torch of liberty fall from our hands? Shall we not take it up, man after man of us, and run that race of freedom which shall end only when the torch is lifted high upon those uplands where no light is needed, but where shines the brilliancy of the justice of God?[3]

T MS (WP, DLC).
[3] There is a WWhw outline of this address (Wilson entitled it "The Abandoned Issues"), with the composition date of Sept. 11, 1912, in WP, DLC.

From Edward Mandell House

Dear Governor: New York City. September 21st, 1912.

It is exceedingly important that McCombs and I see you tomorrow, and I hope you will be able to let me take you to him at your earliest convenience. I will meet you anywhere and at any time and motor you out.

He has some information concerning the New York situation that you should know at once, and he bids me impress upon you the urgency of it.

I would appreciate it if you would not mention the purport of this note to anyone.

Your friend always,   [E. M. House]

TCL (E. M. House Papers, CtY).

To Edward Mandell House

My dear Mr. House   [Sea Girt, N. J., Sept. 21, 1912]

It is *literally* impossible before Tuesday afternoon. I will let you know as soon as possible.

In incredible haste

W.W.

ALS (E. M. House Papers, CtY).

A Speech in Hoboken, New Jersey, Supporting William Hughes for Senator[1]

[Sept. 21, 1912]

Mr. Chairman[2] and Fellow Citizens: It is very delightful indeed to get back from a long journey and face the people that I know and love so well at home, because I got my schooling in practical politics in New Jersey, and I feel when I am in New Jersey exactly like a man who can talk face to face with his own family. For you have honored me with your confidence, and I owe you my allegiance. I have come here, as Senator Towne[3] has said, to talk practical politics to you. We have only one thing to consider in the choice we are to make on Tuesday next, and that is the supremacy of the Democratic party in the councils of the nation.

I have just been over great spaces, among the free people of this great country of ours. And while I feel in the greeting that you have just given me the kind of sympathy and support that makes a man strong, I want to tell you very frankly that that

[1] Delivered in St. Mary's Hall.
[2] Mayor Martin Cooke, who introduced Wilson.
[3] Charles Arnette Towne, senator from Michigan, 1900-1901, and congressman from New York, 1905-1907, at this time practicing law in New York.

same spirit of hopeful looking forward to great things is to be felt all over the United States. Now there is no section of the Democracy in the Union that is more closely watched than that section that resides in New Jersey. Are they going to turn their faces backward, or are they going to keep them forward and united to the victory which can never thereafter be wrested from them? That is the question that we have to answer; and I want you to dismiss from your mind all consideration of persons. As I have just said in another place tonight,[4] if James Smith, Jr., were my most intimate and dearest friend, I would have to oppose his selection as senator of the United States, because of his avowed opinions—not his opinions avowed ten, fifteen, twenty years ago—but his opinions avowed yesterday, avowed in most of the newspapers of this great commonwealth.

For there is one critical question now facing the United States: What are you going to do about the tariff? Mr. Smith stands exactly now where he stood when he was in the Senate before about the tariff. But the tariff means something very different now from what it meant when he voted to sustain the sugar duties half a generation ago. It is not a question of distant record; it is a question of what we are about to do now. He says that he is in favor of the tariff on account of the American workingmen. Now mark you, we are against the tariff because it has built up great trusts which have deliberately fought organized labor in the United States.

One of the chief beneficiaries of the protective tariff in this country is the United States Steel Corporation, one of the few corporations which has systematically and successfully excluded organized labor from its employment. And the two parties that we are facing, the one led by Mr. Taft and the other by Mr. Roosevelt, are taking this attitude with regard to the tariff, for they are standing firm to support the tariff, though they are ready to tinker with some of its details. And the third party is saying not only that the trusts shall not continue to dominate us, but that the trusts shall be put under the shield of the law to be administered according to the direction of the federal government. The federal government will deliberately enter into a permanent partnership with these very monopolies, these very organizations of control, these very beneficiaries of special privilege, which have come into existence because of the protective tariff.

And now a gentleman calling himself a Democrat offers himself for your suffrages with the statement that he is also standing

4 In Dickinson High School, Jersey City. There is a transcript of this speech in the Swem Coll., NjP.

with the party of Mr. Taft and Mr. Roosevelt in favor of the maintenance of the very foundation of monopoly. And what are we to
do in the circumstances? Why, we know what practical politics
is in the year 1912. Practical politics in the year 1912 is this,
that you will give the people of this country progressive politics
or you will go out of business. The Democratic party of the
United States has now got to make its final choice. If its rank and
file everywhere shows its disposition to give the people of the
United States progressive candidates and progressive policies,
nobody can unseat it from power in our generation. But if it de-
clines, if it even hesitates, if it is even halfhearted, the nation
will not only not trust it but it won't deserve to be trusted.

I myself would not trust a party in the year 1912 that hesitated
for a single moment to stand unhesitatingly by the men who
mean to alter the economic conditions of this country in such
ways that the doors of opportunity will again be flung open to the
rank and file of men. Everywhere that I go I talk to groups of
businessmen, to groups of men who are the leaders in business,
and not in a single instance do they even question the statement
that the industries of this country are getting to be in the grasp
and control of small groups of men, and that they are not proposing to allow any new entries in the race. They are not proposing to leave the lists open anywhere. They are proposing to keep
the control and the opportunity in their own hands. For they control credit as well as production, and you cannot set yourself up
in competition with them because they won't let you have the
money to start with.

And any man who does not know the critical choice of this
year does not know practical politics, and he does not know
whereon hinges the success of the great party which I myself
believe will save this country.

When a man, therefore, deliberately takes his stand against
progressive policies along the only lines whereon they are possible, he excludes himself from any consideration as a Democratic
candidate. I am perfectly willing to recognize the fact that a man
bred in another school of politics, with his notions formed and
hardened and crystalized in another generation, with all his associations so interlinked with these very big business enterprises
that he cannot see the horizons of ordinary life, may hold such
notions as Mr. Smith holds with perfect honesty. That is not the
point. The point is that those are not the notions which the people of the United States are going to permit their leaders to hold
and that, therefore, we are now making a choice which has very
little to do with individual character, which in one sense has very

little to do with records that date back a number of years. It has to do with opinion, with character, with purpose formed now and exercised now.

I call those of you, who were in this hall during the gubernatorial campaign of two years ago, to witness that I said that the only terms upon which I wanted any man to vote for me were that they understood that I meant business absolutely with regard to the progressive program of the Democratic party, and that if they did not want me to lead they ought not to vote for me. I said that not only here in this hall, which has now grown so familiar to me, but everywhere in the state. And when the people voted for me they put this obligation upon me—that I should do exactly what I am doing tonight, tell you the absolute truth about the situation, no matter what individual suffers.

If you want to put the Democratic party out of business, if you want to dampen the admiration of the whole United States for the great Democracy of New Jersey which has leaped into the leadership of the Union, then you know how to vote on Tuesday. Vote to go back into another age. Vote to go back to another leadership. Vote to go back to another set of thoughts. Vote to go back to those who stand pat. Vote to go back to those who do not know the promise or the beckoning hand of the future.

It is my duty to say these things to you, and I want to say this: I have set my standard, and I am not going to parley with any man. Men have come to me and professed that they meant to support me. It is not a personal question with me. It is not for a moment a question whether they will support me for office or not. The question is: Will they support the Democratic party in its progressive policies? If they will, I will deal with them. If they will not, I am done with them forever. This is business. This is war. And the question hereafter is going to be, not what did you say, but what did you do? In the parlance of the day, the essential thing is that you should deliver the goods.

But it is not a negative position merely. It is not that we are opposed merely to a particular candidate. It is not merely that we are opposed to him on account of his position and his actions. Anybody in the State of New Jersey had, of course, as it goes without saying, an absolute right to oppose the policies which the Democratic party has put through in this state in the last two years. Nobody objects to differences of opinion or to men fighting for their opinions when they are against one another. But when you know that a man has fought against the policies and the opinions of the majority of his fellow-Democrats through two years of an administration of which the state apparently approved, then you know how singular the circumstance is when that man offers himself as the representative of the party in the United States Senate. I happen to know what Mr. Smith has done during these last two years. He has opposed the progressive program of the Democracy of this state wherever it was possible for him to oppose it. He had a perfect right to do so, but, after having done so, he has not a perfect right to offer himself as the spokesman, the representative, of that party.

There are men, on the other hand, who have done the exact opposite and who have not done it for the first time. There are men who did not have to turn a corner, who did not have to change their views, who have been headed in one direction ever since they got into public life.

One of those men is John Wescott of Camden, a man whom I honor and admire. And John Wescott is so devoted to the objects which he has been seeking all his life that he is willing to do a deeply disinterested thing in order to make sure of the success of the cause that he believes in. That is the supreme test of a man's character, that he is willing to make sacrifices for the things that he believes in. It is not hard for me, with your support, with the confidence of men of progressive minds everywhere in the country, to stand on a public platform and advise the prosecution of these great policies. That is not hard. There is exhilaration in it. But to stand up and say: "Gentlemen, I believe in these things with all my heart, but you had better choose somebody else for leader," is a very hard thing indeed. And this man has been big enough to do that hard thing, and he has made way for another man of the same kind. That is the reason he could do it. He knew that he was not giving up any principle. He knew that he was not stopping any momentum of the party. He knew that he was giving way to a man who, since he was a lad, has fought for the interests of the common man in the State of New Jersey; who has represented the men who did not have special opportunities, who did not have special privileges, who did not have special happy openings upon which they could enter to prosecute their fortunes—a man whose eyes have always been kindly as they looked to his fellow men; a man who has thrust himself forward, but who, coming a modest youngster into the House of Representatives, presently made everybody know that Billy Hughes was sound, was sound to the core; that you never had to guess and speculate where he was going to stand when it came to a vote upon principle; that you never had to ask whether he had the courage to lead; that you never had to doubt that he was willing to stand alone, if it was necessary that he had to stand alone, in order to advocate all things that he believed in—until men of the humblest sort knew that they could go to Washington and get Billy Hughes' ear, and that he would not merely listen to them but after they had talked to him that he would go away and try to do the thing they wanted him to do. And now, by slow degrees, not by any of the arts of the politician, by nothing but by honesty and character and courage and insight, he has come to be one of the leading members of the House of Representatives. And it was his sagacity and his promptness, his character and honesty, that helped untangle some of the most difficult situations in the recent reorganization of the House of Representatives, after the power of the Speaker was thrust to one side and all members were put upon an equality in their efforts to serve the nation in committees.

These things are done quietly, gentlemen. They are not dramatic, they are not histrionic, they are not done in costume, they are not done with gesture and demonstration. They are done in a workaday fashion, as a man goes to his daily duty, to see that no part of it is neglected or scanted.

So the man who Wescott has made way for is a man whom all the country, through its representatives gathered from every part of the Union, knows to be a genuine worker for the things that the country now has at heart. If you nominate Billy Hughes for the Senate, the whole country will say, "Ah, it was no sporadic, spasmodic, temporary impulse in New Jersey. Those men have got together and mean business. They are going to serve the country. They are going to put tested timber forward. They are going to put stuff into this thing that has been tested by some of the hardest trials of practical politics. And we now know that New Jersey stands at the front and leads us in these things upon which the country has set its heart."

I wish I could have taken you to see some of the crowds that I have recently seen. I wish you could see streets lined with men and women of all sorts and the chief enthusiasm coming from the plain fellows, as if they at last saw some hope that somebody was going to think about them and their interests in conducting a great government. I wish you could see the light and confidence and the hope that is reflected in the faces of the people of this country all over. If you did, the image would never fade out of your recollection again, and if you did anything to disappoint that hope you could never forgive yourself as long as you lived. Do you realize how serious a situation a man is placed in, when, by the extraordinary confidence of his fellow partisans, he is put in the position I am in? I heard a man say the other day that he hoped and expected that if I were elected President of the United States, I would be courageous. Do you realize what that means for a man who is a candidate for a great office—that men expect that he will be able to make life easier for them and food more abundant for the people that they love and are dependent upon them?

Why, gentlemen, how in God's name could a man think of anything but the great hurt and necessity and pitiful need of the plain people of this country? It will probably take a long time to make food cheaper. But all I know is that we have got to begin and get at it, until the conditions of life in this country will be so altered that hope will be restored and that bread will again abundantly be made accessible to every man. A great power has its grip upon the Government of the United States, and we are expected to take those steely fingers and break them away from their hold. It will take cooperative strength. It will take the united spirit and confidence of the people of the United States. We are just at the beginning of a great task. And do you wonder that, knowing that feeling—the hope and impulse of the people of the United States—I, when I was asked if I would come and counsel with you with regard to the possibility of your putting something in the way of serving the people of the United States, that I said, "Come? Why, of course I will come. I am tired out. I haven't any voice left to speak that." But great Scott, what difference does that make? If these people will take my counsel, if they believe in me, if they trust me for a moment, I must come and tell them what it is they are about, so they won't, out of weakness or personal sympathy for anybody, make the fundamental mistake of setting back the cause of the people about a generation. For it is nothing less than the cause of the people. We are trying to set the Government of the United States free and make it your government again. Shall we use men who believe that the thing ought to be done, or shall we go back into the hands of those who do not believe there is any necessity that it should be done? There are men connected with big business in this country who believe that big business is the necessary providence to take care of. And we know it is that kind of providence which God in his wisdom will sooner or later crown with a destroying disapproval. For there is a God in the heavens. There is justice in the souls of men. They are not going to be cheated. They are looking to us. Shall we cheat them? Is it possible that we should disappoint their confident hope? Are we not going to carry New Jersey a step further, and with New Jersey hearten the whole United States in the confidence that the day of the people has come when men shall be emancipated from the privilege of those who would rule?

T MS (C. L. Swem Coll., NjP).

To Mary Allen Hulbert

Dearest Friend,   Sea Girt, New Jersey 22 Sept., 1912

I think you can hardly know what pleasure your letter gave me. The only sign of lack of sympathetic imagination I ever saw in you is your failure to realize how *necessary* such letters are to me,—how particularly necessary *now* in the midst of the life I am leading. Can you not imagine how I long for the voice and for the sight of a dear friend in the thronging crowds? And your letters, when you really give yourself leave to write, always afford me the most delightful glimpses of you! This time I see you wandering on the moors, with the light in your eyes that always comes when you let the artist and the poet that is in you look out on Nature, your foster mother; and see you, also, exciting, as usual, the admiration and the wonder of those about you, who feel your charm and yet feel you distant and inaccessible!

I *love* the remarks about you that you quote. Please quote to me everything of the kind that you can recall. Somehow these things subtly minister to my vanity! For *I* found you out, and at once! *I* made you unveil your real self, quit the masquerade and show me the whole of your great, your lovely nature. I fancy that is why you gave me your generous friendship, in a way so much beyond my deserts. It was out of a sort of gratitude for having penetrated your disguise and given you leave to show your real self,—given you release from your self-imposed aloofness and proud isolation. I can see the two selves still, alas! in your letters (I say "alas!" that I should still sometimes be cheated by being shown only the *first*, the unreal self!) When you doubt yourself; when you assume that such a busy man will be bored by anything more than a hasty note; when you are shy and self-distrustful,— then you also distrust and fail to comprehend me; then you are withdrawn again into your shell, look at me as if I were part of the rest of the world and were to be kept suspiciously at a distance. Therefore I will tolerate nothing from you but long letters. In them you *cannot* keep up the disguise. Remember that they are a delight to me, and that I never *needed* them so much as I do now!

That is a generous and delightful idea about Bermuda![1] Thank you for it with all my heart, with all *our* hearts,—for Ellen is as delighted with it as I am. If only it meant also that we were going to visit you! If I am elected we will try to break away and go.

I am very well and very fit and elastic when I can count on letters from my friends. Let your letters seek me here on Sundays, please; and after Oct. 1 please write me at Princeton again. With most affectionate messages from us all,

Your devoted friend   Woodrow Wilson

ALS (WP, DLC).
1 She had offered the Wilsons her rented house, Glencove, in Paget West, after the election.

A Campaign Address in Scranton, Pennsylvania[1]

[[Sept. 23, 1912]]

Mr. Chairman,[2] and fellow citizens: It is with very deep emotion that I face this great audience, because as your near neighbor I know what this audience represents. I know that we have in this great company, representing the rich and beautiful County of Lackawanna, a sort of cross section of the great people of the United States. Because there is represented here not only a very extraordinary variety of industry, but also the very extraordinary variety of population which makes up and enriches the body of our great nation. There are men represented here who have come from many distant lands to seek what America professes to offer. And as I face this audience the first thought that I have is this: It is true that our object in this campaign is to return the government to the people to whom it belongs. But it is very easy to say that, and the task of returning it to the people is a task which we ought to examine very frankly, very candidly and very intimately indeed.

This is not the year in which we can commend our policies by our rhetoric. This is the year in which we must render phrases into reality, when we must change the mist into the bar of iron. We must take counsel together how this great enterprise of freedom is to be accomplished. It is perfectly plain to every man, it always has been plain, what the Government of the United States was intended to be. It is written so plain, is couched in words so often repeated from one end of the world to the other, that no man needs now to be told that this was intended to be a government of the people, and that it was intended to be a government under which, above all things else, men were to enjoy absolute

1 Delivered in the Thirteenth Regiment Armory.
2 Edward James Lynett, publisher of the *Scranton Times*.

equality of opportunity. But it is one thing to say that there shall be equality of opportunity, and it is another thing to see to it that nobody successfully interferes to prevent the existence of freedom of opportunity. The power of the government is one thing, and the power of the forces opposed to the government is another thing. We don't have to determine tonight what the purpose or the power of the government is. We have to determine what the purpose and the power of the people are who intend to see to it that the government serves them and not the people.

I know that the Government of the United States is not a free instrument and that it is our duty to set it free. Very well, set it free from whom? And how to set it free? Because I have always been impatient of the discussion of abstract propositions. That may seem a strange statement to be made by a man whose opponents, whenever they can't answer his arguments, call him academic. But I have always been opposed to the mere presentation to audiences of the abstract conceptions of government.

Of course this was intended to be a government of free citizens and of equal opportunity, but how are we going to make it such— that is the question. Because I realize that while we are followers of Jefferson, there is one principle of Jefferson's which no longer can obtain in the practical politics of America. You know that it was Jefferson who said that the best government is that which does as little governing as possible, which exercises its power as little as possible. And that was said in a day when the opportunities of America were so obvious to every man, when every individual was so free to use his powers without let or hindrance, that all that was necessary was that the government should withhold its hand and see to it that every man got an opportunity to act as he would. But that time is passed. America is not now and cannot in the future be a place for unrestricted individual enterprise. It is true that we have come upon an age of great cooperative industry. It is true that we must act absolutely upon that principle.

Let me illustrate what I mean. You know that it used to be true in our cities that every family occupied a separate house of its own, that every family had its own little premises, that every family was separated in its life from every other family. But you know that that is no longer the case, and that it cannot be the case in our great cities. Families live in layers. They live in tenements, they live in flats, they live on floors, they are piled layer upon layer in the great tenement houses of our crowded districts. And not only are they piled layer upon layer, but they are associated room by room so that there is in each room sometimes in our congested districts a separate family.

Now, what has happened in foreign countries, in some of which they have made much more progress than we in handling these things, is this: In the city of Glasgow, for example, which is one of the model cities of the world, they have made up their minds that the entries, the hallways, of great tenements are public streets. Therefore the policeman goes up the stairway and patrols the corridors. The lighting department of the city sees to it that the corridors are abundantly lighted, and the staircases. And the city does not deceive itself into supposing that the great building is a unit from which the police are to keep out and the city authority to be excluded, but it says: "These are the highways of human movement, and wherever light is needed, wherever order is needed, there we will carry the authority of the city."

And I have likened that to our modern industrial enterprise. You know that a great many corporations, like the Steel Corporation, for example, are very like a great tenement house. It isn't the premises of a single commercial family. It is just as much a public business as a great tenement house is a public highway. When you offer the securities of a great corporation to anybody who wishes to purchase them, you must open that corporation to the inspection of everybody who wants to purchase. There must, to follow out the figure of the tenement house, be lights along the corridor; there must be police patrolling the openings; there must be inspection wherever it is known that men may be deceived with regard to the contents of the premises. If we believe that fraud lies in wait for us, we must have the means of determining whether fraud lies there or not.

Similarly, the treatment of labor by the great corporations is not now what it was in Jefferson's time. Who in this great audience knows his employer? I mean among those who go down into the mines, or go into the mills and factories, and who never see, who particularly never deal with, the president of the corporation. You probably don't know the directors of the corporation by sight. The only thing you know is that by the score, by the hundred, by the thousand, you are employed with your fellow workmen by some agent of an invisible employer. Therefore, whenever bodies of men employ bodies of men it ceases to be a private relationship. So that when a court, when a court in my own state, held that workmen could not peaceably dissuade other workingmen from taking employment, and based the decision upon the analogy of domestic servants, they simply showed that their minds and understandings were lingering in an age which had passed away two or three generations ago. This dealing of great bodies of men with other bodies of men is a matter of public scrutiny and should be a matter of public regulation.

Similarly, it was no business of the law in the time of Jefferson to come into the house and see how I kept house. But when my house, when my property, when my so-called private property, became a great mine, and men went along dark corridors amidst every kind of danger in order to dig out of the bowels of the earth things necessary for the industries of a whole nation, and when it was known that no individual owned these mines, that they were owned by great stock companies, that their partnership was as wide as great communities, then all the old analogies absolutely collapsed, and it became the right of the government to go down in those mines and see whether human beings were properly treated in them or not, to see whether accidents were properly safeguarded against, to see whether the modern method of using these inestimable riches of the world were followed or were not followed. And so you know that, by the action of a Democratic House only two years ago, the Bureau of Mines and Mining was fully equipped to act as foster father of the miners of the United States, and to go into these so-called private properties and see that the life of human beings was just as much safeguarded there as it could be in the circumstances, just as much safeguarded as it would be upon the streets of Scranton; because there are dangers on the streets of Scranton. If somebody puts a derrick improperly erected and secured on top of a building or overtopping the street upon any kind of structure, then the government of the city has the right to see that that derrick is so secured that you and I can walk under it and not be afraid that the heavens are going to fall on us. And, similarly, in these great beehives, wherein every corridor swarm men of flesh and blood, it is similarly the privilege of the government, whether of the state or of the United States, as the case may be, to see that human life is properly cared for and that the human lungs have something to breathe.

What I am illustrating for you is this, and it is something that our Republican opponents don't seem to credit us with intelligence enough to comprehend. Because we won't take the dictum of a leader who thinks he knows exactly what ought to be done for everybody, we are accused of wishing to minimize the powers of the Government of the United States. I am not afraid of the utmost exercise of the powers of the government of Pennsylvania, or of the Union, provided they are exercised with patriotism and intelligence and really in the interest of the people who are living under them. But when it is proposed to set up guardians over those people and to take care of them by a process of tutelage and supervision, in which they play no active part, I utter my absolute objection. Because the proposal of the third party, for example, is not to take you out of the hands of the men who have corrupted the Government of the United States, but to see to it that you remain in their hands and that that government guarantees to you that they will be humane to you.

The most corrupting thing in this country has been this self-same tariff of which Mr. Palmer spoke so convincingly. The workingmen of America are not going to allow themselves to be deceived by a colossal bluff any longer. One of the corporations in the United States which has succeeded in mastering the laborer and saying to him, "You shall not organize; you shall not exercise your liberty of cooperation, though we who employ you are using the power of organization to the utmost point of absolute control," namely, the United States Steel Corporation, paid enormous dividends and still more enormous bonuses to those who promoted its organization at the same time that it was making men work twelve hours, seven days in the week, at wages which in the 365 days of the year would not allow enough to support a family. If they have millions to divide among themselves and get those millions, as they profess to get them, from the opportunities created by the tariff, where does the workingman come in?

Mr. Roosevelt himself has spoken of the profits which they get as "prize money," and his objection is just the objection that I am raising. He says that not enough of the "prize money" gets into the pay envelope. And I quite agree with him. But I want to know how he proposes to get it there. I search his program from top to bottom, and the only proposal I can find is this: That there shall be an industrial commission charged with the supervision of the great monopolistic combinations which have been formed under the protection of the tariff, and that the Government of the United States shall see to it that these gentlemen who have conquered labor shall be kind to labor. And I find then the proposition is this: That there shall be two masters, the great corporations and, over it, the Government of the United States, and I ask, "Who is going to be the master of the Government of the United States?" It has a master now, those who in combination control these monopolies. And if the government controlled by the monopolies in its turn controls the monopolies, the partnership is finally consummated.

I don't care how benevolent the master is going to be, I will not live under a master. That is not what America was created for. America was created in order that every man should have the same chance with every other man to exercise mastery over his own fortunes. Now, what I want to do is to follow the example of the authorities of the city of Glasgow. I want to light and patrol the corridors of these great organizations in order to see that nobody who tries to traverse them is waylaid and maltreated. Because if you will but hold them off, if you will but see to it that the weak are protected, I will venture a wager with you that there are some men in the United States now weak, economically weak, who have brains enough to compete with these gentlemen. And if you will but protect them, they will presently come into the market and put these gentlemen on their mettle. And the minute they come into the market, there will be a bigger market for labor and a different wage scale for labor. Because it is susceptible of absolute proof that the high-paid labor of America—where it is high-paid—is cheaper than the low-paid labor of the continent of Europe.

Do you know that about 90 per cent, I am told, of those who are employed in labor in this country are not employed in the protected industries, and that their wages are almost without exception higher than the wages of those who are employed in the protected industries? There is no corner on carpenters, there is no corner on bricklayers, there is no corner on scores of individual instances of classes of skilled laborers. But there is a corner on the poolers in the furnaces, there is a corner on the men who dive down into the mines. They are in the grip of a controlling power which determines the market rates of wages in the United States, and only where labor is free is labor highly paid in America.

So that when I am fighting against monopolistic control, I am fighting for the liberty of every man in America, and I am fighting for the liberty of American industry. These gentlemen say that the commission which they wish to set up should not be bound too much by laws, but that they should be allowed to indulge in what they call constructive regulation, which amounts to administration. And they intimate, though they do not say, that it will be perfectly feasible for this commission to regulate prices and also to regulate, I dare say, in the long run, though they do not now propose it, the rates of wages. How are they going to regulate them? Suppose that they take the net profits of a great concern—and if you take some of these monopolistic concerns, the net profits are very large—and suppose they say these net profits are too large. How are they going to tell how much of those profits came from efficiency of administration and how much from excessive prices? Now, if you tax efficiency, you discourage industry. If you tax excessive profits, you destroy your monopoly, that is to say, you discourage your monopoly without increasing its efficiency. Because without competition there isn't going to be efficiency.

Do you know that railway rates in the United States came down and came steadily down during the period which preceded the regulation of the Interstate Commerce Commission, and that since the regulation of the Interstate Commerce Commission the rates have steadily, though not rapidly, gone up? That means that the cost of operation of the railways in the competitive period under the stimulation of competition went down, and that the cost of operation since the period of competition was closed has not gone down. I am not going to explain it, but I suspect that nobody brings his operating costs down unless he has to, and that he doesn't have to unless somebody more intelligent and more efficient than himself gets in the field against him. There is instance after instance in the United States of the discouragement of invention, because, if with the machinery that you have, you have got a corner on the market, why should you encourage those who would improve your machinery? There is no reason why you should improve your processes if you have got control of the whole production or so large a proportion of it that you are independent. And if under the present circumstances a man does arise who shows that he can beat you, what do you do? You buy him out at three or four times the value of his business. And then you charge the consumer the interest on the four or five times that you have paid him to get out. And so the process of monopoly is a process of piling up capital, nominal capital, piling up prices and not increasing efficiency.

I want a chance to fight for the liberation of American industry, and I know how to do it. I didn't find it out. I have had no divine inspiration. I do not pretend to have the absolute by the wool, but I have been fortunate enough to live with men who did know how. And I have been docile enough to learn from men who did know. The only advantage that I can claim is that I haven't any notes in bank and therefore am at liberty to look around me. I have always been careful to live on the salary that I have, knowing that that was the only condition of independence. And being at liberty to look around, having the privilege of being associated with men who were in the thick of every kind of affairs, I have had the opportunity of knowing what was going on, and I have had the opportunity of knowing how things can be done which are exactly opposite to those which are proposed in the program I have just been criticizing.

These giant corporations have got their monopolistic power because the processes of competition by which they crushed the small man out were not regulated, and I am in favor of such regulation of competition as will see to it that new entries can come into the race and that the newcomer is allowed to show his paces before he is put out of the race. You can do that. You can say to these gentlemen who are in the driver's seat of these cars of Juggernaut, "You can drive down the highways, but we warn you that if anybody gets run over, the driver goes to jail. We don't care how big the concern is, we don't care how powerful a business you have built up if you don't use your power unfairly. But the minute you use it unfairly, then you come under the ban of the law. Mark you, we are not going to put the car of Juggernaut in jail. We are going to put the driver in jail, because we may want to use the car ourselves. What we want you to distinctly understand is that nobody is going to take a joy ride in that thing; that we recognize in this great thing the majesty and, it may be, the majestic duty of the great conception of property, but we also recognize on the road the great thronging multitudes of mankind. And if you can't drive along the road without crushing men, then we will have to forbid even the road to you, because we are going to protect men."

We believe that the power of America resides not in the men who have made good and gained a great supremacy in the field of business, but in the men who are to make good. Where is the power, where is the distinction of the great office of President of the United States? Is America going to be saved because George Washington was great? Because Lincoln was great? Because men of devoted characters have served in that great office? Don't you know that America is safe only because we do not know who the future Presidents of the United States are going to be? If we had depended upon the lineage of these gentlemen, they might have failed to have sons like themselves. But we are not depending upon anybody except the great American people, and we know that when the time comes some figure, it may be hitherto unknown, from some family whose name and fame the country has never heard, will come a man fitted for the great task by the gift of God and by virtue of his own indomitable character.

I say this with a certain degree of embarrassment because I am a candidate for that great office. And I am not going to pretend to any body of my fellow citizens that I have any sort of confidence that I am a big enough man for the place. But I do feel proud of this, that no law, no rule of blood, no privilege of money, picked me out to be a candidate even. It may be a mistake, but you can't blame your system for it, because it is a fine system where some remote, severe academic schoolmaster may become President of the United States. He is not connected at least with the powers that have been, and he has even upon occasion set himself against the powers that are. Men speculate as to what he might be ignorant or audacious enough to do. But all of that is of the excitement of the democratic game. We are sports. We aren't going to tie up to a particular family. We aren't going to tie up to a particular class. We are going to say, "We have played this game long enough now to be perfectly serene about it, and we are going to take the chances of the game." That is the beauty of democracy. Democracy means that instead of depending for the fertility of your genius upon a little acre long tilled, you are going to depend upon all the wide prairies and the hillsides and the forested mountains, that you don't care whether a man comes from Maine or from Texas, or from Washington or from Florida, or anywhere in between, provided when he comes and you look at him you like him.

And your confidence of the future is in this, that some man of some kind, probably from an uncalculated quarter, is going to come. You see, therefore, that I am simply going about to illustrate a single thing. I am simply trying to hold your attention to one theme, namely this, that America must be fertile, or she cannot be great, and that if you confine the processes of your industry or the processes of your politics to these lines where there may be or has been monopoly, you impoverish the great country which we would enrich. That to my mind is the whole lesson of history.

Men have always, sooner or later, kicked over the traces after they had for a little while lived upon the theory that some of them ought to take care of the rest of them. There is no man, there is no group of men, there is no class of men, big enough or wise enough to take care of a free people. If the free people can't take care of itself, then it isn't free, it hasn't grown up. That is the very definition of freedom. If you are afraid to trust any and every man to put forth his powers as he pleases, then you are afraid of liberty itself. I am willing to risk liberty to the utmost, and I am not willing to risk anything else. So that, for my part, having once got blood in my eye and felt the zest of the active quest for the scalps of the men who don't know any better than to resist the liberties of a great people, it doesn't make any difference to me whether I am elected President or not. I'll find some means somewhere of making it infinitely uncomfortable for them.

Really, the object of public opinion is to make it uncomfortable for the men who don't behave themselves. Because I am very much more afraid of the just opinion of my fellow citizens than I am of jail. Because in jail you are at least safeguarded against the most terrible of all things—the look in the eyes of the people who don't trust you. In those circumstances, the thickness of the wall of the prison is a gracious thing to you. I would a great deal rather be in jail than be hated. If I am a crook, I want to be segregated, because when you are once crooked you don't fit anywhere. And the singular thing about our recent experience is that there are a lot of men who are crooked and don't know it, who will describe themselves to you as having such straight grain in them that they can carry the strain of the whole structure of political life. They don't know that they have been gyrating; they have been dervishes so long that they can't see anything as a fixed point, not even the Decalogue.

So that what I long for, and what I believe you long for, is to return to the simplicity of American life. It's got to be complicated in its structure. You can't go back to the old ways of doing business entirely, but it can be simple again in its moral judgments. It can again establish the standard of morality. We have got very much confused. Our morality is just about big enough to fit my personal relationship to you. It's got to be big enough to fit my personal relationship to all the community in which I live and everybody with whom I am connected, whether I see them or not. And we haven't got up to the job yet. We can get up to it only by threading our way along these intricate corridors, only by taking the patrolman's lamp and going up and down the interior of our great complicated structure of life, through all the passages of the beehive in which we live, and see to it that men are remaining our neighbors and doing their duty as human beings.

That is the reason, my friends, that I am a democrat with a little d. And I am a Democrat with a big D because the divided Republican family doesn't seem to know what to do with us. The regular Republicans and the irregular Republicans are very much more interested in each other than they are in us. And while that is the case, I think we, while they are thus engaged, better go about the busines of the country. I remember being in the city of Springfield, Massachusetts, before the presidential primaries. The day before the ex-President had been there, and the day before that, the President of the United States had been there, and they had been saying a great deal about each other. I was holding a midday meeting, and I wanted to get the attention, at least, of my audience, so I ventured to say to them, "After what you people have been through with here the last two days, perhaps you would like to know what the public questions of the day are." And I feel a good deal that way still. The question of the day is not the division of responsibility, but the method of the liberation of the people.

I am not interested in persons. I can't force myself to be interested in persons. I don't want to say anything about them, and I don't care what they say about me. I simply want to say to them at every point, "Very true, it may be so, let us grant all that, and return to business. What are you proposing to do to put more money in the envelope of the workingman? What are you proposing to do to break up the lines of monopoly in the United States? What are you proposing to do to set this people free again and give them direct access to their own government?" For the vision of America will never change. America once, when she was a little people, sat upon a hill of vantage and had a vision of the future. She saw men happy because they were free. She saw them free because they were equal. She saw them banded together because they had the spirit of brothers. She saw them safe because they did not wish to impose upon one another. And the vision is not changed. The multitude has grown—that welcome multitude that comes from all parts of the world to seek a safe place of life and of hope in America.

And so America will move forward, if she moves forward at all, only with her face to that same sun of promise. Just so soon as she forgets the sun in the heavens, just so soon as she looks so intently upon the road before her and around her that she does not know where it leads, then will she forget what America was created for, and her light will go out, and the nations will grope again in darkness, and they will say, "Where are those who prophesied a day of freedom for us? Where are the lights that we followed? Where is the torch that the runners bore? Where are those who bade us hope? Where came in those whispers of dull despair?"

Has America turned back? Has America forgotten her mission? Has America forgotten that her politics are part of her life and that only as the red blood of her people flows in the veins of her polity shall she occupy that point of vantage which has made her the beacon and the leader of mankind?[3]

Printed in the *Scranton*, Pa., *Times*, Sept. 24, 1912; corrected from the shorthand notes in the C. L. Swem Coll., NjP.
[3] There is a WWhw and WWsh outline of this address dated Sept. 23, 1912, in WP, DLC.

Ellen Axson Wilson to Nancy Saunders Toy

My dear Mrs. Toy,   Sea Girt, New Jersey Sept. 23, 1912.

Many, many thanks for your tempting invitation! I am very sorry that it is not possible for me to accept it, but we are leaving Sea Girt next Tuesday, and the business of closing this house and opening the one in Princeton will make a journey just at this time impractical. It is too bad: but still I have already found that such tours give one no opportunity for human intercourse with friends.

We were extremely obliged to you too for your kind letter with regard to the Cleveland affair. We were pleased to have our suspicions of [Nicholas Murray] Butler's complicity in certain things so directly confirmed! It is an entertaining story and I wish I had time to write it for your amusement. Of course as usual the fine Italian hand of Dean West is at the bottom of it. He had poor old Cleveland, (who failed miserably towards the end, mentally as well as physically) *completely* under his influence. But "Wilson circles" are not at all anxious about the alleged letter because, as your husband says, it would seem to the country now rather irrelevant. I would much prefer to have the letter printed rather than hinted at in this nasty way. I think it does exist & that they meant to print it but were frightened off by Joline's experience. *His* reputation as a gentleman was *destroyed* by his little bit of malice in the same line. The Cleveland letter is said to deal with college affairs. It was, of course, written before Woodrow went into politics.

With thanks and warmest regards, I am
                    Sincerely your friend   Ellen A. Wilson.
Please excuse haste.

TCL (RSB Coll., DLC).

To Edward Mandell House

                                Princeton N J Sep 24 1912
Please expect me at two forty eight.
                                Woodrow Wilson.

T telegram (E. M. House Papers, CtY).

From John Temple Graves[1]

My Dear Governor: New York, Sept. 24, 1912.

It is a real pleasure to send you the enclosed cable just received from Paris.[2] It vindicates the view expressed to you that everything would come right in time from our camp. If we come late, I believe we will come with sufficient strength to make up for lost time. I am sure your message had much to do with it.

This fight is between you and Roosevelt and I am glad to believe that The American of this morning and The Journal of this afternoon and the current Hearst Magazine have dealt Roosevelt the heaviest blow he has so far received. You will note that Mr Hearst intimates he has other guns to unlimber along this line and that it is his hope that you may march through the breach they make to an easy victory.

Will you kindly return the cablegram to me, and believe me, with best wishes and sincere regards,

Very truly yours,   John Temple Graves

TLS (WP, DLC).

[1] Editor in chief of Hearst's *New York American.*

[2] It undoubtedly announced that Hearst was coming into the campaign on Wilson's side.

From the Diary of Colonel House

New York, Sept. 25 [24], '12.

I was with Governor Wilson most of the afternoon. He arrived from Trenton at 2.48. We motored out to Larchmont to see Mc-Combs who was ill. There was some talk of waiting at the Pennsylvania Station for President Taft, (Merely to pay our respect to him) who was to arrive a few minutes later, but as time was pressing, it was decided not to do so.

The New York situation is acute, and it is necessary for some definite policy to be decided upon. The break between Murphy and National Headquarters is becoming wider each day, and the newspapers are printing numerous false interviews which makes it yet wider. I am anxious to hold the party together so that every available means may be used for the common good. My dislike of Tammany and its leaders is perhaps stronger than that of Governor Wilson, yet, having had more political experience, I am always ready to work with the best material at hand. My idea is to have them decide upon some unobjectionable Tammany man for Governor of New York who would not bring discredit upon the party.

We had our interview with McCombs and decided upon either Dowling or Osborne. It took us three hours to make the trip to Larchmont and return. Many things were discussed in the most intimate way, such as the feasibility of having Mr. Bryan as a member of the Cabinet. It was decided it would be best to make him Secretary of State, in order to have him in Washington and in harmony with the administration rather than outside and possibly in a critical attitude. Mrs. Bryan's influence too, would be valuable.

Currency reform was discussed and the Governor explained his ideas. He refused to commit himself last winter, but he now has some views upon the subject.

T MS (E. M. House Papers, CtY).

A Campaign Speech on New Issues in Hartford, Connecticut[1]

[Sept. 25, 1912]

Mr. Chairman,[2] ladies and gentlemen: It is a great pleasure to me to stand on this platform. I like to recall the two very happy years that I spent as your not very distant neighbor at Middletown, in this state. And I want to tell you that, as a consequence of that two years of residence, I am not unacquainted with the character of the audience which I face. I know that there are a great many misguided persons present—persons who, with the best intentions and the clearest consciences, have voted the wrong ticket. I also know that, for the very best of reasons, a Connecticut audience is a conservative audience, because Connecticut has had a great deal to conserve that was worth conserving, and she has arranged her constitution so that she has got to conserve it.

So that, all things taken together, my first thought was almost apologetic. Because I know that, in some quarters, at any rate, I have acquired the reputation of being a radical, and while I might have been expected to apologize to you for coming to you, a conservative community, to present radical points of view, I don't think anybody is any longer very much frightened by the word "radical," and there are all sorts of radicals. It depends upon the kind I am whether I shall have to be apologetic or not.

But to speak seriously, the theme that I want to discuss with you this afternoon is simply this: Are those thoughtful men amongst us who fear that we are now about to disturb the ancient

1 Delivered in Parsons' Theater.
2 Joseph Parsons Tuttle, lawyer of Hartford.

foundations of our institutions justified in their fear? For if they are, we ought to go very slowly about the processes of change. If it is indeed true that we have grown tired of the institutions which we have so carefully and sedulously built up, then we ought to go just as slowly and just as carefully about the very dangerous task of altering them. We ought, therefore, to ask ourselves, first of all: Are we justified in the belief that, at any rate the sober men among us, the leaders of progressive thought in this country, are intending to do anything by which we shall retrace our steps, or by which we shall change the whole direction of our development?

I believe, for one, that you cannot tear up ancient rootages and safely plant the tree of liberty in soil which is not native to it. I believe that the ancient traditions of a people are its ballast, that you cannot take a *tabula rasa* upon which to write political programs. You cannot take a new sheet of paper and determine what your life shall be tomorrow. You must knit the new into the old. And you cannot put new patches on ancient garments without destroying, or endangering the destruction, of the ancient garment. It must be something woven into the fiber, of practically the same pattern, of the same texture and intention. If I did not believe that to be progressive was to preserve the essence of our institutions, I for one could not be progressive.

I have several times used an illustration which to my mind expresses the situation just about as well as a whimsical illustration could express it. I suppose most of you have had the great pleasure of reading that very delightful book of nonsense, *Alice Through the Looking Glass*, the companion of *Alice in Wonderland*. Alice in that book, you remember, is seized by the hand by the Red Queen, the Red Chess Queen, who races her off at a breathless pace until both of them can run no further for lack of breath. Then they stop, and Alice looks around her and says, "But we are just where we were when we started!" "Oh, yes," says the Red Queen, "you have to run twice as fast as that to get anywhere else."

Now, that is, to my mind, the image of progressivism. The laws of this country have not kept up with the change of economic circumstances in this country. They have not kept up with the change of political circumstances in this country. And, therefore, we are not where we were when we started. We are back to the place that we were when we started. And we will have to run, not until we are out of breath, but until we have caught up with our own conditions before we shall be where we were when we started, when we started this great experiment which has been the hope and the beacon of the world. And we would have to run twice as fast as any rational progressive program I have seen in order to get anywhere else.

I am, therefore, a progressive because we have not kept up with our own changes of conditions, either in the economic field or in the political field. We have not kept up as well as other nations because we have not adjusted our practices to the facts of the case. And until we do, and unless we do, the facts of the case will always have the better of the argument. Because if you do not adjust your laws to the facts, so much the worse for the laws, not for the facts, because law trails along after the facts. Only that law is unsafe which runs ahead of the facts and beckons to them and makes it follow imaginative programs and will-o-the-wisps.

Let us ask ourselves, therefore, what it is that disturbs us. In some commonwealths I find a great many conservative men who do not believe, for example, in the direct primary. And they are very diligent in collecting all sorts of evidences that the people do not take very much interest in the direct primary and that it simply creates confusion. I must say, parenthetically, that after yesterday's result of the direct primary in New Jersey,[3] I am re-assured as to its operation. The primary is a means of determin-ing on the part of the people whom they wish to see put into of-fice and whom they wish to exclude from office. And I maintain that the critical part of every political process is the selection of the men who are going to occupy office, and not the election of them. When in the past the two cooperative party machines have seen to it that both tickets had men of the same kind on them, it was Tweedledum or Tweedledee, so far as the voter was con-cerned—that those who managed politics had them coming and had them going, and it didn't make any difference, so far as the interests governing politics were concerned, which of the tickets was elected at the election by the voters.

So that what we have established the direct primary for is this— to break up inside determination of who shall be selected to con-duct the government and make the laws of our commonwealths and of our nation. And everywhere the impression is growing stronger that there will be no means of dominating those who have dominated us except by taking this process of selection into our own hands. Does that upset any ancient foundation? Ah, gentlemen, are we not in danger of being hypocrites, some of us? What do you talk about on the Fourth of July—if you are talking in public? You talk about the Declaration of Independence. Then

[3] Hughes defeated Smith in the senatorial primary by a vote of 62,532 to 33,490.

you back up the Declaration of Independence with those splendid utterances in our earliest state constitutions, which have been copied in all our later ones, taken from the Petition of Rights, or the Declaration of Rights, in the history of the struggle for liberty in England. And there we read this uncompromising sentence, that when at any time the people of a commonwealth find that their governments are not suitable to the circumstances of their lives or the promotion of their liberty, then they are privileged to alter them at their pleasure. That is the foundation, that is the central doctrine, that is the ancient vision of America with regard to affairs, and this arrangement of the direct primary simply squares with that. If they cannot find men whom they can trust to select their tickets, they will select them for themselves. That is what the direct primary means. They do not always do it; they are sometimes too busy. The electorate of the United States is like the god Baal. It is sometimes on a journey; it is sometimes asleep. But when it does wake up it does not resemble the god Baal in the slightest degree. It resembles a great self-possessed power which takes possession, takes control of its own affairs. And I am willing to wait. I am among those who believe so in the essential doctrines of democracy that I am willing to wait on the convenience of this great sovereignty, provided that I know he has got the instrument to dominate whenever he chooses to grasp it.

Then there is another thing that conservative people are disturbed about—the direct election of United States senators. I have seen some thoughtful men discuss that with a sort of shiver, as if to disturb the ancient constitution of the United States Senate was to do something touched with impiety, touched with irreverence for the Constitution. But the first thing necessary to reverence for the United States Senate is to respect the United States senators. I am not one of those who condemn the United States Senate as a body, for no matter what has happened there, no matter how questionable the practices or how corrupt the influences which have filled some of the seats in the United States Senate, it must in fairness be said that the majority of that body has all the years through been untouched by that stain, and that there has always been there a sufficient number of men to vindicate the self-respect and the hopefulness of America with regard to her institutions.

But you need not be told, and it would be painful to repeat to you, some of the processes by which seats have been bought in the United States Senate. And you know, as the whole people of the United States know, that a little group of senators holding the

balance of power has again and again been able to defeat programs of reform upon which the whole country had set its heart;
and that whenever you analyzed the power that was behind those
little groups, you found that it was not the power of public opinion, but some private influence, hardly to be disclosed by superficial scrutiny, which had put those men there to do that thing.

Now, returning to the original principles upon which we profess to stand, have the people of the United States not the right to
see to it that every seat in the United States Senate represents the
unbought influences of America? Does the direct election of senators touch anything except the private control of seats in the
Senate? For you must remember another thing, gentlemen, you
must remember that we have not been without our suspicions
about some of the legislatures which elect senators. Some of the
suspicions which we entertained in New Jersey about them turned
out to be founded upon very solid facts, indeed. And until two
years ago, New Jersey had not in half a generation been represented in the United States Senate by the men who would have
been chosen if the processes had been free.

So that we are not now to deceive ourselves by putting our
heads in the sand and saying, "Everything is all right." Didn't
Mr. Bryce say that the American Constitution was the most perfect instrument ever devised by the brain of man?[4] Haven't we
been praised all over the world for our singular genius for setting
up successful states? Yes, we have, but a very thoughtful English-
man, and a very witty one, said a very instructive thing about
that. He said that to show that the American Constitution has
worked well is not to prove that it is an excellent constitution,
because the Americans could run any constitution[5]—a compliment which is also a comment, a compliment which we lay like
sweet unction to our souls, but a criticism which ought to set us
thinking. And while it is true that when American forces are
awake they can conduct American affairs without serious de-

[4] He meant William E. Gladstone's comment: "But, as the British Constitution
is the most subtle organism which has proceeded from the womb and the long
gestation of progressive history, so the American Constitution is, so far as I
can see, the most wonderful work ever struck off, at a given time by the brain
and purpose of man." "Kin beyond Sea," *North American Review*, cxxvii (Sept.-
Oct., 1878), 185.

[5] He referred to Walter Bagehot, *The English Constitution* (London, 1867),
p. 271: "The Americans now extol their institutions, and so defraud themselves
of their due praise. But if they had not a genius for politics; if they had not a
moderation in action singularly curious where superficial speech is so violent;
if they had not a regard for law, such as no great people have yet evinced, and
infinitely surpassing ours,—the multiplicity of authorities in the American Constitution would long ago have brought it to a bad end. Sensible shareholders, I
have heard a shrewd attorney say, can work *any* deed of settlement; and so
the men of Massachusetts could, I believe, work *any* constitution."

parture from the ideals of the Constitution, it is nevertheless true that we have had many shameful instances of practices which we can absolutely remove by the direct election of senators by the people themselves. And, therefore, I, for one, will not allow any man who knows his history to say to me that I am acting inconsistently with either the spirit or the form of the American government in advocating the direct election of United States senators.

Take another matter, for let's get another step deeper. I hope you won't, any of you, think that I am going too far in even mentioning in your presence those extreme doctrines of the initiative, the referendum, and the recall. It is the last word that makes most men shrink. There are communities, there are states in the Union, in which I am quite ready to admit that it is perhaps premature, that perhaps it will never be necessary to discuss these measures. But I want to call your attention to the fact that these measures have been discussed and have been adopted in those states where the electorate had become convinced that they did not have representative government. Let no man deceive himself by the fallacy that anybody proposes to substitute direct legislation by the people or the direct reference of laws voted in the legislature to the vote of the people for representative government. The most eager advocates of these reforms have always said that they were intended to recover representative government, that they had no place where those who were elected to legislative chambers were really representative of the communities which they professed to serve.

The initiative is a means of recapturing the seat of legislative authority on behalf of the people themselves, and the referendum is a means of seeing to it that unrepresentative measures are not put upon the statute books, but are checked by being submitted to the vote of the people. When you come to the recall, the principle is that if an administrative officer—for we will begin with administrative officers—is corrupt or so unwise as to be doing things that are likely to lead to all sorts of mischief in the future, it will be possible by a sedate and slow process, prescribed by the law, to get rid of that officer before the end of his term. Because you must admit that it is a little inconvenient sometimes to have what someone called an astronomical system of government, a system of government in which you can't change anything until there has been a certain number of revolutions of the seasons. And nobody in New England ought to find any very grave objection to the recall of administrative officers, because in most parts of New England the ordinary administrative term is a single twelvemonth. You haven't been willing in New England to trust any man out of your sight more than twelve months, so that your elections are a sort of continuous performance based on the very fundamental idea that we are discussing—that you will not take your own hands off your own affairs. That is the principle of the recall. I don't see how any man who is grounded in the traditions of American affairs, particularly as they derive their origins from New England, can find any valid objection to the recall of administrative officers.

It is another matter when it comes to the judiciary. I myself have never been in favor of the recall of judges. But now that that has received your approval, let me tell you why. Not because some judges haven't deserved to be recalled. That isn't the point. But because that is treating the symptom instead of the disease. The disease lies deeper, and sometimes it is very virulent and very dangerous. Gentlemen, there have been courts in the United States that were controlled by private interests. There have been supreme courts in our states at which men without privilege could not get justice. There have been corrupt judges; there have been controlled judges; there have been judges who acted as other men's servants and not as the servants of the public. And there can be no moral objection to removing such men from public service.

Ah, there are some shameful chapters in that story! Think of it! The reason you applauded just now was that you feel, as I feel, that the judiciary of the United States is the last and ultimate safeguard of the things that we want to hold stable in this country. But suppose that that safeguard is corrupted, suppose that it doesn't guard my interests and yours, but guards merely the interests of a very small group of individuals, and that whenever your interest clashes with theirs, yours will have to give way, though you represent 90 per cent of your fellow citizens and they only 10 per cent. Then where is your safeguard, and what is it safeguarding, I would like to know? The great processes of equitable thought must control the judiciary, as they control every other instrument of government. But there are ways and ways of controlling. If—mark you, I say if—at one time the Union Pacific Railroad, or rather the Southern Pacific Railroad, owned the supreme court of the State of California, what was the trouble? Would you remedy it by recalling the judges of the supreme court of California? Not so long as the Southern Pacific Railroad could substitute others for them. You wouldn't be cutting deep enough. Where you want to go is to the seat of the trouble. Where you want to go is to the place and the process by which those judges were picked out. And when you get there, you lead to the moral of the whole of this discussion, because the moral of it all is that the people of the United States have suspected, until their suspicions have been justified by all sorts of substantial and unanswerable evidence, that in place after place, at turning point after turning point in the history of this country, we have been controlled by private understandings and not by the public interest, and that influences which were improper, if not corrupt, have determined everything from the making of laws to the administration of justice. They have suspected that the Southern Pacific Railroad owned the supreme court of that great and beautiful state that stretches her fair acres up and down the coast of the Pacific. And because of that they have said, "We are going to go to the heart of this matter and dislodge these men who have been controlling our affairs." And no man who understands anything about liberty, or anything about economic prosperity, ought to find it in his conscience or in his heart to withhold their hands. This thing that grows like a canker in our vitals must be cut out, though I grant you it must be cut out with the skill and the knowledge and the tenderness of the surgeon who will not disturb the vital tissues to which this ugly thing is attached.

Let us keep the integrity and the purity of our whole structure, but let us get rid of those things that are corrupting it, for the people of the United States have made up their minds that they are going to unearth the beast in the jungle. They know that their affairs have constituted a sort of jungle in which, when they hunted, they were caught by the beast instead of catching him. They have determined, therefore, to take an axe and to level the jungle and then see where the beast will find cover, to be ready when the jungle is cut down to bag their game. And I for my part bid them godspeed. The jungle breeds nothing but infection.

Now that, if you choose to call it radicalism, is the kind of radicalism I believe in. If that be radicalism, then the preservation of our life and purity as a nation is a radical proposition. And it is the literal meaning of the word, because, if I am correctly informed, radical means "rootical"—it goes to the root of the matter. But where does it all come from? There is no use, as I have just now said, dealing with the symptoms. Where is the seat of the disease? Where is the fountain of corruption?

For I tell you, my fellow citizens, that the choice of this campaign is not a choice among those things that I have been talking about. I have been using them as illustrations, in order to draw your thought to the central point, where lie the sources of all that we are discussing. The radical circumstance, the circumstance that is the taproot of the whole matter, is that we have not now a free government, that some secret influences are controlling it, and it is absolutely impossible to pursue any program of reform, no matter how handsome and hopeful it may be, until we get an instrument of our own with which to pursue it.

You know where the seat of corruption lies. If you can, or think you can, conduct your business only by getting special favors from the government, if you know that you can carry on some of the enterprises that you are now carrying on only if you can see to it that some of the laws of the United States are not changed, then you are going to do, some of you are going to do, thoughtlessly it may be, but nevertheless rather systematically, what has been done for so many years. You are going to contribute your money to the party that will guarantee to you that these privileges are not taken away.

And the chief seat of privileges in the United States is the protective tariff. I won't say the "protective" tariff, for I deny that epithet to it. A system of protection such as was originally conceived by Henry Clay bears not even a family resemblance to the Payne-Aldrich tariff measure. Almost all the parts of the Payne-Aldrich schedules that most interest those who have usually replenished the coffers of the regular Republican party lie concealed in phraseology which you can't understand and no man can understand until an expert has uncovered their meaning to him. And when representatives of your own in the Senate and in the House of Representatives sought explanations from the chairmen of the Committee on Finance and the Committee on Ways and Means of these very schedules, they couldn't get them. They were to all intents and purposes told that it was none of their business. And the pity of it was that in the circumstances it was none of their business. It was the business of the gentlemen who had seen to it that they had private understandings with those who controlled the deliberations and conclusions of those committees.

This is the part of the country, like the great State of New Jersey, which I have the privilege of representing, the great neighboring state of Pennsylvania, and the great imperial state of New York, where the scarecrow of free trade is being held up in front. Who said free trade? Who proposed free trade? You can't have free trade in the United States, because the Government of the United States is of necessity, with our present division of the fields of taxation between the federal and state governments, supported by the duties collected at the ports. I would like to ask some gentlemen if very much is collected in the way of duties at the ports under the tariff schedules under which they operate. Some of the duties are practically prohibitive, and there is no tariff to be got from them. But that is a matter on one side. What I am trying to point out to you now is that this protective tariff, so-called, has become a means of fostering the growth of particular groups of industries at the expense of the economic vitality of the rest of the country. What the Democrats propose is a very practical thing indeed. They propose to unearth these special privileges and to cut them out of the tariff. They propose not to leave a single concealed private advantage in the statutes concerning duties that can possibly be eradicated without affecting the part of the business that is sound and legitimate and which we all wish to see promoted.

Some men talk as if Democrats weren't part of the United States. I met a lady the other day, an elderly lady, who said to me with pride, "Why, Governor, I have been a Democrat ever since they hunted them with dogs." And you would suppose, to hear some men talk, that Democrats don't share the life of the United States. Why Democrats—I mean simon-pure Democrats who always vote the Democratic ticket—constitute nearly one half the voters of this country. They are engaged in all sorts of enterprises, big and little. There isn't a walk of life or a kind of occupation in which you won't find them; and, as a Philadelphia paper very wittily said the other day, they can't commit economic murder without committing economic suicide. Do you suppose, therefore, that half of the population of the United States, or something of that kind, is going about to destroy the very foundations of our economic life by simply running amuck amidst the schedules of the tariff! Some of them are so tough that they wouldn't be hurt if it did. But that isn't the program, and anybody who says that it is simply doesn't understand the situation in the United States at all. All that the Democrats claim is this, that the partnership ought to be bigger than it is. Just because there are so many of them, they know how many are outside. And let me tell you, just as many Republicans are outside.

The only thing I have against them—my Republican fellow citizens—is that they have allowed themselves to be imposed upon so many years. Think of saying that the protective tariff is for the benefit of the workingman, in the presence of all those facts that have just been disclosed in Lawrence, Massachusetts,[6] where the worst schedule[7] of all operates to keep men on wages

6 He referred to the massive strike of woolen mill workers which had convulsed Lawrence earlier in the year. It began on January 12, 1912, when workers, led by the Industrial Workers of the World, protesting against low wages, stormed

upon which they cannot live! Why, the audacity, the impudence of the claim is what strikes one, and in face of the fact that the workingmen of this country who are in unprotected industries are better paid than those who are in protected industries, at any rate, in the conspicuously protected industries. The steel schedule, I dare say, is rather satisfactory to those who manufacture steel, but is it satisfactory to those who make the steel with their own tired hands? Don't you know that there are mills in which men are made to work seven days in the week for twelve hours a day, in the 365 weary days of the year, and can't make enough to pay their bills? And that in one of the giants among our industries, one of the undertakings which has thriven to gigantic size upon this very system.

Ah, the whole mask of the fraud is falling away, and men are beginning to see disclosed little groups of persons maintaining control over the dominant party, and, through the dominant party, operating the government in their own interest, and not in the interest of the people of the United States. And there comes in your political moral. For these gentlemen don't act directly upon the Government of the United States. They act through an interesting class of persons known as political bosses. Political bosses are not politicians at all. They are the business agents on the political side of certain kinds of business. They are the experts who instruct these gentlemen how they can manage not to be embarrassed either by those who occupy executive or by those who occupy legislative offices. And they are well paid for their services, not necessarily in cash, but by being on the inside of many large transactions.

The trouble with bosses is that they are not politicians. By a boss I would like to tell you what I mean. I don't mean the leader of a political organization. I mean the manipulator of a machine. Now, a machine is that part of a political organization which has been taken out of the hands of the rank and file of the organization and has gone to seed in the hands of a few chosen men. It is the part that has ceased to be political and become a business agency for the determination of the public policy of states and of the nation.

You have your complete series, therefore, of suspicions about

---

two plants and damaged machinery. It ended, after considerable violence, on March 18. The conflict dominated the front pages of all Boston newspapers, received national press coverage, and was the subject of a congressional investigation. See Donald B. Cole, *Immigrant City: Lawrence, Massachusetts, 1845-1921* (Chapel Hill, N. C., 1963), pp. 3-9, p. 231.

[7] Schedule K, the wool and woolen products schedule of the Payne-Aldrich tariff.

nominations for office, about the election of United States senators, about the rejection of laws traced down to the taproot—this
great colossal system of special privilege, on account of which
men feel obliged to keep their hands upon the sources of power.
. . .

But in the meantime the point we should realize is that we are
choosing. The thought I want to leave with you is this: Here is
the choice you have to make. The Democrats are proposing to
intervene and, by lowering those duties which have protected
special privilege, expose special privilege to a very wholesome,
chastening kind of competition, and then to adopt a process of
legislation by which competition will be so regulated that big
business can't crush out little business, and that little business
can grow instead of being built by private understanding into big
business, and put every man who is manufacturing or engaged in
commerce in this country on his mettle to beat, not the capital,
but the brains of his competitors. Whereas, on the other hand,
the leaders of the third party are proposing to you—I would say
parenthetically that the leaders of the regular Republican party
aren't proposing anything—but the leaders of the third party are
proposing that you accept the established monopolies as inevitable, their control as permanent, and undertake to regulate them
through a commission which will not itself be too carefully restricted by law, but will have the right to make rules by which
they will accomplish what the platform calls constructive regulation. In short, it proposes to leave the government in the hands
and under the influences which now control it and which, so long
as they can control it, make it absolutely impossible that we
should have a free instrument by which to restore the rule and
the government of the people themselves.[8]

T MS (C. L. Swem Coll., NjP), with many corrections from the nearly complete
text in the *Hartford Daily Times*, Sept. 26, 1912.

[8] There is a WWhw outline of this speech dated Sept. 25, 1912, in the C. L.
Swem Coll., NjP.

An Address in New Haven Opening the Connecticut State Campaign[1]

[Sept. 25, 1912]

Your Excellency,[2] Mr. Chairman,[3] and fellow citizens: The introduction reminds me, by contrast, of the remark made to me
by a gentleman a good many months ago after I had appeared

[1] Delivered in the Hyperion Theater.
[2] Governor Simeon E. Baldwin.
[3] John E. Doughan, chairman of the Democratic town committee.

before a good many audiences. He said that he ventured to say that if he had an opportunity to add a petition to the litany, it would be "From all introducers and traducers, good Lord deliver us." But I told him, for I had had other experiences like this evening, that I counted myself peculiarly happy in my introducers, and that I could not have more prudently chosen my traducers if I had chosen them myself. Governor Baldwin has certainly, unintentionally no doubt, put me at a certain disadvantage, because it is not an advantage to a speaker to be eloquently introduced. I count the introduction I have just had the pleasure of listening to as unusually brilliant and eloquent, and I feel myself put to my mettle to live up to it.

I am interested to learn from Governor Baldwin that this is the opening of the present campaign in New Haven. That gives me leave to do what I should like very much to do, to introduce to some gentlemen in this audience, who are not well acquainted with it, the great Democratic party, for I know that there are many men sitting before me who are here on the anxious bench. I know that they are now thinking of changing their course of life. I know that they are now "sicklied o'er with the pale cast of thought," and I would if I could commend to their consideration in the choice of their future course in politics the great party which I represent. That party, ladies and gentlemen, is great by recent proof, for the Democratic party has been a minority party for sixteen years in this nation, and during those sixteen years it has grown in power, in clearness of thought, and in determinateness of action. It did not wait for the year 1912 to discover the program which was necessary for the rectification of conditions in the United States. It has foreseen the greater part of that program for half a generation. It has been calling through all these years of discouragement upon the American people to bear witness to the fact that they did not have access to their own government and were not being governed in their own general interest. This steadfastness in principle in the face of adversity is to my mind a proof of greatness, particularly when in the midst of adversity the party has grown stronger and stronger, and its vision clearer and clearer. For there have been many vacillations in politics, and after a while there came a day when the ranks of the Republican party began in part to waver and to break.

We saw the day in New Jersey when there arose a little group of Republicans who called themselves the New Idea Republicans, when the idea of serving the whole people was a new idea with the Republican party. Then there arose in the far state of Iowa another group of men who began to see that the crux of the whole business was the protective tariff, and they began to shake the faith of the West in the time-honored traditions of the Republican party with regard to that policy. Then there arose that sturdy little giant in Wisconsin, who is now such an indomitable, unconquerable champion of progressive ideas all along the line—I mean Senator La Follette. Men who seek expediency rather than pursue principle took him up for a little while and pretended to follow him, and then rejected him, not because he was not the genuine champion of their principles, but because they apparently saw their interest lie in another direction. I do not believe there are many chapters of personal history in the records of parties in this country more difficult to reconcile with principles of honor than that. I feel myself close kin to these men who have been fighting the battle of progressive democracy, for no matter what label they bear, we are of one principle.

I remember hearing a story not long ago. I have told it a number of times, but perhaps you will bear with me if I tell it again, because it interprets my feeling. A very deaf old lady was approached by her son who wanted to introduce a stranger to her and he said, "Mama, this is Mr. Stickpin." "I beg your pardon," she said, "what did you say the name was?" "Mr. Stickpin." "I don't catch it," she said. "Mr. Stickpin." "Oh," and she said, "it's no use, it sounds exactly like 'Stickpin.'" Now, when I talk of men of Mr. La Follette's way of thinking in politics, I feel like saying, "I beg your pardon, what did you say you were?" "A Republican." "A what?" "A Republican." "No use, it sounds to me just like Democrat." I can't tell the difference, and I realize that in the ranks of these men, these men who in the United States Senate for months past have been voting with the Democratic majority in the House of Representatives and showing that we have a government—have had a government—which is neither flesh, fish, nor fowl in respect of party control, because a union of Democrats and so-called Republicans has been sending a Republican President measures which he consistently vetoed.

And the proposition to go on with the regular Republican party is a proposition to go on with this same paralysis upon us; for I don't believe that anybody expects that the majority will be changed in the next House of Representatives. And I believe that most persons expect that the majority in the next Senate will, at any rate, not belong to the regular Republicans; and that with a united pair of progressive houses, it would be folly to have a President that doesn't move with it—the movement of the thought of the country and the representative bodies of the country—no matter how admirable his character, no matter how high and patriotic his purposes.

For I yield to no man in personal admiration of our present distinguished President. I would be incapable of a personal criticism of him, because I am not criticizing him in my thoughts, much less in my speech. I am simply stating to you a situation, and I want to say parenthetically in the same connection, does anybody dream for a moment that there can be a third-party majority in either of the houses that are to be elected on the fifth of November? Does anybody think that it would be wise to have so extremely active a gentleman, so extremely aggressive and versatile a gentleman as is now leading the third party, put alone in Washington, an understudy to Providence?

To turn, then, to the introduction to which I invited your attention, I want to introduce you to the present Democratic party, a party that has come through fire, has been purified, has been shown such errors as it has committed in past years, and is now absolutely and enthusiastically united upon a progressive program, a platform which the whole country is seeking. That is the new Democratic party, new because it never grows old, new because the principles in which it is rooted and grounded never can grow old, new because they are the identical principles upon which, as your Governor has said, the great Declaration of Independence itself was founded, and that other document with which Jefferson had so much to do, the incomparable Virginia Bill of Rights. And so this is the party which is now being questioned with regard to its purposes by the leaders of parties which are either breaking up or have not yet attained to the bone and sinew of manhood. For these gentlemen are saying, "If you give power to the Democrats, you will do all sorts of things. In the first place, you will have free trade." Ah, that ancient bogy! How long will they continue to dress this thing of their imagination in the old clothes of ancient stump orators? There cannot be free trade in the United States as long as the established fiscal policy of the federal government is maintained. The federal government has chosen throughout all the generations that have preceded us to maintain itself chiefly on indirect instead of direct taxation. I dare say we shall never see a time when it can alter that policy in any substantial degree; and there is no Democrat of thoughtfulness that I have met who contemplates a program of free trade.

But what we have been doing, and what we intend to do, what the House of Representatives has been attempting to do and will attempt to do again and succeed, is to weed this garden that we have been cultivating. Because if we have been laying at the roots of our industrial enterprises this fertilization of protection, if we have been stimulating it by this policy originated, at any rate in its present form, by Henry Clay, we have found that the stimulation was not equal in respect of all the growths in the garden, and that there are some growths, which every man can distinguish with the naked eye, which have so overtopped the rest, which have so thrown the rest into destroying shadows, that it is impossible for the industries of the United States as a whole to prosper under their destroying shade. In other words, we have found out that this that professes to be a process of protection has become a process of favoritism, and that the favorites of this policy have flourished at the expense of all the rest. And now we are going into this garden and weed it. We are going into this garden and give the little plants air and light in which to grow. We are going into this garden and pull up every root that has so spread itself as to draw all the nutriment of the soil from the other roots. We are going in there to see to it that fertilization of intelligence, of invention, of origination is once more applied to a set of industries now threatening to be stagnant, because threatening to be too much concentrated. That is the policy of the Democratic party in regard to the protective tariff.

The President said the other day that if the Democratic party was put in power there would come a series of rainy days for those engaged in the industries of the country. I recall the time when he condemned that preposterous Schedule K under which the wool monopoly flourishes, and I want to ask him if he doesn't think that rainy days came long ago to the poor mill hands in Lawrence, Massachusetts. What kind of days are these that are enjoyed by some of the employees of the overshadowing steel monopoly who have to work seven days in the week, twelve hours every one of the seven, and can't, when the 365 weary days have passed and a year is told, find their bills paid or their little families properly sustained? Are they waiting for rainy days? I want to call his attention to the fact that men all over this country in industries not protected see more sun during the day than those who are in most of the protected industries. They get higher wages, they have shorter hours, they are enabled to maintain themselves with a degree of respectability which is denied to the rest.

And I say that the policy of the Democratic party will so variegate and multiply the new undertakings in this country that there will be a wider market and a greater competition for labor, and that the sun will come through the clouds and there will no longer be lead in the skies and a burden intolerable to carry for the servants and creatures of some of the protected industries. I tell you, ladies and gentlemen, the time has gone by for statements which cannot be sustained by the facts, and I very earnestly and respectfully protest against arguments which do not square with the facts. For the fact is that the Democratic party has not proposed to change the established fiscal policy of this country except where it furnishes root for special privilege, and that wherever special privilege grows there American labor languishes.

Then there is another thing it is said will happen if the Democratic party comes in. You know that one of the interesting things that Mr. Jefferson said in those early days of simplicity which marked the beginnings of our government was that the best government consisted in as little government as possible. And there is still a sense in which that is true. It is still intolerable for the government to interfere with our individual activities, except where it is necessary to interfere with them in order to free them. I have long had an image in my mind of what constitutes liberty. Suppose that I were building a great piece of powerful machinery, and suppose that I should so awkwardly and unskillfully assemble the parts of it that every time one part tried to move it would be interfered with by the others, and the whole thing would buckle up and be checked. Liberty for the several parts would consist in the best possible assembling and adjustment of the various parts, would it not? If you want the great piston of the engine to run with absolute freedom, you give it absolutely perfect alignment and adjustment with the other parts of the machine, so that it is free, not when you let it alone, but when you associate it most skillfully and carefully with the other parts of the great structure. And so I feel confident that if Jefferson had lived in our day, he would see what we see—that the individual is caught in a great confused nexus of all sorts of complicated circumstances, and that to let him alone is to leave him helpless as against the obstacles with which he has to contend, and that, therefore, law in our day must come to the assistance of the individual.

The Democratic party does not stand for the limitation of the powers of government, either in the field of the state or in the field of the federal government. There is not a Democrat that I know who is afraid to have the powers of the government exercised to the utmost, but there are a great many of us who are afraid to see them exercised at the discretion of individuals. There are a great many of us who still adhere to that ancient principle that we prefer to be governed by the power of laws, and not by the power of men. Therefore, we favor as much power as you choose, but power guided by knowledge, power extended in detail. Not power given out in the lump in a commission set up, as is proposed by the third party, unencumbered by the restrictions of law to set up a constructive regulation, as their platform calls it, of the trusts and monopolies, but a law which takes its searchlight and casts its illuminating rays down the secret corridors of all the processes by which monopoly has been established, and polices its corridors so that highway robbery is no longer committed on it, so that men are no longer waylaid upon it, so that the liberty of individuals to compete is no longer checked by the power of combinations stronger than any possible individual can be. We want to see the law administered; we are not afraid of commissions.

It is said with a good deal of force, I want frankly to admit, that merely to make laws and leave their application to the present courts with their present procedure is not a very likely way of reform, because the present procedure of our courts means that individuals must challenge the power that is being exerted against them, that an individual must wait until he is injured and then go to the court for redress, and that he must have money enough and courage enough to go to the court and ask for redress. For the worst of our present situation, ladies and gentlemen, is that it requires courage to challenge the power of the men now in control of our industries by resorting to any tribunal whatever. Therefore, I am ready to admit that we may have to have special tribunals, special processes, and I am not afraid, for my part, of the creation of special processes and special tribunals. But I am absolutely opposed to leaving it to the choice of those tribunals what the processes of law shall be and the means of remedy.

And, therefore, the difference between the Democratic and the Republican parties, or rather between the Democratic party and those various other groups that are masquerading under all sorts of names, is that they are willing to accept the discretionary power of individuals, and we are not willing to accept anything except the certainty of law. That is the only thing that has ever afforded salvation or safety.

I want to draw a few illustrations. There is the great policy of conservation, for example, and I do not conceive of conservation in any narrow term. There are forests to conserve, there are great water powers to conserve, there are mines whose wealth should be deemed exhaustible, not inexhaustible, and whose resources should be safeguarded and preserved for future generations. But there is much more than that in the policy of conservation.

There are the lives and fortunes of the citizens of the United States to be conserved. It covers not only forest reserves and forest cultivations and the safeguarding of water powers and mines, but it includes pure food and the public health and the conditions of labor, and all those things which government must see to minutely and courageously if we are not to be sapped of our vitality and disappointed of our hopes. Now, the thing that stands in the way of the proper policy of conservation and makes it impossible to form that policy is that the Government of the United States is now under the influence of men who want to control the forests, control the water courses, control the mines, who will not admit that these are public properties which we hold in trust for future generations as well as for ourselves, and are resisting the efforts of those of us who would extend the threads of law all through these insidious processes which threaten our resources and threaten our lives and vitality.

Then there is the matter of the regulation of the hours of labor, of the conditions of labor, of the sanitation of factories, of the limitation of the work, of work for women and children, of the limitation of hours for men—questions which are in part state questions but also in part federal questions. All of these matters have to be treated by knowledge and pursued by a constancy of purpose which no special interests ought to be allowed to stand in the way of. And the Government of the United States under the Democratic party will attempt to put all through this nation the structural steel of law, so that no man can doubt what his rights are, or doubt the stability of the thing that he is walking on.

Sometimes, when I think of the growth of our economic system, it seems to me as if, leaving our law just about where it was before any of the modern inventions or developments took place, we had simply at haphazard extended the old family residence, added an office here and a workroom there, and a new set of sleeping rooms there, built up higher on the foundations, put out new foundations and new wings, little lean-tos, until we have a structure that has no character whatever. Now, the problem is to continue to live in the house and yet change it.

Well, we are architects in our time, and architects are also engineers in our time. We don't have to stop using a terminal because a new railway station is being built. We don't have to stop any of the processes of our lives because we are rearranging the structures in which we conduct these processes. I say that what we have to undertake is to systematize the foundations of the house, then to thread all the old parts of the structure with the steel which will be laced together in modern fashion, accommodated to all the modern knowledge of structural strength and elasticity, and then slowly change the partitions, re-lay the walls, let in the light through new apertures, improve the ventilation, until finally, a generation or two from now, the scaffolding will be taken away, and there will be the family in a great building whose noble architecture will at last be disclosed, where men can live as a single family, cooperative as in a perfectly co-ordinated beehive, not afraid of any storm of nature, not afraid of any artificial storm, of imitation thunder and lightning, knowing that the foundations go down to the bedrock of principle, knowing that the structure will stand as long as the solid globe, and knowing that whenever they please they can change that plan again and accommodate it as they please to the altering necessity of their lives. That is the figure I have carried in my mind as I have thought of the future. This minute interlacing of ancient life with modern law, such is the program of the Democratic party.

But there are a great many men who don't like the idea. You know that some wit recently said, in view of the fact that most of our American architects are trained in the École des Beaux Arts at Paris, that all American architecture in recent years was either bizarre or "Beaux Arts." I think that our economic architecture is decidedly bizarre, and I am afraid that there is a great deal to learn about the architecture from the same source from which our architects have learned a great many things. I don't mean the School of Fine Arts in Paris, but the experience of France. And from the other side of the water men can now hold up against us the reproach that we have not adjusted our lives to modern conditions to the same extent that they have adjusted theirs. I was very much interested in some of the reasons given by our friends across the Canadian border for being very shy about the reciprocity arrangements. They said, "We are not sure where these arrangements will lead, and we don't care to associate too closely with the economic conditions of the United States until those conditions are as modern as ours." And when I resented it and asked for particulars, I had in regard to many matters to retire from the debate. Because I found that they had adjusted their regulations of economic development to conditions which we had not yet found a way to meet in the United States.

So that all over the country we are facing the same problem. It is a problem not of revolution but of readjustment. And what I want to suggest to you is that the only basis, the only standard, of readjustment proposed or suggested by our opponents is the

standard of expediency, and that only the Democratic party offers a standard of principle. For the expediency of the situation
is merely to see to it that those who receive special privileges behave themselves, whereas our principle is that nobody ought to
receive privileges at all—that every special privilege shall be destroyed, not with a ruthless hand, not in such a fashion as suddenly to upset the conditions of business, but nevertheless with
the firmness and kindness of the judicious parent. The Government of the United States at present is a mere foster child of the
special interests. It is not allowed to have a will of its own. It is
told at every move, "Don't do that. You will interfere with our
prosperity." And we ask, "Where is our prosperity lodged?" and a
certain group of gentlemen say, "With us."

Now, I, for my part, don't want to belong to a nation, and take
leave prettily to believe that I do not belong to a nation, that needs
to be taken care of by guardians. I want to belong to a nation,
and I am proud that I do belong to a nation, that knows how to
take care of itself. If I thought that the American people were
reckless, were ignorant, were vindictive, do you suppose I would
want to put the government in their hands? But the beauty of
democracy is that when you are reckless you destroy your own
established conditions of life. When you are vindictive, you wreak
your vengeance upon yourself, and that the whole stability of
democratic polity rests upon the fact that every interest is every
man's interest. If it were not so, there could be no community;
if it were not so, there could be no cooperation; if it were not so,
there could be no renewal. And that to my mind is the most important part of the whole matter. For what I am anxious about,
ladies and gentlemen, is the conditions which the next generation
will find, for the present generation finds this—that if, for example, you add to the reputation of America for ingenuity by originating a great invention, a great industrial invention, a singular
thing happens to you. If you want, let us say, a million dollars
to build your plant and advertise your product and employ your
agents and make a market for it, where are you going to get the
million dollars? Because the minute you apply for the million
dollars, this proposition is put to you: "This invention will interfere with the established processes and market control of certain
great industries. We are already financing those industries. Their
securities are in our hands. We will lend you the money if you
will make an arrangement with those industries and go in with
them. If you will not, then you can't have the money." I am gen-
eralizing the statement, but I could particularize it. I could tell
you instances where exactly that thing happened. And by the

combinations of great industries, processes are not only being standardized, but they are being kept at a single point of development and efficiency of operation. The increase of the power to produce in proportion to the cost of production is not studied in America as it used to be studied, because if you don't have to improve your processes in order to excel a competitor (if you are human, you aren't going to improve your processes) and if you can prevent the competitor from coming into the field, then you can sit at your leisure and behind this wall of protection which prevents the brains of any foreigner competing with you, you can rest at your ease for a whole generation.

And so I say that I want to see those conditions created which will permit this: Let a man begin his business on never so small a scale and let him be safe in beginning it on a small scale. He is not safe now, because if he enters a field where a great combination has established a market, that great combination will undersell him in his local market, which is his only market, making its necessary profits in other parts of the country until he is killed off. And enterprise after enterprise is nipped in its infancy by the monopolistic control of our industrial markets. So that America is about to see another generation which must be a generation of employees unless it makes up its mind to be a generation of masters. The great militant, fighting, triumphant America is a nation of officers, a nation of men who are their own masters, a nation of men who will originate their own processes of industry and of life. And we shall never see the day, I confidently predict, when America will allow itself to be employed and patronized and taken care of.

I hope I have succeeded, therefore, in introducing to you the present-day Democratic party. It has been here all along, but you weren't paying any attention. You are just now beginning to take notice, because there was a solid phalanx, a solid organized rush line, between you and the horizon. The whole horizon was shut out from you by the towering figures of the men who held so closely and firmly together in order to dominate the situation. And now these lines are broken; a little bit of the horizon can be glimpsed; and beyond these towering figures you see the great resurgent mass of the American people. And you see certain gentlemen, I hope modest gentlemen, trying to speak for them, saying, "We have been waiting for your attention for a long time; now will you be kind enough to listen? Will you be kind enough to realize what our ideals are? Will you be kind enough to open your eyes to the vision which has led us on through dark days for a whole generation?"

For we would not have carried this burden of exile if we had not seen a vision. We could have traded; we could have got into the game; we could have surrendered and made terms; we could have played the role of patrons to the men who wanted to dominate the interests of the country—and here and there gentlemen who pretended to be Democrats did make those arrangements. I could mention some of them. I have known them. They couldn't stand the pace. They couldn't stand the privation. There was too little in it. And you never can stand it unless you have some imperishable food within you upon which to sustain life and courage, the food of those visions of the spirit where a table is set before you loaded with palatable fruits, the fruits of hope, the fruits of imagination, those invisible things of the spirit which are the only things upon which we can carry ourselves through this weary world without fainting. We have carried in our minds, after you had thought you had obscured them, we have carried in our minds what those men saw who first set their foot upon America—those little bands who came to make a little foothold in the wilderness, because the great teeming nations that they had left behind them had forgotten what human liberty was—liberty of thought, liberty of religion, liberty of residence, liberty of action. And so we set up an asylum. For whom? For the world.

Is it not a beautiful thought that there are nations of Europe that have dreamed dreams that they never could realize on their native soil and have sent their vanguards to America to discover? Why, in that ancient Kingdom of Hungary, for example, contemporary with the great Magna Charta, to which we look back as the source of our constitutional liberties, there was proclaimed upon a notable day the terms of the Great Golden Bull which ran almost in the identical terms of Magna Charta. But Hungary never could get a foothold for the execution of those principles until she began to send eager multitudes across the ocean to find in America what they had vainly hoped for in Hungary. Then I can take the great Italian race, going back to the stern Roman days and coming down to the days of Garibaldi and the visionary but practical Cavour, who built a nation out of separated kingdoms, and accommodated the temporal with the spiritual power as they had never been accommodated before, and find them coming in multitudes over to America, pleased that they could find even more than Garibaldi and Cavour could give them. Then those pathetic heroic struggles that mark the dark days in Poland; then the struggling multitudes that came from Poland to find their home in America—why, you could go through the list of the European nations and find in every instance that we had either realized their hopes for them or grossly deceived them. For we are trustees of all the confidence of mankind in liberty. If we do not redeem the trust, if we do not fulfill the pledge, then we are of all nations the most to be pitied, for the more high your aim, the more disastrous your failure to reach it. The more glorious your program, the more contemptible your failure.

Why did we lift this vision of peace before mankind if we did not know the terms on which peace could be realized? And so like an army indomitable, irresistible, we have enlisted in such ways that no prolonged night of darkness and extinguished camp-fires can make us the less confident that the morning will dawn. And when the morning dawns and the mists rise, then men shall discover their manhood again and put on that armor of the righteousness of God, which makes any nation unconquerable.[4]

T MS (C. L. Swem Coll., NjP); with a few corrections from the incomplete text in the *New Haven Evening Register*, Sept. 26, 1912, and from the nearly complete text in the *Cleveland Plain Dealer*, Oct. 12, 1912.

[4] There is a WWhw outline of this address dated Sept. 25, 1912, in the C. L. Swem Coll., NjP.

An Address to Workingmen in Fall River, Massachusetts[1]

[Sept. 26, 1912]

Your Honor,[2] fellow citizens: The minute I came into this room I knew that this was where I wanted to be. I love to have a body of men about me like this, not sitting down like a formal audience, but collected together like a lot of neighbors to talk matters over. I like to be close to the men that I am talking to, so that I can see in their faces. Dr. Coughlin[3] said that it was kind of me to accept your invitation. It was not kind of me—I esteem it a privilege to be here and talk face to face about the matters which concern all of us, for the real difficulty of our nation, gentlemen, has been that not enough of us realized that the matters we discussed were matters of common concern. We have talked as if we had to serve now this interest and again that interest, as if all the interests were not linked together, provided we understood them and knew how they were related to one another. And the burden that is upon the heart of every conscientious public man is the burden of the thought that perhaps he does not sufficiently comprehend the national life. For, as a matter of fact, no

[1] Delivered in the Casino.
[2] Thomas F. Higgins, lawyer and mayor of Fall River.
[3] John William Coughlin, M.D., of Fall River, member of the Democratic National Committee.

single man does comprehend. The whole purpose of democracy is that we may hold counsel with one another, so as not to depend upon the understanding of one man, but to depend upon the counsel of all. For only as men are brought into counsel and state their own needs and interests can the general interests of a great people be compounded into a policy that will be suitable to all.

When I came here tonight I realized that I was coming into a community where a very large proportion of men go daily to difficult labor and are confined all day long at tasks which make them feel that they are right against the adamant of life. You don't want to hear a rhetorical disquisition on politics. You don't want to hear word pyrotechnics. You want to hear the kind of talk that gets down to the interests that are nearest to you. You want what you don't now get. You want political and economic justice, do you not? And our search must be for justice and the means of getting it. I want, in the first place, to record my protest against any discussion of this matter which would seem to indicate that there are bodies of our fellow citizens who are trying to grind us down and do us injustice. There are some men of that sort. I don't know how they sleep o'nights, but there are men of that kind. But thank God they are not numerous. And we are caught in the grip of a great economic system which is heartless because men are not in it. You know, when I hear judges, for example, reason upon the analogy of the relationships that used to exist between workmen and their employers a generation ago, I wonder why they have not opened their eyes to the modern world. Why, in the modern world a man never sees, or practically never sees, his real employer.

I was discussing conditions in one of the best known centers of the textile industry in this country—I mean one of those almost as well known as your own city—and they were saying that the difficulty there was that most of the men who owned the mills didn't live in the town at all; they lived at a great distance. The stock was not owned in the town. And that, therefore, the workman was further off than usual from his employer. He didn't deal with him as an individual, as workmen used to deal with their employers when I was a boy, and I can assure you that that isn't so very long ago. They now deal with great impersonal things called corporations, not with anybody in particular, but with the agents of great powers which you can't even imagine. You never saw a corporation any more than you ever saw a government. You never saw the body of men who are conducting the industry in which you are employed. And they never saw you. What they know about you is written in ledgers and books and letters, in the correspondence of the office, in the reports of the superintendents. You are a long way off from them. And, therefore, what we have to discuss is not the intentional wrongs which individuals do us, for I do not believe there are a great many of those, but the wrongs of the system. We want to get a new light thrown all through the intricacies of this matter so that we may know where we are.

I was illustrating the matter in my mind the other night in this way. You know that one of the best governed cities in the world is the great Scotch city of Glasgow. (Applause) I thought I might strike a Scotchman. Well, I have a lot of it in me myself. And one of the most interesting things about the administration of that city in connection with matters such as we are now discussing is this: You know how in the modern city we don't many of us have the privilege of living in separate houses. At most we have the whole floor of a tenement; the worst we have is one room, and we crowd the whole family into one room in the tenement; and so there is family after family in the same building, in the same house. Now, it is absurd in these circumstances to regard the front door of that house on the street as the entrance to a private place, for it isn't. And the authorities of the city of Glasgow don't pretend to regard it that way. They treat the entries and the staircases and the corridors of those buildings exactly as if they were the streets of the town, as to all intents and purposes they are. They light them, they patrol them, and the whole authority of the city of Glasgow—the part of the authority that keeps order and sees after sanitation and everything of that sort—has free access to everything except the actual residences, behind the closed doors of apartments, just as it ought to be.

Very well, I want the law in respect of all our matters to do something very much like that—to send the representative of the law inside the house, through the corridors, up the staircases, into everything except individual men's private business. And then let us see if we can't understand one another better by knowing the conditions under which we live and what it is that we ought to do in order to help one another. Because, gentlemen, we are upon the eve of a new arrangement in America.

You have only to examine the platforms of all the parties, for they are multiplying fast now, in order to see that they are all realizing more or less distinctly the new duty that is laid upon government. We used to think in the old-fashioned days, when life was very simple, that all that government had to do was to put on a policeman's uniform and say, "Now, don't anybody hurt anybody else." We used to say that the ideal of government was for every man to be left alone and not interfered with, only when he interfered with somebody else; and that the best government was the government that did as little governing as possible. But we are coming now to realize that life is so complicated that we are not dealing with the old conditions, and that the law has to step in and create the conditions under which we live, the conditions which will make it tolerable for us to live. And the reason that you have now to be very careful in the way you are going to vote on the fifth of November is that you are going to choose a method of justice.

All the parties are offering you justice. But it is one thing to offer it to you, and it is another thing to know how to give it to you. In the first place, I want to present this consideration to you: There is only one party that is ready to give it to you. Have you heard anybody predict that the third party is going to have a majority in the House of Representatives? Have you heard anybody predict, in his wildest enthusiasm, that it is going to have a majority in the Senate of the United States? Don't you know just as well as you are sitting there that if the leader of the third party should be elected President, he would be one of the most lonely officials in the United States? In all probability, in a probability so strong as to amount to a practical certainty, he would have associated with him a Democratic House and a Democratic Senate. He would be just as lonely and just as unserviceable as the present President of the United States. I beg that you won't think that that is said with disrespect, for it is not. I am merely stating a fact. The House of Representatives is Democratic; there is a sufficient number of Republicans in the Senate who vote on all important matters with the Democrats in the Senate to make a majority; and the chief legislation of the past session has not been Republican and has therefore not been acceptable to the President; and almost all the chief measures intended for the relief of the voters and buyers of this country have been vetoed by the President. So that you know what I mean. The present President is lonely. He occupies simply a post of resistance. He hasn't got a team behind him; he isn't associated with a team.

And the only President you can associate with a team in the coming years is a Democratic President. Now, I don't know what kind of a captain of the team the candidate would make. I have played quarterback and captain on a smaller team of the same kind, and I found it easy to teach the team the signals, and I found that they responded to the signals with a good deal of spirit. But this is another and a bigger job, and I am not going to pretend to you that I know whether the Democratic candidate would be successful or not. All that I know is that he would have a team back of him, and that no other President you can choose at this juncture would have. Therefore, if you are going to get justice that isn't mixed of all kinds of programs, if you aren't going to keep things at a standstill, if you don't want to wait at least two years, and perhaps four years, to get any program, the only thing you can do in common sense is to elect a Democratic President. Think that over. If I am wrong about it, I want to be corrected.

I don't see any possibility in the existing circumstances of the divided Republican ranks of there being anything but a Democratic House and a Democratic Senate, and therefore you have either got to complete your team or leave it uncompleted. And if you vote to put the leader of the third party in and isolate him, I dare say the next four years would be very interesting, but I don't think they would be very fruitful. We have, therefore, another reason for thinking very carefully over what it is the Democrats propose and contrasting what the Democrats propose with what the third party proposes. I say that because I don't understand that the regular Republican party is proposing anything in particular. I am not confining most of my discussions to the third party because I feel that the regular Republican party can be ignored, for I believe that a very great and solid strength remains with it, but simply that I can't find anything to get my teeth into in the program of the regular Republican party. And I can't find anything in the program of the third party that will bear discussion with regard, for example, to the fundamental matter of the tariff.

Both wings of the Republican party, for they are merely wings of one party, are contented with the tariff conditions except that they think that there are some excessive schedules and that there ought to be some tinkering done in order to reduce some of the schedules. But they are essentially standing pat, both of them, on the tariff, and the only working proposal I find in either of the programs is in regard to the way you are going to treat the men who have taken the chief advantage from the tariff—I mean the leaders and organizers of the trusts. And there we come upon a very interesting question, which I am going to put to you in this way: We want justice. That is where we began. Now do you want it directly from the government? Or do we want it directly from the government through the trusts? Well, that is the difference. Mr. Roosevelt says that the trusts are a natural development of our economic system, that they are inevitable, that they have come to stay, that we must treat them just as we would the railroads, and accepting them regulate them, and then see to it that justice is done, particularly to the workingman, not by the law, but through the regulated trusts.

Now, what kind of friends have the workingmen of the country found the trusts to be to them? Just put that question to yourself. And is the government going to make Christians of these trusts? Is the government going to put bowels of compassion in them? Is the government going to persuade them to be kind and benevolent to us in the use of their enormous and irresistible power? Is that all the government is going to do? Is the government going to take us back a hundred years, nay, 150 years, in our development, and put us in tutelage again? Let me tell you that benevolence never developed any man and never developed any nation. The only way a man is developed is by being put in such a position that he can and will take care of himself. Liberty is the only wine we have ever drunk that has made a real tonic. And if I could be assured beforehand, or rather if I could be so hypnotized as to believe beforehand, that the trusts would be good to us, I would say "No, thank you, I don't want anybody to be good to me. I want a chance to show my mettle, and I don't want any orders. I merely want a fair field and no favor." Because while it might be very convenient to be taken care of, it will make a dwarf of me to be taken care of. And I don't care to lose my growth.

So that we have to ask ourselves this question: Have the trusts been the friends of the workingmen of this country? Why, you know the answer to that question. The trusts are the only power in this country that have broken the power of organized labor. They are the only things in this country that have been strong enough to fight organized labor. Why? This question was put in this debate the other night: One of the speakers of the third party said, "Why is it any more likely that regulated trusts will do an injustice to the workingmen than that regulated railroads should do an injustice to workingmen?" The railroads haven't fought and overcome organized labor. Why should the regulated trusts overcome it? Well, I'll answer the question, because there are some men who can't think, but any man who can think knows the answer. In the first place, the railroads before they were regulated never tried to break up organized labor. That is one answer. And the trusts have tried and have succeeded. So that you started with a different set of circumstances. And then there is this other obvious circumstance, that you can't shut up one part of a railroad and work only another part. And the way the trusts beat organized labor is by shutting up some of their mills and transferring the orders to another at a distance and starving out that installment of the army of labor in order to conquer it; and, further, by dividing it and fighting it here when they don't have to fight it there, make it impossible for them to win.

You can't stop the railways of this country. Public opinion won't permit it. The government won't permit it. The mails have to be carried, and if you can't shut a thing up, you can't beat a strike. Now, are you going to go to the length of obliging these men who own all the plants and assemble in a great trust plants scattered all over the country, to work them all the time? You would have a job at that, because the market doesn't always justify it, and they can fool you to the top of their bent by showing you their order lists and showing you that they are not justified in working all the time. The thing isn't feasible, and the difference between the two cases is so gross and obvious that it is almost a waste of time to point it out. But the point I want to return to is that with this ability to shut shops up, with this ability to shut off labor in certain parts of the country, with unlimited means to live, while the men shut out can't live, because they haven't unlimited means, they have used that awful power to break up the right to organize. That is my point. Because if it isn't a right on the part of workingmen to organize, then there oughtn't to be a right on the part of capital to organize. It is organization that makes capital strong, and it isn't fair from the legal point of view, or any other point of view, to prevent the rest of the men dealing with capital from getting the strength which organization, and only organization, brings.

So that you don't have to defend all the things that organized labor has done. Organized labor has been unwise in some things, but the point is this, that the right of organization on the part of labor is not recognized even by the laws of the United States. And nowhere in the third term platform is it promised that that right will be granted. There is a plank in which it is said, "We are in favor of the organization of labor"—I have forgotten the exact words, but that is what it means—"We are in favor of the organization of labor," that is to say, "We approve of the practice." But it doesn't anywhere promise to buttress that practice with the structural steel of law. And this is the law at present: In most of the states of the Union, so far as I know in all of them, for I haven't been able to examine all the decisions of the courts, any corporation, any employer of any kind, has the right under our laws to dismiss not only one of his workingmen or a group of them, but all of them, for no other reason whatever than that they belong to a union. He doesn't have to show that they are not good workmen; he doesn't have to show that they have been negligent, broken the machinery, or done anything that they oughtn't to do. He can dismiss them wholesale merely because they belong to a union.

Now, a union can't oppose an employer merely on the ground that he is employing men who don't belong to a union. And so the thing is absolutely one-sided. The courts have held that union labor has not the right to boycott a concern because it is employing non-union labor, and yet it says that the concern may boycott them because they are unionized. And I believe that we ought to hold a brief for the right, the legal right, to organize. Of course, we can go to the opposite extreme. We may say that capital shall not organize, but imagine the howl that would create. Do you think you could get through a law that capital couldn't organize? Well, what is sauce for the goose is sauce for the gander, and if capital can organize, then it stands to every standard of justice that I have ever heard of that everybody else who has a legitimate object may organize. And there ought to be an absolute equality in regard to that right. Of course, the law must regulate what capital can do with its organization, and we will all of us agree that the law ought also to regulate what organized labor can do with its organization. But that is another story. At present there is no legal right to organize. That is the extraordinary circumstance.

And these organized bodies of capital have been the very forces which have been fighting the right of the workingmen, and successfully fighting the right of the workingmen, to organize. Now, we will assume that the third party platform is carried out—it can't be carried out so far as I can see for four years anyhow—but we will assume that it is carried out. Then where are we? These organized powers through which organized labor has been defeated are to be the instrumentalities of the government in dealing with labor as in dealing with everything else. For they are to be the accepted and regulated instrumentalities of our economic development.

Gentlemen, we can't afford to have justice, supposing they give us justice, which I very seriously doubt, but even assuming they give us justice, we can't afford to have justice without liberty. We can't afford to have justice as a gift. We must have justice as a right, and we must be in a position to get what is coming to us by our own force. Otherwise, all the fighting power, all the ardor, all the hope of liberty, have gone out. And I, for one, do not believe for one moment that the people of this country are going to put themselves in the hands of a government which does not give them justice directly, but administers justice to them through the instrumentality of powers which have shown themselves unjust.

That is what you have got to choose between, for this is the program of the Progressive party. On the other hand the Democratic party proposes to do a very different thing. It proposes to regulate the use of the power that organized capital can make. It proposes to see to it that they [the trusts] no longer dominate by the means by which they have dominated, for they have dominated by putting all small beginners in business out of the game. You can't now get a foothold in a local market in some of the biggest industries of this country, or in some of the biggest undertakings of this country. You can't set up a rivalry. And you have to begin somewhere. You can't begin in space. You can't begin in an airship. You have got to begin in some community. Your market has got to be your neighbors first and those who know you there. But unless you have unlimited capital, which of course you wouldn't have when you were beginning, or unlimited credit, which these gentlemen can see to it that you shan't get, they can kill you out in your local market any time they try, on the same basis exactly that they beat organized labor. For they can sell at a loss in your market because they are selling at a profit everywhere else, and they can recoup the losses by which they beat you by the profits which they make in fields where they have beaten other fellows and put them out.

Now, you can stop that. Somebody said to me the other day, "Is it fair to dissolve the trusts?" Well, it hasn't seemed to make much difference whether they were dissolved or not that I have seen, that is to say, nominally dissolved. But I would be perfectly willing to let them go without dissolution; because if we can make competition fair and prevent the giants from killing the pigmies, then I am perfectly willing to let the brains of the pigmies compete with the brains of the giants. And I see a time when the pigmies will be so much more athletic, so much more astute, so much more active, than the giants, that it will be a case of Jack the giant killer. I want simply, if these gentlemen believe as they state in their circulars advertising their stock, if they believe as they state that the combination produces efficiency and economy, then I want to see them prove it by beating independent competitors whom they can't put out of business by unfair competition and whom they can't deprive of credit which is necessary for the expansion of the new business! For now, by interlocking directorates, by being members of every kind of thing from banks and railroads and mining corporations to everything else that you can think of at the same time, they can limit credits. And that also can be prevented. I am willing to let Jack come into the field with the giant, and if Jack has the brains that some Jacks I know in America have, then I want to see the giant get the better of him with the load that he, the giant, has to carry, the load of water! For I'll undertake to put a water-logged giant out of business any time if you will give me a fair field and as much credit as I am entitled to, and see to it that the law does what from time immemorial it has been expected to do, stands by me because I am weak and need to be protected until I can take care of myself.

That is the program of the Democratic party, nothing new in it except two items—those items are very new—to see to it that competition is so regulated that you won't have to regulate trusts, because there won't be any. Trusts can't stand competition, let me tell you. "Well," you say, "do you mean to break up big business altogether?" Certainly not. There are different kinds of big business. There is big business spelled with a big B and there is big business spelled with a small b. But the one is inflated, and the other is not. The one belongs to high finance, and the other belongs to everyday, workaday, success and brains. There will be big business in the modern world inevitably, because it is a world of cooperation. It is a world of large operations. It is a world of world-wide operations. But there is a world of difference between the big business that grows by enterprise, by economy, by efficiency, by working capital, every dollar of which is real and is used, and that which is artificially built up by agreements arrived at by gentlemen sitting in rooms where they put together units of every kind, good plants with bad plants, efficient business with inefficient business, and then pay those who get up the scheme such a large bonus for having been kind enough to get it up that they have to carry that bonus in the form of stocks and bonds for the rest of their lives. So that I think I can say that I know that trusts constitute an unsound and uneconomical way of doing business, and that a sound and economical way of doing business will easily supersede them. And America will then be released from her trammels, the trammels that she now suffers under, in a way she has never been released in our time.

Why is it that this party, this third party, that has such a splendid program—I think there are eight or ten things that they promise to do for workingmen—why doesn't it occur to them that there are certain things that we can do, that the people can do for themselves? I tell you the difference in my formula and theirs:

I believe in government by the people, and they believe in government for the people. And government by the people is the only vital kind. I don't know enough to take care of the people of the United States, and I venture to believe that there isn't anybody else that knows enough. Government for the people is sooner or later autocracy and tyranny, no matter whether it is benevolent or not. And only government by the people is liberty and opportunity. And, therefore, it is the most notable circumstance of this campaign that neither of the parties or fragments of parties that are opposing the great united Democratic party has any program whatever of government by the people. They are both of them proposing the old-fashioned government that we have had for the last weary sixteen years of government for the people.

You don't have to go far from Washington to consult the bosses; you don't have to go far from the national capital to consult big business. You can telegraph for them. They will come to see you at a moment's notice from the ends of the country. From all the financial centers they will come down and be very pleased to confer with you and tell you how the United States ought to be governed. But the United States ought occasionally to be consulted. We are not children. We are not wards. Who made these gentlemen our guardians? They are very respectable men, very gifted men. I know some of them and honor some of them. I know some others whom I do not honor. And I know just how they are tied into politics because, of the ones whom I don't honor, they are tied into politics through instrumentalities known as bosses—political bosses, not the heads of great organizations. You cannot have a great political party without a coherent, energetic, splendidly put-together organization. But an organization is a very different thing from a machine. You will notice that bosses do not allow much cooperation in running a machine. The machine isn't run by the organization; the machine runs the organization. And there is a close corporation about it, and you generally do not have to consult more than one or two persons to know what a machine is going to do. And a machine is intended, not to advance a party as an organization, but to advance the interests of the gentlemen who own the machine. And they advance their interests by being very closely and confidentially related with the gentlemen who run high finance and big business with the inflated B's at the top.

So that what the process of our politics has been has become only too painfully and disgustingly familiar; and we want to get rid of it. We want splendid organized forces in this country which will bring recruits in from every quarter, bring the unionists in, bring everybody in to constitute a great irresistible force of public opinion.

For you know, gentlemen, just as well as I do, that the question of wages, for example, is not a question of the tariff. Oh, how long American workmen have allowed themselves to be fooled by a colossal bluff!

Take the wage scales; take any wage scales you choose, and see if they are in proportion, or anything like proportion, to the protective duties enjoyed by the industries in question. You won't find that they match in any instance. Some protected industries do pay good wages; others pay wages with which I dare say some of you are familiar. And they differ in different places, in different cities. For example, the city of Lowell in this state for some reason is a city in which lower wages are paid than are paid anywhere else in Massachusetts, even in the same industries. But those industries there are similar to industries elsewhere. They enjoy the same protective tariff. And you would suppose that if this ancient story about the tariff producing high wages were true, it would produce the same high wages wherever it was in operation. But it does not, and you know it does not. Wages are proportionate to the competition for labor. There is a market for labor just as there is a market for anything else. And if you limit enterprise—as you do by perpetuating the trusts, for they control the large fields of enterprise—if you limit enterprise, you insure the permanency of low wages. The only way to get high wages, aside from the efforts of organized labor, which have succeeded, happily, in many instances, aside from the efforts of organized labor, the only way is to create a varied and increasing market for labor.

Do you see any violent rise in wages now? And yet there is an increasing demand for labor in this country. There is every prospect of Democratic success in November, and yet there is a boom on. Nobody seems to be nervous about the Democrats upsetting business. Because we are beginning to think like grown-up men now, not like silly children. And in this great boom, why is there not an instant increase in wages along with the great demand for labor? Because there is a dead level in wages, in most instances due to the fact that the same persons control over large areas. That is the first reason. And it is competition for labor that produces life in the labor market, just as it is competition in every other thing that produces life and change. And so, if you want enterprise you will not accept trusts as inevitable. And if you don't get enterprise, then the government will have to determine what your wages will be in the long run. And then where will you be? You will simply be where we started in the old days long, long ago, about which we can only read, when men were taken care of by the government and found it so intolerable that they changed absolutely the whole form of their government.

We stand at the parting of the ways, gentlemen. We have got to make a choice on the fifth of November that will last us the rest of our lives. Make the choice that I have indicated, of perpetuating the power of these things that control us, and you cannot turn back. You have got a chance to turn back now, or rather, to turn away in another direction, for nobody proposes to turn back. You have got a chance now to choose the direction which leads to the hills, or you can choose the direction which leads down into the slough, where you will wallow some of these days as the servants of trusts supported by the government.

I know which way you are going. You are not going to be fooled by the present levelness of the country. There is a sign at the crossroads. Look at the sign. Do not take this road that you know eventually leads down hill into the regions of despair. Choose this other road, where there will be displayed at last, when our children are happier than we are, some of the delectable mountains towards which the great American people have been moving all these years of struggle. There will come a time when our children, because of us—because we saw with open eyes, because we had some heroic strength in us—will bless us that we did not condemn them to perpetual subordination; and looking back from the light, from the far places which they have attained, will say, "These men conceived again the vision of liberty, and we, their offspring, are free."[4]

T MS (C. L. Swem Coll., NjP), with corrections from the typed transcript in WP, DLC, and from the partial texts in the *Boston Evening Transcript*, Sept. 27, 1912, and the *Boston Herald Traveler*, Sept. 27, 1912.

[4] There is a WWhw outline of this address dated Sept. 26, 1912, in the C. L. Swem Coll., NjP.

A News Report

[*Sept. 26, 1912*]

TAFT MEETS WILSON FOR PLEASANT CHAT

Rivals in Boston Discuss the Strain of a Campaign
for the Presidency.

BOSTON, Mass., Sept. 26.—At the end of a hard day's campaigning, in which he praised President Taft as a delightful person and criticised him as an unserviceable President, Gov. Woodrow

Wilson met the President and shook hands with him here to-night.

Shortly before midnight the Democratic candidate and the President met in a private suite at the Copely Plaza Hotel, to which Gov. Wilson came as an overnight guest and the President came as a speaker at the dinner of the International Congress of Chambers of Commerce of the World.

President Taft came to the meeting in evening clothes and looked a picture of repose, while Gov. Wilson came into the hotel on foot, carrying two handbags, and looking very travel stained.

From the hotel corridors as Gov. Wilson entered the President could be seen sitting in a box above the diners in the banquet hall. A cheer went up for Gov. Wilson, and another for the President.

An Italian rose to make an address, and Gov. Wilson, suggesting that his hands were soiled, asked that he be shown to a room. Policemen on guard at the banquet hall tunneled a way for Gov. Wilson through the lobby, and he was taken to a room. Word was sent to President Taft that Gov. Wilson did not feel like going to sleep under the same roof without greeting him, and in a few minutes word was sent back that President Taft was very glad of the opportunity for a meeting.

Gov. Wilson slipped into an evening suit and then came down to the State Room, where he found himself with Gov. Foss and a number of his aids in military uniform. President Taft, it was said, would be along in a minute. But Gov. Wilson protested. He said that would look as though the President had sought him out, whereas it was he who wished to greet the President.

While Gov. Foss was rearranging the plan for the meeting, Gov. Wilson slipped away through a side door into the banquet room and took a vacant seat at a table. No one recognized him, and he enjoyed himself chatting with several diners at his table.

Finally President Taft arose from his box, and his opponent, who was present incognito, left the banquet hall at the same moment. President Taft went to a private room on the fifth floor, and there Gov. Wilson, accompanied by Dudley Field Malone and Gov. Foss, called upon him.

"How are you, Mr. President?" remarked Gov. Wilson.

"How are you, Governor?" the President replied. "I hope the campaigning has not worn you out."

"It hasn't done that," said Gov. Wilson, "but it has nearly done so. It has been quite a hard week. How's your voice? Is it holding out?" he asked.

"Yes," replied the President, "and how is yours?"

"It's pretty fine, but now and then it gets a bit husky."

"Well," said President Taft, "there are three men that can sympathize with you, Mr. Bryan, Mr. Roosevelt, and myself. We have been through it all."

The conversation continued for several minutes, and then Gov. Wilson retired to his own room.

"It was a very delightful meeting," said Gov. Wilson as he turned the key to his room. "I am very fond of President Taft."

Gov. Wilson started the day by arising at the Taft Hotel in New Haven in a bedroom which, he said, he had had plenty of room, "because it was built especially for the President." Gov. Wilson knew as the day progressed that he was close to President Taft's campaigning trail.

As his train ran from New Haven to Springfield, Gov. Wilson remarked to his associates on the journey, "This is a very remarkable experience, trailing the Elephant and the Bull Moose in the same territory; they are animals native to such distant zones."

Printed in the *New York Times*, Sept. 27, 1912.

From Evans Tulane Richardson[1]

My dear Governor   Casa Grande, Arizona September 26, 1912

You were courteous enough to answer the letter which I wrote you just after your nomination.[2] But this is written with the understanding that you will not attempt to answer it, with all the demands that must be made upon you at this time.

Arizona is enthusiastic over the news from New Jersey. If you beat Smith on the first memorable occasion, you annihilated him this time. While we can't see anything here except Democrat success in the election in this state, I rather wish we were having a more vigorous campaign. But perhaps that will come. I have seen too many Yale games won or lost in the second half or ninth inning to be able to settle down into the feeling of absolute certainty that seems to prevail out here. Not but that I am satisfied that you will carry Arizona and in fact believe that some people are going to rub their eyes when they wake up on Nov. 6th and find how many states you have carried. But overconfidence doesn't exactly appeal to me. The Roosevelt people are doing the hardest work here. And while he has a large following in the state, he has no license to win. I believe that his speeches in Tucson and Phoenix did him more harm than good. They served to show the real man to many who had never seen him. I suppose his calling you a liar[3] probably did not disturb you any more than when Smith tried to "make it a fight," but it disgusted fair minded people, who want issues discussed and not personalities.

I have just been re-reading Malone's article in the National Monthly.[4] It is very able and most timely. I think it will mean many thousands of votes for you, from people who have honestly believe[d] the silly stuff that has been handed out about you.

Even the most ardent Clark men here seem well satisfied at the way things have gone. They agree with me that you will make a better president and also feel that we can't very well spare Clark from the speaker's chair.

Your definition of a schoolmaster was great. And Malone's picture of your home was very interesting. Altogether he gives the public at large a chance to know you somewhat as we at Princeton already know you. I wish I had 1,000 copies of his article. I have asked for 50, though they may be hard to get.

Working for you out here reminds me of the warm times I used to have in New York and Washington, when the battle was on at Princeton, and which would have meant so much new life and vigor to the institution could they have seen it as you did.

My wife and daughter[5] enjoyed your speech in St Paul and say you had a great ovation. I only hope we may be fortunate enough to have you here before the campaign is over.

With kindest regards to Mrs. Wilson and yourself, believe me
Sincerely yours   Evans T. Richardson

TLS (WP, DLC).
[1] Princeton 1888, editor of the *Casa Grande*, Ariz., *Times*.
[2] It is missing.
[3] He referred to the speech that Roosevelt made in Topeka, Kansas, on September 21, shortly after leaving Arizona. According to the Phoenix *Arizona Republican*, Sept. 22, 1912, Roosevelt said that in his recent speeches Wilson had "directly inverted the truth" about the Roosevelt administration's policies toward the trusts.
[4] Dudley Field Malone, "Woodrow Wilson—The Man," *National Monthly*, IV (Sept. 1912), 91.
[5] Katherine Augusta Mayo (Mrs. Evans Tulane) Richardson and Katherine Beecher Richardson.

To Louis Dembitz Brandeis

Hartford, Conn Sept. 27, [19]12

Please set forth as explicitly as possible the actual measures by which competition can be effectively regulated. The more explicit we are on this point, the more completely will the enemies guns be spiked.   Woodrow Wilson

T telegram (L. D. Brandeis Papers, KyLoU).

A News Report

[September 28, 1912]

Governor Wilson in Princeton Tuesday

Governor Woodrow Wilson was in Princeton Tuesday for the first time since his nomination for the Presidency. He came home to vote in the primary election. He looked in rugged health. Mr. Myers,[1] President of the Woodrow Wilson Club of the University, met the Governor at the Junction and brought him over in an automobile. They arrived about ten o'clock.

The members of the Woodrow Wilson Club marched to the corner of Nassau street and Washington road and awaited his arrival. As soon as the Governor's car appeared at the crest of the Washington road hill the students let loose a volley of cheers for their former President, and as the car turned into Nassau street they formed in line and with much cheering escorted the Governor up Nassau to Chambers street, thence to the polling place in the Engine House, where Governor Wilson votes. At the polling place the Governor got out and the crowd formed a semi-circle and demanded a speech, but Dr. Wilson reminded them that it was unlawful in New Jersey to make a political speech within a hundred feet of a polling place. So the crowd moved up the street and the Governor addressed them from the rear steps of the Second Presbyterian Church. He told them that he was now endeavoring to translate his former teachings at Princeton into action, and then discussed some of the issues of the campaign. One of the things he said which made the crowd laugh was that every time he proves a point he is called academic. The Governor was in fine voice and his speech made a very decided impression. It was followed by general handshaking, and then the Governor went back to the polls to register and vote. When his turn came he gave his pedigree, as required by the direct primary law, which includes the age of the voter. The Governor confessed to fifty-six, and when all the facts were set down he signed the statement. His ballot was No. 9. He spent the rest of the morning visiting friends, leaving on the 1.12 train. He expects to return soon with his family to his residence on Cleveland Lane. After leaving Princeton he went to New England to fill speaking engagements.

Printed in the *Princeton Press*, September 28, 1912.
  1 Paul Forrest Myers, Princeton 1913.

From Louis Dembitz Brandeis

PERSONAL

My dear Governor Wilson: [Boston] September 28, 1912.

Your telegram received.

I am sending you herewith copies of the suggestions for two articles which were sent to Hapgood[1] recently, and to which I referred in our talk yesterday, namely "Concentration" and "Trusts and the Interstate Commerce Commission." Possibly you may find the facts therein stated of service.

Our railroad monopoly hearings[2] continue today. I must defer therefore the preparation of suggestions for the letter until they adjourn, but I hope to have the suggestions in your hands next Wednesday morning, and shall mail them to Sea Girt unless you otherwise direct.

I have a letter today from Raymond W. Pullman[3] of Washington, who was formerly associated with Mr. [Gifford] Pinchot, reminding me of a promise I made him to talk with you, when occasion served, of the National problems of conservation. Our conference yesterday was so brief that this proved impossible, but I have no doubt that if you do speak at the Conservation Congress in Indianapolis, as the newspapers suggest, you will make clear to the Country that, in respect to natural resources, as well as human resources, you are quite as determined as the New Party leaders that a broad policy of conservation shall prevail.   Yours very truly,   LDB

CCLI (RSB Coll., DLC).

[1] Norman Hapgood, editor of *Collier's Weekly*, had invited Brandeis to write a series on the question of monopoly. The first two appeared as L. D. Brandeis, "Trusts, Efficiency, and the New Party," *Collier's Weekly*, XLIX (Sept. 14, 1912), 14-15, and "Trusts, the Export Trade, and the New Party," *ibid.*, L (Sept. 21, 1912), 10-11. The last two, copies of which Brandeis sent to Wilson, were printed as editorials in Hapgood's columns in *ibid.*, L (Oct. 5, 1912), 8-9.

[2] The Interstate Commerce Commission's investigation of railroad rates, services, and financial management. Brandeis was participating as an attorney representing shippers.

[3] A reporter for the *Washington Post* who had written a series of articles on municipal government and civic reform.

A Tribute to William Frank McCombs[1]

[Sept. 28, 1912]

Mr. Toastmaster,[2] Mr. McCombs, Ladies and Gentlemen: The announcement of your toastmaster may have seemed to you to

[1] Delivered at a dinner at the Hotel Astor in New York given by the Woodrow Wilson College Men's League to celebrate McCombs' return to Democratic national headquarters.

[2] William Hanford Edwards, Princeton 1900, commissioner of the Street Cleaning Department of the City of New York.

convey a threat—I am not going to speak until it is time for my train! For I conceive my part in this delightful occasion to be a very simple one, and certainly it is one that affords me the greatest pleasure to perform. I am not here for any other purpose than to render my tribute of sincere admiration and affection for William F. McCombs. If you will reflect upon my relationship with him, you will perceive that it must mean a great deal to a man who has spent most of his life in teaching that one of the men with whom he has been associated as master with pupil, should so believe in him as Mr. McCombs has believed in me, for this, gentlemen, is the highest reward of the teacher. The teacher cannot promise himself that much of what he teaches will remain in the mind of his pupil; he cannot be sure that all of what he has taught his pupil is true or deserves to be permanent—but what he can hope to convey, what it is his highest hope to convey, is that desire for the truth and that respect for the intellectual processes which discover the truth, which ought to be the ideal of every teacher and of every student. So that if I could believe that a great many men have gone out from Princeton feeling about me as Mr. McCombs has felt about me, I would feel that I had been more than repaid for everything that I had ever done in trying to be the sort of a teacher that youngsters would like to have.

I have been reflecting as I have been sitting here upon the relationship that college men bear to public life now. It must be admitted, gentlemen, to our shame, that college men have not borne a very active relationship to public life in this country in the past. Almost all of the men who have most exercised themselves in the field of politics in the United States have been men who have not distinguished themselves, who would not have been picked out by their fellow countrymen because of their connection with a college. It has not been true of other countries. Other countries have tended to pick out their most highly educated men for leadership in the policy of government. You know that some men who either misunderstood or desired to misrepresent some of the views that I have held about those of our fellow citizens who were not born in America represented me on one occasion as saying something very disrespectful of the great Hungarian people, and I mention it because I want to tell you what a Hungarian[3] said to me the other day. He came to see me at Sea Girt and he said: "Sir, we have been very much interested—my people have been very much interested—in your nomination for the presidency because you are the type of university man whom

[3] Geza Kende, assistant editor of *Amerikai Magyar Népszava* (*American-Hungarian People's Voice*), who visited Wilson at Sea Girt on July 22, 1912.

we have been in the habit of raising to public office in our native land."

Think of what a rebuke that would have been to me, how keenly I would have felt it as a rebuke, if I had indeed held the opinions ascribed to me. And yet, as in the case of Hungary, so in the case of other nations: they have looked to their highly trained men for leadership. And I suppose that we have not done so, because many of our public tasks have not in the past been as difficult as the tasks of public leaders in the older countries of the world. We have had a long youth. We have had a long, irresponsible youth as a nation. Our tasks and our lives have been easy; our resources have been abundant; we have been wasteful. We are only just now beginning to realize that our affairs are growing hot with all sorts of complications, and that it is going to need the clearest, most dispassionate sort of thinking to thread our way among the mazes of the difficulties which surround us.

And I expect that in the future we shall be obliged to call upon the men of high and difficult training to lead us along the paths of public policy; but we would never have done so if something had not happened which is now beginning to happen in the United States. What is happening is not that the college man is changing his type exactly in the United States, or is making up his mind of a sudden that he is going to join the nation in its efforts and not stand aloof, but rather that the nation is invading the university.

And I want to say, notwithstanding my own personal connection, that I believe that one of the most influential circumstances of our time has been the fact that the great majority of university men in this country are graduates of state universities, which have constantly felt their sensitive relationship to public opinion. If you will go into some of the great western states, whose state universities are most conspicuous, you will find that a larger and larger proportion of the men in public life in those states are university men. You know that one of the men who has been most conspicuous, and most honorably conspicuous in this country, for leading and giving energy to the progressive sentiment of the people has been Senator La Follette, who surrounded himself with a team of University of Wisconsin men, and who depended upon them for the expert advice which clarified the measures which he proposed and so successfully put into operation in his government. And the idea of what a university has to do is hardly properly discredited because opinion has gone in and taken possession of the university and appropriated it unto itself. And the university man is now beginning to feel what I remember when

I was a youngster he did not feel: he feels the pulse that beats in the great heart of the people themselves. And as he is beginning to feel it, some things are falling away from him.

There is such a thing as the academic point of view. I do not use the word academic in this connection exactly as our distinguished ex-President uses it. I find that whenever I know the facts and know what they mean and say what they mean, he says that I am academic. By which I infer that the only thing that can be stripped of the pretension of the academic mind is unsustained assertion.

But there is an academic point of view, and it is a very unserviceable point of view. I have experienced it again and again in my association with college men. I have found college men just a little unwilling to admit into their reckoning some of the most practical circumstances of life. The college man's point of view is very much like that of the lawyer who told his client who was already in jail that the authorities couldn't put him in jail, and whose client retorted: "Damn it, man, but I am in jail." Now the circumstance of his being in jail was most irrational. It did not square with the provisions of the law or with the spirit of justice, but he was there.

One of the hardest things for the college man to take into his consciousness is the fact that he cannot justify by his reason. One of the facts of life, for example, is public opinion. Sometimes public opinion for a considerable period is not well founded. Suppose, for example, that you are thinking of nominating for office or renominating for office a man who in the general opinion is considered to have failed. Suppose that the fact is that he has not failed. But suppose that the necessity of acting is at hand, and the general opinion is that he has? How are you going to treat that opinion? Are you going to say that it is unjust, that it is unreasonable, it is not founded in the truth? All right, if you are academic, say so and then try to elect him. The minute you have done that you have run your head against a fact—the fact that he was not elected. It becomes one of those stubborn facts that constitutes a piece of history. And then in the study of your sons in college they will accept that as part of their reasoning because it will then be an established fact, so that the next generation of college men will know what you refused to see.

Most college men, therefore, go about reasoning about things and leaving out some of the most important elements, leaving out what are the fundamental and most practical elements in the whole matter. They reason without their feet on the ground. That is what I call academic, and I have met many men with this academic point of view. I have met some public men with this point of view. And I say to you that the business of the college man is to widen his reasoning to see to it that the intangible facts, the unreasonable facts, even the incredible facts—if they be facts—be taken into the foundations of his action, because life does not consist in thinking, it consists in acting. Your life does not consist in the theory of the circulation of the blood, it consists in the circulation of the blood. It consists in the great vital forces that pump this red tonic through you from end to end. And you must, therefore, take life in its practical facts as you find it and climb upon that to the vision that you have had.

It is very fine indeed to think of the meaning of McCombs' name that Finley[4] so beautifully reminded us of—the man of the crests, the man of the uplands. And it is pretty fine to think what looking off from the uplands means. And what the college man finds it most difficult to do is done in the valley—to remember what he saw from the uplands. The thing that he saw was the immortality of truth and of principle. And he knows perfectly well that if he knows life and action embody the truth and principle, he shares that immortality, so that he can afford to sacrifice his physical life. He can afford to go into that country which no man has seen, knowing that there he will wear the purified garment of the men who saw the delectable region before he reached it. And he knows that the dark doors of death lying ahead of him may, if he choose, lead to the region of eternal emancipation. I should say that, if a body of college men had once got the real vision of truth in them, they would make the most incomparable troubles in the world.

You know that we have marveled at the apparent indifference to death shown by that extraordinary nation that has sprung into a leading place in the world in our time—I mean the Japanese nation. And we have supposed that it was a sort of agnosticism on their part. I don't so understand it. I cannot explain the philosophy; I cannot explain the religious enthusiasm which lies underneath it, but I can imagine it. The life of that nation is in the spiritual world. The life of that nation is in the spirit of its ancestors, still immortal. And it has no fear of death, because it believes that death is translation into that state of immortality. If you believe that you win by dying, it is a privilege to die.

Men then may covet it and may think death is sweet and desirable. But they cannot think so unless they utterly believe in

4 John Huston Finley, president of the College of the City of New York, who also spoke.

the ideal. A man who has gone through college and has had no vision, has had no glimpse, has had no certitude brought to him of the things that are permanent, as contrasted with the things that are temporary, has gone through college in vain, has missed something that he ought to have found there.

So that this gathering to my mind is not a gathering of men who have made up their minds that they will indulge in the leadership of the nation. A league of college men cannot say to one another, "Go to. We will run the country." They are just like everybody else. And they have first got to love the country and submit to its processes and feel the pulse of the people and get the enthusiasm of the things to be done, and then let the great forces that have been bred in them by training work to that end. In other words, they have got to subordinate themselves in order to lead.

The whole process of leadership, if it be right, is a process of sympathy. It is a process of insight. It is a process of putting yourself at the point of view of the average man. And the only advantage you have as college men is that you have been trained, if you have been trained at all, to interpret other things than those that are bred in you as an individual, to project yourselves into situations, to substitute yourselves for other individuals, to play into a life that is not your own. That is what your training fits you for if it fits you for anything. That is fine, and so I say that if you will submerge yourselves, if you will immerse yourselves, if you will get the color of this great nation into all your thinking, then you will at last release your individual force. Because what the nation needs at this moment is not men who bend others to think as they do, but men who find out what others think and translate that into the best possible action.

The trouble with the government of this country in past decades has been simply this, that a few men have undertaken to do the thinking for the rest. It is a task which has often been attempted before, and it has never succeeded. It never can succeed. The probabilities of its success do not depend upon the character or even the genius of the little group that attempts it. It is in itself intrinsically impossible, and the only reason we ever set up democracy was that we knew that it was impossible.

The only persons who can vitalize this country are the persons who will be the spokesmen of the whole country, and only as they are spokesmen are they great. They cannot be great in forcing their conceptions upon the nation. They can be only great in making the nation's own thought rise into the region of practicability, by its translation into acts of Congress and the statutes of state legislation, interpreting the best that they find coming to them out of the common thought.

If some of us, therefore, show a little heat in public discussion, if some of us show an ardor that makes our words sometimes run beyond the exact truth of an exposition, it is because we are hammering a crust, we are trying to break through a crystallization—the crystallization of special interests in this country. And we are trying to get this thing so broken into the whole country, so transfused into the thoughts of the whole nation, that it will take on a new energy and a new beauty and a new strength and give us the old hope again. For as we are headed now, we have lost sight of the old hope of America. The old hope of America was that the common thought should be the reigning thought, and the present practice of America is that the thought of some should dominate not only the thought but the fortunes of all the rest.

There is no group of men wise enough to dominate a great free nation. Because if they do dominate it, then it would be proof positive that it had ceased to be free. I would not feel that there was any credit in leading a nation that would follow me without asking any questions. But if it puts me to my test every time by searching questions as to whether I understand it or not, and then trusts me after I have answered the questions, then I have a faint gleam of hope that perhaps I have seen what they intended me to see, and that perhaps I can be a vehicle, not for the realization of my own purposes or ambitions, but for the realization of what the nation desires.

The function of the college man is interpretation, and what greater interpretation could there be than to interpret the thought in the heart of a great people? I tell you, gentlemen, as I go about this country and meet the crowds that gather about me, whether from curiosity or whatever other motive, I feel nothing so much as the intensity of the common man. I can pick out the men who are at ease in their fortunes and who have thought perhaps a little too much in the academic atmosphere by looking at a crowd, because they are standing as if they were at a show. They are seeing a public man go through his stunts, but the other men are not. They are listening as if they were waiting to be fed. They are listening as if they were waiting to hear if there was somebody who could speak the thing that has been dumb in their own hearts and minds, and it makes a man's heart ache to think that he cannot be sure that he is doing it for them; that they are longing for something that he does not understand. He prays God that something will bring into his consciousness what is in theirs, so that the whole nation may feel at last released from its dumbness, feel at last that there is no invisible force holding it back from its goal, feel at last that there is hope and confidence and that the road may be trodden as if they were brothers, shoulder to shoulder, not asking each other about differences of class, not contesting for any selfish advantage, but united in the common enterprise.

Now, the man whom we are honoring tonight is a man who has tried to do just that thing. You know that there is nobody who is more likely to be reduced to the circumstances in which he is working than a lawyer. I mean that the big clients are the ones that he naturally wants, and I mean that the big clients are the very clients that are getting together to see that nobody else gets what they want, and that a lawyer in a great commercial and industrial center who keeps his vision of the common interest and awaits the time when, whether correctly or mistakenly in this case, he can serve it or thinks he can serve it, is a very fine example of what a college man ought to be.

I have allowed myself to wander off into a disquisition about what college men ought to be, but I have really all the time been thinking of this man, because I cannot speak particulars, because a public place is not a place in which to touch on intimate affection, a public place is not proper for the display of your heart. There would be a breach of taste in showing just how I feel about McCombs, and the admiration I entertain for him is of the same sort exactly as the admiration that you entertain, although my admiration is sustained by a more intimate knowledge of the particulars.

I know the burden he has borne. I know the infinite labor which has temporarily put him out of the active field, and I know that it would be impossible for me to find words in which to express my own personal impressions of the man who has so disinterestedly, so persistently, with an enthusiasm which I must frankly say to you I cannot understand, worked for the nomination of the man who has at last been burdened with the responsibility of leading the great Democratic party.

Transcript of shorthand notes (C. L. Swem Coll., NjP).

From Ira Remsen

My dear Governor Wilson: [Baltimore] September 28, 1912

A few days ago I received from a friend a newspaper clipping from the Springfield Republican giving a report of a speech made by you at the Interstate Fair at Sioux City, Iowa. I think I know you well enough to be justified in assuming that you would not knowingly be guilty of a misstatement of facts. It is therefore evident that someone has given you wrong information, and I feel it my duty to send this correction. You say that the Board of Experts appointed by President Roosevelt "were not asked this question: 'Can benzoate of soda be used to conceal putrefaction? Can it be used in things that have gone bad to conceal the fact that they have gone bad and to induce people to put them in their stomachs after they had gone bad?' They were not asked that question because if they had been they would have said: 'Yes, it can be used in that way,' and Dr. Wiley knew that it was so used in that way."

With all due respect for you and your informant this is not a statement of fact. Our Commission looked into that question very carefully and reached the conclusion that benzoate of soda cannot be used to conceal inferiority, and although this was not stated in the official report to the Government, it was stated in the presence of the Secretary of Agriculture and Dr. Wiley in a public address at Denver, 1909, and the Secretary has called attention to this fact on more than one occasion.[1]

You further say: "I want to warn the people of this country to beware of commissions of experts. I have lived with experts all my life, and I know that experts don't see anything except what is under their microscopes, under their eye. They don't even perceive what is under their nose. . . ."

I do not know what your definition of an "expert" is, but according to the definition commonly accepted, an expert is one who knows something of the subject he is talking about, and the world is very dependent upon the work of experts. You know this is true and it is unnecessary for me to make this statement, but the statement in your speech is certainly misleading. I fancy there are just as broad-minded men among experts as are to be found in any other class of the community. I am not defending myself in what I here say, but am trying to help you and not to bother you.

Wishing you all success in your campaign, I remain

                    Yours very sincerely,   [Ira Remsen][2]

CCL (I. Remsen Papers, MdBJ-Ar).

¹ Considerable controversy continued to surround this whole issue. The Denver meeting of the Association of State and National Food and Dairy Departments, August 1909, was characterized by stormy debate and political maneuver. The close vote that endorsed the Remsen board did not end the dispute. Those food processors who did not use preservatives supported Wiley rather than Remsen's board. They asserted that use of benzoate permitted less scrupulous competitors to process inferior foods or employ less than sanitary methods. Consumers' leagues and the American Medical Association's committee on medical legislation also adopted resolutions in support of Wiley's position. See Oscar E. Anderson, Jr., *The Health of a Nation: Harvey W. Wiley and the Fight for Pure Food* (Chicago, 1958), pp. 217-19, 228-31.

² Tumulty acknowledged this letter in J. P. Tumulty to I. Remsen, Oct. 3, 1912, TLS (I. Remsen Papers, MdBJ-Ar). In a speech in McVicker's Theater in Chicago on October 10, 1912 Wilson returned to this subject. He apologized to the canning industry for having said that canners were engaged in preserving food by chemical processes. He explained that they did not need to make use of preservatives. But he made no reference to Remsen's assertions. There is a transcript of this speech in the C. L. Swem Coll., NjP.

From the Diary of Colonel House

September 28, 1912.

Was at Headquarters early. McAdoo for the first time talked without reserve regarding his position in the matter of the Governorship, stipulating that McCombs must not know. I believe McAdoo would be good material for the Governorship. Of course, McCombs is working against it.

Governor Wilson came in last night from New England, leaving at twelve. He asked me to take him out in our motor for a conference. He was particularly anxious to discuss the State situation before making his speech at McCombs' dinner. McAdoo is urging him to come out actively against Dix and Murphy. I urged him not to do this. McCombs is the only link between the bosses and Wilson. The Governor's inclination is to go after them. He finally agreed to give out a letter Monday without mentioning either by name.

We discussed the organization.

A Statement on the New York Democratic Situation¹

[[Sept. 29, 1912]]

I have been looking forward to the Syracuse convention² with the deepest interest, because I realize its critical importance to the party throughout the Nation, and I have made my own opinion with regard to it very plain to every friend from New York who has done me the honor to consult me.

I have not said anything in public about it, or through the newspapers, because I wanted to avoid even the appearance of doing what I condemn in others, namely, trying to dictate what a great party organization should do, what candidates it should choose, and what platforms it should adopt. But the very principle to which I hold myself bound, both in speech and in action, justifies me in saying that the whole country demands and expects that the Democracy of New York be left absolutely free to make its own choice.[3]

I believe that it is ready to choose a progressive man of a kind to be his own master and to adopt a platform to which men of progressive principles everywhere can heartily subscribe, if only it be left free from personal control of any sort. The organized Democrats of the great State of New York are ready to serve the Nation and to serve it with intelligence. They need no direction from the Governor of another State, even though he be the candidate of his party for the Presidency.

It is seldom organizations that are at fault; it is those who attempt to dictate their action. No intelligent party leader can justly or wisely, or even intelligently, condemn or reject the open and honest organization by which alone parties can be held to concerted action, but he can and must do everything in his power to keep them free and unbossed.

The Democracy of New York is at a critical turning point in its history. The whole country awaits its action at Syracuse with deep attention and concern. Democrats everywhere look to it to set an example and vindicate the fair name of the party. They will feel the chill and discouragement very keenly if it should fail them, and will be stirred by added hope and enthusiasm if it should accomplish what is expected of it.

It will not do for the choice of the convention at Syracuse to be any less free than that which gave the third party Mr. Straus and the regular Republican party Mr. [Job Elmer] Hedges.[4]

Printed in the *New York Times*, Sept. 30, 1912.
[1] There is a WWsh draft of this statement in WP, DLC.
[2] The Democratic state convention, which was to meet on October 3.
[3] That is, free from Tammany's dictation and more specifically from Murphy's control.
[4] Murphy did not insist upon the renomination of Governor Dix and permitted the nomination of Congressman William Sulzer. See Link, *Road to the White House*, pp. 496-97.

To Mary Allen Hulbert

Dearest Friend,   Sea Girt, New Jersey 29 Sept., 1912

On Tuesday we move to Princeton, and on Wednesday afternoon I leave for a ten days' absence in the West, going as far as

Denver. That is the reason I am anxious to get a reply to my card of yesterday, from New York before Wednesday P.M. You may imagine how I was affected by the report that a scandal was being fabricated against me. Exactly what I heard was this, that Mr. Elihu Root, the Senator from New York had recently said to some one who was sitting next to him at dinner that he understood that a judge in Pittsfield had in his possession, or had been shown a letter, in connection with an action for divorce, which showed me in some way implicated in the matter. I think the inference drawn was that the letter was *from me*.[1] It at once came into my mind that this might be an attempt to set gossip afloat, if nothing more, which would, no matter how completely discredited later, abundantly suffice, just at this juncture, to ruin me utterly, and all connected with me and I resorted to you at once, in the hope that, if there were any discoverable clue to the infamous thing, you could help me discover it. You will know where and how to institute inquiry. The mere breath of such a thing would, of course, put an end to my candidacy and to my career. It is too deep an iniquity for words!

I am very well, but so tired that I can barely do the thinking necessary for the campaign,—and this new method of attack has made me sick at heart.

I spoke at Fall River the other evening. Is it not from Fall River that the boats ply to Nantucket? I thought that you might have heard of the meeting, and looked eagerly around among the women of the audience in the hope that I might see you there. How jolly, how delightful that would have been! But no such luck! I am pegging away after my own fashion at this weary business of campaigning. There would be no bearing its tremendous burdens if there were not the element of large duty and serviceableness in it. There *are* great issues, the greatest imaginable, issues of life and death, as it seems to me, so far as the sound political life of the country is concerned; and therefore I keep heart and strength. The people believe in me and trust me. If they can only be suffered to continue to do so by my malevolent foes!

All join me in affectionate messages,

Your devoted friend,   Woodrow Wilson

ALS (WP, DLC).
[1] There is nothing in the Papers of Elihu Root and William Howard Taft, both in DLC, relating to this.

To Louis Dembitz Brandeis

Dear Mr. Brandeis,   Sea Girt, N. J. 29 Sept., 1912

   Thank you warmly for the articles and for your letter.

   Please address me, after this, at Princeton, N. J.

   In haste,

            Cordially and faithfully Yours,   Woodrow Wilson

TCL (RSB Coll., DLC).

From the Diary of Colonel House

September 30, 1912.

   McCombs is stopping at the Astor. He has done nothing regarding the New York situation as he promised. The dinner given him Saturday night pleased him. The Governor made only a fair speech. He called me over the telephone Sunday night from Sea Girt and read what he had written to give out to the press. He mentions no names. Dowling has been agreed upon as the best man for the nomination for Governor of New York by Wilson, McCombs and me. McCombs has ascertained that the World will support him. He says he got this assurance from the Editor, Cobb, and Ralph Pulitzer. The Governor desired this before deciding to support Dowling.

   The jealousy between McCombs and McAdoo is acute. Governor Wilson is going West again Wednesday. I am sending messages to Mrs. Bryan by him.

To Charles William Eliot

My dear Mr. Eliot: [Sea Girt, N. J.] September 30, 1912.

   I want to give myself the pleasure of telling you how deeply I appreciate the statement you have issued concerning the pending election.[1]

   Being one of the interested parties, I do not feel that I am competent to assess the conclusion at which it arrives but it seems to me so splendid in its moderation and in every way so strong and so representative of everything that is associated with your name and influence, that, even if I were not concerned in it, I would wish to express my great admiration.

   I hope, with all my heart, that nothing may occur to alter your judgment of me.

      Hoping that you are absolutely restored to health in every way,

         Cordially and sincerely yours,   Woodrow Wilson

TLS (photostat in RSB Coll., DLC).

¹ C. W. Eliot to the Editor, Sept. 20, 1912, *New York Times*, Sept. 24, 1912. Eliot said that there were two principal issues in the campaign—prompt reduction of the tariff and the degree to which the Constitution should be modified by interpretation or practice to permit needed reform. Eliot asserted that Roosevelt's utterances on the tariff were "contradictory and vague." Moreover, Eliot went on, at a time when all parties were inclined to stretch the Constitution, the President ought not to be, like Roosevelt, an "impulsive, self-confident, headstrong man, impatient of restraints and opposition, and given to the use of extravagant language." In contrast, Wilson clearly advocated tariff reduction, and his statements were more "prudent and measured in regard to the proposed changes than those of ex-President Roosevelt." Wilson also possessed qualities of "fairness, sober judgment, and quiet resolution."

From Louis Dembitz Brandeis, with Enclosures

My dear Gov. Wilson: Boston, Mass. September 30, 1912.

I enclose herewith suggestions for the letter, about which we talked, dealing with the difference between your attitude and Roosevelt's on trusts and the remedies you propose to apply. It is not in as good form as I should wish and there are also a number of matters which I should be glad to consider further, but I understand you are to leave for the West on Wednesday, and I wanted to have it in your hands tomorrow so that if you deem it desirable to discuss the matter with me you could wire me tomorrow and I could take the night train to New York and see you Wednesday morning. It would be necessary for me to trouble you to come to New York and be there early as I should have to leave New York on the noon train.

You will note that I have referred to two La Follette bills— The La Follette-Stanley Anti-Trust bill, which was first introduced August 19, 1911, and was in the main drawn by me; the other La Follette Federal Commission bill, was drawn by the University of Wisconsin people practically under the controlling influence of Charles McCarthy, who, I understand, practically framed the plank in the New Party platform. He is a strong supporter of Roosevelt. I have never seen the Federal Commission Bill in print, and I do not know the date when it was introduced; indeed I did not know that it had actually been introduced until I saw it stated in a recent letter of McCarthy's to Hapgood, which letter enclosed also a statement from the La Follette Campaign Committee referring to the Commission Bill. It seems to me important to verify the fact and to ascertain definitely the date of the La-Follette Federal Commission Bill.

I have no doubt that your definite declaration on the lines indicated in this letter will make some enemies, as well as friends, but I assume that you have considered that matter adequately.

I understood that this matter was taken up with you by Mr. G. S. MacFarland[1] while you were in Boston, and I, therefore, submitted this draft to him for his suggestions. He has approved it in its present form, but he states that what he had more particularly in mind was some definite statement from you dealing particularly with the relation of the trusts to labor, and that he thought you ought to express yourself in a letter or otherwise, more fully on that subject.

I understand that you have a copy of my address of Sept. 18, before the Massachusetts State Branch of the Federation of Labor, also of my letter of September 24; but if I could be of any further assistance to you, you will, of course, call upon me.

I have arranged to speak on the trust problem before different organizations in Portland, Me., Boston, Springfield, Providence, New York City, Brooklyn and Rochester, N. Y., within the next ten days, and then to discuss these subjects at different places in Ohio, Pittsburg and Detroit, so that it would probably be impossible for me to meet you at any time after Wednesday morning.

If you find it desirable to have me come to New York please wire my office as early in the day as possible, and if you should not telegraph before evening I can be reached at my home, 6 Otis Place, Boston.

I am sending a copy of this letter to you, also, care of Mr. McAdoo.   Yours very truly,   Louis D. Brandeis

P.S. I have just wired you as follows:

"Am mailing you to Trenton suggestions for letter and am sending copy to you care Mr. McAdoo. If upon reading same you should wish to have conference with me could meet you in New York early wednesday morning but must leave New York on noon train."

I am enclosing you a copy of a memo. on the La Follette Anti-Trust bill which I prepared last December, and which may save you some trouble in considering that bill. The Stanley Bill, which I also drew, is somewhat different in form and omits a number of the sections of the La Follette Bill. Lenroot[2] introduced the La Follette Bill in the House.   L.D.B.

TLS (WP, DLC).

[1] Grenville S. MacFarland, lawyer of Boston, general counsel for the Hearst interests in New England, and editorial writer for the *Boston American*.

[2] Irvine Luther Lenroot, progressive Republican congressman from Wisconsin.

Sept. 30, 1912. L.D.B.

Suggestions for letter of Governor Wilson on Trusts.

You have asked me to state what the essential difference is between the Democratic Party's solution of the Trust Problem and that of the New Party; and how we propose to "regulate competition."

My answer is this:

The two parties differ fundamentally regarding the economic policy which the country should pursue. The Democratic Party insists that competition can be and should be maintained in every branch of private industry; that competition can be and should be restored in those branches of industry in which it has been suppressed by the trusts; and that, if at any future time monopoly should appear to be desirable in any branch of industry, the monopoly should be a public one—a monopoly owned by the people and not by the capitalists. The New Party, on the other hand, insists that private monopoly may be desirable in some branches of industry, or at all events, *is* inevitable; and that existing trusts should not be dismembered or forcibly dislodged from those branches of industry in which they have already acquired a monopoly, but should be made "good" by regulation. In other words, the New Party declares that private monopoly in industry is not necessarily evil, but may do evil; and that legislation should be limited to such *laws and regulations* as should attempt merely to prevent the doing of evil. The New Party does not fear commercial power, however great, if only methods for regulation are provided. We believe that no methods of regulation ever have been or can be devised to remove the menace inherent in private monopoly and overweening commercial power.

This difference in the economic policy of the two parties is fundamental and irreconcilable. It is the difference between industrial liberty and industrial absolutism, *tempered by governmental (that is, party) supervision.*

On the other hand, there is no fundamental difference between the two parties as to the ⟨means to be adopted or the⟩ machinery to be employed in order to "regulate" industry. The differences between the two parties in this respect would doubtless be found to be either differences in detail or such differences as *would*

1 Wilson edited this document in anticipation of issuing it under his own name. The words in angle brackets are in the original version and were deleted by Wilson; his additions are printed in italics.

naturally or necessarily result from the differences in the ends sought to be accomplished. The New Party, in its tolerance of private monopoly, would have no use for legal or administrative machinery by which existing trusts might be effectively ⟨disintegrated⟩ *deprived of their domination and illicit power.* The Democratic Party, while preserving competition, *and preserving it, perhaps, through a special commission,* would have no use for a price fixing board.

The Sherman Anti Trust Act has ⟨, in the past, been little more than⟩ *proved, so far, of little value, except as* a declaration of our economic policy. The experience gained in the twenty-two years since the Act was passed has, however, served ⟨some⟩ *a* useful purpose. It has established the soundness of the economic policy which ⟨it⟩ *the Act* embodies; and it has taught us what the defects in the statute are which have in large part prevented its effective operation. To make that Sherman law a controlling force,—to preserve competition where it now exists, and to restore competition where it has been suppressed,—additional and comprehensive legislation is necessary. The prohibitions upon combination contained in the act must be made more definite; the provisions for enforcing its provisions by the Courts must be improved; and ⟨they⟩ *these* must be supplemented by other adequate machinery to be administered, *if necessary,* by a Federal Board or Commission.

The general character of this new legislation should be as follows:

First: Remove the Uncertainties in the Sherman Law.

This can be accomplished, in large measure, by making the prohibitions upon combination more definite ⟨somewhat as the La Follette-Stanley Anti Trust bills propose⟩. The Sherman Law, as interpreted by the United States Supreme Court, prohibits monopolies and combinations "unreasonably" in restraint of trade. Experience has taught us, in the main, what combinations are thus "unreasonable." They are the combinations which suppress competition. ⟨and⟩ Experience has also taught us that competition is never suppressed by the ⟨greater⟩ *mere* efficiency ⟨of one concern⟩ *of the successful rival.* It is suppressed either by agreement to form a monopoly or by those excesses of competition which are designed to crush a rival. ⟨And⟩ Experience has ⟨tuaght⟩ *taught* us, likewise, many of the specific methods or means by which the great trusts, utilizing their huge resources or *their* particularly favored positions commonly crush rivals; for instance "cut throat" competition; discrimination against customers who ⟨would⟩ *will* not deal exclusively with the combination; ⟨excluding⟩ *the exclusion of* competitors from access to ⟨essential⟩ *indispensable* raw material; espionage; doing business under false names; or *through* "fake independents"; ⟨securing unfair advantage through railroad rebates;⟩ or acquiring, ⟨otherwise⟩ *in any other way* than through efficiency, such a control over the market as to dominate the trade. The time has come to utilize that experience and to embody its dictates in rules of positive law, which will instruct the many business men who desire to obey the statute, what they should avoid—and admonish those less conscientious what they must avoid. By making the prohibitions upon combinations thus definite, the uncertainty of the act about which business men most complain will be in large measure removed, and the enforcement of the law will become much simpler and more effective.

Second: Facilitate the Enforcement of the law by the Courts.

A great advance in regulating competition and preventing monopoly will result from making the judicial machinery efficient. ⟨and several measures, wisely framed to further this end are also embodied in the La Follette-Stanley Anti Trust bills.⟩ Efficient judicial machinery will give relief to the people by effecting a real disintegration of those trusts which have heretofore suppressed competition and will also enable individuals who have suffered from illegal acts to secure adequate compensation. Efficient judicial machinery will be even more potent as a deterrent than as a cure; for inefficient judicial processes ⟨is⟩ *are* the greatest encouragement to law-breaking. Despite the tolerance of trusts heretofore exhibited by the government, it is hardly conceivable that private monopoly would have acquired its present sway in America, if the judicial machinery for enforcing the prohibitions of the Sherman law had been adequate; and it is certain that the lamentable failure of the proceedings against the Standard Oil and the Tobacco Trust could have been averted. For the failure of those proceedings is not due primarily to inability ⟨of⟩ *on the part of the* Courts to prevent or to disintegrate illegal combinations. It is due to ⟨remediable⟩ defects in judicial machinery or methods *which can be and should be remedied.*

The failure of the decrees to restore competition is due mainly to the fact, that the Court in dividing the trust properties into several segments, did not make these segments separate and distinct;—but, on the contrary, provided that ⟨these segments⟩ *they* should or might be owned (and necessarily controlled) by the same stockholders in the same proportions. Such a provision invited certain failure of the declared purpose of restoring competition. Actual disintegration of ⟨each of⟩ these trusts and absolute restoration of competitive conditions could have been attained if the decrees had made a proper distribution of the properties among the several concerns and had ⟨been⟩ provided that these segments should be, not nominally but actually, separate and distinct. That would have been accomplished if for a limited period no person had been permitted to own at the same time stock in more than one of the segments. ⟨The La Follette-Stanley Anti-Trust bills provide, among other things, for this simple but radical change in the methods of "disintegration."⟩

⟨In another respect the Standard Oil and Tobacco Trust suits present an even more glaring defeat in judicial processes, namely, the failure to afford redress for wrongs done in the past. Each of these trusts had extorted hundreds of millions of dollars from the public and in the process had ruthlessly crushed hundreds and possibly thousands of independent business concerns. Upon the admitted facts the Supreme Court declared unanimously that the combinations and their acts were illegal, but the corporation was left in undisputed possession of their ill-gotten gains, and no reparation was made to anyone for the great wrong so profitably pursued by the trusts,—obviously a failure of justice destined to bring into disrepute not only the Sherman Law, but all law.⟩

This failure is not inherent in judicial processes. It is due wholly to a surprising lack of effective legal method and machinery. The judicial determination of the illegality of the combination and its practices should result, under any proper system of law, as a matter of course, in compensation to the injured, and reparation to the public in some form for the profits wrongfully obtained. The Sherman Law contemplated in part such a result, for it provided that anyone injured by an illegal combination might recover three times the damages actually suffered. But that provision has been practically a dead letter; because under the general rules of law the decisions in proceedings instituted by the Government do not enure in any respect, to the individual benefit of those who have been injured. In order to get redress, the injured person or corporation would have to institute entirely independent proceedings—proceedings exactly as if the Government had never acted. In other words the private litigant would derive no legal aid from the decree in favor of the Government.

This rule of general law has afforded to the trusts immunity for wrong done. Few injured individuals or concerns could afford to conduct the expensive litigation necessary to establish the illegality of the trusts. Few could, regardless of expense, obtain the evidence required for that purpose until it was disclosed in the proceeding instituted by the Government. But before the Government's protracted litigation closed, the Statute of Limitation would ordinarily bar any suits of individual concerns to recover compensation for the wrongs done.

The pending bills supply [remedy] these gross defects in the judicial machinery by a very simple device. They provide in substance, that whenever in a proceeding instituted by the Government a final judgment is rendered declaring that the defendant has entered into a combination in unreasonable restraint of trade, that finding shall be conclusive as against the defendant in any other proceedings brought against the defendant by anyone, so that the injured person would thereafter merely have to establish the amount of the loss suffered; and the danger of losing the right to compensation (while awaiting the results of the Government suit) is averted by the further simple device of providing that the Statute of Limitations shall not run while the Government suit is pending.

These are a few of the many improvements in judicial machinery which, if adopted, would go far toward making the Sherman law a controlling force. It is largely by similar improvements in our judicial machinery, and not by the recall of judges, that the inefficiency of our courts will be overcome and a just administration of law be attained.

Third: Create a Board or Commission to Aid in Administering the Sherman Law.

The functions of government should not be limited to the enactment of wise rules of action, and the providing of efficient judicial machinery, by which those guilty of breaking the law may be punished, and those injured, secure compensation. The Government, at least where the general public is concerned, is charged with securing also compliance with the law. We need the inspector and the policeman, even more than we need the prosecuting attorney; and we *probably* need for the enforcement of the Sherman law and *the* regulation of competition an administrative Board with broad powers. What the precise powers of such a Board should be is a subject which will require the most careful consideration of Congress. The bill introduced by Senator Newlands August 21, 1911 and the Federal Commission bill introduced later by Senator La Follette, contain many suggestions of value. It is clear that the scope of the duties of any Board that may be created, should be broad; and it is probable that whatever powers are conferred upon the Board at the outset will be increased from time to time as we learn from experience. But as to some of the powers which may be safely conferred upon the Board, there is, *I should suppose*, little room for difference of opinion.

1. The Board should have ample powers of investigation

In the complicated questions involved in dealing with big business, the first requisite is knowledge, comprehensive, accurate, and up to date, of the details of business operations.

The Bureau of Corporations has, to a ⟨slight⟩ *certain* extent, collected ⟨some such⟩ information of this kind in the past, and a part of it has been published with much benefit to the public. The current collection and prompt publication of such information concerning the various branches of business would prove of great value in preserving competition. The methods of destructive competition will not bear the light of day. The mere substitution of knowledge for ignorance—of publicity for secrecy—will go far toward preventing monopoly. ⟨But⟩ *Quite* aside from the questions bearing specifically upon the Sherman Law, the collection of this data would prove of inestimable advantage in the conduct of business.

2: The Board should co-operate with the Department of Justice in securing compliance with the Sherman Law. The comprehensive knowledge of the different branches of business systematically acquired by the Board would greatly facilitate and expedite the work of the Department of Justice and would enable it to supply the Court with that detailed and expert knowledge required to deal intelligently with the intricate commercial problems involved in administering the Sherman Law.

3: The Board should be empowered to aid in securing compliance with the law, not only in the interest of the general public, but at the request and for the benefit of those particular individuals or concerns who have been injured ⟨by⟩ or fear *immediate* injury ⟨from⟩ *as the result of* infractions of the law by others. The inequality between ⟨the⟩ great corporations with huge resources and ⟨the⟩ *this* small competitor ⟨and others⟩ is such that "equality before the law" ⟨will⟩ *can* no longer be secured merely by supplying adequate machinery for enforcing the law. To prevent oppression and injustice the Government must be prepared to lend its aid.

T MS (WP, DLC).

E N C L O S U R E   I I

Memo on La Follette Anti Trust Bill

LDB Dec/1911

First: Removing Uncertainties.

The Sherman Law prohibits (as interpreted by the Supreme Court) two classes of combinations.

1. Combinations unreasonably in restraint of trade.
2. Combinations securing or attempting to secure a monopoly.

In applying the monopoly provision, no special difficulty is presented on the score of uncertainty. The uncertainties complained of arise in determining what restraint shall be deemed reasonable, and hence permissible, and what unreasonable, and hence illegal. These uncertainties the La Follette bill seeks to remove so far as our experience with combinations and with the Sherman Law enables it to be done. We have had in America nearly thirty years' experience with trusts. We have had the opportunity of observing the incidents of these combinations, their methods and practices.

We are able, in some measure, to determine to what extent these methods and practices are necessarily or generally harmful; how far they are excesses or abuses of trade rights and as such destructive of fair competition. Clearly any combination pursuing practices destructive of fair competition unreasonably restrains trade.

Practices Rendering Restraints of Trade Illegal.

The La Follette bill adds to the Sherman Law as Section 10 an enumeration of certain practices which have been shown by our economic and legal experience to be of that character, and declares that when resorted to by a combination in restraint of trade shall be accepted as establishing conclusively that the restraint in [is] unreasonable, and hence illegal.

The practices there set forth are all practices of unfair competition. Clauses a, b, c, d and e of Section 10 present various efforts which have been resorted to by the trusts to crush competition by utilizing their domination of the trade or particularly favorable conditions to prevent a customer dealing with some competitor. For instance, by refusing to sell to a particular person some necessary or desirable article unless the purchaser agrees to deal exclusively with the seller; or to refuse to sell to the purchaser on fair terms or at a reasonable price, unless he will agree to buy all articles from the seller; or to make to the purchaser some special inducement to prevent his dealing with a competitor where the trade conditions are such that compliance with the seller's demands is practically compulsory. The practices so enumerated in the La Follette bill are obviously unfair competition and have proved most effective instruments for crushing competition.

Thus, the Tobacco Trust through its jobbers offered a special discount to those who purchased all their supplies from these jobbers. The Trust controlled certain practically indispensable brands. The retailer could not carry on a successful tobacco business without these brands, nor could he carry on business successfully without receiving the benefit of the discount which was offered by the Trust, so long as his own competitors had the benefit of it. The introduction of this special discount was effective in destroying the business of competitors and ultimately ruining them. Obviously any combination resorting to such methods restrains trade unreasonably and hence illegally, and the La Follette bill so declares. Indeed this practice pursued by the Tobacco Trust was so clearly destructive of competition that the legislature of Massachusetts prohibited the practice by whomsoever resorted to, not confining the prohibition to combinations in restraint of trade. (See Mass. Revised Laws 56, Sec. 1) The statute was enforced against the Tobacco Trust. (See 188 Mass. 299; 191 Mass. 545)

The United Shoe Machinery Company resorted to somewhat similar devices. That Company, which has practically a monopoly of the most important machines used in the manufacture of shoes, leases its machines, with some form of royalty. There are a number of different machines used in the manufacture of a single pair of shoes. For instance, the Goodyear Welting and Stitching Machine, Lasting Machine, Metallic Fastening Machine. The United Company, for the purpose of preventing its customers from patronizing competitors introduced what has been known as tying clauses in their leases. For instance, in the case of the McKay Metallic Fastening Machine, the company required that the machine should be used to full capacity, limited only to the output of the factory, that new machines should be secured, if the output required, and that these machines should not be used on shoes that had been lasted, welted or turned by machines not hired from the lessor. In like manner the use of the lasting Machine was prohibited in making shoes on which welting or turn machines not hired from the United Company had been used. In respect to certain machines the Company issued what is called independent leases, which did not contain the restrictions above referred to, but introduced in these leases terms so onerous that customers who undertook to operate under them were severely handicapped. The purpose of the United Company was, of course, to prevent competition by requiring its customers to deal exclusively with it, and as it owned a number of machines practically indispensable in the manufacture of shoes it succeeded in crushing all competitors. Obviously a practice so pursued is unfair competition, and a combination using such methods was restraining trade unreasonably and hence illegally, and the provisions of the La Follette bill so declare. Indeed the practice was so clearly destructive of competition that the legislature of Massachusetts by Statute of 1907, Chap. 469, prohibited such action.

Section 10 provides that if those combining in restraint of trade shall be found guilty of violating the Interstate Commerce act, as by the accepting of rebates, such a conviction shall be accepted as conclusive evidence that the restraint exercised in [is] unreasonable. Experience showed in the case of the Standard Oil Trust, of the Beef Trust, and of the Sugar Trust, that the obtaining of rebates from the railroads is one of the commonest forms of unfair competition. The La Follette bill has therefore specified the conviction of rebating as of itself establishing that unreasonableness of the restraint exists.

While the La Follette bill in Section 10 enumerates certain practices of unfair competition, it provides also generally that the resort by a combination in restraint of trade of [to] unfair or oppressive methods of competition make the competition unreasonable.

I suggest that Section 10 of the La Follette bill should be modified by inserting certain other well-known practices of unfair competition like the following:

(1) Espionage of the business of any competitor either through bribery of any agent or employee of such competitor or obtaining information from any public official, or otherwise through violation of a breach of trust or duty. This practice was one effectually used by the Tobacco Trust, and also by the Standard Oil Trust, to crush competitors and is obviously unfair competition.

(2) Giving away, selling at or below the cost of manufacture to aid the distribution of any of its products, or adopting like methods of cut throat competition for the purpose of destroying or crushing the business of a competitor. This, also, is a method of unfair competition extensively practiced by both the Standard Oil and the Tobacco Trust, and effectively used by them to crush competition. It is obviously unfair competition and any restraint

of trade in connection with which this is practiced is an unreasonable restraint, which should be declared illegal.

(3) Doing business directly or indirectly under any name other than its corporate name;—one of the common resources of the trusts in unfair competition has been conducting business ostensibly as an independent; for instance, using some subsidiary concern ostensibly independent as an instrument for crushing competitors. This was one of the commonest as well as one of the meanest methods adopted by the Tobacco Trust for crushing its competitors. It is obviously unfair competition, and a restraint of trade of which this is an incident is unreasonable, and should be declared illegal.

I therefore suggest as covering the above the following additional clauses for Section 10 of the bill:[1]

Practices Presumptively Unreasonable.

The practices above enumerated, frequently practised by trusts and combinations, have been recognized as necessarily harmful, and as therefore making restraint unreasonable wherever found. There are other practices which do not necessarily render combinations or conspiracies in restraint of trade harmful or mischievous, and hence unreasonable, but ordinarily have that effect. In Section 11 of the La Follette bill these conditions or practices which presumptively, but not necessarily, render combinations or conspiracies in restraint of trade unreasonable are set forth. The section therefore makes the practice a rebuttable presumption of unreasonableness.

Thus, if a conspiracy or restraint of trade is established the fact that it enjoyed entire control of at least forty per cent of the business in the market involved renders the restraint presumptively unreasonable. In other words it is declared with legal presumption that the control of forty per cent of an article is unreasonable; but though that probability is given legal recognition an opportunity is offered of establishing that the contrary is true. I am inclined to think that this percentage should be reduced to thirty.

In Section b of article 11 there is set forth as one of the practices creating a presumption of unreasonableness the fact that the vender, with a view to preventing competition, fixes an unreasonably high price on an article which his competitor must use. For instance, in the manufacture of plug tobacco licorice paste is essential. If the combination fixes an unreasonably high price on licorice paste that the competitor must buy, under this class of

[1] Here follows a blank space.

facts it would create a presumption of unreasonableness. I am inclined to think that that presumption ought to be conclusive, and that clause b should be inserted in Section 10 instead of being in Section 11.

It is a well known fact that the Tobacco Trust used this method of unfiar [unfair] competition in respect to both licorice paste and tin foil, and that until the commencement of the prosecution by the Government in connection with its licorice paste monopoly the Trust charged its competitors at an extortionate price for licorice paste.

The method adopted by the La Follette bill of removing a part of the realm of uncertainty as to what conditions render restraint of trade unreasonable, and therefore illegal, finds its analogy in other branches of the law. For instance, in the law of negligence. In early days there was uncertainty as to what conduct would be required of a person crossing a railroad track, in order to avoid the charge of lack of reasonable care. In the course of time experience developed that a man must stop, look and listen. That obligation came gradually to be recognized as a rule of law. It was a part of the law that in case of the dishonor of a note, notice must be sent to the maker within a reasonable time. What was a reasonable time long remained a question of doubt. Gradually the rule of law developed that notice must be sent within twenty-four hours. Our experience is constantly developing for us laws of human conduct, and certain facts, judgment upon which might at one time have been doubtful, later received a certain legal effect.

Second: Making Enforcement of the Law Easier.

This is effected by the La Follette bill, by adding to the Sherman Law Section 9, a provision that whenever it shall appear that there was a combination or conspiracy in restraint of trade the burden of proof to establish the reasonableness of the restraint shall be upon the party who contends that the restraint is reasonable.

At present when either the Government or an individual seeks to enforce the Sherman Law, the burden of proof is upon the prosecutor or plaintiff to establish not only the existence of a restraint of trade, but also that the restraint is unreasonable. In criminal proceedings proof must be made beyond the question of a doubt. Clearly if such a conspiracy is established, the burden of showing that it is not harmful, or at least that it is not unreasonable, ought to be upon him who makes that contention.

Section 9, while recognizing absolutely the rule of reason as enunciated by the Supreme Court, declares the rule of common sence which is to prevail in applying that rule of reason. If it is justifiable to restrain trade the party who does so restrain trade ought to show the justification.

This provision is analogous to the provision introduced in the Interstate Commerce Law in 1910, when it was provided that where a carrier undertakes to increase a rate, and the reasonableness of the rate is question, the burden of proof shall be upon the carrier to establish the reasonableness of the increase. The wisdom and justice of this rule was clearly demonstrated recently in the Advance Rate Cases.

Third: Making the Remedy Adequate.

The inadequacy of the remedies now provided by the Sherman Law, at least as interpreted by the Courts, is obvious. This inadequacy shows itself

(1) in the failure to give redress to those who have been injured by the illegal operations of the combination, and at the same time leaving the combination in the possession of its illegally gotten gains.

(2) in the failure to provide for such a disintegration of the combination as will restore competition.

1. A Remedy for Those Injured.

The inadequacy of the present law is manifested most clearly in its failure either to afford compensation or to administer punishment, even though the violations of the act have been judicially established. The Standard Oil and Tobacco cases afford a signal illustration of this defect. Each of these industrial combinations has been the means by which hundreds of millions of dollars have been extorted from the public, and hundreds, probably thousands, of independent business concerns have been ruthlessly crushed. Hardly one of the consumers, and almost none of the producers or dealers who fell a victim before the illegal practices of these trusts has been or will be compensated as a result of the recent dicisions. All the fruits of the illegal practices are left to the enjoyment of the rapacious officers or stockholders of these companies. No reparation is made for the past wrongs so profitably pursued. Obviously this is a complete failure of justice tending to bring not only this law but all laws into disrepute. Even if these decisions should result in preventing a recurrence of these wrongs, we are nevertheless confronted with the rank social and industrial injustice that there is no remedy and no punishment for past wrongdoing and suffering inflicted. As the wrongfulness of the acts and the illegality of the conspiracies engaged in by these combinations have been judicially established, it would follow, under a proper judicial system, as a matter of course, that those who were injured thereby should be enabled to recover compensation, and that the wrongdoer should be obliged (so far as then feasible) to disgorge profits wrongfully obtained.

The present failure of justice in this respect is due mainly to two causes.

First: While every person injured by the Standard Oil or the Tobacco conspiracies has the right, under the Sherman Anti Trust Law, to bring an action for damages, the expense of bringing such an action would ordinarily be prohibitive, because these companies could and would compel each plaintiff to prove over again the facts on which they were recently found to be guilty. And it will be borne in mind that the testimony in the Standard Oil case alone filled twenty-four printed volumes. A right in the individual of recovery, which existing [exists] only under conditions which permit the company to raise again a question which has been settled against it by final judgment in a proceeding instituted by the Government on behalf of the people,—including the injured individual,—is clearly a substantial denial of the right of recovery. Obviously, under any proper system for administering the law, when once a concern has been declared to have violated the Anti Trust Act in a proceeding in which the Government, which represents all persons except the defendant, was a party, the issue ought to be deemed definitely settled against the defendants for all purposes and for all times.

Second: Even if the circumstances were such as would justify an injured party seeking compensation after these companies had been judicially found to have violated the law by government proceeding, the private individual would, under the present law, probably find his claim barred, in whole or in part, by the statute of limitations, owing to the long period of time which necessarily elapses between the commencement of a proceeding by the government to enforce the law, and the entry of final judgment.

The new bill undertakes to remedy this failure of justice, that is—to make the remedy of the individual more adequate and complete through the following provisions:

Section 12 provides in substance that whenever in any proceeding instituted by the Government, a final judgment is rendered to the effect that the defendant has entered into a combination or conspiracy in unreasonable restraint of trade, that finding shall be conclusive as against the defendant in any proceeding brought against him by any person or corporation. A person injured by the illegal combination who brought suit for damages would, under the new bill, be relieved from proving the wrongfulness of the defendant's act. It would be necessary for him to prove merely the amount of the loss which he has suffered by reason of the defendant's act,—a comparatively simple matter.

Section 13 seeks to further facilitate the remedy of injured parties by enabling them to establish their claim for damages or to secure other appropriate relief in the same proceeding in which the Government obtained its final judgment. The right to file such a petition in the pending suit may often be a much simpler and less expensive course than to institute an independent suit, and it may result in a much swifter remedy by reason of the fact that the petition would come before a court which had already familiarized itself with the complicated facts involved in such litigation.

Section 14 removes the danger of the injured party losing his right to compensation through lapse of time, for it provides that a cause of action should not be barred if begun within three years after the entry of the final judgment declaring the law to have been violated.

The provision above described would not only afford to the injured party an adequate remedy, but would also prove powerful as a deterrent to law breaking, for by making effective the remedy of those injured it would, in connection with the existing provisions of the Sherman Anti Trust Act (under which treble damages, together with an allowance for counsel fees, may be awarded), make real and appropriate the financial punishment to the corporation for engaging in illegal practices. With such provisions and reasonable certainty that the Government would do its duty in enforcing the law, there would be an accounting to be rendered after a decision against an illegal trust, which would make the conduct of its business and the holding of its securities in such a corporation extremely unprofitable. The facilities afforded sufferers are such that they would undoubtedly be widely availed of. If such were now the law, hundreds, and possibly thousands, of petitions would be filed at once in the courts in which the Standard Oil and Tobacco cases are now pending, which would consume a large part of those illegal profits which have been earned through defiance of the law. This provision becomes of increased importance by reason of the fact that the judicial insertion into the anti-trust act of the word "unreasonable" has, from one point of view, greatly added to the difficulty of enforcing a criminal remedy against wrong-doers, it being contended by high authority that a person cannot legally, or at all events properly, be punished criminally for a violation of the law, when the rule of law to be observed was in itself uncertain.

2. Protection of Those Dependent Upon Trusts.

Section 15 provides for the protection of those who through process of monopolization have become absolutely dependent upon a Trust for business existence,—like the Shoe manufacturers upon the United Shoe Machinery Company at present. That Company has so completely extinguished all competition in the supplying of bottoming machines for those that if the United Company refused to lease its machines to a shoe manufacturer, he would be compelled to go out of business. There would be no difficulty in other machines being built, but as there is no market for such machines owing largely to the tying clauses in the United Company's leases, no other machines are being built. Consequently the United Company, having acquired monopoly power the shoe manufacturers ought to be protected until there has been an opportunity for providing a substitute. That means not only time for new machines to be supplied in the market, but also the opportunity to instruct operatives to work the new machines. To-day the United Company might punish a shoe manufacturer by withdrawing its machines on 30 days notice and leave him helpless.

3. To Effectually Restore Competition.

Section 16 provides for power in the Court to do all that is necessary to effectually restore competitive conditions. This is designed particularly to overcome such defective "disintegration" as was practiced in the Tobacco case. The bulk of the Tobacco Company properties were divided among three corporations owned by the same stockholders in the same proportions, and necessarily controlled by the same people. The Independents contended that different parts of the Trust's property should be distributed among different sets of individuals and provision made so that the segments into which the Trust was divided were absolutely distinct each from the other.

Section 16 makes clear the powers which the Court apparently thought it did not possess, and certainly did not exercise.

Section 17 provides for giving to independents and to States interested in the prosecution an opportunity to be heard in the proceedings against the trust.

4. Withdrawing Government Business from Trusts.

Section 18 undertakes to give to Trust prosecutions an added effectiveness through withdrawing from the Trust against which proceedings have been brought the support of the Government which comes through purchase from it. It is an extraordinary fact that the English Government refused to purchase from the Beef Packers while they were under indictment, but the federal government was making purchases from that and other trusts against which proceedings were pending. In other words, while the right hand of the Department of Justice was proceeding against the Trust, all the other departments were supporting the Trust with business and making an effective defense impossible.

Section 18 undertakes to remedy this situation by providing that the Government shall not patronize Trusts against which prosecutions are pending, unless it is necessary to do so, i.e. unless no adequate opportunity exists of obtaining another article of equal utility at a reasonable price.

5. The Patent Monopoly.

Section 19 provides specifically that the possession of a patent gives no greater rights to restrain trade or commerce outside of the precise matter covered by the patent than if no patent existed, and also provides for forfeiting patents used as a part of a combination to illegally suppress competition.

CC MS (WP, DLC).

A Brief Speech in Trenton to the New Jersey Democratic Convention

[[Oct. 1, 1912]]

There are tremendous issues, but we have found the crux of them; we have located the heart of the matter. Our choice is as to whether we shall accept monopoly or destroy the process by which monopoly has been manufactured with all its established dangers and its known control over the affairs of government. We are to decide whether we shall oust our self-constituted masters or accept them permanently.

Make one choice and you will enjoy the confidence of the people for the next generation. Make the other and there will be no chance for the people to free themselves within a generation. This should be the heart of the debate. We have taken an unassailable position and we know now that both branches of the

Republican party are on the defensive—that they have indefensible positions.

I don't think we have to sacrifice anything through our fighting, yet it is a profound satisfaction to know that we are fighting for the right. If the Democratic party throughout the nation will get the fighting ardor into its blood that we have felt here in New Jersey it will have a long and fruitful life ahead of it.

I feel so strongly that I cannot refrain from exhorting you to stand together with a singleness of purpose for the high enterprise in which you are engaged.

Printed in the *Trenton Evening Times*, Oct. 2, 1912.

The Platform of the New Jersey Democratic Party[1]

[[Oct. 1, 1912]]

We, the Democrats of New Jersey, in convention assembled, hereby ratify the platform adopted by our party at Baltimore, and pledge our sincere support to its candidates.

In seeking again the suffrage and support of our fellow citizens of New Jersey, it is proper that we should briefly indicate the policies underlying our party platform, together with a statement of how our past pledges have been kept. The test of future conduct is never better measured than by past performances, and, in setting forth the record of the Democrats of New Jersey, we are confident in the declaration that never before in the history of the state has so large a number of progressive and beneficial legislative enactments been passed as have been passed during the last two years under the administration of the Democratic party. The efforts of the Democratic party for the past two years, in effecting reforms obviously necessary and long desired, upon which opinion in the state had for many years been centered, constitutes a record of achievements without parallel in the political history of the state.

Two years of Democratic administration under Governor Wilson has resulted in the following acts of legislation:

1. A simple and effective direct primary law regulating the selection and nomination of all candidates for public office, including presidential delegates.

2. A stringent corrupt practices act, providing for full and complete publicity of all moneys used in connection with political campaigns.

---

1 While there is no direct evidence about the authorship of this document, internal evidence, vocabulary, phrasing, and style all point to Wilson as the principal author.

3. A practical and human[e] employers' liability act, regulating the relations between employers and employees.

4. An effective and progressive public utilities act.

5. An act prohibiting the employment of children in mercantile establishments during school hours.

6. A semi-monthly pay bill for railroad employees.

7. An act abolishing contract labor in penal institutions, and providing for a state use system.

8. Amendments to the factory laws safeguarding the lives of workers in factories and workshops.

9. An act providing for an eight hour day on state, county and municipal work.

10. Commission government for cities and towns.

Under the progressive policy of the Democratic party the government of New Jersey has been made responsive to the will of the people of the state, and the gates of political opportunity have been opened wide to the humblest of our citizens; the corrupting and blighting influence of money in connection with elections has been greatly lessened; the relation between employers and employees have been improved by humane legislation and laws safeguarding the lives of workmen have been enacted.

The Democratic party, in convention assembled, pledges itself to the continuance of these policies, and to that end, we propose, during the coming year, to set ourselves to the accomplishment of the following objects:

1. We believe in upholding, in all its vigor, the fundamental principle of the direct primary act known as the Geran law, and we pledge ourselves to oppose, and, if possible, to prevent the passage of any act which shall in any way tend to impair its efficiency in operation.

2. We favor the election of United States Senators by a direct vote of the people, and we pledge ourselves to the support of the pending amendments to the federal constitution to that effect.

3. We believe in the speedy administration of the criminal laws of the state and the separation from politics of the instrumentalities for drawing petit and grand juries, so that the possibility of political and other improper influences shall be speedily eliminated.

4. Where certain very important reforms advocated by earnest bodies of citizens cannot be effected in this state without constitutional amendment, therefore, we favor the election by popular vote, under such regulations as may be provided by the Legislature, of a convention for the consideration of all needful amendments to the constitution of the state.

5. The corrupt practices act, passed during the first year of

Governor Wilson's term, designed to eliminate the purchasing power of money in politics, we intend to maintain in all its vigor, believing that the freedom of the voter in exercising his suffrage should be a matter of careful regulation, and that the utmost publicity concerning campaign expenses, together with a speedy and accurate accounting after all primaries and elections, will tend to minimize the possibility of corrupting influence and render the contest for office as free as possible under existing political conditions.

6. As a mode of securing the use of public buildings to the people responsible for their existence, and to lessen the increasing cost of elections, we heartily recommend the use of schoolhouses and public buildings for political and other neighborhood and public meetings, as well as for elections, under proper local regulation.

7. For the purpose of securing to the citizens of the various municipalities within the state the power to govern themselves, we are in favor of such laws as will give them the right to enjoy the greatest home rule possible in all matters affecting their local governments.

8. We call the attention of the people of this state to the enactment of the laws passed during the session of 1912, which laws tend to the simplification of civil procedure in our law courts. We believe that after a fair trial of these measures, the criticism made against the court's delays will disappear, and that the expensiveness of litigation will be minimized; that technicalities will no longer be permitted to stand in the way of justice and of the merits of controversies.

9. We pledge our party to the establishment and extension of the agricultural and forestry schools in rural sections, and to the continuance of the industrial and vocational schools in the cities.

10. We believe in the immediate readjustment of our system of taxation, and to that end favor such changes in our laws in regard to this matter as will provide a more satisfactory means of assessing and equalizing taxes.

11. We believe that our present corporation act has been used as an instrument to create conditions which have resulted injuriously to the public. We favor an immediate investigation of the method of incorporation pursued in this state under our laws, and we pledge our party to the enactment of such salutary checks upon incorporation and increase of capital and merger corporations as will effectually tend to prevent monopolies and have a wholesome tendency to restrict the issuance of securities, unless the issuance is founded upon bona fide valuation.

12. We reaffirm our allegiance to the principle that the natu-

ral resources of the state should be considered as common to our whole people; that the benefits accruing from the proper conservation of these natural resources should result from their development under public control, and that in pursuance of this policy our water rights and other natural resources should not be permitted to be used, whether owned by the state or privately, for any purpose injurious to the public welfare, and we believe that the wilful destruction of forest resources should be prevented by well considered laws.

13. We pledge our party to the continued support of our public utilities commission, together with an extension of its powers of supervision, so that the rights of the people of the state and of the corporations affected by this particular commission shall be justly and impartially guarded. And in this regard we believe that the commission, in addition to having the power to suspend increased rates pending the investigation of the propriety thereof, should have the power to grant or withhold its permission for the issuance of corporate securities for the protection of investors.

14. We believe that any legislative provision which has for its purpose the betterment of conditions, whether in the city or county, is particularly praiseworthy, and we record our approval of the parcels post service, and urge upon our representatives in Congress and in the Senate of the United States, the desirability of securing as speedily as possible an extension of this form of transportation, which is a matter of great importance to the residents of our rural communities, and we favor a constant and well regulated policy of road building and road maintenance, so that the rural counties in this state may enjoy the benefits of a scientific road construction.

15. In calling attention to the work of the Democratic party during the last session in regard to these measures of social and industrial justice, including the workmen's compensation act, and the laws affecting women and minors, we reiterate our sincere desire to exact such legislation as will effectually prevent or minimize industrial accidents and tend to decrease those diseases incident to particular undertakings, an enlargement of the powers of the state labor department, an extension of the workmen's compensation and employers' liability act, complete publicity of the reports of industrial accidents and diseases, and the careful regulation of the hours of labor for children.

16. We believe in the extension of the powers of the department of labor and the state health department, so that those parts of our state government may be properly maintained, believing

that these departments, whose supervision is of a purely humanitarian nature, should be wholly separated from politics; that when their scope is enlarged they should be given an adequate number of inspectors adapted to their increased needs; that the authority to enforce any necessary regulation pertaining to these departments should be of a summary character.

17. We also favor and endorse the efforts which our state and its various institutions are making for the preservation of the public health, and, for the purpose of effectually coping with the problem of tuberculosis, we believe in the establishment of a system of expert medical inspection of all school children, and the enlargement under expert supervision of a sanitarium for those affected with incipient tuberculosis. To those unfortunates who, by reason of defects of intellect, poverty or enforced confinement are at the present time wards of the state, we favor a liberal provision, estimated under proper authority, for their maintenance and the bestowal upon them of all care possible, so that their deficiencies may be remedied, or their condition at least ameliorated.

18. We pledge the immediate enactment of legislation, not less stringent than that in force in other states, whereby, subject to the regulation of the Public Utilities Commission or of such other body as may be designated for that purpose, there shall be promptly undertaken the elimination of every dangerous railroad grade crossing in the state, under such terms as to the distribution of the expense of such work as may be determined by the Legislature. We point to the fact that the Republican party, having control of the Legislature of 1912, despite explicit pledges, made no effort to solve the important problem until the busy closing days of the session, when adequate consideration and debate were impossible. The measure then proposed and forced through by the majority was obviously designed more for political than for practical purposes, and was on its face a lame, ineffective and unstatesmanlike solution of a great state problem.

19. We favor safeguarding railway travel, as far as possible, and therefore pledge ourselves to the passage of a law to accomplish the purposes contemplated in the full crew bill, which for the past two sessions failed to pass the Republican Senate.

20. We denounce the repeated efforts of our Republican opponents at the last session of the Legislature in endeavoring to procure over the veto of a Democratic Governor, the enactment into law of several measures designed to weaken and nullify the provisions of the Geran election law and corrupt practices act, and call the attention of the voters of the state to the action of the

Republican House and Senate in passing over the Governor's veto a large number of bills increasing the salaries of municipal officers without the intervention or concurrent action of the local responsible financial authorities.

21. We call attention to the fact that, under the careful and efficient administration of the state comptroller's department, the receipts of the state from collateral inheritance taxes have been so largely increased that, although the appropriations for the current fiscal year exceed those of 1911 by $400,000, the balance at the close of the current fiscal year will equal, if not exceed, the balance of the fiscal year of 1911.

22. We favor the creation by new legislation of county sinking fund commissions, whose members must be specially qualified and none of whom shall hold any other public office.

23. We favor legislative enactments requiring the installation of a uniform system of accounting for the municipalities and counties of this state.

Printed in the *Trenton Evening Times*, Oct. 2, 1912.

From Alexander Jeffrey McKelway

Dear Governor Wilson: Trenton, N. J., October 2, 1912.

I saw in yesterday's papers that you would be in Trenton this morning, and came by on my way from New York with the bare hope of seeing you.

For the past ten days I have been much interested in the plans at National Headquarters for the organization of the social workers of the country in your behalf. I have been in conference with Mr. John M. Glenn, of the Russell Sage Foundation,[1] Mr. Williams, of the Charity Organization Society of New York,[2] and others, and I had a chat with Mr. Frank P. Walsh[3] yesterday afternoon.

I regret very much that the Social Centre Bureau was organized under that name. It means nothing to the social worker. While the use of the school plant, for social service of various kinds, is universally recognized by social workers as a good thing, there is really no issue concerning this, and the confining of social service interests to this single idea, is rather unfortunate. If it is not too late, I wish that you would suggest to Mr. Walsh a change in the name to the "Social Service Bureau."[4] I agreed to furnish him a list of names from my correspondence which he can reach; he has some other lists, and I think the literature which he is sending out will be of help to your cause.

I suggest that he might consult, to advantage, with Mr. Hastings H. Hart,[5] 105 East Twenty-Second Street, also of the Russell Sage Foundation, who is a brother of Professor Albert Bushnell Hart,—but, unlike his brother, is devoted to your interests, and prefers your candidacy to that of the ex-President from the point of view of the aid you would give, as President, to the various causes of social reform. I am sure that Dr. Hart could place some time at Mr. Walsh's disposal.

May I take the liberty of suggesting, that at a convenient opportunity on your Western trip, you make mention, in your own inimitable way, of what the Federal Government can do and what State governments can do for the promotion of human welfare in the narrower sense of that phrase? The third party'[s] program is a very alluring one to social workers who do not stop to think of the limited powers of the Federal Government to carry out their program. The more intelligent among them, however, fully understand that, in regard to most of these reform movements, the National Government can aid only in the way of investigation and publicity through existing agencies, such as the Bureau of Labor, the Bureau of Education, the Census Bureau and the Children's Bureau, or through special commissions, like the Commission on Industrial Relations, which was passed by the last Congress, and of which Congressman Hughes, of New Jersey,—who, I hope, will soon be Senator Hughes,—was the sponsor in the House. This is a most valuable function of the National Government, in the opinion of those who need accurate and standardized information concerning the problems with which they are dealing;—and the people whom I may be said to represent, have been very impatient with the attitude of most of the reactionary Republicans, and with some of the same kind of Democrats, like Mr. Fitzgerald, of the Appropriations Committee. The other thing that the Federal Government can do, is to set a good example to the states within its unquestioned jurisdiction, such as the District of Columbia, Alaska, Porto Rico and the Philippines, in the line of model laws and model institutions for the promotion of human welfare and the care of the unfortunate.

May I suggest also, that you send out a message to the effect that Progressive Democrats in their several state jurisdictions, should stand for:

Modern principles of prison reform, such as are being worked out by the American Prison Association.

The adoption of the uniform child labor law, which was recently adopted unanimously by the American Bar Association, formulated by the Commission on Uniform State Laws; the New Jersey law very nearly approximates it now.

The establishment of Juvenile Courts and Reformatories.

The proper care of defectives.

The care of dependent children.

And adequate appropriations from the public tr[e]asury for the various phases of human welfare work.

As I may have written you before, the strong hold which Mr. Roosevelt has upon the majority of social workers is their knowledge of his ready sympathy and his willingness to do anything in his power to forward their various hobbies.

To my mind, the fault in the platform of the third party is the failure to call immediately for a National Constitutional Convention to enable the Federal Government to accomplish the ends set forth; but I presume that even Mr. Roosevelt balked somewhat at this.

I trust that you will pardon this over-long communication, and will believe I am thinking only of the good effect upon a large number of worthy people, in their proper understanding of your position upon these questions.

Your address to the college men in New York Saturday night was a most inspiring one, and I hope that a copy cam [can] be put in the hands of every college graduate in the country.

I have the honor to remain,

Your obedient servant,   A. J. McKelway.

TLS (WP, DLC).

[1] John Mark Glenn, director of the foundation since 1907.

[2] Mornay Williams, lawyer of New York, president of the New York Juvenile Asylum, 1897-1909, active in promoting legislation for the improvement of labor conditions and prison reform.

[3] Francis Patrick Walsh, noted reformer and lawyer of Kansas City; at this time head of the Social Center Bureau of the Democratic national headquarters.

[4] McKelway's suggestion was adopted forthwith.

[5] Hastings Hornell Hart, director of the Russell Sage Foundation's Department of Child-Helping.

An Address in Indianapolis on Conservation[1]

[Oct. 3, 1912]

Mr. Chairman[2] and fellow citizens: It is with genuine pleasure that I find myself in this place, facing a company of men and women who are devoting themselves to so disinterested a cause as that to which this congress is consecrated. Your chairman has stated in exactly the terms of my own thought the errand upon which I have come. It would seem presumption upon my part to instruct this congress or to attempt to instruct it in the means of

[1] Delivered in the Indianapolis Coliseum to the National Conservation Congress.

[2] John Barber White, president of the congress.

conservation. I have come here, as he has said, to share in the inspiration of the occasion, to gather into my own thought an impression of the men and women who are working for these great objects in the United States.

When I was on my way out here and was thinking of this occasion, I prepared my talk on the conservation of our natural resources. When I arrived at the station I was told to change the subject, that that was not what the congress was this year devoting its particular attention to, but to the conservation of the vital energy of the people of the United States. I had thought that I would have to apologize to you for wandering off, before I had finished my address, into that very topic, because it seems to me that the more broadly we view the field of obligation, the more clearly it will appear to us that our duty is only shown in respect of the laying of the foundations, when we have conserved the natural resources of America, for those natural resources are of no consequence unless there is a free and virile people to use them.

We are in the midst of a political campaign, and most of the audiences that I have faced have been political audiences. I want to say very frankly to you that it is a comfort to me to face another kind, because in a campaign we take politics, as it were, to the people. But on this occasion the people of the United States are bringing to us the great forces of their thought. A congress like this means something more vital in some aspects than any ordered effort of political parties, for here are represented the men and women from every quarter of the Union, come together to speak that great volunteer voice of America, which is the atmosphere of politics, which creates the environment of the public man, which is the unbidden conscience of a great people asserting itself and instructing those who would hear it what their lines of best service are. All voluntary effort distinguishes a free people from a people that is not free. An effort, an organization, that comes about whether the politician wants it to or not is the kind of effort and organization which shows that the people are ready to govern themselves and to assert their own opinions, whether the men now in the public eye consent to be their public servants or not.

I have often made this boast about America, that dearly as we love our own institutions, proud as we are of the political history of America, if you could imagine our absolutely forgetting overnight the documents upon which our constitutional history rests, in the morning we could make a new constitution. We would not lose our self-possession. We would not lose our long training in self-control. We would not lose our instinct and genius for self-government. Strip us of one government and we would make a new government in which we would shine as much as we shone in the old. If that be not true, then this is not America, for America consists in the independent and originative power of the thought of the people.

And so, when men and women from every part of the country gather in a great congress like this to treat, not of matters of interest so much as matters of duty, you realize at a gathering like this the vitality of the heart as well as of the mind of America. And men of every sort must give heed to the utterances of gatherings of this kind. I know that there are some persons who come to these gatherings representing only themselves. I know that a gathering of men interested in special objects is a great magnet to the crank. I know that all sorts of people with special notions of their own come, sometimes, to exploit them. But, after all, we ought to be very tolerant even of them, because some of the finest notions in the world have lived for a little while very lonely in the brain of a single man or a single woman. It is only by the foolishness of preaching that they get their currency and finally gain their imperial triumph by conquering the minds of the world. So it is these volunteer tributaries of thought, these irresistible currents of the national life, that are the most vital part of every people's history. That is the reason I say that it is a comfort to face an audience that I am not trying to persuade with regard to anything, but with which I am trying to get in sympathy, in order to share the great forces which they represent.

It would be almost like assuring you that I was a thoughtful and rational being to say that I am in profound sympathy with the whole work of this great congress, and that I am in particular sympathy, in keenest sympathy, with that part which affects the conservation of the vital energy of the people of the United States. We have prided ourselves, ladies and gentlemen, upon our inventive genius. We have prided ourselves upon the ability to devise machines that can almost dispense with the intelligence of men. We have become a great manufacturing people because of this genius, because of our ability to make, not only the tangible machinery of great enterprises, but also the intellectual machinery of great enterprises. And we have been so proud of the mere multiplication of the resources of the nation, so proud of its wealth, so proud of the ingenious methods by which we have increased its wealth, that we have sometimes been almost in danger of forgetting what the real root of the whole matter is.

I say, without intending to indict anybody, that it has too often

happened that men have felt themselves obliged to dismiss superintendents who overtaxed a delicate piece of machinery, who
have not gone further and felt obliged to dismiss a superintendent who overtaxed that most delicate of all pieces of machinery,
the human body and the human brain. If you drive your men and
women too hard, your machinery will presently have to go on the
scrap heap. If you sap the vital energy of your people, then there
will be no energy in any part of the life that you live or in any
enterprise that you may undertake, and the energy of your people is not merely a physical energy.

I am glad to say that the great State of New Jersey, which I
have the honor to represent, has been very forward among her
sister states in attempting to safeguard the lives and the health
of those who work in her factories and in all the undertakings
which are in danger of impairing their health. I am glad to say
that our legislature has been to a very considerable extent, though
not so far as it ought to be, thoughtful of the health of children,
thoughtful of the strength of women, thoughtful of the men and
women together who have to breathe noxious gases and who are
exposed to certain kinds of dust bred in certain manufactories,
which dust carries congestion, disease, and danger to the lungs
and to the whole system. We have been thoughtful of these
things, but, after all, we stand in exactly the same relation to our
bodies that the nation stands to her forests and her rivers and her
mines. I have no use for my body unless I have a free and happy
soul to be a tenant of it. We have no happy use for this continent
unless we have a free and hopeful and energetic people to use it.

I know that I have sometimes spoken of how foreigners laugh
at Americans because they boast of the size of America, as if they
made it. And we are twitted with a pride in something that we did
not create. We didn't stretch all this great body of earth and pile
it into beautiful mountains and valleys and variegate it with forests from ocean to ocean. And they say, "Why should you be so
proud of what God created? You were not partners in the creation." But it seems to me that it is perfectly open for us to reply
that any nation is as big as the thing that it accomplishes, and
we have reason to be proud of the size of America because we
have occupied and dominated it. But we have come to a point
where occupation and domination will not suffice to win us credit
with the nations of the world or with our own respect. It was fine
to have the cohesive and orderly power to plant commonwealths
from one side of this great continent to the other. It was pretty
fine, and it strikes the imagination to remember the time when
the ring of the axe in the forest and the crack of the rifle meant

not merely the felling of a tree or the death of some living thing, but it meant the voices of the vanguard of civilization making spaces for homes, destroying the wild life that would endanger human life, or destroying the life which it was necessary to destroy in order to sustain human life; and that the mere muscle, the mere quickness of eye, the mere indomitable, fearless courage of those pioneers that crossed this continent ahead of us was evidence of the virility of the race, and was also evidence of its capacity to rule and to make conquest of the things that it needed to use.

But now we have come to a point where everything has to be justified by its spiritual consequences, and the difficult part of the task is that which is immediately ahead of us. Until the census of 1890, every Census Bureau could prepare maps for us on which the frontiers of settlement in America were drawn. And until that time there had always been an interspace between the frontier movement westward and the little strip of coast upon the Pacific, which had been occupied, as it were, prematurely and out of order. But in 1890 it was impossible to draw a frontier in the United States. It was impossible to show any places where the spaces had not, at any rate, been sparsely filled, sparsely occupied by the populations that lived under the flag of the Union. It was about that time, by the way, or eight years later, that we were so eager for a frontier that we established a new one in the Philippines, in order, as Mr. Kipling would say, to satisfy the feet of our young men. But the United States, ever since 1890, has been through with the business of beginning and now has the enormously more difficult task before it of finishing.

It is very easy, I am told, though I have never tried it, roughly to sketch in a picture, that all the students in art schools can make the rough sketch reasonably well, but that almost all people, except those who have passed a certain point, spoil the picture in the finishing. All the difficulties, all the niceties of art, lie in the last touches, not in the first. All the difficulties and niceties of civilization lie in the last touches, not in the first. Anybody with courage and fortitude and resourcefulness can set up a frontier, but we have discovered, to our cost, that not many of us can set up a successful city government. Almost all the best governed cities in the world are on the other side of the water. Almost all of the worst governed cities in the world, in the civilized world, are in America. And the thing that is most taxing our political genius is making a decent finish where we made such a distinguished beginning. You can feel it under you as you traverse a city. You can feel it in the pavements—they are provisional, most of them, or haven't been laid at all. And in jolting in the streets that are not the main thoroughfares of an American city, you feel the jolt of unfinished America. We haven't had time or we have let the contract to the wrong man, but whatever be the cause, we have not completed the job in a way that ought to be satisfactory to our pride.

You know that we are waiting for the development of an American literature, so I am told. Now, literature can't be done with the flat hand. You can't write an immortal sentence by taking a handful of words out of the dictionary and scattering them across the page. They have to be wrought together with the vital blood of the imagination in order to speak to any other readers except those of the day itself. And as in all forms of art, whether literary or musical or sculptural, there is this final test, can you finish what you began? I believe, therefore, that the problem of this congress is just this problem of putting the last touches on the human enterprise which we undertook in America. We didn't undertake anything new in America in respect of our industry. You will not find anything in the way of industry in America which cannot be matched elsewhere in the world. If the happiness of our people and the welfare of our people does not exceed the happiness and welfare of other people, then as Americans we have failed, because we promised the world, not a new abundance of wealth, not an unprecedented scale of physical development, but a free and happy people. That is the final pledge which we shall have to redeem, and if we don't redeem it then we must admit an invalidity to the title deeds of America.

America was set up and opened her doors in order that all mankind might come and find what it was to release their energies in a way that would bring them comfort and happiness and peace of mind, and we have to see to it that they get happiness and comfort and peace of mind. And we have got to lend the efforts, not only of great voluntary associations like this, but the efforts of our state governments and our national government to this highest of all enterprises, to see that the people are taken care of. Not taken care of in the sense that those are taken care of who cannot take care of themselves, because the best way to teach a boy to swim is to throw him into the water. And too much inflated apparatus around him will only prevent his learning to swim, because the great object in swimming is not to go to the bottom, and many of the devices by which we now learn to swim make it unnecessary to swim because you can stay on top just the same. And I, for my part, do not believe that human vitality is assisted by making it unnecessary for it to assert itself. On the contrary, I believe that it is quickened only when it is put under such stimulation as to feel the whip, whether of necessity or of interest, to quicken it.

But the last crux of the whole matter comes here: I am not interested in exerting myself unless the exertion, when it is over, brings me satisfaction. If I have to work in such conditions that every night I fall into my bed absolutely exhausted and with the lamp of hope almost at its last dying flicker, then I don't care whether I get up in the morning or not. And when I get up in the morning I don't go blithely to my work, I don't go to my work like a man who relishes the tasks of life. I go there because I must go or starve. And there is always the goad at my stomach, the goad at my heart, because those dependent upon me will suffer if I don't go to the work. And the only way in which I can go to my work with satisfaction is by feeling that wherever I turn I am dealing with fellow men, with fellow human beings.

So that we must take the heartlessness out of industry before we can put heart in the men who are engaged in industry. The employer has got to feel that he is dealing with flesh and blood like his own and with his fellow men, or else his employees will not be in sympathy with him and will not be in sympathy with the work. And a man who is not in sympathy with his work will not produce the things that are worth using.

All the stories we tell, all the stories we tell to our children about work, are told of such men as Stradivarius, who lingered in the making of a violin as a lover would linger with his lady, who hated to take his fingers from the beloved wooden box which was yielding its music to his magic touch. And that to our minds, in all poetry and song since Stradivarius, that has been to us the type of the genius of human art that goes into work that is done with affection, with zest. We point to some of the exquisitely completed work of the stone carvers of the Middle Ages, the little hidden pieces tucked away unseen in the great cathedral, where the work is just as loving in its detail and completeness as it is upon the altar itself. And we say, "This is the efflorescence of the human spirit expressed in obscure work." The man knew that nobody, except perhaps an occasional adventurer climbing to repair the cathedral, would ever see that work, but he wrought it for the sake of his own heart and in the sight of God. And that we instinctively accept as the type of the spiritual side of work.

Now, imagine, ladies and gentlemen, imagine as merchants and manufacturers and bankers, what would happen to the industrial supremacy of the United States if all her workmen worked in that spirit of love and sympathy for their work? Would there be goods anywhere in the world that could for one moment match the goods made in America? Wouldn't the American label be a labor of spiritual distinction? And how are you going to bring that about? Why, you are going to bring it about by the work, by such work as this congress is interested in and the work which will ensue. Because the things you are discussing now are merely the passageways to things that are better. Just so soon as you make it a matter of conscience with your legislators to see to it that human life is conserved wherever modern processes touch it; just so soon as you make it the duty of society to release the human spirit occasionally on playgrounds surrounded with beauty, to give it even in cities the touch of nature and the freedom of the open sky; just so soon as you realize, and have all of society realize, that play, enjoyment, is part of the building up of the human spirit, and that the load must sometimes be lifted or else it will be a breaking load; just as soon as you realize that every time you touch the imagination of your people and quicken their thought and encourage their hope and spread abroad among them the sense of human fellowship and of mutual helpfulness, you are elevating all the levels of the national life. Then you will begin to see that your factories are doing better work, because sooner or later this atmospheric influence is going to get into every office in the United States, and men are going to see that the best possible instruments they can have are men whom they regard as partners and fellow beings.

I look upon a congress like this as the indispensable instrument, as one of the indispensable instruments, of the public life. Law, ladies and gentlemen, does not run before the thought of society and draw that thought after it. Law is nothing else but the embodiment of the thought of society. And when I see great bodies of men and women like this running ahead of the law and beckoning it on to fair enterprises of every sort, I know that I see the rising tide which is going to bring these things in inevitably. I know that I see law in the making. I know that I see the future forming its lines before my eyes. And that presently, when we come to agreement, and whenever we come to substantial agreement, we shall have the things that we desire. So that for a man in public life an assemblage like this is the food of his thought, if he lend his thought to what his fellow countrymen are desiring and planning. And all the zest of politics lies not in holding things where they are, but in carrying them forward along the lines of promise to the place where they ought to be.

You are our consciences. You are our mentors. You are our schoolmasters. The men in public life have only twenty-four hours in their day, and they generally spend eight of the twenty-four sleeping—I must admit, generally, to spending nine—and in what remains they cannot comprehend the interests of a great nation. No man that I ever met, no group of men that I ever met, could sum up in their own thoughts the interests of a varied nation. Therefore, they are absolutely dependent upon suggestions coming from every fertile quarter into their consciousness. They are subject, or they ought to be subject, daily to instruction.

A gentleman was quoting to me today a very fine remark of Prince Bismarck. He was taxed with inconsistency, with holding an opinion today that he had not held yesterday. He said he would be ashamed of himself if he did not hold himself at liberty, whenever he learned a new fact, to readjust his opinions. Now, that is what learning is for. Ought any man to be ashamed to have accepted the Darwinian theory because he didn't hold it before Darwin demonstrated it? Ought any man to be ashamed of having given up the Copernican idea of the universe? Ought any man to be obliged to apologize for having yielded to the facts? If he doesn't, he will sooner or later be very sorry, because the facts are our masters, and if we don't yield to them we will presently be their slaves.

I suppose that if I chose to assert the full consistency of my independence, I would say that I was at liberty to jump from the top of this building. But just as soon as I reached the ground Nature would have said to me, "You fool, didn't you ever hear of the law of gravitation? Didn't you ever hear of any of the things that would happen to you if you jumped off a building of this height? Now suppose you spend a considerable period in a hospital thinking it over." And it would be very impressively borne in upon me what the penalties of the ignorance of the law of gravitation were.

Now, it is going to be very impressively borne in upon the public men of this country, if they ignore them, what the laws of human life are. As Dr. Holmes used to say, the truth is no invalid. You needn't be afraid of how roughly you treat her, she will survive. And if you treat her too roughly, there is a certain reaction that will occur in your own constitution which will be the severest penalty you could carry.

I came, therefore, to Indianapolis today to put my mind at your service—merely to express an attitude, merely to confess a faith, merely to declare the deep interest which must underlie all human effort. For when the last thing is said about human effort, ladies and gentlemen, it lies in human sympathy. Unless the hearts of men are bound together, the policies of men will fail.

Because the only thing that makes classes in a great nation is that they do not understand that their interests are identical. The only thing that embarrasses public action is that certain men seek advantages which they can gain only at the expense of the rest of the country. And when they have gained them, those very advantages prove the heaviest weight they have to carry, because they are then responsible for all that happens to those upon whom they have imposed and to those from whom they have subtracted what was their right. So that the deepest task of our politics is to understand one another. The deepest task of all politics is to understand everybody. And I don't see how everybody is going to be understood unless everybody speaks up. And the more unbidden spokesmen there are, the more vocal the nation is, the more certain we shall be to work out in peace, and finally in pride, the great tasks which lie ahead of us.

T MS (C. L. Swem Coll., NjP), with corrections from the ICF transcript in RSB Coll., DLC, and from the complete text in the *Indianapolis News*, Oct. 4, 1912.

A Campaign Address in Indianapolis Proclaiming the New Freedom[1]

[Oct. 3, 1912]

Mr. Chairman,[2] fellow citizens: It would move any man very deeply, I think, to face a vast concourse like this, and certainly it constitutes for me one of the supreme privileges of my life. I cannot see you, and inasmuch as I am not boastful of my beauty, I trust you cannot see me! But I would, if I could, convey to you some of the thoughts that are suggested to my mind by this vast concourse of people.

It is impossible that a great body of people like this has come together merely out of curiosity, merely out of the habit of political rally, merely in order to show their interest in a political campaign of the ordinary kind. I believe that there is abroad in this country a very profound interest in the fundamental issues of this campaign, and I do not wonder that that interest is profound, for those issues are the issues of life and of death.

I do not believe that any speaker can exaggerate for you the critical character of the present political situation. We talk, and we talk in very plausible phrases, indeed, about returning the government of this country to the people of this country. We did

[1] Delivered in the evening before a vast crowd in the Washington Baseball Park.
[2] Senator John W. Kern.

not (interruption from the crowd) I can assure the gentlemen back there, there is nothing to see. My personal beauty is not the kind to excite admiration. (interruption) Perhaps if everybody would sit down there would be less disturbance. I esteem it a great privilege, therefore, to have an opportunity to discuss, even with those of you whom my voice can reach, the fundamental things of our present national interest. Because, as I think of the great Democratic party which has entrusted me with the responsibility of leading it, I ask myself, "What is the thing that is expected by the people of the United States of this great party?"

Because the thing that we are proposing to do, ladies and gentlemen, is, as I have just now said, to restore the Government of the United States to the people. And this issue has arisen because it is sadly true that the Government of the United States has not been under the control of the people in recent decades. We have found something intervening between us and the government which we supposed belonged to us, something intangible, something that we felt we could not grapple with, something that it was impossible to tear away from—a space that lay between us and the government at Washington. And the thing I want to impress upon your thought tonight is merely this: The Democratic party is the only party that is now proposing to take away the influences which have governed the administration of this country and kept it out of sympathy with the great body of the people.

I want you particularly to notice that there are only two parties in the present campaign, or rather that there is one party and two fragments of another party. Because it is not Democrats that have gone over into the new party, it is almost exclusively Republicans. And what we are facing, therefore, is two segments of a great disrupted party, and those two segments are made up in this way. You know that on the one hand are those who call themselves the regular Republicans, and those on the other hand who try to arrogate to themselves entirely the name of Progressives. But what I want you to realize is that these Progressives have not drawn to themselves the old force, the old insurgent force, of the Republican party.

You know that for a long time we have been seeing this split about to occur in the Republican party. For a long time there have been men showing their courage, here, there, and elsewhere, who, though they still called themselves Republicans, protested against the prevalent policy of the Republican party. These men for a long time were called by different names. In New Jersey we called them the New Idea Republicans, when being fair to the people was a new idea among Republicans. And in other parts of the country they were called by other designations, but presently we began to call them insurgents.

Now, what I want to call your attention to is the fact that the new party, the third party, has not drawn to itself the full strength, or even all the principal leaders, of the insurgent Republicans, because this circumstance appeals to every man who thinks the present situation over. The very things that we are protesting against, the very conditions that we are trying to alter, are conditions which were created under the two leaders of the two branches of the present Republican party, because it is true that these conditions were just as much created under Mr. Roosevelt as they have been created under Mr. Taft. There was a growth during his administration of the great monopolies, which we call trusts, upon a scale never before dreamed of and upon a greater scale than has been characteristic of the administration of his successor.

Some time ago, during the campaign which preceded the two Republican political conventions, you remember that there was a very interesting campaign between Mr. Taft and Mr. Roosevelt. And everything that anybody could say against Mr. Taft, Mr. Roosevelt said. And everything that anybody could say against Mr. Roosevelt, Mr. Taft said. And the Democrats were inclined to believe both of them, for the truth was that Mr. Taft was merely the successor of Mr. Roosevelt in the prosecution of policies which Mr. Taft did not alter but merely sought to confirm and establish.

You have therefore this extraordinary spectacle of the two branches of the Republican party, both of them led by men equally responsible for the very conditions which we are seeking to alter. And the reason that some of the insurgent Republicans are not following Mr. Roosevelt, the reason that men like Mr. La Follette, for example, are not following Mr. Roosevelt, is that they have already tested Mr. Roosevelt when he was President and have found that he was not willing to cooperate with them along any line that would be efficient in the checking of the evils of which we complain. So that the leader of the very movement which is proposed for our emancipation is a man who has been tried in this very matter and not found either willing or competent to accomplish the objects that we now seek.

In order to confirm my view of the matter, you have only to read Mr. La Follette's autobiography,[3] and I advise every man who can lay his hands on a copy of the *American Review* to read

[3] Cited in n. 3 to the address printed at Feb. 24, 1912, Vol. 24.

that extraordinary narrative. There, in detail, it is told how Mr. La Follette and others like him carried proposals to the then President, Mr. Roosevelt, which would have made this campaign inconceivable. And after he had, following his first generous impulse, consented to cooperate with them, he subsequently drew back and refused to cooperate with them, under what influences I do not care to conjecture, because it is not my duty and it would be very distasteful to me to call in question the motives of these gentlemen. That is not my object or my desire. My object is merely to point out the fact that the very conditions we are trying to remedy were built up under these two gentlemen who are the opponents of the Democratic party. Therefore, to my mind it is a choice between Tweedledum and Tweedledee to choose between the leader of one branch of the Republican party and the leader of the other branch of the Republican party, because what the whole country knows to be true, these gentlemen deny.

The whole country knows that special privilege has sprung up in this land. The whole country knows, except these gentlemen, that it has been due chiefly to the protective tariff. These gentlemen deny that special privilege has been caused by the administration of the protective tariff. They deny what all the rest of the country has become convinced is true. And after they have denied the responsibility of the tariff policy for special privilege, they turn about to those creatures of special privilege which we call the trusts—those organizations which have created monopoly and created the high cost of living in this country—and deny that the tariff created them. Not only that, but deny that it is possible to reverse the process by which that monopoly was created, because in the very platform of the third party (if I had thought there would be light enough to read it to you, I would have brought it and read it), in the very platform of the third party, it is not said that they intend to correct the conditions of monopoly, but merely that they intend to assuage them, to render them less severe, to legalize and moderate the processes of monopoly. So that the two things we are fighting against, namely, excessive tariffs and almost universal monopoly, are the very things that these two branches of the Republican party both decline to combat. They do not so much as propose to lay the knife at any one of the roots of the difficulties under which we now labor. On the contrary, they intend to accept these evils and stagger along under the burden of excessive tariffs and intolerable monopolies as best they can through administrative commissions. I say, therefore, that it is inconceivable that the people of the United States, whose instinct is against special privilege and whose deepest convictions are against monopoly, should turn to either of these parties for relief when these parties do not so much as pretend to offer them relief.

It is this circumstance that puts me in a very sober mood. It is this process which makes me feel that great bodies of men of this sort have come together, not in order to whoop it up for a party, not in order to merely look at a candidate, but to show there is a great uprising in this country against intolerable conditions which only the Democratic party proposes to attack and to alter. Only the Democratic party is ready to attack and alter these things. Do you see any breach anywhere in the Democratic ranks? Don't you know that wherever you live men are coming as volunteers, recruits into the ranks of the Democrats? Don't you know that everywhere that you turn men are taking it for granted that the country must follow this party or else wander for another four years in the wilderness?

There are some noble people, there are some people of very high principle, who believe that they can turn in other quarters for relief, but they do so simply because there is one of these parties that blows beautiful bubbles for them to see float in the air of oratory, men who paint iridescent dreams of uplifted humanity, men who speak of going to the rescue of the helpless, men who speak of checking the oppression of those who are overburdened, men who paint the picture of the redemption of mankind and don't admit who they are, who are preaching this doctrine. They are the men whom we have seen and tested, and their conversion is after the time when they possessed the power to do these things and refused to do them.

Is humanity burdened now for the first time? Are men in need of succor now who were not in need of succor ten years ago? Are men now in need of protection by the government who did not need protection when these gentlemen exercised the tremendous power of the office of President? Is it not true that when Theodore Roosevelt was President of the United States the people of the United States were willing to follow him wherever he led? And where did he lead them? When did he turn in the direction of this great uplift of humanity? How long was the vision delayed? How impossible was it for him to see it when his arm was strong to come to the succor of the weak! And now he has seen it, when he wishes to regain their confidence, which by his failure to act he had forfeited!

And so I say it is not as if novices had come before us. It is not as if men had come before us who had seen these things all their lives and waited, waited in vain for an opportunity to do them. For we know the men we are dealing with, and we know that there are men in this third party who are following that leader notwithstanding the fact that they do not believe in him. They simply want a third party because they do not yet find themselves ready to trust the Democratic party and yet are unwilling to trust the regulars among the Republican party. So that they are hoping that something may happen, even under a leader whom they do not have full confidence in, that will enable mankind to find an opportunity to cast its masses against the gates of opportunity and at least burst them open by the great rush of their gathering multitudes. They do not look for guidance. They merely hope for the consummation of their united power in a blind effort to escape something that they fear and dread.

Ah, gentlemen, shall they go under such shepherds? Shall they go deliberately so shepherded? Shall mankind follow those who could have succored them and did not?

Now, on the other hand, what can we say in all honesty and truth of the Democratic party? Why, gentlemen, the Democratic party was preaching these doctrines and offering you leaders to carry them out before these gentlemen ever admitted that anything was wrong or had any dream of the hopes of humanity. We didn't wait until the year 1912 to discover that the plain people in America had nothing to say about their government. We have been telling you that for half a generation and more. We have been warning you of the very things that have come to pass, in season and out of season. We have kept a straight course. We have never turned our faces for one moment from the faith that was in us—the faith in the common people of this great commonwealth, this great body of commonwealths, this great nation. And now what is happening? Why, with renewed hope, with renewed confidence, with renewed ardor of conviction, under leaders chosen after the freest fashion that our politics have ever witnessed—chosen freely at Baltimore, chosen yesterday freely for perhaps the first time within our recollection in the Empire State of New York—untrammeled leaders, leaders who have no obligations except to those who have trusted and believed in them, are now asked to lead the Democratic party along those paths of conviction which these other gentlemen have so recently found, which they have found only now that they see that these are the paths perhaps to a renewal of their power.

I would not speak, I would not say, one word of bitterness, but I do utter my profound protest against the idea that it is possible to do these things through the instrumentality of new converts. I say that those who are rooted and grounded in this faith, those

Wilson accepting the nomination, Sea Girt

Wilson and family on the porch at Sea Girt

Reception at Sea Girt

Talking to school children in Minneapolis

New Jersey Day at Sea Girt

William Howard Taft

Theodore Roosevelt

With Mrs. Wilson and Eleanor in Bermuda

who have been willing to stay out in the cold as minorities through half a generation, are men tried to the bottom of all that is in them. Their stuff is tried out in the furnace, and they are now ready to serve you, and they are ready as an absolutely united team. Where will you find any disinclination to take the signals from the leader? Where will you find any clefts in the Democratic ranks? Is it not true that this solid phalanx, with its banners now cast to the wind, is marching with a tread that shakes the earth to take possession of the government for the people of the United States? This is what heartens the men who are in this fight. This is what quickens their pulses. This is what makes everything worthwhile that has to be done in the honest conduct of a frank campaign.

For our object, as we call you to witness, throughout this campaign is to discuss not persons, but issues. We are not interested in persons. I tell you frankly, I am not interested even in the person who is the Democratic candidate for President. I am sorry for him. I am sorry for him because I believe he is going to be elected, and I believe that there will rest upon him the duty of carrying out these fundamental tasks. And there will be no greater burden in our generation than to organize the forces of liberty in our time in order to make conquest of a new freedom for America. It will be no child's play, but I believe that it will be possible. Because a man is not as big as his belief in himself. He is as big as the number of persons who believe in him. He is as big as the force that is back of him. He is as big as the convictions that move him. He is as big as the trust that is reposed in him by the people of the country. And with that trust, with that confidence, with that impulse of conviction and hope, I believe that the task is possible, and I believe that the achievement is at hand.

And you in Indiana have laid the foundation for the things that are to come. With a great Democratic governor and two distinguished Democratic senators,[4] you have already got into the game and made it certain what Indiana is going to do on the fifth of November. You have made it certain that that splendid man, free from every influence that should not control him, whom the Democrats have nominated for the governorship of this state,[5] will succeed the great governor who is to be Vice-President of the United States.

I want to express my great admiration for and confidence in Mr. Ralston, whom I wish I might greet here in person tonight,

4 Thomas R. Marshall, Benjamin Franklin Shively, and John W. Kern.
5 Samuel Moffett Ralston.

but who is very much better engaged in other parts of the state. And I want to say this to you: There are about a hundred thousand Democrats, as I understand it, in Indiana who—let me finish the sentence—there are about a hundred thousand Democrats in Indiana who haven't registered. Now, remember that the seventh of October—next Monday—will be your last chance to register. And I should hate to see the great State of Indiana lag behind in the procession because some men had forgotten to register. So my advice to you is to register so distinctly that your signature can be heard all over the United States, so that you may get ready to release the great force that is lying ready in this state for the service of the nation and release it entire in its magnificent strength as a whole. I say this because I understand it is a new law in Indiana, your first experience in registering, and I believe that some of you rather resent the necessity of registering, as if somebody doubted your authenticity as a voter in Indiana, as if you hadn't been voting time out of mind, some of you. But it is a great deal better to be a regular voter than a questionable voter.

You know, we passed a law in New Jersey about eighteen months ago which had a very interesting effect. It enabled us to find out how many men long buried in the graveyards had been voting in New Jersey. We first had a definite and rigid registration. Then we sent out sample ballots to all the men who had voted at the preceding election. And in one city alone,[6] eighteen thousand sample ballots were returned because there were no such persons resident in the city. I dare say that a great many of them might have been found if the inscriptions upon the gravestones had been properly searched, because we had been largely governed in New Jersey by a spook population. But now we have the satisfaction of being governed by living men. Not all of them are a satisfaction to us, but most of them are. And when we have tested them recently, most of them knew what they wanted. So that I simply cite this as an example so that you will be inspired to enroll among the living, not be relegated to the classification of the dead.

For the business in hand, my fellow citizens, is very serious business indeed. Any state which does not now get into the procession for the renewal of the rights of man will be sorry for it a generation from now. But if their vote is recorded on the right side on the fifth of November, they will sometimes say to their children, "Yes, we took part in the re-emancipation of America on the fifth of November 1912." And I pray God that no man

6 Newark.

whom you trust on the fifth of November 1912 will ever be coward enough to betray you to your enemies, because with this great
people behind them, those who surrendered again to the malign
influences which have been governing the administration at
Washington would indeed be cowards and renegades.

I beg that when you go to the polls on the fifth of November,
you will go with quiet minds and very sober thoughts. For you
are then to make your choice whether you will live under legalized monopoly for the rest of your lives or seek the way of release,
which it is perfectly possible to find, by seeing to it that those who
have oppressed you open again the fields of competition, so that
new men with brains, new men with capital, new men with energy in their veins, may build up enterprises in America. And,
amidst a nation stimulated to every kind of new endeavor, we
shall find again the paths of liberty, the paths of peace, the paths
of common confidence, and therefore the only paths that lead to
prosperity and success.[7]

T MS (C. L. Swem Coll., NjP); with corrections from the ICF transcript in RSB
Coll., DLC, and from the complete text in the *Indianapolis News*, Oct. 4, 1912.
    [7] There is a WWhw outline of this address dated Sept. [Oct.] 3, 1912, in
WP, DLC.

To William Sulzer

[Indianapolis, Ind., Oct. 3, 1912]

My heartiest congra[t]ulations and good wishes. I am greatly
gratified by the action of the convention.

[Woodrow Wilson]

Printed in the *New York Times*, Oct. 4, 1912.

From William Sulzer

Syracuse N Y Oct 3 12

Many thanks for your congratulations   I shall follow you in
the fight for the rights of the plain people to triumphant victory
for true democracy.

Wm Sulzer

T telegram (WP, DLC).

A Portion of An Address in Kokomo, Indiana[1]

[Oct. 4, 1912]

And for my part, in all that I may have to do in public affairs in the United States, I am going to think of towns like Kokomo in Indiana, towns of the old American pattern, and my thought is going to be bent upon the multiplication of towns of that kind and the prevention of the concentration of industry in this country in such a shape and upon such a scale that towns that own themselves will be impossible.

You know what the vitality of America consists of. Your vitality does not lie in New York. Your vitality does not lie in Chicago. Your vitality will not be sapped by anything that happens in St. Louis. Your vitality lies in your own brains, in your own energies, in your own love of enterprise, in the richness of these incomparable fields that stretch beyond the borders of the town, in the wealth which you extract from nature and originate for yourselves by the inventive genius characteristic of all free American communities. That is the wealth of America, and if America discourages the locality, she will kill the nation. A nation is as rich as her localities, she is not as rich as her capitals. The amount of money in Wall Street is no indication of the energy of the American people. That indication can be found only in the fertility of the American mind and the fertility of American industry everywhere in the United States. If America were not rich and fertile, there would be no money in Wall Street. If America were not vital and able to take care of herself, the great money exchanges would break down.

And I believe that I am preaching the very cause of some of the gentlemen whom I am opposing when I preach the cause of free industry in the United States. For I think they are slowly girdling the tree that bears the inestimable fruits of our life, and that if they are permitted to girdle it entirely nature will take her revenge and the tree will die. I do not believe that America is great because she has great men in her now. I believe that America is great in proportion as she can make sure of having great men in the next generation. I believe that she is rich in her unborn children, rich, that is to say, if those unborn children see the sun in a day of opportunity, see the sun when they are free to exercise their energies as they will. If they open their eyes in a land where there is no special privilege, then they will come into a new era of American greatness and American liberty. But if they open their eyes in a country where they must be employees or nothing, if they open their eyes in a land of merely regulated monopoly, where all the conditions of industry are determined by small groups of men, then they will see an America such as the founders of this great Republic would have wept to think of. They would never have set up these institutions to be made such use of as these gentlemen purport to make of them; for neither the regular nor the irregular Republican party even proposes to do away with monopoly in the United States. The only thing that either of them proposes is to accept monopoly and to regulate it, to consent to live under it, and then try to see if they can't keep monopoly from running over us and destroying us. If monopoly persists, monopoly will always sit at the helm of this government as it is sitting now, and I do not expect to see monopoly restrain itself. If there are men in this country big enough to own the Government of the United States, they are going to own it. For what we have to determine now is whether we are big enough, whether we are men enough, whether we are free enough, to take possession again of the government which is our own. We haven't had free access to it. Our minds have not touched it by way of guidance in half a generation. And now we are engaged in nothing else than the recovery of what was made with our own hands and acts only by our delegated authority.

I tell you, gentlemen, when you discuss the question of the tariffs and of the trusts, you are discussing the very lives of yourselves and your children. The Democratic party is the friend of business, but it is the friend only of free business. It is the absolute, declared, implacable enemy of monopoly of every kind. Our platform says that it is absolutely unbearable, and I entirely subscribe to that. But because we are the friends of free industry, it doesn't mean that we are going to so move, so handle, the tariff, so hasten the processes of change as to unsettle anything that is sound in the United States.

There are men in your community, there are men connected with the manufacture of wire and nails in this town, who know that they are not free, who have said to committees of the Congress of the United States that they could beat their competitors with an altered and lowered tariff, if only the grip that the present steel monopoly has on the raw material, particularly on steel billets, could in some degree be released. This isn't the only country in which they have tried this kind of thing. They are trying it now in Germany and finding exactly the same thing. They have a steel trust there which is a trust covering the raw material and the more crude products of steel. Every competitor of the highly manufactured product has to buy from that trust, and they are finding now that that is smothering, straitening, confining, impeding, the free industries of Germany. And the same thing is happening in this country. Every man who is free is opposed to monopoly, and only those are in favor of monopoly who are either politically or economically bound to monopoly. The serious circumstance of our time is that so many men are politically bound to monopoly, and the more serious circumstance still is that so many men are economically dependent upon monopoly.

Gentlemen, it is a privilege to stand in a place like this facing serious men, discussing serious questions. I am not here to exhibit myself as a candidate. I am here merely, if I may have that privilege, to set your minds close to the vital problems of our whole national development and to bid you make your choice on the fifth of November on principle. Make it for yourselves and your children, make it not only for the State of Indiana, but for the great nation of which the State of Indiana constitutes one of the constituent stars.

Yes, every great commonwealth, every commonwealth, has swung into that blue heaven that is in the corner of the flag. What have we rejoiced in? Have we rejoiced merely that a new link was forged in the chain which men could use to bind us? Have we not rejoiced that a free commonwealth had come into existence? And is it not true that here in Indiana again and again you have produced the voices which have proclaimed the liberties of mankind and the men who have fought for the essential principles of American constitutional liberty?

Indiana cannot afford to forfeit her laurels by coming into the columns of those who support monopoly. The only thing she can afford, in consistency with her past, is to shoulder the responsibility of being free. And I can tell you, without any fear of contradiction, that the only national party that is now compact enough and big enough to carry out this program is the party which has honored me temporarily with its leadership.

T MS (C. L. Swem Coll., NjP).
1 Delivered in the courthouse yard.

A Speech to Workingmen in Peru, Indiana[1]

[Oct. 4, 1912]

Mr. Chairman[2] and fellow citizens: I was very much surprised to hear your chairman just now say that this was the opening of the campaign in this part of Indiana. I had formed the opinion that in Indiana you were like we are in New Jersey—we never

1 Delivered near the railroad station.
2 Charles Albert Cole, lawyer of Peru.

close a campaign in New Jersey, we keep it up all the time—and I supposed that there was as much politics to the square inch in Indiana as there is in New Jersey. I wish that all the politics in Indiana were always of the complexion that I understand it is in Peru. I understand it is strongly Democratic here. I find, therefore, surrounded by Democrats, that Peru is not as distant from the United States as I supposed it was. Looking around about you, I do not feel in the least like a stranger. I feel very much at home and cannot realize that I am in a foreign country.

As we came along in the train just now, there were some young friends of mine accompanying me who, perhaps I should say, were indiscreet enough to spread Wilson buttons broadcast from the train as we were moving along. And I was struck by the remark of one man, to whom a button was thrown, so much struck by it, that it has stuck in my mind. He said, "I have no use for that. I am a workingman." Now what can he have meant? Because it would go straight to the heart of any Democrat to hear any man say or feel that the interests of the workingman were not the first in the thoughts of the Democratic party. It has come to a pretty pass in the United States if the party that has always prided itself on being the party of the common people is now to be rejected by any member of the most enormous party of the United States. Because when I hear a man calling himself a workingman, I wonder what I am. I do not want to belong to an insignificant minority. Why, the United States consists of workingmen, and no party that cannot get the confidence, that cannot retain the confidence of workingmen, ought to call itself a national party at all. I am not deceiving myself by believing that this man spoke the general feeling. I am sure he spoke only an individual feeling. I believe, just between you and me, that he spoke that feeling which is making some men break away from all the older parties in the United States. For the great growth of Socialism in this country, ladies and gentlemen, is the growth of protest more than anything else.

I remember, about eighteen months ago, I was in a little town in Nebraska,[3] where the train I was on stopped for some fifteen minutes. I was walking up and down the platform when I met a very pleasing young man in overalls, who told me that he was the mayor of the town and also admitted that he was a Socialist. I said, "What does that mean, does that mean that this town is a Socialistic town?" "No, sir," he said, "I do not deceive myself about that. It was about 20 per cent Socialist and 80 per cent protest." Protest against what, do you suppose? Alas, ladies and gen-

[3] About this incident, see n. 3 to the address printed at June 2, 1911, Vol. 23.

tlemen, I know very well what it was a protest against. I know, for example that in the State of New Jersey, men had been voting the Republican ticket and the Democratic ticket for half a generation and had never seen any of the promises made to them in party platforms redeemed in action. And after men have voted in vain, election after election, I, for one, cannot blame them for flinging away from the parties that have deceived them. I cannot believe in or subscribe to the programs of the parties which they join in their disgust and despair, but I cannot criticize them for the protest. And, therefore, I realize as much as any man living that the Democratic party now stands or falls as it redeems or does not redeem the promises that it has made to the people of the United States. There is to be no self-deception in regard to this. Parties have been held back by the influences which I could easily describe to you, for I have touched them and I have fought them; have been held back from serving the people as they should have been served, and, God helping us, this is the time when the Democratic party must see to it that these restraints are cast off and the people of the United States served as parties have all along professed to serve them.

Now, when I look at the labor situation in the United States, I do not find the laboring men satisfied with that situation. Why, gentlemen, if you look back to the promises that the Republican party has made you, to the assurances that the Republican party has given you in the past; when you look back to their professions that the protective tariff was meant for the benefit of the workingmen of this country and then realize that the discontent of workingmen in this country has been growing more and more manifest as the tariff duties rose, higher and higher, I ask you when you are going to call their bluff? I ask you how much longer you are going to be imposed upon?

You know very well what the leader of the third party said not many weeks ago. He said that his only quarrel with the protective tariff was that the men who got the benefits of it did not divide with the workingmen,—did he not? He said that not enough of the "prize money"—for such was his name for it—went into the pay envelope, thereby admitting the absolute failure of the protective policy as Republicans had always advocated it. For they said that the protective policy was meant for the pay envelope, and you know just as well as I do that no part got into the pay envelope that the men who were paying the wages could prevent getting there. You know just as well as I do that organized labor is almost the only influence that has ever brought about substantial increases of wages in this country. And you also know that, though a Republican administration has presided over the business of this country for half a generation, the organization of labor is not yet legal in the United States. Anything else can organize. Capital can organize and be sustained by the courts, because sustained by the law. But the organization of labor is not recognized by the law. The courts of this country have held that employers can dismiss their employees for the single reason that they belong to a labor union. But they have also held that the labor union had not the right to boycott, I mean peaceably, peaceably boycott that very concern because it employed men who did not belong to organized labor. In other words the thing is not two-sided. You can be shut out because you belong to a union, but you cannot fight in favor of the union and be sustained by the law.

Therefore, I call your attention to the fact that these men who have not put the "prize money" into the pay envelope have been the very men who have fought organized labor, for the biggest trusts in this country are the very instrumentalities that have been most successful in fighting organized labor.

I believe, therefore, that the whole pretense of the protective tariff is a huge piece of humbug so far as the workingmen of this country are concerned. That is not to say that the protective tariff has not had something to do with building up the present wealth and our present economic organization. That is not to say that the Democratic party will pull down any part of the structure that is sound. But it is to say that the main object, as these gentlemen have professed it, of the protective policy has not turned out to be true, does not directly benefit the workingmen. So, the workingmen of this country who are in unprotected industries are at this moment getting higher wages than most of those who are in protected industries. And some of the lowest wages in this country—wages so low that the men and children receiving them cannot live on them—are paid by some of the most highly protected industries.

I was very much grieved the other day when President Taft, who personally I have a great respect for, said that if the Democratic party came into power it would mean a series of rainy years and rainy days for the workingmen of this country. And I asked him in return, what sort of days he thought had prevailed at Lawrence, Massachusetts. One of the most highly protected industries in this country is the woolen industry, and that same industry was paying starvation wages to those poor people in Lawrence, Massachusetts, and the whole scheme of life was for them clouded over. Rainy days indeed! When did these people ever see the fair sun that shines upon the men that are not anxious from morning to night where their food and clothing and shelter will come from.

Ah, gentlemen, it is time we cease to be deceived about these things. It is time we stood up as men and claimed our own rights as against the combined powers which have been fighting us.

You know that some men who wanted to do me as much injury as they could, when I was running for governor in New Jersey, said that I had once said that a dollar a day was enough for any man. Now this contemptible lie was uttered by men who knew that some of the protected industries were paying less than one dollar a day, were paying less than it was possible for any man to live on. And they put into the mouth of a man who has all his life preached this doctrine of freedom for the workingman the opinion that nobody ought to be treated any better than the most highly protected workingmen were treated. So that they were trying to prevent the election of a man who they feared would some day interfere with the protective tariff, by saying that he believed in the things that the protective tariff brings about. A pretty lot of logicians they are! They thrive on that kind of thing, apparently.

One of the hardest fights I had in New Jersey last winter was to get through the legislature a bill providing for fuller train crews on the trains that run through New Jersey, not merely for the sake of the crews themselves, but for the sake of the safety of the traveling public. And that measure was defeated by a Republican Senate, a Republican standpat Senate. And then the very gentlemen who defeated it went out and said that it would have passed if the governor had not vetoed it, after I had told them what I thought of them after they did not pass it. And I am ready to tell them any time what I think of them. It is too far from New Jersey to say what I think of [certain men in] New Jersey, because that is not sportsmanlike. I want to say it to them. If I had anything of the same kind to say to somebody in Indiana, I would wish he was present so that I might say it to him.

At the present time what I am interested in is to have the workingman, like everyone else in this country, go to the polls on the fifth of November and vote according to the facts; not let anybody put it over them; not let them be deceived by assertions not supported by the facts. Because the fact is that there are great combinations of capital in this country which, because they control great bodies of industry, control and limit the market for labor. They determine how many men shall be employed. And one of the grounds of pride that you have in Indiana is that all over Indiana there are towns with industries of their own that they have not allowed any of these combinations to gobble, that are locally owned, that are locally developed, that are locally independent, so that the reputation of Indiana for intelligence is showing itself in the deserved reputation of Indiana for independence. Don't let the rest of the United States, or rather don't let the men who own a large part of the rest of the United States, swallow you up. We were once swallowed up in New Jersey. I could give you a list of the corporations that used to own the government of New Jersey. But they do not own it any longer, and it was not hard to displace them. All you have got to do to reject them once [and for all] is to set them on the platform where they can be seen and describe them and tell the way in which they transact business behind the scenes in the halls and corridors of the state capitol. Before I became governor, there used to be a special room in which a body of gentlemen used to meet whom nobody had elected to conduct the government of New Jersey, but who were looked up to as a board of guardians, for such we always called them, to tell the legislature of New Jersey what it could and what it could not do.

So, what has happened in this country is that those who have controlled our industry and our transportation have tried to control our governments and to our shame, be it said, in too many instances have succeeded.

What I want to lay before great crowds like this, therefore, is not to appeal for myself personally, is not an argument to the effect that only Democrats know how to cure the ills of the country, but an argument to this effect: Find out what it is you want and then make up your minds which set of men are most likely to give it to you. It is perfectly easy to talk about returning the government to the people, but it is going to be a tremendous job to do it. You have got to choose the freest men you can find. You have got to choose the ablest men you can find. And you have got to choose men who know the facts and who do not hesitate to utter them. I find to know the facts and reason from them brings down scorn upon me in some quarters. I could mention one or two gentlemen who, whenever I reason from the facts as everybody knows them, remind the people that I was a schoolmaster, and that I am merely academic, which is another way of saying that I know what I am talking about, because the schoolmaster that doesn't know what he is talking about generally loses his job. And then they, on the contrary, offset the argument of the academic schoolmaster by very vociferous assertion with no facts to support them. Now as between assertion and reason, I feel that I can safely depend on the American people to prefer the reasoning to the assertion, particularly when men like the Hoosier schoolmasters are abroad in this great commonwealth, famous for its schoolmasters, famous for its intelligence.

I come with the utmost confidence and appeal to every voter in Indiana. First of all—for this is a practical detail I must remind you of—get registered, because if you do not register, you do not count. And if you do not count, you will just have to go and look on at the side lines while the game is being played. First of all, register. And I say this, not only to Democrats, because I know a great many gentlemen who are going to vote as I think they ought to vote who have not called themselves Democrats. So, I say, no matter how you are labeled, go and register. And then when you vote on the fifth of November, go into the polling booth and say, each man to himself, I am now a trustee of this vote for the people of Indiana and the people of the United States. I am going to vote according to my convictions. I am not going to vote according to the looks or the antecedents of the candidate. I am going to vote for the things that I believe in. And after I have done that, I can go home with a free conscience.

There are a lot of men going to vote in the United States this year, and thank God nobody knows how they will vote. I know some men rather high in business who are not going to let anybody know how they vote, because they know that if some people knew how they voted, they would get after their scalps. It is not only the little men in this country who are afraid of the big ones, it is some of the big ones that are afraid of other big ones. And the only place they feel safe is in the polling booth, with the door shut and the ballot folded. Then, without any mark of identification on the ballot, they can go home and make believe they have voted as they always voted, but know they have done something that is going to make an absolute change of the atmosphere in the United States.

The air is going to clear on the sixth of November. It is not going to clear up by a cyclone. You won't know what has happened. You will not have heard it. You won't hear anything drop on the fifth. But on the sixth, men will take a fuller lung of air and they will say to one another, "Now we have started out on the new journey, and we are going to see whether we own our own government or not." And if the men that you put into office then go back on you, I, for one, hope that they will be gibbeted for the rest of history and held up to the scorn of mankind.

T MS (C. L. Swem Coll., NjP), with a few corrections from the incomplete text in the *Peru*, Ind., *Evening Journal*, Oct. 4, 1912.

To Louis Dembitz Brandeis

Chicago, Ills Oct 4, [19]12

Please use the letter yourself   deep appreciation of your kindness

W.W.

TC telegram (RSB Coll., DLC).

Remarks to the Women's Democratic Club in Omaha, Nebraska[1]

[Oct. 5, 1912]

Madam Chairman,[2] Mrs. Bryan,[3] and Ladies: I will leave out
the gentlemen this time. They are just sort of a framework. It is
an interesting company that sits in front of me. My voice has
been a good deal damaged by Indiana politics, but what remains
of it shall perhaps serve me to express the very great appreciation
I have of the opportunity of meeting this company, and of knowing what the women of Nebraska are intending to do for the
Democratic party. Because I know that when the impulse comes
from that side, it will be greatly accelerated. And I have just
heard the testimony of one of the seasoned politicians of this part
of the country that, in the short time you have been forming your
plans, you have done more than all the men put together. It
strikes me that when such a number of women get together, they
get together with more than ordinary political interest, because
there is an ardor of loyalty and of feeling that seems to lift the
whole level of the enterprise.

I was privileged to be associated in some degree with the beginning of the National Women's Democratic League,[4] and I
know, from the activity of the eastern portions of the league, how
very busy, and how intelligently busy, the women are in this great
cause. And, surely, it is a woman's cause. Because the thing that
touches me most to the quick in the whole business is that, by
the errors of our economic development, it seems to me that the
doors of opportunity have been too much closed to the coming
generation. For, it has always been my feeling that the strength
of the nation consists in the hope of the next generation, and not
in the success of the present generation. In other words, that
what is going to happen to our boys and to our girls is very much
more the test of America than what has happened to our men
and our women and that, therefore, the Democratic cause, which
is the cause of liberty, of enterprise, and openness of opportunity,

is peculiarly a mother's cause and by that token, therefore, a woman's cause. It is the hope of the future as contrasted with the embarrassment of the future.

I congratulate the Democratic party that they should have such active allies in a quarter where the work is sure to be done with such intelligence and enthusiasm, and I, am sure, with such tact and success. I thank you for this opportunity of greeting you.

T MS (C. L. Swem Coll., NjP), with corrections from the ICF transcript in RSB Coll., DLC.
    1 Delivered in the Paxton Hotel.
    2 The newspapers do not identify her.
    3 Mary Elizabeth Baird Bryan.
    4 It was organized in Washington on June 1, 1910, to promote the election of Democratic candidates.

A Nonpartisan Talk to the Commercial Club of Omaha[1]

[Oct. 5, 1912]

Senator Hitchcock[2] and gentlemen of the Commercial Club: Before I arose I was told that there had been an injunction laid upon me which was first expressed in this way, that the speech was to be nonpolitical; then the orders were modified and I was told it was to be nonpartisan. I am very glad, indeed, to yield to those instructions. Indeed, if I may be very frank with you, I am not interested in partisan discussions. I believe that a new temper has come into our discussions, and that we are ourselves impatient of setting up the records of parties in contrast with one another, or the records of the party candidates in contrast with one another. That, to my mind, at any rate, is not the interesting part of it. The people of the United States have to be served, and the question is how are we going to serve them? And it will make very little difference, except to the historian a few years from now, what sort of fellows we are—I mean those of us who are unfortunate enough to be lifted up to the light to be examined. So that I do not feel in the least hampered by my instructions. For there are all sorts of politics. There is explicit politics and there is implicit politics, and I am going to take the liberty to imply as much politics as the thread of my discourse will naturally involve. And yet, it hasn't very much thread. There is only one theme to talk about in a company of men like this.

I was very pleased to learn that two thirds of you have been Republicans. I say "have been," because you look like honest men who vote according to your opinions; and the opinions of the

    1 Delivered in the club building.
    2 Gilbert Monell Hitchcock, Democratic senator from Nebraska.

country are changing, and I take it for granted you are not going to lag behind them. And I, for my part, don't hold it up against you that you have been Republicans. All of us have committed errors in our youth. All of us look back upon episodes and judgments in our life which we should hope might be overlooked by those who are our indulgent friends. And, really, to speak seriously, I find it very difficult to draw party lines among the men I meet. When a man of genuine interest in advancing the public welfare tells me what he thinks really should be done and then begins to describe himself in party terms, the two things don't seem to have anything to do with one another. And that is for a reason I think we ought all to reflect upon very seriously.

The situation of the United States in respect to public questions is not now what it ever was before. I don't find any one even of the old questions wearing the aspect, now, upon close examination, that it has worn at any previous time. Take the tariff question, for example. The tariff question is very old in its older forms, but it is absolutely new in its present form. The tariff question originally was a question of domestic development; and now the energies of the United States have been such, and her output in the field of manufacture has been such, that we need the markets of the world. If we continue to confine ourselves to domestic development, then we will be kept in a straitjacket. We will find it impossible to release our energies upon the great field upon which we are now ready to enter, and enter by way of conquest. America is straining at the leash to capture the markets of the world, and, therefore, the whole question of domestic development wears another aspect, and the whole tariff question wears another aspect because all trade is two-sided. You can't sell everything and buy nothing. You can't establish any commercial relationships that aren't two-sided. And if America is to insist upon selling everything and buying nothing, she will find that the rest of the world stands very cold and indifferent to her enterprise.

And then there is drawn into that the old question which has been very hard to get America interested in—the merchant marine. In order to get your own markets, you have got to carry your own goods to market. If two department stores, for example, or rather if one department store used the delivery wagons of the other one, I know what would happen. The goods of the other one would be delivered first; not only that, but the routes would be chosen for the convenience of the customers of that store. That, now, that is exactly analogous to what happens in our day whenever we ship beyond the confines of the United States. Except for our coast trade, we are bound to ship in lines, by the use of lines, that have been established for the purpose of developing English or German or French or Italian trade. They, therefore, carry our goods first of all to the markets where English merchants or German merchants have got their foothold and have established their supremacy, and that puts us at a great disadvantage at the very outset. And, then, the routes are the routes which they chose, which they have established, which they have subsidized. Our commercial development outside the United States, therefore, is at the convenience and at the dictation of our rivals, and so long as that is true, we are going to be at a hopeless disadvantage. We have got to develop a merchant marine, or else keep within the confines of our domestic development.

Not only that, but the question of the tariff is an absolutely new question inside as well as outside. It is an absolutely new question because of the very serious curtailment of domestic competition. Now, you don't have to discuss that question as a Democrat or as a Republican. Whether you are a Republican or a Democrat, you know that the old free field of competition in the United States has disappeared, and that it was only domestic competition that kept prices down to a normal level. For nobody can persuade me that there is any partisanship in the laws of the market. The laws of the market are supreme over statesmen, over domestic relationships, and over national boundaries. And competition is the only thing that can keep normal levels in the prices charged for manufactured or any other goods. Competition is the only thing in the labor market that can keep a normal wage average. And just so soon as competition disappears, then prices begin to be abnormal and wages begin to be abnormal, and everything begins to be controlled which once was established by the free competition of the market. Therefore, the old arguments that used to be relied upon to prove to you that we weren't being squeezed by those who enjoyed the benefits of the tariff have disappeared. They have disappeared for the very interesting reason that we are being squeezed. The facts are going to make conquest of every situation in the world, and men who close their eyes to the facts are going to be defeated. For it is only the facts that determine these things.

Now, the warfares of trade are the worst things that can occur. I picture to myself the function of a body of men like this. The function of this body is not to see that any particular group of men in Omaha has an advantage in the industries and the trade of Omaha, but that they are drawn together so that they will understand the interests and the development of the city as

a whole, that they will play into each other's hands and serve
one another's interests and, above all things else, they will let the
rest of the country in on the advantages of locating in Omaha
and of trading in Omaha and of using Omaha as one of the great
distributing and vital centers of the industry of the country. Your
business as a body is a business of accommodation and mutual
understanding and mutual service, is it not? Now just so soon as
you forget that, just so soon as you begin to build up one interest
against another, there is going to be war in your own midst, and
that war will be to the disadvantage of everybody, even to the
person who gains a special advantage, because the atmosphere of
business then becomes an atmosphere of suspicion. And the most
serious thing to my mind about the business situation in the
United States is that the people of the United States, by and large,
are not satisfied in their minds that the thing is done on a fair
basis. And you don't need me to tell you that the atmosphere of
suspicion is the atmosphere which business of all things else can't
breathe.

You don't have to be special students of financial crises and
financial panics, for example, to know that a panic is properly
described as a state of mind, nothing else than a state of mind.
There is just as much money in the country the day after a crash
came as the day before it came; there is just as much wealth in
the country. If everybody could take hope and confidence again,
the thing would be thrown off like a nightmare and move forward, except for this abominable embarrassment that we have in
an inelastic currency. We haven't got the means of freedom until
we get an elastic currency, but, barring that, a panic is a mere
state of mind. Everybody has stopped trusting everybody else, and
all the call loans are brought in in a hurry because you are not
certain that when you call, you are calling anything but a bluff.
Therefore, the atmosphere of suspicion stops, checks, congests
business as any other chill would congest the physical body. And
if you are going to allow the people of the United States to feel
that somebody, some groups of men, are getting an unfair advantage, then you are more and more going to create a hostility to
the very basis of our commercial and industrial prosperity. You
can't have prosperity on that basis. Prosperity is as much psychological as material, and if you spoil the psychology of it, you will
spoil the material of it.

One of the hopeful signs of the times, to my mind, is that,
whereas a very short time ago—I don't know how short, at a guess,
five years—businessmen in this country were very hostile to suggestions of change. You heard everywhere the mere command,

"Let us alone. Business is all right. We will take care of ourselves. Let us alone. Keep your hands off." I don't hear very much of that any longer, and I don't hear it because I find businessmen and their legal advisers everywhere admitting that things are not adjusted as they ought to be, and, until they are, it isn't safe to let business alone.

I used to be a lawyer. I repented early and changed. And I know it has taken me about twenty-five years to get away from a lawyer's point of view. I would speak with the utmost respect of that profession, even if I did quit it, but the lawyer's point of view is this, that he is professionally on the defensive. He must see to it that his client isn't interfered with, isn't embarrassed, isn't brought under fire in any way. And, therefore, he has constantly got his bulwarks out to defend the things that he is connected with. And he refuses to stand outside and look at the thing objectively and form a candid opinion as to how he really thinks it works.

Take the old time before we had begun to find a solution—I don't claim we have found an entire solution yet—of the railway question, of the question of railway regulation. The railway lawyers used to din it in my ears—I have been discussing these things, though I haven't been handling them, for a great many years— used to din it in my ears that all the legislatures of the country were playing hob with the railroads because they didn't know what they were about, and that they were going to ruin the whole transportation business of the country. "Well," I said, "I think a great many of the measures being adopted are very unwise and may be very hurtful, but I would like to know who is to blame. You are the only men who know how these laws should be drafted in a way to regulate and yet not injure the business of your clients, and until you get into this game I haven't any sympathy with you whatever. You are standing outside and saying, 'Don't do anything, gentlemen. Hold off.' And they won't hold off, and if you don't tell them how to do it, they are going to do it their own way, and you will be to blame." I see the same thing now with regard to business. The conditions of business in this country have to be altered, gentlemen, in order that there may be no private monopoly of any kind. That is going to come. If it comes with your assistance, if it comes with your counsel, if it comes with your frank cooperation, then it will come wisely, and I say nobody will hurt. But it is going to come anyhow. And if you don't assist, you are the responsible parties for the injury done to business.

I don't think any of us can escape the moral of the situation.

The moral is that the control of the business of this country is getting into too small a number of hands. Now, we have got to get together to see how to prevent that, and it is only by getting together that we can wisely prevent it. It is only by understanding one another. It is only by counsel. What I would be proud to be would be the spokesman of frank common counsel in this country with regard to its business affairs. I, myself, have had some business experience, but not enough to constitute me a judge. And I don't believe that any man in any one line of business knows enough of the business of the country to constitute himself a judge. But the various kinds of business, if they will frankly speak out what is really in their minds in regard to these matters, can conjointly effect a peaceful revolution in this country, which won't for a moment disturb the growth of our prosperity.

The only thing that alarms me is the number of influential businessmen who confide to me confidentially their agreement with some of my opinions. Why confidentially? Because they are afraid of somebody. Now, it has come to a pretty pass when American businessmen are afraid of anybody. And yet there are men that they had better be afraid of. There are men who will crush them like an eggshell in their hands if they stand in the way of the consummation of their ambitions. There are men who will see to it that they don't get credit for the initiation of any enterprise that will interfere with the enterprises that these gentlemen are interested in. I am not arguing this with you, I am telling you. And I think you know it. I have seen men crushed. I have seen them crushed before my eyes because they dared to vote in a legislature in a way that interfered with the plans of some of these interests.

There is one man[3] I like to think of. He was a skilled workman, merely of a kind for which there is little demand because his specialty was such that only a particular set of men employed such work, only a particular industry employed such work. They were opposed to the defeat of one James Smith, Jr., in New Jersey for United States senator two years ago—we have had to defeat Mr. Smith twice; this was the first time. And they were interested in him on a perfectly nonpartisan basis, because Mr. Smith, I must say for him, has always been very frank in saying that he was not a Democrat when it came to the tariff, and these gentlemen were particularly interested in one schedule of the tariff which they expected him to stand by. This employee of theirs had been

---

[3] Allan B. Walsh, about whom see n. 4 to the address printed at May 30, 1911, Vol. 23.

elected to the state legislature, and so long as he didn't make adventures of his own in the field of voting, they had been perfectly content that he should be there. But he was a man of conviction. He was a man who understood what the people of the state wanted and what they ought to want, and he voted against Mr. Smith. And then their hand began to close over him. And when he voted for certain measures which they disapproved of it shut and he was crushed. He was put out of his business and couldn't find it anywhere else in the United States. A local board elected him as its secretary. And now the people of his congressional district have nominated him for Congress, and he is going to make laws for these gentlemen. And it serves them right. What business of theirs was it to bring pressure to bear upon the member of the legislature of a sovereign state to vote in their special interest? I am not now arguing whether their special interest was legitimate or illegitimate. That has nothing to do with it. Legislatures are not elected to serve special interests. They are elected to serve the general interests; and the man that ought to be guarded by society as if he was their most precious possession is a man who votes according to his conscience. This man did vote according to his conscience, and the last time he voted I saw the tears that ran down his cheeks because he didn't know where the money was going to come from to support his wife and children after he had done that thing.

Now, gentlemen, I have been dealing with realities. I haven't been living in an imaginary world in the State of New Jersey. These are things that my eyes have seen and my hands have handled, and I'll tell you frankly, it is sometimes very difficult to hold my mind back from passion in the presence of injustice and selfishness of this kind. But we must hold ourselves back from passion. You can't do anything wise if you are passionate. You can't do anything wise if you fight men as men and question their motives. You must fight things. You must fight policies. You must fight situations. If you don't, then you skew the whole perspective. You don't see anything in its right relations. I am not interested in men. I must frankly say, with apologies, that I am not interested in the candidates of the other parties, and I find it difficult to get interested in the candidate of my own party. Because the thing to be done is so much bigger than men, transcends all personal considerations by such immeasurable distances, and if we don't get this purified ardor for right things into our minds, we can't do the right things. Now, I believe that this ardor is spreading. I believe that it is contagious. I believe that it is splendidly contagious, and that is the reason it is easy to make a nonpartisan speech. There isn't any party in it. There is mere justice in it. There is mere rectitude. There is mere comprehension of the whole business interest of the country. And, therefore, it doesn't make a peppercorn's difference how many of you were Republicans—you are all going to be patriots.

T MS (C. L. Swem Coll., NjP), with corrections from the ICF transcript in RSB Coll., DLC.

A Talk to Democratic Workers in Lincoln, Nebraska[1]

[Oct. 5, 1912]

Mr. Chairman,[2] Mr. Bryan,[3] and fellow Democrats: It is certainly a high compliment to be thus received, and, as has been aptly said, this is the best body of workers in the Union, and I congratulate you on your opportunity to work for the things that we are now banded together to accomplish.

And I want to express on this the first opportunity that I have had since getting into Lincoln the very deep pleasure it gives me to find myself beside Mr. Bryan. We, gentlemen, are free to serve the people of the United States, and in my opinion it was Mr. Bryan that set us free. I think no one could have followed the course of events in that extraordinary convention at Baltimore without sharing in that opinion. And I believe, as I go around the country, I find everywhere that opinion earnestly and sincerely entertained. So that it is a special pleasure for me to come here and pay my profound tribute of respect to him.

And how are we going to use our freedom? It is a splendid thing to think, gentlemen, that having been set free, there is now no longer any necessary stigma attached to organization. When an organization goes bad, then it becomes a machine. But when it is sound, when it is made up of men who really entertain the convictions of the party, when it is a body of men organized to see that the full expression of public opinion is brought out in behalf of measures intended for the advancement of the cause of the people, then it becomes a thing of splendid dignity, then it has all the glory of a peaceful army, then it has all the strength of men who are banded together with a sympathy that ties them into a single brotherhood. I think that men are so often mistaken in disparaging party organizations. Why, gentlemen, that is the only way we can pull together—by a common understanding. And I want to congratulate the Democracy of Nebraska on the way it has knit itself together into a single body.

One of the most convincing signs of a new day and a new hope is that everywhere men are giving up their personal attitudes of antagonism and getting together in a spirit that gives them happiness. For I have seen some of these men who have sacrificed, it may be, something of their particular point of view, have seen the look of relief and happiness in their faces. They are glad to be shoulder to shoulder with men with whom their differences were artificial, not fundamental.

And there is now beginning to dawn all over the United States the confident expectation of a victory for the people. I don't know what Mr. Bryan's observations may have been, but I think that I have seen that change within the last ten days. At any rate, it has been a very peculiar and to me an amusing change, if I may be personal, with regard to myself. A great many people in the United States have regarded me as a very remote and academic person. They don't know how much human nature there has been in me to give me trouble all my life. And I have been perfectly aware that at first the crowds that gathered to hear me gathered in a critical temper to see this novel specimen, to see this newcomer into national politics, to see what the animal looked like, and what his paces were, and what his tones of voice and attitudes of mind were. And I am glad now to see this attitude changing. They have apparently adopted me into the human family. And I like to see the enthusiasm of the plainest sort of men as they approach me, for I consider that the deepest compliment that I can be paid. And when they call me "Kid" and "Woody," and all the rest of it, I know that I am all right.

I have always said that I remember the exact moment when I first became a candidate for office in New Jersey. They had been looking me over in New Jersey in the same critical way, but finally one day the ice seemed to break and one great husky fellow slapped me on the back and said, "Doc, you're all right!" And I knew from that moment that I was adopted into the family, and that I needn't be afraid that my fellow citizens in New Jersey would have any suspicions of me.

I have sometimes suspected that I was taken up as an innocent, and that some persons were disappointed that I turned out to have had as much of human experience as they had. They have been complaining of it ever since. But, after all, gentlemen, what would you think of a man who went dry, who became a hull of a man, after associating for twenty-five years with the young men of America, who have, I suppose, as much red blood in them and as much undirected mischief and as much enthusiasm for ideals as any part of the population that you can find. And the thing to rejoice over at this moment is the multitudes of young men who are turning to the Democratic party, for we cannot make an immortal party with one generation. Because immortality consists in its constant recruiting out of the ranks of the generations coming on.

And there was a time, a time through which we had to live with such patience as we could command, when practically all young men turned to the Republican party as the party of opportunity, until they found upon a certain day that the Republican party, whether intentionally or unintentionally, was slowly closing the doors of opportunity against them, and making it necessary that they should submit to the discipline of a mastery which was to them intolerable. And seeing that there was no future in that direction for men of ambition and initiative, they have naturally turned to us, who have been waiting for them to recognize us as their friends for half a generation and more.

Because, as I was pointing out to an audience in Omaha today,[4] we are not new to this business. Certain gentlemen on the Republican side have just discovered what the programs of humanity are, and we have known them for a long time. We have laid down, to use the illustration I was using today, these specifications for the new building for eighteen years. And now the other contractors are beginning to look critically at our proposals and adopt such pieces of them as they think fit to adopt.

I congratulate you, therefore, that you have now come out of the wilderness and are in sight of the kind of success which we shall make permanent if we never for a moment falter, if we never for a moment forget that we are not working merely to keep a party together, but working to serve a people. The minute we forget that, we shall lose; and when we lose for that reason, we shall deserve to lose. There is no reason for being for a party except to conduct a great polity, and there is no possible foundation for a great polity except a body of immovable convictions. So that if we move forward with conviction, we can move forward with enthusiasm.

It is a privilege to come into touch with a body of men like this, who are in contact with the practical conditions of politics in an age, in a year, when all the heart has grown tonic, when discouragement has disappeared. And the only thing I have to warn you against is not to be fooled by the too prosperous promises of the time. I don't think that the army that has the liberty of America in its charge can afford not to keep watch at every turn and see that the enemy nowhere surprises them.

T MS (C. L. Swem Coll., NjP); with corrections from the ICF transcript in RSB Coll., DLC, and the text in the *Lincoln Daily Star*, Oct. 6, 1912.

A Campaign Address in the Lincoln Auditorium

[Oct. 5, 1912]

Mr. Bryan, ladies and gentlemen: I shall have to ask you to be a little patient if you cannot at first distinctly hear what I say, because I left the best tones of my voice in the State of Indiana, where I foolishly attempted, night before last, to make myself audible to 35,000 people. But if you will only give this patient voice of mine time, it will come up, I believe, to the occasion.

I want to say that I have been profoundly touched by the extraordinary reception accorded me by the generous-hearted people of Nebraska. I suppose that you would naturally imagine that a reception such as you have given me today fills me with a sense of elation, with a sense of enjoyment, with the joy of a man who is riding upon the waves of popularity. But I want to assure you that the feeling predominant in my mind is one of serious responsibility. It is no light matter to be received by a free people as you have received me, because you would not have received me in this way unless you believed in me, in the sincerity of my purpose, and in the rectitude of my intentions. And what this reception means to me is that I am put under bonds to live up to the standards which you yourselves have created for me.

Moreover, in coming to Lincoln, I am coming, as it were, to the Mecca of progressive Democracy. I know that the standards to which you will hold me in Nebraska are the highest standards to which a Democrat can be held. The thought that must come into every man's mind who has any responsibility in public affairs now is that there are tremendous questions to be settled, and that the way to settle them is to make use of the incomparable force of great bodies of men and women like this. And yet I know that the force of men and women such as this before me cannot be made use of except by a free government, and the

Government of the United States during the last few decades has not been free. The parties of the United States have, in recent years, not always been free. There have been forces at work, forces with which I have come into personal contact, fighting in such commonwealths as New Jersey, for example, that had a grip that had to be broken, fastened upon the Democratic party as they had a grip also fastened upon the Republican party. Those forces have again and again tried to assert themselves in the national councils of the Democratic party, and I am proud to come to Lincoln and render my tribute of respect and admiration to the great champion of liberty who set the Democratic party free at Baltimore. Mr. Bryan was not the champion of any candidate. Mr. Bryan, with the tact which ought to characterize a great leader, did not attempt to dictate what the choice of the Baltimore convention should be. But he did attempt, and did splendidly succeed, in preventing the control of that convention by those interests which are inimical to the rights of the people of the United States. If I, as the result of the freedom of that convention, was the man of their choice for leader, my responsibility is all the greater to live up to the standards to which he brought that great body of representative Democrats.

I am proud to stand shoulder to shoulder with him. Now, ladies and gentlemen, what is there to do? (A voice: "Vote for Wilson!")

That, I admit, ladies and gentlemen is the proper first preliminary, but that is only a preliminary, because Woodrow Wilson, if elected, will only be as strong as the support that men and women like you give him, and therefore it is merely a preliminary to choose a President. Then we have got to mass the forces behind that President who know what the country needs and, thinking clearly, purpose irresistibly. It is therefore very important in this campaign that we should distinctly understand what we want to do, because you cannot choose the men to do it unless you know what there is to do.

And I am afraid that some of my fellow citizens are inclined to choose gentlemen to do new things who are only in the habit of doing the old things. You can't teach an old dog new tricks, and the Democratic dogs never knew the old tricks. And it is important that we should realize this very clearly, because I wish to assist in the process of conversion which is now so hopefully in progress in the Republican party. I do not believe in emotional conversions. I believe in rational conversions. And I want to convince, if I may, some of the Republicans present—assuming that any Republicans have ventured into this place—that the only course they can pursue in this new age, if they entertain with us the new purposes, is to turn in a new direction for the instrumentalities upon which those purposes are to be accomplished.

For I want, in the first place, to call your attention to the fact that there is now only one national party; that there was another but it is now so divided into many varieties that there are no single terms in which to describe it. I am going to speak of the third party as Republicans, because practically all of them were Republicans, and I am going to speak of the regulars backing Mr. Taft as Republicans, because they still admit it.

The third party has not recruited itself from the ranks of the Democrats, and I need not add that the other party has not hoped to recruit itself from that direction. It is a very serious thing to do when you choose a leader, because a leader is of no use to you unless he can translate a program into action. Therefore, the program that he believes in is the man himself.

Now, we are not going to discuss tonight the sympathies, or susceptibilities, the enthusiasms, of the several men who are seeking your suffrages for President of the United States. I am perfectly ready to believe, and will admit for the sake of argument, that Mr. Roosevelt's heart and soul are committed to that part of the third term program which contains those hopeful plans of human betterment in which so many noble men and women of this country have enlisted their sympathies and their energies. I am not here to criticize anybody who has been drawn to that party because of that part of the program. But I want to call their attention to the fact that you can't have a program that you can carry out through a resisting and unsuitable medium, and that the thing that is absolutely necessary for every candid voter to remember with regard to the third party is that the means of government—the means of getting the things that this country needs—are exactly the same on that side as they are on the side where Mr. Taft seeks the suffrages of the country. Because, while the party of Mr. Taft says in its platform that monopoly ought not to exist, the section of the Republican party that is following Mr. Roosevelt subscribes to the statement that monopoly ought to be adopted by the law and by regulation should be the governing force in the development of American industry. So that all that the third party asks of the monopolists is that they should cooperate, and the only hope of a program of human uplift from that party is that the monopolists will cooperate.

Have you got any hopes in that direction? Don't you know what the Republican party has provided you with up to this time?

I have taken special pains to clear from my own mind, at any rate, the Republican conception of government. That conception is that the people cannot organize their opinion in such fashion as to control their own government, and that, therefore, it is necessary constantly to consult those whose material interests in the development of the country are larger than anybody else's, and then through the hands of these trustees administer the government, not through the people, but for the people. I am perfectly ready to believe—knowing some of the men concerned as I do, I must believe—that a great many men now engaged in the promotion of monopoly in this country really wish to see the United States prosperous and really desire to adopt the means that will make it prosperous. But they are not willing to let anybody else determine the means of prosperity except themselves. I wonder at the frame of mind which makes them believe that they are the trustees of political discretion in this country, but I am willing to admit for the sake of argument that that is their candid and deliberate judgment. And what we have to fight, therefore, is not a body of deliberate enemies, it may be, but a body of mistaken men. And what I want to point out to you is that Mr. Roosevelt subscribes to the judgment of these mistaken men as to the influences which should govern America. That is the serious part of it. Mr. Roosevelt's judgment has been captured. Mr. Roosevelt's idea of the way in which the industries of this country ought to be controlled has been captured. He does not propose to set us free. He proposes to use monopoly in order to make us happy. And the project is one of those projects which all history cries out against as impossible.

The Democratic platform is the only platform which says that private monopoly is indefensible and intolerable, and any man who does not subscribe to that opinion does not know the way to set the people of the United States free and to serve humanity. All that Mr. Roosevelt is asking you to do is to elect him president of the board of trustees. I do not care how wise, how patriotic, the trustees may be, I have never heard of any group of men into whose hands I am willing to put the liberties of America in trust. And, therefore, I am not, in this campaign, engaged in doubting any man's motives. I merely want to point out that these gentlemen are not proposing the methods of liberty but are proposing the methods of control. And control amongst a free people is intolerable.

I have been very much interested the last day or two in having described to me the industries of some of these smaller western cities. I know, in Indiana, for example, town after town was pointed out to me that still has the American characteristic, in which there are factories upon factories owned by men who live in the place—independent enterprises still unabsorbed by the great economic combinations which have become so threateningly inhuman in our economic organization, and it seems to me that these are outposts and symbols of the older and freer America. And after I had traveled through that series of towns and met the sturdy people that live in them, I ended at the city of Gary, just a little way outside of Chicago, and realized that I had come from the older America into the newer America, for this was a town owned and built by a single monopolistic corporation. And I wondered which kind of America the people of America, if they could see this picture as I saw it, would choose.

Which do you want? Do you want to live in a town patronized by some great combination of capitalists who pick it out as a suitable place to plant their industry and draw you into their employment? Or do you want to see your sons and your brothers and your husbands build up businesses for themselves under the protection of laws which make it impossible for any giants, however big, to crush them and put them out of business, so that they can match their wits here in the midst of a free country with any captain of industry or master of finance to be found anywhere in the world, and put every man who now attempts to control and promote monopoly upon his mettle to beat them at initiative, at economy, at the organization of business and the cheap production of salable goods? Which do you want?

Why, gentlemen, America is never going to submit to monopoly. America is never going to choose thralldom instead of freedom. Look what there is to decide! There is the tariff question. Can the tariff question be decided in favor of the people of the United States so long as the monopolies are the chief counselors at Washington? There is the great currency question. You know how difficult it is to move your crops every year. And I tremble, I must frankly tell you, to think of the bumper crops that are now coming from our fields, because they are going to need enormous bodies of cash to move them. You have got to get that cash by calling in your loans and embarrassing people in every center of commercial activity, because there isn't cash enough under our inelastic currency to lend itself to this instrumentality. And are we going to settle the currency question so long as the Government of the United States listens only to the counsel of those who command the banking situation in the United States? You can't solve the tariff, you can't solve the currency question under the domination which is proposed by one branch of the Republican party and tolerated by the other.

And then there is the great question of conservation. What is our fear about conservation? The hands that are being stretched out to monopolize our forests, to pre-empt the use of our great power-producing streams, the hands that are being stretched into the bowels of the earth to take possession of the great riches that lie hidden in Alaska and elsewhere in the incomparable domain of the United States are the hands of monopoly. And is this thing merely to be regulated? Is this thing to be legalized? Are these men to continue to stand at the elbow of government and tell us how we are to save ourselves from the very things that we fear? You can't settle the question of conservation while monopoly exists, if monopoly is close to the ears of those who govern. And the question of conservation is a great deal bigger than the question of saving our forests and our mineral resources and our waters. It is as big as the life and happiness and strength and elasticity and hope of our people.

The Government of the United States has now to look out upon her people and see what they need, what should be done for them. Ah, gentlemen, there are tasks awaiting the Government of the United States which it cannot perform until every pulse of that government beats in unison with the needs and the desires of the whole body of the American people. Shall we not give the people access of sympathy, access of counsel, access of authority to the instrumentalities which are to be indispensable to their lives? When I think of the great things to be accomplished, and then think of the danger that there is that the people of the United States will not choose free instruments to accomplish them, then I tremble to think of the verdict that may be rendered on the fifth of November.

But when you look around, when you go through America, as I have recently been going through it, your heart rises again. Why, two years ago, when I was running for governor in New Jersey, I used to come away from public meetings with a certain burden on my heart, because I knew I was not mistaken in feeling that I had seen in the faces and felt in the atmosphere of the great meetings that I addressed a certain sense of foreboding and anxiety, as a people who were anxious about their future. But I haven't seen anything of that kind in the year 1912. The people of the United States now know what they intend to do. They intend to take charge of their own affairs again, and they see the way to do it. Great outpourings like this are not in compliment to an individual. They are in demonstration of a purpose. And all I have to say for the Democratic candidate for the presidency is that I pray God he may be shown the way not to disappoint the expectations of such people.

Only you can show him the way. You can't do it by proxy. You must determine the interests of your own lives and then find spokesmen for those interests who will speak them as fearlessly as men have learned how to speak in Nebraska. The great emancipation which has been wrought for you by the fight for progressive democracy, which has gone on from splendid stage to splendid stage in this state, is that it has raised up for you men who fearlessly speak the truth. And that is not true of all parts of the country. Why, there are parts of the country where I am considered brave if I speak in words what every man and woman in the audience knows to be true. Now, I have never known what it was to exercise courage when I knew that the stars in all their courses were fighting my way. Do you suppose a man needs to be courageous to speak the truth, to attach his puny force to the great voice of God, which is the truth itself? A man would be a coward that wouldn't speak the truth. A man would be a fool who didn't see that the only puissance in human affairs was the irresistible force of the truth itself. And men are weak in proportion as they are mistaken. They are weak in proportion as their judgments are misled. They are weak in proportion as they do not see the practical terms into which the truth can be translated. But they are not courageous when they merely tell the truth, because if they lie because they were afraid, do you suppose they would have very comfortable moments when they withdrew into the privacy of their own family?

I wonder how some men sleep o'nights because they deceive themselves and deceive others all day long and then actually go home and go to sleep. I don't know what their dreams can be. And they speak the things that they know are not true because they are afraid of something. Fear is abroad. In free America there are men who dare not undertake certain business enterprises because they know they would be crushed. There are men who dare not speak certain opinions because they know they would be boycotted in influential circles upon which their credit and their advancement in their business depend. Do you suppose that it is singular that men should rise up and fight through half a generation, as your own champions have fought, in order to dispel that fear? The only way to dispel fear is to bring the things that you are afraid of out in the open and challenge them there to meet the great moral force of the people of the United States. So that if these gentlemen will come out and avow their

purposes, they will destroy all possibility of realizing those purposes.

One of the fine things of our time is that the whole game is
disclosed. We now know the processes of monopoly; and we therefore know the processes of law by which monopoly can be destroyed. They have shown their hands, and we know how to stay
their use of illegitimate power. Will we do them any damage?
I tell you frankly that if I thought that any considerable portion
of the enterprising men of America would be injured by the policies that I am interested in, I would hesitate. But I am clear in
the conviction that to set the people of the United States free is
to set the big enterprises free along with the little ones.

Because I have never heard of any business conditions which
were dependent upon the subservience of great bodies of enterprising businessmen. If you have to be subservient, you aren't
even making the rich fellows as rich as they might be, because
you are not adding your originative force to the extraordinary
production of wealth in America. America is as rich, not as Wall
Street, not as the financial centers in Chicago and St. Louis and
San Francisco, but it is as rich as the people that make those
centers rich. And if those people hesitate in their enterprise,
cower in the face of power, hesitate to originate designs of their
own, then the very fountains which make these places abound
in wealth are dried up at the source. So that by setting the little
men of America free, you are not damaging the giants. You are
merely making them behave like human beings.

Now, a giant ought to have more human nature in him than
a pigmy, and we want to really read the Decalogue to those
big men who may not have heard it in some time. And by moralizing, we are going to set them free and their business free.

It may be that certain things will happen, for monopoly in
this country is carrying a body of water such as no body of men
ought to be asked to carry. And when by regulated competition,
that is to say, fair competition, competition that fights fair, they
are put upon their mettle, they will have to economize in their
processes of business, and they can't economize unless they drop
that water. I do not know how to squeeze the water out, but they
will get rid of it if you will put them on their mettle. They will
have to get rid of it, or those of us who don't carry tanks will
outrun them in the race. Put all the business of America upon
the footing of economy and efficiency, and then let the race be
to the strongest and the swiftest.

So that our program is a program of prosperity, only it is a
program of prosperity that is a little more pervasive than the

present program; and pervasive prosperity is more fruitful than that which is narrow and restrictive. I congratulate the monopolists of the United States that they are not going to have their way, because, quite contrary to their own theory, the people of the United States are wiser than they are. The people of the United States understand the United States as these gentlemen do not. And if they will only give us leave, we will not only make them rich, but we will make them happy. Because, then, their consciences will have less to carry. They are waking up to this fact, ladies and gentlemen. The businessmen of this country are not deluded, and not all of the big businessmen of this country are deluded. Some men who have been led into wrong practices, who have been led into the practices of monopoly, because that seemed to be the drift and inevitable method of supremacy of our times, are just as ready as we are to turn about and adopt the processes of freedom. Because American hearts beat in a lot of these men just as they beat under our jackets. They will be as glad to be free as we shall be to set them free. And then the splendid force which has led to things that hurt us will lead to things that benefit us. We are coming to a common understanding, and only a common understanding is the tolerable basis of a free government.

I congratulate you, therefore, ladies and gentlemen, that you are now coming to that point of fruition of which you have dreamed and for which you have planned in Nebraska for more than half a generation. I suppose you have felt very tired sometimes waiting for the rest of the United States to see the point, and I want to say very frankly in this presence that some parts of the point I was very slow to see myself. But you only have to throw a man in the water to make him realize how cold it is, and, when they chucked me into the water two years ago in New Jersey, I knew exactly what the conditions were in American political and economic life. I had thought that I understood them before; since then I know that I understand them. Because I lived in a state that was owned by a series of corporations. They handed it along. It was at one time owned by the Pennsylvania Railroad. Then it was owned by the Public Service Corporation. It was owned by the Public Service Corporation when I was admitted, and that corporation has been resentful ever since that I interfered with its tenancy. But I really don't see any reason why people should give up their own residence to so small a body of men to monopolize. And, therefore, when I asked them for their title deeds and they couldn't produce them, and there was no court except the court of public opinion to resort to, which had already ruled against them, they moved out. And now they eat out of our hands and aren't losing flesh either. They are making just as much money as they made before, only they are making it in a more respectable way. They are making it without the constant assistance of the legislature of New Jersey. They are making it in the normal way, by supplying the people of New Jersey with the services in the way of transportation and gas and water that they really need. And, therefore, I do not believe that there are any thoughtful officials of the Public Service Corporation of New Jersey that now seriously regret the change that has come about. . . .

What we propose, therefore, in this program of freedom, is a program of general advantage. Almost every monopoly that has resisted extinction has resisted the real interests of its own stockholders. And it has been very, very slow business convincing those who were responsible for the business of the country that that was the fact. After the fourth of March next, therefore, we are all going to get together. We are going to stop serving special interests, and we are going to stop setting up one interest against another interest. We are not going to champion one set of people against another set of people, but we are going to see what common counsel can accomplish for the happiness and redemption of America.

T MS (C. L. Swem Coll., NjP); with corrections from the ICF transcript in the RSB Coll., DLC, and from the complete text in the *Lincoln Daily Star*, Oct. 6, 1912.

To Ellen Axson Wilson

[Lincoln, Neb., Oct. 6, 1912]

Fine Sunday rest after strenuous day yesterday. Am perfectly well and feeling quite equal to the task. Enjoyed my visit with Mr. Bryan very much indeed. Dearest love to all.

[Woodrow Wilson]

ICFT transcript of CLSsh notes (RSB Coll., DLC).

To George Darius Kilborn[1]

Personal

My dear Mr. Kilborn: [Lincoln, Neb., Oct. 6, 1912]

Knowing how generous you have been in your support of me, I venture to turn to you as to a true friend to urge this point. It is absolutely indispensable if the Democratic policy is to be carried out during the next administration that the Executive should be supported by a favorable majority in both houses. The only present hope of the opposition is to retain its control over the Senate, and they are concentrating their strength upon the mountain states in their struggle to accomplish this object. I am particularly anxious, therefore, about the election of both Mr. Pittman and Mr. Tallman.[2] I do not know what your own views upon their candidacy are, but I venture to send you this word because I feel so strongly my responsibility as the leader of the party and am so convinced of the necessity of having a Democratic Congress.

With warmest regards and deep appreciation of your generous attitude towards myself.

Cordially yours,   [Woodrow Wilson]

ICFT transcript of CLSsh notes (RSB Coll., DLC).
[1] Owner and publisher of the Reno *Nevada State Journal*, the largest newspaper in the state.
[2] Key Pittman, lawyer of Tonopah, Nev., was chosen senator by popular vote on November 5 and was unanimously elected by the Nevada legislature on January 29, 1913. Clay Tallman, also a lawyer of Tonopah and a member of the Nevada Senate, lost his race for congressman by 69 votes.

Two Letters from Charles Willis Thompson[1] to Berenice Morrow Thompson

On board the Wilson train, out of Lincoln, Neb.,
Dearest: 3.50 p/m., Central time Oct. 6, 1912.

. . . I like the Governor more than I expected to. He has a sense of humor that appeals to me. When I was introduced to him I said, "You don't remember it, Governor, but I've met you a couple of times. When you were Presidebt of Princeton I went to you to get an interview telling your plans." "Did you get it?" asked Wilson, with a dry smile; he knew darned well I didn't.

When Wilson heard that I was to join the party he tried to place me, and among other questions asked, "What sort of looking man is he?" "He looks," said Roscoe Mitchell,[2] "like Opper's cartoons of the Common People."[3]

The first time I heard the Gocernor speak was at Creighton University in Omaha. Of course his speech was old, but it was all new to me, and I noticed that every time he got off anything humorous he would glance at me to see how it struck the new man in the party. I observed, too, that he had a hard job to keep from laughing when he heard himself extravagantly eulogized. When the man who made the first speech called him "one of the greatest educators of this or any other age" Wilson had to bite his lips and bite thwm hard to keep from making an unseemly display. Once when he got off his "Red Queen" joke he winked at Hamer and Lawrence.⁴ This is the story from Alice Through the Looking Glass, where Alice and the Red Queen run very fast and Alice says at the end of the run, "Wbhy, we're back just where we started." "Certainly," says the Queen; "you'd have to run twice as fast as that to get anywhere else." He has told this so often that it has become a stock joke in the party, as Roosevelt's "Little Bull Mooses" did with his crowd. . . .

Yours lovingly,   Charley.

❖

On board the Wilson train, somewhere in Nebraska,
Dearest: 7 p.m., Oct. 6, 1912 (Central time).

The arrangements on this trip are different from what they were on the Roosevelt one. We all dine together in the Goverbor's car, the Federal, ours (the Jemez) being a compartment car. The Governor, of course, takes the head of the table, and he is a jovial companion. He is a good story-teller and not sensitive. The fact that along the line sight-seers say, "He may be all right, but he ain't good-looking," turned up as a subject of discussion to-night, and it reminded the Governor of an occasion when he was running for Governor. "I stopped," said he, "in ftront of a billboard that had my picture on it. As I stood there I became conscious of tw[o] workingmen who were passing, and staring at me. One of them said to the other, 'Bill, damned if them two ain't enough alike to be twins.' "

The Governor, I am surprised to find, cusses as much as Roosevelt, or even more, and nearly as much as Taft. Mitchell informed him yesterday that the Evening Post had refused to support Sulzer on account of his Tammany record. The Governor was mad. "There's no use," said he, "in being so damned ladylike."

They lined us all up on Bryan's porch today and photographed us, with Bryan and Wilson in the van. I didn't ask what paper it was for, for I am convinced that I never will see any of these pictures as long as I live.

At the table the Governor asked me a lot of questions about Roosevelt and was much interested in finding out that the Colonel dictates his important speeches in advance. "I wish I could do that," he said. "I've tried to do it over and over again, but I can't." He also wanted to hear about the time when they howled at T.R. in Atlanta and was immensely tickled with how the Colonel subdued the crowd by the absurdly simple device of jumping on a table, which distracted their attention. He and Measday and I got into an argument about Hearst's merits as a speaker, the Governor and I taking the ground that he was a good one, with Measday in opposition, and incidental to the argument I told about Hearst's first speech, the one he made before the Judiciary Committee in Washington. . . .

Your loving husband,   Charley.

TLS (C. W. Thompson Papers, NjP).

[1] Political correspondent for the *New York Times* and other newspapers, author of *Presidents I've Known and Two Near Presidents* (Indianapolis, 1929).

[2] Correspondent for Hearst's *New York American*. In 1914 he resigned in protest when fabricated material was inserted in his dispatches by Hearst editors. See Isaac Russell, "Hearst-Made War News," *Harper's Weekly*, LIX (July 25, 1914), 76-78.

[3] Frederick Burr Opper, artist and illustrator for *Puck* and the *New York Journal*, famed for his cartoon characters of tramps and political figures.

[4] Wesley Hamer, reporter for the Hearst newspapers, and David Lawrence, Princeton 1910, Associated Press correspondent.

An Address in Colorado Springs, Colorado[1]

[Oct. 7, 1912]

Mr. Chairman[2] and fellow citizens: Ordinarily I would esteem it cruelty to animals to inflict two speeches on one town,[3] but I comfort myself by the reflection that you did not undergo the other speech. I am also stimulated by the information that a very considerable number of those present represent the educational interests of this community and of this state. And, therefore, I feel very much at home, not only, but I know that you are disciplined to attention and that, therefore, you are very tame under the infliction of public speakers. I know, moreover, that you will sympathize with me in my present uncomfortable position, for whenever we use any conclusive arguments in public debate, you and I are complimented by being called academic. And, therefore, I will expect your sympathy in the things that I may have time to lay before you in the brief interval that is at my disposal this afternoon.

An educational body, a body of people thoughtful of the permanent interests of the country, ought to be the body most easy to convince that we are about to make a very critical choice in the United States. But there is one thing in my thoughts just now which quite overcrowds anything that might concern myself in the coming election. You can't carry out a great policy without the assistance of the Congress of the United States, and I must

[1] Delivered in the Opera House.
[2] Mayor Henry C. Hall.
[3] Wilson had just spoken in the Temple Theater in Colorado Springs.

say that I am even more interested in seeing both houses of the national Congress Democratic than I am in seeing the presidency occupied by a Democrat, because if both houses are Democratic, the next occupant of the President's chair, if he be not a Democrat, will be a very lonely and helpless person. I will take it for granted, therefore, that if the houses are Democratic, the President will be Democratic. And the critical matter in Colorado just now is that you have the choice through your legislature of two senators of the United States. I came out to Colorado chiefly to urge the selection of a Democratic legislature, in order that we might have a Democratic majority in the Senate of the United States. Because the houses of Congress are the places where policy is hammered out, where all the various views converge, where the real volume of competitive energy is set forth, where all the forces of the United States concentrate.

Your presiding officer has referred to one of the most difficult of these public questions. I mean the question of conservation and the relations of the national policy of conservation to local development. I realize, ladies and gentlemen, even though I have not had personal contact with the administration of these grave matters, that there has been a comparative failure on the part of the Government of the United States always to adjust its conservation policy to the needs of local development. And I believe that a little conference, a little frankness, a little care to see that everybody's needs are understood, will lead to a very different policy on the part of the authorities at Washington, and that we can safely promise that, if the Democratic party is in control, the conservation policy to which we are all deeply committed will not be so administered as to interfere with local needs and development. That ought to go without saying, that ought to go as a matter of course, but that is a mere matter of common sense.

But what I want to call your attention to is that you can't have a conservation policy in which you yourselves are to have any voice whatever unless the present character of the Government of the United States is changed. You know what has been the embarrassment about conservation. You know that the federal government has not dared relax its hold because, not bona fide settlers, not men bent upon the legitimate development of great states, but men bent upon getting in their own exclusive control great mineral, forest, and water resources, have stood at the ear of the government and attempted to dictate its policy. And the Government of the United States has not dared relax its somewhat rigid policy because of the fear that these forces would be stronger than the forces of individual communities and of the public interest. What we are now in dread of is that this control will be made permanent. Why is it that Alaska has lagged in her development? Why is it that there are great mountains of coal piled up in the shipping places on the coast of Alaska which the government at Washington won't permit to be sold? It is because the government isn't sure that it has followed all the intricate threads of intrigue by which small bodies of men have tried to get absolute and exclusive control of the coal fields of Alaska. The government stands itself suspicious of the forces by which it is surrounded. And whatever other direction you turn, you find the same situation.

Turn in the direction of the great tariff question. There are interests, for example, in Colorado which will have to be safeguarded, but who is going to safeguard them? The men who are establishing monopoly, or the free voice of the people of Colorado? Do you want these things absolutely controlling and your lives subordinated to that control? Or do you want a real local voice in the development of your own resources and the use of your own soil and the variation of your own industry? So long as the Government of the United States is chiefly influenced by the promoters of monopoly, you dare not stir in your development for fear of falling in their hands. Why, all this western country has written all over it the annals of monopolistic control. What are you going to do on the fifth of November? Relieve yourselves of this incubus, make yourselves free to settle conservation questions and tariff questions and currency questions and questions of foreign commerce? Then to which of the competing candidates for your confidence are you going to turn?

I am not now speaking of the candidates for the presidency; they are merely the spokesmen of different groups having definite programs. And I want to call your attention to the fact that neither branch of the Republican party (for the other two parties are merely branches of that party), neither branch of the Republican party even proposes to break the partnership which has so far embarrassed every action of the federal government. The third party merely proposes that we accept the domination in commerce and in industry of the trusts that have already built themselves up, accept them as facts, just as we accept our railways as facts, and proceed to regulate them, make them tolerant of our lives, make them the instruments of our development, make them gracious and beneficent. In other words, they are going to change the temper of the trusts but are going to leave us in the hands of the trusts.

Now, I don't trust any promises of a change of temper on the part of monopoly. Monopoly never was conceived in the temper of tolerance. Monopoly never was conceived with the purpose of general development. It was conceived with the purpose of special development. And we now have this whole program laid bare, for we know that it is the men who have promoted the trusts who have conceived the policy written into the program of the third party. It may be that they conceived it in what they believed to be the interest of the nation. I am not now impeaching their motives. I am saying that they are trying—whether honestly or dishonestly is of no matter—they are trying to perpetuate the system through which their control is maintained, and that the third party is lending itself to that project.

But a great many of you will say—and I dare say a great many of the women of Colorado will say—"This platform also contains things that our hearts have desired for more than a generation and we have found no party to espouse. And this third party has written into their platform those projects of human uplift, those plans of humane consideration for the men, women, and children who toil in America, which lie nearest and dearest to us." Yes, they have written these things into their platform, but who is going to give you the consummation of these plans? A government acting through the instrumentality of regulated monopoly? Has monopoly been very benevolent to its employees? Have the trusts had a soft heart for the working people of America? Have you found trusts that cared whether women were sapped of their vitality or not? Have you found trusts which are very scrupulous about using children in their tender years? Have you found trusts that were keen to protect the lungs and the health and the freedom of their employees? Have you found trusts that thought as much of their men as they did of their machinery? Then who is going to convert these men into the chief instruments of our benevolence? And how is a leader who has surrendered to the judgment of these men as to how the Government of the United States ought to act to carry out these things which can be carried out only by those who are absolutely disinterested? If you will point to me the least promise of disinterestedness on the part of the masters of our lives, then I will concede you some ray of hope; but only upon this hypothesis, only upon this conjecture, that the history of the world is going to be reversed, and the men who have the power to oppress us will be kind to us and will promote our interests, whether our interests jump with theirs or not.

We are going to make the most critical choice of American history on the fifth of November next, and I appeal particularly to the women of Colorado to see that the humane purposes of the nation are not put in the hands of pitiless giants, for that is the choice that you have to make. It may be that Mr. Roosevelt is entirely sincere; I am quite ready to concede that he is. But I am more afraid of a sincere man who is mistaken than of a scoundrel who is trying to mislead us, because the force of sincerity is more formidable than the force of iniquity. You can find a rascal out, but you can't smoke a sincere man out. And if he is sincere and mistaken, then he is all the more dangerous. And I believe, as profoundly as I believe anything, that the program he proposes is a program by which we would reverse all the processes of free industry in America.

I, therefore, am engaged against the program, not against the man. He is at perfect liberty to say anything about me that he pleases, provided he will answer my argument. That is the only condition of the battle. For the immortality of truth lies in the fact that you can't kill it by abusing the men that utter it. You have got to convince the people of the United States in this turning point in their career, and I am happy to say that I say these things with all the more freedom and force in a community reputed to have had Republican inclinations than I would say them in a community known to be overwhelmingly Democratic. Because the Democrats are going to vote the Democratic ticket anyhow. They are more absolutely united and more hopefully militant now than they ever have been in my recollection. You can't break into their ranks, and you can't resist their ranks.

But for the rest of you the choice is this: Are you going to sit on the side lines and witness the game, or are you going to get into the game? Are you going to put your force to the wheel, or are you going to stand off and say, "Well, we will not vote this time. We don't like the other branch of the family. We can't vote for that. We don't hope to do anything for our branch of the family, and we are not going to assist the men who aren't in the family."

Why, I am very much puzzled when I talk with some Republicans and match my ideas with theirs. They have got exactly the same ideas that I have, and yet they call themselves Republicans, and I call myself a Democrat. And I would like to know where the difference comes in. I think I have discovered it. They believe that the tariff ought to be revised, and revised downward. But they remember that their fathers revered the tariff, and, therefore, they think it is an act of impiety to speak disrespectfully of the tariff. Now, I have never entertained any feeling of reverence for the tariff. Either it is good for the United States, or it isn't. It is a mere question of fact, a mere question of circumstance. And circumstances change. So that the tariff may be good for the United States in one year and not good in the next generation. All that I revere are the facts of the case. And I have no belief in the doctrine of protection any more than I have a belief in the doctrine of free trade. What I have a belief in is trying to find out what is good for the United States, and, therefore, I don't speak respectfully of the tariff. And that is what divides me from my so-called Republican brothers. It is a matter of etiquette. They think it is impolite to speak as I sometimes do of the tariff, and I think it is perfectly pardonable manners. And I ask them, "Are you going to divide yourselves from us on a point of etiquette?"

I left a meeting the other day, and a friend of mine overheard two gentlemen who were known to be Republicans exchanging views as to myself. One of them said to the other, "Are you going to vote for him?" He said, "Well, I am going to try to." Which is a most interesting point of view to me. He meant, "If I can only forget my dear father, if I can only forget that myth that I have been following ever since I was a boy, namely, that the wealth of the United States does not consist in the genius of the American people, but in the protection of the American government, why, then I may vote for this man. Otherwise, he is too heterodox, he is too dangerous; I should fear that I was making my dear old father turn over in his grave." Now, I hope that, with due apologies to your ancestors, you will really sit up and take notice and judge according to the facts of the case. For I don't like to see people voting in the last generation. This is the year 1912, and it isn't like any year that has preceded it. The commercial, industrial, social, economic circumstances of the age are not remotely like the circumstances under which your fathers voted. Now, why not do your fathers the justice of doing what they did, namely, thinking for yourselves? Why not come out and say, "We are not going to ask whether this is a Republican ticket or a Democratic ticket. We are going to ask what we are voting for and whether we believe in it or not." Because conviction is the only thing that is now going to save the people of the United States from a colossal blunder. You say, "What conviction?" The conviction that liberty is the only road that America can follow.

I am not going to stop now, for fear my train should leave me, to show you how I think the progress of monopoly could be absolutely blocked in the United States. But there is a way of absolutely blocking it by the regulation of competition, and all that we propose to do is this: nobody proposes to take these trusts and squeeze the water out of them. All that anybody proposes is to put them on their mettle and tell them that if they carry that water in a free competitive market, they are welcome to carry it. But if they cannot, they will have to get rid of it in ways which they themselves are at liberty to devise, but that they have got to earn what they get, and not get it by monopolistic agreements and by monopolistic practices and cutthroat competition. That will settle the question of watered stock in a generation, and I don't believe that they will run out so suddenly as to drown anybody. It won't resemble one of the sudden floods that we are trying to prevent by a system of reservoirs. Perhaps they can build a graduated system of reservoirs by which to control this water so that it will irrigate and fertilize the valleys below instead of overwhelming them. But that is their own engineering job; that is none of our business. But they put the water up there, they dammed it up. Now, they have got to see to it that the dam don't break, because if the dam does break only their own people will be drowned.

And so I say open a competitive market into which newcomers are welcome, into which newcomers may come with their capital down to hard pan and their energy down to hard pan—their courage down to hard pan—and in a free market challenge these gentlemen to keep their supremacy by the mere means of efficiency. I, for one, don't care how big any business gets by efficiency, but I am jealous of any bigness that comes by monopoly. And, therefore, the test of efficiency is the Democratic test, and it is the only test which a democratic country can afford to put to the energies of its people.

I am speaking, ladies and gentlemen, in very plain terms about very practical matters, in order that you may realize that your action on the fifth of November ought not in conscience to be a matter of sentiment, but it ought to be a matter of clear-sighted opinion. And when once you have examined the programs of the parties, I know only too well that this compact, hopeful, militant Democratic team can break through the lines of monopoly and set you free. Not because any one of us is wise enough to do the job, but because all of us are willing to heed the counsels, the common counsels, of a great and free people.

T MS (C. L. Swem Coll., NjP); with corrections from the ICF transcript in RSB Coll., DLC, and from the partial text in the Denver *Rocky Mountain News*, Oct. 8, 1912.

A Call in Denver for a "Second Emancipation"[1]

[Oct. 7, 1912]

Ladies and Gentlemen: What shall a man say in the presence of so splendid a welcome as you have given me? I need not tell you that it moves me very deeply, indeed, to have this evidence of your friendship and of your welcome. And I am all the more moved because it seems to me that a great concourse like this is, as it were, a picture of the nation which we are attempting to serve. It, therefore, fills me with very deep emotion as I think of the opportunity of addressing to this vast assemblage some of the matters that are in my mind with regard to the future of the United States.

As I approached your beautiful city today I had placed in my hands a copy of the *Rocky Mountain News* of this morning, bidding me a welcome that I felt I was not worthy to receive and yet suggesting in the course of the editorial some of the thoughts which I wish most sincerely to present to you tonight. That editorial said that the time had come in the United States when the classes were arrayed against the masses. And I asked myself, "Can it be true that we have come to a point of critical conflict?" Is it not rather true that the classes and the masses alike have learned in the United States to understand one another, to vie with one another in the service of a common cause? Who are the classes in the United States? I do not believe that it can be justly said that there are any distinctly marked social classes in the United States though there are, I am sorry to say, very distinctly marked economic classes in the United States. There is a social class in the United States, but it does not count politically. It is that class which has been said to devote itself to expense regardless of pleasure, a class which I venture to say is negligible in weighing the forces in the field of politics, a class that merely spends and in turn is spent for nothing that is valuable in life. But there has been a process by which classes have been created in the United States, and that process the present year of politics is intended to check.

I want, if I may ask the indulgence of your attention for a little while, to describe to you what seems to me the choice that we have to make in the United States in this critical year. Some small bodies of men in the United States have in recent years developed a power which has threatened to control the economic and political fortunes of our whole great free population. And the processes by which that power has been created we ourselves have witnessed. We know that in the lobbies of Congress there have assembled men who have tried through the Ways and Means Committee of the House of Representatives and the Finance Committee of the Senate to obtain for themselves special and permanent privileges which would distinguish them in power and influence from all the other men striving for mastery in America.

We know that there is one name which we have learned to associate with this process by which mastery was sought to be created. I don't mention that name with any desire to bring a single individual into undeserved disrepute, but as we speak of Cannonism in the House, we have spoken of Aldrichism in the Senate. And the gentleman who was until recently the senior senator from Rhode Island was known to be the spokesman and representative of those men who were seeking special privilege through the legislation of the United States. By the special privileges which were there built up it became possible for men by great, sometimes secret, combinations of capital to establish a domination over the economic development of the United States which we sum up when we speak of the trusts, when we speak of the monopolies which have been established amongst us. Now, what is very much in my heart as I face a great assemblage like this is the question: Is there any political process which can set this great people free from the thralldom of monopoly? For if we cannot escape monopoly, we cannot set up a free government in the United States. I want to ask gentlemen of this great western country who are interested in its development to ask themselves what has stood in the way of that development. You know that one of the critical questions in which you are interested is the question of conservation. You know that you are fretful and dissatisfied because great forest areas, great water courses, great mineral resources, are held back from use by the Government of the United States, and that your local development seems to be checked by the stiff policy of restriction observed by the government at Washington.

But why does the government at Washington preserve this policy so stiff and rigid and inflexible? Because there are special interests which are stretching out their hands to monpolize these great resources which the people of this region ought to enjoy and ought to use. And the Government of the United States dares not release its grasp for fear these special powers that have been built up by the special legislation at Washington should become the masters of your development and of the nation's development itself. You are looking forward to the time when commerce shall change its course. You know, ladies and gentlemen, that just so soon as that great ship canal is opened through the Isthmus of

Panama, the blood in our veins will run in other directions. The great courses of commerce will be altered. Great ports will spring up which have hitherto had only little rivulets of commerce reaching their doors. New lines of railway will be necessary. And a thrill of movement will go through this western country such as it has never felt yet, and it will find itself near to some markets which are the markets of the world and which have seemed only too remote from it.

But the Government of the United States is at this moment afraid that the whole benefit of that great change will come only to those who already control the transportation facilities of this continent. So that in every direction you turn, whether it be the question of tariff or the question of trade, or the question of conservation, there is some power that we fear. Shall a great people consent to be fearful lest there are powers springing up in its own midst which it cannot control? We are not free to move in the settlement of any one of these questions until we have settled this preliminary, fundamental question, Is the Government of the United States free, or is it not?

At present the Government of the United States is not free. It is dominated by those men who have set up an economic control in this country. For monopolies in this country do not stand single and separate. They stand united in their force to resist all change. And this united force is all but too great for the government itself. Therefore, ladies and gentlemen, you have to choose on the fifth of November next what the future development of the United States is going to be. There are two proposals before you.

I am not going to discuss the proposals of the regular branch of the Republican party, because I don't discover that it has any. But I do discover that there is a very frank and very explicit and a very interesting proposal on the part of the third party. Wait until you understand it and then vote for it.

You will observe that this is our problem. All the world knows that this is our problem. First of all to change the tariff laws of the United States so that no special privilege will find cover underneath it at any point. Neither the regular Republicans nor the irregular Republicans propose any fundamental change whatever in the tariff. All the world knows that springing out of the tariff question is the great question of the trusts, which is the question of established monopoly. And the only proposal with regard to that comes from the third party, which proposes to make monopoly permanent and legal and to regulate it in our interest. To regulate it in our interest? If you say no, you haven't read the platform itself. The platform states that their object is to accept the existing conditions and set up a commission which shall have, without too much restriction of law, the right of constructive regulation, that is to say, discretionary regulation, over the exercise of these monopolistic powers. And all the newspapers that are supporting that program explicitly profess that purpose. Therefore, we have in this third party not even a proposal to change the existing partnership between big business and the Government of the United States.

On the other hand stands the proposal of the Democratic party to do the thing which, if it had been done when the Democratic party first proposed it, would have prevented the creation of monopoly, namely, the regulation of competition. What was it that made monopoly? (A voice: Roosevelt.) No, that isn't fair. He simply sat by helpless while it grew up.

But we know the processes by which monopoly is created. Just let me mention a few of them. One is that a lot of gentlemen, representing amongst them a majority of those engaged in a certain line of manufacture, get together and agree that they will amongst them control the output and determine the price. That is to say, they make a monopolistic agreement. They have an understanding which isn't necessarily a legal combination. Then when they have the understanding, this is the way they carry it out. If any rival with brains enough and enterprise enough to make them uneasy arises in any locality in the United States, they go into his local market and undersell him, so as to kill him before he gets big enough to be formidable, in the meantime selling at a profit throughout the rest of the Union and so recoup themselves for the losses which he cannot stand because he has only the local market. If anyone of you has tried it you know that is the way you have fared.

Then, in the third place, they agree among themselves that if any merchants refuse to buy exclusively from them they will cut them off entirely and so make it impossible for them to afford to buy a portion of their supply from the competitor.

Then, in the fourth place, they manage to get hold of so much of the raw material in the mines or on the backs of the cattle of the country or in whatever other source, that they can shut off the supply of raw material from those who dare to come into the field of manufacture against them. They set up a system of espionage throughout the country to find where new men are daring to come into the field against them.

Now, this unregulated competition has built up monopoly in the United States. And at any time that we had cared to step in and regulate the competition by stopping these practices we could have prevented monopoly. And in the meantime what has monopoly entailed upon us? When these gentlemen could not kill a great rival they bought a big one, and after they had bought the big one at three and a half times what his business was possibly worth, they have had to pay interest and dividends on the four or five times what they would otherwise have put into their business by way of sound and legitimate capital. And the people of the United States have had to pay the prices in order to enable them to carry the water.

Just so soon as you regulate competition and oblige these gentlemen to depend upon efficiency and efficiency only, you make it impossible for them to carry the water. I am not interested in squeezing the water out myself. I don't know how. I am only interested in making them carry it in a free market. If in a free market, where we have made it possible for independent competitors to enter the lists against them, they can carry this handicap, they are welcome, so far as I am concerned, to carry it. But I know how the competition of brains goes on well enough to know that the fresh competitor, working on real capital, economizing his processes, improving every invention that he uses, can beat the giant carrying the tank of water in any race he sets out upon.

I challenge these gentlemen to come into a fair field against the United States to beat independent competitors. They cannot do it. But they are going to have to try. I am not of that hopeful disposition to believe that we can teach the trusts to be pitiful and good and righteous. And knowing as I do, and as every thoughtful man in the United States knows, that these men have been masters of the government, I am not hopeful of [their] making the government masters of them.

Now, there was applause a moment ago when I mentioned the third party, and I think I know why. These people were not thinking about the perpetuation of monopoly. They were thinking of what the third party promises monopoly will do for us if we only give it a chance. If monopoly, forsooth monopoly, will shorten the hours of labor, will be regardful of the weakness of women, will be pitiful towards little children, will safeguard its machinery, will improve all its processes, will raise its wages and lower its prices, I should be less harsh. I am not of the sanguine disposition of the leaders of the third party. I have seen these giants close their hands upon the workingmen of this country already, and I have seen the blood come through their fingers. And I am not hopeful to believe that they will relax their grasp and lift these victims into the hopeful heavens. Ah, ladies and gentlemen, when you are starting out on a program, when you are starting on a journey, look beneath you and see the beast you are riding. You cannot get to any goal by that vehicle. Why, I was saying today that I had an image in my mind of the great trusts of this country, impersonated as you please, standing upon a great stage. There would not be so many of them as there are on this stage, and in front of them Mr. Roosevelt leading them in the Hallelujah Chorus. I don't know whether he thinks he can teach them the tune or not, but I think I see the cynical smile on their faces as they would try to learn it from him. Leave the government and the industry of the United States under the control and in the possession in which it now is, and the Hallelujah Chorus will sound like bitter mockery in our ears.

This is not a campaign against individuals. It is a crusade against powers that have governed us, that have limited our development, that have determined our lives, that have set us in a straitjacket to do as they please. This is a second struggle for emancipation. I could, if I chose, ladies and gentlemen, amuse you with the humors of this campaign. I could, if I thought it proper, lead your minds off by way of illustration into many a pleasant path of discussion. But I tell you, when I came into this room and felt the electric atmosphere of this great assemblage, I knew that I didn't dare tell you anything but the solemn truth. It is an infinitely solemn truth. I wish that I hadn't left a reasonably good voice in Indiana so that I might have the strength and the lungs to make every man and woman in this assemblage understand the issues of life and death which turn upon the election in November; not because you are going to choose a particular man President, because, contrary to opinions in certain quarters, there is no indispensable man.

I have the honor to represent, for the time being, the principles and the purposes and the impulses of what I believe to be a majority of the American people. But I want to say to you with perfect sincerity that some other man could do it just as well, provided he had this passion, this passion for the right settlement of the question whether we are to be dominated by economic monopoly or not.

There are a great many interesting things to discuss in this campaign, and I have tried to make speeches along other lines. And my mind swings back to this line as if it were following a magnet, for when I see great masses of uplifted faces like this, I know this: we are now going to determine what the hope and the opportunity and the achievement of the next generation in

America is going to be. We are trustees for our children, we are trustees of that great inheritance of American liberty which expresses itself not merely in song, not merely in flowers of rhetoric, not merely in emotional outbursts, but in those stern principles and programs of action which only thoughtful men can work out in quiet, under the impulse of universal sympathy with the struggle of mankind.

Suppose we depended upon these gentlemen who have the trusts in their control for the future development of the United States? Are nations, I ask you, developed from the top? Every nation is like a great tree. It may display a beautiful foliage. It may produce excellent fruit upon its branches, but its strength lies down in the dark, hidden, and fertile soil. And the future masters of America, if we are true to America, are coming from the unknown quarters. If this is a true democracy, no man can predict where the leaders of America are coming from. I suspect that it is harder for a leader to be born in a palace than to be born in a cabin. I suspect that it is harder for men at the top to understand the ardors, the hopes, the terrors of America than for men at the bottom. I suspect that men in the ranks who are struggling for a mere foothold, who are fearful lest their health should give way and their children should starve, know more of what America has to do than any other men in the country.

A friend of mine told me this evening that he had recently met a very highly educated gentleman from China who had only been ten days in this country, and that he asked him after his ten days what was the thing he regarded as most remarkable in America. "Why," he said, "much the most remarkable thing I have noticed is the expression of hope that is upon the faces of all the people." For you know in the Oriental countries, if you have traveled there, there seems to have settled upon the countenances of men and women a sort of acceptance of the inevitable. They are born into a certain stiff regime of life from which they do not hope or expect to be extricated. And as I think of that, I think, what are we to do for the hope of the average American man and woman? Are we to make these people look forward for permission to come into the field of activity? Are we to make them accept monopoly or the hopefulness of free enterprise? If America is not to have free enterprise, then she can have freedom of no sort whatever.

Ladies and gentlemen, is it of no consequence in this discussion that the Democratic party is the only national party now consolidated with a single purpose? I marvel that men retain such stiff traditions as not to see that the Republican party is now in absolute dissolution, and that the reason for this dissolution is that men in its own ranks have revolted from the things from which we are now trying to escape. I am not expecting Republicans to vote for me in this election because of any special confidence in me, but because they must see that if they want to escape from the things which their judgments condemn, there is only one team ready for the game.

I don't see any team ready for the game except the great Democratic team. It understands the game; it is eager for it and it can beat any scrub team in existence. And what a splendid game it is! How fine it is to believe that we have an opportunity to vote the United States free again! I want to say, as I say on every occasion, that I am not indicting or throwing any suspicion upon the character of the gentlemen whose judgments I am opposing. I have a great respect for the characters of the men, but if they were my dearest friends I would feel myself obliged to set myself like steel against their purposes. They don't see the character of the age. They have despaired of meeting the forces with which we must contend. And therefore I stand before you, not as a representative of the Democratic party, merely, but in my firm conviction as a representative, however unworthy, of the new day, the new purpose, the new life of achievement in this great country which is devoted to disinterested achievement.

I thought, as I crossed these beautiful valleys today, how clear the air was and how it suggested the unimpeded vision by which men might see the distant hills of achievement to which our great people have been struggling through all these hopeful years. And, as I, in imagination, looked back down the slopes of the continent to the great valley of the Mississippi and beyond to that eastern country where the great forces of the nation are in such hot and close and eager contest, I thought to myself that this western land, lifted high to the heavens, is a sort of coign of vantage from which one may look out and see what were the original purposes of America. We may here see the map of life spread before us, see the weary roads that men have traveled in order to gain the vision which has been the inspiration of American public men time out of mind. And when I know that out of this western country has come so much of the progressive sentiment and progressive force of our day, and how that force has been thrown back to the release of privilege and the revival of hope in the eastern country, I feel as if here I stood, not upon this little pulpit, but upon a great pulpit of the Rockies, looking back and crying to my brethren in the East, "Here are these clear-sighted hosts of the West who are going to show you the way now, as they have oftentimes in the past, by which America may once again be liberated." The air will be tonic in that new land. We are coming yet to that land of promise towards which the feet of America have been pressing through all the ages. And then we can look our brethren of other peoples in the face and say, "We haven't broken our promises to you. We have not brought you here to be servants and slaves. We have brought you here to share in a great inheritance of liberty. We have kept our promise to ourselves and our promise to you."

Who will volunteer for the great army of emancipation? Who will come to the polls in the spirit of soldiers of liberty and see to it that America never again faces so much as the fear of subjection on the part of all of her people to an insignificant group of her principal men? And our emancipation will include them. We will set them free from their own mistaken judgment. When they speak of the people they do not include themselves. When we speak of the people, we are more generous and include them. When they have been set free, when they have been shown the dignity of service, as contrasted with the disgrace of mastery, then they will for the first time find the zest of power, the zest of serving their fellow men and reaping a reward which will be sweet to the taste and give them such dreams at night as those have who care for little children and are mindful of the mercies of human life.

And so my appeal is the old appeal—as old as the history of human liberty. When I look at this great flag of ours, I seem to see in it alternate strips of parchment and of blood. On the parchment are inscribed the ancient sentences of our great Bill of Rights, and the blood is the blood that has been spilled to give those sentences validity. And into the blue heaven in the corner has swung star after star, the symbol of a great commonwealth —the star of Colorado along with the star of ancient Virginia. And these stars will shine there with undiminished luster only so long as we remember the liberties of men and see to it that it is never again necessary to shed a single tear or a single drop of blood in their vindication.

ICFT transcript of CLSsh notes (RSB Coll., DLC), with many corrections from the nearly full text in the Denver *Rocky Mountain News*, Oct. 8, 1912.
    1 Delivered in the Denver Auditorium.

From Nathan Straus

My dear Governor Wilson,   New York. October 7, 1912.

Enclosed please find an additional campaign contribution.[1] For obvious reasons[2] I do not want to give any more in New York State. For the same reasons, I should prefer not to have you use this check in the New York campaign. I don't think you need much help here. You will carry New York anyhow.

I hope you will be elected. I shall do everything in my power to help you, and I think there is no doubt but that you will win out.

Very sincerely yours,   Nathan Straus

HwLS (WP, DLC).
   [1] Of $5,000.
   [2] Because his brother, Oscar, was running for governor on the Progressive ticket.

A Campaign Address in Topeka, Kansas[1]

[Oct. 8, 1912]

Mr. Mayor,[2] Ladies and Gentlemen: It is very delightful indeed to find myself in Kansas again, because you know that Kansas has always been looked to by the rest of the country for leadership in things progressive. It is pleasant, therefore, to come and drink at some of the fountains of inspiration which are to be found in this state. And I will confide to you this anxiety, the fear lest Kansas should not pick out at this time the genuine breed of progressive. There are a great many breeds now. The variety is positively confusing, and I want, if you will be patient with me—and you have been infinitely patient in waiting for me —to expound to you what it seems to me that Kansas ought to discriminate about in the approaching election. Because I have my very serious doubts whether the party that has labeled itself "Progressive" is really progressive at all or not. I have entertained a very warm admiration for some of the progressive Republicans in Kansas. I have had the privilege of knowing some of them personally and knowing how sincere their interest in the advancement of the public welfare was. And it would distress me to see them ally themselves, as they seem about to ally themselves, with a party which cannot with its present program serve the progressive cause.

I say with its present program, because I want to be perfectly frank with every audience I face. I know the purposes of these

   [1] Delivered in the Topeka Auditorium in the afternoon.
   [2] Julius Benoit Billard.

men, and I sincerely fear that they are mistaking the method by which progressive measures can be put into operation in this country. Let us discuss for a little while, if you please, what it is that we are after, because in the little time that is left me I must omit preliminaries and plunge into the heart of my matter.

What gave rise to the progressive movement in America? I will not stop now to pronounce a eulogy upon the Democratic party and to point out to you that the Democratic party has not recently adopted a program of progressivism. Ever since the modern movement in economics, the Democratic party has warned you that the so-called protective policy was affording a covert for all sorts of special privileges, and that if you did not withdraw those special privileges, they would some time come back to haunt you and to dominate you. The Democratic party, ever since the creation of the great trusts which are now monopolizing some of the lines of industry and economic activity in this country, has warned you that these men who now seemed your servants might some day become your masters.

And when the progressive movement began in the Republican party, how did it begin? What were these new-line Republicans afraid of? The thing did not begin only in the West, though the West showed the most manifest signs of it. It began, though some people find it very hard to believe, also in the State of New Jersey. We had in the State of New Jersey, a good many years ago, a group of Republicans in the state—they never got on the national stage—who called themselves the New Idea Republicans, when the idea that the Republican program was not serving the country was a new idea. And these gentlemen separated themselves, very decisively separated themselves, from their companions in the Republican party in the State of New Jersey. Then came the movement—I am not stating them in order—there came the movement in Ohio, there came that great movement in Wisconsin, there sprang up in that northern state that redoubtable champion of progressivism, Robert La Follette. Robert La Follette has discriminated. He has not followed the third party, because he sees deeper into the program of the third party than some gentlemen hereabouts have looked. And I want to warn you of just the mistake which Robert La Follette avoided by knowing, by intimate association, just how close to and just how far from the progressive temper and the progressive program the present leader of the third party stood. For the danger that these men were engaged against was the danger of the domination of our development by those who had taken special advantage of the financial policy of this government and had established monopoly in many lines of industry. La Follette has always said what Democrats have always said, "These forces will overcome your government if your government does not overcome them."

Therefore, the test of progressivism is that you see the danger of the tariff and that you see the menace of monopoly. I ask you, which branch of the Republican party has seen either? They both stand pat on the tariff. They admit that some duties are too high and ought to be reduced, but they don't tell you upon what principle they are going to reduce them. They just have a notion that here and there somebody has been extravagant, and they are going to try to reduce the extravagance of the claims that special interests have made upon us. But they don't intend to cut at the heart of the special interests. On the contrary, the utterances of Mr. Roosevelt with regard to the tariff are practically the same as the utterances of Mr. Taft, and if you look at the Saratoga program, the Saratoga platform,[3] which Mr. Roosevelt himself endorsed, you will find there an unqualified endorsement of the Payne-Aldrich tariff, just as unqualified as Mr. Taft made in his Winona speech.[4] And in recent months, in recent weeks, Mr. Roosevelt has brushed the tariff aside and has said the tariff is not what ails us.

Now, what has he done with regard to the trusts? I suppose that there are a great many gentlemen here who are interested in currency reform, and you know that the opinion of the country in general has rejected the plan of currency reform offered by the so-called Aldrich Monetary Commission.[5] I am not sure that they have not turned from it chiefly because it bears Mr. Aldrich's name. But there are two parts to that plan. One part offers a new basis for an elastic currency, and the other proposes a method of control, and the method of control confirms the present power of small groups of American bankers to dominate the new system. Now, just as that plan proposes the control of those already controlling, so the plan of the third party with regard to the regulation of trusts proposes that we shall act through those already in control. For it does not propose, as the Democratic party does, to see to it that there is no such thing as private monopoly; but it proposes to regulate private monopoly. So that Mr. Roosevelt cannot divorce his thought from the idea that the chief business-

[3] The New York state Republican platform of 1910.
[4] Taft's speech in Winona, Minn., of September 17, 1909, defending the Payne-Aldrich tariff.
[5] For the origin and work of the National Monetary Commission, see n. 3 to the address printed at March 19, 1909, Vol. 19, and n. 3 to the interview printed at Aug. 26, 1911, Vol. 23.

men of this country are the only men who understand the business of this country.

Now, I absolutely dissent from that proposition. I believe that the rank and file of the businessmen in this country understand the economic conditions of the United States, and that this small group of men do not understand that condition. I understand from the newspaper press that Mr. Roosevelt was distressed by my suggestion the other day that the United States Steel Corporation was back of his plan for controlling the trusts.[6] He interpreted my remark to mean that they were supporting him with their money. I wasn't thinking about money. I don't know whether they are supporting him with their money or not; it doesn't make any difference. What I meant was, they are supporting him with their thought, and their thought is not our thought. I meant, and I say again, that the kind of control which he proposes is the kind of control that the United States Steel Corporation wants. I am perfectly ready to admit that they think it is best for the country. My point is that this is a method conceived from the point of view of the very men who are to be controlled, and that that is just the wrong point of view from which to conceive it.

These gentlemen in Kansas, therefore, who are supporting the third party are supporting a party whose fundamental program is agreeable to the monopolies of this country. And yet how these gentlemen, some of whom, as I have said, I know, have been fighting monopoly through all their career, and how they can reconcile the continuation of the battle under the banner of the very men they are fighting, I cannot imagine. I challenge the program in its fundamentals as not a progressive program at all. Now, gentlemen, this is a matter which you can judge for yourselves. Why did Mr. Gary propose this very method when he was at the head of the steel trust? Why is this very method commended here, there, and everywhere by the men who are interested in the maintenance of the present economic system of the United States? Why do the men who do not wish to be disturbed urge the adoption of this program, and why do men who wish to disturb them get back of this program? Why, it is because they read the rest of the program and forget what is at the heart of it. The rest of the program is very handsome; there is a great pulse beating in that platform of sympathy for the human race. But

[6] "As far as I know," Roosevelt said in a statement issued in Albany, N. Y., on October 7, "the only big man connected with either the Steel Corporation or the Harvester Trust who is supporting me is Mr. Perkins. As far as I know, all the others in both the Steel Corporation and the Harvester Trust are supporting either Mr. Taft or Mr. Wilson." *New York Times*, Oct. 8, 1912.

I don't want the sympathy of the trusts for the human race. I don't want their condescending assistance. And I don't want their assistance which they give at the compulsion of the federal government.

Every day I read over that plank of the third party in order to be sure that I am getting it right. All that they complain of is that these gentlemen exercise their power in a way that is secret. Therefore they want publicity. In a way that is arbitrary, therefore they want regulation. In a way that does not suit the general interests of the community, therefore they want them reminded of those general interests by an industrial commission. But at every turn it is the trusts who are to do us good, and not we ourselves. And I absolutely protest against being put into the hands of trustees. Mr. Roosevelt's conception of government is Mr. Taft's: that the presidency of the United States is the presidency of a board of directors. And I say, for my part, that if the people of the United States can't get justice for themselves, then it is high time that they should join the third party and get it from somebody else! The justice proposed is very beautiful. It is very attractive. There are planks in that platform which stir all the sympathies of the human heart. They propose things that we all want to do. But the question is, who is going to do them? Through whose instrumentality? Why, I want to say to the workingmen here that the platform proposes various measures of justice to the workingmen. Through whom, gentlemen?

Have you dealt with the United States Steel Corporation? Don't you know that that corporation and others like it have been the most successful and implacable enemies of organized labor? Don't you know that they stand against the right of workingmen to organize? And all that they do for their workingmen by way of making them comfortable, by way of making them happy, they do in order that their discontent may not reach outside the mills and organize the force of labor against them? I do not mean that there are not public-spirited and philanthropic men among the directors of the United States Steel Corporation, for there are. But I do mean that these gentlemen are of the temper to control the laboring men of this country, just as they are of the temper to control the markets of this country. And they want to get the whole economic development of the United States subject to the kind of control which they can suggest to the Government of the United States. And if Mr. Roosevelt is willing to have Mr. Perkins suggest how the corporations ought to be regulated, why will he not be willing to take suggestions from the same quarter as to the detail of the regulation? Mark you, ladies and gentlemen, I am not discussing individuals. I know Mr. George Perkins; I have no quarrel with anything except his judgment. He does not look at these things the way men who do not wish to accustom their minds to monopoly look at them.

Now, I take my stand absolutely where every progressive ought to take his stand—on the proposition of the Democratic platform that private monopoly is indefensible and intolerable. And there I will fight my battle. And I know how to fight it. What these gentlemen do not want is this: you know that you cannot stand competition unless you can beat your competitors by fair means or foul. I am perfectly willing that they should beat any competitor by fair means; and I know the foul means they have adopted; and I know that they can be stopped by law. Now, if they think that coming into the market upon the basis of mere efficiency, upon the mere basis of knowing how to manufacture goods better than anybody else and sell them cheaper than anybody else, if they can carry the immense amount of water that they have put into their enterprises in order to buy up rivals, then they are perfectly welcome to try it. For I have no fear of efficiency. I have only a fear of those things which they have been doing. When the gentlemen who represent a large proportion of a given industry get together and agree that they will all sell at the same price, that they will do everything together to control the market; then when they proceed to squeeze out every beginner who tries to go into the field against them; then when they begin to discriminate against those in the retail business who buy from the competitor; then when they begin to restrict the amount of raw material which can be bought by the competitor, then I know what is going on, and I know the methods by which those things can be stopped. All the fair competition you choose, but no unfair competition of any kind. And then when unfair competition is eliminated, let us see these gentlemen carry their tanks of water on their backs. All that I ask, and all I shall fight for, is that they shall come into the field against the merit and brains everywhere. If they can beat American brains, then they have got the best brains.

But if you want to know how far brains go, suppose you try to match your brains in a local market against these gentlemen and see them undersell you before your market is any bigger than the locality and make it absolutely impossible for you to get a fast foothold! If you want to know how brains count, originate some invention which will improve the kind of machinery they are using, and then see if you can borrow enough money to manufacture it without going into partnership with these gentlemen and pooling your interests with theirs. I know men who have tried it, and they could not get the money, because the great moneylenders of this country are in the arrangement with the great manufacturers of this country. And they do not propose to see their control of the market interfered with by outsiders. And who are outsiders? Why, all the rest of the people of the United States are outsiders.

Then, we have an inside to our government and an outside. And Mr. Roosevelt wants to patent the inside. He says it is a good enough inside for him, provided he can use it. I do not mean use it for his own aggrandizement, but provided he can use it for the people of the United States. For I am not aspersing Mr. Roosevelt's motives. I have nothing to do with them. They are postponed until the judgment day. But if he is allowed to patent the present processes of industry in this country and direct them with regard to the way in which they treat the United States, then he will see that his old classifications are realized. For he used to tell us there were good trusts and bad trusts; and he will guarantee to us that all trusts will be good. I dare say that he believes what he says. But in spite of his extraordinary capacity, I do not believe he can play Providence to the human race quite so successfully as that, and I am strengthened in that doubt by the fact that they have fooled him on one or two notable occasions already. He will not admit that he was fooled, but it is evident that he was taken into camp,[7] as any man might be taken into camp who does not understand the whole business of the United States. I certainly do not; and if men experienced in these things come to me and declare upon their honor that so and so has to be done in order to avoid catastrophe, I have no knowledge sufficient to match their information. I am not blaming a man because he has been taken into camp, but I do blame him for proposing to perpetuate an arrangement which will make it dangerous lest he should be taken into camp again.

And I warn every progressive Republican in Kansas that by lending his assistance to this program he is playing false to the very battle in which he has enlisted, for that battle is a battle against monopoly, against control, against the concentration of power in our economic development, against all those things that interfere with absolutely free enterprise. And I believe that some day these gentlemen will wake up and realize that they have misplaced their trust, not in an individual, it may be, but in a pro-

[7] He referred, among other things, to Roosevelt's approval of the acquisition of the Tennessee Coal and Iron Company by United States Steel during the Panic of 1907.

gram which is fatal to the things that we hold dearest. And so I have come into Kansas as into one of the homes of progressivism to ask you to test your progressivism. Put it in the fire. Test it with fire. Do not test it by label. The third party platform may be labeled "fireproof," but you put it in the fire and see. And if it will undergo the fire test in your consciences, in your knowledge of men, in your knowledge of the men who are backing that program, then by all means vote the third ticket. But if not, beware of voting the third ticket.

I say the third ticket because there are so many that they have to be numbered. And ever since I got into Kansas, early this morning at six o'clock, I have been trying to understand the variety of arrangements which are either consummated or contemplated in Kansas. Because, after your political leaders have conferred, and your courts have decided, and people have withdrawn, and others have been substituted, and there have been new tickets, and all that kind of thing, I do not know how you can tell where you are. The only safe thing is to give the conundrum up and vote Democratic. There is no doubt where the Democrats stand. They have not the least doubt where they are bound; and they are going to get there. They are going to get there by the votes of Kansas. For I have not come into Kansas for the first time. I have had the privilege of conferring with Kansans in their own homes more than once. And I have seen the rising tide in this redoubtable old commonwealth. Why, you were born in order to set some people free! Now, why not go on and set everybody free! You were born in order to make a territory into which human slavery could not come! Why not enact that economic slavery cannot come into Kansas! Why not enact that monopoly shall never rear its head in this soil fertilized by the blood of martyrs in the cause of liberty! I challenge you to read the history of your state and make it impossible for anybody ever to ask again, "What's the matter with Kansas?"[8]

T MS (C. L. Swem Coll., NjP).

[8] The title of William Allen White's famous editorial, about which see n. 4 to the news report printed at Feb. 17, 1904, Vol. 15.

An Address in Kansas City, Missouri[1]

[Oct. 8, 1912]

Mr. Speaker,[2] ladies and gentlemen: I never imagined that a crowd as big as this would come together merely to look at me.

[1] Delivered in Convention Hall.
[2] Champ Clark.

Evidently you are not in the humor to hear a speech, but there are some things that I want to say to you. In the first place I want to express my very deep gratification at meeting so many of my fellow citizens of Missouri, and I want to say to them what a profound satisfaction it affords me to find myself here on this platform, shoulder to shoulder with the great Speaker of the House of Representatives, a man whom I have long honored and admired and whom I consider myself specially fortunate to find myself in harness with.

I think that there is nothing the Democrats ought to be prouder of at the present moment than the extraordinary unity and solidity of their great forces. I don't wonder that when they see great outpourings like this they take heart to believe that a great conquest is in store for the Democratic hosts. The distinguished Speaker gave a very interesting description of the connections of the several candidates for the presidency. I believe that one of the most interesting circumstances about the third party is this, that it is a great body of personal followers rather than a great political party. Because I cannot explain otherwise some of the followers that Colonel Roosevelt has drawn to himself. I find that he has drawn into his personal following a number of men who seem to have forgotten the objects which they have in view. They are men who, for a great many years, have devoted themselves very intelligently and very energetically to the promises of a progressive program of legislative reform. This program of legislative reform has grown out of definite conditions which every man ought to understand in order that he may vote intelligently on the fifth of November. Those conditions hinge upon two particular problems in our national life—problems which we must face with the greatest possible frankness and the greatest possible independence of judgment.

In the first place, there are the problems which connect themselves with the so-called protective tariff; and what must strike everyone who discusses the tariff at all is the fact that the third party does not even profess to be dissatisfied with the tariff policy of the government except in certain details. The program of the third party is a program of correcting certain excessive duties, but it is not a program of condemnation of any policy whatever connected with the tariff legislation of the United States. Our objection goes to the essence of the matter. We say that it has turned out to be, not a policy of protection, but a policy of special favor, and that under the cover of these special favors there have grown up the great monopolistic combinations and undertakings in this country. Now, the third party, made up of men who banded themselves together originally to fight the tariff, is no longer fighting the tariff; made up of men banded together to oppose monopoly, is not any longer opposing monopoly, because the third party proposes, instead of abolishing, to adopt and regulate the monopolistic enterprises of this country. And, therefore, I ask any man who is genuinely progressive to examine himself very carefully and to ask whether this indeed be a progressive party.

I am not going to waste very much argument on that because I know which side of the river I am on. I know how Missouri thinks. I know the ancient faith of this great commonwealth. I know how in instances such as their support of the great Speaker of the House of Representatives, they have again and again shown, when they could see the right man, they would marshal themselves behind the progressive forces of Democratic policy. Therefore, I have come here tonight, not to make you an argumentative speech, not to do anything except to declare to you that I stand ready to serve you in the spirit of these men who have already shown that they can bear the test in your service. What I desire is to be their collaborator. It honors me to be spoken of as their leader, for the time being, in the great matters to which they have always been devoted. I know the whole Union has again and again thought of this central valley as the home of those who look forward in the policies of the United States, who are not content to walk with their eyes over their shoulders, who know that the country is to be served only by the shaping of its policy from year to year. Men must keep their eyes open, open to the future, comprehending the present duties, and correct those things that are wrong, desiring to see that each generation, as it comes on to the stage, may come with a new hope and a revived courage. So that the great Democracy, now for the first time in our generation, is going to have a chance to show whether it can return the government to the people or not; for this is the enterprise to which, time out of mind, the great Democratic party has been devoted. Ever since the great Jefferson spoke the immortal truths which are the foundation stones of our doctrine, this party has devoted itself with singleness of heart, through adversity of the most prolonged sort, to that cause which lies dear to every man's heart, which is upon every man's lips, but which only some serve, in season and out of season,—I mean the cause of the common people of the United States.

For when I look forward to the future of the United States, I know that it is not going to be framed by the chosen and privileged few, but that in proportion as the great mass of people in the United States are hopeful and happy and have their ambitions released, so is America to be great, so is America to realize the great ambitions of achievement which have always lifted her high to the view of the envious world. I know the government of the future will not be that of the favored few. And so I am here tonight merely to say to you that I feel profoundly honored that hosts of men who believe in the rights of man should stand behind the great party which has honored me as its standard-bearer in this contest.

Individual men rise and fall. Individual men are of little consequence except as they voice in all sincerity the best aspirations of their fellow citizens. No President of the United States, as your great Speaker has just intimated, is any stronger than the people that are back of him. And when I think of the two branches of the Republican party, neither of them proposing to separate that party from the special backing which it has had in those particular groups of men who are advancing the interests of combined capital, and then think of the great hosts of Democracy, I know that the thing to be decided on the fifth of November is this: Shall the people march to Washington, or will they leave Washington in the hands of trustees? Shall they elect a President of the United States, or shall they elect a president of the board of directors?

Now I, for my part, cannot dream of any doubt as to the choice the American people will make when it is clearcut in their consciousness that they are now choosing between two paths. Shall they live under the old regime of freedom of enterprise, or shall they live under the new regime of enthroned, though regulated, monopoly? You cannot use monopoly in order to serve a free people. You cannot use great combinations of capital to be pitiful and righteous and just. The judgments of justice, the standards of righteousness, arise out of the consciences of great bodies of men enlisted, not in the promotion of special privilege, but in the realization of human rights. And when I read those beautiful portions of the program of the third party devoted to the uplift of mankind, and see noble men and women attaching themselves to that party in the hope that regulated monopoly may realize these dreams of humanity, I wonder if they have studied the instruments through which they are going to do these things. The man who is leading the third party has not changed his point of view since he was President of the United States. I am not asking him to change it. I am not saying that he has not a perfect right to retain it. But I say that no man who had the point of view with regard to the government of this country which he had when he was President ought to be President again.

I said not long ago that Mr. Roosevelt was promoting a plan for the control of monopoly which was supported by the United States Steel Corporation. Mr. Roosevelt denied that he was being supported by more than one member. He was thinking of money. I was thinking of ideas. I did not say that he was getting money from these gentlemen; it is a matter of perfect indifference to me where he gets his money. But it is a matter of a great deal of difference to me where he gets his ideas. And he got his ideas with regard to the regulation of monopoly from the gentlemen who control the United States Steel Corporation. Now, I am perfectly ready to admit that the gentlemen who control the United States Steel Corporation have a perfect right to entertain their own ideas about this and to urge them upon the people of the United States. But I want to say, right now, that their ideas are not my ideas, and that I am perfectly certain that they would not promote any idea which interfered with the monopoly of the United States Steel Corporation. And inasmuch as I hope and intend to interfere with monopoly just as much as possible, I cannot subscribe to these arrangements by which they know that it will not be disturbed. Therefore, we are fighting out in this thing, not a battle between persons, but a battle between ideas, a battle between non-American and American ideas. For Jefferson did not utter the creed merely of the Democratic party, he uttered the creed of the American people. Because every time you put even standpat Republican orators to the test of doctrines, they profess to agree with Abraham Lincoln and Thomas Jefferson, who agreed with one another. But when it comes to practice, they forget their doctrine. And I insist that the prestige, the greatness, the dignity, of the Democratic party consists in this—that it has always tried to match its practice with its principles.

Now, I see in this great company, in its uneasiness, in its unrest, not only that it is disquieted by the hot atmosphere of this hall and does not want any more hot air added to it, but that it is impatient to march to the polls and decide the verdict of the American people. Because I know just how you feel. When I spoke just now about the candidate of the third party somebody over here said I need not worry. And I am not worrying.

This is not a meeting to make up our minds. This is a meeting to ratify our purposes. We know what we are going to do. We are going to get together in overwhelming numbers, and by a tremendous majority of the American people the future development of America is going to be settled. When I go away from this beautiful city tonight I shall have an image in my mind of great gathering hosts and of free American voters, each man with his eye lifted to the horizon, where he sees the light of a new day beginning to spread its blush along the heavens. I shall feel as if this whole mass in front of us were a type, were an embodiment, of the great American democracy, that I had seen that democracy rise in its might and manifest its irresistible purpose.[3]

T MS (C. L. Swem Coll., NjP), with a few corrections and one addition from the incomplete text in the *Kansas City Times*, Oct. 9, 1912.

  [3] There is an undated WWsh outline of this speech in WP, DLC.

Abram Woodruff Halsey to Ellen Axson Wilson

My Dear Mrs Wilson,   New York Oct. 8, 1912

A letter came to the Board[1] Rooms yesterday. It was from Japan and gave the straw vote of the American missionaries for President. I am sure it will interest you. There were 171 votes cast as follows:

Wilson	122
Roosevelt	35
Chapin[2]	10
Taft	4

What do you think of that for Japan? I trust you are all well. I thought the Governor was in fine physical condition the night he spoke at the College Club in New York. The pace is pretty rapid but he seems to keep up with the procession[.] Sorry not to have seen you in New York. I had a few words with your daughter. Remember me to her and the sisters as well.

                                  Cordially   A. W. Halsey

ALS (WP, DLC).

  [1] That is, the Board of Foreign Missions of the Presbyterian Church, U.S.A., of which he was a general secretary.

  [2] Eugene Wilder Chafin, presidential candidate of the Prohibition party.

Remarks in Springfield, Illinois, on the Main Issue of the Campaign[1]

[Oct. 9, 1912]

Mr. President,[2] ladies and gentlemen: I feel that I owe an apology to the people of Illinois and the people of the United States for conducting a campaign during a week when the World Series of baseball is on.[3] I am sure you would rather hear the score, and I am so confident what the score is going to be on the fifth of November that I am very much interested in the score

from day to day. Moreover, I would like you to understand that
the Democratic battery is getting on to Mr. Roosevelt's curves,
and they are knocking out a home run every time they go to
the bat. In my innocent youth I used to play baseball, and I have
pursued it with ardor ever since. And I believe that every college
man, at any rate, must understand me when I say that it is difficult for me not to allow my own attention to be distracted from
politics, because, after all, who wins that pennant is a very important national question.

I feel very much honored, ladies and gentlemen, to stand in
this place because I know the associations with which this place
is connected. I know the extraordinary number of great men
which in a particular generation Illinois contributed to the guidance of this nation. And I know that those men, in their lives,
spoke the very lesson which it is now imperatively important that
the people of the United States should learn, namely, that their
health does not come from the top, but that it comes from the
rank of the people themselves.

I feel profoundly impressed as I stand in this historic place,
so near the spot where men have spoken of the issues of life and
death for the great country which we love. And I hope that you
will not think I am speaking the language of exaggeration when
I say that I believe we are again face to face with the issues of
life and death—not with the issues of life and death that turn
upon sectional strife, not upon those issues which are explicitly
based upon questions which threaten to divide a nation, but upon
very much more subtle questions than that. Because now we
have to determine whether we are going to master the economic
powers that have absolutely dominated our life, or whether we
are going to control our own affairs directly through the voice
of the people themselves. I say that that is the issue of life and
death, for no nation can remain free, gentlemen, in which small
groups of men determine the industrial development, and by
determining the industrial development, determine the political
policies. Because the trouble with this country has not been that
there has been big business, but that big business has closed its
hand upon politics, and that the politics of this country has been
dominated by the men who had the chief stake in maintaining
those policies, which afforded them special privileges and made
us their bond servants in the development of the country. Because when the greater movements of credit, when all the greater
developments of industry, when all the currents of commerce,
are controlled by little groups of men, then the rest of us must

look around between their legs to see what chance we may have, what outlook we may have upon life and enterprise and achievement and the initiation of great things.

And so the people of the United States on the fifth of November are going to choose the form of government they will live under. They are going to choose whether they will live under a government which will take care of the weak, or a government where the strong will dominate the weak. And I, for my part, have not the least doubt as to what the verdict is going to be.

I have not traveled from one part of this country to the other and failed to observe how the people of this country have awakened to the real circumstances of their life and of their country and of their government. And I know, if I know anything, that they are going to resume that sway which they resumed long ago when this government was set up. I know that I do not have to appeal to the men who have been Republicans in the city of Springfield and in the State of Illinois to absolutely repudiate those methods of government which the great founders of the Republican party would have been the first to repudiate.

When gentlemen proposing to legalize monopoly profess to speak in the name of Lincoln, it is as if those who professed and intended to perpetuate human slavery should have dared to speak in the name of the Great Emancipator. We are going to repudiate all this slavery just as emphatically as we repudiated the other. And we are not going to look to the gentlemen who established that slavery in order to accomplish our liberty. We know the voice. The voice is the voice of Esau, though the touch may be the touch of Jacob. But we are not going to be touched. We have grown a little too familiar with the eccentric orbit of the gentlemen who are now trying to swing into the course of the people to be misled. We are not gazers upon an empty heaven, for we know where the fixed constellations are, and we are going to follow the old stars of liberty.

T MS (C. L. Swem Coll., NjP), with corrections from the complete text in the Springfield *Illinois State Register*, Oct. 10, 1912.

[1] Delivered at the Sangamon County Courthouse.

[2] Ben Franklin Caldwell, congressman from Illinois, 1899-1905, 1907-1909; president of the Caldwell State Bank of Chatham, Ill.

[3] The Boston Red Sox and the New York Giants played in the World Series between October 8 and 16. The Red Sox won the series, four games to three, with one tie game.

A Brief Speech in the Coliseum in Springfield

[Oct. 9, 1912]

Mr. Chairman[1] and fellow citizens: It is with very genuine emotions that I face a great company like this, and your presiding officer has unwittingly touched the very nerve of my feelings in what he has said about the association of this place with the life and the career of the immortal Lincoln. Because, gentlemen, we are face to face with a very profound change in American politics, and the career of Lincoln suggests to us just the sort of change that is going to take place.

You know that in the time of Lincoln there were a great many men associated with the Government of the United States whose patriotism we are not privileged to deny or to question, who intended to serve the people of the United States, but had become so saturated with the point of view of a governing class that it was impossible for them to see America as the people of America themselves saw it. And then there arose in this great State of Illinois that interesting figure, that immortal figure, of the great Lincoln, who stood up and said, "The politicians of this country, the men who have governed this country, do not see affairs from the point of view of the people of the United States." When I think of that tall, gaunt figure rising in Illinois, I have the picture of a man free, unentangled, unassociated with the governing influences of the country, ready to see things with an open eye, to see them steadily, to see them whole, to see them as the men he rubbed shoulders with and associated with saw them, standing up and facing men like Douglas and the others who were opposing him with this message: "You are looking at the situation as another generation has looked at it. You are looking at rights, at human rights, as another generation has looked at them."

I tell you that this generation looks at them with a clarified vision. We are coming on. Then there came a day when the great hosts sang, "Yes, Father Abraham, we are coming on." The great body of the American people, seeing this man, said to each other: "He has our heart under his jacket. This man has our thought in his mind. This man has our vision in his eye."

I tell you, gentlemen, that progress comes in every great nation only by a complete alteration of the point of view, only by what I might call a shake-up and a reformation, and the great shake-up comes when all the foundations of established authority are shaken by the moving mass of the irresistible force of the great commonwealths.

Now, the trouble with our present political conditions is that we need some man who has not been associated with the governing classes and influences of this country to stand up and speak for us, a voice from the outside calling upon the American people to assert again their rights and their prerogatives in the possession of their own government.

My thought about both Mr. Taft and Mr. Roosevelt is a thought of entire respect, but these gentlemen have been so intimately associated with the powers that have been determining the policies of this government for almost a generation that they cannot look at the affairs of the United States with the view of a new age and of a changed set of circumstances. They are unable to speak. They sympathize with the people. Their hearts, no doubt, go out to the great masses of unknown men in this country. But their thought is in close habitual association with those who have framed the policies of this country during our own lifetime. And those who have framed those policies have framed the protective tariff, have developed the trusts, have coordinated and ordered all the great economic forces of this country in such fashion that nothing but an outside force breaking in can disturb their domination and control. And, therefore, the Democratic party stands up in the presence of these gentlemen and says, "We are not denying your integrity, we are not denying your purpose, but the thought of the people of the United States has not yet penetrated to your consciousness. You are willing to act for the people, but you are not willing to act through the people."

The Democratic party, time out of mind, has believed that every country is rescued from unfavorable conditions by a self-assertion on the part of the neglected portions of the community. The community in the United States has not been brought within the councils of the nation.

It is impossible for me, ladies and gentlemen, with my impaired voice, that I have impaired in your service, to expound to you at any length today—and the circumstances render it unsuitable that I should explain to you at any length today—the issues and the intricacies of the present campaign. But what I want to leave with you is this suggestion: You furnished the nation with the judgment, with the discrimination, to pick out a man from the ranks who would go in and give the Government of the United States a new point of view. And I want to ask you if it is not time that the Government of the United States should be renewed with fresh blood from the outside. And I ask you if it is not suitable that you men who knew Lincoln, you men of the same breed with Lincoln, you men of the same sympathies with Lincoln, should assert yourselves in a declaration of independence which it is necessary for this nation now to pronounce against the economic forces which have been governing it?

I have come here touched with the spirit of the place, filled with reverence for the associations connected with a great name. You gave the country this great man. Now, can you not, at this critical stage of the nation's history, back the party which stands for the things which Lincoln loved and try to see things from the point of view where Lincoln stood?

I do not for one moment believe that Lincoln would admit that the party which is seeking to legalize monopoly was the same party that he had belonged to. I won't pretend to say what a great man like Lincoln would have done in this day, but I have my shrewd guess about the matter. And I believe that with that infallible instinct of his, that invariable sympathy with the general body of the people, he would have lined himself up with the men who were striving for a new order of things in the United States.

We have a very, very erratic comet now sweeping across our horizon. But we have our eyes upon the stable constellations, and we are not going to follow the erratic course of an incalculable body, even though it be in heaven. For we are going to reckon by the course of the stars and live in the light of the undying sun which shines alike upon all men, the just and the unjust, which uncovers the crusts and brings up the crops. And when the men who cultivate the crops of this country, when the men who make up the real bone and sinew of this country, make up their minds that they are going to be the rulers of this country, then we won't need any erratic comets to lead us. We shall follow the old stars and live with them in their eternal majesty and serenity.

T MS (C. L. Swem Coll., NjP), with corrections from the complete text in the Springfield *Illinois State Register*, Oct. 10, 1912.

[1] John Montgomery Crebs, president of the Illinois State Board of Agriculture, banker of Carmi, Ill.

Remarks to Democratic Newspapermen in St. Louis[1]

[Oct. 9, 1912]

Mr. Toastmaster[2] and gentlemen: The campaign has not been very kind to my voice and, therefore, I cannot speak to you very long, but there are too many important matters at issue for me to decline to speak at all to so influential a company as this.

[1] To the Democratic Press Association of Missouri at the Hotel Jefferson.
[2] H. J. Blanton, president of the association and editor of the *Monroe County Appeal* of Paris, Mo.

In the first place, I want to express the very sincere pleasure which I feel in finding myself shoulder to shoulder with the great Speaker of the House of Representatives, and there was only one word in the toastmaster's introduction at which I would quibble, and that is the word "rival." Mr. Clark and I are not rivals. We are comrades, and I feel infinitely strengthened in having the experience and counsel of such men as he. The whole of the problem that we now face, gentlemen, is a problem with which you are yourselves intimately connected. Because I feel that the newspapers of this country, and perhaps I may say particularly the county newspapers of this country, are responsible for the exact slant which opinion is to take with regard to public matters—because the daily or the weekly impression after a while becomes indelible, and it is only by the reiteration of the things that we all of us see that we shall be able to form opinion and to mold it permanently as we desire for the welfare of the country.

There have been numerous revelations within the last few days as a result of the investigation of the Clapp committee in Washington.[3] You have not been taken by surprise by those revelations. You cannot say that there is anything in them that you did not know before except their detail. You know just as well as if it had been part of your familiar thought all along that these corporations, these great interests, were contributing to the success of the Republican party. I dare say that corporations have upon occasion contributed to Democratic funds, but never in anything like the same proportion with which they have contributed to Republican funds. You have known always, if you have known anything, that the big business interests of this country supported the Republican party with the expectation and the exaction that the Republican party should take care of them. That is the system with a big S upon which the Republican party has been maintained. I am not saying this by way of indictment. I am not saying it by way of blame. It is merely an accepted and acknowledged fact. And now we are face to face with this problem—how to convince public opinion that a party based and sup-

[3] The Clapp committee began a new round of hearings on September 30. Between that date and October 8, the testimony produced a number of sensational revelations. It came out that, of the total reported expenditure of $2,195,000 by the Republican National Committe in the presidential campaign of 1904, 73½ per cent had been contributed by corporations or individuals on behalf of corporations. J. P. Morgan gave $150,000; the Standard Oil Co., $100,000; Henry Clay Frick, $100,000; and E. H. Harriman, $50,000. Testifying on October 4, Roosevelt admitted knowing in 1904 that *some* corporations were aiding his campaign, but he denied that he knew at the time of the contributions from Morgan and the Standard Oil Co. Moreover, he repeatedly asserted that no special favors had ever been requested or extended to any of the contributors. *Campaign Contributions*, 1, 197-681.

ported upon that system can rescue the country from the very things which that system has set up.

To turn back, as in some quarters it seems likely that independent opinion in the Republican party will turn back, to Mr. Taft and the regular organization is to turn back to the inevitable consequences of the system. Mark what the results will be. There isn't a great problem in this country which can be solved unless that old understanding and partnership is absolutely broken up. You can't solve the conservation question. Why is it that the people of the State of Washington, for example, can't buy coal out of Alaska? Why is it that great mountains of coal are piled up at the shipping places in Alaska under the ban of the government, not salable even. It is because the government doesn't know how yet to prevent the Guggenheims and men like them from closing their hand over the resources of Alaska. And it doesn't dare move, either, because it isn't independent enough to move or because it doesn't know in which direction to move. The same is true with regard to the forest resources, with regard to all the mines within the older territory of the United States, with regard to the leasing and control of the water powers. Now, when you think of this great body of water that ought to be the chief highway of trade throughout the United States that runs at your very doors here, do you suppose for one moment that you are going to have a system of caring for and developing the inland waterways of this country under the domination of special interests, out of the coffers of a government which is controlled by special interests? And how does any man entertain a reasonable hope that the Republican party will ever release itself from the alliance it has already made and so long maintained. Can any resident of the Mississippi Valley expect an independent and beneficial development of the inland waterways of this country through a Republican administration? They cannot reasonably expect it; they may unreasonably expect it.

And so we are face to face with nothing less than this—unless we can get a free government, we can't get anything else. So that the problem you have to put to your leaders and the American people today, and every day, is this, not what these gentlemen propose to do, but can they do it through the instrumentalities which they are sure to use? Why, what gave rise to the independent movement, to the insurgent movement in the Republican party? They revolted from such outrageous extremes of policy as the Payne-Aldrich tariff bill, for example, because it was a covert and hiding place for special privilege. But does either branch of the Republican party now even propose any radical changes in the tariff policy? They are both standing pat, standing pat in the very heart, within the very citadel, of the special system which I have just now alluded to. And why did these gentlemen who revolted from the Republican policy revolt from it? Because they supposed that the development of the United States was being hastened? No, because they believed it was being retarded by these special privileges, because they were opposed to trusts and monopolies.

Now the regular Republicans say they are opposed to monopoly. But all that they suggest by way of opposing it they narrate among the things that they have already done, and I haven't seen any noticeable decline in the processes of monopoly. The other branch of the party proposes to accept monopoly and to see to it that by governmental regulation it is made gracious and righteous and good to us. So that both branches of the Republican party stand pat on both parts of the system. There isn't any place within the Republican ranks to which the independent voter can turn who expects to see this country released from the incubus of centralized and special control under which it has labored. So that the Democratic party ought to regard itself as a party sacredly devoted, devoted in the spirit of Christianity, to nothing less than a great war of emancipation.

Think of it, gentlemen, if you, through your columns, if we who are privileged to make public speeches, if the hosts ordered throughout the ranks of the Democratic party, don't set this government free, there is no one else who so much as proposes to set it free. And, therefore, the burden is upon our consciences. And, ah, what a reward it will be if through intelligence, if through unswerving devotion to a cause like this, we can return the Government of the United States to the people! All generations will call us blessed, and we shall recover again our spirit in affairs, our self-respect, our poise. We shall free ourselves from fear and emancipate ourselves from thralldom. It is a great cause worthy of every great effort, and it is a privilege, in my opinion, to be able, either by writing or by speech, to stand in the breach against those who would still further enchain and debase us. I consider it more than a pleasure, a great privilege, to have had the opportunity of saying even these few words to so influential a body as this. And I am sure that when this campaign is over and we have released the Government of the United States, we shall look forward to a new age in America, because those that we have opposed will profit as much as we ourselves. And men who have sought the wrong courses will join us in a great rejoicing that again we can look each other in the face as

American citizens and say that again we are respecting ourselves and respecting our neighbors and assisting the great cause of human liberty.

ICFT transcript of CLSsh notes (RSB Coll., DLC).

From William Green[1]

Dear Sir: Indianapolis, Ind., Oct. 9, 1912.

My absence from Indianapolis when you were here recently leads me to write you about a matter concerning which I had hoped at that time to confer with you.

The miners of this country feel that the needs and the importance of the great industry with which they are connected are not appreciated by the public and that the industry has received from neither the Federal nor the State governments, the recognition and aid to which it is entitled.

As representing one of the Nation's two great foundation industries, the miners long ago asked for the establishment of a Department of Mines. After several years of pleading we had to be content with the establishment of a bureau of mines, with an appropriation much below what was needed and concerning which John Mitchell[2] said in a recent letter to the chairman of The Congressional Committee on "Mines and Mining."

"The inadequacy of the facilities tends to bring discredit on the work, and thereby discourage both those associated with it and those for whose benefit the movement was inaugurated. I fear it also indicates a failure to comprehend the importance and magnitude of the undertaking and the difficulties involved."

In view of the fact that the present Congress made a larger percentage increase in the appropriation for the mining investigations than for the work of other bureaus, and, in view of the plank in the National Democratic platform which promises the needed enlargement of this work, we are led to believe that if elected to the Presidency, you will cooperate with us not only in securing the fulfillment of this promise, but also in pushing forward the movement, both for better safeguarding the lives of miners and for lessening the waste of resources necessary for the country's welfare.

For I may add in conclusion that the miners of this country are as patriotic and as anxious for its permanent welfare as are any other class of its citizens; and their interest in the mining industry is not limited to matters pertaining to their own safety, but includes also measures to secure this wiser use of our resources upon which will depend both the future and the present welfare of our industry and of our country.

Very Truly Yours, Wm. Green.

TLS (WP, DLC).

[1] Statistician of the United Mine Workers of America, concerned with gathering data on mining accidents, accident prevention, and occupational diseases; Democratic member of the Ohio State Senate.

[2] President of the U.M.W., 1898-1908; at this time a professional lecturer on trade unionism.

A Campaign Address in Chicago[1]

[Oct. 10, 1912]

Mr. Chairman[2] and fellow citizens: I very warmly appreciate the generous introduction which I have just listened to, and I only wish that I could borrow my introducer's magnificent voice. I left the best tones of my voice in the State of Indiana. (Voice from the audience: "Good place!") A very good place. When I came here this evening, I asked where it was I was going to speak; and when I was told that it was to be in the armory of the Fighting Irish Seventh, then I knew that that was where I wanted to be.

I have in me a very interesting and troublesome mixture of bloods. I get all my stubbornness from the Scotch, and then there is something else that gives me a great deal of trouble, which I attribute to the Irish. At any rate, it makes me love a scrap; and so I knew that if I was to be privileged to speak in this armory, I would be forgiven for speaking in a somewhat militant manner.

As I reflected upon the great bodies of people that have come to this great country of ours, with the love of liberty in their hearts—not only the great Irish people, but the great liberty-loving men and women from every civilized country on the globe—the great people of liberty-loving Poland, where so much blood has been spent in the cause of human rights; the ancient Italian people, whose love of liberty runs back to the days of the Roman Republic; the great Slavic people; the great peoples out of Sicily; the great peoples from every quarter of the globe who have come to America in order to be free—I reflected upon this question: what did they come to be free from? What was there that they wanted to get rid of in the countries which they left and hoped to find in the country in which they took refuge and made a new home for themselves? What was it that these militant people

[1] Delivered in the 7th Regiment Armory.

[2] James J. Townsend, former president of the Chicago Stock Exchange and a lieutenant of Roger C. Sullivan.

came to fight for? Why, they came to fight for a release from arbitrary power of every kind and of every degree. They came to fight against the arbitrary power of governments, the arbitrary control of aristocracy, the arbitrary privilege of classes that did not allow their privileges to be interfered with by the general interests of the people. And, when I thought whether they had found what they came to seek or not, I reflected upon the present circumstances of our political life. And I was glad that I was to be with some representatives of the Fighting Seventh, because it seems to me that there is a great deal to fight for if we are to satisfy the expectations and the hopes of mankind.

While these people have escaped the open and avowed tyranny of special classes and of arbitrary governments, they have not escaped in America the private power of privilege and of narrow and exclusive power. For in America we have found this—that privilege has crept upon us in the dark; that privilege has laid its hand secretly on the government; that men who grew powerful because of the very freedom of the land in which we live, men who grew powerful because of the very opportunities which the world has sought to share with us, found presently that under the shadow of the government's patronage they could control the government itself, found that the secret ways of power were possible in America, where public ways of power would have been impossible in America.

You know the system by which they have maintained their power. These men have found elections an inconvenience, but, nevertheless, not a bar to their power. They have gone through the forms of election because they knew they could control tickets. They knew they could control the personnel, not only of our executive offices, but of our legislative chambers, and, sometimes to our shame, be it said, even of our courts; and that all they had to do was to keep under cover in order to exercise the absolutely arbitrary powers of government.

So that what I have to ask myself, as I face the possible future of the United States, is this: Do the people of the United States see distinctly what it is that they have to fight, and have they made up their minds that they are going to fight it to the finish? For my own part, it is perfectly evident what there is to fight in the United States. I am not one of those who believe that those who have maintained secret power in America are all bad men who mean to do a malevolent thing and to change the character of government in the United States. Many of them are men who have been bred in a system, now perfectly obvious and patent to the eye of every man, to which they have grown so accustomed that they have honestly come to believe that the Government of the United States is safe only under the aegis of their influence and of their guidance. You know what the system is. It is being uncovered every day at Washington. Nobody need be surprised, I dare say nobody was surprised to find that the chief contributions to campaign funds had come from particular corporations, because it had become obvious that, whether these corporations intended to corrupt the government or not, they had grown in the habit of controlling the government, and that this was the recognized means by which they got influence over the councils, not only of the executive at Washington, but also of the committees of Congress.

For a long time we knew these things and did not rise up in arms against them, and it is only now that we are beginning to realize how deeply significant the whole thing is. We are jealous now who makes contributions to political campaigns, because we know that those who make contributions expect to get the chief consideration of the government, and that they levy tribute of special privilege in order as a guarantee that they will be justified in continuing to support the party to which they give their contributions. I dare say that corporations have contributed in times past to Democratic campaign funds. But they have done so only as an anchor to windward; they have done so only because, contributing a great deal to the one side, they thought they had better contribute a little to the other, and so hedge on their bets.

They have done so, not by the direct implication of the public leaders of the two parties, but by the direct implication of the private managers of both parties. For we live, ladies and gentlemen, we have lived in too many parts of this country, under a system of secret management, and secret management which was conducted through the astuteness, through the power, through the sleepless activity of men who acted as the go-betweens between politics and business. A great many businessmen in this audience will bear me witness that they have been the victims of this system as well as the beneficiaries of it, that they have a tribute levied on them as the price of protection just as often as they have contributed money in order to get favors, and that therefore the whole bad system is against the interests of all of us alike and is something that, for the common benefit, we ought all to unite against.

Very well then, if we are to redeem the promises of America to mankind we must redeem the Government of the United States from private control. I know something of this business because about two years ago I was put at the head of a government which had been under private control. I know exactly the kind of influences that have to be fought, and I know, also, and am glad to know, that some of the men who exercised the control were very much ashamed of it and were glad to get rid of it. Because the general revival of conscience in this country has not been confined to those who were consciously fighting special privilege. The awakening of conscience has extended to those who were enjoying special privileges. And I thank God that the businessmen of this country are beginning to see the economic organization of this country in its true light—as an aristocracy of privilege which they themselves must escape from if they are to exercise the real freedom of enterprise.

And, therefore, when I began my speech by saying that I was glad to be in a place whose associations were with a fighting regiment, I wasn't thinking about the spilling of blood, I wasn't thinking about violence, I wasn't thinking about setting class against class, I wasn't thinking of any enterprise which ought to disturb American society in regard to any of its sound foundations. I was thinking of that enterprise which every man of a clear and enlightened conscience must wish to take part in, in liberating the government which he loves, which he serves, and which must save him from every kind of private control and thralldom.

It is a theme which ought to stir the blood and quicken the mind of any man who has the spirit of public service. I wish that I had a voice in which to express to you the great theme that is in my mind and in my conscience and in my imagination. For, as I look forward to the future years of the United States, they seem to me to be years brightening with increasing happiness, years clarified by a better and better conscience in public affairs, years wherein the government will be set free, years in which all the various populations of the United States will be welded together into one blood and kindred and thought. And we shall have a renaissance of the rights of man. The rights of man used to be conceived in the terms of selfish individual liberty. But in this later age we are conceiving the rights of man in the terms of united liberty, where we are bound together by common enterprises, understand our own interests because we understand the interests of others, serve ourselves because we are willing to serve mankind.

I stand here tonight merely to challenge the attention of this great audience to the purpose, to the hope, to the conviction of the great free Democratic party. Because, if I may say so without any intentional aspersion upon any other candidate, I will say that the Democratic party (applause)—you caught the sentence in the middle, but you were about right—is the only party which has no entangling alliances, the only party whose candidates have no bonds, either past or present, the only party of national proportions, the only team ready to serve the nation. Because you know that, whereas there used to be two national parties, there is now only one. I do not know whether the pieces of the other will ever come together or not; but I do know that such dismembered pieces of national parties as are lying around belong to the Republican party.

I do not anywhere find any division, any lack of unity, any lack of fighting courage and of fighting confidence in the ranks of the Democrats of the United States. You only confuse your thoughts by turning to the Republicans; you can clarify them only by turning to the Democrats. I have been traveling to various parts of the country in recent months, and it seems to me that I am witnessing a great uprising of the people of the United States. And I know that they are turning their faces towards a new age, under the leadership of a party which, more than any other party, has seen the light and the command of the new age; and that in the time to come men will look back and be glad that there was a united host which could take the leadership of the American people in a time of critical change, when old things were not to be forgotten, when old principles were to be revived, when old principles were to be suited to the conditions of a new age, calling upon the common counsels of a whole people to unite in liberating the great Government of the United States.[3]

T MS (C. L. Swem Coll., NjP).
    [3] There is a WWhw outline of this address, with the composition date of Oct. 10, 1912, in WP, DLC.

A Campaign Address in Cleveland[1]

[Oct. 11, 1912]

Mr. Chairman,[2] Ladies and Gentlemen: It is indeed tantalizing not to have the full power of my voice tonight in the presence of an audience so worth addressing as this, for I feel very much stimulated when I come into this great state and particularly put upon my mettle when I come into this great city. Because I know how this city has set itself free, and it is delightful to me to keep

    [1] Delivered in the Central Armory.
    [2] John Hessin Clarke, lawyer of Cleveland, prominent in Ohio Democratic politics.

comradeship with men whom I so honor, and men so willing to follow, as your distinguished mayor,[3] men of whom you feel that you can lay your mind alongside of theirs and know that you are touching true stuff, that they will tell you the truth, and that they will act upon the truth as they know it. For a free nation should be served only by free men.

Perhaps you will forgive me if I recall the circumstance that my own father was born in the State of Ohio, and that there is a certain touch of filial romance connected with this state as I look on the things that he told me of his youth and of his manhood in this great commonwealth, some things that he did not wish his son to repeat but other things which his son has been very proud to emulate. Moreover, I have always thought of Ohio as the first territory into which the freeing forces of America seemed to go and encamp, as that region of the country into which the fighting strength of many movements came in the early days and set up a commonwealth which was in the later years to furnish so much fighting strength and so much of the origination of leadership to the country which it had enriched by its establishment. But it is a circumstance that appeals to my imagination that so many of the foreigners who have settled in the United States have crowded into the cities of Ohio, because I dare say they came into those cities to find what the men who had established those cities had established them to realize.

I remember attending, not long ago, a meeting of men very much interested in foreign missions,[4] and they were very much encouraged by the circumstance that the different denominations which are conducting missionary enterprises at the ends of the world were drawing together and forgetting their denominational differences. And I could not help thinking that if they succeeded in this handsome enterprise in the missionary field, I hoped they would not come to America and induce their converts to look at us in our multiform division of creed and find in us Christians who could not agree with one another after we had induced them to agree with each other. I shouldn't like America to be looked over for her Christian unity; and yet, when I think of what these people who have come to us from foreign countries came to find, I cannot but ask myself: Did they find in the field of politics what they had expected to find?

That was a very interesting, and to my mind, a very pathetic

---

[3] Newton D. Baker.
[4] About this meeting, a "China dinner" on Jan. 14, 1909, and Wilson's remarks, see W. H. Grant to WW, Dec. 19, 1908, Vol. 18, and the news report printed at Jan. 28, 1911, Vol. 22.

remark that was made by one of our fellow citizens who had been only ten years resident in this country. He said that, except for the fortunes which had attended his children's schooling, he had not found in America what he expected to find, until one evening he was going down the street and saw one of the schoolhouses lighted and went in and found, not that the school was in session, but that the neighborhood was in session, that men out of all the homes in that section of the community had crowded into the schoolhouse to discuss the matters which concerned them, just as you have discussed them in those meetings—an allusion to which you have just greeted with applause—in the tents in which your mayor meets you and lays before you municipal matters.[5] And when he got into that meeting, he said: "Ah, for the first time, I have found America. I have found the neighbors in conference. I have found the forces of local pride set afoot by men without distinction of social position, without distinction of official authority, without distinction of the power either of wealth or of political influence."

And so it seems to me that we are under the indictment of not affording those who come to join our citizenship the things which we ourselves pretend to prize and which they had confidently expected to find. When they came to America they expected to find that all men had an equal voice in the government of this great country, and they found nothing of the kind. They found that if they wanted to exercise any but a negligible influence in the field of politics there was some unofficial person to whom you had to go. What do you suppose that the people who come into most of our cities, into the cities that have not set themselves free as Cleveland has, find when they try to exercise political influence? They find that there is a boss to consult, and that that boss is not the leader of a political party, but the arranger of those matters which interest the men that get contracts, those matters which interest those who wish favorable municipal ordinances and those who make the largest contributions to political campaigns, those who exercise this, that, or the other underground influence. So they find that, although in America there are no kings that are crowned as despots, there are masters to whom the great and the small alike must resort if they would see political plans put into execution. And when you extend the view, when you enlarge the stage upon which these things are exhibited, then what do you discover? You discover that the President of the United States finds, as your mayor

5 A practice begun by Tom L. Johnson because all halls were closed to him, and carried on by Baker.

has explained to you, that Mr. Aldrich and Mr. Cannon are stronger than all the promises made to the American people, that they are stronger because they represent the influences that have the policies of the Government of the United States within their private grasp. Ah, if you will examine never so casually the *Congressional Record* you will find that in the debate on the Payne-Aldrich tariff, the debate upon that tariff, the schedules of which the President could not change, Mr. Aldrich refused to reveal to the Senate of the United States the information upon which many of those schedules were constructed. And that the members of the Senate were obliged to take the schedules blindly upon the assurance that the powers back of the Republican party were back of Mr. Aldrich, that he was their spokesman, that they must take their orders from him, that not only they, but the President, must take their orders from them. For it is self-confessed on the part of the President that the forces of private influence were stronger than his own convictions and stronger than the mandates of the American people. But when we turn to the gentleman who preceded him in office, we find that those influences were equally strong.

I have no fear of the money back of Mr. Roosevelt, but I do very much fear the ideas back of Mr. Roosevelt. For those ideas were bred in the very company which has debauched and debased the Government of the United States, not, it may be, intentionally, for there are great excuses for the love and exercise of power, and I dare say that many of these men who have sought absolutely to control economic development in the United States believe that they are controlling it in the general interest of the people of the country. It is not my purpose to impugn their motives, but my point is that the whole plan of government set forth in the platform of the third party is conceived in the terms of those and in the thought of those who have promoted and maintained monopoly in the United States.

This is a battle, ladies and gentlemen, for emancipation, emancipation from mistaken friends, it may be, but nevertheless emancipation from men who have conceived the development of the United States in the terms of their own private and selfish power. I would be loath to go into a contest in which the only question was: Which party shall be entrusted with power? I would be loath to go into a contest in which the only question was: Which man do you think would be the better and stronger President of the United States? I am not interested in those questions.

I am interested in this question: What set of principles are you going to enthrone in the Government of the United States? And I am proud at this juncture of national affairs to stand as the representative of the Democratic party; because through all its vicissitudes that party has kept the lamp of its principles burning clear and undefiled. Do you not realize that this great party has been purged as by fire? Do you not realize that through more than sixteen years it has gone forward undaunted through defeat after defeat, holding up the very principles, and some of the very remedies, which now at last its opponents have discovered and put forth? The principles set forth in the third party platform are the principles of converts and tyros; whereas, the principles set forth in the Democratic platform are the principles for which they have sacrificed power, to which they have devoted themselves through adversity, knowing that some day the United States would turn its face again to those ancient lamps which shone upon its path when the little nation set out upon its errand of liberty, in the days when the government was set up. If I did not believe that monopoly could be restrained and destroyed I would not believe that liberty could be recovered in the United States, and I know that the processes of liberty are the processes of life. I wish that I had the voice, for one thing, and the brains, for another, to expound to you, to introduce to you, the Democratic party as I see it, not as I see the people that compose it, because we are of all sorts and conditions of men. I would not commend us to you personally, for that would be immodest, but I would like to introduce to you the Democratic party as it stands as the spokesman of certain principles and processes in our life.

For example, the President said the other day that if the Democratic party came into power every workingman in the United States would regret that he had voted for that party, and that there would come rainy days in which the skies would be overcast and hope would seem to flicker out in his life; that we would bring about that great bogy with which you have been frightened all these years in your innocence—the bogy of free trade. Have you never reflected that the Democrats constitute about half of the United States, and that, as a Philadelphia editor said, they could not commit economic murder without committing economic suicide? Do you believe that half the nation is going to put the other half out of business on terms which will make it necessary for them to go out of business also? Do you suppose that Democrats have not lived in the United States and do not understand the business conditions in the United States? Why, there isn't a business in the United States that isn't in greater or less degree sustained by the activity and intelligence of Democrats. We are not as innocent as we look. I have nowhere heard a thoughtful Democrat propose to lay so much as a disturbing touch upon any sound part of the business of the United States. But I have seen Democratic surgeons getting their knives ready for the unwholesome growths that have attached themselves to the economic body politic. And these things are going to be cut out for the sake of the sound tissue and not at its expense, in order that the sound tissue may carry the blood more blithely, in order that the sound tissue may build new tissue and bring on a greater and more expanding life, in order that the intelligence of many men, instead of the intelligence of a few men, should direct and advance the industrial undertakings of the United States.

There can't be free trade in the United States if we are to pay the bills, because the Government of the United States has committed itself to a fiscal policy which makes it necessary to sustain it for the most part by indirect instead of direct taxes.

But have the rainy days not come? Have the workingmen, who have spread over them these heavenly wings of protective policy, never felt a little chilled under the shadow? Have they not found it impossible to pay the bills? And have their wages ever borne any direct proportion, that you have heard of, to the amount of protection granted the industry in which they were engaged? One of the things that Mr. Taft denounced, even in his Winona speech, in which he gave his approval to the Payne-Aldrich tariff bill, was that infamous Schedule K, upon which are perched all the cormorants of the wool schedule. He said that that schedule was absolutely indefensible. There are the heaviest duties in that schedule that are to be found in the tariff. But have you heard that those poor toiling multitudes in Lawrence, Massachusetts, have found the days bright because of the protection of that schedule? They have been ground between the upper and the nether millstone, and the particular trust that was employing them effected its combination by the method which your mayor has described, after multiplying its capital five times above any possible correct valuation of the properties, and is paying handsome dividends on the five times its legitimate capital, and is, besides that, accumulating from year to year surplus enough to build new factories, and paying on an average not more than eight dollars a week to its employees. I say that because I have seen hundreds of the pay envelopes, and if they contained what they were said to contain, the average was below eight dollars a week.

So I say, do not be afraid that the Democratic party will disturb this intolerable thing so as to make it any more intolerable for them. They could not go below rock bottom. And, as your affairs grind upon that rock bottom, I hope you realize the solid foundations of this splendid protective policy! Why in the name of the intelligence of the American people have the workingmen of this country not called this bluff long ago? Mr. Roosevelt says that some duties are too high—he doesn't say which—and that when they are high, and it is discovered that those who get the benefit do not divide fairly with their workingmen, then they should be taken off. In other words, his tariff policy is a penalty policy; whereas, our tariff policy is this: If you are taxing the American people to pay dividends on money that you never had, then we are not going to make arrangements which will allow you to continue that interesting business. And when we have broken up your monopoly, as we will, the other competitors will come into the field, there will be a more active bidding for the work of the workingmen of the country, and, with an enlarged market for labor, there will be an elasticity in the wage market that there never has been before. A new enterprise of rock bottom of capital, upon the solid foundations of intelligence and efficiency, will put these gentlemen to their mettle and see whether in a race of efficiency they will be the swift or the slow. For they are carrying an enormous handicap; every undertaking has strapped on its back a tank in which the water will slop and under which no man can run straight. If these giants are so great and strong that they can carry the handicap, I'll stand on the sidelines and applaud. But I want to see them carry them in competition with those who are swift of foot and honest of equipment.

And, therefore, there is another thing that you must not believe about the Democratic party. These gentlemen say that if the Democratic party gets into power it will follow the old Jeffersonian idea of taking its hands off, that what we need is more power, not less power. Why, Mr. Roosevelt has had a great deal of amusement expounding what he believes to be my political philosophy. He is going a long journey, and I bid him welcome to that jungle. I am not interested in my political philosophy. I am interested in what he is going to do and in what he is thinking about, and I would invite him to be interested in what I am thinking about and am going to do.

He says, for example, that I am not the friend of the workingmen. I am perfectly willing to leave that to the jury. I am perfectly willing that he should consult the workingmen of the State of New Jersey, and I'll abide by their verdict. I am not interested in any assessment of character. What I want to know is: how is the business going to be conducted? Now, when you talk about power, all that I have to say is this: power is something which, according to the Democratic theory, ought to be exercised by law and not by personal discretion. Under the Democrats, you will find this social structure of ours penetrated and sustained by the structural steel of law, wherever law is necessary, but you won't find that we are going to put in the hands of individuals or commissions the right to build the house according to their own plans and specifications. We are going to insist upon an architecture so certain, so definite, so based upon the right engineering principles of liberty, that we can be sure we can live there and not have the roof fall in. We are not going to depend upon the special Providence of any President or of any commission appointed by any President to see that the powers that we fear are good to us and don't hurt us. I never saw a savior of society, and I never expect to see one; but I feel about it as Mr. Burgess felt about the purple cow:

> I never saw a purple cow,
> I never hope to see one.
> But this I'll tell you anyhow:
> I'd rather see than be one.

And about saviors of society, I feel the same way. I never saw one, I never hope to see one, but, I'll tell you, I would rather see than be one. The responsibility is too serious. The probabilities of failure are too large; the possibilities of disgrace are too terrible. Because the whole crux of our difficulty is this, that these gentlemen have insisted upon doing the thinking for the people of the United States; and I want to see a time when the people of the United States do their own thinking. We haven't got to the point of intellectual bankruptcy where we have to appoint receivers for our intelligence. And the whole situation in the United States might be summed up by saying that the Republican party has put the intelligence of this country into the hands of receivers in Wall Street offices. Very able receivers they are, and they have received a great deal! No doubt they are making the business pay, but the partners are sorely disappointed, the stockholders are growing very impatient, because the business isn't put upon its feet again and their profits once more returned to them. And what Mr. Roosevelt desires to be authorized to do is to appoint the receivers, unless he had already been vested with that divine function himself.

And so, ladies and gentlemen, when I look forward to the choice to be made on the fifth of November, I tell you very frankly that it does not seem to me to center upon individuals. It seems to me to center upon ideals, upon principles, and I cannot think that I am exaggerating when I say that there hangs upon the choice of that day the issues of life and death. For we shall upon that day choose our form of government. We shall choose whether we shall continue to have our affairs dominated and determined by small groups of men, who have been allowed to acquire the great economic power of this country into their own hands, or whether we shall again assert the individual independence, the aggregate majesty, the aggregate capacity, of the American people in the conduct alike of their business and of their politics. That is what we shall have to choose on the fifth of November. And I, for my part, do not doubt the choice. How can there be any doubt when we know what we are dealing with? It is very awkward to discuss politics nowadays, because there is only one party that you can talk about. The other fragments lying around have such a miscellany of makeup. For example, the third party consists of gentlemen who would stand pat if anybody would endure their society, but who, being rejected of those who were once the elect, have gone over into the new camp. Then there are gentlemen who used to be progressives, and allied with such genuine progressives as Robert La Follette of Wisconsin, but who suffered themselves to imagine that the leader of the third party is a real progressive and will lead them in the direction in which they started, forgetting where they started for.

You know, it makes a great deal of difference. I remember a friend of mine asking an old fellow in Scotland, who was breaking stones by the road, if this was the road he sought. He said "Whaur ye came frae?" My friend said, "What business is it of yours where I come from?" "It's as muckle as whaur ye gangin' tae." His question was a very honest question; because if I start from there to there, that is the right road, but if I start from there to there, this isn't the right road. Where I started from and where I intended to go is the whole moral of my story.

Now, these gentlemen started as insurgent Republicans in order to lower the tariff and get rid of the trusts, and they have allied themselves with the party which tolerates the tariff and proposes to legalize the trusts. Therefore, I classify them as progressives who have lost their way. Then there is a large body of very interesting and very attractive men and women whose hearts are full of pity for the human race and who like all that iridescent part of the platform which promises to redeem us from all our ills, and who believe that a man who is willing to sanction the tariff and make the trusts permanent can find the instruments through which to relieve us of the burdens of our economic existence. I admire their faith, but I cannot entertain it. Then, finally, there is a lot of flotsam and jetsam that has floated that way, because there seemed to be in all the maelstrom of our politics a little current set in that direction.

Then, on the other side, there are all those gentlemen who have a vague notion that something is happening, but they don't know exactly what it is. They would like to move, but they have no leader. And so they think the easiest thing is to consult their grandmother and do nothing. Those are the gentlemen who are following Mr. Taft. So, what are you going to do, stand still with the standpatters, gyrate with the gyrators, or move with the solid mass, millions strong, that constitutes the Democratic party, and has had its eye on the horizon for sixteen years?

We aren't novices, we aren't recent converts, we haven't found out something in the year 1912 that we didn't know before. Nineteen twelve has only confirmed our opinions of what has all along waited to be done and no Republican leader has even yet proposed to do, namely, to cut all special privilege out of the tariff and remove monopoly from the United States. Determine what you want to have, and then determine by what means you are most likely to get it. The Democratic party has no entanglements. Those who lead the Democratic party are not embarrassed by any partnership whatever. We are free to serve you. It would be embarrassing to ask you to determine whether we are intelligent enough to do it, but we are not depending wholly on our own intelligence. We have had this whole course mapped out for us by gentlemen ever since America was founded, and unless we are fools, we cannot lose our way. We have had this star set in our firmament and have been steering by it ever since we were boys.

I remember how, when I was a boy, I used to be thrilled by reading the mere sentences of Thomas Jefferson. I did not know distinctly what they meant, but somehow they quickened my blood, somehow they stirred everything that was within me, somehow they made me feel freer as I read. And there began to dawn upon me the vision of America—the nation that had eschewed private power, that had turned its back upon the control by individuals of the fortunes of great masses of men, that had begun to believe in the immortality and in the immortal freedom of the human soul, and had set a stage for that liberty here in America—an unbounded continent, a continent which in its beauty and in its majesty was a proper setting for the jewel of human liberty.

Transcript of shorthand notes (C. L. Swem Coll., NjP); T transcript (WP, DLC).

From Henry Lee Higginson

My dear Governor Wilson: [Boston] October 11, 1912

Will you forgive me for calling your attention to a matter of much importance, as it seems to me?

Mr. Brandeis, as well as many men, is helping you to your election. I have known Mr. Brandeis many years, and know his reputation here. He has done various things which have brought on him the contempt of many good people, both of his own profession and of other callings. Some years ago he attacked vigorously the New Haven Road, and made written statements about it which made it appear that it was bankrupt.[1] Accordingly, the State made a Commission,—of which a Mr. George F. Swain, LL.D., then a professor at the Institute of Technology, and now at Harvard University, together with the tax commissioner and the bank commissioner were members,—to study the accounts and property of the New Haven Railroad. They made a report, which was called the "Validation Report," and which is before me. This showed the property to be in excess of what the New Haven Road claimed.

Mr. Brandeis' attack on the railroad might well have frightened many holders of these bonds and also the savings banks which held them largely through the States of Connecticut, Rhode Island, Massachusetts, and New York, and might well have started a panic among the depositors in those banks. It was a public injury, as well as an injury to the New York, New Haven & Hartford Railroad, and his accusations were absolutely false and without justification. He attacked a purchase which the New Haven Road made of Boston & Maine shares and which the Governor ordered investigated by a commission of three excellent men here. One of these men, a leading lawyer, in speaking of the case before the Railroad Committee of our Legislature, spoke of Brandeis as "the counsel who casts slime over everything that he touches"; and many people agree entirely with those words.

During some years Mr. Brandeis was counsel for the United Shoe Machinery Corporation, and last year he shifted to the other side and sided in the attack on that corporation.[2]

I know no reputable lawyer here who has a good word for him. I do not care to censure him, and should not do so if the newspaper reports did not indicate that he is looking for political position, and if he did not continually pose as a friend of the people, a man who helped the underdog &c., and if I did not feel that he might produce a wrong impression on you. I think you will understand my meaning.

I am expecting your election, and hoping for you a very strong Cabinet and a fortunate administration. It is to the greatest advantage of any citizen of the United States that our President should not only be able and honest, but also should have strong helpers, for a terribly difficult task lies before him.

Naturally, what I say to you in this letter is as from one comrade who wishes another well, and I ask leave to sign myself "a comrade." I am, with great respect,

Very truly yours,   Henry L. Higginson

TLS (Letterpress Books, H. L. Higginson Papers, MH-BA).

1 On the subject of Brandeis and his controversy with the New Haven Railroad, see Alpheus T. Mason, *Brandeis: A Free Man's Life* (New York, 1946), pp. 177-214, and Richard M. Abrams, "Brandeis and the New Haven-Boston & Maine Merger Battle Revisited," *Business History Review*, XXXVI (Winter 1962), 408-30.

2 About Brandeis and his relations with the United Shoe Machinery Co., see Mason, *Brandeis*, pp. 214-29.

From the Diary of Colonel House

October 12, 1912.

Governor Wilson came in from the West today. I went with him to the Vanderbilt Hotel where McAdoo wanted to confer with him. Reporters had an interview from a former student of Princeton saying that Governor Wilson believed in an aristocratic government similar to that of England, and that he did not believe in democracy. The Governor is to write a letter denying this, saying the student was refused a degree, hence his animus.

We decided also about the question of the McCormick contribution and that we would be frank about it, the Governor taking all responsibility for its acceptance. I agreed with the Governor that it would not be well for him to attend a number of small celebrations tonight; it would not be dignified.

I took the Governor to the Plaza Hotel to see McCombs and Judge Dowling; B. M. Baruch,[1] Samuel Untermyer came to the hotel during our visit. The Governor was doubtful about meeting Baruch, a Wall Street broker, and insisted that I remain during the entire conversation. Much gum-shoe method was evidenced in McCombs' dealings.

I offered our motor to the Governor and he used it all the evening.

1 Bernard Mannes Baruch, Wall Street speculator. For his later memories of his first meeting with Wilson, see Margaret L. Coit, *Mr. Baruch* (Boston, 1957), pp. 136-37, and Bernard M. Baruch, *Baruch: The Public Years* (New York, 1960), pp. 8-9.

To Mary Allen Hulbert

Dearest Friend,   Princeton, New Jersey 13 Oct., 1912

Thank you with all my heart for your letters sent me while I was in the West. The second one, by the way, was opened by one of my Secretaries, who pays not the slightest attention to what is written on the envelope. I dare say there is nothing substantial behind what was told me, though it was told so circumstantially and came to me so direct that it still gives me ground for much speculation and concern. You have been very fine and sweet about it all.

I am so much interested to learn that you may be in New York this week. Please telephone if you come in before Thursday,—for I expect to be at home, or near it, till then, and should so like to run in with Ellen to see you. This is one of the few intervals I am to enjoy of exemption from campaign duty.

I got back home this morning at one o'clock. After attending two dinners in New York last night, I caught an express which was stopped for me at the junction at 12:30, and drove home in a cab, too sleepy and tired for words. For I dare say you have read what I went through in the West and know more about it than I do. For I do not get time to read the papers at all and always find when I get back from a trip that the family and my intimate friends know much more about what happened than I do,—and so there is nothing to tell! I am still very tired—but perfectly well. It is wonderful how tough I have turned out to be, and how much I can stand—for the physical strain of what I went through this time is all but overwhelming; and yet I lost nothing but my voice—and not all of that. I was fool enough to try to make thirty-five thousand people hear me out-of-doors, and after that the old instrument, usually so sound and reliable, went wheezy and had no volume or resonance in it. It is slowly coming back now, under the kindly influences of silence. "The trouble with me is I talk too damn much."

All join me in the most affectionate messages. The quiet and freedom of Princeton are delightful and healing. I dread starting out again—and hope the *first* occasion will be to see you in N.Y. Love to all.   Your devoted friend   Woodrow Wilson

ALS (WP, DLC).

To William Green

Dear Sir: [Trenton, N. J., c. Oct. 13, 1912]

I am glad to receive your letter of the 9th inst., as it affords me an opportunity to express more clearly than I had occasion to do in the recent past my own appreciation of the miner's work and my desire to contribute in any possible way toward the betterment of the conditions under which he labors.

You are doubtless correct in your statement, that in the past the importance and the needs of the mining industry have not been fully appreciated. But this cannot long be the case; for the people of this country are already coming to recognize the fact that the products of the mine as well as the products of the farm enter into the increasing cost of living; and that mining and agriculture are the two great indispensable foundation industries of the nation. Furthermore, there is, fortunately, a growing public recognition of the fact that mining deserves special consideration at the hands of both the federal and the state governments because of its dangers and the heavy loss of life among those who labor underground, and because of the fact that of our mineral resources we have but the one supply, which we cannot increase but which we continue to decrease by both what we use and what we waste.

The inspection of mines, of course, comes under the police control of the several states, but the investigative and educational work, such as the federal government has properly and liberally provided for in behalf of American agriculture, and which has contributed so largely to the prosperity of our farmers and to the upbuilding of the nation, should be provided for by the federal government with proportionate liberality in behalf of the mining industry; and this work should be enlarged without delay, and should be pushed forward with all possible zeal, as it has to do not only with the better development of a great industry, but with the saving of human life.

You may rest assured of my earnest cooperation in pushing forward this important work, whether it be as the chief executive of the nation or as a private citizen.

[Cordially and sincerely yours, Woodrow Wilson]

TCL (WP, DLC).

Two News Reports

[*Oct. 15, 1912*]

WILSON SENDS SYMPATHY

Mrs. Wilson Also Telegraphs to Mrs. Roosevelt
in Chicago.

PRINCETON, N. J., Oct. 15.—Gov. Wilson was up early this morning, and the first thing he asked the newspaper men was about the progress Mr. Roosevelt was making toward recovery.[1] He showed plainly the relief he felt when told that the early reports were favorable. On his arrival at the State House he sent this telegram to Col. Roosevelt in care of the National Progressive headquarters in Chicago:

Please accept my warmest sympathy and heartiest congratulations that your wound is not serious.

To-night a telegram was sent by Mrs. Wilson to Mrs. Roosevelt. It read:

Mrs. Theodore Roosevelt, Mercy Hospital, Chicago

My heartfelt sympathy in your anxiety and distress. Mr. Wilson and I have been shocked beyond expression and await each item of news with deep solicitude.

Mrs. Woodrow Wilson.

Gov. Wilson asked the newspaper men to keep him in touch with Chicago and tell him immediately of any reports received from the Mercy Hospital.

"I want you to let me know everything about the condition of Col. Roosevelt just as soon as you can," he said. "I am immeasurably shocked and saddened."

Friends of Gov. Wilson expressed deep concern to-day about his safety as a result of the attack upon Col. Roosevelt, but this had not occurred to the Governor until it was mentioned to him by the newspaper men. Then he said that he would take no added precautions during the campaign.

"There is nothing that can be done to guard against such attacks," he said. "It seems to me that police and secret service guards are useless if a madman attempts to attack a man in public life."

[1] Theodore Roosevelt was shot in the chest by a fanatic as he left his hotel in Milwaukee on the evening of October 14 on his way to a speaking engagement. He insisted on making the speech, and physicians later determined that the wound was not serious, the force of the bullet having been largely spent before it entered his body. After two weeks of recuperation, Roosevelt made a final campaign speech in Madison Square Garden on October 30.

WILSON WON'T SPEAK WITH ROOSEVELT ILL

PRINCETON, N. J., Oct. 15.—Gov. Woodrow Wilson is going to cut short his active campaigning, as a result of the injuries sustained by Col. Roosevelt at the hands of an assassin last night. The Governor will go into Delaware, West Virginia, and Pennsylvania, starting tomorrow night, as scheduled. His trip will then be brought to an end unless Col. Roosevelt is able to get out on the stump again. At 11 o'clock tonight, after receiving the latest reports from Chicago, Gov. Wilson issued this statement at his home, in Cleveland Lane:

I cannot cancel the engagements which are immediately ahead of me without subjecting those who have arranged them to very serious embarrassment and great unnecessary expense, but I shall cut the series at the earliest possible point.

Mr. Taft has at no time taken an active part in the campaign, and I have no desire to be the single candidate on the stump, engaged against no active antagonist.

"Will your engagements in New York be canceled?" the Governor was asked.

"Yes," said he, "I have asked my managers to arrange to cancel the engagements in New York and Brooklyn for this Saturday night."

Before issuing his statement Gov. Wilson talked over the long-distance telephone to Democratic National headquarters in New York.

Printed in the *New York Times*, Oct. 16, 1912.

From Benjamin McAlester Anderson, Jr.[1]

My dear Sir: New York Oct. 15, 1912.

This letter is, in effect, a joint letter from Professor John B. Clark and myself, as it is written after an extended conference with him, and with his authorization of the use of his name. We were both greatly interested, and not a little concerned, by the enclosed statement in the New York *Times* of Saturday last,[2] which quotes you as holding, in effect, that all that need be done in connection with the problem of monopoly is to remove the special favors and unfair methods of competition which have built up the trusts, and then "natural law" will take care of the situation: that there is no danger in size as such: that, if they can be made to fight fairly, you are willing for them to remain as big as they can. We were not sure that this meant that you would not make use of the Sherman Law—or a strengthened Sherman Law—to break up some of the existing combinations, and are very anxious not to misinterpret you. If, however, such is your present opinion, we most strongly urge that you suspend judgment upon the point, and do not commit yourself to the policy indicated. While Professor Clark and I are disposed to agree that if the race were started *de novo*, no firm using only legitimate methods could obtain a dangerous power, the significant fact is that there now exist great monopolies which by unfair methods have got so big that their very size enables them to dominate the situation. To use a phrase which Professor Clark repeated with approval, we must use "some dynamite" to break the crust. Not necessarily a great deal, but it is surely not well to close the door to this possibility in case, after all, the theory should not work. We do not ask you, in the midst of your campaign duties, to reinvestigate the matter or to change your well matured opinions without such investigation, but we do most strongly request that you suspend judgment, and that you do not, in other speeches, commit yourself to a policy which we are both convinced will not go far enough.

Professor Clark, I may add, held substantially the view attributed to you when he wrote his *Control of Trusts* in 1901.[3] He has since found it necessary to abandon this view. It is not enough, he now maintains, so to regulate competition that "potential competition" may exist. There must be *actual* competition, on a considerable scale, and in all important markets. And size, as such, is often a tremendous factor in preventing this. Professor Clark has written for the *Independent* of this week (the next issue, that is) an article[4] endorsing your policy as he understood it before this note appeared in the *Times*. He hopes that his original interpretation is correct. I may add that, while he waives the question of details, he is disposed to believe that a Federal Commission, issuing licences to corporations doing interstate business, and having power to revoke them, will be an effective means of handling such parts of the problem as call for direct Federal action.

May I, in conclusion, tell you of the warmth of admiration which Professor Clark manifested toward you in the conversation, and of the high hopes and high confidence we have in your career as the next President of the United States? While I have not had Professor Clark's opportunities of knowing you personally and well, I still feel a keen personal interest in you and your success which will, I trust, in part excuse this intrusion upon the time of a busy man.

Very sincerely yours,   B. M. Anderson, Jr.

TLS (WP, DLC).

¹ Instructor in Economics, Columbia University.

² The enclosure is missing, but he referred to the news report, with long quotations, of Wilson's speeches in Cleveland, Canton, and Orrville, Ohio, in the *New York Times*, Oct. 12, 1912.

³ John Bates Clark, *The Control of Trusts: An Argument in Favor of Curbing the Power of Monopoly by a Natural Method* (New York and London, 1901). See also John Bates Clark and John Maurice Clark, *The Control of Trusts* (New York, 1912).

⁴ J. B. Clark, "The Parties and the Supreme Issue," *The Independent*, LXXIII (Oct. 17, 1912), 891-94.

From the Diary of Colonel House

October 15, 1912.

Everything is upset today over the attempted assassination of Theodore Roosevelt. Governor Wilson was uncertain as to his procedure with his speaking engagements, etc. He called me over the telephone, or rather asked that I speak with him when Mc-Adoo had him on the wire. He wants to curtail his speechmaking very much as he is tired. McAdoo is anxious that he should continue as planned. The Governor left the matter to me to arrange.

McCombs was to have gone to headquarters today in order to take charge, but he did not put in an appearance and could not be found at his hotel. Both McCombs and McAdoo were on the witness stand in Washington yesterday regarding campaign funds. McCombs was a poor witness.

Congressman A. S. Burleson took dinner with me and remained until eleven o'clock. I telephoned Governor Wilson at Princeton while Burleson was here, urging him to cancel all engagements until Roosevelt was able to get out again. Wilson was at first doubtful but wrote out a statement, which he read to me over the telephone, following my suggestions as to what to say. All of the Campaign Committee were against me in this. They wanted the Governor to continue speechmaking and so advised him. My thought was that if he continued to speak after T.R. had been shot, it would create sympathy for T.R. and would do Wilson infinite harm. The situation is a dangerous one and needs to be handled with care. The generous, the chivalrous and the wise thing to do, so it seems to me, is to discontinue speaking until his antagonist is also able to speak. I am glad Wilson sees it as I do. He suggested that we might delay a decision until tomorrow and get the opinion of the full Committee, but I disagreed to this and said that the delay would be disadvantageous. Then, too, it would make it embarrassing if the Committee differed from him as they certainly would, for their individual opinions have already been expressed. Burleson thinks I took too much responsibility in advising contrary to the rest of the Committee.

To Nathan Straus

My dear Mr. Straus: [Trenton, N. J., Oct. 16, 1912]

You are very generous in sending your check for $5,000 with characteristic modesty and simplicity. You may be sure that the money will not be used in New York.

With the most cordial appreciation and sincere regard,
                    Faithfully yours,   [Woodrow Wilson]

T ICF transcript of CLSsh notes (RSB Coll., DLC).

To George Foster Peabody

My dear friend: Trenton, N. J. October 16, 1912

It was very thoughtful and characteristically kind of you to suggest a vacation for us after the election at Lake George,[1] and I thank you with all my heart. Our plan is to go, if possible, to Bermuda, but we have been saying this to no one. We picked out Bermuda because Mrs. Wilson is such an inveterate Southerner that she wants to go to a warm place, the warmer the better, and I must say for myself that warmth rests me more than a bracing temperature does.

There is no limit to your generosity, and I have in a sense enjoyed Abenia already, because the chief enjoyment of it would be the thought of your kindness and friendship.

I am delighted that you think my speeches worth while.
                    Cordially and faithfully yours,   Woodrow Wilson

TLS (G. F. Peabody Papers, DLC).
[1] G. F. Peabody to WW, Oct. 9, 1912, ALS (WP, DLC), and G. F. Peabody to EAW, Oct. 9, 1912, ALS (WP, DLC).

From Edith Gittings Reid

Dearest of Governors   [Baltimore] October 16th [1912]

Seven wise women of Baltimore tell me that they have implored you to come and make an address of cheer to the suffering ones.

Please do so, and bring with you Mrs Wilson and Jessie[.] We will have such fun! Mrs Wilson, Jessie, & I. And you will be happy too, though not in the same way.

I have plenty of room to make you all comfortable, and I terribly want to see you.

Do you know I truly believe that you are the best loved man in America to-day? Even the fat old men at the Maryland Club cannot dislike you though they sadly fear that you may decrease their poker earnings.

Oh! Come down, Prophet of Reason, of good things. Come down to us.

Love for you all   Your devoted friend   Edith G. Reid

ALS (WP, DLC).

Joseph Patrick Tumulty to Henry Lee Higginson

Dear Mr. Higginson: Trenton, N. J. October 16, 1912

Before Governor Wilson left for Delaware tonight he read your letter of October 11th with reference to Mr. Louis D. Brandeis with a great deal of interest, and requested me to thank you for the information which you have been good enough to give him. The Governor thanks you sincerely for the deep interest you have taken in him.   Very truly yours   J. P. Tumulty

TLS (H. L. Higginson Papers, MH-BA).

From the Diary of Colonel House

October 16, 1912.

There was a full meeting of the Committee today. McCombs kept them waiting for nearly an hour. He has forced McAdoo to give up his, McCombs' room, and the force in McAdoo's room was moved into mine. McAdoo refused to go with Governor Wilson on his speaking tour and is pretty sore over the way he has been treated. The Governor called up the last thing before leaving to ask about Secret Service men accompanying him on the trip and the advisability of same. I told him that I had already seen to it and that men in plain clothes would be with him constantly. Captain Bill McDonald[1] will be here tomorrow. I wired for him the day Roosevelt was shot and he will be with the Governor from now until after the election. I had asked Governor Wilson to allow me to send for Captain McDonald. I had already told him of Captain Bill, and no explanation was necessary as to his fitness. I sent this despatch to Bill: "Come immediately. Important. Bring your artillery." Bill thought I was in some trouble and replied "I am coming."

1 William Jesse McDonald, captain in the Texas Rangers, 1891-1907, and, more recently, a Texas state revenue agent. In April 1905, he served as body-guard for President Theodore Roosevelt during a coyote hunt in Texas and Oklahoma Territory. A colorful character with a talent for self-publicity, he had already been the subject of a biography—Albert Bigelow Paine, *Captain Bill McDonald, Texas Ranger: A Story of Frontier Reform* (New York, 1909). The biography, which included a prefatory letter from Roosevelt, was inspired by Colonel House, who had known McDonald since the 1890s. For a more balanced appraisal, see Walter Prescott Webb, *The Texas Rangers: A Century of Frontier Defense*, 2nd edn. (Austin, Tex., 1965).

An Extract from a Speech in Georgetown, Delaware

[Oct. 17, 1912]

Mr. Chairman,[1] ladies and gentlemen: It is with the greatest pleasure that I find myself in Delaware and yet with a certain re-luctance that I continue the campaign just at the present time, because I think the whole country must yet feel very deeply the shock and indignation with regard to the attack on Mr. Roosevelt. I myself have been very much saddened by it because I have not at any time felt any personal opposition in this campaign. I have been fighting issues, and I am very sorry to see the chief spokes-man of one great set of issues, for a very short time, we hope, taken out of the campaign.

T MS (C. L. Swem Coll., NjP).
1 Unidentified.

An Extract from a Speech in Dover, Delaware

[Oct. 17, 1912]

I do not predict trouble in the United States. I rejoice to believe that America is a singularly self-possessed nation. It is averse from nothing so much as violent disorder. I believe that part of the sadness we now suffer from, because of that atrocious assault upon Mr. Roosevelt, is a feeling that there is anybody in the United States who would dare attempt to interrupt the orderly course of politics and the public affairs of this country by the violence of his own hand. We deeply resent it. We resent the thought that there should be any citizen of the United States that should raise his hand against the peaceful, the orderly, the just, the open de-termination of public affairs.

I have come out to fulfill the engagements of this week with a very great reluctance, because my thought is constantly of that gallant gentleman lying in the hospital at Chicago. Mr. Roosevelt did a vast deal to wake the country up to the problems that now have to be settled, and that he should have been stayed in his attempt to discuss the settlement of these questions by a hand of violence is a thing which every American must deeply deplore and feel ashamed of.

T MS (C. L. Swem Coll., NjP), with corrections from the complete text in the *New York Times*, Oct. 18, 1912.

A Campaign Address in Wilmington, Delaware[1]

[Oct. 17, 1912]

Mr. Chairman[2] and fellow citizens: You have indeed made me feel very much at home by your gracious greeting, and it was very delightful to hear Mr. Saulsbury say that I came here as Delaware's choice. It was partly on that account that I gave myself the pleasure of spending today in Delaware in order that I might speak, not for myself, but for the state ticket in whose fortunes I am so deeply interested. I know against what odds Senator Monaghan[3] has fought for the people's cause in the legislature of Delaware. I know how long and against what discouragements he fought, the very fight that we fought at such weary lengths in New Jersey before we accomplished anything, and I confidently believe that, as your [next] governor here relates, Delaware is turning from the things that have bound her.

I have come here to give myself the pleasure of rendering him such support as I can and also to remind you that the national stage is set, and that it is your privilege either to assist or to refuse to assist. You can add a congressman and a senator to the force that is there going to advance progressive policy in the United States.

You have not, permit me to remind you, sent a senator to Washington in a great many years who advanced anything except his own interests. And the rest of the Union is now waiting for stout little Delaware to join the procession. Nobody has ever doubted that the hearts of the people of Delaware were with the cause of the people. Nobody has ever doubted that the purposes of progress resided in the minds of thoughtful men in Delaware as well as elsewhere. And yet all the country has looked on in amazement

[1] Delivered in the Opera House.
[2] Willard Saulsbury.
[3] State Senator Thomas M. Monaghan, Democratic candidate for governor. He was not elected.

that Delaware has permitted herself to be held in the hollow of the hand by a few conspicuous interests which she could outvote, but to which she submissively submitted herself. It is amazing, but the end has come. Delaware is now going to assert her independence. Delaware is now going to issue an edict of emancipation and join the forward movement that is sweeping over the United States.

As I have traveled from one part of the country to the other, it has been something to quicken the blood, something to illuminate the imagination, to find the attitude of the people of the United States. As I was traveling on the train the other day, I saw a great placard. In the middle of it was a picture of President Taft. On either side was reading matter addressed to the voters of the United States, and one phrase stuck in my memory: "It is better to be safe than to be sorry." It is also safer to hug your base than to steal a base. You never won a single battle of human liberty by playing safe. Every battle, everything that is worthwhile in life, has been won by taking risks, and I would rather be courageous than be sorry. I would rather espouse a great cause than be ashamed that I did not espouse it. I would rather risk my fortunes than sell my liberty. What do these gentlemen think that America has come to? Do they think that she has lost her ancient spirit? Do they think that she has forgotten the thing for which she was created? Do they suppose that America is going to be content to let things alone, when there isn't a man in the United States who doesn't know that it would be desperately dangerous to let things alone?

I, for my part, ladies and gentlemen, am not disturbed by some of the symptoms of our life. I rejoice that there was a protest in the city of Lawrence, Massachusetts, against some of the transparencies that were displayed at a little procession there. When men deny that there is a God and propose that there should be no law, when men reject the flag of the United States and carry only a crimson symbol, which is a symbol of revolt against that flag and against every other, I am glad that men should rise up and protest against their actions.[4] But I am not afraid that the

---

[4] Wilson referred to two incidents, both of them outgrowths of the Lawrence strike led by the Industrial Workers of the World. Feeling continued to run high there despite a settlement satisfactory, for the most part, to the workers. On September 30, anarchists from Lawrence and elsewhere led a large parade in honor of Annie LoPezzi, the only person killed during the strike. There were some fifty red and black flags, as well as banners with the slogan, "No God, No Country." Native and immigrant groups who had been opposed to the strike and its radical leaders organized a huge counter parade on Columbus Day, October 12. Some 32,000 people, including some of the earlier strikers, marched under banners reading "For God and Country." Cole, *Immigrant City*, pp. 195-96.

red of that flag of protest represents the real spirit of the people of the United States. I am not afraid of revolution. It has been the privilege and the pride of America to settle her own affairs without, in De Tocqueville's fine phrase, drawing a single tear or a single drop of blood from mankind. But I do say this—that any body of men that seeks to hold the United States at a standstill for four years risks action at the end of the four years which might be averted now if we undertook the calm courses of constructive statesmanship.

For the program of the Democratic party is a program of constructive statesmanship. It is a program by which it is proposed not to disturb the foundations of anything that is honest and legitimate, by which it is not proposed to set any pace that it will be impossible for a conservative people to follow, but it is a program which proposes to meet what every man in the United States knows has to be met.

This is a great business city. It is a great manufacturing city. I would be perfectly willing to leave it to any jury of businessmen in this country whether they thought the present organization of business in the United States was satisfactory. There isn't a single man coming up in business who doesn't feel the chill of the shadow of the overtowering trusts of this country. Mr. Brockson, your candidate for Congress,[5] used a very brief and sufficient description of a trust today. He said, "A trust is a corporation that has grown so big that it can determine the prices of the things that it manufactures." That is a very compendious definition of what, in practice, a trust is. And just so soon as a corporation gets so big and controls so large a part of the product of the country that it can determine prices, you know what it means to compete with it. . . .

The Government of the United States must intervene to do what only the Democratic party proposes to do, namely, to take care of the beginner, to take care of the new businessman, to take care of the little businessman and see that any unfair interference with the growth of his business shall be a criminal offense. No other party proposes that. It is amazing to me that the people of the United States should not see that the counsels of the Republican party are counsels of despair. They say: "Don't stir. If you move in any direction you may get into trouble. Just trust to Providence and the liberality of American history and think in the terms of the Republican party, and it will be perfectly safe never to do anything without consulting your grand-

[5] Franklin Brockson. He was elected and served a single term.

mother." And the Republican party sits like a complacent old grandmother and twirls its thumb and says, "My dears, so long as you sit perfectly still, you are perfectly safe and you won't be sorry."

Why, the great world of human affairs is moving with tremendous force. We are at the opening of a new age. These gentlemen have not seen the dawning. These gentlemen have not seen the light in the eyes of men of new generations. Do they know whom the first voters of this country are voting for in this campaign? They are supporting the Democratic party. Men of middle age everywhere tell me that though they themselves have voted the Republican ticket, the younger generation is getting away from them. And some of them admit, rather sheepishly, that the young generation has won them over, and that they themselves are going to do an incredible thing for them. They are going to vote the Democratic ticket.

The Republican party bases its only hope upon the inveterate habit of a large number of gentlemen of voting the Republican ticket. And any country that votes by habit is a country that sooner or later is going to find itself in profound difficulties, because habit belongs to the past, but the policy of the Democratic party belongs to the future. And any nation that has its eyes to the front is a nation that cannot vote by habit, cannot vote by prepossession, must be voting according to the facts or else overridden and overcome by the facts. For there is not a policy characteristic of the Republican party that is now suitable to the circumstances of 1912. The tariff policy was conceived in a time utterly unlike the year 1912. The trouble with some Republicans is that they waited until 1912 to discover that they were in a new age. It has been in slow process of discovery for a long time. You wouldn't suppose that part of the progressive movement, at any rate in the ranks of the Republican party, originated in New Jersey, would you?

New Jersey had been supposed to be one of the backward states of the Union until recently, when she got a move on her. But it is a good many years now since that interesting figure of young Senator Colby of Essex County arose in the City of Newark and started a movement among the Republicans known as the New Idea Movement. I have never had that name explained to me, and I have simply assumed that it meant that the idea of the Republican party understanding and serving the people was a new idea. For that was Senator Colby's idea. He was tired of seeing New Jersey and the Republicans in New Jersey serve a narrow group of special interests, and he led a hopeful little band that determined to serve the people instead of the special interests. Then the movement spread, or perhaps it was widened at the same moment. I am not meaning to claim for this little group in New Jersey the origination of the movement, but about the same time there sprang up in Iowa a group of men who saw that the tariff policy of this country was not in the interest of the people, or even of the rank and file of the manufacturers of the country.

Then there arose in Wisconsin that indomitable little figure of Bob La Follette. I tell you, ladies and gentlemen, I doff my hat to Bob La Follette. He has never taken his eye for a single moment from the goal he set out to reach. He has walked a straight line to it in spite of every temptation to look on one side.

Do you remember that story in the Arabian Nights of the man who was sent on a quest to the top of a great mountain to bring an enchanted bird that was there singing lonely in a cage, and how he was warned that he must not heed any voice by the wayside, that he would find the wayside strewn with great stones, that every one of those stones was some traveler in quest of that enchanted bird who had allowed himself to be drawn aside and had turned back at the call of some voice—for the very stones cried out—that just so surely if he looked aside or turned back he himself would be transfixed and transformed into a stone?

And I have sometimes thought of Senator La Follette climbing that mountain of privilege in order to take away the only precious thing that was in it, namely, the rights of the people of the United States. And the stones, the standpat stones, crying out to him, "Bob, look around, you are on the wrong journey. This isn't the way. You are betraying us." Taunted, laughed at, called back, going steadfastly on and not allowing himself to be deflected for a single moment for fear he also should hark and lose all his power to serve the great interests to which he had devoted himself.

I love these lonely figures climbing this ugly mountain of privilege, but they are not so lonely now. I am sorry, for my part, that I didn't come in when they were fewer, and there was no credit to come in when I came in. The whole nation had awakened. All of New Jersey, at any rate, was tired of the game and was willing to try an unsophisticated schoolmaster, because it was in search of somebody that didn't know how to play the old game. He was allowed the privilege of coming in. And now I see all the forces of the United States gathering in irresistible numbers, not misled by these old cries, laughing at the predictions of disaster if men are given power who mean to do something, scoffing at the men who tell them the old tale—the protective system was intended for the benefit of the underpaid workingmen of America—not allowing themselves to be drawn aside by the threat that the factories would close, knowing that all that threat means is that the factories may deliberately be closed as a means of controlling their votes, for that is all that it has ever meant.

For my part, I challenge these gentlemen to close the mills. They are not going to intimidate the workingmen of this country any longer. The workingmen have figured out how admirably they share in the benefits of the protective tariff, and it is almost as easy to pay their bills with the mills shut as with them open. I was speaking a moment ago about Lawrence, Massachusetts. Why, that town is under the shadow of the highest mountain of privilege that has been erected on that pre-empted territory of the protective tariff, that is, here Schedule K towers to the clouds. Schedule K is the woolen schedule, and under the shadow of that schedule the working people get less than an average of eight dollars a week. And they cannot live on their wages, and the men who enjoy the benefits of Schedue K pay dividends on a stock that is watered five times over and have a surplus sufficient to build an extra mill occasionally out of their savings.

Suppose that the mills of Lawrence sometime close to show these poor deluded people, no longer deluded, however, what the power of the trusts is? Don't you see that it would only be the extravagance, the audacity, the brutality of power to do a thing like that, when I have been told by woolen men themselves that the schedule was iniquitous, that they didn't need it?

A man high in the woolen trade came to me the other day and said, "Governor, I am going to vote the Democratic ticket." "But," I said, "I thought you were under the care of Schedule K." "Yes," he said, "I am, and I am ashamed of it." And, thank God, there are men who are ashamed of robbing the people of the United States. Let them utter their threats. Let them dare play any longer with the people of the United States. We are not children. We have been schooled in this school of privation too long. We have seen the prices rise so much faster than our earnings could rise. We have seen our wages pursue so hopelessly the bills that we have had to pay that we aren't afraid of change any longer. And it is better to risk our fortunes than to be cowards and sit still.

And so I have every confidence that the people of the United States have at last seen the point. It is for that reason that I have taken the liberty of coming to Delaware to enjoy the feeling, which I have had all day today, that Delaware is going to take part in the great undertaking. I want to say this, ladies and gentlemen. I just now said something very disrespectful about the gentlemen who represent you in the United States Senate. I don't wish you to understand me as being disrespectful to them as individuals. I am sorry for them, just as I am sorry for a blind man, just as I am sorry for any other ignorant man. They serve special interests because they see by them blindly. They don't see anything but the old road they have traveled. They have no vision. They have no comprehension of what ordinary men are striving for in this world. They believe—and it is that believing that renders them dangerous—they believe that they are the only safe custodians of our prosperity. And I want to get rid of them, agreeable gentlemen though they are, because I don't believe they understand the United States or its interests. They have never shown any great comprehension of the interests of Delaware. If they had, there are several things you might have obtained by this time. You might have obtained a public utility commission, for example, for the state. Why didn't you get one? Because a particular railway[6] has you absolutely at its mercy so long as you don't have one.

I sympathize with you. New Jersey used to be owned by the Pennsylvania Railroad Company. Then it was owned by another corporation, the Public Service Corporation. I don't know how they transferred the title, but the title was transferred. And it was only a year ago that New Jersey got a public utility commission that had powers of regulation; and it didn't get it until the representatives of these corporations were turned out of the State House and out of the Senate. There would be an amazing difference in your freight rates, there would be a noticeable difference in the development of your agricultural towns, and, more than that, there would be a notable increase in the business of these very corporations.

Why, the State of Wisconsin began this business years ago, and every public service corporation, every railway, every gas company, every water company, every trolley company in the State of Wisconsin fought the measure as they would have fought destruction, and what are they saying now? They are saying they have fought with united force against any attempt to change the policy of the state, because by public regulation they have come from under the cloud of public suspicion. And, by the publicity that has resulted, everybody knows how sound their business is. And their securities are practically guaranteed to be good

[6] The Pennsylvania Railroad.

by the State of Wisconsin and command a premium in the bond and stock market such as they never commanded before.

If I believed that by fighting for the cause of the people I was doing irreparable injury to great interests in this country, I might hesitate. But I am fighting these gentlemen because I take leave to believe that I know more about their interests than they do. They will scoff at that, but that doesn't make any difference. I have been scoffed at before. A simple-hearted schoolmaster though I be, these gentlemen will sooner or later thank God that in the year 1912 the United States took charge of its own affairs. I venture to say that ten years from now, if I should live, they will be very good friends of mine. And how free they will be! It is all very well to have political bosses in your employ, but these same political bosses can levy dues on you. And a boss is almost as oppressive to the people he serves as he is to the people whom he exploits.

These gentlemen will enjoy a freedom, a self-respect, a free scope in the world of enterprise, such as they do not now enjoy. They are now timid, fearful of any change, looking around lest somebody should do them harm, saying, "For pity's sake, don't let anybody interfere with us." And we are rearing a generation of men who will sooner or later at this rate have nervous prostration because you have to watch the people of the United States very narrowly to prevent their doing anything. And if you have to have them in your mind all the time, why you will sooner or later have nervous prostration or go to an insane asylum. You will think that somebody has a conspiracy against you, when the only conspiracy is the popular invitation to make common interest with your fellow men and enjoy the liberties of a free country. I am proud that that old party, for the illumination of whose pathway Jefferson held aloft the lamp of his clear mind three generations ago, should now come to the front and lift this same ancient symbol of liberty above its head and say, "Friends and fellow countrymen, we have not forgotten our great heritage. Follow us and America shall rediscover her own liberty."

ICFT transcript of CLSsh notes (RSB Coll., DLC), with corrections from the partial text in the Wilmington, Del., *Every Evening*, Oct. 18, 1912.

A Public Letter

To the Voters of America:　　　　Sea Girt, N. J., Oct. 19, 1912.

I am glad to have an opportunity to state very simply and directly why I am seeking to be elected President of the United

States. I feel very deeply that this is not an ambition a man should entertain for his own sake. He must seek to serve a cause, and must know very clearly what cause it is he is seeking to serve.

The cause I am enlisted in lies very plain to my own view: The Government of the United States, as now bound by the policies which have become characteristic of Republican administration in recent years, is not free to serve the whole people impartially, and it ought to be set free. It has been tied up, whether deliberately or merely by unintentional development, with particular interests, which have used their power, both to control the government and to control the industrial development of the country. It must be freed from such entanglements and alliances. Until it is freed, it cannot serve the people as a whole. Until it is freed, it cannot undertake any programme of social and economic betterment, but must be checked and thwarted at every turn by its patrons and masters.

In practically every speech that I make, I put at the front of what I have to say the question of the tariff and the question of the trusts, not because of any thought of party strategy, but because I believe the solution of these questions to lie at the very heart of the bigger question, whether the government shall be free or not. The government is not free because it has granted special favors to particular classes by means of the tariff. The men to whom these special favors have been granted have formed great combinations by which to control enterprise and determine the prices of commodities. They could not have done this had it not been for the tariff. No party, therefore, which does not propose to take away these special favors and prevent monopoly absolutely in the markets of the country sees even so much as the most elementary part of the method by which the government is to be set free.

The control to which tariff legislation has led, both in the field of politics and in the field of business, is what has produced the most odious feature of our present political situation, namely, the absolute domination of powerful bosses. Bosses cannot exist without business alliances. With them politics is hardly distinguishable from business. They maintain their control because they are allied with men who wish their assistance in order to get contracts, in order to obtain special legislative advantages, in order to prevent reforms which will interfere with monopoly or with their enjoyment of special exemptions. Merely as political leaders, not backed by money, not supported by securely intrenched special interests, they would be entirely manageable and comparatively powerless. By freeing the government, therefore, we at the same time break the power of the boss. He trades, he does not govern. He arranges, he does not lead. He sets the stage for what the people are to do; he does not act as their agent or servant, but as their director. For him the real business of politics is done under cover.

The same means that will set the government free from the influences which now constantly control it would set industry free. The enterprise and initiative of all Americans would be substituted for the enterprise and initiative of a small group of them. Economic democracy would take the place of monopoly and selfish management. American industry would have a new buoyancy of hope, a new energy, a new variety. With the restoration of freedom would come the restoration of opportunity.

Moreover, an administration would at last be set up in Washington, and a legislative regime, under which real programmes of social betterment could be undertaken as they cannot now. The government might be serviceable for many things. It might assist in a hundred ways to safeguard the lives and the health and promote the comfort and the happiness of the people; but it can do these things only if its actions be disinterested, only if they respond to public opinion, only if those who lead government see the country as a whole, feel a deep thrill of intimate sympathy with every class and every interest in it, know how to hold an even hand and listen to men of every sort and quality and origin, in taking counsel what is to be done. Interest must not fight against interest. There must be a common understanding and a free action all together.

The reason that I feel justified in appealing to the voters of this country to support the Democratic party at this critical juncture in its affairs is that the leaders of neither of the other parties propose to attack the problem of a free government at its heart. Neither proposes to make a fundamental change in the policy of the government with regard to tariff duties. It is with both of them in respect of the tariff merely a question of more or less, merely a question of lopping off a little here and amending a little there; while with the Democrats it is a question of principle. Their object is to cut every special favor out, and cut it out just as fast as it can be cut out without upsetting the business processes of the country. Neither does either of the other parties propose seriously to disturb the supremacy of the trusts. Their only remedy is to accept the trusts and regulate them, notwithstanding the fact that most of the trusts are so constructed as to insure high prices, because they are not based upon efficiency but upon monopoly. Their success lies in control. The competition of more efficient competitors, not loaded down by the debts created when the combinations were made, would embarrass and conquer them. Trusts want the protection of the government, and are likely to get it if either the Republican or the so-called "Progressive" party prevails.

Surely this is a cause. Surely the questions of the pending election, looked at from this point of view, rise into a cause. They are not merely the debates of a casual party contest. They are the issues of life and death to a nation which must be free in order to be strong. What will patriotic men do?

Woodrow Wilson

Printed copy (Harry A. Garfield Papers, DLC); also printed in the New York *World*, Oct. 27, 1912.

A Campaign Address at the Academy of Music in Brooklyn

[Oct. 19, 1912]

Mr. Chairman[1] and fellow citizens: It is with the greatest interest that I find myself facing this magnificent audience. And I have come here tonight in order to discuss the question, just where do we stand in this campaign? For all the preliminary parts of the campaign have been fought, the lines are drawn, the field is ordered, the armies have gathered for the final contest. And now we ought to take account of the principles and purposes which we mean to set forward. I want, if you will be patient with me, to lay before your minds the circumstances which brought on the present campaign.

This campaign is in many respects unprecedented in American history, because it has been preceded by a realignment of forces such as has never been witnessed before in a campaign in the experience of the country. You know that for more than sixteen years the Democratic party has been pointing out to the country that certain things were going on. And about the middle of that period, there began to be shown an awakening in the line of opposition. What preceded this campaign and made it very significant was the going to pieces of the Republican party. That going to pieces did not wait for the assembling of the first convention at Chicago. It had been going on for at least a decade. We know the leaders. We know the issues. We know the causes. So that what has been happening in the United States is that by slow degrees, but with accumulating force, the leaders of the Repub-

[1] Andrew McLean, editor-in-chief of the *Brooklyn Daily Citizen*.

lican party have come to see that the course they were steering was impossible and led straight to difficulties which, it might be, could not be remedied if they went too far.

I want you to realize what these difficulties were, because campaigns, in my opinion, ladies and gentlemen, are not for the display of oratory or for the eulogy of parties. I regard politics as a stern piece of business. The people of the United States are going to assemble at their various voting places on the fifth of November to determine the course of the nation, and they ought to know the grounds upon which they are determining it. They ought to determine it with the distinct purpose of seeing to it that they know what they want and are finding the means of getting what they want, else it is a mere review of the troops, else the war is not joined, else nothing is accomplished.

Too many a campaign has been like that. Too many a campaign has simply consisted of every Republican voting as his party leaders told him, and every Democrat voting as his party leaders told him, voting for a ticket which he had no part in choosing, voting for issues which he had no part in formulating. Most of our campaigns have consisted in going through the motions. But we can't afford to go through the motions any more, because the issues of life depend upon what we are about to do. We are either going to recover and put into practice again the ideals of America, or we are going to turn our backs upon them and lose them. What was it that cut into the ranks of the Republicans? What was it that quickened the consciences of some of the most thoughtful leaders of that party? What was it that made us presently distinguish that stout litle figure of Bob La Follette in Wisconsin? For I want tonight to pick out some of the men who have done the progressive thinking of this country outside the ranks of the Democrats as well as inside.

While I am proud to claim for the great party I have the honor to represent that it has been progressive from the first, I want to point out to you how the leaven of conviction has been working in the ranks of the other party and turning some of its leaders in the other direction so far as to face the very light that has been leading the Democratic party through all these years of waiting and discouragement. Those men, when they got to Washington, and before they got to Washington, in dealing with state governments, saw certain things happen. They saw certain powers closing around the governments with which they were dealing. Closing around, do I say? They had already closed. The hand had been set upon the throttle, and the whole machinery of the government was under the control of small bodies of men.

I speak of what I know, because just across the river in that stout Commonwealth of New Jersey, which I have very near at my heart, there was a body of men, so small that you could get them into one room, that absolutely controlled the course of affairs in New Jersey and determined what the legislature could do, and what the legislature could not do. And they were not all of them of one party. That is the pity of it. For your characteristic boss isn't a party man. Your characteristic boss is a man who has alliances with both sides—I was about to say, I would have said, with all sides—for his threads and alliances and partnerships spread into everything. What America likes, what America believes in, what America cannot dispense with, is coherent, loyal party organization. And America has no quarrel whatever with those men who devote their time so loyally, and with so much intelligence, to keeping the ranks of party columns closed and organized and disciplined.

I never want to speak of party bosses without speaking of the legitimate leaders and organizers of parties of which there are many. But a boss is a man who has begun to use the forces of a party under private direction, under the direction of small groups of men who mean to use government for their own purposes, and not for public purposes. Just so soon as that kind of boss gets hold upon a community nothing is determined by opinion; everything is determined by private control.

Very well, then, this was the sort of thing which those gentlemen in Washington found closing around the Government of the United States. How singular that figure used to be, how impudent that figure was, of the one-time senior senator of Rhode Island[2] telling the Senate of the United States what tariff schedules they must, and what tariff schedules they must not, adopt! And how audaciously he dictated without condescending any information whatever! How impudently he withheld the information which was necessary for public action upon important matters of that sort! And when men associated with him in the Senate saw that they were not permitted to know the influences which determined the action of the government, and that the machinery of the Senate and of the House alike were subject to secret discipline, then their consciences began to prick them. They said, "If the power of the Republican party has come to this, in God's name in whose interest are we acting? In the interest of the people of the United States? Why, the people of the United States are not admitted to these councils. You don't see any attorneys for the

[2] Nelson W. Aldrich.

people in the lobby. You don't see individuals who represent the rights and interests of communities waiting for audience before the Ways and Means Committee of the House and Finance Committee of the Senate. This is not politics, this is business, and it is very narrow, selfish business at that."

I have had some businessmen say to me, "All that we want, all that we businessmen want, is to be let alone. Politics ought not to interfere with business." And my reply invariably is this: "Politics will not interfere with business when politics ceases to be business. Take your hands off, come out into the open with us, and we will take our hands off." But just so long as there is some private influence at work to control the government, then the conscience of every public-spirited man who loves America will be set against the men who are trying to control the Government of the United States after that fashion. There is a bigger monopoly than any monopoly that is ordinarily mentioned on the stump, the monopoly of the—

We have no right to be rude to a woman.[3]

Mr. Wilson, you just said you were trying to destroy a monopoly, and I ask you, what about woman suffrage? The men have a monopoly on that.

Woman suffrage, madam, is not a question that is dealt with by the national government at all, and I am here only as the representative of a national party.

I appeal to you as an American, Mr. Wilson.

I hope you will not consider it a discourtesy if I decline to answer this question on this occasion. I am sure that the lady will not insist when I positively decline to discuss that question now.

Why do you decline?

I was trying to draw your attention to the circumstances which brought about the present political situation, an unprecedented situation in the experience of the country, the great monopoly in the United States.

Ladies and gentlemen, this is a serious matter. It was very much against my will and wish that the lady should be ejected.[4] I would rather have the meeting broken up, because I respect the right of every person holding strong convictions to put questions, however inopportune. The question was not pertinent to what I was discussing and, of course, it is not pertinent to the national campaign, but I am sincerely sorry for the incident.

I would like, if I might, to have your attention while I recover

[3] At this point, Maud Malone of Brooklyn, a militant suffragette, stood up and interrupted Wilson. Their colloquy now follows.
[4] The police had just removed Miss Malone and hustled her off to jail.

the thread of what I was saying. I was trying to point out to you, my fellow citizens, what is a very serious matter now—that a monopoly of manufacturing is not to be compared with that root monopoly of all, namely, the monopoly of the influence which controls the government, and that men in Washington were beginning to realize more and more from year to year, that there was not a wide enough field of conference, that too few persons controlled the councils of the Government of the United States. That was the first thing they discovered. Then they discovered that the purpose of this control was to get special favors from the government, and that that ancient policy that so many Americans have come almost to revere—I mean the policy of protection—was being distorted to very illegitimate and outrageous uses. For it was being employed, not to stimulate industries all along the line, not to support American industry where it needed support, but to hide special favors, hide all in the phraseology of particular schedules of the tariff, in order that an illegitimate and special profit might be reaped by the men who had the private ear of the government itself.

For you will notice that the very Republicans who first in Iowa, for example, turned against the protective policy of the United States Government, turned against it, not because they found some duties too high, as the Republican platform now says, but because they found the system by which duties were levied to be a system of private patronage and not of public protection. So that they saw that this monopoly of government was maintained for selfish purposes, in order that particular groups of men could profit to such a degree that they were more and more getting their hands upon the whole industrial structure of a great free nation. And that accompanying all this were the backstair methods, the secret processes, those influences, those pulls, as we say in the language of the street, which some men had and some men did not have. So that if you wanted to get at the government of the country you had to get at it through certain privileged channels and knew you couldn't get at it by any other ways. And by all these means of control and private influence and tariff preference, there was being built up in this country something against which all the wars of liberty chronicled among mankind have been waged, namely, private monopoly.

I tell you there is not to be found in the history of mankind a single case where the rights insisted upon by human beings in the field of politics were not resisted by those who had entrenched themselves behind the favors of the government and built up private monopolies for their own benefit. Therefore, when we hurl ourselves against that apparently formidable but really weak force of private monopoly, we are simply taking up the history of liberty where it was left off. We are taking out of the hands of those who have fallen by the wayside that torch, that only torch which has ever illuminated the path of men who would be free. And so we have come to this juncture. All the while that this was going on, all the while that this leaven of conscience, this illumination, was working among the Republicans, there had stood that unbroken solid phalanx of the Democrats who had said all along that they were arrayed and would remain arrayed against those forces until the end, until upon some happy day they would have the right to draw their columns up in open battle and rout those forces that had set themselves against the liberty of mankind.

And now we have come to a time when, with broken forces against us, we have united forces with which to redeem America. Is it not something to quicken the blood? Is it not a happy circumstance for any man to be engaged in the national field of politics at this time? I sometimes feel as if I were reaping an unearned usury. While I looked on, perforce indeed, but nevertheless comparatively inactive, these forces gathered. And then, when they had gathered, I was given the privilege of leading them. I do not claim to deserve it. I only claim to be unaffectedly proud of the privilege that is mine of leading these forces! And now what are we going to do? Are we going to look about among our neighbors and say, "Here, what are you doing? Vote the Democratic ticket!" Are we going to look suspiciously upon the new alliances, the new legitimate alliances of politics?

Why, it is perfectly obvious what every public-spirited American ought to do. He ought to use every means in his power to draw together men of like minds in every community and say, "Men and brethren, there is no difference between us if our minds agree, if we love the country in the same terms, if we wish to accomplish the same purposes." But we must certainly have a concerted plan of action and be clear in our thinking in order that there may be the same thought in all our minds. . . .[5]

ICFT transcript of CLSsh notes (RSB Coll., DLC), with additions and corrections from the complete text in the *Brooklyn Daily Eagle*, Oct. 20, 1912.

[5] There is a WWhw outline of this address, with the composition date of Oct. 19, 1912, in WP, DLC.

A Campaign Address in Carnegie Hall

[Oct. 19, 1912]

Mr. Chairman[1] and fellow citizens: I would indeed be lacking in sensibility if I were not moved by the presence of so great an audience as this. And I count myself particularly fortunate in being here under the presidency of my distinguished friend, Mr. Herman Ridder, a man who has served the Democratic party so much longer than I have and has served it with so much loyalty and distinction. And I can't myself forget also in this circumstance that you were rather late in naming a state ticket in New York, and I am glad to be here as the campaign is in full swing and I can speak for somebody else besides myself.

It is a genuine pleasure for me to speak a very cordial word of support, a very urgent word of support, for the men who have been named on the state ticket. I think New York will be fortunate in having, I think New York will certainly have the good fortune of having Mr. Sulzer for governor, and I like to find myself associated with sturdy Democrats such as he has proved himself to be. And Mr. Glynn[2] will stand alongside of him as of the same quality.

So that we are privileged tonight to talk not about candidates for the presidency, for that would be very embarrassing, but about the great Democratic cause. And I cannot but be reminded by the special circumstances of this meeting—that it is under the auspices of a man who stands for one of the great solid, energetic elements of our people. I will not call them the German Americans, but I will call them those Americans who proudly look back to a lineage that finds its beginning in the Fatherland.

I should now like to think of America in the terms of these men who have made their homes here in comparatively recent times, because America has, so to say, opened its doors and extended its welcome to men who were Americans everywhere in the world. She has invited all the free forces of the modern civilized peoples to come to America where men can be free, and where all free forces can unite and forget all their differences of origin.

I, for my part, should be sorry to see the Government of the United States adopt any niggardly immigration policy, because when you reflect upon the largess of genius, the infinite variety

[1] Herman Ridder, president and publisher of the *New-Yorker Staats-Zeitung* and long active in local and national Democratic politics.

[2] Martin H. Glynn, Albany editor and lawyer, Democratic nominee for lieutenant governor.

of capacity, which other nations have conferred upon America, it would seem certainly an act of self-denial, an act of folly, to shut our doors against such enrichment.

There is in America an extraordinary variety of national origins and, therefore, this interesting circumstance—that men of many origins are united in a common view, in a common ideal. And if all sorts of literatures as a background, all sorts of imaginations as the vehicle, carry the vision of America, how great is that vision! It is then the vision not of a single people, but the vision of mankind holding itself free and set at liberty to realize all its energies at their best. And what do the free people of the world come to America to find? That is the question we ought to lay to our consciences. What do they come to find, and do they find it?

We all realize that every man, free to make a home for himself elsewhere, who turns his eyes towards America, says to himself, "There is the place where men are not forbidden to do or prevented from doing anything that their native energies suffer. There is the land where we shall not be bidden what we shall do or forbidden what we shall not do, but shall be free to release our energies in an air with which we can gratefully fill our lungs, fear no man, and serve no man."

They also have another conception of America which has been very dear to us and which has excited the imagination of the world. They have had that idea of America as a place of close knit communities, where men think in terms of the common interest, where men do not organize selfish groups to dominate the fortunes of their fellow men, but where, on the contrary, they, by common conference, conceive the policies which are for the common benefit. Well, when they come to America do they find these things?

Why, ladies and gentlemen, in recent years since I entered politics I have chiefly had men's views confided to me privately. Some of the biggest men in the United States in the field of commerce and manufacturing are afraid of somebody, are afraid of something. They know that there is a power somewhere so organized, so subtle, so watchful, so interlocked, so complete, so pervasive, that they had better not speak above their breath when they speak in defiance and condemnation of it. They know that America is not a place of which it is as true as it used to be that a man may choose his own calling and pursue it just as far as his abilities enable him to pursue it because, if he enters certain fields, men will use means against him which will guarantee that he doesn't build up a business that they don't want to have built up, which will guarantee that the ground is cut from under them and the markets shut against them. For if they begin to sell to certain retail dealers, to any retail dealers, the monopoly will refuse to sell to those dealers, and those dealers will be afraid and will not buy the new man's wares. And so Americans look about for the place in which they can begin without fear or favor. And this is the country which has lifted to the admiration of the world its ideals of absolutely free opportunity, where no man has any limitation except the limitations of his character and of his mind, where there is no distinction of class, no distinction of blood, no distinction of social status, but men win or lose on their merits.

I lay it very close to my own conscience as a public man whether we can stand at our doors and welcome all newcomers upon those terms. And I regard the present campaign as a choice on the part of the American people whether they are going to have that kind of life or are not.

We are at the parting of the ways. We have not one or two or three, but many established and formidable monopolies in the United States. We have not one or two, but many fields of endeavor into which it is difficult, if not impossible, for the independent man to enter. We have restricted credit. We have restricted opportunity. We have controlled development, and we have come to see, worst of all, a controlled and dominated government, not government by free opinion, not government by the opinions and the votes of the majority, but government by the opinion and by the duress of the power of small groups of men. And we are here to determine whether on the fifth of November we shall emancipate ourselves or not, and whether we shall emancipate the very men who have put this yoke upon us. For the men who exercise illegitimate power are killing the energies of the American people, and their own profits will be limited if they are the profits of monopoly, and not the profits of efficiency.

The only thing that ought to live in a free air is the thing which is itself free. The only thing that ought to succeed in a free country is the energy which is indomitable and which can conquer a place for itself without the assistance of the government. My indictment against the protective policy in the United States is that it has weakened and not enhanced the vigor of our people, until American manufacturers, who know that they can make better goods than are made elsewhere in the world, and sell them cheaper in foreign markets than they are sold in those very markets of domestic manufacture, are yet afraid to venture out into the great world on their own merits and on their own strength. Think, a nation full of genius and paralyzed by timidity!

The timidity of the businessmen of America is to me nothing less than amazing. They are tied to the apron strings of the government at Washington. They go about to seek favors. They say, "For pity's sake, don't expose us to the weather of the world. Put some home-like government over us, protect us, see to it that men don't come in and match their brains with ours." And, no doubt, to enhance these pecularities, the strongest men get the biggest favors. The men of peculiar genius for organizing industries, the men who could run the industries of any country, are the men who are strongest in the lobbies, demand the highest rates in the schedules of the tariff, and they are so timid that they dare not stand up before the American people but conceal those favors in the verbiage of the tariff schedules itself—concealed jokers. Ah, but it is a bitter joke when men who seek favor because they are strong, are so afraid of the just judgment of their fellow citizens that they dare not expose those favors.

My indictment against the protective policy is that it has not stimulated America, and that it has led to a system of patronage and favors, and on top of that to a system of secret, indirect, intriguing control throughout every portion of our government. I have dealt with one part of our government in one of the states of the Union. I have seen that government owned, and I have seen it liberated. And the interesting thing is that it hasn't suffered one moment in prosperity by being liberated. When that very ancient, that very absurd threat is made to the American people that if the malevolent Democrats get into power there will be an immediate chill running throughout the whole body of American business, and that the Democrats who constitute something like half the country will commit economic suicide by stopping the business of the other half of the country, then I wonder how long the Republican bill posters are going to try to impose on the intelligence of America. They have to put this grand imposition on bill posters because nobody who has more time than to read a bill poster could possibly be imposed on. Pass these handsome pictures on the train and you may see enough of it to believe it, but stop and read it and it is incredible.

There is one phrase of which they are particularly fond. It is better to be safe than to be sorry. It is better to stand still than to move. It is better to endure anything than to try to get rid of anything. It is a great deal more comfortable, and a great deal more ridiculous, I would add, to stand still than to attempt to realize the aspirations of the life of a great country. These gentlemen have indeed gone to seed. I beg to state that the standpat disposition has induced but a cessation in the circulation of the blood. Stand still and do nothing, indeed, when the great world is catapulting through space and human affairs is going just as fast as the world is itself, changing under our very eyes, and we declining to take any part in the guidance of the change for fear some blunder should be made, for fear we should accidentally get rid of our shackles and stand up and be free!

I don't believe that the American people are going to be imposed on by predictions which can be verified only by the deliberate neglect of their business on the part of the businessmen of the United States, because if any shops and mills are closed they will be deliberately closed, just as they were immediately before the election, the election, mark you, of Grover Cleveland. The American people were not imposed upon then, and they are not going to be imposed upon now. Because the interesting thing about the gentlemen who fear the Democratic party is that they take particular pains not to read all that the Democratic leaders say. I am asked every day to quiet the fears of some timid businessman who thinks that, if I get into the presidency, I, all by myself, of course, will absolutely destroy American business. I wish I thought I were big enough to do that, for if I were big enough to destroy it, I would be big enough to set it free.

Not one single legitimate or honest arrangement of American business is going to be disturbed. But every impediment to business is going to be removed. Every illegitimate kind of control is going to be destroyed. Every man who wants an opportunity, and has the energy to seize it, is going to be given a chance to do so. And all that we are going to ask these gentlemen who now enjoy monopolistic advantages to do is to match their brains against the brains of those who will then compete with them. We are going to see that the little fellows are not crushed, and then we are perfectly willing to see what happens to the big fellows, because the little fellows, give them but half a chance, will grow. And these gentlemen are not big by growth, they are big by promotion; they are big by agreement; they are big by arrangements; they are big by all sorts of secret understandings and polite correspondence. And it isn't wise to let the whole be any bigger than the sum of the pieces.

Just so soon, therefore, as we can get American business on the basis of efficiency, what shall we have done? We shall have turned our faces again towards those ancient ideals of American life without which America is not America. I had a great deal rather live under a king whom I know than under a boss whom I don't know. And a boss is a very much more formidable master than a king because a king is an obvious master, and the hand of the boss is where you least expect it to be. If bosses were elected in order to simplify things! But they are not even elected, they are carefully selected for a particular purpose—for the purpose of organizing those private forces in politics which make us wonder after election why the things didn't happen that we voted for.

Always distinguish a boss from a political leader. Party organization is absolutely legitimate and absolutely necessary, and I honor the man who makes the organization of a great party thorough and impregnable in order to use this great instrument for a public service. But that is not a boss. A boss is a man who uses this splendid open force for the secret processes of selfish control, and, therefore, I would rather live under a king than under a boss. . . .

What we have to do, therefore, is to turn the whole interesting business inside out. I have seen the inside of one government and described it to the persons to whom it belonged. It may be that in the Providence of God I will see the inside of another government, and then I will describe it, all of it, to the people to whom it belongs. And every enlightened man will be pleased to abide by the verdict, for if he were not absolutely confident of the superiority and fairness and conservative moderation of the American people, he wouldn't believe in the American form of government. I have never found average judgments departing from the courses of righteousness and fair play, because an average judgment is a disinterested judgment.

The trouble with these little groups of gentlemen who control our government is not that they are bad, but that they are all seeing the same thing from the same point of view. And if you get a population to judging, you can't get a judgment uttered from a single point of view; but you get a judgment as various as the nation and, therefore, suitable to the variegated needs and conditions of a nation.

What we are going to do on the fifth of November, therefore, is to proceed to business. We have been going through the motions of government. We have been having a mock game. We have been having a rehearsal. We have been working out the plot and having a mimic representation of it. We have been going to the polls and saying, "This is the act of a sovereign people, but we won't be sovereign yet. We will postpone it. We will wait another time. The managers behind the scenes are shifting the whole business. We aren't ready for the real thing yet."

And I propose that we stop sitting in the seats and watching the mimic play, that we get out and translate the ideals of American politics into vivid action. So that every man, when he goes to the polls on the fifth of November, will feel the thrill of executing a judgment and say, "We are not now going to leave matters to men who are deputized by their own choice to control us, but we are going to execute a purpose of our own." But you can't do it unless you have a single purpose. You can't do it unless you have concerted action, and you can't carry out concerted action unless you have a body to carry it out through. So your practical dilemma, ladies and gentlemen, is this—when you vote on the fifth of November, where are you going to find the force through which to exercise your purpose? The only solid, united, enthusiastic, thoroughly prepared body in the United States is the Democratic party. Just put us into the field against the two scrub teams and see us roll up the score. That will be a world series worth looking at. And only the men who are giants in principle will win.

I jest about these things, but they are very serious. I tell you, ladies and gentlemen, that the issues of life and death for free government in the United States depend upon the verdict of the fifth of November. Because we have now to choose between our roads—either to recover freedom of enterprise in the United States or else to give it up for our generation. Nobody but the Democratic party proposes to attempt to regulate competition in such fashion that it shall be free. Nobody but the Democratic party proposes to regard private monopoly as indefensible and intolerable. Nobody but the Democratic party has the courage to tackle the central problem of all, namely, how to take the shackles off of the private man in the United States and renew all the energies of America upon a free field. And, therefore, I invite you to this verdict. It is not merely a matter of candidates. I should be abashed if I supposed that it was a matter of wisdom or the discretion of individuals. I don't believe in government that depends upon the ability and discretion of a few individuals. If I am fit to be your President, it is only because I understand you. And if I do not understand you, I am not fit. If I am not expressing in this speech tonight the aspirations and the convictions of the men who sit before me, I beg that you will not vote for me. I do not wish to be your master. I wish to be your spokesman and I rejoice to say, I rejoice to say—As I wait for your gracious applause to cease, I realize that in that sentence I have summed up my whole philosophy and my whole desire, and I thank you for your attention.[3]

ICFT transcript of CLSsh notes (RSB Coll., DLC), with corrections from the partial text in the *New York Times*, Oct. 20, 1912.
    [3] There is a WWhw outline of this address, with the composition date of Oct. 19, 1912, in WP, DLC.

From the Diary of Colonel House

October 20, 1912.

The Wilsons are all in New York at the Hotel Collingwood, and they are delighted with Captain Bill, taking him to church with them. In the afternoon I took Mrs. Wilson and the girls down to call on some friends and then drove the Governor down lower Broadway to the Aquarium. We had a pleasant time together.

We discussed Cabinet places and the fitness of the different ones. I tentatively mentioned Henry Roberts[1] as Secretary to the President, and spoke of the importance of this place. I also mentioned Lehman[2] and Judson[3] as material for the Attorney Generalship. The Governor said that Judson was not fit, that he was a brilliant lawyer but he was very narrow. I think he has some idea of McAdoo as Secretary of the Treasury. I told him that Gore would like to be Secretary of Agriculture offered him but that it was his intention to decline. The Governor did not seem to take to the idea enthusiastically and said it would be all right if he was certain he would really not accept.

I took them to the train, and they have promised to come over some day soon to go to a matinee. Captain Bill went with them to Princeton.

[1] Henry Chalmers Roberts, a Texas-born resident of London, editor of the British edition of *World's Work* since 1906. Roberts had recently corresponded with House and apparently was considering a return to the United States at this time. As it turned out, he remained with the British *World's Work* until 1932.

[2] Frederick William Lehmann, lawyer of St. Louis, president of the American Bar Association in 1908; an independent in politics, he was at this time Solicitor-General of the United States.

[3] Frederick Newton Judson, corporation lawyer of St. Louis, author of numerous legal treatises, special counsel for the federal government in important railway rebate and rate cases.

To Alexander Walters

My dear Bishop Walters:　　　　　Trenton, N. J. [Oct. 21, 1912]

It is a matter of genuine disappointment to me that I shall not be able to be present at the meeting on Saturday night,[1] but inasmuch as I am cancelling every possible engagement, in view of the distressing assault upon Mr. Roosevelt, I do not feel that I can properly add others. I am fulfilling only those to which I have been bound for many weeks.

It would afford me pleasure to be present, because there are certain things I want to say. I hope that it seems superfluous to those who know me, but to those who do not know me perhaps it is not unnecessary for me to assure my colored fellow-citizens of my earnest wish to see justice done them in every matter, and not mere grudging justice, but justice executed with liberality and cordial good feeling. Every guarantee of our law, every principle of our Constitution, commands this, and our sympathies should also make it easy.

The colored people of the United States have made extraordinary progress towards self-support and usefulness, and ought to be encouraged in every possible and proper way. My sympathy with them is of long standing, and I want to assure them through you that should I become President of the United States they may count upon me for absolute fair dealing and for everything by which I could assist in advancing the interests of their race in the United States.

Very cordially yours,   Woodrow Wilson.[2]

Printed in Alexander Walters, *My Life and Work* (New York, 1917), p. 195; checked against the CLSsh notes in RSB Coll., DLC.

[1] A mass meeting of the National Colored Democratic League to be held in Carnegie Hall on October 26, 1912.

[2] Most of this letter was published in the *New York American*, Oct. 23, 1912.

To Norman Hapgood

My dear Hapgood: [Trenton, N. J., Oct. 21, 1912]

What has happened in regard to *Colliers*[1] is in my opinion nothing less than a national calamity. As you were managing the great force of that journal, it was clarifying and purifying everything it touched. Indeed, you constituted its force and I am grieved more deeply than I can say that it should have sacrificed everything to the demands of the advertising department. It will, of course, lose now very steadily and will not even be a good investment if it really follows that course.

Your personal influence, of course, will not be lost because openings of every kind abound for you.

In the meantime let me tell you how genuine a pleasure it has given me and how much of a sense of added strength to have your confidence and support.

Cordially and sincerely yours,   [Woodrow Wilson]

ICFT transcript of CLSsh notes (RSB Coll., DLC).

[1] Hapgood's resignation as editor of *Collier's* was made public on October 18, 1912. The resignation was followed by an acrimonious dispute in the newspapers between Hapgood and the magazine's publisher, Robert Joseph Collier. Collier, a personal friend and political supporter of Theodore Roosevelt, asserted that the break was due to Hapgood's editorial support of Wilson. Hapgood insisted that the rupture came over efforts of the advertising department to control editorial policy. Collier resumed the editorship, which he had held from 1898 to 1902, and the issue of November 2, 1912, anounced his support of Roosevelt and apologized for the pro-Wilson stance of *Collier's* earlier in the campaign.

To Cyrus Adler[1]

My dear Dr. Adler: [Trenton, N. J., Oct. 21, 1912]

Allow me to acknowledge the receipt of your letter of yesterday[2] and to express my sincere appreciation.

I feel that there is a certain impropriety in my expressing opinions regarding pending bills in Congress so long as there is an "if" connected with my election. But I need not hesitate on that account to say that I am in substantial agreement with you about the immigration policy which the country ought to observe. I think that this country can afford to use and ought to give opportunity to every man and woman of sound morals, sound mind, and sound body who comes in good faith to spend his or her energies in our life, and I should certainly be inclined so far as I am myself concerned to scrutinize very jealously any restrictions that would limit that principle in practice.

I, moreover, beg to assure you that I should never consent to any treaty with a foreign country which made any discrimination whatever among American citizens on the ground of creed or race or religion. I put myself very squarely on record to that effect at the Carnegie Hall meeting[3] and of course did so with the greatest pleasure.

Cordially and sincerely yours,   [Woodrow Wilson]

ICFT transcript of CLSsh notes (RSB Coll., DLC).
1 President of Dropsie College for Hebrew and Cognate Learning, Philadelphia.
2 It is missing.
3 See the news report and address printed at Dec. 7, 1911, Vol. 23.

To Robert Stephen Hudspeth

My dear Judge: [Trenton, N. J., Oct. 21, 1912]

My own judgment is with your "secret thought." I do not believe I ought to make any statement on the negro question. I think it ought to suffice Bishop Walters that he himself distinctly knows my mind in this matter and can count on my impartiality.

Cordially and faithfully yours,   [Woodrow Wilson]

ICFT transcript of CLSsh notes (RSB Coll., DLC).

An Interview

[Oct. 22, 1912]

WILSON, TOO, WANTS CLEAN CAMPAIGNS
Joins President Taft in Condemning Mud-Slinging and Lack of Dignity.

PRINCETON, Oct. 22.—Governor Wilson agrees with President Taft that personalities have no place in a Presidential campaign.

He made this very plain in an exclusive interview granted the United Press today in which he discussed the questions answered by President Taft in his interview with the United Press correspondent at Beverly [Mass.] yesterday.

The Democratic candidate made it clear also that he believes the voters are satisfied with the manner in which he has conducted his present campaign. Governor Wilson believes the rank and file of Americans demand dignity in their high office holders.

"Governor Wilson," he was asked, "how do you believe Presidential campaigns should be conducted?"

"I hope that I have made it very clear," said the candidate, "by the way in which I have conducted my own campaign how I think campaigns ought to be conducted. I think they should be conducted and decided by a very frank and open discussion of the issues involved; of the interests to be served, and of the available means of doing what is proposed. They should be regarded as a very great and serious matter of national life and business."

"What is the effect of personalities in a Presidential campaign?"

"The effect of personalities in a Presidential campaign is not only to inject bitterness but to obscure the issues. In my opinion personalities have no place in such contests. It is, of course, pertinent to discuss the public record of the candidates in order to test the soundness of their position and judge their capacity to do what they purpose doing, but that is a very different matter from indulging in personalities. To excite mere prejudice against the individuals you are opposing is to show your own weakness."

"Do the people still look for dignity in high office?"

"I think the people do look for dignity in high office, and are deeply chagrined and disappointed when they do not find it."

Printed in the *Trenton Evening Times*, Oct. 22, 1912.

A News Report

[Oct. 22, 1912]

WILSON'S FINGERS NIMBLE ON KEYS

PRINCETON, Oct. 22.—Governor Wilson has qualified as an accomplished typewriter as well as an expert stenographer, and as a result he was able to go to Trenton to attend to state business with the satisfaction of having cleaned up most of the mass of correspondence which had accumulated here in his absence.

After the Governor had dictated to his stenographer[1] nearly all day yesterday, he dismissed the young man who had to go to Trenton to transcribe his notes. This left Governor Wilson with several hours on his hands. After reading his letter he would jot down the answers in short hand and then turn to his old typewriter[2] and transcribe his own notes, address the envelopes, sign the letters, seal the envelopes and lick the stamps.

Governor Wilson uses a typewriter with an old style keyboard which no modern typist understands. He much prefers it to the universal keyboard.

"The keyboard on the modern typewriter," he said, "must have been invented by a left handed man. All the letters that you use the most are on the wrong side."

Printed in the *Trenton Evening Times*, Oct. 22, 1912.
[1] Charles L. Swem.
[2] A Hammond typewriter.

To William Gibbs McAdoo

Dear Mr. McAdoo: Princeton, N. J., October 22, 1912.

My attention has been called to the statement that I have become a member of the Knights of Columbus. This is, of course, not true. I have not been asked to join the order either as an active or an honorary member, and am not eligible because I am not a Catholic.

I must warn my friends everywhere that statements of this kind are all campaign inventions, devised to serve a special purpose. This particular statement has been circulated in selected quarters to create the impression that I am trying to identify myself politically with the great Catholic body. In other quarters all sorts of statements are being set afloat to prove that I am hostile to the Catholics.

It is a very petty and ridiculous business. If all these fabrications could be brought together they would make very amusing reading. They would leave a very flat taste in the mouth, for they would entirely neutralize one another and prove that I was nothing and everything.

I am a normal man, following my own natural course of thought, playing no favorites, and trying to treat every creed and class with impartiality and respect.

Very sincerely yours, Woodrow Wilson.

TCL (WP, DLC).

From Theodore Roosevelt

[Oyster Bay, N. Y., Oct. 22, 1912]

I wish to thank you for your very warm sympathy.

[Theodore Roosevelt]

Printed in the *Trenton Evening True American*, Oct. 23, 1912.

A Religious Address[1]

[Oct. 23, 1912]

I have a simple thought in my mind tonight. One cannot stand in the presence of two hundred years without solemnity and without reflecting upon the things that are permanent and the things that are transient. This church is much older than the Constitution of the United States, which seems the foundation of our life. It is much older than the liberty of the nation, and yet it is not as old as the seed from which it sprang, as the great church of which it forms a recent part. For the Presbyterian Church is very much older, as a great organization originating in the desire of men to find God by their own way, than any church established in America. All the traditions of the Presbyterian Church run back through the processes of hardihood and liberty that seem interwoven with the structure and the creation of nations. So that we obviously, in thinking of the history of this particular congregation, are thinking of something that transcends the circumstances of a particular age.

If you go back two hundred years, you go back to a time utterly unlike our own. That, indeed, is not difficult. If you go back a single generation, you go back to a world utterly unlike our own in social, economic, and political circumstances, and, for that matter, in circumstances of faith and belief. So that the most noticeable thing about the life of men is the number of things

[1] Delivered in the First Presbyterian Church of Trenton, on the occasion of the celebration of the two hundredth anniversary of its founding.

that change, the number of things that are transitory, the number of things that alter, not only their form, but seem in some instances to alter their very substance.

When you see a great measure, thrown across the ages, that stretches two hundred years, you know that that is not part of something that is transient, but part of something that is permanent. For if it is two hundred years long, it is apt to be very much longer, to have connections that make it an intimate part of the structural part of humanity. For the church does represent a structural part of humanity. It represents that spiritual part which does not seek expression in the forms of government or even in the forms of society, but seeks expression in its search for God, in its search for the ultimate explanation of life, in its search for the ultimate fountains of the human spirit.

The things that are outside of us and beyond our control and higher than we are, are the things by which we seek to measure ourselves. And every church is a sort of attempt to discover a standard. We know that that standard cannot be discovered in our own lives, because we see how our own lives change and alter under the very impulses of our own changing conclusions and varying temptations. We know that life without something like the standard of the church is a mere quicksand in which we walk, not only with faltering and stumbling footsteps, but with a sinking sense that we have nothing under our feet. So that when I think of this church, I think of it as one of the expressions, one of the many expressions, of the permanent side of life. I say "one of the many expressions," because, as Dr. McKelway[2] said about Dr. Hall,[3] Dr. Hall has not found a denominational heaven. Dr. Hall has found a heaven in which denominational differences are not only insignificant but unknown, where all the ultimate things are alike, where there are no theological controversies.

A theological controversy arises out of doubt. It arises out of a difference of opinion; it arises out of a difference of information. Somebody has said that the church a man belongs to is largely a question of temperament, largely a question of his spiritual approach to the angle from which he looks at a thing. Some people enjoy the service. Presbyterians have an inordinate taste for sermons. They come to be instructed; they come to hear things discussed, they come to hear life expounded and the standards applied to life upon some high plane of exposition, whereas, others wish to have their emotional sides appealed to in preference to their intellectual sides. But, however the variation may

2 St. Clair McKelway, who also spoke.
3 The Rev. Dr. John Hall (1806-1894), pastor of the First Presbyterian Church of Trenton, 1841-1884.

go, no matter what the ephemeral feature may be, no matter what the external form may be, they are all looking for a foothold, they are all looking for some firm ground of faith upon which to walk. This church has witnessed many changes—the rise of a nation, the birth and death of political parties—it has seen everything change except this search for God.

Therefore, every community ought to realize, it seems to me, that the search for God takes precedence over everything else. When it looks at a church as it passes down the crowded street, it ought to say, "There is one of the permanent interrogation points in our lives." What is the foundation of our life? What is the source of our strength? Where is our salvation? Not in ourselves, but in something external to ourselves and greater than ourselves, from which we are to rise. So the first thought that I have in standing here tonight is that these walls have witnessed the permanent impulses and instincts of human life, that they are greater than the walls of cities. And the second thing that I have in mind is this, that this search is fruitless if it issues in mere conclusions, if it issues in mere intellectual certitudes. It is fruitless unless it gets embodied in men.

What I greatly enjoyed and liked the taste of was Dr. McKelway's description of Dr. Hall. I knew nothing of Dr. Hall before I came here tonight, but I recognized in Dr. McKelway's description a translation into life, an embodiment in flesh and blood, of what the church is looking for. And I realized that the only stable things in communities are men whom those communities can tie to, and that there is no use tying to any man if his foundation does not go beneath his feet, if he is not rooted and grounded in something greater and more permanent than himself. I venture to say that the majesty—the gentle majesty—that surrounds a man like Dr. Hall comes from the fact that he is not playing a part that centers in himself, but that he is a sort of deputy of the truth: He is commissioned to represent things great and permanent and fundamental.

I remember once, when I was a lad, being deeply impressed with this simple instance in the life of a great clergyman[4] whom I knew: he was in the presence of a number of men who were rather eagerly debating some subject of local excitement, and one of them, forgetting his presence, uttered a profane word, and then recollecting himself and turning to the clergyman, he said, "Doctor, I beg your pardon; I forgot that you were present." And with the greatest and most beautiful simplicity, he said, "Ah, my dear sir, it was not me whom you offended." He seemed at that

---

[4] His father.

moment to stand there as the ambassador of God, offended merely because his Master had been offended, and thinking not only of himself but of his Master. His dignity was not touched, but the dignity he wore as the representative of One who made him, Who was greater than he, and Who is the standard of all things. If a man, therefore, can bring into a community this eternal thing, he stands there rooted, storms can break around him, mutations of every kind can come, and he is not moved. And sooner or later the community will turn to him almost as they would turn for salvation, go to him for those deep counsels which transcend all circumstances.

I have seen this beautiful thing happen. And I know that the salvation of a church and the salvation of a community and the salvation of a state is to be found only in those men who are thus rendered greater than themselves, and greater than their age, and greater than anything that can happen to them. Those old martyrs who went to the stake smiling and singing songs of praise were terrible fellows—terrible because their very gaiety in going to the stake was evidence of the fact that this was an incident, not an end, that this meant nothing, and that after them their ashes would seem to speak the condemnation of those who put them to the stake, and stand up and condemn the generation that dared interfere with the processes of Divine Providence. That, I suppose, is the foundation of all confidence. I cannot imagine anything like self-confidence. A man who is self-confident is leaning on a broken reed, or a reed that will break if he leans too hard. His confidence, if he be unconquerable, is in something that he knows has never been conquered, that cannot be conquered by his being put out of the world, that will spring up like dragons' teeth and make armies over night to fight the battles of the Lord.

Always look out for the man who has that in him. Always be afraid of the man who is indifferent to his own success and certain of the success of the thing that he represents. Stand out of his way, for he has behind him the hosts of the Almighty. So in proportion as this church has produced men of that quality, she has produced the fruit that makes the church permanent. Most church members, I dare say, are insignificant to the church. They are not of the stuff that I have been describing. But, for my part, I think it is enough for the salvation of the world if any particular congregation produces one such man a generation. If it produces two, that is largess; if it produces three, that is the revolution of the community; if it produces four, the millennium is approaching. One is enough for a generation, because your generation cannot get away from that.

Dr. McKelway said that Dr. Hall was saluted by everybody who passed him on the streets of Trenton, whether they knew him or not. That figure, that modest man, was the hope and permanence of the town. They were taking off their hats to the majesty of Trenton, to its hope, to all the things that pointed to a long future and deliverance from things that were impure, and the raising of the levels of life.

There was a similar example in the city of New Orleans, the more remarkable perhaps, because at the time that the example was exhibited, New Orleans was very much larger than Trenton was at the time that Dr. Hall lived in it. There was an old gentleman there who had lived to be nearly ninety years old—Dr. Benjamin Palmer—to whom everybody of every denomination in that town ultimately turned as the leading central figure of New Orleans; not because of his extraordinary gifts, though he could bring any body of people to their feet with his eloquence, not because of his lovable nature, but because he was the embodiment of the grace of God. And by long residence there everybody knew that he was untainted and untouched and unimpeachable. When you get a man like that, then there is an ideal resident and in the flesh, and only those ideals that are resident and in the flesh will rescue a people.

We ought to bless our churches. We ought to think of them as the instrumentalities by which these miracles are wrought, these miracles of regeneration. The example of consecrated men is better than all the books and precepts that the world contains, except perhaps this book that I am touching, which seems something more than a book. It seems to contain something more than words and printed pages, because everything in it is so concrete, the men it speaks of are so real, and the truths it utters are so compelling. Read in this air, they are familiar, but they are not redeeming words unless they vibrate beyond the walls of the churches and walk the streets and are seen in the households and are translated into the public life of the community.

T MS (C. L. Swem Coll., NjP), with a few typographical corrections from the partial text in the *New York Times*, Oct. 24, 1912, and from the full text in the *Trenton Evening True American*, Oct. 24, 1912.

To John Hanson Kennard, Jr.[1]

My dear Kennard: [Trenton, N. J., Oct. 23, 1912]

Mrs. Wilson has handed me your letter of October 21 with the accompanying article.[2] I am sure you know without my saying it that I sincerely appreciate your desire to help me in any way, but I have the most deep-rooted objection to the publication of private letters of any kind during a man's lifetime. I am opposed to the whole principle and I believe that the effect of it is almost always bad. I feel, therefore, that I must beg that you will, if you publish anything, not publish the letters. There is, of course, nothing in them that would embarrass me but their publication would very much indeed.

Sincerely yours,   [Woodrow Wilson]

ICFT transcript of CLSsh notes (RSB Coll., DLC).
[1] An old acquaintance of Wilson's from his graduate student days at The Johns Hopkins University. At this time a lawyer and president of a truck sales agency in New York.
[2] Kennard's letter and its enclosure are missing.

To Carolyn Wells[1]

My dear Miss Wells: [Trenton, N. J., c. Oct. 24, 1912]

I wish I could send you something that was worthwhile in response to your interesting letter of yesterday.[2] The fact is that I am a somewhat indiscriminate reader of detective stories and would be at a loss to pick out my favorites. My real criticism of many of them, even including Anna Katharine Green's,[3] is that the mechanism of the whole thing too much subordinates the characters, and the characters are apt to be mere dummies with a very conventionalized way of talking and very little human nature except such as sets the plot forward. On the whole I have got the most authentic thrills out of Anna Katharine Green's books and Gaboriau's.[4]

Cordially and sincerely yours,   [Woodrow Wilson]

ICFT transcript of CLSsh notes (RSB Coll., DLC).
[1] Of Rahway, N. J., prolific author of mystery and detective stories, humorous articles, and nonsense verse.
[2] Her letter is missing.
[3] Anna Katharine Green (Mrs. Charles) Rohlfs, author of many detective and mystery stories.
[4] Émile Gaboriau, the originator of the detective novel in France.

To Harry B. Davison[1] and Grace Walcott Davison

My dear Friends: [Trenton, N. J., Oct. 24, 1912]

I am deeply gratified by the high compliment you have paid me in naming your son[2] after me and want to express my genuine appreciation. I sincerely hope that nothing may ever happen which will make you regret this choice of name.

Cordially and sincerely yours,   [Woodrow Wilson]

ICFT transcript of CLSsh notes (RSB Coll., DLC).
[1] Mechanical draftsman of 204 Becker St., Schenectady, N. Y., employed by the General Electric Co.
[2] Woodrow Wilson Davison, born Oct. 16, 1912.

A Draft of a Statement

[Oct. 25, 1912]

Gov. Wilson to-night confirmed Mr. Bryan's statement, reported from Oxford, Mich., that the $12,500 contributed by his classmate, Mr. Cyrus H. McCormick to his pre-convention campaign fund had been returned.[1] "Mr Cleveland Dodge and Mr. McCormick arranged the return between them, in order to relieve me of embarrassment in case anything might occur in the future which might remind me of a personal obligation when some question of the performance of a public duty arose."

"The whole transaction," he said, "simply confirms what I have always thought of both Dodge and McCormick, my classmates and life-long friends. I did not know until a couple of weeks before the opening of the Clapp committee's investigation that McCormick had contributed anything; and I feel sure that he never intended that I should know. That was the way he used to contribute to university funds; keeping himself entirely in the background; and I have now still another proof of the quality of the group of men who stood by me so loyally and so without thought of themselves—at a great personal cost to themselves, indeed, when I was making my fight for scholarship and democracy in the University,—for they were fighting men who had been their friends even longer than I had and were fighting against social standards which too many men of their class in the business world were willing to see fastened upon the life of the place. All of the men on Mr. Dodge's list[2] were in college with me—three of them my classmates; and all of them had been trustees of Princeton during my presidency there. I had dealt with them too long and too intimately to feel bound, by any assistance they might lend my candidacy, to anything but the performance of my duty. And now their quality is shown again by sample. Mr. Dodge and Mr. McCormick have relieved me entirely of any possible embarrassment I might have felt in the future by reason of my knowledge of Mr. McCormick's contribution. They have closed the incident in the spirit of generous friendship."[3]

WWhw MS (WP, DLC).
[1] Bryan is reported to have said on October 25 that Wilson himself had "directed" that McCormick's contribution to the prenomination campaign be returned, and that Wilson had written to McCormick that "he could not afford

to be under the slightest obligation to anyone connected with any enterprise which might be involved in litigation with the Government after he became President." *New York Times*, Oct. 26, 1912.

2 For this list, see C. H. Dodge to WW, Sept. 5, 1912, n. 2.

3 There is a WWsh draft of this statement in WP, DLC. Instead of this statement, Wilson and his advisers decided to issue a more general report on the return of McCormick's contribution. It stated that Dodge had initiated the return subsequent to McCombs's testimony before the Clapp committee on October 14, in which the names of the contributors and the amounts contributed had been made public, and that he had done so without consulting Wilson. The report included a brief direct quotation from Wilson regarding Bryan's reported statement which ran as follows:

"Mr. Bryan must have been in part misquoted. The money was returned, but not at my request. It was done upon the initiative of Mr. Dodge and Mr. McCormick themselves. It was characteristic of them. They have illustrated again what they illustrated so often while they were trustees of the university during my presidency here. They have always tried to act in such a way as to help me and yet leave me free." New York *World*, Oct. 26, 1912.

To Thomas Pryor Gore

My dear Senator: Trenton, New Jersey October 26, 1912.

I am intensely gratified because of the splendid efforts which you report are being made by the Democratic workers everywhere.

I not only appreciate that this is being done by them, but I especially appreciate the necessity for such work.

One of the greatest essentials now is to get every voter who is favorable to our cause out to the polls on Election Day.

There is no more effective factor in accomplishing this end than the precinct and club workers. They are, in the last analysis, the ones upon whom we are absolutely dependent for getting our voters to the polls, and I cannot urge too strongly the importance of their work.

You have a splendid organized force of loyal Democrats who love our cause and are making sacrifices for it, and I commend them heartily.

I look with assurance upon the result on November 5th because I believe that every one of our workers, those who are members of the various committees, and those who are doing things in an individual capacity, will prove worthy of this confidence which we all feel in them.

Sincerely your friend,   Woodrow Wilson

Printed facsimile (received from Mrs. John Woodruff).

To Mary Allen Hulbert

Dearest Friend,   Princeton, 27 Oct., 1912

It was terrible—it was tragical—that you should have been put through that intolerable ordeal in Boston. I should like to break that young Davis's neck! The Judge should have shielded you more than he did.[1]

I am told *now* that Mr. Root did *not* speak of a letter, but said that another judge had told the judge who sat in your case that T.D. had alleged certain things to *him*: I wonder if T.D. is lying to you now? I [He] seemed very straightforward about it all in these notes you sent me. By the way, do you know where that young Lawrence[2] is who was Allen's tutor in Bermuda, and what he is doing. Is he, too, inclined to lie vindictively? He seemed a very gentlemanly sort.

I took it for granted that you went to New York, as you had planned, last Monday, and called up the Manhattan on the telephone Tuesday, Wednesday, and Thursday—never dreaming, of course, that you had gone to Boston! I wish you had not gone! My mind dwells on the intolerable experience and is very sad. But it was like you to go! It was generous—to help others out—and you deemed it your duty on Allen's account,—and of course you went! You would have gone if you had known beforehand what you had to go through! You are as steadfast as heroic and intrepid—and unfortunate! My heart applauds you and bleeds for you. It is like a Greek tragedy, noble and inevitable. But it cannot and will not last. That I believe and pray.

I have spent a whole week at home; but to-morrow start out "on the road" again to get into the fray—now that Mr. Roosevelt is so much better and again in charge of his own fight. I shall speak in New York on the evening of Thursday, the 31st., go "up state" on Friday, and be in New York again on Saturday, the second. Will you be accessible there that day, to receive a call from Ellen and me? Please answer this question in a note sent to the University Club, 5th Ave. and 54th St., where I can get it on the 31st.

It is dreadful to think of what you must have suffered. I hope that rest and the delightful home quiet of Sandanwede have acted as a cure and tonic by this time and that closing the house and getting away will not "take it out of you" again. I wish you were at Hot Springs without the journey and all that precedes it!

I am persist[ent]ly well, in spite of everything. All join me in affectionate messages. Love to Mrs. Allen and Allen.

Your devoted friend   Woodrow Wilson

ALS (WP, DLC).
   1 Evidence about this matter is missing in the Boston newspapers and elsewhere.
   2 He is described but not identified in WW to EAW, Feb. 4, 1908, Vol. 17.

A Campaign Address at West Chester, Pennsylvania[1]

[Oct. 28, 1912]

Mr. Chairman[2] and fellow citizens: It is a great pleasure to find myself in West Chester again. The last time I came here as a schoolmaster.[3] This time I come here upon an errand which I would not like to characterize as the errand of soliciting your suffrages, but rather for the purpose of seeking the privilege of discussing with you some of the greatest issues of our national life.

I am glad to remember that this is a part of the great State of Pennsylvania in which there is an unusual proportion of men who vote according to their own thoughts and their own convictions. This part of Pennsylvania has the distinction of being one of the most independent parts of the state, and that, I want to say, is a distinction for any part of any state. The men who vote as they think are the men who govern the nation, and men now are taking leave to think for themselves about the affairs of the United States. Parties seem almost to have lost their hold both upon the conviction and upon the imagination of men. Certainly, if the Republican party has kept its hold, it will have to determine which half of it has the hold.

I am interested to know that this part of Pennsylvania has been represented in the state legislature by Democrats who have fulfilled their pledges and voted as they had promised their constituents to vote upon the great state questions, and that you have been represented in the state Senate by a man of singular independence and courage. So that everything shows that West Chester votes as she thinks. You know that it is an interesting reflection, my fellow citizens, to contrast the numerous straw votes with the actual vote at election. There is always a considerable difference when the straw vote is taken. Every man who declares his preference realizes that he is really speaking for the man who in his judgment would make the best public officer. But I am sorry to say that when it comes to the actual voting at election, many of those same men will say to themselves, "I believe in Mr. A, but my interest, my narrow, peculiar, special,

   1 Delivered at the Opera House.
   2 John V. Craven.
   3 See the news item printed at Jan. 13, 1906, Vol. 16.

personal interest, probably lies with Mr. B. At any rate, those who support Mr. B have me more or less in their power, and they are putting the screws on me to vote for Mr. B. I cannot afford to vote according to my preference."

There used to be times in America when presidential elections were settled by the screws that were put on men. There used to be presidential elections in which men voted because they were threatened and knew that those who made the threats would be audacious enough to carry them out in the face of every circumstance of public policy and of public interest. But I am happy to believe that the time has come when America is not going to vote as she is told, when America is going to vote as she thinks. Because all about me in New Jersey, all about you in Pennsylvania, all over the United States, the number of men who have taken the veil away from their eyes and have insisted upon seeing things as they are, has been multiplied and multiplied and multiplied, campaign after campaign, until men are not any longer to be deceived by the ancient shibboleths, the worn-out cries, the forgotten panics, the old threats that have been used again and again and again. Why, Pennsylvania expects, New Jersey expects, the country expects, the Democratic ticket to win. And as the expectation grows, the prosperity of the country is not checked for a moment. There is not a thoughtful businessman in America who has any real dread of any serious interruption of his business affairs if the Democratic ticket is elected—unless he has been breaking the laws of the land and the laws of honor. I hope that those men are afraid, and their fear will be justified.

But there is a very interesting thing happening in America. And I want to point out to you gentlemen here, who are going to vote, and you ladies, who are going to determine how some of you men vote, that it is necessary to do a great deal more than to elect a President. It is necessary to have a Congress that will back him up at every point in carrying out the reforms which are necessary for the liberation of this country, for the freeing of its enterprise from the shackles by which it is now bound. The interesting thing that is happening is this: America has got out of her great middle class—of merchants; men with a little capital; men who could, if they could be but assisted by credit, begin new enterprises; men who have the scope and the view, at any rate in particular communities, to press forward the enterprises of these communities—this great middle class from which the energies of America have sprung is being crushed between the upper and the nether millstones. There is a weight above them— a weight of concentrated capital and of organized control—

against which they are throwing themselves in vain. And beneath them the great body of working people, the great majority of people in this country, upon whom that control is directly exercised by the determination of the industries of the country and the determination of the share that the working people shall have in the industries of the country.

So that the originative part of America, the part of America that makes new enterprises, the part into which the ambitious and gifted workingman makes his way up, the class that saves, that plans, that organizes, that presently spreads its enterprises until they have a national scope and character—that middle class —is being more and more squeezed out by the processes which we call the processes of prosperity. They are sharing prosperity, no doubt, but what alarms me is that they are not originating prosperity. No country can afford to have its prosperity originated by a small controlling class. I am looking forward to the treasury of America. The treasury of America does not lie in the brains of the small body of men now in control of the great enterprises that have been concentrated under the direction of a very small number of persons. The treasury of America lies in those ambitious thoughts, those energies that can not be withheld, those plans that are conceived in quiet. It depends upon the invention of unknown men, upon the origination of unknown men, upon the ambition of unknown men. Every country is renewed out of the unknown ranks, not out of the ranks of those already famous and powerful and in control.

Therefore, I feel like saying—I wish I could say it to America —we are banded together, my fellow citizens, we Americans, to see whether we can restore America again by getting rid of that absolutely un-American thing which enables a small number of men who control the government to get favors from the government, by those favors to exclude their fellows from similar opportunity, by those favors to extend a network of control which will presently drive out every industry in the country, and so make men forget that ancient time when America lay in every hamlet, when America was to be seen in every fair valley, when America displayed her great forces on the broad prairies, ran her fine fires of enterprise up all the mountainsides and down into the bowels of the earth. And eager men were captains of industry everywhere, not employees, not looking to a distant city to find out what they might do; looking about them, organizing companies among their neighbors, finding credit according to their character, not according to their connections, finding credit in proportion to what was known to be in them and behind them, not in proportion to the securities that they held that were approved where they were not known. You have to be authenticated now in order to start an enterprise, in a perfectly impersonal way, not according to yourself, but according to what you own that somebody else has earned. And you cannot begin the great enterprises that have made America until you are so authenticated.

I do not feel that this is an ordinary political campaign, and it does not make any difference to me now whether a man is a Democrat, or has been a Republican, or is something now for which he has not found a label. Because I find a good many men confused to find out what they are by description. They are, as a friend of mine said, between sizes in politics, and nothing seems to fit them. That is because we have come into a new age in which we must do new things, and think new things, and get together in order to agree upon a common policy, no matter what party we have belonged to. I would rather, therefore, have an audience like this, made up, as I believe, of men ready to vote according to their convictions, than speak to a body of mere partisans who already know how they are going to vote, or rather do not know anything except that they are going to vote as they were told to vote. I do not want anybody to vote for me because somebody else told him to vote for me. I want him to vote for me because he believes this. And every man in his senses in America believes this because he believes that we have come to a time of imperative change, that to wait for that change for four years would be folly, because the change, when it came at the end of four years, might not be thoughtful and deliberate, —that we have got to have change now.

It is better to have it now under an organized force, moderately and intelligently guided, than to have it four years from now under forces which we cannot foresee or calculate. Where but in the Democratic party will you find a force big enough, organized enough, united enough, to do this work for you now— while we are still calm, while we are still deliberate, while we are still under the leadership of men who have been thoughtful about affairs, and who have taken the pains to understand the business of the country? Where else will you find a force? Everywhere I go, I find men admitting that the next House of Representatives is going to be Democratic. Nobody doubts that. Very few people doubt that the next Senate is going to be Democratic. Well, then, is it not wise that you should have a Democrat as President also? Because only a Democrat can drive that team. Where else, I ask you in candor, are you going to find a President who can manage the forces that are going to assemble in Washington in the next Congress? The present President has not even tried to manage them. A very honest man, he has felt that his honesty was safest when safeguarded by absolute inactivity. He has thought that a House that was Democratic and a Senate that was not entirely standpat Republican ought not to be trusted to do anything, and that, therefore, the only safe thing was to save the United States and veto everything. Do you want a policy of inaction like that for another four years, with all the forces gathering that you have seen in your own communities, that any man with vision sees all over the United States? The people of this country are infinitely impatient that they have been unable to get what their consciences and their principles demand. And if you make them wait another four years, or if you give them a four years in which they will be guessing every month which way they are going, why, at the end of those four years, you will have something that you cannot control, and that no man can now calculate or foresee.

I do not mean to intimate to you that we will have revolution. America is not a country of revolutions. America is not a country that resorts to force. America is distinguished for keeping her head, for keeping her self-possession, and doing things deliberately. But America may do extreme things four years from now if she cannot do moderate and sensible things now. Therefore, upon the mere principles of dynamics, upon the mere calculation of forces, I urge every independent man to consider what his vote means next week. Does it mean postponement? Does it mean uncertainty? Or does it mean something definite? Is he ready to lodge his faith in some particular set of men and to back up some particular line of policy, or is he not ready? If he is not ready, then he ought to vote one or the other of the Republican tickets. If he is ready for action, and believes in anything, believes in anything that he thinks can be done, then he ought to vote for the Democratic candidates. . . .

So, ladies and gentlemen, I have had the pleasure in the few minutes that I have had at my disposal here to lay what I conceive to be the heart of the matter before you. We are trying to release the average man in America to be master of his own fortunes again. And the average man can release himself only by allying himself at this present moment with that party that has determined upon the program which does not treat with monopoly upon any terms whatever. For we offer, not palliation, not mere control, but remedy. And I, for my part, will not stop short of remedy itself.

T MS (C. L. Swem Coll., NjP), with a few corrections from the partial text in the *Philadelphia Record*, Oct. 29, 1912.

A Campaign Speech in Montclair, New Jersey[1]

[Oct. 29, 1912]

Mr. Chairman[2] and fellow citizens: It is with unaffected pleasure that I find myself speaking in dear old New Jersey again. You are my neighbors and my friends, and I do not have to introduce myself to you. In some other parts of the country I have a settled feeling that the people are looking to see what this specimen looks like. They are looking at me as they would upon a rare species of horse that is being led around the ring. But here I have no such uncomfortable feeling. You have seen me, not too often, I hope, but often enough to know what sort of a fellow I am.

I undertook a particular commission when I became your governor, and I remember one of the things I stated on the occasion to which Mr. Livermore referred. I said that I was always going to speak to you with absolute frankness about public affairs. Fortunately, that does not cause me a great effort. The only effort I ever experience in public speaking is the effort not to speak too frankly. Therefore, I have come to speak very frankly to you about the situation in Essex County. I have come upon a national errand, not a local one. I have some good friends on the local ticket in Montclair, and it would afford me a great deal of pleasure to speak of some of them, for example, Mr. Rockwell, your candidate for mayor.[3] But that is not my errand here.

We are now in the last week of a great national campaign. Something very important, something very systematic, something very organic, has to be done for the American people. It cannot be done by a President only, but by a President plus a Senate of the United States and a House of Representatives. Many people seem to think that Mr. Hughes has already been selected as a senator from New Jersey because there was such an emphatic vote for him at the primaries. But those were the primaries of a party, ladies and gentlemen. That was not the vote of the whole electorate of New Jersey, and Mr. Hughes cannot go to the United States Senate unless there is a Democratic majority in the joint session of the next legislature of New Jersey. I have come here to speak for the Democratic legislative

[1] Delivered in the Hillside Grammar School.
[2] John Robert McDowell Livermore of Montclair, head of a ship and freight brokerage firm in New York.
[3] William Locke Rockwell, lawyer of Newark. He was not elected.

ticket in the county, because the men on it have pledged themselves to me personally, and to the convention of their party, and in every way possible to pledge themselves, that they will stand by the program of that party and vote for William Hughes.

My errand here, therefore, is chiefly this: I know you are going to vote for Mr. Townsend,[4] and, therefore, since I have only a little while I am not going to talk about elections to the House of Representatives. I feel reasonably assured that that is safe, else it would give me great pleasure to say more about Mr. Townsend and what I think about the necessity of having a strong body of thoughtful men to sustain the policies of the Democratic party in the House of Representatives. But do you realize that a majority of the states of this Union now have Democratic governors; that a large majority of the chief cities of the United States now have Democratic mayors; and that if you put all of the legislatures of the states of the Union in a single body, there would be a majority of two hundred for the Democrats; that the Democrats now control the national House of Representatives; and that, in the processes of our politics the hardest things to capture and the last things to capture are the Senate and the presidency?

The people of the United States have declared their preferences in politics again and again, but they are not represented by the Senate of the United States or the President of the United States. I show that by the figures. If you want, therefore, to carry out any organic purpose whatever, through the instrumentality of a Democratic majority, you must assist us to get a Democratic Senate and put a Democrat into the presidency. And I want to call the attention of this audience to what it is that lies before us, for I consider politics as a form of national business, not as a form of party sentiment. I belong to a party because I believe in its ancient principles which, if properly translated into action, will be for the uplifting of the United States. So long as I believe in the principles of that party and see an opportunity to put them into realization, I am going to stand by the legitimate organization of that party. But I look upon the party as an instrument, not as an end. I do not limit my view by the Democratic party, but I look through the Democratic party to the destinies of the United States. And if that party does not serve you, does not satisfy your principles and your ambitions for America, after you have tried it and rejected it, I will join with you in rejecting it.

4 Edward Waterman Townsend of Montclair, author and congressman, 1911-1915.

Men are instruments, parties are instruments, and therefore we ought to know what it is we mean to do.

I want to call your attention to the fact that there is one division of the Republican party which is now dwelling with a great deal of subtlety and a great deal of persuasiveness upon a program of social justice, and of social uplift, and of the improvement of the condition of the working women and children and the rank and file of workingmen. There is not a right heart in any of our communities that does not jump with every purpose of that program. There is no quarrel about that, there is no difference of purpose, of principles. The question is, when do you want it done, and how are you going to get it done? Suppose you want it done now. What will you do? Elect here and there, for that is all you can hope to do, a few candidates of that party, with the certainty that the several branches of the federal government cannot be put into its hands immediately, and so vote for a program and postpone its carrying out? Is that your idea of practical politics? I have no patience whatever with voting for abstractions, for general ideas, for nothing renders me more impatient than to discuss obvious principles when we all agree on them. I want to know how you are going to get these things done— by whom and when?

Look about you: an absolutely demoralized and divided Republican party, neither branch of which can hope to control the several branches of the federal government within the next four years; a program, therefore, if you vote for them, of postponement, a program by which you will say that we cannot do anything now except satisfy ourselves in the choice of a few individuals whose speeches and promises we like. And, therefore, we will fool the people again with postponed hopes. On the other hand, what have you? A reorganized, rejuvenated, united and triumphant Democracy ready to do things; led by men so pledged to do these things that, if they do not exercise their utmost endeavor to do them, they will go down to dishonored graves, recorded by the historian as men who betrayed a great faith and deceived the people.

The only organization through which it is possible in the immediate future to control and guide and use the great instrumentalities, by which alone political reforms can come—if you are practical people and want to vote upon the principle of dynamics, upon the principle of getting things done—is the Democratic party, and there is no choice but to vote the Democratic ticket. That is not an illogical conclusion. It is an obvious, practical fact which every candid man will have to admit. Now, what do you want to do? Upon my word, one of the greatest evidences of the weakness of the regular branch of the Republican party is its manifestations of despair. Who but men in despair would utter manifest misrepresentations upon every billboard along the line of the railway, and upon every dead wall in every city. Better to be safe than to be sorry; better to do nothing than to venture upon the lines of righteousness, justice and reform; better to break all promises of the Republican party itself, which are promises of reform, than to touch anything or to change anything. And if these pestiferous Democrats get in, if this wild-eyed schoolmaster becomes President, then we shall have free trade. Governor Wilson does not sufficiently define his position on the tariff. The only thing that you have to do to know Governor Wilson's position on the tariff is to be able to read the English language. Not once, but again and again and again, in every speech, until I was ashamed to look into the faces of the reporters who followed me around, I have defined my exact position on the tariff, and these gentlemen know that I have. I made a speech only last night in Philadelphia, in which I made that thing perfectly clear again, and this morning one of the papers of Philadelphia said that I had announced for free trade.[5] Fortunately, it quoted my speech and therefore proved that I had not. Only this evening, at the hotel in Montclair, I got a telegram from Wisconsin saying that the *Detroit Free Press* reported that I had declared for free trade last night in Philadelphia, and wanted to know if that was true. Now, it is awkward to answer that telegram without characterizing the management of the *Detroit Free Press*, but I have confined myself to polite language in this campaign. For the sake, therefore, of those who cannot read the English language, or for those who tonight for the first time have become curious as to my position on the tariff, I will state it again. I have not heard any thoughtful Democrat declare for free trade. I have heard every Democrat declare for what I have—going through the tariff with as fine a tooth comb as is necessary to find all concealed and illegitimate special privileges and cut every one of them

---

[5] The Philadelphia *North American*, Oct. 29, 1912, included on its front page an editorial statement with the headline, "Governor Wilson Declares for Free Trade." The editorial sought to prove this charge with quotations lifted from Wilson's public letter of October 19, 1912 (printed at that date in this volume). As Wilson indicates, the *North American* of October 29 also printed copious extracts from his two speeches in Philadelphia on October 28, both of which indicated clearly that he favored lowering tariff rates rather than free trade.

out, and leave absolutely safe every sound and healthy fiber of American business.

I have always used the same figure of speech about it. I have imagined myself what I am not, a skillful surgeon. I have imagined myself about to perform an operation upon a patient for the most part perfect, lusty, and well, but troubled with growths upon the vital parts, which have to be cut with such a nice and discriminating skill that no healthy fiber will be touched or damaged. If there are foreign growths upon the body politic, they are diseased, not healthy. They check the wholesome courses of the blood. They reduce the vitality. They make a nation which was meant to be vital from end to end, vital at a very small top, and likely to go to seed at that.

And, therefore, our program with regard to the tariff is a program by which American business will be liberated and not embarrassed. And if a crisis or panic, which these gentlemen dare to predict, comes on top of that, it can come only by the deliberate act of those who control the credit of America. It is not a prediction, it is a threat, and I want you to mark it and watch it as a threat on the part of men who, if they dared, can show their hand and show that they hold the credit of America in the palm of their hand. Only deliberate betrayal of the interests of this country by them can bring panic upon us in the midst of abundance, and when the President of the United States makes himself responsible for the statement that the panic of 1893 was due, among other things, to a tariff bill which came a year afterward, and that it came because of Mr. Cleveland's administration, I can only express my deep regret that the President of the United States has not read the history of the United States. Any statement that Mr. Taft makes I believe to be made in honesty, but this statement, if he made it, was made in ignorance.

I happen to have read the history of the United States, and the crisis of 1893 can be demonstrably shown to have arisen out of currency legislation out of a government absolutely controlled by the Republican party. The panic of 1893 was on its way, as every man of business who remembers back as far as that knows, before Mr. Cleveland's administration began. And it matured merely in the first months of his administration and would have been stopped if the Senate of the United States had yielded to the advice of the administration more promptly than it did. It did not yield until it was necessary for the government to do extraordinary things to stay it. Any man in Wall Street, or any man connected with financial affairs, will remember the circumstances to which I allude. Therefore, I say it is impossible to connect Democratic administrations, by the process of cause and effect, with financial panics. But the thing, moreover, my friends, is unworthy. It is unworthy of men in public life to try to mislead public thought after such a fashion.

We have things to do, therefore, wholesome things to do, things that we have long known had to be done; if we had not known it there would have been no division in the Republican party. How did it begin? By the stirring of conscience amongst those several factions in the ranks of the Republican party itself. There are those men we used to call insurgents down in the city of Washington, and that stout little figure of Bob La Follette up in Wisconsin. Where did they come from? They came from the profound observations of conscientious men who saw what was going on, on the inside, in the city of Washington. How special interests were more and more closing their power about this great government supposed to belong to us. What are you going to do about it? Which branch of the Republican party, which brought this about, would you like to see cure it, and which branch of the Republican party proposes to cure it?

The very branch of the Republican party which promises to give you this splendid program of social justice, which I do not say in irony, promises to govern you through the instrumentality of regulated monopoly. Now, it may be pleasant to live under monopolists who have got religion and turned to philanthropy. It may be pleasant to live under monopolists who are pitiful. But, for my part, I would rather be governed by a law which governs them as well as me. I do not want government by law which contemplates them. I would rather have justice than mercy, rather righteousness than commiseration. And I would rather own my soul than to be taken care of by benevolent powers which do not belong to me, and which I admit I could not control. Either this is our government or it is not. If it is, I suggest we go and take possession of it.

I am offering myself to you and to the other people of the United States, not as your master and leader, but as your spokesman; as a man who will do his best to put into language and action the common impulses and the common sense of justice of the American people. I can conceive of no higher commission. I can conceive of no more exalted honor than that. And I know that in the processes of our politics the very people I long to speak for are being put out of business. That middle class, if we have any classes in the United States, which consists of the men capable of setting up in business for themselves, who have saved enough money to begin, who see opportunities, and who can organize beginnings which will grow into bigger things, if you give them a chance, are being squeezed out by the intolerable pressure of this thing which presses them from above—this control of organized industry and this absolute control of large credit —so that the originative class, the class from which the genius and the leaders of America have always come, is being slowly and more slowly depressed, until it is just conceivable that if we let things alone we will be made up of two sections of people— those who are our masters and those whom our masters employ. God forbid that America should ever come to such a pass!

But I must tell you frankly that I do not have the least fear that she will. I have been from one end of this country to the other, and I know the spirit of the American people, and I do not doubt the verdict on the fifth of November. I am perfectly willing that you should regard me, so far as I am connected with this movement, as a happy accident, because I did not bring this thing about. I happened to be nominated at the right time. But I believe in these things as you believe in them. My heart is in them, as the common heart of America is in them. And I would glory in the opportunity of trying to put my small powers to the test in seeing whether, as Americans, we cannot get together and restore America; get the old ideals in our hearts again; get the old freedom in the air; breathe the tonic of liberty, and see men go to the polls, not with suspicion, not with cynical doubt, but knowing they went there in their puissance and in their sovereignty, as men who are determining the course of a great nation. That is the spirit, that is the light in the eye which we shall carry to the little booth. And there will seem to be no roof to the polling place, but the blue heavens will be above us, and we shall dream of the hills of the countryside and the free spaces of America, where no man is afraid and where every man knows he lives under God's heaven, and where there is law and righteousness and truth.

T MS (WP, DLC).

Two Campaign Addresses in Cape May County,
New Jersey[1]

[Oct. 30, 1912]

Mr. Chairman[2] and fellow citizens: It is very delightful to feel at home here again, because I have come to feel very much at home in Cape May County, and I remember with the greatest pleasure the visits that I have made to this particular building surrounded by so many associations of your life. This is going to be a very interesting day for you, because I understand that, later in the day, two gentlemen[3] are going to assist in an ante-mortem examination of what remains of the Republican party. There are a great many gentlemen connected with that lingering organization for whom I have the highest respect and a very warm personal regard, and I certainly wouldn't say anything disrespectful of Governor Stokes or of the senator who accompanies him. But I do want to call your attention to the record of the Republican party in the State of New Jersey for the sake of asking you if you feel that, while they were in control, you had any very vital connection with the government at Trenton. You know, for example, the experience that we went through. You know how a law was passed with regard to the fishing interests of this county,[4] which you didn't know anything about, which both your senator and representative voted for. And the only question I asked before I signed it was whether they had voted for it or not. Then I found, in spite of promises to let you know exactly what was going on that affected your interests, they had done nothing of the kind, and that I had to come down here after the legislation was passed to find out in what way it affected your interests and then go about to assist others—not your representatives—to bring about a repeal of the law.

Do you think you were organically connected very intimately with the councils of the Republican party when those things were going on? I simply know that your representatives have never done what they were told to do and not told to do by people in Cape May County. They were told to do it by that very small

1 Delivered in the court house, Cape May Court House, and in the Hippodrome, Wildwood, respectively.

2 Frederick J. Melvin, sheriff of Cape May County.

3 Edward Casper Stokes, Republican Governor of New Jersey, 1905-1908, and Isaac T. Nichols, Republican state senator from Cumberland County, were following Wilson on the campaign trail through South Jersey.

4 For a discussion of this law (Chapter 263, *Laws of New Jersey*, 1911) and of Wilson's visit to the fishing area on August 14, 1911, see the news report printed at Aug. 18, 1911, Vol. 23. The law was amended in Chapter 193, *Laws of New Jersey*, 1912, enacted on March 27, 1912.

body of men, not a dozen in number, who have habitually determined what should be done in this state, whether the people voted for it or not—people we used to call the Board of Guardians until we showed them the door and turned them out of the State House at Trenton. You did not have representative government in New Jersey, and you did not have representative government in Cape May County.

These are things that are matters of record and experience. For I have seen the operation of things at Trenton, and I came here when I was a candidate for governor and discussed that. I was going to tell you exactly what I saw and knew. Very well, then, what I have come for now is this. I haven't come to commend myself to you as a candidate for the presidency, because I feel very much in the position that Mr. Hughes says he is in. My record is made up, and you can judge for yourself what it is, and I am willing to abide by the judgment. I certainly am not going to excuse myself or commend myself, but I do want to point out to you an opportunity to be an organic part of the United States. There is only one great force in this country now, my friends, that can govern the nation and strike out a line of policy. That is the Democratic party. You may say that it is a matter of accident because our opponents are divided, but why are our opponents divided? What brought about the division in the Republican party? Why, the operation of the consciences of certain men in the ranks of that party, who saw that the government at Washington, as well as the governments in many of the states, had been used for the promotion of special selfish private interests and who made up their minds that that thing had to stop. The division in the Republican ranks is not a mere factional division. It is a division which has been brought about by this— that a very considerable number of Republicans have come to agree with the Democrats, without being willing to call themselves Democrats, because what they found out was what the Democratic party had been preaching to the country for half a generation. Therefore, all that has happened in the Republican ranks is that those have fallen away from that party who could no longer stand the things that were being done.

Men like Bob La Follette, as everybody calls him affectionately in Wisconsin, haven't got out of the Republican party for nothing. Mr. La Follette hasn't in a literal sense got out of the Republican party, because he hasn't joined the other branch of it. But he is fighting all the ranks of the Republican party because he utterly condemns the policy that they pursued under President Taft. He utterly repudiates also the claims of the other half of the party to represent those things which he represents and has fought for so indomitably in a way to attract the attention and the admiration of the whole country. A man who will not abandon a single inch of his principles is a man that we must all admire, whether we call ourselves by the same name or not. It is men who are fighting for principle who have broken up the Republican party. Men in the ranks of the Republican party aren't fighting for people who have broken it up, but it is broken. It isn't possible in the next two years, or the next four years, for either branch of the Republican party to get such strength or such extended organization or so many men in office as to control the several branches of the federal government.

There is only one organization big enough, united enough, clear enough in purpose to do that, and that is the Democratic organization. And what do you think of the Democratic organization? You have seen a sample of its service in the State of New Jersey. Has it dealt candidly with you? Has it tried to carry out the things that you voted for again and again and again before you voted for it in 1910? The Democratic party didn't have anything new to offer you in 1910. It had only those things that both parties had been promising you for a generation almost. But the difference was that you voted for the Democrats in 1910, and they carried out the program which you had voted for in other instances and commanded the Republican party to carry out, and they had not carried out. That is the plain record of the state. The Democratic party in New Jersey has served you according to its word and has redeemed every promise that it made.

Now it happens that the Democratic party in the nation is led by the same man who led the Democratic party in New Jersey, and I am not aware of having changed my point of view or my purposes in the slightest degree. I feel in talking to you home folks that I must tell you the real things that lie in my heart. I am interested in parties, my friends, only as instrumentalities. I am devoted to the Democratic party because I believe that, amidst a multitude of blunders, no doubt, it has been trying to steer by the standards set up in the ancient days when our conception of democracy was so clear-eyed and simple, and that no party has approximated more nearly than it has the effort to serve the people rather than to serve the special interests.

But if the Democratic party does not do that in fact as well as in theory, I am not going to criticize anybody that deserts the Democratic party. It won't be desertion. There is only one thing, my friends, that you can desert, and that is your principles. You can't desert a party. If it won't let you use it to carry out your principles, then it is nothing and ought to be thrown aside. But you can desert your principles, and the whole art of politics is to find the most effective means of putting your principles into operation. Where are your men? Where is your organization that can do it? When can you do it? How can you do it? Those are the practical questions. Now, as practical men in the year 1912, how are you going to join the great body of millions of people in the United States who are trying to restore the government to its simplicity and to integrity again?

There is only one organization that you can support. You don't have to join it to support it. Do you think that Bob Hand[5] ever belonged to an organization that dreamed of the interests of the people of the United States? I never saw the slightest [evidence] of it.

Do you believe that Cape May County has been a vital part of the great war in the United States against wrong? Do you feel braced? Do you feel as if you had tonic in you because you have had part in the fight? If you have had part in the fight, who was your instrument? You had a much more vital part with contracts for roads in Cape May County than you have had with the people of the United States. Politics is a stern business, my friends. There is no use fooling ourselves. You haven't had any connection with any noble cause in the field of politics in the United States in my experience. And it is just about time that every man in the State of New Jersey examined himself upon this question: What can I do to add my moral force and my convictions to the forces of America?

I am infinitely interested, therefore, in the choice of an assemblyman and in the choice of a senator from Cape May County because I want the ranks of Trenton to be solid, not only, but I want to see the ranks in Washington solid. There is one thing that the nation hasn't captured yet. The nation is not represented in the chamber of the United States Senate. The United States Senate has not yet been taken away from the special interests in this country. We have got to capture it. There is no possibility of capturing it through the divided Republican ranks, but there is a possibility of capturing it through the united Democratic ranks. And if you men will assist that united body by assisting in creating a majority of Democrats in the legislature at Trenton, then we will send an honest man and a man of the people to represent us in the Senate of the United States in the person of William Hughes.

[5] Robert Edmonds Hand, state senator from Cape May County.

Hughes is a very modest man. He stands up here and tells you that you are anxious to hear the Governor, and he gives way and all that sort of thing, but when he is at Washington he is on the job all the time. There isn't a man who is more trusted in the United States to speak wise counsel as to what legislation is just and possible for the plain working people of this country than William Hughes. Any man in Washington will tell you that, and any man in Washington who knows the organization of the present House of Representatives will tell you how influential Hughes has been in bringing that organization together, not only, but in making it efficient and in guiding it wisely and sanely. A man who doesn't lose his balance, a man who keeps his head, a man who knows human nature, a man who loves the people and knows how to serve them—that is the kind of man that I know Hughes to be. And I, for one, as a Jerseyman, would be proud to see William Hughes in the Senate of the United States. I know that he represents the principles that I am ambitious to represent. I know that he has the sympathies in his heart that I have in my heart. I know that he comprehends the struggle, the strain, the burden of life the plain men have to carry. . . .

It is delightful to find Cape May County wide awake. It is delightful to find this old county, which has been so systematically neglected, so systematically forgotten by the other parts of the state, now coming into the running, and saying, "We, too, are part of the new force, of the new age, and we are going to take part in a rejuvenation of American institutions which will be worthy of the great founders of this ancient county." Think of those simple days when this county was set up and how well, then think of the principles which made those men steadfast; think of what they would have said of little groups of men who served their own interests instead of serving the people of the county.

And by just men whom you know, like Thompson Baker,[6] just men who have been tested in your own county and then in Trenton and in Washington, Cape May will lift its voice and say, "The day has come when the people shall rule. We know who are our friends. We know who comprehend us. We know whose hearts beat with our hearts. We are not examining party labels. We are choosing men and measures, and the men we believe in are the men we are going to follow. The party that serves us is the party we will acknowledge so long as it serves us. When

---

[6] Jacob Thompson Baker, mayor of Wildwood and Democratic candidate for Congress. He was elected.

it stops serving us, we will reject it and try to find another party, if there isn't a party already in existence, that can serve us."

The Democratic party has been predicting the year 1912 for nearly sixteen years, and now the year 1912 has not taken the Democratic party by surprise. We knew that the time would come when you would have to turn to us and when we should have the honor to represent the people of the United States in their sovereign majesty, with their eyes lifted to the old standards and the old ideals. And I believe that the country will win a very wonderful thing on the Tuesday of next week—an entire re-assertion, from one end of this country to the other, of the independence, the individual judgment, of the American voter.

✧

Mr. Chairman[7] and fellow citizens: The scene is very much changed since I was here last time. When I last spoke in this building, there was a sawdust ring in the middle, and I felt as if I had joined the circus. Now there is a stage with scenery, and I feel as if I had joined a dramatic company. And the play we are about to put on the boards is a play very novel in America, for it is a play, not made up of stars, but participated in by the American people—a play in which the great forces of the plot come out of the pulse beats of the great average body of American citizens.

I have come down into this sunny county with the greatest pleasure, because I know of nothing more pleasant than to summon people who have sat on the side lines and looked on to come in and take part in the game. This is a very beautiful and very fertile and very prosperous county, and most of New Jersey thinks of it as a remote spot of sand on the seashore, where you can always count upon what is going to happen, where you can always be sure that the Republican candidates are going to be elected whether they deserve it or not. You haven't even played a part in the calculations of the politicians of New Jersey. And the county that has the least power in any state is the county that can be relied upon to vote the way it is told by the leaders of the party. Where do we look for the changes of politics in the United States? We look to the debatable states, do we not? Where do we look for the changes in New Jersey? We look to those counties where men vote individually and as they think. We do not look anywhere else.

Now, in this fine peninsula, thrusting her coasts out into the

7 The chairman of the Wildwood meeting cannot be identified from the available news reports.

sea, bathed by the fresh waters of the ocean, rendered tonic by the free airs of an unobstructed heaven, why have the people slept all these years politically? Why have they allowed themselves to be mastered and have never taken charge of their own affairs? I observed, when I was elected governor, that only one man was ever asked what Cape May County was going to do. That was the senator in Trenton from Cape May County. And I have learned since then that he very seldom consulted Cape May County as to what his answer was going to be. On occasion he spoke for them without knowing what their will was. And I suspect without caring what their will was. For again, again, and again, they had accepted their fortunes from him.

What I want to impress upon you, my friends of Cape May County, is this—that you haven't counted in the politics of New Jersey, and no county is going to be reckoned that doesn't vote independently, the majority of whose citizens do not go to the polls their own masters, not to be bidden by any party expediency, and not to be controlled by any past party affiliations.

I am a stout party man. I believe in party organization. I do not see how, without legitimate organization, men can get together and keep together. But I want to say this—that any party organization that can count upon support because of its name, regardless of what it does and of what it gives the people, will sooner or later be discredited and rendered unworthy of the confidence of the people for whom it speaks. Therefore, I come to point out to you that the Republican party in Cape May County, like the Republican party in the Union, has been ruined by its own unquestioned successes. It has been ruined by having the people of the county, and the people of the country, put their affairs in its hands and then ask no questions that were inconvenient either between elections or at elections.

I have come down here to speak for the local candidates. You know that Mr. Hughes just now said to you that his name will not appear upon the ticket that you vote next week. Neither will my name. You will either vote for the electors who are going to vote for me or for the electors who are going to vote for somebody else. That is, electors are not always labeled. They need not be labeled except Democratic or Republican or Progressive or Prohibition or Socialist. You only know by inference whom you are voting for after you have voted for them, and they are not bound by law to vote for the men whom you expect them to vote for. Under the Constitution of the United States, the electors can vote for any citizen of the United States they choose to vote for. All they are bound by is their honor as party men to accept the nominations of their party. It is just the same with the members of the legislature. They are bound not by law but merely by their honor to vote for the candidate for United States senator who has been named by the majority of their fellow partisans in the polls at the primaries. You vote for Hughes, therefore, exactly as you vote for me—by voting for the men who will vote for him. And there are two men, Mr. Wheaton[8] and Mr. Porter,[9] honorable men, men who live in your midst, men who know your characters, men who are in touch with your life, honest men, honorable men if I may judge by listening to their speeches, quick-witted men who know what they are about, who, if you will send them to Trenton, will form part of that force which will serve the people of the Commonwealth of New Jersey and the people of the stout old County of Cape May. It is a pleasure to be able to speak for and to support candidates of this quality.

And then, there is that fine gentleman who is offering himself for your suffrages, for whom you can vote directly for membership in the Congress of the United States. It is always a pleasure to me to be associated with Mr. Thompson Baker. There is a spontaneity, a fervor, a genuineness in that man's utterances of the old time principles of American life that it quickens my blood to hear. For when I hear a man talk about the rights of the people, when I hear a man talk against special privilege and for the common right, it does my heart good to hear fire in his voice. I have heard a lot of men talk about those things. Some talk about them because they love the sound of the handsome rhetoric in which the phrases run, but here is a man whose heart seems to kindle when he speaks of these things that are in themselves abstract. Because I was sitting behind him today, for example, at lunch, and he was telling me about a man in Wildwood who earns two dollars a day and who said to him that in his family they did not have meat to eat once a week. Every Saturday night he gets his twelve dollars, but no part of his twelve dollars can buy meat. That is a luxury in his family. The tears came into Mr. Baker's eyes as he talked of this; and he said, "My God, Governor, isn't there something that we, as a national party, can do to make life more tolerable for these men?" And when I see a man's eyes kindle that way, when I hear that kind of throb in his voice, it seems to me that I feel the thrill of the whole

---

[8] Harry C. Wheaton, former blacksmith, mayor of North Wildwood, and Democratic candidate for state senator. He was elected.

[9] William Porter, druggist, musician, local officeholder of Cape May City, Democratic candidate for the Assembly. He was elected.

American people calling unto us. Is it not time, men and brethren, that we got rid of these little groups who do not know us, who do not feel the necessities of our lives, who do not realize the pressure that is upon us? And is it not time that men that speak of us and for us should have charge of the government of this great country?

Why, when I go about this country and meet great crowds of people and some plain fellow seizes me by the arm and says, "Governor, God bless you, I wish you well," my throat fills up. I say to myself, "Do I know how to serve that man? Do I know what his life is? Do I know how it is possible to lift men working, as he is working, into more light, more hope, more freedom, more opportunity?" And I go and sit down and question myself, whether I am worthy of the confidence of men who address me in that fashion. For we have nothing less in hand now, my friends, than the recovery for the government of that intimate sympathy with the people, which is the only possible rule and foundation upon which right and righteous policy can be built.

And so when I come to speak for Mr. Baker and Mr. Wheaton and Mr. Porter, I come to speak as if I were saying to you, "We are drawing recruits into the people's army. Are you going to give them to us? Are you going to enlist them? Are you going to commission them? Is Cape May County going to be part of the great general change which is going to lift the United States upon new levels of achievement and of opportunity?" My heart burns as I look upon my own people here in New Jersey.

Think back a couple of years, my friends. Are you prouder of New Jersey now than you were then? God knows that nobody that has served you in those two years has done anything more than his duty, and no man ought to brag of his duty. I subscribe to that old passage in the scriptures, "We are unprofitable servants; we have done that which was our duty to do." But I would like to know whether you had that kind of unprofitable servants before? I would like to know why you are prouder of New Jersey now than you were two years ago. Simply because, at last in New Jersey, you have seen promises fulfilled. You have seen commonplace morality put into the places of government once more.

It is no jest. It is no fancy picture that your guest, the candidate for the state Senate,[10] drew before you just now. That

10 That is, Harry C. Wheaton.

figure of Mr. Gardner,[11] sitting alone in the grandstand without human companionship, is a very solemn picture, indeed, because the man who serves special interests will sooner or later be absolutely lonely, unloved, desolate, left without the regard and without the support of his fellow men. It doesn't make any difference whether the time comes now or comes when he is going down to the grave, the historian will write upon his epitaph: "He betrayed the confidence of those who had elevated him to a high place of responsibility and of trust."

I am not here to attack the character of Mr. Gardner. The tribunal that should judge him is not yet sitting. We are not worthy to attempt to assess the motives of our fellow men. It behooves us to take care of our own motives and see that they are all right. But we are here to assess the performance of public men. I would be ashamed of myself if I said anything against a person, a public man as a private person, as a private soul, but I have a right to speak of his public record. And I say that the member of Congress from this district has not served the people of New Jersey, but has served the special interests of New Jersey. Now, does Cape May County want to take part in that kind of thing, or does Cape May County want to clean the slate, to begin all over again, and to see to it that the man she gives in cooperation with the other citizens of this congressional district is a man blameless, devoted to the public interest, afire with those intentions which alone can make a man great in public service?

I am here not at the bidding of any man, but of my own wish. Mr. Baker was kind enough to say to me that he was very much obliged to me for coming down into Cape May County. I can't imagine why any man should be obliged to the governor of the state for coming to any part of the state to which he belongs and uttering his earnest plea to his fellow citizens. I wanted to come to Cape May County particularly because Cape May County has so seldom given herself the indulgence of independent voting. And I believe that Cape May County will grow more and more proud of herself, more and more prosperous, as she devotes herself disinterestedly to the public welfare and undertakes to judge of men independently of their party affiliations.

I wish that I had voice enough at this stage of the campaign to put before you all the things that struggle for utterance in me against the obstructions of my hoarseness as I face this great company. Gentlemen, you don't live in great cities, you are not

11 John James Gardner (1845-1921), New Jersey Republican state senator, 1878-1893; congressman, 1893-1913.

tempted by the heat and passion of the modern time. You live in these free fields. You stand upon the brink of the ocean and of the river. You go out in boats under the free heaven, and your sails bow to the unbidden winds that blow across the face of the waters. You are in constant, immediate, simple touch with the great forces that made and govern the world. Surely, if any clear thinking can be done anywhere, it can be done in this incomparable air of this lovely peninsula. And I seem to myself to be summoning you to exercise the ancient liberties of America in summoning you to join the forces which are now going to act to set America free again. For I am devoted, as I am sure you in your secret thoughts are devoted, to those permanent ideals which have always lured America onward, those ideals set up long ago at the making of the government, when Cape May lay, as she lies now, open and untainted to the heavens. For this county is older than the Union, older in the institutions of American liberty. She came in at the birth, and she will never consent to be in at the death. She will never consent to betray those high ideals of individual judgment and of public confidence to which she owes her own prosperity and the prosperity of the great country of which she forms so beautiful and so chosen a part.

And now I want to say in conclusion, just between you and me, that I haven't the slightest doubt how you are going to vote next week. Before I came down here, a man who lives in Cape May County, not present today, I am sorry to say, said to me, "Governor, what are you going down into Cape May for? You needn't go down there. They are all Wilson men down there."

"Well," I said, "that is a very delightful thing to hear, and I hope it is so. But if it is so, that is all the more reason why I should go down there. Because I want them to be Baker men, and Wheaton men, and Porter men, because I am not standing alone. I am not the Democratic party. I can't as President, or as governor, do anything but what great bodies of free men assist me to do, and if they are Wilson men in Cape May County they will vote the Democratic ticket." If you cannot vote for these gentlemen, don't vote for me. I am not a candidate for a pedestal. I am not a candidate to be set up in lonely dignity, to suffer the intolerable disappointment of being left alone, unable to do the great things which the American people will expect of me if they honor me with their suffrages. If you cannot back me up, don't put me up all by myself and then desert me. If you believe in me, make it possible for me to do something.

No man in a great commonwealth or in a great nation can do anything by himself except talk, and if my voice comes back to me I shall continue to talk. But talking is not business unless it means that men are going to be drawn together by the public discussion of great questions into a common, cooperative, irresistible force. Don't elect me captain unless you are going to give me a team. For if I am captain, and either of those Republican scrub teams is put alongside of me, I cannot do anything at all. They won't know what there is to be done, and they won't believe me if I tell them.

What I leave with you, therefore, is this suggestion: It is team or nothing. Is that a bargain? You will go back on me, you will go back on your governor, if you vote for me and don't give me a team. And, therefore, my bargain, my exhortation, to you today is, go to the polls and vote by this rule—either give him a team or vote for somebody else.

Partial T transcripts (C. L. Swem Coll., NjP); ICFT transcripts of CLSsh notes (RSB Coll., DLC); with corrections and additions from the partial texts in the *Philadelphia Record*, Oct. 31, 1912.

A Campaign Address in Burlington, New Jersey

Mr. Chairman[1] and fellow citizens: [Oct. 30, 1912]

It is a very great pleasure to me to find myself in Burlington County again; and as I stand before you tonight, my mind and my heart are full of the things that concern New Jersey. For, after all, a man's patriotism must have, if it be vital, a deep local rootage. My love for my country seems to me to center in my love for New Jersey. There are things that I desire for her perhaps more than I desire them for any other commonwealth in the United States. And what I have been thinking about as I have been sitting here tonight is this: You, I have reason to believe, are proud of the change that has come over the position of New Jersey in the United States within the last two years. You know that two years ago it was supposed impossible that progressive legislation should come out of New Jersey. She was known as the home of the trusts. She was thought of by the rest of the world as a commonwealth contented to live under the domination of special privileges. But she emancipated herself, and now she is proud to stand at the front of those states that mean to serve the nation with openness of mind, loving the things that are just, loving the rights that are equal, purposing the things that are for the common good. What did you do to bring that about?

I want to talk to you in very plain and practical terms about this, because I think it will help our thinking in regard to what

1 Thomas Howard Birch.

you are—we are—going to do next Tuesday. Burlington County in 1910 voted for me for governor, but it didn't vote for anybody to support me as governor. Remember that! It merely, so far as it was concerned, sent me lonely to Trenton. It said, "Now, let us see what *you* can do." I was honored by that personal preference, but I was weakened by that lack of support. Burlington County wasn't willing to go any further than to try an experiment with the governorship. And what did the governor find when he got to Trenton? A Democratic House and a Republican Senate. That Republican Senate would not have consented to the progressive measures of the session of 1911 unless the members of that house had thought that the people of New Jersey at last meant business, and that, whether they had changed the complexion of that body that time or not, they would change it next time if it did not yield to the impulses of popular thought.

Well, what did you do next time? You not only did not change the complexion of that body, but you gave me a Republican Assembly. You deprived me of such support as I did have, and you checked the wheels of progress. I am not now talking about Burlington County merely, but about the State of New Jersey. Was that as far as you wanted to go?

What did you get in the session of 1911? You got laws that set you free to make your own choices for office. You got a corrupt practices act that, so long as local officials are honest and faithful, will make your elections absolutely pure and clean, though only this day I have heard of the use of money in Cape May County in ways in which it ought not to be used. Only the integrity of your local officials will make your corrupt practices act effective, and I have just written a letter to every prosecutor of the pleas in New Jersey, calling his attention to the fact that I, so far as I can, will hold him personally responsible for the enforcement of that law.

You got a law which took off of you the grip of the Public Service Corporation and destroyed the domination of the transportation, of the organized transportation agents of this state. In other words, by the legislation of 1911 you were set free to conduct your own government and, so far as the laws of New Jersey permit, to conduct your own business. And then what did you do? You then made it absolutely impossible to follow that up with anything else, because I tell you frankly that the men you sent to the Assembly and the Senate were not in sympathy with progressive legislation. Burlington County, except for her vote, for which I shall always be grateful, for me personally, has not yet done anything to set forward the progressive program which will re-establish constitutional as well as popular government in the United States.

What are you going to do next Tuesday, then? Are you going to vote for me for President and then see to it that nothing else happens as you did in the state arrangement? Do you think I desire that? You are sufficiently acquainted with me to have me ask the question. Do you think that I believe that single-handed, without the assistance, without the consistent support, of my fellow citizens, I can accomplish anything for the nation? All that I can do is to make everybody partners with me in what I know. All I can do is to tell the people of New Jersey and the people of the United States what I find is going on. But what good will that do if there stands a Senate stiff against me? What good will that do if it is impossible to give the people the laws which alone can rectify the mischief which has been wrought by mistaken legislation in this country? Mr. Baker is perfectly right in his characterization of the inequalities of the present laws under which you live, but who is going to make them equal? The President? The President can't make them equal. Nothing except the organized and unified force of the Government of the United States can make them equal.

When you are asked to vote for Mr. Magee,[2] therefore, you are not only asked to vote for an honest man who believes in a progressive program for this state, but you are asked to vote for a man who will vote for William Hughes for senator and see to it that New Jersey has two senators who always think on the side of the people and always vote for the programs of the people.

Senator Briggs does not do that. I have nothing against Senator Briggs personally. I do not allow myself to attack persons. I have a very warm personal feeling for Senator Briggs. But he would admit very freely that he does not agree with me in public policies, and that he intends, in every circumstance where he has the opportunity, to stand against me in public policies. He does not believe in the policies of the people. So far as he does not, we must respect him for voting according to his beliefs. But he will stand, so far as his single vote is concerned, against the progress that we propose. And, therefore, you would have this nice condition if you sent Mr. Briggs or if you sent anybody else except a member of the Democratic organization to be associated with a Democratic President. You would have the whole process of reform and progress either diverted or arrested.

2 John D. Magee, Democratic candidate for the Assembly. He lost narrowly to his Republican opponent.

And you would have set up what no wise businessman would possibly set up—one part of the government which would check and neutralize the other part, so far as New Jersey is concerned.

What is the use of calling New Jersey progressive if New Jersey can't be progressive all along the line? If you don't send a Democratic Assembly and a Democratic Senate to Trenton this year, you are going to show to the United States that all you did was foolishly to take a fancy to a single man and make him governor, and that, with that, your whole impulse of progressiveness was all exhausted and you didn't want anything else. That would make me feel very foolish, and it would not be doing justice to your own characters.

I know the people of New Jersey. I know that you are as truly progressive as any other people in the United States. And what I dread is seeing anything done which will discredit that character in the view of the country at large. For while it is very delightful to be trusted as an individual, it is a great deal more delightful to be the spokesman of people whom you believe in. Don't you realize the difference? Suppose that you trust me enough to put me in a great office and let me speak for myself? Am I half as big a man in those circumstances as I would be if I spoke for you? I want to be a typical Jerseyman. That is all I want to be. I want people to believe that the voice of the presidency is, among other things, the voice of New Jersey, and that New Jersey shows that it is by putting alongside of the President a Democratic senator and Democratic representatives in the lower house.

Think of the representation in the lower house of this congressional district! Why, Mr. Gardner looks to me like a piece of ancient history. I don't mean the outside of him, but the inside of him. Mr. Gardner's opinions are to me so antiquated as to be incredible. I don't believe them. I sometimes venture to suspect that he does not believe them, because he is a man of brains; and how a man of brains can stand by the program that he stands by, I, for one, cannot comprehend. I, therefore, regard him as an antique. Now, antiques are too precious to be used. They ought to be put on a shelf. They ought to be reserved among the curios, so that when you see Mr. Gardner you may say, "There goes a piece of ancient New Jersey, not a sample of the commonwealth, not a sample of the thinking of this congressional district."

Let us imagine a procession down Pennsylvania Avenue in Washington City of the men from New Jersey. Just imagine a procession. Let us suppose that the President is at the head of

it. And then there come two senators; and then there come the
congressmen. It would be a very odd assortment, and the man
at the head of the procession would have to turn around to the
people on the streets and say, "Don't think that all of this is a
sample of New Jersey. You see that the cloth is patched, that
the pattern is variegated. There are some old things in this collection that New Jersey may, in the Providence of God, outlive!"

I advise you, therefore, to bring this congressional district
up to date, up to sample. Make it a real piece of the general
pattern of the life and thought of the people of New Jersey who
tonight here swarmed to fill the hall. Ultimately, I will have to
consult some of the gentlemen from New Jersey, and not all of
the gentlemen from New Jersey. And I will feel very much as if
I were untrue to the people of New Jersey if I can't believe in the
thinking of all the men associated with me from New Jersey.

The critical business of this year, therefore, is not merely the
election of a President, because this country may be put in a
very serious case if you don't now make a homogeneous government at Washington. If you are going to have a President of one
party and one set of opinions, and a Senate of another, why,
then, you are going to have an arrested development which may
increase the uneasiness, increase the impatience in this country
to such an extent that the breaking up of party lines will be a
great deal more serious two years from now, and four years from
now, than it is at present. These things that you witness among
the Republicans are not accidental. This division in the Republican party is not a mere factional fight. It is a great breaking
up of the deep. It is the rejection by nature, so to speak, of the
policies which the Republican party has tried to perpetuate.
Standpatism is just as impossible in this modern age as it is impossible for a thin crust of the earth to keep its place above a
flaming volcano. Why, all the blood in this nation is now running into the vital courses of reform. And the men who stand
against reform are standing against nature—standing against all
the impulses, all the energies, all the hopes, all the ambitions of
America. The enterprise is desperate, and they know that it is
desperate.

What are they advising you to do? Why, ladies and gentlemen,
this last week of the campaign brings to the surface some things
that are to me almost incredible. I read the other day again the
platform of the regular Republican party. That platform proposes reforms all the way through the scale, and yet what is happening during this week? You are being warned not to change
anything. You are being advised to stand still. You are being

advised to shun the advice of those who advise radical reforms, some of which this party has pretended to propose itself. There is a sort of paralysis that has crept over the party. It comes to the brink of action and then draws back. It promised you, four years ago, a downward revision of the tariff. By everything that was solemn, they pledged themselves to undertake such a revision. And they did not undertake it. They have not undertaken a single reform which they promised you they would undertake. And the whole motto—the whole moral—they are trying to enforce upon you now is that change is dangerous, that it is a great deal better to be safe than to be sorry. Ah, what a counsel of ineptitude! What a counsel of incapacity! What a counsel of timidity! What a counsel of ignorance—not to know that this great people is straining at the leash and, if it cannot get reform from one of the regular parties, will find some other way to get it. Here you have an ancient, tested, definite, organized, united party, led by men who know what has to be done and are ready to do it in moderation, with a just regard for every legitimate interest of the commonwealth, standing ready to redeem the nation from its impatience and to set it forward upon the path which it is so eager to tread. And do you hold back from the party?

I said in Cape May today, and I repeat it to you, if you are not going to vote to support me in Washington, don't vote to send me to Washington. I am not covetous of a lonely position. I am not covetous of impotence. I want men back of me who think as I do. If I get men back of me who think as I do, we shall in God's Providence bring about a prosperity and an open door for all the men coming on in this country, such as they have not known in a generation. This is our vision. This is our pledge. This is our purpose. I did not use the word that it is *my* ambition and pledge and purpose, for that is futile. Mine is a single voice amongst the 90,000,000. It is *our* purpose—that great body of free men who are not in thralldom to special interests, who owe a debt to no man, who are bound by promises to no interest or individual, who know that we are free and rejoice that our freedom unites us with the great body of common people in America.

I would rather be the voice of a nation than the voice of a class. I would rather serve; I would rather interpret the common feeling; I would rather know the common impulse of America than to originate. I would rather be the spokesman of the men who have confidence in me, and who I know will stand behind me in any crisis, than to pride myself in the belief that

I alone could devise a plan to redeem and restore the strength of the human race. I would rather know what plain men are thinking about than pride myself that I was showing the human race the way of progress and redemption. The human race lives its own life. It knows its own suffering. And in the soil of that suffering will spring up those growths and fruitages of faith which are alone the history of mankind. And it will work out its own salvation, if once the channels of government are free of access and unclogged by the interest of a favored class.

Ladies and gentlemen, I wish I had the language in which to express to you the longing that is in the heart of men who, like myself, are offering to attempt the interpretation of the common thought and the redemption of the common man in America. If I could make you see what we long for, I believe that men would forget what parties they have been associated with. They would look one another in the face and say: "Have we been dreaming a dream? Have we actually been voting for men because they belonged to a party and not because they belonged to mankind?" Ah, how deeply I sympathize with what Mr. Baker was saying! How deeply I sympathize with the shame that we can't talk politics without losing our fairness, our deep sympathy with one another as human beings, without misrepresenting one another, without letting petty party passion determine what we shall say and what we shall do, and the representation we shall make of other men! How pitiful it is to have men misinterpret history itself in order, by discrediting a party by false representation, to discredit honest men who are trying to lead the nation without regard to party, but only with regard to human rights! How pitiful a comment it is! And I believe that, after the vote of next Tuesday, men will feel a sort of relief that they have come out of a nightmare. They have stopped suspecting one another. They have looked candidly at each other's minds and characters and have banded themselves together to bring about a great restoration, a great emancipation, a new age of opportunity and achievement for America. When I ask you the commonplace question, therefore, whom are you going to vote for for senator from Burlington, and whom are you going to vote for for representative in the Assembly from Burlington, I am asking you nothing less than this—what is to be your interest and participation in the fate of fair, elevated politics in America? For there is no other way for you to express it.

It doesn't make any difference to the United States what you think about the candidates in the next county or in the next state. It doesn't make any difference what you think about the candidacy of Mr. Sulzer in New York. All that makes any difference to the United States, or to your consciences, is what do you think of the candidate for the Assembly and the candidate for the Senate in the County of Burlington? You can't transact business with the other people of the United States except by your votes, and your votes can only be for these gentlemen or against them. Therefore, interpret yourselves on the fifth of November. Let me know—for I will speak of myself—let me know what my relations are going to be, not as an individual, but as a party leader, with the great enlightened County of Burlington. I would like to know. I would like to feel that the next time I came here I might say, "Now, my friends, we are working together for a common cause. Burlington has supplied me with the men that I needed for the work that Burlington wants done. She has supplied me with men out of Burlington to do the thing that has to be done."

I come from Mercer County. Now vote for your Burlington men and see whether you agree with the County of Mercer or not. Let us see if we can't draw New Jersey together into an irresistible phalanx, so that men will think of New Jersey as they think of Wisconsin, as they think of Oregon, as they think of the great states whose populations unite to support now men of one party, now men of the other, because they believe in them.

Don't you know what Oregon did, for example? Oregon is ordinarily a Republican state, or it was before it got religion. And yet Oregon, while it was voting Republican, compelled a Republican legislature to send a Democrat to the United States Senate,[3] showing that Oregon wasn't in leading strings; Oregon wasn't in party harness. Oregon believed in Chamberlain and said, "There is the man we want to send to Washington," and obliged a Republican legislature to send him to Washington. And that attracted the attention of the whole nation, nay, the attention of the whole thoughtful world—that America was coming out of the leading strings of parties and was beginning to transact the great business of humanity. Men and measures are the only things that are worthy of the thought of a great free people who are not going to school to politicians, but going to school to their own consciences, following their own visions, realizing their own dreams of what American manhood means and must achieve.

ICFT transcript of CLSsh notes (RSB Coll., DLC), with corrections from the full texts in the *Trenton Evening True American*, Oct. 31, 1912, and the *Newark Evening News*, Oct. 31, 1912, and with additions from the partial text in the *Philadelphia Record*, Oct. 31, 1912.
3 George Earle Chamberlain, elected in 1908.

A News Item

[*Oct. 30, 1912*]

WATSON QUITS WILSON.

ATLANTA, Oct. 30.—Thomas E. Watson[1] has served notice that he will decline to vote for Woodrow Wilson and that he will ask his Georgia following to back him up and stay away from the polls.

Mr. Watson quotes the New York Times as saying that Wilson has joined the Knights of Columbus and, therefore, Watson says he will quit the Wilson camp. There is some apprehension felt among State politicians that Watson's attitude may affect the Georgia situation dangerously. Watson is supposed to command about 15,000 votes in Georgia.

Printed in the New York *World*, Oct. 31, 1912.
[1] Thomas Edward Watson, former Populist; leader of a number of small farmers in Georgia; notorious racist and religious bigot.

A Campaign Address in Madison Square Garden[1]

[October 31, 1912]

Fellow citizens: No man could fail to be deeply moved by a demonstration such as we have witnessed tonight. And yet I am the more thrilled by it because I realize that it is the demonstration for a cause, and not for a man. All over this country, from one ocean to the other, men are becoming aware that in less than a week the common people of America will come into their own again.

There is no cause half so sacred as the cause of a people. There is no idea so uplifting as the idea of the service of humanity. There is nothing that touches the springs of conscience like the cause of the oppressed, the cause of those who suffer and need not only our sympathy, but our justice, our righteous action, our action for them as well as for ourselves. And so, when I look about upon this great company, the thought that moves me is

[1] Wilson spoke to an audience variously estimated by the newspapers at from 12,000 to 16,000 persons. For some two hours before Wilson arrived, the throng listened to speeches by Cleveland H. Dodge, Thomas M. Mulry (the chairman of the meeting), William Sulzer, Martin H. Glynn, Augustus Thomas, and Oscar W. Underwood. Underwood's speech came to a sudden end with the appearance on stage of Wilson. This set off a tumultuous ovation which lasted for more than an hour. Wilson was so moved that he forgot his prepared speech, stating later: "It was a wonderful demonstration. The thing completely rattled me and I forgot my speech. I didn't deliver the speech I had thought out so carefully." *New York Times*, Nov. 1, 1912. For other details of the affair, see Link, *Road to the White House*, pp. 521-22.

that government is an enterprise of mankind, not an enterprise of parties, that parties are but the poor servants of the cause of mankind.

As election day approaches, a greater, greater, and greater feeling of solemnity comes over me, because I know that the American people are now about to make one of the most vital choices of their lives. I know that there are some features of this campaign which have been disappointing to serious-minded men all over the Union. We started out to discuss, like frank and honest men, the deepest concerns of a great nation. For a little while —for a few weeks—swords were crossed in gallant controversy with regard to the great fundamentals of government and of national development. And then there seemed to be a recession, a falling back, a dying away of the ardor of frank discussion.

And men began to speak, to speak uncharitably, of one another and of one another's motives. And the great party which has for so long governed the Union seemed to draw back from its own purposes. For what has struck a great many men in America is that, while the regular Republican party started out upon this campaign apparently with a clear vision that there were great reforms to accomplish, and with a definite program by which they purposed to accomplish them, the same thing happened as the end of the campaign approached that has happened again and again on the part of this very party. They drew back from their own purposes. They said: "We have builded a structure which we do not know how to change, and which we dare not touch. We fear that the men in whose interest we have built it up, the men who control credit from one end of the nation to the other—if they are not pleased with our action, will do something to destroy the prosperity of the nation."

They feared the very power they had built up! They feared the very thing their own hands had created! And again in the history of America, this party, once brave to strike out actively for itself, drew back from its own purposes and hesitated to act at all. So that from one end of the country to the other advertisements are spread upon the billboards and upon the dead walls, whose counsel is this: "If you do anything, you do it at your own peril. We advise you to do nothing. We advise you to have no commerce with the men who have definite programs of reform and the courage and character to carry them out."

And then, on the other hand, there is the other branch of the Republican party. I don't know how to characterize it, because where it can capture the regular ticket, it is regular; and where it can't, it is irregular. It is particularly irregular because—no, don't put anybody out. It is inconvenient to have more than one man speaking at a time, but this is a free country. I speak of this third party without disrespect as the irregular Republican party, because I know from reports coming from all parts of the Union that that party has not drawn from the ranks of the Democrats, and therefore it must be made up of those Republicans who are dissatisfied with the regular organization and its avowed purposes and program.

They are irregular in this. They are looking about as adventurers, discoverers of new ways of performing old duties. The duty to humanity is a duty which every party owes and has owed, from the foundation of the American government until now. But the processes of duty have never been obscured. The processes of oppression have never been hidden. The processes of special privilege have all along been disclosed. The channels of legislation were open. The obligations of executive action were obvious to the eye. And these gentlemen, without proposing new duties, go about to propose new methods of performing old duties. And how do they propose to perform them? I believe that it is of the utmost importance that the American people should examine this purpose in the most critical fashion. The program is doubtful because it changes its aspect every time we have a new interpretation or explanation of it.

But the method is not doubtful. The method is that we shall turn away from the old processes of law to new methods of executive supervision and regulation. For when you approach, with the leaders of this party, the great tariff question, what is it that they say they mean to do? Look around and see if prices are too high? No, that is not the trouble. Look around and see if trusts are combining to control the markets? No, that is not the trouble.

The trouble is that the beneficiaries of the tariff, according to these gentlemen, do not equitably divide their spoils. And the proposal of this party is this: Let those enjoy these special benefits who divide, and take them away from those who do not divide. Government does not propose to intervene in order to relieve the community of its burdens, but it proposes to intervene in order to change the methods and the processes of doing business on the part of those who enjoy special privilege.

And when you turn to the other side of it, it is proposed that the great trusts shall have the law so changed that they are to admit competition, that they are to cease from the processes by which they have imposed upon us and burdened us, and if they don't, what are we to do? Why, there are some plain and old-fashioned methods of enforcing the law with which every lawyer, every layman, every tyro is acquainted. Those processes are that when a man breaks the law, he must personally take the penalty.

If the law will but exercise a little scrutiny of the methods of the modern trusts, it will find that the trusts do not impersonally break the law, but break the law through the instrumentality of well-known individual officers. And just so soon as these officers find themselves subject to the law, the law will be obeyed, and not before.

But by the processes proposed by the leaders of the new party, just so soon as a trust ceases to observe the letter and the spirit of the law, the government is to take charge of it and administer its affairs, because we are now told that it is to be put into the hands of a receiver. Every lawyer knows what a receiver has to do. He has to take the business and the assets of an insolvent concern and try to get the most possible out of the business for the sake of the creditors, in order that the business may be put upon its feet again.

But now we are to have a new kind of receiver—a receiver whose object it is to discipline the corporation, to chasten the owners. For we are told that after the corporation has been brought to its senses by being administered by a receiver appointed by the government, it is then to be returned to its owners in their chastened and rectified consciences. The government is to administer business for the sake of chastening the owners of the business.

My friends, it is a very serious matter to propose to reverse all the processes of law. And it is a very futile matter to propose to change all the centers of energy and origination in the Government of the United States from the combined organs of the government to the discretionary action of the executive.

I do not believe that it is safe to put the disciplining of business in the hands of any officer of government whatever. When business is once free it will not need the hand of discipline. It is not now free, and the great enterprise of politics in our day is to set the average businessman free again.

What the Democratic party proposes to do is to go into power and do the things that the Republican party has been talking about doing for sixteen years. There is a very simple way of doing it—to direct the provisions of your law against every specific process of monopoly which has, by crushing competition, built up the control of small numbers of men, and then direct the punishment against every individual who disobeys the law. If this is done with clearness and steadiness of purpose, and with absolute fairness and courage, there will be no more monopolies in the United States.

No one desires to discipline business because it is big. All that we need to do is to check those who use big business to crush little business, who use power to prevent anybody coming into competition with their power by a power and an intelligence of his own. For when we talk of restoring the government to the people, we are talking of nothing more than this—of having the action of the government based on the interests of the average man and the rank and file of the people. It doesn't mean that the people are to go down to Washington and sit in superintendence on the government. But it means that the people won't have to go to Washington in order to have the government know what they are thinking about, because all the channels of counsel will be open, all the channels of sympathy. And when we have set the government free, what do we mean to do? Do we mean to try to change men's hearts and so direct and modify men's business that they will be kind to one another?

That is an impossible enterprise. What we are going to try to do is to see that nothing more than justice is done. Our standard is not pity, but justice. For, my fellow citizens, you are not bene-fited by the pity of your employer or the pity of your party leader. You are benefited and elevated by having your rights respected.

Government is based upon right, not benevolence. And so when I look abroad and see the great things that are to be done, when I know the things that must be done in order to protect women, in order to protect children, and in order to protect the great masses of men who carry the sometimes intolerable burdens of our daily industry, I say to myself, "We are proposing nothing for these people except what is their due as human beings." We are not proposing to go about with condescension; we are not proposing to go about with the helping hand of those who are stronger to lift up the weaker. But we are going about with the strong hand of government to see that nobody imposes on the weak, to see that nobody lowers the levels of American vitality by putting on the working people of this country more than flesh and blood and nerves and heart can bear. And this, not because we are trying to do something more than govern, but because government is meant for the conservation of the national life. And if you depress the levels of vitality, you depress the will power and hope and achievement of the nation.

The nation does not consist of those who direct industry. The nation consists of those who carry on industry by their daily labor. And when I look about upon a great company like this, I know that they come to this great gathering only in the evening, because from the rising of the sun to the going down of it, they must be intent upon those tasks without which they cannot eat and be fed, or take care of those whom they love and are dependent upon them, and the real problems of their day are between sunrise and sunset. They don't come to a hall like this to hear merely flowers of rhetoric. They come to see if it is possible to find honest men who understand what ought to be done.

There are some things that ought not to be done. That man ought to be ashamed of himself who sets passion or one class of society aflame against another class. And the task of every honest leader of the people is the task of convincing his fellow citizens that that man who regards himself as in a class apart is an enemy to the progress of mankind; that where there are classes in point of privilege there is no righteousness, there is no justice, there is no fair play; and that to lift the masses, to safeguard those who are weak, to set forward the hopes of those who are merely beginning to come in on the great enterprise of life, is to help those at the top just as much as it is to help those at the bottom.

No man's heart is right unless he feels it beat upon the same level with all other hearts in God's world. Now, it is a very serious enterprise, my friends, to pretend that you are going to set up justice and rectify wrong in a great nation of ninety million people. Do you know what we have to do? This government was set up for a little handful of people on this Atlantic coast, mustering only three million strong. Opportunity lay at every man's door. No man who had the least gift could fail of the full opportunity of development. And now we have to make these institutions of ours, sacred to the cause of liberty, work for the benefit of ninety millions of struggling men as well as they worked for three millions of men just beginning life in a virgin continent. And how are we going to do that unless we realize that every one of the ninety million must count in the solution that we are going to propose? And how is every man going to count if he doesn't go to the polls on the voting day with this at his conscience—that he isn't voting for himself, that he isn't voting for his own business, that he isn't voting for his own prospects, but has in his eye that first vision that burst upon the world when America was born, that vision that the free men of America will go to the polling booths to vote the rest of the world free with themselves?

And all they have to do in order to do that is to realize that the common enterprises of life are the enterprises of politics; that a man isn't voting an abstract political creed, but is voting a program of justice and of right when he votes at the polls.

Now, if you want that program, what are you going to do next Tuesday? (A voice: "Vote for Wilson.") I appreciate the compliment, but I want to say this, that unless you people put yourselves into Wilson he won't be worth anything.

The only thing that will set reform forward in this country, my friends, is a united government, and a united government doesn't consist of a President. A united government consists of a House of Representatives, of a President, and of something that in my time the people have not yet captured—a Senate. And it consists of something more. If you have a Democratic government at Washington and don't have a Democratic government in New York, you haven't got any conducting medium by which to signal to Washington. You have got to have a vital organization of purpose, spreading throughout the United States, in order that great bodies of men may unite together for the great project of emancipation. And the only possible chance of having a great united organization after the fourth of March next is to vote the Democratic ticket.

If you vote for the regular Republicans, you will only postpone the obsequies. If you vote for the other branch of the Republican party, you are only making a prediction that after a while a power may be built up which will control the three branches of the government. Your only chance for immediate action is to vote for the single, united, cohesive, clear-sighted power that is within your reach—that great combined, rejuvenated, absolutely confident body of men who are now going to take charge of your government at Washington. You know what they propose to do, and you know what they don't propose to do.

I get telegrams about every second hour now asking me to deny that I am a free trader, showing that there are some persons in the United States who believe that the Democrats don't understand the business structure of the country in which they live. How many Democrats were there at the last election? Not enough to elect a government, but almost half the voters in the United States were Democrats even then—more than half of them are now. And unless these gentlemen are all going out of business, they aren't going to vote to destroy business or to touch any sound or stable thing in the United States.

But I am wasting my breath. Nobody believes for one moment that the Democratic party is going to upset honest business in the United States. The real trouble is that some gentlemen know that it is going to upset dishonest business in the United States. And they themselves will be glad of it after the operation is over. I have seen the patient lie on the table in New Jersey. I have seen him rise from the table, astonished that he is still alive, and rejoicing that he felt better than ever he did in his life. The period of convalescence was extraordinarily short. And there isn't a man in large business in New Jersey who would wish to see the government of New Jersey again owned by the large corporations of the state.

A corporation that has to pay campaign contributions in order to avoid hostile legislation is also obliged to pay blood money in order to be permitted to live. And the freedom that they get by mere reform is a freedom which promotes their own prosperity and happiness. But I haven't come here to reassure you. I felt like saying, if I could have been heard while you were cheering, that it would be a very good idea to make it unanimous to go home and go to bed, and the thing that I envied most was your voices.

Evidently you have not been campaigning or you could not possibly have shouted as long as that. But what is the shouting? The shouting will soon be over. These scenes will soon cease. After next Tuesday we shall know, not what men are going to proclaim, not what men are going to profess, but what men are going to do. God be pitiful on the man who promises the American people what he is not ready to perform!

The case is made up; the case is before the jury. I, myself, do not doubt the verdict, but I want to say to you that if the verdict shows that the people of the United States have voted upon their individual convictions as free men, I, for my part, am ready to accept the verdict, whether it is for me or against me. For unless you believe in the things that I believe in and purpose the things that I purpose, it will be of no avail if you elevate me to an isolated and lonely office. I come here, therefore, not to expound to you, not to argue with you, but just to confer with you with regard to the matters upon which we have been thinking for the last three months.

Ladies and gentlemen, what are the liberties of a people? I have often had an image of liberty in my mind, an illustration of it. You know that when a great engine runs free, as we say, its freedom consists in its perfect adjustment. All the parts are so assembled and united and accommodated that there is no friction, but a united power in all the parts. So I speak of political liberty. When we understand one another, when we cooperate with one another, when we are united with one another—then we are free. And when the American people have thus joined together in the great enterprise of their common life, they will wonder how it ever happened that they permitted the great special interests to grow up and overshadow and smother the wholesome growths of the garden. Then they shall wonder that it was ever necessary to summon them to the conclusions of the ballot. I propose that men now forget their individual likes and dislikes, their individual sympathies and antipathies, and, drawing together in the solemn act of a sovereign people, determine what the Government of the United States shall be.

ICFT transcript of CLSsh notes (RSB Coll., DLC), with corrections from the complete texts in the New York *Evening Post*, Nov. 1, 1912, and the New York *World*, Nov. 1, 1912.

A Message to Democratic Rallies

[Nov. 2, 1912]

Friends and fellow citizens: We stand face to face with a great decision, a decision which will affect the whole course of our national life and our individual fortunes throughout the next generation. We must make that decision on the fifth of November. It cannot be postponed. We cannot vote without making it; and if we do not vote, those who do will make it for us. The next four years will determine how we are to solve the question of the tariff, the question of the trusts, the question of the reformation of our whole banking and currency system, the conservation of our natural resources and of the health and vigor of our people, the development of our means of transportation, the right application of our scientific knowledge to the work and healthful prosperity of our whole population, whether in the fields or in the factories or in the mines, the firm establishment of a foreign policy based upon justice and good will rather than upon mere commercial exploitation and the selfish interests of a narrow circle of financiers extending their enterprises to the ends of the earth, and the extension of the assistance of the government to those many programmes of uplift and betterment to which some of the best minds of our age have turned with wise hope and ardor.

There is much to be done, and it must be done in the right spirit and in the right way, or it will deepen our troubles, not relieve them. The tariff question must be solved in the interest of those who work and spend and plan and struggle, those who are finding a foothold and working out a career, those who touch the sources of strength and are quick with the pulse of a common life, for the sake of "the power that tills the fields and builds the cities" and not for the sake of special groups of men who dominate and control their fellows and regard the toil of millions of men merely as an opportunity to make use of their established advantage. It must be handled very prudently, so that no honest toil may be interrupted, no honorable or useful enterprise disturbed; must be dealt with by slow stages of well-considered change,—change whose object shall be to restore and broaden opportunity, and destroy nothing but special privilege and unwholesome control. Those who handle it, therefore, must be men who understand the general interest and have devoted themselves to serving it without fear or favor.

The trust question must be dealt with in the same way with this distinct and single programme, to destroy monopoly and to leave business intact, to give those who conduct enterprise no advantage except that which comes by efficiency, energy and sagacity, those only fountains of honorable wealth, every man rewarded according to his insight and enterprise and service, his mastery in an open field. Currency and banking questions must be discussed and settled in the interest of those who use credit, produce the crops, manufacture the goods, and quicken the commerce of the nation, rather than in the interest of the banker and the promoter and the captain of finance, who if set off by themselves in the management of such things too easily lose sight even of their own intimate and inseparable relation to the general needs and interests of the rank and file. Forests and mines and water courses must be renewed, husbanded and preserved, as if we were trustees for all generations, not merely for our own, for the sake of communities and nations and not merely for the immediate use of those who hasten to enlarge their enterprises and think only of their own profits. The government must employ its powers and spend its money to develop a whole people and a whole continent, and at the same time keep them free and alert and unhampered, its eye always on the common use and purpose, its thought constantly of what will happen to the average man and of what will be prepared for the next generation.

We must consider our foreign policy upon the same high principle. We have become a powerful member of the great family of nations. The nations look to us for standards and policies worthy of America. We must shape our course of action by the maxims of justice and liberality and good will, think of the progress of mankind rather than of the progress of this or that investment, of the protection of American honor and the advancement of American ideals rather than always of American contracts, and lift our diplomacy to the levels of what the best minds have planned for mankind. We must devote the power of the government to the service of the race and think at every turn of men and women and children, of the moral life and physical force and spiritual betterment of those, all of those for whom we profess to have set government up.

None of these high things can be done, because none of them can be conceived, from the point of view of those who at present exercise power over us at Washington. No established policy of the Republican party can be used for such ends. "The black magic of campaign funds" cannot work these miracles. The government at Washington has not in half a generation been conducted from the point of view or by the counsel of the nation as a whole, but by the advice and with the consent of those who have extorted special favors from it, a very small number of persons with their own objects constantly in view, it may be unconscious of their selfishness, certainly unconscious of the interests of the vast majorities whom they ignored in their scheme of prosperity. The great task that waits to be done can be done only by a free government with its eyes upon the whole people, and such a government we have not had since the Dingley and Aldrich tariffs began to be built up, favor by favor, and trusts began to multiply under the very prohibitions of the law. The Republican party is irretrievably committed and bound to go in the very opposite direction from that in which release and freedom lie. It has become a party of special points of view.

The country has already perceived this. Everywhere there has been a steadily gathering revolt by the voters. Twenty-six of the forty-eight state governments are now under Democratic Executives. In the Legislatures of the forty-eight states the Democrats outnumber the Republicans by a majority of two hundred. Seventy-three of the one-hundred and twenty chief cities of the country have Democratic Mayors. There are now two-hundred and twenty-seven Democrats in the National House of Representatives and only one-hundred and sixty-one Republicans. The tide gathers in greater and greater volume. Only the Presidency and the Senate lift their heads a little above it, those citadels of power which the Constitution makes it hardest for the people's majorities to capture and occupy. Until these are taken, the great task will halt and wait, the great task of putting the government at the service of the people.

Shall we not move forward to the final conquest? An organized, united, and enthusiastic force stands ready, the only united and militant force to which the people can turn with any prospect that they will be served, promptly, effectively and upon a clear principle of action,—the great Democratic party, now at last solid and of clear purpose. To it all who are full of hope and of the vigor that makes tomorrows are flocking,—the young men of the nation, the noble and devoted women who wish to see better days for their children and for all who are oppressed, the men who never grow old but always press forward to enterprises of the new age, all who desire free opportunity and love the public course that is just and righteous and quick with the hopes of mankind. A great people is turning its face to the light, not desiring a revolution, but loving the right and determined to set it up, wisely, temperately, honorably, with prudence and patient debate, not in irritation or in haste, but like men, not like children. It is a great day and a propitious. The responsibility is ours, and we shall assume it knowing what it means. The decision of the fifth of November will usher in, if we be true, a new day of confidence, freedom and prosperity. It will be no niggardly triumph of a party or a faction, but the triumph of a people. The Democratic party will be, not the selfish victor, but the trusted instrument, and the years that follow will test every principle of the great Republic; God grant we shall be worthy to prevail.[1]

T MS (WP, DLC).

[1] There is a WWsh draft of this message dated Nov. 2, 1912, and with the composition date of Oct. 21, 1912, in WP, DLC.

A Portion of a Campaign Speech in Long Branch, New Jersey[1]

[Nov. 2, 1912]

Now, there is only one thing that ever has helped the workingman, or anybody else under any government that ever has been invented, and that is justice and fair play. All that any American worth his salt needs is to be given a fair show and chance to sell his labor in the best market, to carry his skill where it will profit him most, and to be left absolutely free, when he comes to the point of advantage where he could do so, to set up more business for himself. That is the American process. The American principle is: "Don't make a crust above us through which we can't break. Just leave things open for us to get to the top, and we will get to the top."

Now a crust has been stiffened over American society by the domination of the trusts in certain of the greatest industries of this country. They can determine how many laborers are to be employed. They can determine by agreement what wages are to be paid. They can dominate the labor market just in the same way that they can dominate the market that controls prices of commodities. And so long as that is true, men are not given the opportunity to work their way up, are not given release of their faculties in that free field of opportunity which has always heretofore been characteristic of the United States.

What the Democratic party proposes to do, therefore, is not to interfere with business in the United States, but to set it free again. And if that doesn't bring happiness and prosperity, then it is only because the American people have lost their initiative, their extraordinary inventive power, their famous independence of character. I, for my part, know that the minute the shackles are taken off, the world will stand by in wonder to see this giant grow into a colossus. Why, I look forward with rising pulse to the future of emancipated America. We have lived under masters long enough. I have lived under masters. I have seen money control things that money ought never to be allowed to touch. These are things which my eyes have seen and my hands have handled; and the whole ardor of my nature is now enlisted in this enterprise to see to it that selfishness in high places is not controlling the destinies of the average man in America. The average man, indeed! Where did all of us come from except from the ranks of average men? Why and for what reason is a man more than the average in America? There is no aristocracy in America. There are no social classes in America. There isn't a class in America so high that men haven't climbed into it from the bottom, if there is any bottom. We don't think in America there will be a bottom. We think of the free channels of life, that is what we think of. And America has been enriched by the springing up in every class of men who were born masters of their own destinies and fit to rule industries and govern nations.

That is the pride of America, and if out of the average men we can't get our great men, then we have destroyed the very springs of renewal in this America which we built in order to show that every man born of every class had the right and the privilege to make the most of himself.

The example that everybody likes to go back to is the example of Abraham Lincoln. If you can find more humble and more hopeless circumstances than those which surrounded the birth of Abraham Lincoln, I wish you would point them out to me. And yet there was born in a hut one of the rulers of mankind. And there can be no greater glory for a nation than to know that any hut in it may gleam with the gold of the crown of an undiscovered prince. We get our princes not from royal families, but from unknown families. The great credit in America is not to belong to a family that somebody else founded, but to found one; not to be descended from somebody but to furnish the means for somebody to ascend, to lift one's shoulders so that the next generation can climb a little higher and so, ascending from the bottom of the levels of society up and up, until no man shall feel that he is hopelessly in the valley, but that every man shall feel that that light on the hills is a light unto which he himself can ascend and there work conspicuous among his fellows, not because of anything that was given him, but because of something that he did, some service that he rendered, some majesty of genius that was in him. Every man is unhappy and feels that his faculties are imprisoned, and America is maintained to open all the channels of life so that there may be no prison for any man, but that every man who is honest and honorable and respects the rights of his fellows and seeks the ways of service may some day feel the thrill of a great nation in him as honor comes to him for what he did and what he has done.

We don't want to lose that day in America. We shall lose it if we are not careful. Powers are being built up in this country which, if they are allowed to grow much stronger, may be stronger than the Government of the United States combined. And they are combined in the persons of a very small number of men. But I speak as if I feared them. I couldn't stand in the presence of all the men and women I address and look in their faces and see their vitality and know the springs of youth that are in them and fear these things for a moment.

All that America has to do is to believe that something is necessary, and they will do it. The point for you to remember is that the clock has struck. It is time to do it. And you can't do it in the year 1912 unless you vote the Democratic ticket. There may come a time when there is some other instrument ready at hand, but the only instrument now ready by which there is any hope of immediate control of the Government of the United States as a whole is the Democratic party. We won't hold you bound to vote the Democratic ticket next time. Try it this time. I am now addressing myself to those Republicans who are so orthodox that they have some doubt of the next world if they should vote the Democratic ticket. I believe that if they do it this time their action will be looked upon with compassion in the next world, because it is clearly a providential arrangement that if they vote the Republican ticket this time they will throw their votes away.

And I don't think that Providence will hold any man to an act of futility. I don't think Providence would exact it of any man, even though his father was a Republican, which seems the strongest argument I have yet heard. Even though his father was a Republican, I don't think the old gentleman will turn in his grave. The old gentleman will say in his spirit: "When I was your age I voted the Republican ticket because I believed in what the Republican party was doing. Now, if you would be my son, follow my example and vote for something that you want done, and vote for the only men who can do it."

ICFT transcript of CLSsh notes (RSB Coll., DLC).
    ¹ Delivered in the Long Branch Theatre.

From the Diary of Colonel House

November 2, 1912

I went over to see McAdoo at the Vanderbilt Hotel at half past ten and found him nervous and impatient. From there I went over to see the Governor at the Hotel Collingwood as Bill [McDonald] had rung me up at the house asking me to come. Governor Wilson and I had a long talk. He was very critical of McCombs and he does not believe that he can give him a Cabinet position. I told him of speaking to Mrs. Bryan and the suggestion of Mr. Bryan as Ambassador to London.

Someone wished the Governor to give out a last message to the papers. He said he had given out so many that he did not know what to say. He asked me about it and I practically dictated the letter he is to give out Monday.¹ He says his mind is somewhat confused at present but that they will find his will is firm enough later. I asked him not to consider individuals when making his appointments, that he was under obligations to no one, since they were all getting enough out of it in the way of publicity to repay them. He said he intended to consider the good of the country alone in making appointments. I asked him again to be sure to see McAdoo as he was a little hurt at the seeming neglect.

Governor Wilson came to see me at our apartment just as we were finishing lunch. I had lunch brought in for him and he remained until after five o'clock. McAdoo and Dudley Field Malone both came in to see him for a moment. I suggested to him the advantage of making a statement as suggested by Wallace² and he agreed to do so. He asked my advice as to the advisability of

making an address on November 12th at some Confederate un-
veiling. I strongly advised against it on account of it's being his
first official utterance. I also advised him to make a general statement regarding [John Francis] Fitzgerald, Mayor of Boston, who
wanted it to use to promote his ambition to become Senator. The
Governor did not want to do so but I advised him to make a
general statement regarding his desire to have the next Senate
democratic, and not mention Fitzgerald's name. He did so.

1 November 4.
2 Hugh Campbell Wallace, banker and financier of Tacoma, Wash., and
Washington, D. C., long active in national Democratic politics; later an adviser
and informal diplomatic agent of President Wilson; Ambassador to France,
1919-1921.

Two News Reports

[Nov. 4, 1912]

GOV. WILSON HURT BUT WILL SPEAK DESPITE INJURY

Gash on Head, Sustained by Auto Hitting Bump at Hightstown, Will Not Prevent Candidate's Appearance at Passaic and Paterson.

FAREWELL TO STUMP TODAY

Princeton, Nov. 4.—Governor Woodrow Wilson, Democratic
candidate for President, is nursing a four-inch scalp wound, the
result of being thrown against the top of an automobile while on
his way home early yesterday morning after making a speech
at Red Bank.

The Governor got home and went to bed without telling Mrs.
Wilson or his daughters of the accident, fearing that they would
be too much alarmed.

They did not know of the accident until the Governor told
them at the breakfast table. They were shocked, but became
calm when they found it was not serious.

Governor Wilson said that the automobile was going at a speed
of about fifteen miles an hour. He said a shadow had evidently
concealed the mound from the chauffeur—a mound, he said,
apparently caused by the filling in of an excavation.

"We struck the mound at right angles," he said, "and I struck
the roof of the automobile at the same moment. It was a very
hard blow. There is no doubt about that. But, fortunately, I am
hard headed. I had my hat on, and that acted as a cushion but
not as a defense. Captain McDonald, who was by my side, went
through the same contortions. My glasses were knocked from my

nose, and I afterward found that the left lens was broken. I had another pair of glasses with me.

"I felt the top of my head with my hands and was astonished to find that it was bleeding profusely. Some of the blood got on my overcoat. I knew it would not be wise to go on in that condition, so I called to the chauffeur to stop the car. Then I told him I was cut and that he had better find a doctor.

"There were still some people in the street, and the chauffeur called to two boys and asked where he could find a doctor. The boys got on the front of the car with the chauffeur and guided him to Dr. Titus's[1] office, a few blocks away. The boys were the first to get to the doctor's door."

Dr. Titus, Governor Wilson said, found some hairs imbedded in the wound, and these he carefully cleared. "I must say that Dr. Titus showed rare judgment when he decided not to sew the wound. He found that by drawing the edges together and painting the cut with collodion the same effect was had," the Governor said. "Then he adjusted a finishing of gauze, and I was as good as new.

"My family physician, Dr. Carnochan,[2] was eloquent in his praise of Dr. Titus's skill when he made an examination of the wound later. Dr. Carnochan redressed it, but that would have been necessary in any case."

Captain "Bill" McDonald, the Texas Ranger, who for the last few weeks has served as a bodyguard for Governor Wilson, was with him at the time of the accident, and he also received a number of slight bruises.

The Governor was passing through Hightstown, when the automobile, which was going at a rapid rate, struck a mound in the road, bounded a couple of feet and threw the Governor out of his seat and against one of the supports of the top of the car.

Blood began to trickle down Governor Wilson's face and over his shirt and collar when he resumed his seat, and Captain McDonald, greatly alarmed, ordered the automobile stopped at once.

Two physicians shaved off a small patch of hair near the top of his head and found a painful scalp wound, four inches long, from which blood was flowing freely.

After washing and cauterizing the wound the physicians dressed it with gauze, adding a small piece of court plaster. The Governor absolutely refused to allow the wound to be dressed with a bandage. "I don't want to go home with my head tied up," he said, adding that if he did so his wife and daughters would be seriously alarmed before he had time to explain to them the nature of the accident.

One of the first things the Governor did when he arose yesterday was to call up Democratic headquarters in New York and assure them that his injuries were not serious.

He said they would not prevent him from keeping his engagements to speak in Passaic and Paterson tonight.

News of the accident to Governor Wilson seemed to travel like wildfire, and all the afternoon telegrams and telephone messages poured into this town containing inquiries as to the Governor's condition. They came from all parts of the country, and were so numerous that late in the afternoon he humorously said that he had been so busy answering inquiries that he had not had time to shave.

Printed in the *Trenton Evening True American*, Nov. 4, 1912.
   [1] George E. Titus, physician of Hightstown, N. J.
   [2] John McDowell Carnochan, Princeton 1896, physician of Princeton, N. J.

✧

WILSON LAUGHS OVER BALD SPOT
Bare Crown, Shaved After Auto Mishap, He Calls
His "Private Property."

PRINCETON, Nov. 4.—Attempts by the brigade of photographers on duty here to get a "snap" of Governor Wilson's "premature bald spot," caused by the surgeon's razor, following his accident of yesterday morning, failed today. The Governor laughingly, but nevertheless positively, refused to pose. He insisted that plaster covering the gash, made when his head bumped the top of an auto that hit a mound at Hightstown, while he was homing from his Saturday night meetings, was "private property." He declared that it was only a scratch anyhow.

Governor Wilson arose at 8:30 this morning feeling none the worse for the mishap. He said he felt no ill-effects from the accident and that the wound had given him no trouble during the night.

"I can feel the wound going through the process of healing," he said, "and this causes a slight burning sensation, but that is all."

The physicians who attended the Governor ventured to say that there is practically no chance of blood poisoning, as the wound was promptly taken care of.

The Governor cleaned up a mass of correspondence before leaving this afternoon for Paterson and Passaic, where he will wind up the campaign tonight by an appeal for Democratic votes for the Legislative ticket.

The Governor will also urge the election of "Fighting Bob" Bremner,[1] the newspaper man, who is a candidate for Congress.

"I am particularly glad to go to Passaic and speak for 'Bob' Bremner," said Governor Wilson, "because he is one of the most courageous men I ever knew. In the face of intense physical suffering, and what at times has looked like certain death, Bremner has fought vigorously on for what he believes is right, and has been cheerful through it all." . . .

The Governor's speeches Saturday night were delivered before large audiences at Long Branch, Freehold, and Red Bank. He spoke particularly in behalf of the re-election of Congressman Scully and the election of the Democratic Assembly ticket, so as to make sure of the selection of William Hughes as United States Senator.

At Long Branch, the Governor indicated that he will, if elected President, remain as Governor until the convening of the Legislature in January.

"I have not stopped being Governor yet," he said, "and it is my ambition to be associated with the Legislature of New Jersey which meets next January, in doing some further things in setting the people of New Jersey free from private and special interests."

In his Red Bank speech the Governor said that the country would be emancipated tomorrow if the electorate would choose the Democratic candidates.

Here, the Governor called Mr. Hughes "Billy," and Mr. Scully "Tom." By way of explanation he said "It is apparent that we can't manifest our love for a man unless we call him by a nickname."

Printed in the *Newark Evening News*, Nov. 4, 1912.

[1] Robert Gunn Bremner, editor and publisher of the *Passaic Daily Herald*. He was elected to Congress.

A Statement to Voters

[Nov. 4, 1912]

The issue is now clearly made up, and goes to the people. I, for one, do not doubt the verdict. The voters must take one or another of three choices:

First, intrust the government to the regular Republican party again, which always begins a campaign with promises of action, and then always at the end draws back and warns against change, dreading to attempt anything at all, for fear it should not satisfy those who control credit and who it has so long permitted to act as trustees for the people in every matter of policy.

Second, place the guidance of their affairs in the hands of men who are searching about for some new way in which to perform old duties, all along plain and imperative, which can easily be performed without the invention of new methods—for example, without shifting the whole energy and initiative of the law to the executive branch of the government.

Third, go forward, without postponement or experiment or confusion, to effect the reforms which the whole country waits for, and which all parties profess to believe necessary, through the instrumentality of a great established and undivided party, clear and explicit as to its purpose, willing to effect them by the ordinary process of legislation; willing to be guided by the common counsel of the Nation as a whole, the plain people with the rest, regardful of every interest, the little as well as the big, because connected with every interest by sympathy and comprehension, and soberly determined to obey the voice of though[t]ful men everywhere by a carefully considered course of moderate yet courageous reform. The mere wise statement of the choices is a predication. We shall trust ourselves and let the little groups of discoverers who would have us vest our powers in them learn, in their turn and at their leisure, to trust us also.

Woodrow Wilson.

Printed in the *Trenton Evening True American*, Nov. 4, 1912.

From George Brinton McClellan Harvey

Dear Mr. Wilson   New York Monday [Nov. 4, 1912]

I shall be busy getting out a paper tomorrow night, so I am going to write a line now.

First, I want to compliment you upon your canvass. I can recall none to equal it in effectiveness. Never before to my knowledge has *every* utterance of a candidate added strength. That surely is an achievement.

My congratulations go naturally to our country. To my mind, it is probably unnecessary to say, your election is the greatest thing that has happened since Lincoln's. Nor am I am sure that it was not *essential*—as probably his was.

A mighty task confronts you, of course. As to that, I have no fears. I have more than hope—I have implicit faith in *you*. It is most comforting, I assure you, to feel that way. And I am more eager, I truly believe, for your great and enduring success as President of the United States than you yourself can possibly be.

So with full confidence I tender my best will and wishes to you and my felicitations to the first Southern-born lady to occupy the White House since Eliza McCardle.[1]

Most sincerely yours   George Harvey

ALS (WP, DLC).
[1] Wife of Andrew Johnson. He forgot Ellen Lewis Herndon (Mrs. Chester Alan) Arthur, a seventh-generation Virginian.

A News Report of the Last Speeches of the Campaign

[Nov. 5, 1912]

WILSON'S LAST CAMPAIGN TALK

Urges Jersey to Remain Steadfast, Avoiding the Ruts of Former Days.

PASSAIC, Nov. 5.—Before the people of his own State, those who started him on the road to the Presidency two years ago, Governor Wilson last night brought his Presidential campaign to a close. He spoke to two big, hearty audiences, one at Paterson and one in this city.

Hearers of the Governor were struck, uniformly, by the thought underlying both his speeches. They impressed one as a sort of valedictory to the citizens of New Jersey, and, further, as a charge to the electorate to see to it that there be no slipping, no sliding back into old ruts, where the system could again control the State's destiny after he had gone on to Washington.

In both speeches, in substantially the same words, the Governor had this to say to the people of the State:

"I am not thinking tonight of the Presidency. I am here wondering what the State of New Jersey is going to do with herself.

"Suppose I should have the honor, with the support of New Jersey, to go to Washington, and there look back on the State I love and see that the voters of this State have not maintained the things I love and the things I believe in. It would be a distressing thing to look back on the State and see many of the things you had bidden me to strive for spoiled by the men whose operations I know."

The Governor, in appealing for the election of the legislative and Congressional ticket, used unmistakable terms in characterizing the old Republican State machine and in declaring Speaker Thomas F. McCran, the Republican nominee for the Senate, as an unfit representative of the people. McCran is being opposed by County Register [Registrar] Peter J. McGinnis.[1]

Then the Governor made an affectionate allusion to Robert

Bremner, the nominee for Congress. Bremner, he said, was an inspiration, was a man who would put new life into officialdom at Washington.

Governor Wilson again lauded Judge William Hughes, candidate for United States Senator, and said he was one of the best gifts that Passaic County has made to the nation. It was Hughes's home folk who heard the laudation and they liked it immensely.

Leaving the Jersey situation aside for the moment, Governor Wilson went into a brief discussion of the situation at large and affirmed with great emphasis that business would be perfectly safe with a Democratic administration.

Every panic since the Civil War, he added, had occurred during Republican administrations, but he knew economic laws and economic history better than to say that those administrations were to blame. He would not descend, he said, to the levels that the Taft supporters had in saying the panic of 1893 was caused by the Cleveland administration. . . .

The two meetings were held in high school auditoriums. Before the first speech, which was at Paterson, the Governor was entertained at a dinner in the Hamilton Club. Mr. Hughes presided, and he was assisted by John Hinchliffe, Prosecutor Michael Dunn, Mayor McBride and other lights of the county Democracy.[2]

During the dinner Joseph P. Tumulty, the Governor's secretary, entered the room, smiling and as happy as man could be.

"It's a boy,"[3] was his simple but none the less ecstatic announcement to the assemblage, whereupon there were long cheers, much hand-clapping and universal congratulations for Mrs. Tumulty[4] and the prospective voter.

Governor Wilson left the head of the table and went to the rear of the room, where stood the smiling Tumulty.

"I congratulate you, my boy," said the Governor, gripping his secretary's hand. Tumulty's family now consists of six children.

Of course, right away everybody started in to christen the youngster, and, strange as it may seem, every one agreed on Thomas Woodrow Wilson Tumulty, taking the Governor's full name for the handle to the surname. Mr. Tumulty wasn't quite sure that the suggestion would be binding on the family.

"You know," he said, with a deferential smile, "I'll have to consult with his mother. His grandfather, too, has been asking to have his name perpetuated, so you see how I'm fixed."

Printed in the *Newark Evening News*, Nov. 5, 1912.
¹ Peter James McGinnis, lawyer of Paterson, defeated Thomas Francis McCran, also a lawyer of Paterson, in the race for state senator from Passaic County.
² John Hinchliffe, president of a brewing company of Paterson, former mayor of Paterson, and former state senator from Passaic County; Michael Dunn, prosecutor of the pleas of Passaic County; and Andrew Francis McBride, M.D., mayor of Paterson.
³ Philip Anthony Tumulty, born November 4, 1912.
⁴ Mary Byrne Tumulty.

To George Brinton McClellan Harvey

My dear Colonel Harvey: Trenton, N.J. November 5, 1912

Your letter of yesterday has given me a great deal of pleasure. It is in the highest degree generous, and I want to thank you for it very warmly indeed. It has given me especial pleasure. I feel that the hardest task ahead of me is to justify the praise of my friends. I shall be content if I can save them from disappointment.

I think I feel in an almost overwhelming degree the sense of responsibility involved in this great contest for the rights of the people, and I am sure that if I am elected today I shall appreciate to the very depths of my heart the gravity and difficulty of the duties that lie before me. I pray God I may be equal to the responsibility.   Sincerely yours,   Woodrow Wilson

TLS (WP, DLC).

From Walter Hines Page

Garden City, New York
My dear Mr. President-Elect: Election-Day. 1912

I write you my congratulations a few hours before I shall know how great your victory is. Even if you were defeated, I should still congratulate you on putting a Presidential campaign on a higher level than we have had, I think, since Washington's time. And your grip became firmer and your sweep wider every week. It was inspiring to watch the unfolding of the deep meaning of the contest and to see the people's grasp of the main idea. I followed you about in four or five middle-Western States, talking with editors and other persons who could take a somewhat detached point of view; and I could see the public mind in the act of grasping as a hope what it had long believed to be a dream. The fight has been fairly, honorably and freely won, and now we enter the Era of Great Opportunity. Thousands of men have a new interest in public affairs and a new hope that you have aroused—men who were becoming hopeless under the long-drawn-out reign of privilege

To the burdensome volume of suggestions that you are receiving, may I add these?

1) Call Congress in extra session, mainly to revise the tariff and incidentally to prepare the way for extending rural credit.

Mr. Taft set the stage right in 1909 when he called an extra session to revise the tariff; but he let the villain conduct the play. To get the main job in hand immediately will be both dramatic and effective, and it will save time. Moreover, it will give you this great tactical advantage: you can the better keep in line those who have debts or doubts before you have answered their importunities for office and favors.

The time is come when all our good land must be developed by the new agriculture and farming be made a business. This calls for money. It requires capital just as manufactures require capital and on at least as favorable terms. Every acre will repay a reasonable long-time loan at a fair interest and yield a profit; and group-borrowing develops men quite as much as men develop the soil. It saved the German farmer and it is remaking Italy. And this is the proper use of much of the money that now flows into the control of the credit-barons. This building-up of farm-life will restore the equilibrium of our civilization, and, besides, it will bring the solution of one-half our currency and credit problem.

2) The time is short and the public expectation will be high. Set your trusted friends immediately to work, every man in the field he knows best, to prepare briefs for you, with suggestions, on such great subjects and departments as will demand early action—such as, the Currency, the Post-Office, Conservation, Rural Credit, and the Agricultural Department. This last has the most direct power for good to the most people, to make our farmers as independent as Denmark's and to give our best country folk the dignity of the old-time English gentleman; and it bristles with insistent problems of reorganization. Such expert and independent information from men who receive no pay— would you not find it interesting to compare with your own knowledge and with the information that is going to be brought to you through regular channels? You can command now the unpaid service of all men who are friendly to your aims.

3) The President reads his Inaugural to the people. Why not go back to the old fashion of reading his Messages to Congress? Would that not help to restore a feeling of comradeship in

responsibility and make the Legislative branch feel nearer to the Executive? Every President of our time has sooner or later got awry with Congress.

I can't keep from saying what a new thrill of hope and tingle of expectancy I feel, as of a great event about to happen for our country and for the restoration of the people's government and for the vindication of the great principles which were set before us in our youth; for you will keep your rudder true.

This is a very glad holiday and I write this with my family about me talking of its meaning; and we every one pray for the safety and good health and happiness of you and of every one of yours.   Most heartily,   Walter H. Page

ALS (WP, DLC).

Two News Reports

[Nov. 5, 1912]

MR. WILSON JOKES WHILE VOTING AT PRINCETON HOME

"I'm Governor and Can Enforce the Law," He Laughingly Tells Photo Men, Who Crowd Polling Place in Engine House, While Taking a Snapshot.

Princeton, Nov. 5.—At 10.15 o'clock this morning, Governor Wilson deposited his ballot in the National presidential election at the village voting place in the First Engine station. He voted ballot number 112.

That he voted for himself was indicated, when he came out of the booth, and laughingly remarked to the election officials:

"Whoever arranged that ballot made the Democratic electors as hard to find as possible. They are almost concealed."

The Democratic ticket appeared in the middle and half-way down the big sheet.

When Governor Wilson arrived at the polling place, he found a battery of cameras trained on the ballot-box waiting to "snap" him. Waving his walking stick toward the photographers, he said to the election officials:

"I'm Governor and can enforce the law if you want me to."

The New Jersey law prohibits loitering about the polling places, but the officials had allowed the photographers to set up their machines and take a flash-light picture of the candidate as he curned [turned] in his ballot.

While waiting his turn to vote Governor Wilson joked with the officials and newspaper men.

"All right, go ahead," he said, as he sat down to give his name and address and receive his ballot.

"We're going to wait till you put it in the box," one of the photographers remarked. "Very well," said the governor, "anything you say; I'm getting very meek about about [sic] having my picture taken."

One of the officials said:

"The man in the middle booth can be called out."

"Oh no," replied Governor Wilson. "Everybody must take his turn.["]

The official replied he was overstaying his time.

"Well don't hurry him," said the governor. "You know we want him to take time to vote right."

While strolling to the voting booth, Gov. Wilson stopped and pointed out a certain little Princeton house to Captain "Bill" McDonald, his bodyguard, and Walter Measday, his secretary.

"I took my meals there when I was a freshman," he said, "and one day I got a fish-bone stuck in my throat. See that porch there? I jumped off that six times trying to shake the bone out."

Printed in the *Trenton Evening True American*, Nov. 5, 1912.

❖

[*Nov. 5, 1912*]

KISS FROM WIFE TELLS WILSON HE'S PRESIDENT-ELECT

PRINCETON, Nov. 5.—As the big grandfather's clock in the library of the Wilson home in Cleveland lane chimed out the hour of ten, Mrs. Woodrow Wilson placed her hands upon the shoulders of her husband and kissed him.

"My dear, I want to be the first to congratulate you," she said.[1]

The Governor was standing with his hands folded and his back to the open log fire. It was the first definite word that he was the President-elect of the United States. The bulletins that removed all doubts of the verdict were given to Mrs. Wilson by "Jack" Mendelson, the telegrapher, who received the news off the leased wire.

Next to congratulate the Governor were his three daughters, Misses Margaret, Bessie [Jessie] and Eleanor Wilson. Bubbling over with happiness, the President-elect fondly embraced each of his daughters.

"Joe" Tumulty, the Governor's secretary, James Woodrow, his cousin, and Charles Swem, personal stenographer, danced with glee. From the time that "Joe" Tumulty had telephoned the first returns from the Princeton Club, New York, at 6.15 o'clock, not a line of discouraging news reached the Governor.

The Governor was at dinner with his family when the telegraph instrument, which had ticked off the news of victory to Grover Cleveland twenty years ago, first sounded. The first bulletins were from up-state counties in New York and showed that the Governor had a big lead over Roosevelt and Taft.

"Jack" Mendelson then copied the returns faster than they could be read aloud by Dudley Field Malone, a personal friend of the Governor, who was a guest at dinner.

James Woodrow and Walter Measday read the returns to the newspaper correspondents in the library. Even after the New York Tribune and other Republican papers had conceded his election, the Governor refused to make a statement for publication.

Throughout the evening the Governor was the centre of a happy group in the parlor. He told stories and laughed at those told by his daughters and others who were in the happy circle about the good fire. His comments on the bulletins were brief.

"That is encouraging," he would say.

"Those figures are surprising," he said when Mr. Malone read a bulletin from New York.

From 8:30 until nearly 10 o'clock the Governor stood with his back to the fire and faced those who were scanning the typewritten bulletins as they came from Mendelson's typewriter. Only two or three times during the evening did the Governor adjust his eyeglasses and read the bull[e]tins for himself.

Others who spent the evening with the Governor and his family not already mentioned were Prof. Stockton Axson, a brother of Mrs. Wilson; Capt. George H. McMasters, U.S.A.;[2] FitzWilliam Woodrow[3] and nine newspaper correspondents who have been with the Governor since the Baltimore Convention.

The Governor walked into the library at 9:30 o'clock and called out to Mr. Tumulty that he was wanted on the telephone. Newspapermen were writing about the big library table.

"You gentlemen will ruin your eyes," he said. "I'll get you a better lamp."

He disappeared into another room and returned within a minute or two with an oil lamp.

"Perhaps this will be better," he said.

The Governor's cottage is in the northwestern part of Princeton. The streets about were quiet to-night except for the constant stream of messenger boys who were kept busy delivering telegrams to the President-elect. A score of the Governor's neighbors called and offered their congratulations in person.

About every twenty minutes the Governor was called to the telephone which is in the diningroom. As this is being written he was just heard to say:

"That is very kind of you. I thank you very much."

Printed in the New York *World*, Nov. 6, 1912.
¹ The popular vote was Wilson, 6,293,019; Roosevelt, 4,119,507; Taft, 3,484,-956; and Debs, 901,873. The vote in the Electoral College was Wilson, 435; Roosevelt, 88; and Taft, 8.
² George Hunter McMaster, captain, U. S. Army, at this time stationed at Fort Slocum, N. Y. He was a member of the McMaster family of Columbia, South Carolina. His sister, Katherine McGregor McMaster Woodrow, was the wife of Wilson's first cousin, the late James Hamilton Woodrow.
³ Fitz William McMaster Woodrow, son of James Hamilton Woodrow. Fitz William was at this time a "student qualifying for regular standing" at Princeton University. He was graduated with the Class of 1913.

Remarks to Princeton Students and Neighbors[1]

[[Nov. 5, 1912]]

Gentlemen, I am sincerely glad to see you. I got up on this chair so that you couldn't see the patch on my head. When I see the crowds gather it carries me back to the days when I labored among you. I can't help thinking this evening that something has only just begun which you men will have a great part in carrying forward.

Prosperity has taken us into devious paths. There is so much to reconstruct, and the reconstruction must be undertaken so justly and by slow process of common counsel, that a generation or two must work out the result to be achieved.

The lesson of this election is the lesson of responsibility. I believe that a great cause has triumphed for the American people. I know what we want, and we will not get it through a single man or a single session of Congress, but through the long process extending through the next generation.

I have no feeling of triumph tonight, but a feeling of solemn responsibility. I know the great task ahead of me and the men associated with myself. I look almost with pleading to you, the young men of America, to stand behind me in the administration. The purest impulses are needed. Wrongs have been done, but they have not been done malevolently. We must have the quietest temper in what we are going to do. We must not let any man divert us. We must have quiet temper and yet be resolute of purpose. But let us hear them all patiently, and yet, hearing all, let us not be diverted.

You men must play a great part. I plead with you again to look constantly forward. I summon you for the rest of your lives to support the men who like myself want to carry the nation forward to its highest destiny and greatness.

Printed in the New York *Evening Post*, Nov. 6, 1912; *New York Times*, Nov. 6, 1912; and *Princeton Alumni Weekly*, XIII (Nov. 6, 1912), 32-3.
   1 "When the news of Wilson's election was publicly announced, President Hibben ordered the bell in Nassau Hall rung and announced that November 6 would be a University holiday. A great crowd of students soon gathered on the campus and went to Prospect, where Hibben greeted them. Then, armed with flags and torches, they marched to Cleveland Lane. The cheers of the students brought Wilson to the front porch; he stood there, bareheaded, while the shouts of the undergraduates mingled with the sound of the bell ringing in old Nassau." Link, *Road to the White House*, p. 523.

From William Howard Taft

Cincinnati, Ohio, Nov. 5, 1912.

I cordially congratulate you on your election, and extend to you my best wishes for a successful administration.

Wm. H. Taft.

T telegram (Letterpress Books, W. H. Taft Papers, DLC).

From Theodore Roosevelt

[Oyster Bay, N. Y., Nov. 5, 1912]

The American people by a great plurality have conferred upon you the highest honor in their gift. I congratulate you thereon.

Theodore Roosevelt.

Printed in the New York *World*, Nov. 6, 1912.

From Thomas Riley Marshall

Indianapolis Ind. Nov. 5, 1912.

I salute you my chieftain in all love and loyalty.

Thos. R. Marshall.

T telegram (WP, DLC).

To Thomas Riley Marshall

[Princeton, N. J., c. Nov. 5, 1912]

Warmest thanks for your generous telegram. Your part in the campaign was a source of great strength and stimulation. Now for the deep pleasure of close association in a great work of national service.   W.W.

WWhw draft written on T. R. Marshall to WW, Nov. 5, 1912.

From William Jennings Bryan

[Lincoln, Neb., Nov. 5, 1912]

I most heartily congratulate you and the country upon your election. Your splendid campaign has borne fruit in a great victory. I am sure your administration will prove a blessing to the nation and a source of strength to our party.

[W. J. Bryan]

Printed in the New York *World*, Nov. 6, 1912.

From William Frank McCombs

[New York, Nov. 5, 1912]

My warmest congratulations to you, our next President. You have won a splendid and significant victory. At this hour you appear to have received the largest Electoral vote ever given to a Presidential candidate. The indications are that your Administration will be supported by a Congress Democratic in both branches.

Wm. F. McCombs.

Printed in the *New York Times*, Nov. 6, 1912.

To William Frank McCombs

[Princeton, N. J., Nov. 5, 1912]

I deeply appreciate your telegram and wish to extend to you and the members of the Campaign Committee my warm congratulations on the part you have played in the organization and conduct of a campaign fought out upon essential issues. A great cause has triumphed. Every Democrat, every true progressive of whatever alliance, must now lend his full force and enthusiasm to the fulfillment of the people's hopes, the establishment of the people's rights, so that justice and progress may go hand in hand.

Woodrow Wilson

Printed in the *New York Times*, Nov. 6, 1912.

From John Grier Hibben

[Princeton, N. J., Nov. 5, 1912]

In the name of Princeton University I extend to you the congratulations and best wishes of your alma mater upon your election to the presidency of the United States.

[John Grier Hibben]

Printed in the *Brooklyn Daily Eagle*, Nov. 6, 1912.

A News Report

[*Nov. 6, 1912*]

WILSON ENDS TALKS; TAKES TIME TO THINK
No More Statements from Him, He Says, One Issued Earlier
Being His Last.

PRINCETON, N.J., Nov. 6.—"I'm not going to give out any more statements. The time has come now to do a lot of thinking."

That was President-elect Wilson's reply to-night when he was asked for his point of view after a day to think things over. He had issued a brief statement earlier in the day. The Governor took a five-mile walk that kept him away from home for two hours in the afternoon. He received few visitors. To the newspaper correspondents the Governor talked freely about the election, but made joking remarks whenever he was asked about his future plans. As far as his Cabinet was concerned, the Governor said that there would not be anything from him for some time to come. He was told that several of the newspapers had already picked a Cabinet for him.

"Well, then, you will have to forbid me reading the newspapers," he said, "for they might prejudice me."

The Governor is planning now to get away on a vacation just as soon as he can, but he will remain in Princeton until the end of the week at least. Where he was going on the vacation he said he did not know himself and would not be ready to announce it until the day before he left here. It has been said that he would go to Bermuda for about three weeks.

"It will be a short vacation," he said and added that he would not resign as Governor of New Jersey before he left at any rate.

It seems certain, however, that he will continue as Governor at least until January when the State Senate will pass into the control of the Democrats. The President of the next Senate will serve out the unexpired term. If Gov. Wilson resigned now, Prof. John D. Prince, a Republican, would move into his offices at the State House, as the Republicans now have a majority in the Senate.

Gov. Wilson did not want to talk politics to-day except as politics might be associated with the result of the election yesterday and he told all his visitors so frankly.

The President-elect was up at 9 o'clock this morning, but even before that hour many neighbors had called to offer their congratulations.

"My election didn't give me insomnia," he explained. "I had to pull myself out of bed by the hair of my head," he remarked.

And then he noticed that one of his visitors was glancing smilingly at the plaster which covered the shaved spot on his head, and he added:

"That was a cruel smile."

"I can hardly realize that it is true," he observed gravely.

"It has not quite dawned on me. I had been in an impersonal atmosphere for the last three months, reading about myself, reading that I was to be elected, and now I can hardly believe that it is true."

The first thing that the Governor wanted to know when he got up was not about his own success, but whether the victory had been pronounced enough to assure the control of the United States Senate by the Democratic Party. He was told that there seemed to be no question about that and he plainly showed his happiness. Later in the day National Chairman McCombs appeared to offer his congratulations and add his assurances.

It was after this conference with Mr. McCombs that Gov. Wilson dictated a short statement, the last of a formal nature that he expects to make for some time. It read:

The result fills me with the hope that the thoughtful Progressive forces of the Nation may now at last unite to give the country freedom of enterprise and a Government released from all selfish and private influences, devoted to justice and progress.

There is absolutely nothing for the honest and enlightened business men of the country to fear.

No man whose business is conducted without violation of the rights of free competition and without such private understandings and secret alliances as violate the principle of our law and the policy of all wholesome commerce and enterprise need fear either interference or embarrassment from the Administration.

Our hope and purpose is now to bring all the free forces of the Nation into active and intelligent co-operation and to give to our prosperity a freshness and spirit and a confidence such as it has not had in our time.

The responsibilities of the task are tremendous, but they are common responsibilities which all leaders of action and opinion must share, and with the confidence of the people behind us everything that is right is possible.

My own ambition will be more than satisfied if I may be permitted to be the frank spokesman of the Nation's thoughtful purpose in these great matters.[1]

1 There is a WWsh draft of this statement in WP, DLC.

The Governor said that he felt in the best of health and spirits, but did want to get away by himself for a time. Chairman McCombs, he added, placing his hand on the shoulder of his friend, looked in pretty good shape, too. Some one suggested that the sweeping victory had been about the best tonic that McCombs could have had, and the Governor agreed that such was the case.

Mr. McCombs was asked what the campaign had cost.

"Oh, about a million," he said. "We expect to finish with money in the treasury."

When the camera men clustered about the front of his home the Governor was ready to pose for them, saying that he supposed he could not escape it. He led out Chairman McCombs for another picture.

At just 3:15 o'clock in the afternoon the Governor, accompanied by Capt. "Bill" McDonald, his bodyguard, started out for the five-mile tramp. Every minute or two some one hurried forward to congratulate him, and the Governor stood the assault well. One professor, whom he had known when he was President of Princeton University, spoke of his injury Sunday night, and the Governor removed his hat so that his friend might see where the hair had been shaved off and the pink plaster substituted.

The Governor and Captain "Bill" stopped at the Princeton football field and sat down in a corner of the grandstand to watch the practice. Two or three of the graduate coaches were the first to see him, and ran over to shake hands. The football players kept at their scrimmage and kicking just as if the next President of the United States wasn't looking on.

After leaving the football field the Governor continued on toward Carnegie Lake. A great log obstructed the sidewalk a little further on, and the Governor and Capt. McDonald stopped to move it. It was about all they could do by pushing and shoving and kicking to get the log out of the way, but they worked until they had moved it to one side. Then the Governor knocked the dirt off his hands, smiled at Capt. "Bill" as if he had greatly enjoyed it all, and quickening his step set the pace to Carnegie Lake.

Halfway up a hill the Governor stopped abruptly and pointed with his cane to a grass snake about a foot long that was wriggling its way toward him. Capt. "Bill" grabbed the Governor's cane out of his hand and aimed a sturdy blow at the snake, hit a rock, and the cane snapped in two. The Governor couldn't help smiling as he saw the embarrassment of the ex-Texas Ranger.

The Governor did his best to console Capt. McDonald, saying

he didn't like the cane, anyway, and had just been presented with a new hickory stick. He picked up the broken piece and fitted it on the steel bar which extended through the cane.

"See, it can be fixed all right," he said. The Captain wouldn't hear of that, and he solemnly insisted that he would send the Governor a new cane.

Printed in the *New York Times*, Nov. 7, 1912.

To William Howard Taft

Princeton, N. J., Nov. 6, 1912.

I warmly appreciate your kind message and wish to express my sincere personal regards.   Woodrow Wilson.

T telegram (W. H. Taft Papers, DLC).

To Theodore Roosevelt

[Princeton, N. J., Nov. 6, 1912]

My sincerest thanks for your kind message. Pray accept my cordial good wishes.   [Woodrow Wilson]

ICFT transcript of CLSsh notes (RSB Coll., DLC).

To William Jennings Bryan

[Princeton, N. J., Nov. 6, 1912]

My heartfelt thanks for your generous telegram. Your own splendid work in the campaign has commanded universal admiration and I want to send you my own warmest personal thanks.   [Woodrow Wilson]

ICFT transcript of CLSsh notes (RSB Coll., DLC).

To Walter Hines Page

My dear Page: Trenton, N. J. November 6, 1912

Just a line to thank you for your splendid letter. As I have told you more than once, you always set me thinking, and along fertile lines. I deeply appreciate your friendship, and your thought of what I must be thinking about as well of what I am doing.

In haste

Cordially and gratefully yours,   Woodrow Wilson

TLS (W. H. Page Papers, MH).

To Florence Jaffray Hurst Harriman

My dear Mrs. Harriman: [Trenton, N. J., c. Nov. 6, 1912]

Your kind letter of November 1[1] gives me a sort of pang. I feel as if I had interfered unreasonably with your plans in respect of the ball[2] and entirely without meaning to do so. I was thinking and speaking only of my own daughters attending and not of the event itself. I beg you to believe that I did not intend the least criticism even by implication. Everything that you have planned and done has seemed to me admirable, and I can not tell you how much I have admired your pluck and your devotion to the cause. It has been a splendid example of wise thoughtfulness as well as of energy and enterprise. It would grieve me very much to have you think that I have been critical at any point or of any detail. I understood the purpose of the ball perfectly and had no thought of its being out of the way. I must have written hastily and stupidly to leave any other impression on your mind.

It is delightful that you should be getting well again and I hope that nothing will prevent your getting the rest and recuperation you must so much need.

Mrs. Wilson joins me in the warmest messages of regard and admiration.

Cordially and sincerely yours,   [Woodrow Wilson]

ICFT transcript of CLSsh notes (RSB Coll., DLC).
  [1] Her letter is missing.
  [2] A costume ball held in the Waldorf-Astoria on November 4, 1912, under the auspices of the Women's Wilson and Marshall League to raise funds for the Democratic presidential campaign. See the *New York Times*, Oct. 28 and Nov. 3, 1912.

To George Wilkins Guthrie

My dear Mr. Chairman: [Trenton, N. J., Nov. 6, 1912]

It grieves me that you should have been disappointed about Pennsylvania[1] and I must admit that my own hopes had risen high in that direction but there is certainly nothing to regret or explain. The fight was splendid and I feel like congratulating you on it. Your message[2] gave me the greatest pleasure.

[Sincerely yours,   Woodrow Wilson]

ICFT transcript of CLSsh notes (RSB Coll., DLC).
  [1] The vote in Pennsylvania was Roosevelt, 447,426; Wilson, 395,619; Taft, 273,305; and Debs, 83,164. Roosevelt thus won thirty-eight electoral votes.
  [2] It is missing.

To Richard Evelyn Byrd

My dear Byrd: [Trenton, N. J., Nov. 6, 1912]

The message of congratulation[1] signed by yourself and your son[2] gave me peculiar pleasure. It is very delightful to think of the long fight, the many fine friends, and the great ending.

[Sincerely yours,   Woodrow Wilson]

ICFT transcript of CLSsh notes (RSB Coll., DLC).
   [1] It is missing.
   [2] Harry Flood Byrd.

To the Postmaster of Sweetwater, Texas[1]

My dear Sir: [Trenton, N. J., Nov. 6, 1912]

A little girl[2] living in Sweetwater, Texas, wrote to me on October 31 sending me a dollar for the campaign fund. In opening the envelope the part of her letter containing her name was accidentally torn off and I do not know how to write to her to acknowledge the contribution. I wonder if it would be possible for you to attend to this matter and let me know her name. I enclose the letter.   [Sincerely yours,   Woodrow Wilson]

ICFT transcript of CLSsh notes (RSB Coll., DLC).
   [1] Morus B. Howard.
   [2] Thelma Howard.

From Louis Dembitz Brandeis

My dear Governor Wilson: Boston, Nov. 6th. 1912

Your great victory, so nobly won, fills me with a deep sense of gratitude; and I feel that every American should be congratulated, except possibly yourself.

May strength be given you to bear the heavy burden.

Most Cordially   Louis D. Brandeis

ALS (WP, DLC).

From Samuel Untermyer

Dear Mr. President-Elect: [New York] November 6th, 1912.

Money Trust Inquiry.

I realize the demands upon you and hesitate to intrude at this time but there are important questions of policy in connection with the pending Money Trust Inquiry requiring immediate decision before the hearings which are fixed for the end of this month are resumed. The questions include proposed legislation to require the incorporation of and to regulate Clearing House Associations, Stock Exchanges, National Banks and the currency and are accordingly of surpassing National importance.

It does not seem to me wise or proper that the Committee should make recommendations to Congress or should even shape its further line of inquiry and policy without the knowledge and approval of the head of the party that is to be held responsible for its action.

The occasion for a decision at this time arises out of the fact that I am now in negotiation with the authorities of the Clearing House Association and the Stock Exchange in the effort to agree on legislation that would require that those two institutions, which are now being conducted as unincorporated, irresponsible private clubs, shall be required to incorporate and be subjected to legislative and judicial control.

This is illustrative only of the questions that are req[u]iring solution and with which the incoming Administration is seriously concerned. I regard the Inquiry as on the whole the most ambitious and far-reaching in its possibilities for good or evil ever undertaken by Congress but the many questions involved are exceedingly technical and complicated and will accordingly require considerable explanation and study for a proper understanding.

If you feel that you care to take up the subject at this stage and that it is of sufficient importance to justify your giving to it the better part of an entire day of your precious time I will be pleased to attend upon you at any time and place you will be good enough to designate if you will give me a few days notice. It would be quite useless and wasteful to ask you to burden your mind with this topic at this time unless it so happens that you achieve the well-nigh impossible task of giving to it some hours of your undivided attention.

Awaiting your instructions, believe me

Very respectfully yours   Sam'l Untermyer.

To Champ Clark

My dear Mr. Speaker: [Trenton, N. J., Nov. 7, 1912]

Thank you warmly for your message of congratulation but more for your efforts in behalf of the ticket. It was delightful to see you and be with you when I was in Missouri. I note with great pleasure the increased majority by which you were re-elected to Congress.

[Sincerely yours,   Woodrow Wilson]

ICFT transcript of CLSsh notes (RSB Coll., DLC).

To Edward Mandell House

My dear friend: Trenton, N. J. November 7, 1912

I need not tell you with what feelings I read your message of congratulation.[1] You know how I have depended upon your friendship and counsel throughout. I feel that no small part of the result is due to your own wise counsel.

You will know without my telling you how full a freight of affectionate regard these lines carry. Mrs. Wilson and my daughters join me in the warmest messages to you all.

Sincerely yours,   Woodrow Wilson

TLS (E. M. House Papers, CtY).
[1] It is missing.

To Cyrus Hall McCormick

My dear Cyrus: Trenton, N. J. November 7, 1912

Thank you with all my heart for your message.[1] I am sure that you know with what deep affection and admiration I regard you. You have acted in everything in the way I knew you would act, and my gratitude is very deep and genuine.

Affectionately yours,   Woodrow Wilson

TLS (WP, DLC).
[1] C. H. McCormick to WW, Nov. 6, 1912, TC telegram (C. H. McCormick Papers, WHi).

From Carter Glass

Personal.

Dear Governor Wilson: Lynchburg, Va., November 7, 1912.

Accept, if you please, my very earnest congratulation on your remarkable victory at the polls last Tuesday. It betokens the re-establishment of real representative government at Washington; and many people are praying that the wholesome influence of your election may reach Virginia and aid in its redemption.

I am writing especially to inquire when you think I may have a brief interview with you concerning the matter of revising our currency system. I am chairman of the House Committee to which has been referred the bill and report of the Monetary Commission and which is charged with the consideration of the entire subject of a reorganization of the banking and currency system. While we did not think it would be prudent to complicate the Presidential contest by taking any definite action at the last session of Congress, the committee has not been idle. With the assistance of Prof. H. Parker Willis,[1] formerly of Washington & Lee University, we have gone into much work of detail and have, indeed, formulated, tentatively, a substitute for what is known as the Aldrich bill. I think the committee would not like to proceed without some suggestions from you as to the nature of the work already done and as to what you think should be done. The probability is that we shall not be able to pass a bill in the 62d Congress, but that you will have to approve or disapprove currency legislation by the 63d Congress. For this and other obvious reasons it seems to me that it is essentially important that the matter should be brought to your attention as early as possible by Dr. Willis and myself.

I know that you are now overwhelmed with correspondence; but I would be glad to hear from you at your convenience.

With cordial regards,   Sincerely yours,   Carter Glass.

TLS (WP, DLC).
[1] Henry Parker Willis (1874-1937), adjunct professor and professor at Washington and Lee University, 1898-1905; Professor of Finance at George Washington University, 1905-1906 and 1907-12. At various times after 1901 he was a financial writer and correspondent for the New York *Evening Post, Springfield Republican,* and New York *Journal of Commerce.* He was consultant to the House Ways and Means Committee in 1911 and to the House Banking and Currency Committee in 1912.

From James Bryce[1]

Private

My dear Governor   Washington. Nov. 8th 1912

Though I am debarred from congratulating a victor in a political campaign, there is nothing to prevent me from sending sincere good wishes and earnest hopes to an old friend who, being a scholar and a man of learning has obtained a rare and splendid opportunity of showing in the amplest sphere of action what the possession of thought and learning may accomplish for the good of a nation in the field of practical statesmanship[.] This opportunity is yours, and I may wish you joy the more heartily because I feel confident that your attainments and character promise success. Few have ever reached your high office equally qualified, in both respects, to discharge its duties worthily

I have a message to deliver to you which can be delivered only by word of mouth. Will you kindly let me know whenever you are coming to Washington, or to Baltimore, in order that we may meet, even if only for a few minutes?

My wife[2] joins with me in cordial good wishes and warm regards to Mrs. Wilson.

Believe me   Very sincerely yours   James Bryce

ALS (WP, DLC).
[1] At this time British Ambassador to the United States.
[2] Elizabeth Marion Ashton Bryce.

From the Diary of Colonel House

November 8, 1912.

McAdoo and I had a long talk in which he spoke very freely. I advised him against going to Princeton or bothering the President-elect. He confessed to having telephoned him and said he had been over once at the insistance of Daniels. He promised to remain away but it will nearly kill him to do so for he is intensely interested in the situation.

Old Bill arrived and after talking with him I think it is best for him to return home for the present. The Wilsons were sorry to see him leave. He looked over the Secret Service men to see if he thought them fit. He told me that they did well enough but that he did not like their carrying 38's. When he said this to the Secret Service men, they did not like it and replied: "A 38 will kill a man all right." "Yes," said Bill, "if you give him a week to die in." I find that he has talked much of me and my political work in Texas to Wilson. The Governor wanted to know whether I had been successful in all my political campaigns and what kind of men I had chosen.

To William Jennings Bryan

My dear Mr. Bryan: Trenton, N. J. November 9, 1912

I must give myself the pleasure of adding a more extended line than I could send you by telegraph. I have thought of you very constantly throughout the campaign and have felt every day strengthened and heartened by your active and generous support. I was greatly refreshed also by my little visit to you in Lincoln.

We have won a great victory, and it is now our privilege to show that we can live up to it. It is delightful to see the forces of the party united, and their union should now bring fruit of the richest sort.

Mrs. Wilson was greatly distressed that illness should have prevented Mrs. Bryan from coming to Princeton. I sincerely hope that she is entirely herself again. Mrs. Wilson enjoyed so much meeting her in New York. She joins me in sending most cordial messages of regard to you both.

Faithfully yours,   Woodrow Wilson

Thank you warmly for the account of the convention.[1]

W.W.

TLS (W. J. Bryan Papers, DLC).
[1] It is missing. Bryan had probably sent a copy of his *A Tale of Two Conventions* (New York, 1912).

To James Bryce

My dear Mr. Bryce: [Trenton, N. J. c. Nov. 9, 1912]

Your letter has given me deep pleasure and I thank you for it with all my heart. Its generous words of personal confidence and of friendship are more gratifying to me than I can say. I was deeply distressed this morning to learn from the newspapers that you had tendered your resignation as Ambassador. One of the first thoughts I had upon learning of my election was that I should enjoy the pleasure of being associated with you in Washington and now that pleasure apparently is going to be denied me.

I wonder how long you are going to linger in the country. I am planning to get away to Bermuda on Saturday next for a vacation and shall be gone until the 16th of December. In the meantime it seems impossible for me to get to Baltimore or Washington. Will it be too late for me to see you when I return?

With deep appreciation of your generous letter and with warm regards for both Mrs. Bryce and yourself from Mrs. Wilson and myself,

Cordially and sincerely yours,   [Woodrow Wilson]

ICFT transcript of CLSsh notes (RSB Coll., DLC).

To Thomas Pryor Gore

My dear Senator: [Trenton, N. J., Nov. 9, 1912]

Your message[1] went straight to my heart because I know how large a part of the success your own splendid work constituted and that I am only the leader of a noble band of gentlemen who are ready to serve the country to the utmost. I want to send you my special thanks for your part in the campaign and to express the hope that you will now get some genuine rest and refreshment before you pitch in again at Washington next month. I am off on the 16th for a month of very much needed rest.

Cordially and faithfully yours,   [Woodrow Wilson]

ICFT transcript of CLSsh notes (RSB Coll., DLC).
   [1] It is missing.

To John Grier Hibben

My dear President Hibben: [Trenton, N. J., Nov. 9, 1912]

I need not tell you how gratifying it was to me to receive through you the congratulations of my Alma Mater. I hope sincerely that she may never have occasion to be ashamed of her son.

[Sincerely yours,   Woodrow Wilson]

ICFT transcript of CLSsh notes (RSB Coll., DLC).

To Ralph Pulitzer

My dear Mr. Pulitzer: [Trenton, N. J., Nov. 9, 1912]

It was delightful to receive your message of congratulation.[1] I have been particularly proud of the generous support the *World* has given me and I think I look back with peculiar pleasure to your little speech at the dinner which the New York Press Club gave me. You have throughout proved yourself a most generous friend and supporter. I thank you with all my heart.

[Sincerely yours,   Woodrow Wilson]

ICFT transcript of CLSsh notes (RSB Coll., DLC).
   [1] It is missing.

To Addie Worth Bagley Daniels

My dear Mrs. Daniels: [Trenton, N. J., Nov. 9, 1912]

It was very sweet of you to send a message of congratulation.[1] Our hearts and thoughts have been with you throughout the terrible strain you have been through and we were particularly distressed to learn that you had yourself had an attack of the fever. Mrs. Wilson joins me in warmest sympathy and in congratulations on the recovery of the dear patients.

[Sincerely yours,   Woodrow Wilson]

ICFT transcript of CLSsh notes (RSB Coll., DLC).
1 It is missing.

To Harvey Washington Wiley

My dear Dr. Wiley: [Trenton, N. J., Nov. 9, 1912]

Thank you most heartily not only for your thoughtful kindness in sending me a message of congratulation[1] but also for all the fine work which you did during the campaign. It was a great source of strength to us all.

[Cordially yours,   Woodrow Wilson]

ICFT transcript of CLSsh (RSB Coll., DLC).
1 It is missing.

From Abbott Lawrence Lowell

Dear Mr Wilson: [Cambridge, Mass.] November 9, 1912.

I want to congratulate you most heartily on your election, or rather not you so much as the country, for although you have vast opportunities for usefulness, and will have the joy that comes with making a firm and wise use of them, the path is not without brambles. But I rejoice in your overwhelming victory, and I am glad that you carried our State.

You may remember my writing you in the summer a caution about the selection of your principal advisers and officials from this State.[1] I did so because I felt that it was important for the standing of your administration here to put in your cabinet—if you take a Massachusetts man at all—a man who would be universally respected if possible; and what I feared was that you might suppose that Louis Brandeis was held in more general esteem than is the case. You know the opinions here of Governor Foss, but I felt that you might have heard a one-sided view of Brandeis; and, unlike others, he is not in the position where political exigencies may force him upon you. It is not agreeable to write this, but I think I should do so.

To speak of another subject: W[illiam]. Cameron Forbes, Governor-General of the Philippines, would be very glad to have a talk with you and explain his views of the situation; but he does not feel that he can do so unless you send for him. I feel that he has been doing a great work there, but in any case you would probably like to hear his point of view. He is now here recovering from a serious illness contracted in the Philippines.

Yours very truly,   A. Lawrence Lowell

CCL (A. L. Lowell Papers, MH-Ar).
[1] A. L. Lowell to WW, Sept. 7, 1912, TLS (WP, DLC).

From Felexiana Shepherd Baker Woodrow

My dear Tommy: Columbia, S. C., Nov. 10, 1912.

I cannot tell you how overjoyed we all are at your great victory.

And now, if the Committee[1] can persuade you to spend at least a part of your vacation, in your old home, you may feel assured of a most hearty welcome from all, especially from me.

With love to all,   Affectionately,   Aunt Felie.

ALS (WP, DLC).
[1] A committee of Columbia residents had purchased the former Wilson home in that city. The group visited Wilson in Princeton on November 12 and offered him the use of the house as a winter home. *Newark Evening News*, Nov. 12, 1912.

Remarks at the Dedication of Wilson Cottage[1]

[[Nov. 12, 1912]]

Mr. Anderson and ladies and gentlemen: I am sorry if Mr. Anderson or Mrs. Mansell abbreviated their interesting remarks upon the idea that I had come here to entertain you with an address. I came here, on the contrary, merely to show my very great and genuine interest in the work that is being done in this school, and also to say a word or two about the general responsibilities which seem to me to be suggested by the work of institutions of this sort. Of course, we are casting about, as you have seen from what has already been said, for some definite foundation for action. The Justice of the Court of New York,[2] who was quoted by Mr. Anderson, assumed as a settled fact that more of what we become is due to environment than to heredity; but Mrs. Mansell and the investigations of the psychology department of this institution would seem to suggest that more comes from heredity than from environment. And, indeed, if you look at these

[1] At the New Jersey State Home for Girls in Trenton, a corrective institution for females between the ages of ten and nineteen. It had 225 inmates at this time. Robert M. Anderson, assistant treasurer of Princeton Theological Seminary and president of the board of trustees of the home, presided; Mrs. Elizabeth V. H. Mansell, matron, reviewed its work; and Anderson then introduced Wilson.
[2] The editors have been unable to identify him.

tables on the wall on either side and see the black spots where some flaw in moral heredity has shown itself, you will see that there is a great deal to show for that thesis.

And yet the whole basis of society is individual responsibility. If you can't hold the individual responsible for what he does, then you can't punish him; and if society is responsible for what he does, there is no means that I know of of punishing society. The very fact that crime exists, the very fact that moral dereliction exists, is in itself a sort of penalty upon society, and there are those who say that these are simply symptoms that society is sick and that we must cure it. Yet all the fabric of criminal law, for example, would fall down if there were no personal responsibility. It is not just to incarcerate an individual or to punish him with the extreme penalty of death if he is not responsible for what he did. The truth of the whole matter seems to lie, as usual, just about half way between the two extremes. Undoubtedly there is a great deal, a vast deal, for which society is responsible, and that is the justification for the existence of institutions of this sort.

The legislature of New Jersey would not be justified in making large appropriations for work of this kind here and elsewhere if the State of New Jersey were not in some degree responsible for the social conditions which make these things possible. We have no right to spend the public money for the benefit of a few, or for the relief of a few, unless by doing so we confer a general benefit and reach a general public object. And we, of course, satisfy our own consciences and our own scruples as public servants by the reflection that we are attempting to do the very thing that Mrs. Mansell suggested, attempting to carry this work far enough, so far that it will reach a point where it will begin to contract again, because we will have then almost caught up with the evil and checked some of the chief forces which are producing it. But all that simply means that the study of politics, as well as the study of social development, is a study in the give and take, the play and interchange, of moral forces.

The great argument, if you will not suspect me of touching upon a party question, but the great argument against special privilege is simply the argument that it gives one set of people an advantage that others do not enjoy, and therefore is not a basis of moral equality or of equality of opportunity. So that society is constantly studying its moral responsibilities. Public questions would be almost uninteresting if they were merely business questions, if they were merely material questions. America would be deeply uninteresting if it did not have its life and being in a conception. The men who founded this country had a vision. They said: "Men are brethren. You have no right to supervise or to dictate their religious opinions. You have no right to draw distinctions between them that nature has not drawn. You have no right to set up one class upon a basis of privilege upon which the other classes are excluded. We have had a vision of brotherhood, of mutual helpfulness, of equal rights; we are going to spread a great polity over this continent which will embody these things and make them real. We are going to keep our doors wide open so that those who seek this thing from the ends of the earth may come and enjoy it."

And what makes us proud of America is that she has had these visions. These are moral visions. There is no money to be made out of these visions. America has not grown rich by having them. She has grown great by having them, but that is another story. And, therefore, her greatness lies in the way she expresses herself, not only in her general polity, but in undertakings like this, which we are showing our sympathies with this afternoon. For here we do this; we say we are going to take those whom the wrong moral processes of our social development have crushed or jeopardized or injured, and we are going to take them and put them into a more wholesome moral atmosphere, and we are going to direct upon them the best forces of society instead of the worst forces of society in order that the next generation may be better, in order that this generation may have some example of purity and of rectitude.

For, after all, morals sadly need buttressing in all of us. We are very much more trustworthy when we are amongst good people than when we are amongst bad people. A bad example is dreadfully contagious, even with the best of us. And it wouldn't do for any of us to live too long in the environment from which some of these poor girls have been rescued. We are susceptible of damage in our morals. It is almost terrible to think, aside from the providence and grace of God, of how much of our morals depends upon the watchful eyes of our neighbors.

Now, it is as if we took these young women and these young girls away from those eyes that were indulgent of evil and put them under the observation of eyes that were less indulgent of evil, that exacted right things of them, and exacted them, not by way of compulsion only, but by way of sympathy also, and more potently still by way of example. The world is lifted by example. The world is purified by its saints. And its saints are still exceptional. It is purified by the rare instance, the conspicuous instance. Biography, so to say, contains the seed of all great improvements. The beauty of the biographies of the Old Testament seems to me to be that there are real men in them. When we write the biography of a saint we leave out all of his sins, but the sacred biographers did not. They included his sins, and then showed how, by the grace of God, he had become exalted over his sins and got them under his feet. We don't do that because, I dare say, of the scruples of etiquette or we don't want to offend their friends and acquaintances. And all truthful biography is locked up to be published in the next generation. But not so with these vital biographies; they are men of flesh and subject to temptation like our own, who have sinned, and who have overcome their sin.

And so these children and young women are shown the way by which they can overcome the things amidst which they have been bred. In brief, to bring the whole thing to a head, this is the expression of the intelligent sympathy and helpfulness of sympathy. We say, "We know how this happened. We don't condemn you. We are going to help you by sympathetic understanding and by setting before you those fairer examples of conduct which, after all, are the salvation of the world."

Printed in the *Trenton Evening Times*, Nov. 13, 1912, with corrections from the ICF transcript of CLSsh notes, RSB Coll., DLC.

A News Report

[Nov. 12, 1912]

WILSON'S BOYHOOD HOME PURCHASED FOR HIS USE

PRINCETON, Nov. 12.—President-elect Wilson was invited yesterday to spend his winters in Columbia, S. C., his old home.

William G. [Elliott] Gonzales, editor of The Columbia, S. C., State; Mayor W[ade]. H[ampton]. Gibbes, Dr. S[amuel]. C[hiles]. Mitchell, president of the University of South Carolina; J. E. Swearing,[1] State superintendent of education, and James Woodrow, a cousin of the President-elect and an instructor in the University of South Carolina, officially informed the Governor of the purchase by the State of his boyhood home, and that it was being remodeled for his use in winter. It is said to be probable that the Wilsons will spend part of their winters there.

"It's a very pretty sentiment," said the President-elect. "When I was a half-grown boy, my father built a house in Columbia, which my mother altogether planned,[2] and of course I remember all the details of the building and the development of the little piece of property.

"These gentlemen today came to tell me that my friends in South Carolina had interested themselves to get control of that house, which they would fix up in any way convenient for me for use in the winters, if I wanted to go South while President.

"The house is just near a very big and comfortable hotel, built since our time, that will make it quite convenient for the secretaries and their families to live within easy reach of me. It seemed to me it was an ideal suggestion and that it embodied a very pretty sentiment. In that little Southern home I had perhaps the largest number of my boyhood associations. Of course I expect to have my same old room when I return to the old homestead."

Printed in the *Newark Evening News*, Nov. 12, 1912.
  1 John Eldred Swearingen.
  2 There is a picture of it in Vol. 1.

To William Jennings Bryan

My dear Mr. Bryan: [Trenton, N. J., c. Nov. 12, 1912]

I find myself, after two years of continuous strain, rather completely fagged out. I am, therefore, going to run away for a four weeks vacation in Bermuda, starting on Saturday. People have been pouring in here to see me but I have been holding no conferences with anybody and therefore they have come (though very welcome) without invitation. I want to get my head cleared for what is to follow before I ask for final counsel or form any judgments of my own aside from the big essentials.

I write this just as a message of warm greeting and to express the hope that as soon as possible after I get back on the 16th of December I may be able to get hold of you for a long and intimate conference.

Mrs. Wilson joins me in warmest messages to Mrs. Bryan, with warm regards and in the hope that Mrs. Bryan is feeling quite herself again.

      Cordially and faithfully yours,   [Woodrow Wilson]

ICFT transcript of CLSsh (RSB Coll., DLC).

To Felexiana Shepherd Baker Woodrow

My dear Aunt Felie: [Trenton, N. J., c. Nov. 12, 1912]

Your message made us very happy. Fitz William [Woodrow] had told us how interested you were in all the circumstances of the election and our thought has been with you very constantly.

We send in return our warmest love. I wonder if it is within the possibilities that you should be in Washington in March.

[Affectionately yours,   Woodrow Wilson]

ICFT transcript of CLSsh (RSB Coll., DLC).

To Abbott Lawrence Lowell

My dear Lowell: Trenton, N. J. November 12, 1912

Thank you heartily for your letter of congratulation not only but for the candid advice which it gives concerning Mr. Brandeis. I know with what good conscience you speak, and therefore know how to value your opinions.

It surprises me very much to learn that Brandeis does not in your judgment stand very high in the opinion of the best judges in Massachusetts. I had formed a very high opinion of him, and many of his ideas have made a deep impression on me. Warned by you, I shall be very careful to look into all Massachusetts reputations critically. It is hard to see any man from a single angle.

Cordially and sincerely yours,   Woodrow Wilson

TLS (A. L. Lowell Papers, MH-Ar).

To Alfred McCalmont Wilson

My dear Alfred: [Trenton, N. J., c. Nov. 12, 1912]

Thank you warmly for your letter of November 8th.[1] You know how glad we always are to hear from you and your cordial allegiance to us all makes us very happy. I would be very glad indeed if you would do what you suggest and write me a letter telling me what you think of the men who have worked for the cause in Oregon. We just had the great pleasure yesterday of having your father with us for half the day. It was thoroughly delightful. He is looking, I am happy to say, very well indeed. All unite in warm love and sincere appreciation of your generous letter.

Faithfully yours,   [Woodrow Wilson]

ICFT transcript of CLSsh (RSB Coll., DLC).
[1] It is missing.

To Robert Stephen Hudspeth

My dear Judge: [Trenton, N. J., c. Nov. 12, 1912]

Thank you with all my heart for your letter of November 11th.[1] It has made me very happy. It so obviously comes from your heart and so much has been pent up in your heart for a long time about our affairs that I felt highly honored by it and my thanks are from the bottom of my heart.

Your own part in the great work has been so constant, so faithful, so intelligent, so watchful that I want to convey to you not only my warm thanks but my most cordial and heartfelt congratulations. God send we may be long associated in the work to which we have put our hands.

[Cordially and sincerely yours,   Woodrow Wilson]

ICFT transcript of CLSsh notes (RSB Coll., DLC).
[1] It is missing.

To Joseph Rucker Lamar[1]

My dear Justice Lamar: [Trenton, N. J., c. Nov. 12, 1912]

It is hard for me to write this letter without beginning it, "My dear Joe," so vividly do I remember the many times when you and Philip[2] and I played together.[3] I thank you with all my heart for your line of congratulation[4] and shall look forward with the greatest interest to renewing our old acquaintance when I come to Washington.

Cordially yours,   [Woodrow Wilson]

ICFT transcript of CLSsh (RSB Coll., DLC).
[1] Associate Justice of the United States Supreme Court.
[2] Joseph Lamar's deceased brother, Philip Lamar. The Lamar brothers and Wilson attended Joseph T. Derry's Select Classical School in Augusta, Ga., 1867-70.
[3] The Lamars lived next door to the Wilsons in Augusta.
[4] It is missing.

To Samuel Untermyer

Personal   [Trenton, N. J., c. Nov. 12, 1912]

My dear Mr. Untermyer:

Thank you sincerely for your letter about the money trust inquiry. Unfortunately it turns out to be out of the question for me to devote the time that would be necessary to really grasp the matter before I get away for my vacation. I shall look forward with the greatest interest to taking it up with you at the earliest possible time after I return.

In the meantime pray believe that my entire confidence goes with the committee in its work and inquiry.

[Sincerely yours,   Woodrow Wilson]

ICFT transcript of CLSsh notes (RSB Coll., DLC).

From Alexander Jeffrey McKelway

Dear Mr. Wilson: Washington, D. C., Nov. 12, 1912.

I was very proud to receive your kind letter concerning my reply to a letter from Prof. Albert Bushnell Hart.[1]

I really believe that the Social Service Committee[2] did a great deal of good in showing the country that a large number of us "humanists" were heartily for your election and were able to give a reason for the faith that was in us. May I say here that I am one southern Democrat who does not belong to the appetite end of the Party and who does not want any office for himself or for his relatives; but I am so intensely interested in the success of your Administration that I am only afraid of boring you with my suggestions.

As I have just written to Mr. Frank Walsh of Kansas City, I believe that the best part of the National Progressive Party can be absorbed by the Democratic Party by the wise handling of the Progressives in Congress and by the adoption of the human welfare programme of that party within the necessary restrictions of the Federal Constitution. I would much rather see a reactionary party in opposition than a Progressive Party.

I believe it would be a good idea for you, a month or so after the inauguration, to call a conference in Washington of those distinguished in different lines of social reform to determine just what, in the opinion of the conference, the Federal government can do and should do to promote these reforms. Of course everything would depend on the personnel of such a conference, but there undoubtedly could be selected a group of people whose names alone would create confidence in any programme adopted, with the advantage of giving such a programme very influential backing in every part of the Nation.

Also, among your many titles I do not want you to forget that you are Mayor of Washington, having the appointment of Commissioners and the veto power over Acts of our Board of Aldermen, that is, Congress. We have an intolerable situation here in many ways. I hope that the questions as to assessment and taxation, for example, will be thoroughly thrashed out during the short session of Congress. I have no idea that the Senate, under the leadership of Senator Gallinger,[3] Chairman of the Committee on the District of Columbia, will agree to any substantial reforms initiated by the House. There is no reason on earth why this city should not be a model to the whole country in its institutions and laws. It is very far from that now and the reason is the same as that which has held back other communities, namely, legislative power has been prostituted to selfish interests. I feel sure that all that is going to be changed.

Presbyterian Washington is greatly excited as to where you and your family will put their church letters. If I may give disinterested advice again, since my family belong to a little Southern Presbyterian Church that ought never to have been established, but which we feel bound to help, I would recommend the Church of the Covenant. Dr. Charles Wood, the pastor, was, I think, a protege of Mr. Cleveland's. Mr. Cleveland attended his church, then a mission church in Albany, when he was Governor of New York. Dr. Wood was later pastor of the Walnut Street Presbyterian Church in Philadelphia. I regard him as the best preacher in Washington and sneak off to hear him whenever I can. His sermons are always interesting and inspiring, and the President of the United States will feel that he can escape the cares of state by going to church, which he could not do in some churches.

I vote for an early extra session of Congress; for Louis Brandeis for the attorney-generalship, and for the rest of the Cabinet to be made up without disturbing the Democratic organization in the House or Senate; and for the retention of Miss Julia Lathrop as Chief of the Children's Bureau, which she has managed to organize with absolute indifference to political influence.

I see that my good friend, W. B. Wilson, of Pennsylvania, is among those mentioned for the new position of Chief of the Department of Labor. I fear he is not of Cabinet size. I know the members of Congress so well, as well as some outside of Congress from southern states, and I have such high ideals for your Administration, that not many of those who have been prominently mentioned for various Cabinet positions seem to me to fit exactly.

The new Administration ought to have the help of a Democratic paper in Washington. The Post is without character, being one of very few journals in the United States with the reputation that its principles are for sale. The Star is as mean as the New York Sun without even being smart. The Herald started out as an independent paper but succumbed to the financial interests that have been dominant in Washington during this Administration. The Times belongs to Mr. [Frank] Munsey. The Herald could probably be bought for a reasonable figure though it has to use the news service of the New York Sun, the Post and the Star controlling the Associated Press Dispatches.

Wishing you a quiet vacation, undisturbed by office-seekers or social reformers, I remain,

Cordially yours,   A. J. McKelway.

TLS (WP, DLC).
  1 This exchange is missing.
  2 Of the Democratic National Committee. During the campaign, it published, among other things, *Woodrow Wilson Places Human Rights Above Property Rights* (New York, 1912).
  3 Jacob Harold Gallinger, Republican senator from New Hampshire, 1891-1918.

To Louis Dembitz Brandeis

My dear Mr. Brandeis: [Trenton, N. J., Nov. 13, 1912]

You were yourself a great part of the victory. I know, therefore, how to thank you for your thought of me in sending me your gracious message of November 6th. It now remains for us to devote all our strength to making good.

In haste,   Sincerely yours,   [Woodrow Wilson]

ICFT transcript of CLSsh (RSB Coll., DLC).

To Charles Spalding Thomas

Personal and Private

My dear Governor Thomas: [Trenton, N. J., Nov. 13, 1912]

I have been thinking very carefully and very earnestly about my duty in the matter of making the suggestion you indicate[1] to Governor Shafroth and must admit that I feel as yet like too much of a novice in the difficult situation I find myself in to know exactly what is the wise thing to do. I think that as a general rule it is a perfectly sound principle that the leading and influential Democrats of each state should be allowed to determine their own course of action without interference from the national leader of the party unless some unusual exigency should arise. This is my present judgment and I am reinforced in it because I know how difficult it is to deal with some of the elements which are likely to disturb the harmonious councils of the party in Colorado. I feel very strongly that you and the other thoughtful men in the state are very much better able than I am to work out the desired and desirable result.

Perhaps, as I grow older in this task, my view will change in these matters but at present I have a rather painful consciousness of inexperience and feel that I ought to act upon the doubt. It is quite inconceivable to me that should the general interest of the party demand a special session of the legislature, Governor Shafroth would hesitate to convene it.

With warmest regard,

Cordially and sincerely yours,   [Woodrow Wilson]

ICFT transcript of CLSsh (RSB Coll., DLC).
1 In a missing letter, Thomas had written, suggesting that Wilson urge Governor Shafroth to call a special session of the Colorado legislature to elect a senator to fill the unexpired term, 1913-15, of Charles J. Hughes, deceased. Thomas was elected on January 14, 1913.

To Edward Joshua Ward[1]

My dear Dr. Ward: [Trenton, N. J., Nov. 13, 1912]

It is not merely the selection of my Cabinet, it is the preparation for and guidance of everything that must go with the successful opening of the administration that is restraining me from accepting invitations[2] of any kind, but I have this to suggest. No one who knows me will for a moment doubt my sincere devotion to the Social Center Movement, and I shall be very pleased indeed when I come back from Bermuda (which will be on the 16th of December) to prepare a message to be read to the conference which will speak in no doubtful terms. My presence at the conference would involve me in embarrassments which I think you cannot realize. I can, because I have declined invitations of the first consequence and in connection with some of the best movements in the country, and have declined them out of a sheer sense of duty. I have all too brief a time in which to prepare for what is before me. I would not take the vacation I am about to take if it were not imperatively necessary for me to do so in order to render myself fit.

I am sure that all connected with the great Social Center Movement will understand and agree that my decision is the right one.

I am delighted with what you tell me of what Miss Jane Addams has said. It will be delightful to cooperate with her. I know her spirit and her high principle.

Cordially and sincerely yours,   [Woodrow Wilson]

ICFT transcript of CLSsh (RSB Coll., DLC).
1 Presbyterian minister; supervisor of the Social Center Development, Rochester, N. Y., 1907-10; since 1910, state adviser on civic and social center development in the Extension Division of the University of Wisconsin.
2 It is missing.

To Carter Glass

My dear Mr. Glass: Trenton, N. J. November 14, 1912

I warmly appreciate your letter of November 7th. Letters descended upon me in such a flood that it has been impossible even to sort them according to their importance, and therefore I have just turned yours up from the pile too late, alas, to arrange for an interview with you before I go away to Bermuda on Saturday.

I shall seek an opportunity as early as possible after my return to commune with you, because the question of the revision of the currency is one of such capital importance that I wish to devote the most serious and immediate attention to it.

It is very delightful to know that I am going to be associated with you in the work at Washington. I shall look forward to it with genuine pleasure.

Cordially and sincerely yours,   Woodrow Wilson

Facsimile printed in Carter Glass, *An Adventure in Constructive Finance* (Garden City, N. Y., 1927), p. 75.

To Ira Remsen

My dear Dr. Remsen: [Trenton, N. J., c. Nov. 14, 1912]

Before I go off for a short vacation I want to get something off my mind that has been very much on it. Ever since you announced your intention to retire from the Presidency of The Hopkins (a resolution which I, along with all other university men, sincerely deplore) the man I have had in my mind as ideally qualified to succeed you and to attempt the particular tasks which now lie immediately ahead of the University, is Henry B. Fine, my long time colleague here. He was Dean of the University throughout my administration as President of Princeton. I have, therefore, seen and tested his qualifications as an executive in the most intimate and thorough fashion. Not only that, I have also been so familiar with his ideals and his academic interests and purposes that I want to urge his name, through you, upon the consideration of the board with the greatest earnestness.

I believe that university service throughout the country would profit by his elevation to such a position of authority and peculiar influence.

With warmest regards,

Sincerely yours,   [Woodrow Wilson]

ICFT transcript of CLSsh (RSB Coll., DLC).

To John Milton Waldron

My dear Dr. Waldron: [Trenton, N. J., Nov. 14, 1912]

Thank you sincerely for your letter of November 7th.[1] The support of the colored people of the country accorded me at the election has given me genuine gratification.

Sincerely yours,   [Woodrow Wilson]

ICFT transcript of CLSsh (RSB Coll., DLC).
[1] It is missing.

From Morus B. Howard

Personal

Sweetwater, Texas.
My dear Mr. Wilson: November 14, 1912.

I have your letter of November 5th, with reference to a letter containing a dollar received by you from a little girl living in Sweetwater, but the name of the sender being torn off accidentally in opening the envelope. I beg to advise you that the letter was sent by my little daughter Thelma, and I feel that a few words of explanation is necessary that you may receive the letter in the spirit in which it was sent.

Our superintendent of city schools, Professor M. B. Johnson, has been a strong admiror of you even before you were elected Governor of New Jersey. He has studied your books and knows you possibly better than any other man in these parts. His scholarship, his wide knowledge of men and affairs, all combine to make him a strong Wilson man. Being naturally drawn to you pedagogically, he has so thoroughly studied your ideas of conditions and progressiveness that he has done a great work for you in this state; or putting it in his own language, "Wilson's fight is the fight of the people," and he has never missed an opportunity to make you votes.

During the last three months of school last spring and during the fall term he lectured to the children in all the schools on your life and your greatness as an American citizen until every child knows more about you than possibly any great American citizen now living. So you easily understand why the dollar came. And not only have the children learned to think of you as an ideal American citizen, but many others of us.

I wish you most splendid success in your administration of National affairs, and pledge you most loyal support.

Faithfully yours, M. B. Howard
Postmaster,
Secretary School Board.

TLS (WP, DLC).

To Davison McDowell Douglas[1]

My dear Mr. Douglas: Trenton, N. J. November 15, 1912.

I do not know of anything that has given me greater pleasure than the splendid way in which college men have rallied to my support. Your kind message of congratulation[2] brings this to my mind very vividly, and I thank you with all my heart.

Sincerely yours, Woodrow Wilson

TLS (D. M. Douglas Papers, ScU).
[1] President of the Presbyterian College of South Carolina.
[2] It is missing.

From Newton Diehl Baker

My dear Mr Wilson: [Cleveland] November 15, 1912

I appreciate most heartily your generous note[1] of this morning. My place in your army is out here where I can interpret you to the virile but somewhat impatient people who are making a wonderful city of Cleveland and I shall follow your course with the most loyal delight and understanding. . . .

With every hope for your health and strength and happiness,
Faithfully yours, Newton D. Baker

ALS (WP, DLC).
[1] It is missing. Wilson no doubt had expressed a desire to have Baker in his administration in some capacity.

From William T. Ferguson

Mr. Wilson: Washington, D. C., November 15/12.

There is an attempt on the part of some colored men, who supported Mr. Taft and Mr. Roosevelt, to create a panic here among the colored citizens. A large number of our colored citizens live by employment in the Departments, and they are being led to believe that the same kind of a wholesale dismissal will take place when you come in as was made under Mr. Cleveland. They are being advised not to have an inaugural ball—to sell their property—to send their families home and such other foolish things. They have always joined in the festivities of the inauguration, and there is no reason why they should not do so now. As I stated in a letter to you a few days ago[1] I have spoken in the most positive way of your Christian character and friendliness to colored people. May I have a letter from you which will put at rest these ugly rumors? I am to be one of a committee of colored citizens to welcome visiting friends and am to meet a committee on the 30th inst. to arrange for an inaugural ball and if I could have the pleasure of reading a letter from you it would have a gratifying effect. If your colored friends are permitted to do so they are going to make inaugural week a gala week and not one of mourning. With best wishes,

I am yours truly,   Wm. T. Ferguson.

TLS (WP, DLC).
[1] It is missing.

From the Diary of Colonel House

November 16, 1912.

Governor Wilson telephoned me early and asked if it would be convenient for him to come over at ten o-clock. He remained for an hour or more and we went over all matters in the most confidential way. Cabinet material was discussed and he eliminated Huston Thompson whom he knows well. We discussed what to do with McCombs and McAdoo. He said he would give the former a first class foreign appointment in order to get rid of him. He said he would be willing to give him the Collectorship of the Port of New York if it were not that he could build up a formidable political machine. I told him McCombs would not think of accepting the Collectorship. I suggested McAdoo as Secretary of the Treasury, Burleson as Postmaster General. He thought Daniels would be better for Postmaster General but I thought he was not aggressive enough and that the position needed a man who was in touch with Congress. He agreed that this was true.

We talked again of James C. McReynolds[1] as Attorney General. We practically eliminated Brandeis for this position ⟨because he was not thought to be entirely above suspicion and it would not do to put him in such a place⟩. He asked again about offering Mr. Bryan the Secretaryship of State or Ambassadorship to England, and I advised him to do so. He said that he would. I gave him a copy of Philip Dru[2] to take with him on the trip to Bermuda.

1 James Clark McReynolds, Assistant Attorney General of the United States, 1903-1907. See also E. M. House to WW, Nov. 22, 1912.

2 Edward M. House, *Philip Dru: Administrator, A Story of Tomorrow, 1920-1935* (New York, 1912). For an analysis and description, see Rupert N. Richardson, *Colonel Edward M. House: The Texas Years, 1858-1912* (Abilene, Tex., 1964), pp. 252-70.

Remarks Upon Arriving in Bermuda

[[Nov. 18, 1912]]

Your Worship[1] and Gentlemen of the Corporation of Hamilton: It is very gratifying to me to be received in such a cordial and neighbourly way; and I wish to express my sincere pleasure at getting back to Bermuda, for some of the pleasantest days of my life have been passed here. As soon as I knew that I had been sentenced to four years hard labour my first thought was to get away to Bermuda and enjoy my liberty while I might.

I think that what His Worship has remarked about the relations at present existing between the United States and the British Empire are particularly true. The relations between these two great nations are warm and natural, and I hope that during my term of office nothing shall arise to disturb them.

Having expressed my warm appreciation of the way in which I have been received I should like to express the hope that having so received me you will let me go about among you as if I were no one in particular.

I want to renew the many delightful relationships I have enjoyed in your beautiful Islands, and I thank you most sincerely for the courtesy you have bestowed upon me.

Printed in the Hamilton, Bermuda, *Royal Gazette*, Nov. 19, 1912.
1 Musson Wainwright, mayor of Hamilton.

To Edith Gittings Reid

My dear dear friend: BERMUDA, November 20, 1912

At last we are away from the crowd down here in this calm clear land, where it seems possible to detach oneself from all kinds of distracting thoughts and think freely again. It was impossible while we were at Princeton to answer any letters written by those we really cared for, but now a little leisure and peace have sufficed to mend our spirits and it is a delight to turn to those we love most.

Your letters[1] gave us very deep pleasure. I do not know how to thank you for your affection and your confidence. They are like springs to me in a dry land, and it will be no small part of my pride in trying to do right that I am trying to satisfy you and those who like you trust me utterly.

We are going to spend three or four weeks down here, and I hope to get back with a clear head and a sound judgment. How I wish you might be down here also to enjoy with us this incomparable little land!

Ellen joins me in most affectionate messages, and we both wish to be remembered most warmly to Mr. Reid.[2]

Sincerely yours,   Woodrow Wilson

TLS (WC, NjP).
[1] Edith G. Reid to WW, Sept. 29, 1912, ALS (WP, DLC), and Edith G. Reid to WW, Oct. 16, 1912.
[2] Harry Fielding Reid, Professor of Geology, The Johns Hopkins University.

To William Gibbs McAdoo

My dear McAdoo: BERMUDA, November 20, 1912

Here we are settled in a little cottage[1] ideally situated for refreshment and rest, where I hope to get the kind of strength and zest I shall need for the things that lie ahead of me.

At this first moment of leisure for correspondence I want to express to you once more the feeling I have had throughout the campaign of deep and growing satisfaction at the generous and efficient part, the self-sacrificing and sometimes painful part, you have played in pushing forward the common cause in which we both so earnestly believe. The records of my memory in these matters will be records to which I shall most often turn for satisfaction and encouragement. I wanted to send you at least this line of affectionate regard and appreciation.

Pray, never feel that there is anything that has to be explained to me. I think I understand, both by knowledge and intuition, both your motives and your feelings.

Faithfully yours,   Woodrow Wilson

TLS (W. G. McAdoo Papers, DLC).
[1] Glencove, in Paget West.

To William Goodell Frost

My dear friend: BERMUDA, November 20, 1912

I tried hard to reply to the delightful messages of my friends before leaving home but was prevented, and am giving myself the pleasure of writing from Bermuda.

Your letter[1] gave me peculiar pleasure. I know your sincerity and your deep devotion to duty, and therefore any sort of expression of confidence on your part strengthens and refreshes me in anything that I have to undertake. Now that I am about to face the most difficult duties that any man could attempt to perform, I feel that I particularly need the support and confidence and prayers of men like yourself.

I thank you with all my heart.

Cordially yours,   Woodrow Wilson

TLS (W. G. Frost Papers, KyBB).
[1] It is missing.

To Hiram Woods

My dear Hiram: [Bermuda, Nov. 20, 1912]

Delightful as it was the other night to see you and the other old fellows at the dinner,[1] it was tantalizing merely to sit at the table and look at you and have no chance to have personal and intimate chats.

You may be sure that I shall never desire you in any circumstances to drop the old epithets of intimacy. On the contrary I should miss them very sorely if you did. I have now at last at least a little leisure in which to turn to the men I have known and loved so long and express to them my deep and continuing affection.

Faithfully yours,   [Woodrow Wilson]

ICFT transcript of CLSsh (RSB Coll., DLC).
[1] Given in his honor by members of the Class of 1879 at the University Club of New York on November 15, 1912.

To Richard Heath Dabney

My dear Heath: BERMUDA, November 20, 1912

There was certainly no occasion for your apologizing for not saying good-bye to my brother. We all understood perfectly.

I wish I could look forward to the pleasure of seeing the old University again, and I shall certainly make it possible at the time I visit Staunton[1] unless something prevents which I do not now foresee. I hope with all my heart that I can do it under circumstances of as little ceremony as possible. I love the old place for its memories and its simplicities, and not for the trouble that I have subsequently got into.

We are settled here for a little period of rest and recreation, and I hope to come back with new zest and refreshment for my work.

With warmest affection, I am

Faithfully yours,   Woodrow Wilson

TLS (Wilson-Dabney Corr., ViU).
¹ He was to speak at Staunton on December 28, 1912.

To Solomon Bulkley Griffin

Personal

My dear Mr. Griffin: [Bermuda, Nov. 20, 1912]

No letter brought me greater pleasure than yours written on election night.¹ I have been strengthened and made very happy throughout the campaign by the splendid and discriminating support of the *Republican*.

My long delay in acknowledging your letter would not seem to indicate great appreciation but you will readily believe that so long as I was home it was simply impossible to get at my correspondence. I have brought the letters I most wished to acknowledge off with me to this remote little island and here I can give myself liberty to write to those whose friendship I deeply value.

Cordially and sincerely yours,   [Woodrow Wilson]

ICFT transcript of CLSsh (RSB Coll., DLC).
¹ It is missing.

To Charles Henry Grasty

My dear Mr. Grasty: BERMUDA, November 20, 1912

I fear you must have thought that I took very lightly your thoughtful courtesy in having that remarkable scrapbook¹ made up for me, which you were kind enough to send me by the hand of Mr. Jenkins, but of course I did not. I have simply had to postpone to the comparative leisure of this short vacation the pleasure of telling you how sincerely and how highly I appreciated it. It is exactly the kind of thing which I wanted, and I shall keep the book as one of my chief treasures. It contains many things of which I learned for the first time in turning its pages. How is a man ever to know even the circumstances of his own day?

Cordially and sincerely yours,   Woodrow Wilson

TLS (WP, DLC).
¹ A scrapbook (WP, DLC) entitled "The Campaign For Wilson," which Grasty presented to Wilson on behalf of the editorial department of the Balti-

more *Sun*. It contained clippings of editorials, cartoons, and news stories from the *Sun* from March 31, 1910, to November 8, 1912. It is, in effect, a chronicle of Wilson's rise to the Presidency.

To Norman Hapgood

My dear Mr. Hapgood:　　　　BERMUDA, November 20, 1912

At last in this remote island I can command a little of my own time, and I want to tell you how deeply and sincerely I valued your thought of me at the time of the election and afterwards. It is cheering to me to think that I can turn to you in moments of perplexity for some clarifying word of opinion and counsel. I know that what has happened to change your plans and your work will in no wise affect, except perhaps to enhance, your influence, and I hope that you will have the happy opportunity to choose just what you would most like to do.

With warm regard and sincere confidence, I am

Cordially yours,　Woodrow Wilson

TLS (WC, NjP).

To Jerry Bartholomew Sullivan

My dear Sir:　　　　　　[Bermuda, Nov. 20, 1912]

It has been impossible before now for me to reply to your letter of November 6th.[1] I simply was not permitted to have any time of my own so long as I was in the United States.

I need not tell you that it will be very delightful to me to have a conference with you after my return home. I am expecting to be back in New York on the 16th of December. If you would be kind enough to drop me a line about that time, we can easily arrange for a meeting and I shall look forward to it with the greatest pleasure.

I want to congratulate you with all my heart on the result in Iowa. Splendid work was done there and it is heartening to know how many faithful friends I had though there are not many like yourself.

Cordially and sincerely yours,　[Woodrow Wilson]

ICFT transcript of CLSsh (RSB Coll., DLC).
1 It is missing.

A News Item

[Nov. 22, 1912]

WILSON SAYS HE WILL USE FISTS ON PHOTO MAN

HAMILTON, BERMUDA, Nov. 22.—President-elect Wilson "flared-up" today when a newspaper photographer "snapped" him in disregard of his expressed objection.

"You're no gentleman," he exclaimed warmly, "and I'll thrash you if you do that again."

The photographer apologized profusely, but the President-elect was not much mollified—considering that the photographer still had the plate notwithstanding the remorse he professed.

This happened in the President-elect's own yard, where he evidently felt his wishes ought to be respected. There were two photographers there at the time, but one of them did as he was requested and got an approving smile—but no picture—as a reward for it.

Later the President-elect and his daughters took a long bicycle ride.

Printed in the *Trenton Evening Times*, Nov. 22, 1912.

To Mary Allen Hulbert

Dearest Friend,   Glencove, Paget West. 22 Nov., 1912

It seems as if it ought to be the other way around: *you* ought to be writing to me on this paper[.] I feel all the while as if you might walk in at any moment,—or *out* of any one of the rooms, —the whole place seems so like you—so pervaded by you—the furniture, the hangings, the *little* things as well as the big! I never saw you in these rooms, but Shoreby[1] itself could not make me more constantly conscious of you than this place does. Your astral self must be here. Nothing could have been more happy than our arrival at the dear little house—after a calm and delightfully easy passage. Mrs. Eels[2] & Mrs. Parrish[3] had filled the rooms with flowers and with every little thing that we would immediately need, like soap and ink, and Mr. and Mrs. Young[4] *more* than lived up to your eulogy of them. They are real friends and *true* and kind in everything. We feel already an affectionate enthusiasm for them—and are somehow dumb to tell them so. We came *home*,—every one made us *feel* that we were doing so! And Ellen and the girls love Bermuda as I had wished they would —love everything about it—as they should. It is wholly delightful to be their guide to the beauties of the dear place! And *your* thoughtfulness crowned all[.] The house could not have been better or more completely fitted for our needs. We all unite in enthusiastic and affectionate thanks! We have exchanged calls with Government House and are well on the way to more. The Governor and his Lady[5] are *very* nice. We have taken a genuine liking to them. Everybody has been most gracious and kind and —in short, we are deeply content!

I feel I am sending this a bit at a venture, merely addressing it Hot Springs; but I *hope* you are there and in the midst of the cure[.] Pray have a good time withal and think as often and as affectionately as you can of your friends at Glencove.

Your devoted friend   Woodrow Wilson

ALS (WP, DLC).
[1] In Paget West, which Mrs. Hulbert had rented in 1908.
[2] Mrs. Stillman Witt Eells.
[3] Who owned Glencove.
[4] Unidentified.
[5] Lieutenant General Sir George Mackworth Bullock and Lady Amy Isabel Thomson Bullock.

From Edward Mandell House

Dear Governor: New York City. November 22nd, 1912.

I have some accurate information in regard to Edgar Farrer.[1] He is a man of high character and one of the most accomplished lawyers in America. He drinks, but not often to excess now. He has had two distressing domestic tragedies within the year that have saddened his life; a daughter suicided in Paris[2] and a son was killed by burglars.[3]

He is irascible and does not easily get along with men. He was the instigator of the movement to exclude the Negro, Lewis, from the American Bar Association.[4] His private and corporate practice has been unobjectionable.

Do you know a Philadelphia lawyer by the name of William A[nderson]. Glascow Jr.?

He is about forty-eight years old—is a democrat and was born in Virginia. He has been employed by the Interstate Commission at different times.

I do not know him personally but I am told he is a man of high character and great ability. He might be worth investigating.

James C. McReynolds of Tennessee, but more recently of New York, is also worthy of consideration. Although a democrat, Mr. Roosevelt made him special counsel for the Government in the suit against the Tobacco Trust and the Anthracite Coal Trust.

He won the Tobacco suit and he has won the suit against the Coal Trust as far as it has gone. It is now in the Supreme Court.

McReynolds severed his connection with the Government because of his disagreement with Mr. Wickersham[5] regarding the dissolution of the Tobacco Trust. He contended that Wickersham's plan nullified the effects of the victory.

He is about fifty years old. He is considered radical in his views by a large part of the New York Bar. His character and legal attainments are of the highest.

I lunched with Mr. Brandeis yesterday. His mind and mine are in accord concerning most of the questions that are now to the fore. He is more than a lawyer, he is a publicist and he has an unusual facility for lucid expression.

There comes to the surface, now and then, one of those curious Hebrew traits of mind that makes one hold something in reserve.

A large number of reputable people distrust him but I doubt whether the distrust is well founded and it would perhaps attach itself to any man who held his advanced views.

Norman Hapgood lunched with us and I found in him an enthusiastic admirer of Brandeis. They are both going to Hot Springs for a few days as guests of Mr. Charles R. Crane.

Franklyn K. Lane, Democratic Interstate Commerce Commissioner from California was with me a large part of yesterday. Lane is fine material but he is contented with his present position and would not change it.

I talked with him and another Californian concerning Phelan. I was told that Phelan was a man worth from four to ten million dollars, a bachelor, a fine after-dinner speaker, able but cold blooded. He is popular in California outside of San Francisco where he has some enemies on account of the stand that he took against Patrick Calhoun.[6]

You will have some difficulty in selecting your Secretary of the Interior. The West wants him but it would perhaps be a mistake to select him from there.

In the first place, he could not maintain himself with his own people and satisfy the East. If he satisfied the East the West would rend him. It would also be well not to put an ultra Eastern man in that position for the West would resent such action.

As you know, the East is all for conservation and the far West is for it in a limited way—that is where it does not conflict with their material interests. The West is anxious to have the forest and mines, etc. etc. opened up and used to an extent that would aid them commercially.

They are also largely wedded to the idea of state versus national control, which I think is wrong but which we need not go into here.

There is one other thing I want to say and that is this—You can never build a Cabinet that will please everybody. When you seek advice you will find but few agreements, even amongst your friends. When you have about concluded that you have the proper man some one will come along and condemn him so vigorously that it will make you doubt. Therefore in the end, you will have to largely determine their fitness yourself.

Please do not bother to answer my letters unless there is something you want me to do.

Your very faithful,   E. M. House

The N. Y. Sun, The American and some other papers are trying to excel one another as trouble breeders.

TLS (WP, DLC).
  1 Edgar Howard Farrar, corporation lawyer of New Orleans with the firm of Farrar, Jones, Goldsborough and Goldberg. In 1882, he was selected as overseer of a $1,000,000 fund for the establishment of Tulane University and was later involved in the municipal reform movement in New Orleans and in the prosecution of the local Mafia. He was president of the Louisiana Tax Commission, 1906-1908, and of the American Bar Association, 1910-1911.
  2 Lucinda Farrar, a piano student, committed suicide on October 27, 1910.
  3 Edgar Howard Farrar, Jr., a lawyer with his father's firm. He was shot and killed by burglars on November 1, 1911.
  4 He referred to the secession, on September 2, 1911, of 1,000 southern members of the association in protest against the election to membership of William Henry Lewis, Assistant Attorney General of the United States.
  5 George Woodward Wickersham, Attorney General of the United States, 1909-1913.
  6 A grandson of John C. Calhoun, he was a corporation lawyer and prominent in the consolidation of the Southern Railway System and street railways in Pittsburgh, St. Louis, Baltimore, and San Francisco. At this time he was president of the United Railroads and director of the United Railways Investment Co., both of San Francisco.

To William Jennings Bryan

My dear Mr. Bryan: BERMUDA, November 23, 1912

I have just received and read with the greatest appreciation your kind note of November 17th.[1] We shall be down here in Bermuda until the 14th of December, when we sail, expecting to reach New York on the 16th. I shall hope to get into communication with you very promptly after that date.

I appreciate more warmly than I can say the generous terms of your letter, and am looking forward with the greatest pleasure to the opportunity of consulting with you, not now only but often.

Mrs. Wilson joins me in warmest regards both to Mrs. Bryan and yourself.

Cordially and sincerely yours,   Woodrow Wilson

TLS (W. J. Bryan Papers, DLC).
    1 It is missing.

To Henry Burchard Fine

My dear Harry: [Bermuda, Nov. 23, 1912]

I cannot tell you what deep pleasure your letter of November
6th[1] gave me. It reached me last night here in faraway Bermuda
to which we have run away for four weeks of rest and escape
from the turmoil, and I read it aloud to the family. I need not
tell you, my dear fellow, how my affection leapt to meet yours
as I read the generous sentences in which you expressed your
delight at my election. The old days in Princeton, days of strain
and pain, were days when men were bound together by something more than ordinary affection. The affection seemed to have
iron put into it by the influences of strong conviction. Nothing
gave me deeper satisfaction and happiness than the way in which
you always, in your invariable, straightforward, unequivocal way,
sustained the best things in the University. Your deanship was
the center of my strength in the administration of the standards
of the place and I shall always look back upon my association
with you as one of the happiest circumstances of my life. You
may judge, therefore, what it means to me to have you say what
you have said about my election. My heart goes out to you across
the waters and we all join in hoping that your year abroad will
bring you every kind of refreshment and strengthening.

It delights us to hear of Suzanne's[2] recovery of her complete
strength and tone again. Our thoughts will follow you throughout
the winter and I hope that, if anything out of the way happens
to you, you will not fail to let us know. Mrs. Wilson and Jessie
and Nellie (Margaret is not with us) join me in most affectionate
messages to you all.

[Affectionately yours,   Woodrow Wilson]

ICFT transcript of CLSsh (RSB Coll., DLC).
    1 It is missing.
    2 His daughter, Susan Breese Packard Fine.

To David Hunter McAlpin Pyle[1]

My dear Mr. Pyle: [Bermuda, Nov. 23, 1912]

When I wrote you the little note that went off this morning
I had not received your note of November 16th.[2] I want to tell
you how deep and genuine a pleasure I derive from such mes-

sages. Not that I receive a great many of that kind but I do receive some which make me very proud in the consciousness that I have been of some use to the men who studied with me and under me at Princeton. I covet their good opinion perhaps beyond that of any others. This is the kind of reward and the only kind of reward which men in my position seek or care for, and the peculiarity of it is that it cannot come if it is too consciously sought. Such assurances of confidence and friendship make me very happy.

With best wishes,

Cordially and sincerely yours,   [Woodrow Wilson]

ICFT transcript of CLSsh (RSB Coll., DLC).

[1] Princeton 1908, lawyer of New York, and nephew of Charles Williston McAlpin.

[2] It is missing.

To Joseph Patrick Tumulty

My dear Tumulty: BERMUDA, November 25, 1912

We have been here a week now, and I have thought very constantly of you who are so generously and unselfishly pulling away at the laboring oar at home in order that I might have this vacation. All unite in sending you the most affectionate messages.

There is nothing to relate of our stay here. The newspaper men who came down with us are quite in despair at the lack of news and yet are evidently enjoying their outing. I am sure they already agree with me that this is an ideal place for a vacation, and I dare say that by the time the four weeks are out they will be content to have no news to send home. Because, it is a sort of lotus land, where one gets content with doing nothing.

Just at the moment of writing I am a little under the weather because of indigestion, but I shall presently work that off, and I feel confident the remaining three weeks will set me up in fine condition. I have caught up with the letters I brought down with me, and am now free to do some of the quiet thinking and reflecting that was my main purpose in coming here.

I hope that all the family are well, and that the little Philip and his mother come on famously. Our warmest messages to them all.   Affectionately yours,   Woodrow Wilson

TLS (J. P. Tumulty Papers, DLC).

From Edward Mandell House

Dear Governor: New York City. November 25th, 1912.

I have a letter from Mr. Underwood in which he says:

"It is my earnest desire to do everything I can to make Governor Wilson's administration a success and I shall do all in my power to uphold his hands."

I also have a letter from Senator Gore in which he says:

"Colonel Bryan took dinner with me on Sunday. The Colonel is in fine humor and these press dispatches are simply wild and irresponsible guesses. He seems disposed to do team-work and contribute with might and main to the success of the administration.

"I find a strong disposition among Democratic Senators to line up and to back the administration. Those who have been classed as reactionaries seem disposed to march now instead of to mark time. If the situation is handled diplomatically I believe that splendid service can be secured."

I am going to Washington this morning in order to look into the situation myself so as to be able to give you my point of view.

I am enclosing you a letter written by a man[1] whom Mr. Mc-Combs attached to the Headquarters during the last days of the campaign. I think Carmichael has always been a republican and that he has recently been in the employ of the railroads. However, he says some things that may perhaps interest you.

He is a man that has had a great deal of experience in politics and public affairs.

I am leaving in a few minutes and will therefore not be able to sign this letter.

Your very faithful,   E. M. House, per. D.[2]

TLS (WP, DLC).
[1] The enclosure is missing, but it was from Otto Carmichael, a New York financier. Carmichael was Washington correspondent for several newspapers, including the *Detroit Journal*, the *Boston Herald*, and the New York *World*, from 1897 to 1904, and was managing editor and publisher of the *Detroit Free Press*, 1904-1909.
[2] His secretary, Frances Denton.

A News Item

[Nov. 26, 1912]

HIS EXCELLENCY GOVERNOR WILSON.

It was the intention of Governor Wilson, to occupy a seat among the visitors at the House of Assembly yesterday, in order to witness the procedure and hear the debating. An attack of indigestion, however, prevented him from carrying out his intention. He crossed the ferry to Hamilton from Glen Cove, his temporary residence, but was obliged to return without proceeding to the House.

Printed in the Hamilton, Bermuda, *Royal Gazette*, Nov. 26, 1912.

From Edward Mandell House

Dear Governor: New York City. November 28th, 1912.

I spent two strenuous but interesting days in Washington.

While there I had an hour with Chief Justice White, by appointment, and was with him at dinner later.

Among those that called upon me were Speaker Clark, Hoke Smith, Gore, Culberson, Bob Henry, Burleson, Carter Glass and many others. I mention these by name for each of them had something interesting to say.

Mr. Clark has not gotten over his defeat. He is inclined to be friendly with you but his hatred of Mr. Bryan amounts to an obsession, and it is not unlikely that there will be a personal difficulty between them when they meet.

Almost at the beginning, Clark asked me what you intended to do. I replied "about what?" He said "About anything or everything?" I told him that was a pretty leading question and asked him to be more specific. I finally told him that you intended to carry out the democratic policies, as far as you were able, with the aid of such leaders as himself and others. Before he left he was telling me the story of his life and we were on very cordial terms. I think he would like to be invited to see you when you return and I believe it would be a wise thing to do so.

Senator Smith told me a good deal about Bryan and his talks with him upon his recent visit to Washington. He said he was sure that Bryan would accept an appointment to the Cabinet provided he was asked.

Senator Smith is trying to get on the Finance Committee and he is arranging with Gore and others to control that Committee so that the reactionaries, like Martin, will not be able to block progressive legislation. He told me that he, Gore and some others were determined to have harmony if they had to fight for it, and in the fight had to kill a few of their friends.

I talked to him about Currency Reform and I found his mind in a very nebulous condition. He has no conception of what a sound, economic measure is and rather admitted it before I finished with him. He went off into almost as many vagaries as Mr.

Bryan but I hauled him back and when I left I believe that his mind was in a receptive condition for any measure which you might approve.

Senator Gore, I think, you may count upon to aid you in every way possible. So far, he seems to me to be the most practical and efficient of your friends in the Senate. His Populistic tendencies seem to have disappeared and I see an earnest desire to think straight upon all the leading questions before the Nation.

He is growing more rapidly than any man that I have found within the Party. It is true that he had far to come but it seems to me, that he has arrived.

I had a most interesting hour with Mr. Glass. He candidly confessed that he knew nothing about banking or the framing of a monetery measure. I congratulated him upon this for I told him that it was much better to know nothing than to know something wrong. He, too, indicated a willingness to do everything in his power to give, as speedily as possible, a sound economic bill, and upon lines advised by you.

It was interesting to hear him tell of Bryan and the suggestions made by him. I ran over briefly what I considered might be a satisfactory measure. He replied that it seemed all right but it looked as if I had in mind "central control." I told him that no measure could be efficient that did not have a central control. He then said that the platform forbade it. In this, however, I think he is mistaken.

The platform says "We oppose the so called Aldrich plan for the establishment of a central bank." This does not mean, I take it, that the central banking idea is opposed but that the Aldrich plan for a central bank is opposed.

He expressed a desire to see you soon afer your return and I think the quicker you see him the better it will be. You will find him ready to cooperate with you to the fullest extent.

Harvey was there for the purpose of furthering his plan for a single term.

Mr. Taft favors this and so does Mr. Bryan. Mr. Taft favors a six year term and Mr. Bryan leans to four years. Harvey told me that Bob Henry was working with Bryan along this line and that was going to be our first difficulty. He was very pessimistic. He said that no one knew your viewpoint concerning the matter and that your friends were apathetic and that before they realized it a measure would be passed through both branches of Congress and be ready for submission to the people.

It does not require the signature of the President but if it did Mr. Taft would sign it.

Harvey is mistaken about your friends not being alert in regard to it because I talked to Burleson and others and told them to watch every move.

Harvey thought it would be a wise thing to compromise on a six year term which would include you.

In talking with Gore about it afterwards he said the difficulty there was that the Republican States would hesitate to lengthen the term of a Democratic President two years longer than was necessary. If the republicans refused to lengthen the term of a Democratic President then the Democratic States would, in turn, refuse to lengthen the term of a Republican President.

I suggested that the matter should be so arranged that a President should have two terms of four years each which is far better from either viewpoint and which, I am sure, comes nearer meeting the approval of the people.

Both Gore and Burleson are heartily in favor of this and will work along this line. That, however, is one of the first things that we should take up when you come back because the machinery is already in motion and Bryan and Taft, from different motives, are back of it.

The general concensus of opinion amongst those with whom I talked and who had met Bryan, was that he would work in harmony with your administration if he went into the Cabinet but they all thought that there were two difficulties which should be met at the outset—the question of a second term and the further question of currency reform.

I have something to suggest to you along these lines when I see you but which had best not be written.

I obtained a great deal of valuable information from the Chief Justice. He talked to me frankly with the understanding that what he said was to be repeated to no one excepting you.

He cheerfully slaughtered nearly all the gentlemen about whom I wrote to you in my last letter. And this reminds me that I heard today, from another source, that the Philadelphia lawyer, of whom I spoke, had been guilty of some unprofessional practice a few years ago. Whether this is true or not remains to be demonstrated.

Burleson had occasion to see the President yesterday morning and he told him that he would like for Mrs. Wilson and you to come down sometime, at your convenience, and pay Mrs. Taft and him a visit for a few days. He said it would be well worth your while for the reason that they would be able to explain some things that would be of inestimable value to you in connection with the administration of the White House. He told Burleson to please get an expression from you as to whether it would be pleasant for you to come and in that event he would send you a formal invitation. He did not want to send this in advance for fear that you would accept through courtesy to him.

Burleson asked me to convey this information to you and to get an expression from you so that he may in turn convey it to Mr. Taft.

It is rather a round about method but you will understand.

Mr. Taft told Burleson that he had been able to save $100,-oo[o].oo out of his salary since he has been President.

Your very faithful,   E. M. House

Underwood was not in Washington. He is still in Alabama.

TLS (WP, DLC).

To Joseph Patrick Tumulty

My dear Tumulty: [Bermuda, Nov. 30, 1912]

Thank you again and again for what you are doing. The newspapers have told everybody where I am so the letters are pouring in upon me here in a flood but Swem and I are managing to cope with them.

I am glad to hear your report about the speakership.[1] I hope sincerely that Hennessy may be selected as you expect. Any other solution would make the session very difficult for me.

We are getting on all right and I expect to get back in good shape.

Always affectionately yours,   [Woodrow Wilson]

ICFT transcript of CLSsh (RSB Coll., DLC).

[1] It is missing. He referred, however, to the struggle for the New Jersey Assembly speakership between Charles O'Connor Hennessey, the candidate of the Wilson forces, and Leon R. Taylor, supported by the Smith-Nugent machine. With the entire Essex County delegation behind him, Taylor was elected on December 3. The fact that Hennessey was a local optionist also contributed to his defeat because the brewery lobby threw its support to Taylor. Arthur S. Link, *Wilson: The New Freedom* (Princeton, N. J., 1956), pp. 29-30.

To Edward Mandell House

My dear friend: BERMUDA, November 30, 1912

Thank you warmly for your letters, which reached me last night by the steamer. They contain just the kind of items and memoranda which are most useful to me. Above all, they prove your thoughtfulness and friendship, and that makes me very happy.

We are all well and could rest with very equable minds if the kind American people did not unload their correspondence upon us. Letters come in by the score from people we never heard of, and those whom we know and want to hear from write only as you do with something really to say and with the kind of information and advice that really serves my thinking.

I am delighted that you are making a visit to Washington. You can see so much more than other men do and report it so much better, always getting the right point.

With warmest regard, I am

Affectionately yours,   Woodrow Wilson

TLS (E. M. House Papers, CtY).

To Martin Wiley Littleton[1]

My dear Mr. Littleton: [Bermuda, Nov. 30, 1912]

Not until I reached Bermuda did your interesting letter of November 12th[2] come under my eye. I was obliged to bundle it off with a lot of letters which it had been impossible for me to examine in the rush of the days which followed the election.

I read your letter now with a strange feeling because I have acted just contrary to what you had hoped I would do in the matter of the extraordinary session.[3] I hope sincerely that as the months show what they have in store for us, your fears will turn out to be unfounded. There is a great deal in the reasoning of your letter but I cannot help feeling that the bold and straightforward course leaves no choice but that which I have made.

With much regard,

Sincerely yours,   [Woodrow Wilson]

ICFT transcript of CLSsh (RSB Coll., DLC).
1 Democratic congressman from New York, 1911-13.
2 It is missing.
3 Wilson had announced on November 15 that he would call an extraordinary session of Congress not later than April 15, 1913, in order to redeem party pledges and, "in the interest of business," to remove "all uncertainty as to what the particular items of tariff revision are to be." *New York Times*, Nov. 16, 1912.

To Melancthon Williams Jacobus

My dear Dr. Jacobus: BERMUDA, November 30, 1912

Your two letters gave me genuine pleasure.[1] Your faith in me is very touching to me and contributes greatly, I want you to believe, to my strength as well as to my happiness. To be sustained by friends who have known me is half the battle for any man, and I am grateful for it beyond expression.

I am profoundly interested in what you tell me of the plans of the seminary. I am ashamed to say that I had known little or nothing of them. I shall seek an opportunity to read the pamphlet you sent me, and hope we may be able to talk it over when I get back. It is splendid to know of the chances for an adequate endowment which now lie ahead of you. It shows that a seminary which really wakes up to its opportunity need not lack financial support.

Mrs. Wilson and my daughters join me in most cordial messages, and I am as always

Affectionately and gratefully yours,　Woodrow Wilson

I return the enclosed[2] because my knowledge of you makes me free to do so. There is no expense that can be called political that I can devote it to. I am deeply grateful. You are an ideal friend. God bless you.　　　　　　　　　　　　　　　W.W.

TLS (RSB Coll., DLC).
　[1] M. W. Jacobus to WW, Oct. 2 and Nov. 4, 1912, both ALS (WP, DLC).
　[2] Jacobus had enclosed a check in his letter of Oct. 2, 1912.

To Ambrose White Vernon

My dear Vernon:　　　　　　　　　　　　　[Bermuda, Nov. 30, 1912]

Mrs. Wilson and I were more than gratified, we were very deeply touched, by your letter of November 7th.[1] We have been a long time replying to the letters which came to us after the election but you may be sure that we have never for a moment forgotten those which came so straight from the heart as yours did. We thank you for it very deeply and are particularly grateful that there should be those who have this deep faith in us.

We are off here seeking, and I am happy to say, finding a very grateful rest. Bermuda is an ideal place in which to throw burdens off, burdens of thought and preoccupation. All our little household join in the warmest messages to you both.

Affectionately yours,　[Woodrow Wilson]

ICFT transcript of CLSsh (RSB Coll., DLC).
　[1] It is missing.

To Joseph R. Wilson, Jr.

My dear Brother:　　　　　　　　　　　　[Bermuda, Nov. 30, 1912]

It was delightful to get your letter of the 16th[1] giving us fresh news of you all (at least news as fresh as any that reaches us in this distant place).

You may be sure that our thoughts turn to you and Kate and Alice very very often and with deepest affection.

I cannot help being amused, though sympathetic, about what you tell me of the additions to your mail as a result of the election. I am very much interested in what you tell me about the dinner to be given you. It is thoroughly deserved and I hope will have turned out to be a very happy occasion before this reaches you.

We are all very well. This is an ideal resting place and I could rest completely if people whom I don't know would not do me the left-handed kindness of writing me hundreds of letters even here in my retreat. We are getting refreshed and renewed in spite of them, and I hope that by the time the 14th rolls around, when we are to sail back, we shall be in fine fettle.

All join in warmest love to all,

Affectionately yours,   [Woodrow Wilson]

ICFT transcript of CLSsh (RSB Coll., DLC).
¹ J. R. Wilson, Jr. to WW, Nov. 16, 1912, TLS (WP, DLC).

To James W. Bones

My dear Uncle James: [Bermuda, Nov. 30, 1912]

Your letter gave me unqualified pleasure.¹ It has just been forwarded to me here in Bermuda where I am seeking a little rest and recreation before plunging into the formidable duties which await me.

It was delightful to hear from you and to learn that you were in good health. It renewed so many memories and gave me a vivid impression once more of the old days in Augusta and Rome, which I remember so vividly and with such deep pleasure. May God bless and keep you.

Ellen and the girls join me in most affectionate messages.

Affectionately yours,   [Woodrow Wilson]

ICFT transcript of CLSsh (RSB Coll., DLC).
¹ It is missing.

To Jessie Bones Brower

My dear Jessie: [Bermuda, Nov. 30, 1912]

I actually never saw your letter¹ until today. Here it is with a big bundle of stuff that has been forwarded to me from Trenton by my secretary there.

It gives me a great deal of happiness. I need not tell you how delighted I was to hear from you. It would make me very happy if I might see you and talk things over with you. Your letter seems to express my own feeling. I am a bit frightened myself to think of the terrible responsibilities ahead of me and I need all the confidence and affection I can have to sustain me. I wish that you were still in Chicago for I am coming out there in January[2] and I might have a chance to see you if only for a few minutes.

All join me in warmest messages and I am as ever,
Your affectionate cousin,   [Woodrow Wilson]

ICFT transcript of CLSsh (RSB Coll., DLC).
  [1] It is missing.
  [2] On January 11, 1913, when he was to speak to the Commercial Club.

To Anita McCormick Blaine

My dear Mrs. Blaine: BERMUDA, November 30, 1912

Your gracious letter of the 16th of November,[1] written the very day I sailed for Bermuda, reached me only last evening. I want to thank you for it very warmly. It is the voice of a friend not only, but of a friend whose good will and whose opinions I peculiarly value, for I know how sincerely you think and how candidly you speak.

The spirit of the letter is just what I would have expected from you, and I hope with all my heart that its counsel will be practicable to live upon. Unfortunately, the President can do only what the men he is acting with will join him in doing, but at least a beginning can be made in the direction you point out, and I shall try with all my might to make it.

With warmest appreciation, I am
Cordially and sincerely yours,   Woodrow Wilson

TLS (Anita M. Blaine Papers, WHi).
  [1] It is missing.

To Homer Stillé Cummings

My dear Mr. Cummings: [Bermuda, Nov. 30, 1912]

Anybody who speaks in behalf of Josephus Daniels[1] speaks to my heart as well as to my head. I have a real affection for him as well as a very high opinion of him and you may be sure that suggestions such as yours carry great weight with me.

With much regard,
Cordially and sincerely yours,   [Woodrow Wilson]

ICFT transcript of CLSsh (RSB Coll., DLC).
  [1] Cummings' letter is missing.

To James L. Curtis[1]

My dear Sir: [Bermuda, Nov. 30, 1912]

I very much appreciate the invitation of the banquet committee of the National Colored Democratic League to be present at a banquet to be tendered the Right Reverend Alexander Walters, LL.D., D.D., in recognition of his service to the Democratic forces in the recent campaign but my absence from the country will make it impossible for me to be present.

I formed the highest opinion of Bishop Walters' ability and public spirit during the campaign.

[Sincerely yours,   Woodrow Wilson]

ICFT transcript of CLSsh (RSB Coll., DLC).
 [1] Lawyer of New York, secretary of the executive committee of the National Colored Democratic League.

To Francis James Grimké[1]

My dear Mr. Grimké: [Bermuda, Nov. 30, 1912]

Thank you sincerely for your letter of November 20th.[2] It has given me genuine pleasure. I believe with you that only the Christian spirit can clear up the doubts and difficulties that have surrounded the life of our colored fellow citizens.

Sincerely yours,   [Woodrow Wilson]

ICFT transcript of CLSsh (RSB Coll., DLC).
 [1] Negro leader, pastor of the 15th Street Presbyterian Church of Washington, and trustee of Howard University.
 [2] It is missing.

From William Frank McCombs

[New York, Nov. 30, 1912]

Associated Press dispatch from Bermuda makes statement you desire that you be formally sworn in as President on March 4, but that you have decided or prefer the inaugural exercises to take place on April 24. The newspapermen have interviewed me and I have stated that I have not received any word from you in the matter. The short session of Congress must pass before Christmas certain necessary bills affecting the arrangements and many members are urging an immediate action. Is interview authentic? I think it would be advisable if you would cable me your wishes fully.   William McCombs

ICFT transcript of CLSsh (RSB Coll., DLC).

To William Frank McCombs

My dear McCombs: [Bermuda, Nov. 30, 1912]

I have just received your cablegram. I assure you the reporters here have been so short of material that they have drawn upon their fancies. In a conversation the other day with them I did say that I thought that it would be much better and that certainly it would be most agreeable to me if the formal or rather public inauguration might take place later than March 4, but I expressed no wish in the matter and never dreamed that this expression of personal preference would be cabled to the United States. It is extremely annoying to me to have these men constantly exciting comment in the United States over my casual remarks.

I am having a very restful and profitable time down here by not only doing nothing but getting many kinks out of my head.

Always,   Faithfully yours,   [Woodrow Wilson]

ICFT transcript of CLSsh (RSB Coll., DLC).

To Magnus Fraser Peterson

My dear Friend: [Bermuda, Nov. 30, 1912]

Your letter of November 15th[1] has found me here in this little resting place in mid-ocean. I thank you for it with all my heart. It came as the voice of a friend for whom I have a genuine affection as well as a great admiration and you may be sure it cheered me accordingly. I seem to need my friends now for my spiritual support more than I ever did before and it is delightful to have them think of me and turn their thoughts towards me at this time of test and responsibility.

How delightful it would be if I could have a fortnight on the "Fells" but I fear it is past praying for. Mrs. Wilson joins me in all cordial messages to Mrs. Peterson[2] and yourself and the boys.[3] I hope that everything goes well with you and that Grasmere is as rewarding a parish as it is a resting place.

With warmest regards,

Faithfully yours,   [Woodrow Wilson]

ICFT transcript of CLSsh (RSB Coll., DLC).
  [1] It is missing.
  [2] Emily O'Hanlon Peterson.
  [3] John Magnus Peterson and Geofrey Fraser Peterson.

To Mary Allen Hulbert

Dearest Friend, "Glencove," 1 Dec., 1912

I wonder if my last letter (addressed, after all, to Nantucket)[1] reached you? I was very uncertain about your movements and whereabouts.

Allen[2] arrived, with his boat. I dare say he was quite anxious about her on the way down, for they had an exceedingly rough passage and *anything* on the deck, no matter how well secured, must have had a hard time to hold on. There must have been a few hours of real anxiety for everybody, the captain and all old hands included. The Bermudian shows salt stains to the top of her funnels. Allen looks very well indeed. He got his boat off all right,—after a good deal of trouble, it seems,—and turned up this morning with her at this little landing, looking very handsome in his tweeds and shorts. I tried to keep him for dinner but he was promised to the Trimminghams[3] (*what* an ass Tom T. is, and yet what an amiable good fellow!) We were just starting out for church and saw him only for a moment. The boat looks very stout and businesslike in the water,—but a bit dark and piratical!

I shall try to see a good deal of Allen, though we are getting caught in the whirl down here, despite our efforts to keep out, and letters which have to be answered come pouring in by the hundreds with every boat. It is a merciful dispensation of Providence, for us, that the boats are as yet few and far between! My stenographer has intermitent fever in the distribution of his work and will hardly see the sun now till the boat goes out on Tuesday. And the "Oruba" comes in to-morrow (Monday)!

Yesterday there was a great garden party at Government House, an exceedingly pretty sight, though the sky was overcast and a chill wind blew out of the East. The Governor and his Lady are simple, delightful people and the A.D.C.[4] is a delightful chap, too, naïve and diverting.

I am so glad to think of you as at the Hot Springs. It is just the place to get the fatigue out of muscles and mind. You will feel like a new creature and be made ready to enjoy your dear Bermuda,—how dear it is! It never loses or abates its charm and my dear ones love it as much as I do. No small part of our enjoyment is due to your own generous kindness, for this charming cottage gives us a real home, of which we [were] instantly fond, and we are deeply grateful to you for it.

I do not believe a team of horses or all the king's horses and all the king's men could detain Ellen and the children in New York when we go back, but we shall see you, of course, if you are there. Are you giving yourself the full time for the "cure." *Please* do so! All join me in affectionate messages. My love to Mrs. A.

Your devoted friend   Woodrow Wilson

ALS (WP, DLC).
 [1] That is, his letter of Nov. 22, 1912. It was forwarded to Mrs. Hulbert in New York.
 [2] Her son.
 [3] Thomas Darrell Trimingham and Elizabeth Fenton Trimingham. He was owner of Trimingham Brothers, Ltd., the leading Hamilton department store.
 [4] Lt. P. R. B. Laurence.

To William Howard Taft

My dear Mr. President,   Bermuda, 2 Dec., 1912

Your gracious letter, written on Thanksgiving Day,[1] reached me by the steamer that came in to-day.

You are exceedingly kind and we thank you, Mrs. Wilson and I, most warmly for your thought of our pleasure. But, alas! when my remaining two weeks here are over I shall have exhausted my liberty. The legislature of New Jersey meets early in January and I am pledged to devote all my energies between now and the fourth of March to putting through important business there. This, with what I must do to get ready for my duties in Washington, will consume every hour at my disposal. I feel that, in the circumstances, I ought to deny myself the trip to Panama,[2] greatly as I should enjoy and benefit by it, and that it is doubtful whether I ought to give myself even the indulgence of a day off at Washington to enjoy your hospitality, so graciously offered. I shall have my nose to the grindstone!

Mrs. Wilson and I deeply appreciate your kindness. We are denying ourselves a real pleasure. But I know what a legislative session at Trenton means and it seems a clear duty not to leave the task.

May I not express also my admiration, as well as my deep thanks, for your generous reference to me in your speech at Arlington?[3] It gratified me deeply. It was characteristic of you!

With warm regard,

Sincerely Yours,   Woodrow Wilson

ALS (W. H. Taft Papers, DLC).
 [1] It is missing in both the Wilson and Taft Papers, DLC.
 [2] There had been much discussion in the press about a contemplated trip to inspect the Panama Canal.
 [3] He referred to Taft's speech on November 12, 1912, to the United Daughters of the Confederacy at the opening session of their annual convention at Constitution Hall in Washington. Taft said that the Wilson admihistration would give the South a greater feeling of participation in the government than there had been during the Republican regime, and that that would do much toward

eliminating sectional feeling. Taft had helped to lay the cornerstone of a monument to Confederate veterans at Arlington National Cemetery.

Remarks to the Bermuda House of Assembly

[[Dec. 2, 1912]]

I had hoped I might forget, during my stay in Bermuda, that I was able to make a speech, but I cannot refrain from expressing my extreme pleasure at the courtesy with which I have been received. I was interested in the debate and wondered if we every year went through the items of expenditure and revenue for the twelve months there would be a continuous performance which would exceed all the theatres could ever produce, but the idea is an admirable one because it affords the House constant opportunity to review the changing circumstances of the Colony. One of the Members told me he was sorry I had hit upon so dull a sitting. I did not consider it so. I have been a student of parliamentary procedure for years and the slight difference in the procedure to what I am used to was very interesting to me. I admired the businesslike manner of getting through the estimates of expenditure and revenue. I had almost begun to feel Bermuda were one of my homes, and therefore it is all the more delightful to me to be received in this manner. I thank you.

Printed in the Hamilton, Bermuda, *Royal Gazette*, Dec. 3, 1912.

From the Minutes of the Faculty of Princeton University

[Princeton, N. J.] December 2, 1912

Mr. Ormond, chairman of the Special Committee appointed to draw up resolutions of congratulation to President Elect Woodrow Wilson, read the following resolution, which on motion of the Dean of the College was adopted:

"We, the Faculty of Princeton University, take pleasure in congratulating you on your election to the Presidency of the United States, and in expressing our sense of the honor reflected on this University by the elevation of one of its graduates, so long and prominently associated with its life, to the highest office in the gift of the American people.

"We desire to assure you of our continued interest and sympathy in the difficult and responsible work to which you have been called, and to extend to you our best wishes for a distinguished and successful administration of the affairs of the Nation."
V. Lansing Collins   Clerk

"Minutes of the University Faculty of Princeton University, Beginning September, 1902, Ending June, 1914," bound minute book (UA, NjP).

To Sun Yat-sen[1]

My dear Sir: [Bermuda, Dec. 3, 1912]

It was with peculiar pleasure that I received your gracious telegram of November 16th[2] and I beg that you will attribute my long delay in acknowledging it not to neglect but only to the extraordinary demands upon my time and energies since the election.

Permit me to say that I have watched with the keenest interest the recent course of events in China and have felt the strongest sympathy with every movement which looks towards giving the people of the great Empire of China the liberty for which they have so long been yearning and preparing themselves.

With sincere personal respect,

Cordially,   [Woodrow Wilson]

ICFT transcript of CLSsh (RSB Coll., DLC).
   [1] A leading figure in the Chinese Revolution of 1911 which brought down the Manchu dynasty. He served briefly as Provisional President of the new Chinese Republic, resigning in 1912.
   [2] It is missing.

To Edward Mandell House

My dear friend: BERMUDA, December 3, 1912

Your memoranda from Washington are most interesting and helpful. They set my thought going, and I hope I shall have thought something out by the time we meet again and have one of our profitable talks.

Everything goes well with us here and we think constantly of dear and faithful friends.

Affectionately yours,   Woodrow Wilson

TLS (E. M. House Papers, CtY).

To Curtis Guild, Jr.[1]

My dear Mr. Guild: BERMUDA, December 3, 1912

Allow me to acknowledge the receipt of your letter of November 6th[2] apprising me of your generous intention to set me entirely free in the matter of the representation of the United States at the Court of Russia, and to say that I appreciate very sincerely your thoughtful courtesy and public spirit in the matter.

I realize very fully the critical character of the situation with regard to the relations between our own government and the government of Russia. Of course, I have no acquaintance with details and I should welcome the opportunity to acquaint myself very fully with what is in your own mind and has fallen under your own observation while in St. Petersburg. Indeed, I feel it essential that I should know these matters in order that my thought and purposes may not go astray.

I feel that it is absolutely inconsistent with either the dignity or the principles of our own government to enter into any treaty relations with the government of Russia which would permit the treatment of one class of our citizens in one way and all other classes in another,[3] but the difficulties to be faced and overcome in working out the right agreement it is indispensable that I should understand very thoroughly.

I will very seriously consider the question whether I shall ask you to return to the United States before my inauguration for consultation or not, and so hope to write to you later.

With much regard,

Sincerely yours,   Woodrow Wilson

TLS (C. Guild, Jr., Papers, MHi).
   [1] United States Ambassador to Russia.
   [2] It is missing.
   [3] About the matter of Russian discrimination against American Jewish citizens, see WW to H. Bernstein, July 6, 1911, Vol. 23, n. 2.

To Champ Clark

My dear Mr. Speaker: [Bermuda, Dec. 3, 1912]

Your kind letter of November 25th[1] forwarded to me here gave me a great deal of pleasure, and I thank you for it most sincerely. I am expecting to land in New York again on the 16th of December and I want to have if possible a conference with you very soon after that date. I am going to give myself the pleasure of dropping you a note within a short time after my landing in order to find out when and where it will be most convenient for us to meet. There are many things to be talked over.

Cordially and sincerely yours,   [Woodrow Wilson]

ICFT transcript of CLSsh (RSB Coll., DLC).
   [1] It is missing.

To Ira Remsen

My dear Dr. Remsen: [Bermuda, Dec. 3, 1912]

Thank you for your letter of November 16th.[1] I feel so earnestly what I wrote about Fine that I hope the trustees will give me an opportunity to say something about him whenever they take the matter up.

You may be sure that I shall be delighted to talk public matters over with you at any time that we can get together.

Unfortunately I had to decline the alumni invitation. I have denied myself the pleasure of going to any public function between now and the fourth of March next except two to which I had imprudently committed myself months ago. I am heartily sorry that I had to decline in this case.

Cordially and sincerely yours,   [Woodrow Wilson]

ICFT transcript of CLSsh (RSB Coll., DLC).
   [1] It is missing.

To George Fred Williams

My dear Mr. Williams: [Bermuda, Dec. 3, 1912]

Your letter of November 14th[1] has at last reached me here after passing through the flood of letters at Trenton. It gratifies me very much indeed and I want to thank you for it most sincerely. I must confess that I was genuinely puzzled by your one-time complete misunderstanding of my character and impulses and I am very much reassured by what you write.

[Sincerely yours,   Woodrow Wilson]

ICFT transcript of CLSsh (RSB Coll., DLC).
   [1] It is missing.

To Thomas Dixon, Jr.

My dear Dixon: [Bermuda, Dec. 3, 1912]

You may be sure that what you say[1] about Josephus Daniels appeals to my heart as well as to my head. I have known him long enough to love him. He is pure gold and I shall think very seriously about what there is for us to do in connection with the next administration.

It is very gratifying to me that you should feel as you do about me and about what there is for me to accomplish and I can tell you that it went straight to my heart that you should have thought of dedicating your book to me.[2]

Faithfully yours,   [Woodrow Wilson]

ICFT transcript of CLSsh (RSB Coll., DLC).
[1] Dixon's letter is missing.
[2] Dixon's *The Southerner: A Romance of the Real Lincoln* (New York and London, 1913) had the following dedication: "Dedicated to Our First Southern-Born President since Lincoln, My Friend and Collegemate, Woodrow Wilson."

To George Howe III

My dear George: BERMUDA, December 3, 1912

I would have acknowledged your cable[1] long ago if I had not forgotten or misplaced your address. I did not like to send a letter at a venture, like an arrow shot in the air.

I need not tell you, my dear boy, how happy your feeling about me makes me. Ellen received your letter to her and wants me to join her messages to mine. She, dear lady, will not as yet consent to learn to dictate letters and is quite overwhelmed at trying to write everything with her own hand.

We think of you often and most affectionately. I hope that you will not curtail your stay abroad, because I feel it is so valuable to you for refreshment and renewal, but we shall count upon you when you are on your way home again to stop with us as long as you can in Washington. There will be a very warm welcome for you there.

I look forward to the duties awaiting me in Washington with many grave thoughts, but having sought the opportunity I must face it and meet it with the best that is in me. In such circumstances I feel particularly grateful for affection and confidence such as you so generously extend to me.

We are all very well and are off here in Bermuda seeking a little rest and an entire change of scene before plunging into the maelstrom ahead of us. All unite in the most affectionate messages, and I am as always

Yours most affectionately,   Woodrow Wilson

TLS (WP, DLC).
[1] It is missing.

To Joseph Patrick Tumulty

My dear Tumulty: BERMUDA, December 3, 1912

Thank you for your memorandum of November 28th.[1] The situation with regard to the treasurership is indeed extraordinary,[2] and I have tried to give an intimation of my own feeling in the matter confidentially to the editors of the Newark Evening News. It is very unpalatable to me to fight Edwards in any way, for

I have a very cordial feeling towards him, but it seems to me imperatively necessary that we should put Grosscup into this position.

I sincerely hope that your anticipations as to the speakership fight are well grounded, as I dare say they are. I should be very much mortified to lose in that contest.

Everything goes serenely with us here so far, and we think very often of you and your little flock.

Affectionately yours,   Woodrow Wilson

TLS (J. P. Tumulty Papers, DLC).
¹ It is missing.
² He referred to another clash between the Wilson and Nugent forces—this time over the election of a state treasurer. On January 15, 1913, the Democratic legislative caucus overwhelmingly approved Wilson's candidate, Edward E. Grosscup, over Nugent's man, Edward I. Edwards. Legislative confirmation followed thirteen days later. Link, *The New Freedom*, p. 32.

To Royal Meeker

My dear Professor Meeker: BERMUDA, December 3, 1912

I like your suggestion very much indeed,¹ and if you could put together something like a collation of opinions on the part of really competent economists throughout the country with regard to the character and particulars of a currency and banking bill, it would serve my thought in just the way in which it needs to be served. It is generous of you to suggest that you undertake it.

Sincerely yours,   Woodrow Wilson

TLS (WP, DLC).
¹ It is missing.

To Walter N. Alexander¹

My dear Sir: [Bermuda, Dec. 3, 1912]

In reply to your letter of November 19th² I would say that in my opinion your true stuff will be shown when you come out again. It ought to be as possible then as it was at any other time to show the man that is in you. If you really believe in God and in the performance of duty that plain path will lie before you. You will know better than I do whether the community in which you have lived is the right community in which to begin over again or not, but the moral and the hope are the same in any case. I trust with all my heart that you will see it in this light and go forward.

[Sincerely yours,   Woodrow Wilson]

ICFT transcript of CLSsh (RSB Coll., DLC).
    [1] At this time incarcerated in the county jail in Marietta, Ohio.
    [2] It is missing.

To Albert Shaw

My dear Shaw: BERMUDA, December 6, 1912

This little line of grateful acknowledgment will not sufficiently express my feeling about your fine and candid letter of November 27th,[1] but it is all I will write at present, because I shall hope some day to have a long talk with you about the things that are ahead of me. I thank you with all my heart. It was just the kind of letter I like to receive, and it was full of the feeling of the genuine old friendship.

Faithfully yours,   Woodrow Wilson

TLS (A. Shaw Coll., NjP).
    [1] A. Shaw to WW, Nov. 27, 1912, TLS (WP, DLC), an affectionate letter saying, among other things, that in spite of their friendship he had voted for Roosevelt.

From Edward Mandell House

Dear Governor: New York City. December 6th, 1912.

Your letter of December first comes to me today.

I feel guilty of having done my share towards breaking in upon your rest, and although I have much to say I will leave it until we meet and content myself with thanking you for your words of appreciation.

They quicken my already keen desire to have your administration succeed beyond that of any other, and my endeavors are leavened by an affection for you deeper than I can well express.

Your very faithful,   [E. M. House]

CCL (E. M. House Papers, CtY).

From Joseph Patrick Tumulty

My dear Governor: Trenton, N. J. December 6, 1912.

The salient facts that will interest you in the speakership controversy which resulted in the selection of Mr. Leon Taylor, of Monmouth county, are the following:

Nugent came to the State House early on Tuesday morning and informed me that his twelve men were willing to support Hennessy if we would support Martin[1] for leader of the majority.

I told him that we would much prefer going down to defeat than to support Martin, or in any way counternancing his selection, and that it would be far more important for the friends of Governor Wilson to see to it that Martin was beaten for the leadership than to seek the speakership by any deal or compromise of this character.

Nugent was exceedingly decent about it all and labored with Martin for over an hour to get him to release him (Nugent) but Martin was obdurate and insisted upon holding Nugent to his promise. Nugent finally yielded to Martin and Taylor to enter into a combination on the leadership and speakership, and they corraled enough votes to put their slate through as far as it affected the speakership.

The counties that supported Nugent are as follows: Essex, Hudson (three Wedin[2] votes), Hunterdon, Mercer, Monmouth (Crater)[3] Passaic (Hinchliffe), Sussex, Union (Collins),[4] Warren.

The counties that stood by you in the controversy are: Bergen, Camden, Cape May, Cumberland, Hudson (nine votes—Wittpen's friends), Middlesex, Morris, Salem, Somerset.

Since your departure I had held frequent conferences with the State Chairman,[5] your friends in New Jersey, and U. S. Senator Hughes, and they all agreed to lend a helping hand, although Billy Hughes frankly admitted that he was afraid that any part that he might play in this fight would injure his chances for the senatorship.

I was informed by the State Chairman that everything was all right on Monday night, and exacted from him and Judge Hudspeth a promise that they would be in Trenton early on Tuesday morning to aid in making the fight against Nugent and his allies. I arrived in Trenton at nine o'clock on Tuesday morning and was surprised to find that up to 11:30 none of the above gentlemen appeared, and in sheer desperation I called to my aid Job Lippincott, Jim Kerney of the Trenton Times, and Barney Gannon of Middlesex County[6] to help me. To those who came to me asking for advice I clearly defined the issue. It was Progress against Reaction—Governor Wilson against Jim Nugent, Smith and his allies. It was for the upholding of that issue, which soon developed into a fight, that I agreed to lead where others refused to follow.

Nugent was insistent upon putting Mr. Martin over for the leadership, but after a desperate struggle we succeeded in beating Martin. It is impossible for me at this writing, my dear Governor, to picture to you the scenes that were enacted in the State

House that morning and to find that your friends whom you treated with such generosity were afraid to make a fight because they feared the antagonism of Mr. Nugent.

Taylor, I think, is pretty sick of the plight he finds himself in and would undoubtedly have done what we expected him to do, but for the insistence of his ardent friends who kept him in the fight to the finish.

The thing of real importance to us, I feel confident, was the defeat of Martin. Had we been willing to yield on this question we could have won the speakership easily.

The papers have exaggerated, as they generally do, the meeting between Mr. Martin and myself. This was an incident that I regretted very much, but it was something that I feel free to say I could not have avoided and have retained my own self-respect. While I was talking to Sheriff Wedin, Martin, who had been engaged in bulldozing members for the past week, came along and asked me what I was saying to Sheriff Wedin with reference to him. I turned and told him that Sheriff Wedin had asked me what the Governor's attitude was toward him (Martin). I frankly told Martin to his face that he had not shown himself to be your friend and that after you had treated him so generously at the primaries he had attacked you personally. He denied that he had been against you at the primaries, and followed this brazen denial up by telling me that he would assault me and raised his fist to carry out his threat. It was then that I simply defended myself.

Taylor is so nervous over the lacing that is being given him in the various newspapers that he will lean backwards in his efforts to do what is wanted.

Since the caucus I have been criticised for having been "too aggressive" by the gentlemen who did not have nerve enough to take part in this fight on Tuesday in an effort to sustain you and your policies. I shall not attempt to defend myself against this charge, because I feel that my conduct as your representative is justly open to criticism at all times, but unless that criticism comes from your real friends I shall consider it as an attempt on the part of those who deserted us to rid themselves of a responsibility which is properly theirs.

I can only say in defense of myself that I made the best fight I could, with motives that no true friends of yours can justly question. I had to fight like a rat in a corner. If I had yielded at all it would have been to compromise with the men who are your enemies and against popular government in New Jersey.

I cannot speak too highly of the loyalty in this fight of such men as Mr. Griffin of Hoboken,[7] Barney Gannon of Middlesex County, and Mayor Wittpen; they never yielded for a moment and were our consistent friends through[ou]t. Jim Kerney was also our loyal friend throughout and left his business that morning to take part in the fight.

I am sending you herewith copy of letter from Mr. Hennessey in reference to the speakership.

You need not answer this letter.

Very sincerely yours,   [J. P. Tumulty]

CCL (J. P. Tumulty Papers, DLC).
    [1] That is, Assemblyman Thomas F. Martin of Weehawken.
    [2] The votes of friends of Sheriff Nicholas P. Wedin of Hudson County.
    [3] David S. Crater of Freehold, surrogate of Monmouth County.
    [4] Dennis F. Collins of Elizabeth, member of the Democratic State Committee. He was not in the legislature.
    [5] Edward E. Grosscup.
    [6] Bernard M. Gannon, county clerk.
    [7] Thomas F. A. Griffin, assemblyman from Jersey City.

Two Letters to Joseph Patrick Tumulty

My dear Tumulty: BERMUDA, December 11, 1912

I hope with all my heart that you will not distress yourself about the outcome of the caucus. I approve and applaud what you did in every respect, and am deeply sorry and disappointed that you should have been made to carry the fight practically alone. No one can justly criticise anything that you did and I shall say so when I get home.

This is just a line to catch you, if possible, before I myself do. I enclose you a check for $500 for the office expenses. You may be sure it would have gone sooner if there had been any boat to carry it.

In haste   Affectionately yours,   Woodrow Wilson

TLS (J. P. Tumulty Papers, DLC).

❖

My dear Tumulty: [Bermuda, Dec. 11, 1912]

May I impose upon you a little task? The enclosed letter excites my sympathy and I hope it will be possible for you to put it in the hands of somebody in or near Surf City who can clear it up and enable us to ascertain whether the poor woman can be helped or not in her difficulty. We all join in warmest messages.   [Sincerely yours,   Woodrow Wilson]

ICFT transcript of CLSsh (RSB Coll., DLC).

To Josephus Daniels

Personal

My dear Friend: [Bermuda, Dec. 11, 1912]

The editorial[1] about the make-up of the next Senate was exactly what I had been looking around for and I had not been able to find and serves my thought admirably. I thank you for it heartily.

I am deeply rejoiced to learn that Mrs. Daniels and the boys[2] are really well again. I congratulate you with all my heart, and Mrs. Wilson joins in every cordial message.

[Cordially and faithfully yours,   Woodrow Wilson]

ICFT transcript of CLSsh (RSB Coll., DLC).

[1] "How the Senate Stands," Raleigh *News and Observer*, Dec. 3, 1912. This editorial contained a table of the make-up of the Senate in the next Congress, showing forty-nine Democrats, forty-five Republicans, with the two Illinois seats in doubt. The editorial predicted that most progressive Republican senators would be found working with Wilson and their Democratic colleagues for genuine reform legislation, and it concluded: "The fear that the Senate—so long the Citadel of Privilege—would thwart the reform policies that President Wilson and the Democratic House will favor seems to have no foundation to give anxiety to the forces that have enlisted for the war against Privilege and Monopoly and Favoritism."

[2] Addie Worth Bagley (Mrs. Josephus) Daniels, Josephus, Jr., Worth Bagley, Jonathan Worth, and Frank Arthur Daniels.

To Joseph R. Wilson, Jr.

My dearest Brother: [Bermuda, Dec. 11, 1912]

Your letter of December 4th[1] distresses me a bit for I had already written to you from here and the letter must have miscarried or been strangely delayed. You know we cannot send out mail whenever we please. There is a boat only every five or six days and the boats run to no port but New York.

There is no way, therefore, alas, of returning home by way of Nashville to be present at the dinner on the 13th.[2] Indeed I could not if I would get back by that time because the next boat sails on the 14th, there being an unusually long interval between boats this week.

I have sent a short cable which I hope will get there in time and you may be sure that I shall think of you that evening. It is delightful that your friends should pay you this attention and you certainly have earned their admiration.

It was delightful to hear something from you about the dear family. Our thoughts turn to you again and again with deep and lasting affection.

We are all well. I have not been permitted to do very much resting down here but I have at least got away from some things that would have gripped and captured me and feel that the trip has been of a great deal of benefit to me and to all of us.

[Affectionately yours,   Woodrow Wilson]

ICFT transcript of CLSsh (RSB Coll., DLC).
  1 It is missing.
  2 A dinner to honor Joseph R. Wilson, Jr., for his part in the campaign.

To Nicholas L. Piotrowski

My dear Mr. Piotrowski: [Bermuda, Dec. 11, 1912]

The contents of your letter of December 3rd[1] gave me, I need hardly tell you, deep and genuine pleasure. The Polish vote was certainly most extraordinary, and I think in no small part due to your own unselfish efforts. I feel like congratulating you upon it as an evidence of your own insight and your own extended influence. I know how enthusiastically and unsparingly you worked in the matter. It is an inspiring record of loyalty and good work.

Cordially and faithfully yours,   [Woodrow Wilson]

P.S. I enclose the interesting letters you were kind enough to let me see.

ICFT transcript of CLSsh (RSB Coll., DLC).
  1 It is missing.

To Varnum Lansing Collins

My dear Mr. Collins   Bermuda, December 11, 1912.

Allow me to acknowledge the receipt of your letter of December 3d containing a copy of the resolutions adopted by the Faculty of the University at a meeting held December 2, 1912, concerning my election to the presidency of the United States. I need hardly tell you that there is no body of men from whom I would rather have received a message of friendly congratulation, and I wish that there were some adequate means of expressing my deep appreciation.

Sincerely yours   Woodrow Wilson

HwCL in "Minutes of the University Faculty of Princeton University, Beginning September, 1902, Ending June, 1914," bound minute book (UA, NjP).

To George Lockhart Rives[1]

My dear Mr. Rives: [Bermuda, Dec. 11, 1912]

I can not resist the very gracious invitation signed by yourself, Mr. Choate, Mr. Brownell[2] and others of my fellow members of the Round Table Club and beg to say that I shall confidently hope to give myself the pleasure of attending the meeting of the Club on January 31st next. It will be very delightful to look forward to the meeting particularly since I know that it is altogether private and there will be none of the publicity about it from which I am now suffering so many things.[3]

   Cordially and sincerely yours, [Woodrow Wilson]

ICFT transcript of CLSsh (RSB Coll., DLC).
 [1] Lawyer of New York and director of several banks and title and mortgage companies.
 [2] Joseph Hodges Choate of New York, Ambassador to Great Britain, 1899-1905; William Crary Brownell, literary adviser for Charles Scribner's Sons.
 [3] About Wilson's discussion at this meeting with Choate and Elihu Root concerning the Anglo-American dispute over Panama Canal tolls, see Link, *The New Freedom*, p. 306.

From William Jennings Bryan

My Dear Gov,   Miami, Florida Dec 12 [1912]

In compliance with your invitation[1] I shall be pleased to call at Trenton at any time after Thursday that will suit your convenience. I shall be at Wilmington N. C. on next Monday evening at Winston Salem, N. C. on Tuesday evening, at Ashville N. C. on Wednesday evening and at Richmond Va on Thursday evening. I can leave Richmond & reach Trenton Friday morning. Shall be at your service Friday & Saturday &, while I would like to spend Sunday in Washington & start back to Florida on Sunday night I can stay North longer if I can be of any service to you. Please wire me at one of the places named informing me of your pleasure.

I hope you have had an enjoyable rest but I fear the office seekers have been on your trail. From the number of requests I have rec'd your mail must be a great burden.

I attend the Sulzer dinner in N.Y. evening of 21st[.] Mrs. Bryan joins in regards to your family.

     Yours truly W. J. Bryan

ALS (WC, NjP).
 [1] It is missing.

Charles Willis Thompson to Reuben Adiel Bull[1]

Dear Rube: [Bermuda] Dec. 12, 1912.

. . . We're going back to the States next week, so don't you write me any letters here. And I'm sorry to go. I'd like to stay in this lotus land another month. I've got to the feeling that nothing matters a hang, and I don't care whether school keeps or not. The Governor was expatiating on that the other day. "This is an unreal country," he said. "It's a land of witchcraft, a fairy land, a land of make-believe. Why, I give you my word, sometimes when I've been down here and have wanted to get my attention on prosaic matters of business I haven't been able to think of them until—I'm speaking the literal truth—I'd close down all the blinds so that I couldn't see Bermuda and turned on the electric lights. Then I could imagine myself back in the United States, and get back to realities by creating what in fact was an unreal and artificial atmosphere."

He was talking to Van Slyke,[2] Mitchell and me. Van and I mentally registered a telling point for our mail stories; but Mitchell incautiously asked, "Can we print that, Governor?" A look of alarm overspread his face. "Lord, no!" he cried. "If the people who read it were down here and could get the atmosphere it would be all right and they would understand it. But anybody outside of Bermuda and in a more prosaic land would simply think I had gone crazy." Another good story gone wrong. . . .   Be good,   Chas.

CCL (C. W. Thompson Papers, NjP).
   [1] Of Brooklyn, an employee of the Pennsylvania Railroad.
   [2] George Martin Van Slyke, political correspondent of the *New York Herald*.

From Carter Glass

Dear Governor Wilson: Washington. December 14, 1912.

I am reluctant to add to your burdens or to contribute to the annoyances with which I know you are beset; but I feel obliged to again draw your attention to the matter concerning which I wrote you just before your departure for Bermuda. If we are to have a reformation of the currency at the extra session of Congress which I assume will be called, it is imperative that the sub-committee of the Banking and Currency Committee of the House, of which I am chairman, shall proceed as expeditiously as the great importance of the subject will permit. The committee has been meeting and exchanging views and has arranged for a series of hearings beginning with the week of

January 6th. As I have already stated, it is the judgment of the committee that we should not proceed far with the work of constructing a currency bill before we shall have learned something of your views. I would, therefore, be glad if you will, at your earliest convenience, indicate when I may have an interview with you on the subject. Should you assent to the interview, I would like to bring with me Prof. H. Parker Willis, whose services as a currency expert thoroughly familiar with the subject have been engaged by the committee.

Trusting that you enjoyed your brief vacation and may be able cheerfully to withstand the perplexities of the great task before you, I am,   Sincerely yours,   Carter Glass

TLS (WP, DLC).

A News Report

[Dec. 16, 1912]

TANNED BY SUN, WILSON RETURNS IN FINE HEALTH

NEW YORK, Dec. 16.—The steamship Bermudian, with President-elect Wilson and family on board, arrived safely early today, but was held at Quarantine until nearly 8 o'clock. The vessel then proceeded to her dock. There was the usual crush of curiosity seekers to see the Governor leave the pier.

The steamer warped into the pier on time and the Wilson party was greeted by Miss Margaret Wilson, the daughter who had not accompanied her parents; Mr. and Mrs. Dudley Field Malone, and Joseph P. Tumulty. The customs officials had made arrangments to expedite the baggage of the party through the lines and there was no delay.

All had the usual tropical tan, and the Governor declared that he is more than satisfied with the trip. He said he had rested well and felt fine. It was a "real vacation," he said, "and we all feel ready for anything.". . .

Governor Wilson and his family went in an automobile to the Waldorf and the members of the family will stay there until after the Southern Society's dinner tomorrow night. The Governor will go to Trenton on the 4 o'clock train this afternoon and will be at his desk in the capital all day tomorrow. He will come back here late in the day and will attend the dinner as the chief guest of honor.

He positively refused to discuss public matters at the pier and said that he had no appointments to announce and did not know when he would have. While in Bermuda, he answered 700 letters that he had received and which had demanded his personal attention.

The Governor was inclined to be angry when his attention was called to reports from Washington that the campaign against Bryan has collapsed; that Sir [Senator] Martin of Virginia and other conservative Democratic Senators were quoted as saying that Wilson had asked Bryan to become Secretary of State and that Bryan should accept.

"If you want my attitude on this question and on the question of any cabinet appointments," said the Governor somewhat impatiently, "I will refer you to the newspaper men who have been putting the question of who shall be named for the cabinet up to me for six weeks and who have been told repeatedly that I positively will not discuss the subject."

Printed in the *Trenton Evening Times*, Dec. 16, 1912.

From Samuel Gompers

Sir: Washington, D. C., Dec. 16, 1912.

There is a matter of great importance which not only I am directed, but it is my own personal desire to present to you for consideration. I should prefer to lay it before you in person rather than at this time to make it a subject of correspondence. Of course I realize how many requests are made of you for personal interviews, and how much your time is taken up with communications. From what you know of me, I feel that you will understand that I would not ask for a conference were the matter other than of great importance, and which should be at least at first presented to you orally.

If you will accord me the courtesy of an interview for the purpose above indicated, may I suggest that Friday, December 20, or any day of the week after January first, would be suitable for me.[1]

Thanking you in advance, I have the honor to remain,
                    Yours very respectfully,   Saml. Gompers.

TLS (WP, DLC).
[1] See S. Gompers to the Executive Council, Dec. 21, 1912.

A Statement to New Jersey Democrats

[Dec. 17, 1912]

I have been surprised by numerous inquiries as to whether I would continue to "take interest" in the political affairs of the state after assuming my duties as President, and yet I realize the significance of these inquiries. Last summer I warned the voters of the state very explicitly that the men who formerly controlled and discredited our politics were awaiting their opportunity to recover their control and were expecting to find it. What I then said has been abundantly verified by what has happened in the interval. I am keenly aware of the fact that these men have so little respect for the voters of New Jersey that they think all they have to do is to wait to come back into power.

They will be sorely disappointed. They cannot again impose upon the voters of New Jersey. If they should in some evil moment recover control of the party machinery they will only ruin the party and put it permanently out of power. Every step they take, therefore, to re-establish their power should be at once exposed and stopped. The people of the state need not fear that I will become indifferent so long as their confidence encourages me to believe that they wish my aid and counsel. I shall in the future use every proper and legitimate power I have and every influence at my disposal to support and assist the new forces which have regenerated our life during the past two years. I shall not go slack in this business, for I understand my duty to be to stand back of the progressive forces in the Democratic party everywhere and at every juncture, and I feel that in these matters I am under particular obligations of conscience and gratitude to the people of New Jersey.

Printed in the *Trenton Evening Times*, Dec. 17, 1912.

A News Report

[Dec. 17, 1912]

WILSON MEANS TO KEEP FIGHT UP IN JERSEY

TRENTON, Dec. 17.—"Under particular obligations of conscience and gratitude to the people of New Jersey," as he says in a statement he gave out today, Governor Wilson intends to do everything he can to maintain the standard that the Democratic party has attained in the State under his leadership. The statement which means a declaration of war on the old bosses was in response to an inquiry for an expression of the Governor's intentions.

"I intend to use all the powers there are in me to this end," said the Governor, in his direct reply to the query, and he added that he might make a statement later. As soon as the conference with the newspaper men was concluded the Governor set to work on the statement. . . .

The Governor also stated that he intends to remain a resident of New Jersey, despite reports that after he became President he would go to Virginia or some other place in the Southland. It was told to him that certain politicians who had been opposed to his policies had circulated statements that the Governor would accept proffers of a residence in the South and that when he left the State for Washington next March he might be considered almost a negligible factor in the State.

"Certain politicians are hoping that this is so," the Governor was told.

"Well," responded Governor Wilson, "those hopes are going to be disappointed. I intend to keep my residence in New Jersey."

This declaration was emphasized this afternoon when the Governor declined an invitation to make his winter home in Augusta, Ga. The invitation was made through a delegation from the Chamber of Commerce of that city, where the Governor resided as a boy. He said his fighting blood would not permit him to leave New Jersey.

"I want to state the difficulty," he exclaimed to the Georgians. "There's a very interesting political situation in New Jersey. Back of that are a number of persons who used to own New Jersey and whose title has been questioned.

"They have ardent desires to get rid of me—I believe some of them voted for me for President for that reason. The Governor of New Jersey, under the State Constitution, cannot be re-elected to succeed himself, and they saw a chance to get rid of me after two years instead of after three, the full term.

"It is very important that the people should feel that I am still connected with New Jersey. The Democratic party in the State has arrived at a point where it must choose whether it shall continue to be progressive or not.

"I see no vacations before me for a long time. My conscience forbids me, and, having a mixture of Irish and Scotch blood in me, I don't feel as if I wanted to take a vacation where there is a fight on.

"After a few more elections these persons may realize that the progressive program is complete, even to the dot above the i. I cannot break away from New Jersey."

Printed in the *Newark Evening News*, Dec. 17, 1912.

To Oscar Wilder Underwood

My dear Mr. Underwood: [Trenton, N. J.] December 17, 1912.

Being just fresh from Bermuda, I have not yet learned upon what date Congress expects to adjourn. I suppose you would hardly be free to come up to Trenton while the House is in session, but I am very anxious to to [sic] learn your convenience in this matter and your liberty, because I am impatient to have a full talk with you about things pending and to come. Would you be generous enought to let me know the dates upon which it would be possible for you to visit me at Trenton?[1]

Cordially yours,   Woodrow Wilson

TLS (O. W. Underwood Papers, A-Ar).

[1] Underwood's reply is missing in both the Wilson and Underwood Papers. However, Underwood came to Trenton on December 31 for a conference on tariff legislation and cabinet appointments. *New York Times*, Jan. 1, 1913.

An Address to the New York Southern Society

[[Dec. 17,1912]]

Mr.Toastmaster,[1] ladies and gentlemen, I can say to you, without the slightest affectation, that I arise feeling a very great embarrassment, because when a man is made to think about himself that is the profoundest cause for embarrassment.

When you voted for me, if you did, you were thinking about what you wished to see accomplished; but tonight you are looking upon the work of your hands, and I say to you, in order to divert your thoughts and perhaps your attention, that I am not thinking of what I wish to be; I am thinking of what I wish to do. And unless you think the same way, just that much strength will be subtracted from the government of the United States, for the important thing, in the present day and at this particular moment, is what you think.

A nation is not made of anything physical. A nation is made of its thoughts and its purposes. Nothing can give it dignity except its thoughts. Nothing can give it impulse except its ideals. You will be laid away in some grave to sleep, with or without expectation of resurrection, but you will leave behind you a living nation, and you will have contributed to it nothing permanent except the thoughts which you spoke to your neighbors, which you spoke in private to those to whom you unbared your real soul.

[1] Walter Lee McCorkle, Wilson's old friend, president of the New York Southern Society.

And so it seems to me that what we ought to think about tonight is not that the Democratic party has won a victory, is not that a particular combination of men have put into office those whom they regard as their representatives in a political contest, but that there is a vast deal to do in the United States, and that it can be done best by forgetting that we are partisans of anything except the honor and prosperity and integrity of the nation itself.

We cannot be jealous of the nation's honor unless we are jealous of our own, and we cannot understand what constitutes the honor of a nation unless we understand what constitutes the honor of a man. The honor of a man does not consist in consistently serving himself, but in spending some of the fine energy in him on something that has nothing to do with his own personal fortunes. You are patriotic in proportion as you prefer the nation to yourself, and in proportion as there are large numbers of men, or small, who entertain that preference, and entertain it with a passionate sincerity, in that proportion is the nation strong and great, weak or contemptible, in that proportion is hope magnified or chilled for years to come.

What has interested me, therefore, in recent years, has been the change in the thought of the men who have been in a position to do the large things in this country. The thought of some of them has not changed as fast as I should like to see it, but the thought of most of them has changed. It has been my function in the past, perhaps because of a naturally combative nature, to stand often in this room and say to the audiences before me what I knew beforehand they would not like to hear, and to say to them what I believed they would not agree with me in thinking. I have been very disagreeable in this room, not of set purpose, but because I believed at the time that I was speaking what the men before me would ultimately think; and I have seen, not because of any leadership of mine, but because of the steady movement of the moral tides in this country, I have seen the time come when men will cheer sentiments which were once received in chilly silence. I have seen the time come when the business men of New York knew that in the past they had been conducting the business of this country in the wrong way because in the wrong spirit; because in that spirit which makes it impossible for any man to be useful, the notion that he is the appointed trustee to do the thinking for the rest of mankind, and that prosperity consists in the building up of wealth according to his plans and in conforming with his purposes.

The great difficulty with New York has often been that it thought that all the thinking was done in New York, and in that spirit you can neither have sympathy nor respect for the rest of the United States. That sort of intolerance which is natural on the part of men bent with all their energies upon a particular task no longer characterizes an audience like this as it used to characterize it, because, whether by one sort of influence or another, we have been made conscious of the great powers that lie dispersed throughout America. I used to be a hopeless provincial and I always would have remained a hopeless provincial if I had always stayed in one place. The only way you can get other atmospheres into your head is to move into other atmospheres. The only way you can believe that other men know as much as you do is by finding that they know more than you do. The only way to find the variety of the truth is to come into contact with the variety of mind that contains the variety of truth. And so an audience like this has this significance. You have imported the thought of another part of the country into this great port into which so many things are imported. You have imported the thought of the South into New York.

I am happy to concur with one of the distinguished gentlemen who preceded me, in the thought that there is no longer any serious consciousness in this country of sectional differences, but that that consciousness has disappeared not merely by the healing processes of time; for if the circumstances of America had remained the same, time would not have accomplished the thing which we now see brought about. The world has changed about us. America is not what it was when the Civil War was fought. We have come into a new age. There can be no sectionalism about the thinking of America from this time on, because no hard-headed man can prove to you that there are any separate, sectional interests anywhere. The nation in our day and all nations in our day have been so interlaced, they have been so mixed not only by mixture of population but by the union of interests that sectionalism is impossible. But there is something that is different in the makeup of a company like this from the makeup of an ordinary company ordinarily assembled in this hall.

What have you brought out of the South? You may have lost some of it; you may have loved the South without desiring to live in it. You may do what I have seen so many New England Societies do: Worship the Puritans at a very respectful distance. You may believe that the South was a good place to come *from*. You may have a reverence for times which you thank God have gone by; but, having lost all this and being perfectly content to live in New York, what have you brought that you have not thrown away?

The South is an idea with most Southerners, and I have sometimes asked myself, as a Southerner, What is the idea? I find that
some people think that America was settled at the time the
Puritans came over, but it was settled several years before that in
a colony known as Virginia. And when the American Revolution
came on, Virginia showed this singular characteristic: She was
willing to fight for something that had nothing to do with her own
material interests. The Navigation laws, the restrictions of trade,
cut very deep at the port of Boston, but they did not cut deep on
the James River. There was nothing that seriously interfered with
the material prosperity of Virginia in the cause that was made
the cause of the Revolution, and the only greatness of Washington and the other men who stood with him there was that they
thought in terms that were not the terms of their own lives and
interests; and unless the South can continue to do that, she will
cease to have any claim to distinction whatever.

Having come out of the South, are you willing to fight for other
people's causes, or are you not? I would not be understood as
detracting in the least degree from those equally great men who
sternly set their faces to right the wrongs that touched their own
people in New England. I dare say that if the circumstances
had been reversed they would have joined their brethren in
Virginia to defend the rights of the people of Virginia, but I am
saying that the South has again and again fought against her
own material interests for something which she believed to be a
common cause.

There were thinking men in the South who knew it was against
the material interests of the South to fight for slavery. Slavery
is not for the material interest of any nation. They were fighting
because of a certain stubborn pride, that said: "We must insist
upon choosing our own way of life." That is all they were fighting for. They were fighting to put themselves at a permanent disadvantage in the economic development of the United States.

Now that may be a good idea or it may be a bad idea, but it is
an idea. It is not a thing. And men who have lost the capacity to
feel a passion so great for an idea that they are ready to lay down
their lives for it, have ceased to be of the kind of stuff that unconquerable people are made of.

Mr. Thomas[2] quoted a remark of mine that the man knew
the strength of the stream who was swimming against it. I have
been swimming against it all day in New Jersey, and therefore
I have come here in a somewhat grim and solemn humor. Yes,

---

2 Augustus Thomas, well-known playwright and after-dinner speaker.

we straightened things out in New Jersey, but they are not going to stay straightened out of themselves, and the happiest circumstance in the minds of some gentlemen in New Jersey to-night is that they can now count the day when they can get rid of me. That is the reason I informed them to-day that they were not going to get rid of me.

A man can live in Washington and know what is going on in New Jersey, and a man can say from Washington what he thinks about what is going on in New Jersey, and he can say it in the only way which is effectual by mentioning the names of the gentlemen concerned. This anonymous authorship of iniquity ought to stop; the authors ought to be obliged to sign their products. It is all very well to insist it shall be made publicly known who owns this, that, or the other journal, but it should be made publicly known as well who owns this, that, or the other idea or purpose, and if it cannot be produced by law, it can be produced by conversation and by speechmaking, and by doing the only thing which, so far as I know, has ever rendered me effective, talking in specifications.

They are the only things I am interested in. I suppose that as a college man I am thought to be interested only in those large and general ideas on which one can float without ever getting his feet on the ground, but I am not. I prefer to have my feet on the ground.

Now the journey we have to take cannot be taken unless we take it together. There is no use telling you who is doing this mischief unless you disapprove of it after you have heard of it, and I must say that there is no sport in telling you unless you disapprove of it after you have heard it. I have gone through a campaign in which I have endeavored to speak of things, and not of persons, but you speak of persons by implication when you speak of things and the plainer you make the implication, the more effective you make the moral. The only way to keep out of trouble, in the years to come is to see that your names are connected with the right things.

I say that not as a threat to this company, because, of course, there is nobody here who has the least nervousness about the future, but I say it in order to convey more or less playfully— *more-or-less-playfully*—this intimation, that men have now got to stand up and be counted. Men have got to stand up now and be counted, and put their names down on this side or on that, and I believe that there is going to come presently, just so soon as men see that this is business and not amusement, that there is going to come enthusiasm for right things, which will result in this amazing and delightful discovery, that honor and integrity and public purpose breed more prosperity than any other things in the world.

God knows that the poor suffer enough in this country already, and a man would hesitate to take a single step that would increase the number of the poor, or the burdens of the poor, but we must move for the emancipation of the poor, and that emancipation will come from our own emancipation from the errors of our minds as to what constitutes prosperity.

Prosperity does not exist for a nation unless it be pervasive. Prosperity is not a thing which can be consumed privately or by a small number of persons, and the amount of wealth in a nation is very much less important than the accessibility of wealth in a nation. The more people you make it accessible to, the more energy you call forth, until presently, if you carry the process far enough, you get almost the zest of a creative act. A nation seems to rise under your wand, and rise up and produce things greater than the minds of men have yet conceived. That comes from a universal hope, and it comes from nothing else. It comes because men know that they are free, and so long as with bowed heads and doubting hearts they are wondering if they ever shall be free, this marvel cannot be wrought. The marvel is the marvel of the confident mind and the light heart and the eye that sees the vision not so distant but what it may be hoped for and attained.

Now America has seen visions and has attained unto the realization of visions, and then for a little while she has slidden back and lost herself in a mist, and fought for things not worth fighting for and created antagonisms that need not have existed, and misunderstandings which were due to ignorance. She is lifting her head again and saying men are brothers after all and until they be brothers they cannot accomplish the great work of civilization.

The task ahead of me, so far as it is a task of appointment to office, is wholly hateful, but the task ahead of me, so far as it is the leadership of the United States in thinking out its own affairs, is full of nothing but what is bright and touched with confidence, because I *know* that you have only to appeal to the people of the United States on the right grounds to put those who resist out of business, always provided they think you mean what you say. A single evidence that you do not is dangerous. More than one is almost fatal.

It is not the matter of whether you are always right or not. It is not the question of whether you always succeed or not. It is a question of whether you always are moving in the same direction or not, and are always showing the same courage or not.

I am not a brave man, because I do not know anything to be afraid of. You may beat a man temporarily in politics, but if he is right he can go down smiling in your face, and saying, "It is not necessary that I should live to wreak my revenge upon you. That revenge will come in proportion as I have spoken the truth, for you never can silence that truth after it is spoken, and I can smile better than you can if any slightest portion of that kind of immortality is vouchsafed me."

If it can be remembered that you said something that freed the thought of the nation, then you can afford to die to-morrow, because your happiness and your power are safe. That is the kind of moralizing that comes into my mind when I think of the things to come. People make all sorts of sinister predictions as to the trouble we are going to get into down at Washington. I do not think they need give themselves any concern about that because it is going to be public trouble and the great jury is always going to know what the evidence in the case is.

I was warned the other day by the newspapers that I had committed an indiscretion in saying I was going to keep an absolutely open door in the executive offices at Washington, because there were so many people who would want to come in at the door. Perhaps I had better say for my own protection that I meant it would be open only to those who had business to transact, because I want to say to you before I sit down, that I may make myself very unpopular in the months to come by insisting upon preferring business to etiquette. When I take the oath of office I shall deem myself bound to transact the business of the nation, so far as it falls to the Executive, and I shall feel bound to cut out everything that does not touch that business. But that business has to be buttressed and supported and comprehended, and therefore I shall not be obliged to stay at Washington and not go about and converse with my neighbors, and the conversation perhaps will be more vital for me than it will be for my neighbors, for the object will be to learn what the neighbors are thinking about. It is a great deal more important to the country what you think than what I think.

You, as representing the great people of the United States, will do the effectual thinking, and my thinking will be effectual only in proportion as it really interprets the general thinking of the country at large. I must trouble you, therefore, to do a great deal of talking. I must trouble you to say what you really think, and the real difficulty about a community like that of New York is that so few men say in public what they really think. I know what a great many gentlemen here really think, but they have said it to me privately, and many of them have requested me not to mention the fact that they said it. There is somebody in New York, and there are some things in New York that make them afraid. Well, if you are going to be afraid, we cannot help you down in Washington at all, but if you cannot say it any better, come and say it in private, provided you always say what you really think.

There is too much manners in politics. Good taste often stands in the way of public morals. It is not good taste to say what you really think of a man when it is not complimentary, but it is immensely serviceable, and the mere point and punctilio of manners ought not to restrain you. That is the reason so many politicians who are honest seem crude. They actually block out for you their real thoughts as they are, and unfavorable thoughts are not always artistic. They are not always beautiful, and they sometimes have to be framed in language for which the dictionary is quite insufficient.

You know in the trial of Judge Chase,[3] so long ago that to refer to it is no aspersion upon the courts, one of the counts in the indictment against the judge was that he had been profane in charging jurors, which was manifestly at least an impropriety, but the only word affirmatively proved that he had used was the word "damn," and Mr. Luther Martin, who was counsel for Judge Chase, undertook to prove to the Senate of the United States that the word "damn" was a necessary word of emphasis. If you were cataloging fools and spoke of fools, natural-born fools, and—where would you go next? In this presence, I would hesitate to say where to go next, but you know perfectly well where to go. And how would you classify that supreme category of folly otherwise than by the use of words, which, when we pronounce them, do not seem even to be correctly spelled?

A very curious thing has fallen under my observation since I left academic walks and got into political high roads, and that is the increased temptation to profanity.

I suppose it would be physically dangerous to bottle up in yourself without releasing some of the things that you are obliged to think, but of course you can avoid the release in public, and there are places and persons in the presence of whom it is appropriate and wholesome to release these natural and very human impulses of your spirit. I think that the recording angel

[3] That is, the impeachment and trial of Associate Justice Samuel Chase in 1804-1805.

probably does not listen, not only because it offends his taste, but because he knows that such things have to happen in order that the business of the world should go on, for there is such a thing as righteous anger, and without righteous anger I don't know how the conduct of the world can be pushed forward.

Those dilettante gentlemen who never get angry about anything never get enthusiastic about anything, and without enthusiasm there is no spirit in the world.

I have been wandering in my talk to-night because I did not want to talk politics as "sich," and I, of course, would not consent to talk about myself except as perhaps hoping to be the spokesman of men like yourselves in some of the better impulses of the country; but all of my talk has circled about this thought: We ought to be discontented with any occasion of this kind which does not contribute to the general impulse. If men do not go away from an occasion like this purposing to put more force into the best things in the nation, then they have wasted the evening.

I want to appeal to you, gentlemen, to conceive of yourselves as trustees of those interests of the nation with which your personal interests have nothing to do. There are men sitting here who have done this, and from a worldly and material point of view, some of them have lost by it, but they will be mentioned after some of the rest of us are gone; and I suppose that it is better to have lost a fortune and gained an immortal thought than to have lost the thought and lived on the fortune, because you can exhaust the fortune, and you cannot exhaust the thought.

The world has too many people in it who devote themselves to expense regardless of pleasure. Indeed, most people who have a great deal of money seem to take it very hard, being obliged to think of ways to spend it, but no man ever felt jaded or blasé who spent his time thinking how to expend his thoughts on great undertakings.

They say that business is going to be disturbed by the changes which are going to be undertaken by the Democratic party in the economic policy of the country. Business cannot be disturbed unless the minds of those who conduct it are disturbed. A panic is described in all the books on political economy that are not thought out in the presence of actual fact as merely a state of mind, because obviously when a panic occurs there is just as much wealth in the country the day after the panic as the day before. Nothing in material circumstances has changed, but the whole state of mind of the financial community has changed. They dare not part with their money. They call in their loans. They are excited, and they do not always know exactly why. That is a natural panic, but you know there are unnatural panics, and sometimes panics occur because certain gentlemen want to create the impression that the wrong thing is going to be done. I am so remote from these things and so innocent that I do not know whether this is true or not, but I have heard that it is, and I can conceive that it is perfectly possible that it should be so, for the machinery is in existence by which the thing can be deliberately done. In my ignorance of Wall Street, I do not know about this. But I do know that the machinery is in existence for the creation of such panics. But I am not afraid of them. But, frankly, I do not believe there is a man living who dares use that machinery. If there is, I promise him, not on my own behalf, but on behalf of my countrymen, a gibbet as high as Haman. I don't mean a literal gibbet, but a figurative gibbet on which he will be punished as long as his quivering soul is capable of feeling a sense of shame.

These are the punishments which cut to the quick, and America with her eyes open is not going to let any man do this thing.

But I speak as if I expected it. I do not. I speak as if I feared it. I do not. I do not fear anything that won't be more dangerous to the man who attempts it than to the men upon whom it is attempted.

Mr. Thomas made that capital quotation from Emerson about the impudence and the terror. Well, all the terror nowadays seems to me like Greek fire; there is nothing in it; it has all been invented; it is stage property.

The cure for that sort of thing is to have an audience who knows it is all make-believe, that no lives are involved, that nobody is going to be seriously hurt, that the slain are going to revive just as soon as the curtain goes down, and if you applaud enough their extravagant performance they will come out before the curtain and thank you.

I am very happy to believe that the future of America is assured. The recent election did not mean anything, if it did not mean that. America did not say that there was a particular man who was better than anybody else for that particular office. If it did it was a mistake. But it did say that there were certain things that it was not going to stand for, and that inasmuch as one party had given them a chance to support a man who also thought that these things ought not to be stood for, they were going to vote for him. That is what the recent election meant.

I shall be, of all men, most honored if I in any degree speak that common impulse; and there are men upon whom my eye falls, as I look around this company, who are going to tell me how to do it, who are going to stand at my side and tell me of these things and explain to me the things that I do not understand, and then enable me to serve the United States and try, through their wisdom, to intepret the general wisdom of the country itself.

I thank you, gentlemen, for this patient audience of a rambling discourse, and beg that after you go away you will not think of the imperfect way in which I expounded a great theme, but only of the theme itself.

Printed in *Twenty-Seventh Annual Dinner of the New York Southern Society* (Washington, 1918), pp. 39-56, with corrections from the complete text in the New York *World*, Dec. 18, 1912.

Joseph Patrick Tumulty to Edward Mandell House

Trenton N J Dec 17-12.

Governor Wilson will be pleased to take lunch with you tomorrow Wednesday at one oclock at the University Club.

Jos P. Tumulty

T telegram (E. M. House Papers, CtY).

From Cone Johnson

My Dear Sir: Tyler, Texas. December 17th, 1912.

Victory is always perilous. The Democratic Party is now in a most perilous situation. The danger lies largely in the Southern States and arises out of the fact that a large element of the Party in those states are not Democrats in reality, but stand-pat Republicans, sailing under the colors of Democracy, and others who, having no political convictions, are machine gangsters. A number of Senators and Congressmen from the Southern States are the representatives of these elements.

The situation in Texas is in some respects like that existing no doubt in other Southern States; but in other respects it is peculiar. The fight against the reactionery element of the Party in this State began in 1908, in a contest for Delegates at Large to the National Convention. In that fight it fell to my lot to occupy a somewhat conspicuous place. The fight was renewed in 1910 and in 1912, resulting in a Wilson delegation from this State to the Baltimore Convention. This victory was made possible by the previous struggles in behalf of real Democratic principles and integrity in official life. The body of those who made the fight for your nomination in this State was composed of those who had steadfastly and unyieldingly opposed Senator Bailey, of this State, after the disclosures showing his alliance with corrupt in[t]erests;[1] but they were aided by many of those who had formerly been attached to his political fortunes, and these deserve a full measure of appreciation for their loyalty to that which is best in Democracy.

I do not subscribe to the doctrine that "to the victor belongs the spoils." There should be no "spoils" to divide. And yet we have, and are to have, government through party organization, and I see no escape from the general principle, patriotically and broadly administered, that recognition and prestige, which comes from official station, must in the main be extended to those who have fought the battles for the policies which the people have endorsed.

Now more directly to the point: It is going the rounds that the naming of Post Masters in States like Texas will be left to the Congressmen, in their respective districts; and that the larger and wider offices will be appointed largely, if not wholly, on the recommendation of the Senators. If this policy is pursued, then in this State, many, if not a majority, of those who are friends of your administration and the policies you have championed, who seek appointments, will "fall outside the breastworks," to use a current expression in the absence of a better one. Particularly will this be the case in the appointment of Post Masters. Quite a number of the Congressmen from this State were unfriendly to your nomination, and some of them vigorously opposed it, because they were opposed to the policies to which you are attached, and to the so called "socialistic tendency" of the present Democracy. These men are usually followers and supporters of Senator Bailey. The latter, while announcing his retirement from public life at the end of his term in March next, has not, according to his plans, retired, but merely withdrawn from public notice for the time being. He has a large following in this State, of very active, aggressive and assiduous supporters, who have no sympathy whatever with the policies and program adopted by the Democracy at Baltimore, which marked our party as truly progressive. The battle in Texas is not concluded. We must continue the struggle with a compact organization or, at the first reverse which may come to your administration, these will be found joining in the attack. I would not ask at your hands the appointment of any man as a reward for his services to your cause or of friendship to me, for my own interest and activity in your nomination and election was, I assure you, entirely disinterested. I wanted you nominated and made President, because in your candidacy I "saw the best expression of the hopes and aspirations of the American people." But it is to be expected that in the Southern States especially, where the Federal offices great and small have been held by a handful of office seekers and office holders, claiming to be a Republican Party, who do not represent the people whom they serve, the Democrats are expecting to be put in these positions, and it is natural that your friends are exepcting [expecting] that they will not be discriminated against, where they live in districts whose representative in Congress will pass them by. I have had almost numberless solicitations to give my endorsements to applicants from amongst your friends for positions under your administration. To all these I have had to reply that I did not know how these matters would be handled, and that if appointments to these positions must have the endorsement of the Congressmen and Senators, my own influence, if I have any, would be greatly shut out, as in some instances my recommendation would have but little, if any, weight with the Congressmen.

I do not wish that your administration shall be marked by any narrow spirit of partisanship, or that these appointments be made in such a manner as will justify a charge that none but those who were for you are to be appointed; but the situation in this State is such that unless the way is open for your friends to lay these matters to your attention, I fear the opposition will be strengthened and our own folks disheartened. Several of those who were most active as workers in this State for your nomination have expressed to me this same thought. We are far removed from the scene of political activity, some sixteen hundred miles from "headquarters," and our anxiety is therefore the more acute.

In the larger and greater problems on your hands, this matter of patronage, I am sure, will be one of annoyance. Still it is one of the burdens of the great office of President; and my anxiety is that it may prove a proper opportunity to strengthen the cause of Democracy. I am at a loss just how to bring this matter to your attention except in this way, and have hesitated to break in on your labors with this suggestion. But as I was made Chairman of the Delegation to Baltimore, many of your friends in Texas are looking to me, in some measure at least, for suggestions and assistance. So far I have had to satisfy them with my own lack of knowledge of the situation, and have so far given no endorsements.

I assure you of my continued good wishes and prayers that your administration may fulfill the expectations of the people.

With great respect, I remain, my dear Governor,

Very truly your friend,   Cone Johnson.

TLS (WP, DLC).

¹ Johnson here referred to the close ties of Senator Joseph Weldon Bailey to the Waters-Pierce Oil Company and their corporate interests, the rumors and revelations about which shadowed his political career from 1900 until his retirement from the Senate in 1913. See Lewis L. Gould, *Progressives and Prohibitionists: Texas Democrats in the Wilson Era* (Austin, Tex., 1973), pp. 16-23.

From James Bryce

My dear Governor   Washington. Dec. 17th 1912

Your letter reached me just as you were leaving for Bermuda, so it seemed better to await your return before replying to tell you that the time of my departure for England is quite uncertain. My Government have asked me to stay on here to try to dispose of (if possible) this unfortunate question which has arisen regarding the Panama Canal tolls.¹ I have promised to do so, and thus may be detained for weeks and weeks yet, possibly even until March 4, in which case I may hope for the pleasure of welcoming you to Washington. If you should be here any time in January or February, would you let me be apprised, that I might see you and deliver orally the message with which I am charged for you.

It would have been a real joy to my wife and myself to have been living here while you were in the White House, and it adds to our regrets at leaving the U.S. that we are not to have such opportunities for frequently meeting and talking over the subjects which interest us as specially connected with our studies. Well: I hope I may live to have some such opportunities later when your experience has been still further enlarged

With our best wishes for you both,

Always sincerely yours   James Bryce

ALS (WP, DLC).

¹ A controversy between the United States and Great Britain over Congress' exemption of American coastwise ships from tolls for using the Panama Canal, which the British government claimed violated the Hay-Pauncefote Treaty of 1901. There will be numerous documents in following volumes concerning this controversy and its resolution.

From Alexander Walters

My dear Mr. President: New York City, December 17, 1912

Accept my congratulations on your safe return to your home. I am glad to learn through the press that you have greatly improved in health by your visit to Bermuda.

I have heard so much of late through the press and by statements of some of the leaders of the Democratic Party, that positions now held by Negroes under the Republican administration, would be taken away from them and given to White men, that I have thought it wise to write you that in case such an action is contemplated, that this should not be done for the following reasons:

First: It would give the Republican press and the Democratic Press which is friendly disposed to the Negro an opportunity to open up the whole Negro Question and precipitate a controversy which I think would greatly hamper your administration. Things are running along smoothely now, and if possible, it ought to remain so.

Second: The offices now held by Negroes are but a bagatelle in comparison to the offices held by white men. Not of sufficient importance to in any way jeopardize the success of your administration. I am sure that the Democratic Party can do with impunity what the Republicans would hardly dare to do in the way of the appointments of Negroes. The criticisms in such matter have come from the Democratic side. I am sure that our friends of the South will allow you considerable latitude in your appointments of colored men to office.

Congressman Burleson of Texas told me last week that he is willing for you to give a whole governmental department to Negroes, and that he would be glad to discuss the matter with you, if, at any time, you desired him to do so.

I have spoken with a large number of the influential men of the Party and they have expressed themselves as being willing to allow the offices now held by Negro Republicans to go to Negro Democrats.

Third: As a political expediency I think it is wise for the Negroes to keep the positions that they now have. We have a voting population of 750,000 which is increasing annually. These voters are scattered throughout the North, East and West, and in the states like New York, New Jersey, Pennsylvania, Ohio, Illinois, Indiana, and others, the Negro vote is an influential factor that will have to be reckoned with, and since it is now divided, having in some states given you as much as 30 and 40% of the total colored vote, I think that we ought to encourage it.

Fourth: In the last six or seven years we have succeeded in building up a strong Negro Democratic organization. I am sure it would be greatly injured by taking the offices now held by colored men and give them to white men unless you give them offices of like importance, and in that case, you would have to start by giving them such offices before you had taken the old positions away from them.

Of course, with me, the offices are a secondary thing and not a primary thing. The moral, religious and industrial uplift of my people are the primary things to me. But, since the air is full of the other thing and the Negro papers are on the qui vive to have you do something that would make trouble, I am taking the liberty to write you just what is in my heart. I had a talk with Judge Hudsbeth yesterday on the subject and I find that he entertains the same views on the question.

My interest in my race, and the success of your administration induces me to write you this letter.

Again, wishing you great success, I beg to remain,

Yours most respectfully,   Alexander Walters

TLS (WP, DLC).

From Carter Glass

Dear Governor Wilson: Washington. December 18, 1912.

Responding to yours of December 17th,[1] I would make the matter of our conference on the currency question altogether subject to your convenience. The House adjourns for the holidays tomorrow evening. It would suit me to come to Trenton immediately thereafter or on any day of the following week except Christmas and December 27th. I have written Dr. Willis to hold himself in readiness to meet me there on any day that you may designate. Should you decide to confer within the next few days, I would be obliged if you will wire me on receipt of this letter, as I purpose leaving for my home in Virginia tomorrow night unless we may confer this week.

Sincerely yours,   Carter Glass.

TLS (WP, ÐLC).
[1] It is missing in both WP, DLC, and the Glass Papers, ViU.

From George Foster Peabody

New York City

My dear Governor Wilson: December 18th, 1912.

I very seriously hesitate to intrude upon you even a line at this time, when you have so much on your mind and heart. I have, though, the feeling, some how, that perhaps it will not seem a real intrusion if I enclose to you a copy of a personal communication from Mr. Louis F. Post, Editor of The Public, Chicago. I wrote to him in criticism of his editorial expression of desire that Mr. Bryan should decline the Secretaryship of State, if it should be offered to him. His letter indicates to me so definite a temper of hope from your administration, that I think you may not be averse to taking the time to read it. I am, unfortunately, laid up with an attack of the grip at my brother's house in Brooklyn, and the copy of my letter to Mr. Post and his editorial are at Saratoga Springs. I do not think, however, you would need to take the time to read them even if you had them. I endeavored somewhat to suggest the point that if Mr. Bryan were outside of the Cabinet with the necessarily profound interest in the actual work of the administration, it would be almost impossible that he should not be continually claimed to be sympathetic with the various disaffected groups. It is impossible, of course, that Mr. Bryan should continually deny such claims, which would of course be "whispered about" in that most unfortunate official political atmosphere of Washington.

It was a grievous disappointment to me that a temperature of 102 and 2/5ths, which developed on Monday evening, prevented my attendance upon the dinner on Tuesday evening. I was to have met Mr. Hale there also, which would have been another satisfaction following his return from Bermuda.[1] I have heard from my nephew[2] a most enthusiastic account of your noble words of incitation to our fellow-southerners, and I have had the New York Times report read to me this morning. I again congratulate the Country.

I am, with profound admiration,

Very respectfully yours,   George Foster Peabody

TLS (WP, DLC). Enc.: typed extract.

[1] William Bayard Hale had gone to Bermuda to go over with Wilson the proofs of *The New Freedom* (New York, 1913), which Hale had compiled from Wilson's speeches during 1911 and 1912. The book was serialized in *World's Work*, xxv and xxvi (Jan.-July 1913).

[2] Charles Samuel Peabody, architect of New York.

From Norman Hapgood

Dear Governor: [New York] Dec 18 [1912]

I much appreciate your note,[1] saying you would like to know the impressions I received on my little trip to Washington. I was confirmed in the view that the most formidable danger lies in the so-called Progressives. Some of them are eager to find points of attack. Others wish you well, and have been discussing the question of how radical a leader you are to be. Your speech of last night, superb in all ways, is exactly what will attach this group to you. With them on your side I do not think the reactionary democrats would put up a very hopeful fight.

The conservation situation, of course, is only one thing in many, but it seems to be this point at which there is most likely to be some sudden outbreak.

Yours sincerely   Norman Hapgood

ALS (WP, DLC).
¹ It is missing.

From the Diary of Colonel House

December 18, 1912.

Governor Wilson came at half past one. I talked to him about Morganthau and suggested him for Turkey. He replied "there aint going to be no Turkey," and I said, "then let him go look for it."

I talked to him about Tumulty and I asked him if he had considered him for Secretary to the President. He said "yes, but the trouble with Tumulty is that he cannot see beyond Hudson County, his vision is so narrow." I assented but thought he had the political instinct which would be an essential asset. I asked if he had anyone else in mind, and he said yes, Newton Baker of Cleveland. I thought if I were in Wilson's place I would take only men I knew, that in making a selection it was like walking in the country—one could always imagine that something better was beyond, but upon reaching the given point the view was still in the distance like the rainbow.

It was decided that he would suggest to McCombs that he take either Italy or Austria on account of his health, and with a tentative promise of calling him to the Cabinet later. I advised firmness in dealing with McCombs, he talked big but was a man of but little courage. The Governor is to see him at half past three and will let me know tonight or tomorrow what has been done. Bryan was also discussed freely. I advised him to offer Bryan the Secretaryship of State, but afterwards to suggest that it would be of great service if he would go to Russia at this critical time. He thought Bryan would want to discuss with him the personel of his Cabinet and that they could never agree. I argued that there were many people and things that they could agree upon as their object was really the same only their ways of getting at it were different. He might, I thought, mention the names of Burleson, Daniels and others he was considering for the Cabinet who are also friends of Mr. Bryan

We discussed again the Attorney Generalship and he asked about Brandeis. I told him that it was with much regret that I had to advise against him, that I liked him personally but he was not fit for that place. I told him that I had run down all the material in the country and that Wigmore,[1] Dean of the Law School of Northwestern University, was the last, but after meeting him he would probably prove like the rest. We went back to McReynolds and I thought he seemed to understand the different phases of the situation better than anyone I had talked to. He asked if I considered McAdoo suited for the Treasury and I thought he was. Under ordinary conditions I should say an Eastern man would be a bad choice but that in this instance I heartily approved McAdoo. I informed him of the trouble which McAdoo was having with the financial affairs of his tunnel, but I thought he should not be prejudiced by that.

We took dinner with Janet[2] who had McReynolds and McAdoo. I told McAdoo of the conversation I had with the Governor concerning him. The Governor called me over the telephone as promised, but I had just left the house so I have not heard about his talk with McCombs.

[1] John Henry Wigmore, Dean of the Law School of Northwestern University, 1901-1929; prolific author of legal works, most notably, *A Treatise on the System of Evidence in Trials at Common Law* . . . (4 vols., Boston, 1904-1905).
[2] Janet House (Mrs. Gordon) Auchincloss.

From William Gibbs McAdoo

CONFIDENTIAL

Dear Governor: [New York] December 19, 1912.

I received today a letter from your brother dated December 17th, in which he tells me that he has sent a copy of it to you.[1]

Some time ago I suggested to some of our friends in Tennessee that I thought your brother's election to the Senate would be a very happy solution of the existing difficulties. I believe that it will do more than anything else to bring about harmony between the contending factions in the State. Aside from this, it would give me peculiar pleasure to see your brother in the Senate. I think he is admirably qualified for the position (and I say this from my observation and knowledge of his work at Headquarters during the campaign, and my personal contact with him) and it seems to me that he could be of very great service to you and to your administration in the Senate. I know, of course, that some things can be said on the other side, but I do not feel that they count very much against the advantages of having him there.

Before going further with this matter, however, I should very much like to know what your own feeling is about it.

Always, with warm regards,

Sincerely yours,   W G McAdoo

TLS (LPC, W. G. McAdoo Papers, DLC).

¹ J. R. Wilson, Jr., to W. G. McAdoo, Dec. 17, 1912, CCL (WP, DLC), enclosed in J. R. Wilson, Jr., to WW, Dec. 17, 1912, TLS (WP, DLC).

From Joseph R. Wilson, Jr.

My dear Brother: Nashville, Tenn. Dec. 19, 1912.

I have received both of your good letters from Bermuda and it is needless for me to say how glad I was to receive them.

I have delayed writing you about my personal plans because I know how your mind has been occupied. I have, however, reached the point when it appears I will have to make a decision and I am unwilling to act without consulting you for I am anxious to be placed in a position which will enable me, if possible, to be of some service to you and your administration.

I wrote you yesterday sending a copy of a letter I have sent to Mr. McAdoo regarding the Senatorship from this state. There have been no developments along this line since and that letter acquainted you with all the facts I have.

I find that some of your best friends in New York, and men who were friendly to me during the campaign, also, have been considering my case and have some plans which have not yet been revealed to me for my betterment. One of these plans was an election as Secretary of the U.S. Senate. This, however, they seem to have abandoned for the time, at least, because of the fact that the Senate promises to be so close. I am informed that Mr. Gates,¹ a well known Washington newspaper man, is an announced candidate for this position but in a letter from a friend in Washington this morning I am told that he has expressed a willingness to withdraw in my favor should I be a candidate.

I today received a confidential letter from Woolley of the Publicity Department,² you will remember, stating that I have been slated for historian of the Democratic party during the coming four years at a salary of $5,000 per annum. This he told me in strict confidence, for no announcement will be made for some weeks yet, as I understand it.

Several other plans have been suggested to me by friends who are taking an interest in me which I deeply appreciate. Their idea seems to be not only to benefit me personally, but to place me in a position where I will be able to render assistance to you if such be needed. I feel that the time is approaching when I must make a decision and let these friends know what I prefer.

There is one feature of the situation, unfortunately, I must consider. Should duty call me to Washington I must receive a sufficient salary to enable me to meet certain obligations which will of necessity fall upon me as the brother of the President. I do not mean, of course, that we will have to become high livers and do the big society act. This is not our way and would be distasteful, but the obligations mentioned will come nevertheless. They are being felt to some extent even here in Nashville where I find myself called upon to do things which have never before been required of me.

Now I want your candid opinion. I dislike to ask you to give these matters thought at a time when you are so pressed with your official duties, but, as I said, I want, if I can, to assist you in your work for the splendid cause you represent, and yet at the same time I must consider the fact that two precious ones depend upon me for support and I have a first duty to perform for their sakes. After many years of hard newspaper grind, I find myself anxious to leave the newspaper field for a time, at least, and the plans proposed by friends seem to be opening an opportunity. I crave your advice.

Kate and Alice join me in great love to you all. Please let me hear from you as soon as at all possible.

Yours aff.   Joseph.

TLS (WP, DLC).

¹ Robert Moores Gates, Washington correspondent of the Memphis *Commercial Appeal*.

² Robert Wickliffe Woolley, former journalist; chief investigator for the Stanley Committee in its examination of the affairs of the United States Steel Corporation, 1911-1912; chief of the Bureau of Publicity of the Democratic National Committee, 1912.

From Richard Heath Dabney

Dear Woodrow: [Charlottesville, Va.] 19 Dec., 1912.

Just a line to welcome you back from Bermuda and to express the hope that you feel refreshed and ready to tackle your gigantic task.

It causes me regret, of course, to learn that you cannot stay with us as much as twenty-four hours, but we are looking forward most eagerly to your visit, however brief it may be. Please let me know as soon as you decide whether you will come to my house on your way to Staunton or on your way back from there. Let me know the day and train on which to expect you.

Faithfully & affectionately,   R. H. Dabney.

P.S. I sent you a couple of letters to Trenton[1] the other day in regard to positions in the Cabinet.   R.H.D.

ALS (WP, DLC).
  [1] R. H. Dabney to WW, two letters, Dec. 17, 1912, ALS (WP, DLC).

From the Diary of Colonel House

December 19, 1912.

Governor Wilson called me over the telephone and said that McCombs was distinctly disappointed at the ambassadorial offer made him yesterday,[1] and no decision was arrived at. He wanted to know again about Bryan and my advice about it. I advised being cordial in making the offer, and to make it plain afterwards that he would appreciate his taking the foreign post. . . .

I called up Governor Wilson to talk things over and he asked if I still held to my advice about Mr. Byran and I answered, "yes." This is the third or fourth time he has asked me this. It shows how distrustful he is of having Mr. Bryan in his Cabinet.

  [1] Wilson had offered McCombs the ambassadorship to Austria. See the extracts from the Diary of Colonel House printed at Jan. 8 and 24, 1913, Vol. 27.

Samuel Gompers to the Executive Council of the American Federation of Labor

Colleagues: [Washington] Dec. 21, 1912.

In compliance with the direction of the Executive Council at its meeting in Rochester after the convention, instructing the undersigned to lay before the President-elect Wilson the resolutions adopted by the convention upon the subject matter of legislation, and particularly the bill creating a Department of Labor, with a secretary at its head, I communicated with Mr. Wilson, and eleven o'clock yesterday, Friday, December 20th, was set for the conference at the Capitol at Trenton, New Jersey. I asked Secretary Morrison[1] to accompany me and he did. The conference was intensely interesting and cordial.

I presented to Mr. Wilson our legislation in regard to the bills having passed the House upon the following subjects:

Clayton bill to regulate and limit the issuance of injunctions;
Clayton bill to provide jury trial for indirect contempts;
Sulzer bill for the creation of a Department of Labor.

We urged him to do what he could in securing the passage of the bills in the Senate and in any event in having them brought to a vote before the Senate. Of course he declared that there were the proprieties to be observed in the premises, but left the definite impression on both Mr. Morrison and me that he will do what he can. I gave him a copy of the preambles and resolutions of the convention, Resolution #62, page 258 of the printed proceedings, and urged the appointment of a labor man to membership in the cabinet and particularly to the secretaryship of the Department of Labor when the bill creating that Department shall become law. We discussed a number of men and laid particular stress upon the service, ability, and the faithfulness of our friend William B. Wilson. Governor Wilson was greatly interested during our entire conference.

In today's papers I noted a statement which because of an incident which occurred at the conference, made an impression upon my mind. In an interview with a newspaper man, Governor Wilson was asked whether he had given the names of certain men consideration for appointment in his cabinet. He answered, so the paper said, that he never considers men unless he writes their names down. Mr. Wilson wrote the name of William B. Wilson on a memorandum.

We expected the conference with Governor Wilson to last perhaps ten or fifteen minutes. It lasted over an hour and a half.

The above report is made to the Executive Council for the interest it may have and for the archives of the offices of the members of the Executive Council.

Wishing you the compliments of the season, and with best wishes for a Happy and prosperous New Year and success for the year to come, I am

Fraternally yours,   Saml. Gompers.

TLS (Gompers Letter Books, AFL-CIO Archives).
[1] Frank Morrison, Secretary of the A.F.L.

To Mary Allen Hulbert

Dearest Friend,   Princeton, New Jersey 22 Dec., 1912

Our thoughts have been constantly with you since we saw you just before you sailed: we have thought of your first sight of "Glencove" and of the first sadness to be overcome as you thought of the brave and noble lady who is gone,[1] and then, as we hope, of the soothing and healing influence of that dear corner of the world, where all nature calls to you to clear the mind and set the spirits free and meet her half way in beauty of act and impulse. I should be very happy if I could think that my own recent experience there would go a little way towards cheering you. Those four weeks were an unmixed blessing to me and Glencove was the seat, for me, of happiness and renewal. The dear place will always be associated in my mind with days of refreshment and with everything that is worth while aside from the big, absorbing, overtowering duties of life,—with friends—*real* friends—with quiet contemplation, with pure airs that seemed to clear the mind as they cleared the lungs, and with calm hours in which the world looked right again, looming out in its large proportions—simple and as God made it;—but above all with things that lie deep and touch the affections, the things that make life good and worth living! Bermuda gave me a great and noble friendship—and Glencove was the home of the friend whom I had found when those I had deemed my friends were falling away from me, and all the world looked gray and bleak. *Please* write to us soon and tell us *all* about the arrival and all about how you have fared—above all in your heart! We are all well. Those healing days in Bermuda gave us a great store of peace and vitality upon which to live in the months to come,—and we owe it all to your kindness. I have been terribly driven since I got back but seem to have lots of elasticity in me now. There is no news. All join me in affectionate messages. Love to Allen.

Your devoted friend,   Woodrow Wilson

ALS (WP, DLC).
  [1] Her mother, Anjenett Holcomb (Mrs. Charles Sterling) Allen died on December 2, 1912.

From William Jennings Bryan

My Dear Gov,   Washington D. C. [Dec. 22, 1912]

I enclose a speech made by Mr Creasy,[1] whom I mentioned[2] in connection with the agricultural department[.] While speaking of Pa I am reminded that Hon W. H. Berry lives at Chester Pa. He was treasurer of Pa once and has been the candidate for Gov once of [or] twice. He is a high class man & I may give him a letter of introduction to you.

In view of your remarks about locality of Sec of Interior it occurs to me that Mayor Baker of Cleveland is worth thinking about. He is a man of ideals and capacity.

I will see what I can learn about Houston of St Louis. The

papers report that the breakfast tendered Mrs Wilson[3] was a delightful affair. The Sulzer dinner was "progressive."[4] I leave for Miami tonight.   Yours truly   W. J. Bryan

ALS (WP, DLC).
[1] William Trenton Creasy, farmer, member of the Pennsylvania House of Representatives from Columbia County, 1895-1910, former chairman of the Pennsylvania Democratic State Committee.
[2] Bryan and Wilson had conferred for three and a half hours at the State House in Trenton on December 21. As this letter reveals, they discussed cabinet appointments, among other things. Wilson offered the Nebraskan the Secretaryship of State, and he accepted.
[3] Ellen Axson Wilson and her daughters were the guests of honor at a "victory breakfast" given by the Woman's Democratic Club of New York at the Waldorf-Astoria Hotel on December 21, 1912. Fifteen hundred women and a handful of men filled the main ballroom for the event. *New York Times*, Dec. 22, 1912.
[4] Bryan was the featured speaker at a dinner in honor of Governor-elect William Sulzer at the Waldorf-Astoria on December 21, 1912.

To Albert Shaw

Personal.

My dear Shaw: [Trenton, N. J.] December 23, 1912.

You may be sure that I will seek am [an] opportunity to chat with you just as soon as I can get a breathing space. But with the big job still remaining to be done in New Jersey and a bigger thing looming up ahead of me, I am fairly distracted to find space enough in twenty-four hours to do what is absolutely necessary, but I shall make an interval soon, if necessary.

I shall read Professor Garner's article[1] with the greatest interest for I should like mightily to discover what I do think about the Presidency. His collation of my former views may or may not embarrass me.

In haste,   Faithfully yours,   Woodrow Wilson

TLS (A. Shaw Coll., NjP).
[1] James Wilford Garner, "Woodrow Wilson's Ideas of the Presidency," New York *Review of Reviews*, XLVII (Jan. 1913), 47-51. Garner was Professor of Political Science at the University of Illinois. His article was based upon the chapter on the Presidency in Wilson's *Constitutional Government in the United States*, printed in this series in Vol. 18.

To William Gibbs McAdoo

My dear Mr. McAdoo: Trenton, N. J. December 23, 1912.

The suggestion about my brother not only interests me, but excites me. It would indeed be delightful if this could be brought about, particularly when I had nothing to do with it and the thought has originated with generous friends who have begun to appreciate his worth, but I think that in any position he would resort[1] the confidence of those who trusted him.

Thank you also for the letter from Congressman Kent[2] which you were kind enough to let me see. Unless you want the letter back, I am going to take the liberty of keeping it.

In haste,

Cordially and faithfully yours,   Woodrow Wilson

TLS (W. G. McAdoo Papers, DLC).
[1] Wilson undoubtedly said merit or deserve.
[2] This letter is missing.

To Walter Hines Page

Personal.

My dear Page: [Trenton, N. J.] December 23, 1912.

I am going to urge upon our Legislature here in New Jersey in my annual message, legislation in favor of agricultural demonstration work. Could you put your hand on a suitable bill under which a beginning could be made, or could you have such a bill drawn up for me?

In haste,   Faithfully yours,   Woodrow Wilson

TLS (W. H. Page Papers, MH).

From William Frank McCombs

My dear Governor: New York Dec. 23, 1912.

Senator Obadiah Gardner of Maine, whom you no doubt remember as having been one of your staunchest aides and supporters in the Pre-nomination Campaign and afterwards, has more than a fair chance, by a staunch and firm stand of the Democrats, to be returned to the Senate. It is claimed by Senator Gardner and others, and I am inclined to think with more than a degree of truth, that the Maine Democratic members now in Washington are not as zealous as they might be for his return, because of the patronage question. With their staunch and concentrated interest in him it is my opinion that he may go back to the Senate. I am doing everything I can to aid him.

It has occurred to me that if you would write a letter to Senator Chas. F. Johnson and to Congressman Daniel J. McGillicuddy, in which you would state that you were very much interested in Senator Gardner's return to the Senate and that you presumed

they were doing everything possible to that end, a very good effect might be produced. From Senator Gardner's point of view
this would be very valuable. I see no reason why you should not
write such letters, couched as you think best.[1]

This sort of thing has happened in a number of states. With
our very narrow margin in the Senate and the friction which may
come up there, especially between the old members and the
young members, it is my opinion that everything possible should
be done to have the working majority increased as much as possible.

On last Thursday, after having continued my usual work for
several days with a heavy cold, I was seriously threatened with
pneumonia. My physician confined me to my room and refused
to let me communicate with anyone; otherwise I should have
come to Princeton and continued the discussion of the matter
which we took up when you were here.

I hope to-morrow (Tuesday) I shall be able to run down to
Princeton and talk with you, if you are free. I am perfectly well
again.   Yours sincerely,   Wm. F. McCombs

TLS (WP, DLC).
[1] Wilson got in touch with Johnson and McGillicuddy and conferred with
them in Trenton about the Maine senatorial situation on January 6, 1913. *New
York Times*, Jan. 7, 1913. Whatever plans they made, they were futile. The
Maine legislature, in mid-January, elected a Republican, Edwin Chick Burleigh,
to the Senate. Several standpat Democrats joined the Republicans to give Burleigh a majority. *Ibid.*, Jan. 18, 1913.

From Giles B. Jackson[1]

Honorable Sir: Richmond, Va., Dec. 23rd., 1912.

On behalf of the committee representing the National Negro
Woodrow Wilson League and the National Independent Political
League, I presume to address you at some length upon a question that has no doubt already occupied some of your thought,
the attitude of your administration toward the great Negro Question of the Country.

Two things are perfectly apparent, first, that the Negro vote of
the Country played no insignificant part in your triumphant
election to the highest office in the gift of the Nation, and sec-
ondly, there must be some well defined policy with regard to your
dealing with this great question; your vast experience has certainly given you a broad knowledge of this question, and yet
I feel that you can plainly see that the negroes themselves who
are in close touch with the situation can be of great help to you
in this great question. The attitude that you may assume must

be based upon a well defined plan, a plan that being thoroughly thought out in the beginning will require little readjustment on your part.

To this end we are seeking a conference with you bearing on this point. You can readily see that no amount of written communication can give a clear and perfect conception of the things that so seriously affect us. You have been kind enough to acknowledge my personal help, for which I am exceedingly grateful, and I want to assure you that this was given because I honestly believed your election would result in the greatest possible good to my race. We believed you to be a man far above petty political scheme and who honestly believed in justice to all mankind irrespective of race, color or previous condition of servitude. We have been more than delighted with the results thus far obtained, and we are seeking this interview with the broadest mind of citizenship and the desire to be of real service to you as well as to our race and the two political organizations that we represent.

If convenient to you, we shall be glad to have this conference on the 30th or 31st of December, so that should you desire to make any reference to the Negro Question in your forthcoming inagural address, you will have ample time to sift and investigate such suggestions and information that we may be able to give.

The committee we desire to have meet you will be composed of the real representatives of the race, men who have for years studied every phase of the problem, whose positions in life are assured and independent. The committee we propose to send will be Rev. J. Milton Waldron, D.D., Pastor of one of the largest churches of Washington, D. C., a man who has for years worked for the political freedom of his people, whose name must be even familiar to you; Rev. Chas. S. Morris, D.D. LL. D., Pastor of one of the largest churches of Norfolk,[2] Va., and prominently connected with the Baptist National Convention, having served that convention as missionary to Africa to investigate the foreign mission work; W. H. C. Brown, a prominent banker of Norfolk and Newport News, Va., who resigned a splendid federal position to engage in the banking business[3] that he might be perfectly independent in his action; Prof. D. Webster Davis. A.M. D.D., Pastor of the Second Baptist Church, Manchester, Va., an author of four books that have large sale in this Country and abroad,[4] and one of the editors, together with myself, of The Industrial History of the Negro Race of the United States,[5] recently adopted by the State Boards of Education of Virginia, West Virginia and

North Carolina for use in the public schools, along with myself of whom I think it unnecessary to write, except to say that I think my extensive law practice places me above any mercenary motives.

We will esteem it a special favor to give us an early reply.[6]

Very respectfully,   Giles B. Jackson

TLS (WP, DLC).

[1] Prominent Negro lawyer and businessman of Richmond, Va., former Republican, who had organized the National Negro Wilson League in 1912 to supply southern Negro speakers for the Democratic National Committee in the North. See Andrew Buni, *The Negro in Virginia Politics, 1902-1965* (Charlottesville, Va., 1967), pp. 39-41, 63-66.

[2] The Rev. Dr. Charles Satchell Morris, pastor of the Bank Street Baptist Church, Norfolk.

[3] William H. C. Brown, vice-president and general manager of E. C. Brown, Inc., and Brown Savings and Banking Company.

[4] Daniel Webster Davis, author of volumes of poetry and biography.

[5] Giles B. Jackson and D. Webster Davis (eds.), *The Industrial History of the Negro Race of the United States* (Richmond, Va., 1911).

[6] This letter bears the following in shorthand: "Governor Wilson requests me to reply to your letter of December 23 to tell you that he will not be able, because of many engagements made weeks ago, to confer with the delegation as generously suggested by your letter. If you will get in touch with me after the new year, I will try to arrange."

From the Diary of Colonel House

December 23, 1912.

Governor Wilson telephoned about Mrs. Stephen N. Ayers[1] who has gotten up a "Womans National Democratic Club." She was in Princeton yesterday for his advice as to its organization and its officers and he referred her to me. He commends her highly, stating that both he and Mrs. Wilson had received a favorable impression of her. He also said that he had had a delightful interview with Mr. Bryan on Saturday, and that he would tell me about it as soon as we got together. He did not wish to discuss it over the telephone.

I advised "going slow" on the Tennessee Senatorial matter and to leave it to us. He said he had done nothing except to write his brother. I asked him to do nothing further and to see that his brother made no mention of his letter. I regard this as a delicate and dangerous proposition and one which must be handled with care. The senatorial candidates in Tennessee would not look with favor upon any interference from the outside, and I have misgivings as to the propriety of his brother entering the race.

We discussed senatorial matters and I explained that the situation was becoming critical in Kansas.[2] I hardly knew how to proceed, that action should come from the National Committee, and that with McCombs sick and in an ugly mood, it was difficult to do anything.

1 Harriet Margaret Bower (Mrs. Stephen Beckwith) Ayres. See n. 4 to the speech to Democratic women in Omaha, Oct. 5, 1912, Vol. 25.

2 The critical situation in Kansas involved the gubernatorial race in which the Democratic candidate, George Hartshorn Hodges, defeated progressive Republican Arthur Capper by a margin of twenty-nine votes. After the announcement of the official count in early December, the matter was taken to the courts because of voting irregularities in several counties. The state supreme court ruled that Capper's only recourse was a recount by the state Senate. However, since the Democrats had won the legislature in the November election, Capper decided not to press the issue further.

It would appear that Colonel House believed that the confused gubernatorial situation in Kansas might affect the selection of a new United States senator by the state legislature in January 1913. Actually, there was never any doubt about the senatorial race. Democrat William Howard Thompson had defeated progressive Republican Governor Walter Roscoe Stubbs by nearly 21,000 votes in the popular vote. Moreover, the two candidates had agreed before the November election that the loser would not allow his name to be put before the legislature. Accordingly, Thompson was elected by the legislature on January 28, 1913. See Robert Sherman La Forte, *Leaders of Reform: Progressive Republicans in Kansas, 1900-1916* (Lawrence, Kan., 1974), pp. 202-206, and William Frank Zornow, *Kansas: A History of the Jayhawk State* (Norman, Okla., 1957), pp. 221-22.

From William Jennings Bryan

My Dear Gov,   Miami, Florida Dec. 25 [1912]

In our hurried (considering the number of subjects discussed) conference we referred briefly to some subjects upon which I beg to add a word

1st. As to the Atty Gen. I share your high opinion of Brandeis & I do not know that a better man can be found. He has a standing among reformers & I am quite sure that all progressives would be pleased. You can doubtless find some one who will look up his record as a lawyer, but it must be remembered that business is now so monopolized that nearly all the *big* lawyers are *corporation* lawyers—and these become so *biased* by environment that they unconsciously take the corporations side—and the more honest they are the more hurtful is the bias. The corporation lawyers, too, can get endorsements all over the country. Such information as I have leads me to believe that Mr Glasgow of Phil. is of this class. Senator [Hoke] Smith could give you information on this subject. I am not sure but your Atty Gen. will do more than any other cabinet officer to make or unmake your administration. It is more important that he be *at heart* with the people *against the special interests* than that he shall be a brilliant lawyer—brilliant lawyers can be hired but the right kind of man for Atty Gen is not so easy to find.

2nd. I am thinking with increasing pleasure of association with

McAdoo. He is a lovable fellow & I am not surprised that you feel an attachment for him. The only question in my mind has been his financial connections and I know nothing of these except from unfriendly sources. If on investigation you should doubt the wisdom of putting a N. Y. man at the head of the treasury there are other cabinet positions to which the objections raised to him would not lie.

3d. I am glad you are favorably impressed with Burke[.][1] If there are any questions connected with the Interior Dept which might not fit into his line of thought there are other cabinet positions for which he is equally well fitted. If for any reason he is eliminated, Mr. Phelan of California & ExGov Higgins of R. I.[2] represent the same element. So do Gov Dunne of Ill.[3] & Jerry B. Sullivan of Ia.

4th. My thoughts have been engrossed with questions connected with our diplomatic Service & I would like your opinion, when you have time to consider the matter, on this question: Do you think it would tend to improve our foreign relations to send naturalized citizens to represent us in the lands from which they came? We have Sweedes Norwegians & Danes who have gained prominence in this country & who would feel honored to go back in a representative character. We have a man of Cuban descent—Hon W. E. Gonzales of S. C. His father was one of the early Cuban patriots & W. E. & his two brothers[4] served in the Spanish-Am war. He has the most influential paper in his State & was one of your first & most influential friends in S. C. It occurs to me that he might make an admirable minister to Cuba. I forgot to say that he was born in the U.S. of an American mother and his father fought in the Confederate Army.

I wonder if you have thought of Ex V. P. Stevenson of Ill? I do not know that he is strong enough for any active work but he is one of our best & biggest men & you may find some honor that will please him.

Have you ever thought of [William A.] Jones of Va for the War Dept? He is a very substantial man of great legislative experience & has for years been deeply interested in Philippine & Porto Rican questions. I have wondered, too, whether House of Texas would accept any thing. I know you are fond of him. He is competent for any thing. I was gratified to learn of your good opinion of Daniels. He is of the Salt of the Earth. But pardon so lengthy an intrusion upon your time—my only excuse is my deep interest   Yours truly   W. J. Bryan

ALS (WP, DLC).

[1] John Burke, Governor of North Dakota, 1907-13, a Bryanite.

² James Henry Higgins, Governor of Rhode Island, 1907-1909.

³ Edward Fitzsimons Dunne, Governor-elect of Illinois.

⁴ William Elliott Gonzales, editor of the Columbia, S. C. *State*. His father, Ambrosio José Gonzales, a long-time advocate of Cuban independence, never had a settled occupation during his many years of residence in the United States. The brothers here referred to were Ambrose Elliott Gonzales, president and publisher of *The State*, and Narciso Gener Gonzales, editor of *The State* from its founding in 1891 until his assassination in 1903. For an excellent study of the Gonzales family and their journalistic enterprises to the death of N. G. Gonzales, see Lewis Pinckney Jones, *Stormy Petrel: N. G. Gonzales and his State* (Columbia, S. C., 1973).

To William Jennings Bryan

Princeton N J Dec 26 [19]12

Mrs Wilson and my daughters join me in warmest greetings of the season to Mrs Bryan and yourself.

Woodrow Wilson.

T telegram (W. J. Bryan Papers, DLC).

From Thomas Bell Love

My dear Governor Wilson: Dallas, Texas, Dec. 27, 1912.

While I know of nothing tangible on which it can be based, the rumor is persistent in Texas that Congressman Burleson is to be a member of the Cabinet under the new administration, and I have concluded after mature deliberation to candidly express my views in the premises in this letter.

In the first place, permit me to say that in so far as I can conceive there is absolutely no reason why Mr. Burleson's selection for a Cabinet post should be in any way objectionable to me on any personal grounds. Our relations have always been cordial, and we have in common many close personal and political friends. Nevertheless, I cannot escape the belief, all things considered, that his selection would not be for the best for a number of reasons:

1. While he is a tireless and indefatigable worker and is peculiarly able in the matter of keeping his political fences in good repair, I do not believe him to be possessed of the capacity for construction which I think essential to the best type of governmental departmental head, nor do I believe him sufficiently disposed to divest public affairs of personal considerations to meet the peculiar needs of these times. In this I do not mean to reflect upon him in the slightest degree. What I mean to say is that I am fearful that he is too much devoted to the old fashioned and as I think pernicious idea, although it is historically

altogether honorable, of the propriety and importance of a public official taking care of and standing by his friends.

2. I do not think that he is or would be considered altogether representative of the rank and file of the progressive Democracy of Texas. Altogether the most powerful and militant special interest in Texas politics is the liquor interest. Whatever may be one's views as to the merits of the prohibition question, the fact undoubtedly is that in Texas the great majority of progressive Democrats are Prohibitionists, and the great majority of reactionaries are anti-Prohibitionists. It is my judgment that easily seventy-five percent. of the Wilson supporters in Texas in the pre-Convention contest were Prohibition Democrats. Mr. Burleson is a well known anti-Prohibitionist. The head and front of the reactionary and anti-progressive element in the Democratic Party in Texas is the present Governor,[1] who lets pass few opportunities to proclaim his opposition to the essential things for which all progressives stand. He was elected Governor in 1910 because of the division of the progressive forces among three candidates, receiving a large minority of the votes cast in the Democratic primaries. He was renominated in the primaries of 1912 by some forty thousand votes, solely because and in recognition of the time honored custom in this State of giving all elective officers a second term, and in the same prinary [primary] a majority of more than fifty thousand votes was cast against every other reactionary candidate for office from United States Senator down. I have no doubt whatever that nine-tenths of the Wilson supporters in Texas were opponents of the renomination of the present Governor. Mr. Burleson is generally understood to have been one of his supporters.

3. Having eliminated every other vestige of reactionary power in official place in Texas, it is the sincere and determined purpose of the progressive Democrats of Texas to elect a genuine progressive Governor in 1914, and this they regard as of the highest importance. The progressive Democrats are fearful that Mr. Burleson's selection for a Cabinet post, in view of the alignments mentioned, would necessarily militate against their efforts in this direction, by reason of the influence which a Texas Cabinet member would very naturally and must necessarily have in all patronage matters arising within the State. This feeling on their part is somewhat accentuated by the glee with which some of their opponents are receiving the suggestion that he is likely to be selected. Personally I do not believe that Federal or other patronage should ever be used to promote any political end, however meritorious, and I am confident this view is shared largely

by the progressive Democrats of Texas. While they do not desire that the patronage be used against them, neither do they desire that it be used in their behalf or for any purpose other than the good of the public service.

4. I believe that an additional reason why no member of Congress should be selected for any Cabinet post lies in the fact that such a selection is necessarily so likely to incite jealousies on the part of other Members of Congress not so selected. Whether it may be known or not, it is nevertheless a fact that there exists at this time such a jealousy between Mr. Burleson and Congressman Henry of this State. I have too high a regard for both of these men to believe that either of them wittingly would permit any such feeling to influence him; but that it exists and that the selection of either of them would cause some disappointment to the other I have absolutely no doubt.

Writing this letter has not been an altogether pleasant thing to do. Personally I derive the greatest pleasure from commending and assisting the promotion of others, but I feel so sure of my ground that I believe it to be my duty to candidly submit my views for your consideration.

I want you to know that I fully appreciate that such matters must be determined by yourself, and that I have the fullest confidence in your capacity as well as in your disposition to determine them aright, and that whatever you may think best to do in the premises will receive my cordial and hearty approbation and support, for whatever it may be worth.

Sincerely yours,   Thos B Love

TLS (WP, DLC).
1 Oscar Branch Colquitt, Governor of Texas, 1911-1915.

An Address at Mary Baldwin Seminary, Staunton, Virginia[1]

[Dec. 28, 1912]

Dr. Fraser, ladies and gentlemen: I need hardly tell you that there has never been an occasion in my life when it was harder for me to make a speech than on this occasion. The theme seems to be myself, and I have always found that a very dull theme. I have never been inspired to speak upon it. And I must say that

1 Delivered from the steps of the main seminary building as part of the ceremonies in celebration of his birthday by the town of Staunton. Wilson spoke in response to a brief speech of greeting by his host, the Rev. Dr. Abel McIver Fraser, pastor of the First Presbyterian Church of Staunton.

I cannot refrain from reminding you at the outset of the first sentences that I shall attempt to utter that I came to you as the executive of a sister state in the great Union which we all love.

(Mrs. Wilson: "Put on your hat.")

(Voices in audience: "Put on your hat.")

I thank you for the suggestion. That was a suggestion from in front and a command from behind.

I cannot forget at this happy moment the confidence that has been reposed in me and the privilege of service that has been accorded me by the great State of New Jersey; and I want to give myself the pleasure of bringing to the great State of Virginia the greetings of the great State of New Jersey. And I believe that in doing so, I suggest an added significance to this occasion, because a son of the South brings the greetings of the North. I would fain believe that my selection as President by the people of the United States means the final obliteration of everything that may have divided the great sections of this country. A great northern state did not hesitate to put the executive responsibilities of the commonwealth in the hands of a Southerner, and the United States has not hesitated to put in the place of chief power in the country itself a native of Virginia. I should be happy indeed if I should be permitted to deem myself in some degree the instrument in drawing together the hearts of all men in the United States for the service of a nation that has neither region, nor section, nor North, nor South.

You will readily believe that today my thoughts are more of the past than of the future. I have no vivid recollection of the first two years that I spent in Staunton. But I have some vivid recollections of subsequent years when I was permitted to visit this, my birthplace. For I have visited here a number of times, when you paid me no attentions whatever. I cannot fail to recall the embarrassment upon which on one occasion I stood in the place where I am now standing when I was a student of law at the university at Charlottesville. I had the very singular good fortune of having five cousins studying at this seminary.[2] I was very fond of those cousins;[3] and I paid them many attentions, and there were numbers of my confreres at the university who accompanied me—out of courtesy—upon my visits. And on one occasion, when I brought a somewhat numerous company of friends to the spot upon which I am now standing, I remember the great

[2] Jessie Woodrow Bones, Marion McGraw Bones, Jeanie Wilson Woodrow, Harriet ("Hattie") Augusta Woodrow, and Marion Woodrow.

[3] Particularly of Hattie. He fell in love with and later proposed to her.

embarrassment with which I submitted to the cross-examination which preceded my entrance at these portals. I have, therefore, not always been welcomed to this spot with open arms.

I remember that I have played many a time in the yard of the little house[4] opposite. I remember flowers that I have picked there —in the present presence I will not say with whom. And so, first and last, I have had many associations with Staunton; all, however, of a boyish, and as compared with the present circumstances, a trivial character. And my thoughts of necessity look forward, because I was struck the other day by a question which was put to me by a newspaper representative. He said: "I suppose, Governor, next Christmas (meaning the Christmas of last week) will be the happiest Christmas of your life." I said: "My young friend, evidently you have never been elected President of the United States. Can you see how a man can have a light heart looking forward to the responsibilities of that great office, particularly at this time?" Because, my friends, we are clearly entering upon a new age. I do not mean merely "we" of the United States. I mean that the world is facing the future with a new attitude and a new outlook upon the opportunities of life.

It is singular how the drama of the world is cast, as if each century were an act in the drama. In these early years of the twentieth century we are again assuming the attitude which we assumed in the beginning of the nineteenth century. The nineteenth century, with all its associations of the setting up of a free government in America, looked forward to an age in which humanity, the rank and file of men, should be served, and honestly served, by the institutions of government. But we had set up this happy experiment in a country so abundantly furnished with wealth, so extraordinarily provided with opportunity for all sorts and conditions of men, that suddenly we got drunk with the mere wine of prosperity, and for a little while forgot that our mission was not to pile up great wealth, but to serve mankind in humanity and justice. But through this long century, during which it has seemed time after time as if we were forgetting what America was set up to do, the world has slowly come about to the point of view which the fine men who set up the Government of the United States had in the beginning. We are now aware that we are not going to be served by institutions; that mere finely conceived constitutions do not constitute the body of liberty; that the body of liberty can be had only in the use of institutions to serve the permanent needs of the rank and file of men.

[4] That is, the manse where he was born.

So that we are learning again that the service of humanity is
the best business of mankind, and that the business of mankind
must be set forward by the governments which mankind sets up,
in order that justice may be done and mercy not forgotten. All
the world, I say, is turning now as never before to this conception of the elevation of humanity, of men and women, I mean,
not of the privileged few, not of those who can by superior wits
or unusual opportunity struggle to the top, no matter whom they
trample under foot, but of men who cannot struggle to the top
and who must therefore be looked to by the forces of society, for
they have no single force by which they can serve themselves.
There must be heart in a government; there must be a heart in
the policies of government. And men must look to it that they
do unto others as they would have others do unto them. This
used to be, and has long been, the theme of the discourse of
Christian ministers, but it has now come to be part of the bound-
en duties of ministers of state.

This is the solemnity that comes upon a man when he knows
that he is about to be clothed with the responsibilities of a great
office, in which will center part of the example which America
shall set to the world itself. Do you suppose that that gives a
man a very light heart at Christmas? I could pick out some
gentlemen, not confined to one state, some gentlemen likely to
be associated with the Government of the United States, who
have not yet had it dawn upon their intelligence what it is that
government is set up to do. There are men who will have to be
mastered in order that they shall be made the instruments of
justice and mercy. This is not a rosewater affair. This is an
office in which a man must put on his war paint. Fortunately,
I have not such a visage as to mind marring it; and I don't care
whether the war paint is becoming or not. And it need not be
worn with truculence. A man can keep his manners and still
fight. Indeed, I have found that he sometimes dismays his opponents by keeping his manners and fighting, because they apparently do not know how to fight with affability. But the nice
thrust of the sword that is delivered with a smile is more dis-
concerting than the thrust delivered with a scowl. And there
must be some good hard fighting, not only in the next four years,
but in the next generation, in order that we may achieve the
things that we have set out to achieve.

The word that stands at the center of what has to be done
is a very interesting word indeed. It has hitherto been supposed
to be a word of charity, a word of philanthropy, a word which
had to do with the operations of the human heart, rather than

with the operations of the human mind and the human ingenuity. I mean the word "service." The one thing that the businessmen of the United States are now discovering, some of them for themselves, and some of them by suggestion, is that they are not going to be allowed to make any money except for a quid pro quo, that they must render a service or get nothing; and that in the regulation of business, the government, that is to say, the moral judgments of the majority, must determine whether what they are doing is a service or is not a service, and that everything in business and politics is going to be reduced to this standard: "Are you giving anything to society when you want to take something out of society?" is the question to be put to them. A large part, too large a part, of the fortune making of recent decades has consisted in getting something for nothing. I do not include brains in the category of "nothing." I believe a man is entitled to earnings for the suggestions of his brains, but he is not entitled to anything when he creates for his brains a sort of air-tight isolation which makes it impossible for anybody else to suggest anything in that field. And, therefore, while I would be liberal in interpreting the service, I want to proclaim for my fellow citizens this gospel for the future, that the men who serve will be the men who profit.

Now, society has always had its revenges. Society has never consented to remember with honor the men who thought only of themselves. The honors of the world have not been distributed upon the basis of wealth. They have been distributed upon the basis of moral worth. I mean, of course, the permanent honors, the honors that are supplied by the judgments of others and not by the judgments of the men themselves. A man can make himself powerful, but he cannot make himself honored, by serving his own interests. And one of the only things that ever makes a state great is the number of men whom it has contributed to the service of the commonwealth or of the nation who thought of the people they were serving before they thought about themselves.

I was speaking just now of the obliteration of sectional lines. Do you not know that long ago the time came when the people of the North honored the men who had served in the ranks of the Confederacy in the Civil War—honored them because they believed that they were laying their lives down for things that they believed in? Such men never fail of honor, even from those who were opposed to them. Of course, there was a special reason why the South should have honored itself. You remember the quaint story of the man who was trudging home—the old Confederate who was trudging home after the surrender—and who was heard to mutter to himself: "Well, I'm not sorry I went in. I believe I was right. I would do it again because I love my country; but I'll be hanged if I'll ever love another country." It came high in the circumstances, and I think that is the reason we have valued it so highly in the years that have followed.

But it is an interesting circumstance to my mind, ladies and gentlemen, that even in this age of peace a household will hang a sword or a musket up above the mantelpiece, that would never think of hanging a spade or a yardstick. And that is not because we believe in war, not because we would not prefer peace, but because we know that the man who handled that sword or handled that musket did not handle it for himself. He stood for a state or a nation; he was fighting for a cause, and his size is measured by the cause, not by himself. Therefore, those of us who love peace honor the emblem of the sword, for it is the emblem of service, that great word which is going to redeem mankind. We believe that we are finding out more and more ways by which service can be rendered without the spilling of blood. But whether with or without the spilling of blood, it is service that dignifies, and service only.

Therefore, I am happy only in this solemn thought in the present circumstances, that I am permitted to serve a little more than some other men have yet been permitted to do. And I am glad that you Virginians are glad to see a Virginian lent to the service of the United States. For it must be remembered, and perhaps we may be forgiven the pride of remembering it, that Virginia has lent an unusual number of men to the service of the United States, and that many a dispassionate thing, many an unselfish thing, has been conceived in this great commonwealth for the benefit, not so much of Virginia as for the benefit of the United States and of mankind.

A great many people praise what Mr. Jefferson said without knowing exactly what it was that he did say. But what they are really praising is the spirit which they know permeated everything that Mr. Jefferson said. That little house, for it is a little house, with all its dignity, that caps the hill at Monticello and stands at the end of the spur of the hills and looks down upon the beautiful valley below, was the coign of vantage from which he looked forth and saw the fertile fields of Virginia and beyond them saw with his mind's eye the spreading acres of the United States. There he thought what it was that mankind should derive from the thinking done at Monticello, tried to divest his mind of the prejudices of race and locality and speak for those permanent issues of human liberty which are the only things that render human life upon this globe itself immortal. Races are immortal in proportion as they think the thoughts of humanity, and until humanity ceases to exist, the world will be debtor to Virginia for the thoughts conceived at Monticello. And so that is one of the thrones of Virginia, where was set up one of the kings of mankind, kings who have won their own elevation to the throne by thinking for their fellow men in terms of humanity and unselfishness.

These are the things which I should prefer to have associated with this day. I pray you, think not of me, for I am an imperfect instrument in trying once more to do what Virginians have, time out of mind, tried to do for the country and for the world.

Transcript of CLSsh (RSB Coll., DLC), with one addition from the text in the *New York Times*, Dec. 29, 1912.

An Address at a Birthday Banquet in Staunton[1]

[Dec. 28, 1912]

Mr. Toastmaster and gentlemen: I can't pretend to hope to rise to the role which has been outlined for me by the very charming, if imaginative, introduction of your toastmaster. But this occasion does afford me an opportunity which it seemed to me this afternoon hardly afforded, to express my feeling about the extraordinary reception which has been accorded me in my birthplace. It would have been easy, I suppose, almost anywhere to get up as much display, but I believe that there must be very few places in the United States in which the display and every exercise would have been marked by so much excellent taste. There was everywhere a touch of simplicity and of personal feeling which I must say made it very difficult for me to speak this afternoon, because it was hard for me to divest myself of the emotions of the occasion.

The day began with one of the prettiest gifts in its conception that I could have imagined. A committee of gentlemen,[2] as you perhaps know, visited me and presented me with beautifully

[1] The event took place at the Staunton Military Academy. The toastmaster was Allen Caperton Braxton, a lawyer of Staunton and Richmond. The other speakers included Governor William Hodges Mann, Representative Henry De La Warr Flood, Richard Evelyn Byrd, and William Frank McCombs. Wilson responded to the toast, "Our Next President." Richmond *Times-Dispatch*, Dec. 29, 1912. For discussions of this occasion and the significance of Wilson's remarks, see Link, *The New Freedom*, pp. 25-26, and Allen W. Moger, *Virginia: Bourbonism to Byrd, 1870-1925* (Charlottesville, Va., 1968), pp. 283-84.

[2] Headed by Charles Catlett, proprietor of a chemical laboratory in Staunton, on behalf of the city.

wrought miniatures of my father and my mother,[3] and it seemed to me that they had interpreted my own wish and preference; not that I had thought of that gift, but I had wished to be received as a person, a neighbor, as a man who loved the people from whom he had sprung. It was a subtle and delicate compliment, as if they had interpreted my own feeling and my own thought; because I have often said that while I walked, so far as is known, a pretty straight road while I was in college, I did not feel that it was due to any natural and innate virtue of my own. I know again and again, when I was tempted to do things that I knew I ought not to do, I was restrained, not so much by the precepts of morals, as by what I knew the folks at home would think of me if I did those things.

It is astonishing how much of a man's morals is in other people's keeping. There is a story which I have told once or twice—not a funny story but a very touching one, it seems to me, and a very instructive one—which illustrates the thing perfectly. When Mr. Webster was at the acme of his career, he went back after a very fatiguing session of the Senate to his town home in Boston. He reached there in the early afternoon and went immediately to his room and to his bed; (for journeys were more fatiguing then than they are now) and he bade his servant not to venture in any circumstances to interrupt his rest. He had hardly sunk off into that first delicious loss of consciousness which precedes sound sleep when there was a knock at his door. His orders were immediately disobeyed, and his servant roused him; and he angrily asked him why he dared to do that. "Well," he said, "Mr. Webster, I wouldn't have ventured to do it, sir, but there are some gentlemen downstairs from your old home in New Hampshire who wouldn't go away, sir, and they said it was a case of life and death that they had to see you about." Webster, with many complainings and grumblings, got on his clothes and went down, to find a group of plain men from his old home in New Hampshire, who told him that there was a boy, their neighbor, a son of a friend of his, who was charged with murder and caught in a net of circumstantial evidence which seemed absolutely to be conclusive. "But," they said, "Mr. Webster, we have known that boy ever since he was born; he did not commit that murder, and we don't know any man that can unravel this skein of evidence but yourself. You must come." He said, "Gentlemen, I can't. It wouldn't avail the boy anything; I am so worn out that

[3] Executed by Ellen Douglas Stuart, former art teacher at Stuart Hall, a private girls' school in Staunton.

I have no wits to put at his disposal now. I can't come." They pled with him, and finally he said he wouldn't come. And then they rose and the spokesman said, half to Mr. Webster and half to the others, "Well, I suppose we must go home; I don't know what the neighbors will say." "Oh, well," said Mr. Webster, "if it comes to the neighbors, I'll go."

That is the greatest compulsion I know of—what the neighbors would think. A very witty English writer[4] says, "You may talk of the tyranny of Nero and Tiberius, but the real tyranny is the tyranny of your next-door neighbor." The obligation of doing what he does and being what he is is sometimes very onerous indeed. And yet that is what directs the course of most of us, and particularly the moral judgments of the neighbors. Now, I am glad in some respects that you do not know everything that has transpired since I left Staunton, but I am conscious in coming back to this, my native place, of having attempted to square a great part of my life with the standards established in the olden time in the great Commonwealth of Virginia. It is as if a man came back to drink at some of the original fountains of political impulse and inspiration in this country. For in spite of what other gentlemen may claim, Virginia, after all, was settled first, and we did begin to set aglow the lamp of liberty in this colony before it was lighted elsewhere.

I was in Bermuda the other day—as some of you may have heard—and my politeness was put to a great test, because I sat in the little parliament as a guest there and said nothing while the speaker of the assembly told me that theirs was the oldest representative assembly on this side of the water, and added that it had its first session in the year 1620. I knew that the first session of a representative assembly had been in the Commonwealth of Virginia in the year 1619. Although that was only a year's difference, it was a good lead! But I am proud to tell you that I remembered my manners and said nothing—again showing my Virginian training. As an historian, I was outraged, but as a gentleman I had to sit silent.

So, I feel that I am the man that has got something out of this occasion. I am the man that has derived, not, I will say, perhaps the chief pleasure from it—for I think the old Scripture maxim is profoundly true, "It is more blessed to give than to receive"—but certainly the chief profit from it, for I shall go away with all the things renewed in me that may, peradventure, keep me straight. And, after all, the only things that will tell in the years im-

4 Walter Bagehot, in "The Character of Sir Robert Peel."

mediately ahead of us are moral forces. There are some gentlemen in New Jersey wondering yet what struck them. And I
can't explain it to them, because it isn't in their vocabulary. They
supposed, and they suppose yet, that politics is a game, whereas
politics is part of the life of the nation, and any man who doesn't
interpret that life cannot conduct that game. A man, therefore,
who constantly forgets that the judgments of a nation vary and
rise with the circumstances of its life, just as the judgments of
an individual do, is not fitted for the great stage upon which
public affairs are settled.

Their surprise in New Jersey reminds me of a very grotesque
story—perhaps I may call it—in the old frontier days, when there
was a frontier. (The Philippines are our present frontier, and
we don't know what rich things are happening out there, and are
presently, I hope, to deprive ourselves of that frontier.) But when
there was a frontier, when there were rough frontier communities, where civilization had not yet got its complete
ascendency, a man who wished to improve his circumstances
went from an eastern community to a frontier settlement. He was
a very plain man—he was a blacksmith by trade—and a very
peaceable, quiet man. He did not care to carry firearms—indeed
he was unfamiliar with the use of them—but he realized he would
have to have some kind of weapon in the new life he was going
to lead. So he chose the thing most deadly that was most familiar
to him, namely, a rasp about that long and carried it in the only
part of his person that was permanently straight, namely, his
back, where he could reach the handle of it in the loose collar
of his shirt. And finding that in order to make acquaintances in
his new home it was advantageous to sit around with the loafers
in the afternoon in the barroom, he sat there making acquaintances, but not drinking, for his habit was that of a sober man.
And nothing happened until about the third day he was there,
when a bully, who had been off on a spree of about a week, came
back to town and immediately made for the headquarters of his
operations. And seeing this stranger sitting there, he at once
said, "Hello, stranger, come up and take a drink." "No," said
the man, "I don't drink," which, if you remember, was a deadly
insult in those days. The man said, "What!" and reached for his
revolver, and our friend the blacksmith saw there was no time
to be lost. He sprang at this man, and as he sprang drew and
struck, and his victim fell in a heap upon the floor. And the blacksmith was very uneasy; he was afraid in his excitement he had
struck too hard and had killed the man, and was about to go off
when the man said, "No, stranger, don't go off. Stay around."

They picked his victim up and carried him to a sort of drugstore across the street and worked on him. For half an hour or so our friend the blacksmith walked uneasily up and down in front of the barroom, waiting to see what was happening, until the victim emerged with his face held together in every direction with courtplaster, and approached him again; whereupon, the blacksmith thought the attack was going to be renewed and reached for his weapon again. The man said, "No, hold on, stranger, hold on, stranger. I don't hold any ill will agin ye, but," he said, "you will pardon my curiosity, what kind of a dern weapon was that?"

I think that was a reasonable curiosity. And that is the kind of curiosity that is now felt in New Jersey. And it was an unusual weapon of peace that was not like the dirks that are used in the dark. It descended as the heavens would descend, and I hope had something of the heavens about it. But we must reflect, gentlemen, that the country is full of men who do not know how to wield that weapon. Thank God, they don't know how to resist it either, but they don't know how to wield it. Thought is going to dominate this country, because there are lots of things to think out, and nothing will save this country except straight thinking. Morals will save this country because we have changed our lives faster than we have adjusted the Decalogue. We have gone into great transactions which we didn't see how to square with the simple morals of individual action. Many an honest man, many a man who would be unimpeachable in his individual conduct, has, nevertheless, engaged in transactions sometimes in this country which would not square with the principles to which he held himself individually—partly out of ignorance, partly out of haste, partly out of the exigencies of doing great things in a short space of time. I do not feel that you can draw an indictment against any part of our business community. They have largely sinned in ignorance and in thoughtless haste. But they have got to square the biggest things with the simplest standards of morality and obligation.

It isn't a task for the casuist. It isn't a task for the man who will draw fine-spun distinctions. You have got to lay down the great measurements of morals, and square by them. It has got to be done slowly, because some men need a lot of education. It has got to be done tenderly, because if you can educate a man there is no use killing him before you have educated him. It has got to be done in such a way as not to tear and destroy the economic fiber of the nation, and so stop the processes of life. But it has got to be done, and it has got to be done with an absolutely inflexible will. I dare say the patient won't always like it. I dare say that there are some gentlemen who will be criticizing the processes of change until they die; but some of them are elderly, and so the criticism of the processes of change may not be as long as we fear. Because, just so soon as the air clears, men will once more see the horizon. Just so soon as the mists are blown away by the new forces of our time, men will see the road behind them and the road in front of them, and will know in what direction they are going, and whether they are going uphill or downhill.

I sometimes figure to myself what has happened to us now by what happened to me once in the mountains of Wales. I was bicycling, and I had started out from Bangor to go through the mountains by Betws-y-Coed and its exquisite valleys. And I rode for four or five miles with great discontent with my bicycle, because it went abominably hard. I was traveling what appeared to be an absolutely level road. I got off and looked at the adjustments of the machine, and it was all right, and I got on and pedaled and pedaled, and sweated and sweated. I got off again and oiled the thing at every joint, and again pedaled and sweated and pedaled and sweated. After I had gone about five miles, the road, which had been going around the shoulder of a great mountain, swung the other way, and I saw the valley behind me. And I had been coming uphill for five miles and had supposed myself on a level road.

How often that happens to you, particularly where the engineering is as ingenious as the engineering of some things we know have been! The road looks to be the road of civilization, and you swing around some corner of the mountains and get into a keener, finer air; and look back and you see the obstacles that you have been struggling with, and you know what you are up against, and then for the first time you know what it is necessary to do. And so the one thing images in my mind the other: we are not now deceived as to the circumstances of our times or as to what it is necessary to do; and, moreover, we are chagrined to find that America saw the moral somewhat later than some other countries saw it, somewhat later in respect to several important matters than our own immediate neighbors in Canada saw it, for the Canadians have forestalled certain things which we did not even know were in danger of happening.

And so, then in every direction you turn it is a matter of information, of guidance, of moral rectitude, and of inflexible courage, and I believe that the happiest circumstance of our time is that this isn't a thing which a few men have seen. The men who voted the Democratic ticket were rather numerous, and the men who would have voted the Democratic ticket if they hadn't been confused by the circumstances would have added a great many millions more. Because, enormous sections of public opinion of this country are perfectly clarified. There is no doubt in the mind of the nation what has to be done, and there is to no going back whatever. I may blunder, the men who have so far been picked out may not be the right men, but whether they succeed or not, the right men are going to arise, and the thing is going to be done. And there will be a good deal of fun in having a shot at it. Because I feel my temper to be perfectly good. I am not excited. I am not opposed to anybody. I haven't got my gun out for anybody. Some men may accidentally get in the way of the gun, you know! That will be their fault, and not mine, because the level of the gun is established and the range is well known, and the trajectory is calculated. So that I shall feel that I am not responsible for accidents. But I haven't got it in for anybody.

I remember that that was the first thing that I had to preach when I was candidate for governor in New Jersey. I remember saying to an audience made up entirely of workingmen, "Of course, I am the friend of the workingmen, but not against anybody else. I am the friend of capital legitimately employed, but not against the workingmen." The thing we have got to realize is that the right is not partisan, and that what is for the good of one class, if properly understood, is for the good of all classes, and that our cause is a common cause. Until we have seen that, and until we have accumulated brains of common counsel enough to work it out, we haven't seen the thing in its real habit as it is.

There are certain gentlemen—I dare say one of them[5] is present tonight—who have frankly told me that there was a time when they were afraid of me, because they thought I had some screw loose or that I was rather wild. For example, Virginia herself in the convention showed no great enthusiasm for my nomination. But these gentlemen now say to me that in view of things that I have said since I was nominated—which are exactly the same things that I said before I was nominated—they are no longer afraid of me. By which I draw this simple conclusion—that they did not read the things that I said before I was nominated, and that after I was nominated it became worth their while really to find out what I did actually say. I have been uttering, so far as I know, nothing but the original doctrines of liberty as understood in America. And those doctrines have nowhere been better understood or better illustrated than in this ancient Commonwealth of Virginia.

5 Flood, who was a close political ally of Senator Thomas Staples Martin.

The trouble with some gentlemen was that they had ceased to believe in the Virginia Bill of Rights. That is an extremely plainspoken document. It says nothing less irreverent of constitutions than this, that whenever a people finds its institutions unsuitable for its circumstances, it has an inalienable right to change them. We have said that ever since this commonwealth was set up, and it ought not to give us cold feet now. And it is just as true now as when it was said, only some gentlemen have thought that a great many convenient obstacles had been put in the way of acting upon the Virginia Bill of Rights, whereas, I, in my simplicity as a student of affairs, have always believed that the Virginia Bill of Rights meant what it said. If it doesn't, I don't understand the English language not only, but I don't understand English liberty. For the Virginia Bill of Rights didn't say anything new. The Virginia Bill of Rights said what the Declaration of Rights and the Bill of Rights had said in those old days when England was fighting to get a foothold for human rights. It is no discovery made on this side of the water; it is merely a transplantation of the tree of liberty into a soil more wholesome, more virgin, more suitable to know the simple rights of life in dealing man with man.

So I am not in the least afraid of being regarded as a heretic, provided you know the standards of orthodoxy. There are some advantages in reading history. You have got longer lines to measure by. You know you can't set two posts in a row; you have got to have three posts at least to make a row. Because you don't know whether you are going north or going south if you have only two posts, but once set up your third post, and you have got your line. And if you have more than three posts, if the posts run like antique landmarks back into the ancient days when men held these things like religious convictions, then you have got a line which you can't deflect from, so long as you know where to find these landmarks of the progress of mankind.

I was speaking of certain gentlemen in New Jersey. One singular thing happened in New Jersey when I was running for governor. A great many gentlemen who had never read the history of the United States began reading my history of the United States—not for the purpose of learning the history of the United States at all, but for the purpose of finding objectionable things that I might have said. And the incidental advantage was that there was a certain natural increment of historical information in the State of New Jersey, and it became known that certain things had not been discovered by the author of that history but had been commonplace when he wrote them—a very useful thing for some men to remember. It is commonplace where men are free for the right ultimately to succeed. It is not a strange thing, it is a normal thing.

And as I look around upon the audiences that I have had the privilege of facing, there has been something very touching about the campaign that has just closed. Why, gentlemen, a heart has come to common men once more. Men believe now that sooner or later their wrongs are going to be righted, and that a time is going to dawn when justice will be the average and usual thing in the administration of public affairs.

You may imagine the pleasure, therefore, that it gives me to come back to a place where these standards cannot be questioned, for these standards were first established, so far as this side of the water is concerned, in Virginia. And no Virginian can stand up and look the history of Virginia in the face and doubt what the future is going to be. If I have any advantage as a Virginian, it is merely that I have got a running start. A man that ties in with communities of this sort began further back, and the further back you got your start, the greater the momentum. And all that is needed is momentum. It doesn't need any cunning tongue, it doesn't need eloquence. It just needs the kind of serenity which enables you to steer by the stars, and not by the ground.

Transcript of CLSsh (RSB Coll., DLC), with two corrections from the incomplete text in the Richmond *Times-Dispatch*, Dec. 29, 1912.

From Warren Worth Bailey

My Dear Governor,   Johnstown, Pa., Dec. 28 [1912].

I cannot refrain from offering my congratulations on two things—your opening article in World's Work on "The New Freedom" and your protest against the barbaric show being planned at Washington in connection with the coming inauguration.[1] It seems to me in the worst of bad taste for a democracy to imitate the examples of royalty and imperialism in the transfer of an office; and if ever we needed to set an example of Jeffersonian simplicity it is now. I most especially abominate the militaristic savor which is given to these gaudy and garish shows and it seems to me that a popular chord would be struck were this civil function relieved of every martial trapping and every suggestion of military display.

"The New Freedom" is fine in conception, bold in execution and inspiriting in the promise it gives for the next four years. For two years of that period I have been commissioned to work with you along democratic lines[2] toward that goal which you so plainly point out in the article named and it is my earnest hope that in a small way it shall be my good fortune to be of real help in redeeming our great and vital pledges. I grow prouder every day of the fact that it was given to me to vote forty-six times for you at Baltimore and to have shared modestly in writing the great platform upon which your election was achieved; and more and more I feel that a new era is opening up, that better things are appearing above the horizon, that the old order is indeed changing and that in you our historic party has a leader worthy of its past and a guaranty of its future.

It is not for me to proffer advice, but you will pardon me for saying that in my judgment the less we delay in performing the work to which we have been called the better it will be for the country, the smaller the opportunity for the work of those marplots whom you have promised to gibbet as high as Haman.

Hoping at some time to have the privilege of paying my personal respects and becoming better acquainted with your plans for the future and feeling that the mission of Democracy is inspiring, I remain, with every cordial sentiment,

Respectfully yours,   Warren Worth Bailey

TLS (WP, DLC).

[1] During a brief stop of his train at Washington, en route to Staunton, on December 27, Wilson conferred briefly with William Corcoran Eustis, the recently appointed chairman of the committee on arrangements for the presidential inauguration. Wilson was quoted in the press as having told Eustis: "The thing has been overdone in the past. I wish you would have the ceremonies as simple as may be consistent with dignity and order." *Newark Evening News,* Dec. 28, 1912.

[2] He had been elected to the House of Representatives in November.

From Carter Glass

Dear Governor Wilson: Lynchburg, Va., December 29, 1912.

I have been thinking much about the subject of our interview at Princeton on Thursday[1] and am trying in my mind to reduce the suggestions there made to something tangible in order that the hearings before my sub-committee, beginning January 7th, may be directed to a definite, even though tentative, plan of currency reform. I am a little afraid that the embarrassment of being between the fire of two learned professors was somewhat confusing on Thursday; but I have some very distinct notions about the lines we should pursue and especially about the situation that will confront us at Washington. On this latter point there is some illumination in a letter I have just received from one of the great New York bankers invited to the hearings of my sub-committee. There is this paragraph:

"The American Bankers Association, as a body, at its meeting in New Orleans a year ago, endorsed the Aldrich bill. It would seem, therefore, impossible for us as members of the Currency Commission of the American Bankers Association, to take any other position or do anything else before your committee than to endorse that bill, if we were to appear before you officially."

I felt certain before receiving this letter that we would encounter this difficulty. The bankers intend to fight for the Aldrich plan as it is drafted in order to get the same thing in a different form. They do not intend that the $350,000 expended by the Monetary Commission and the additional $300,000 expended by the Citizens League in "educational work" shall be wasted. I much apprehend that "educational work" with some of these gentlemen means ability to organize influences and to bring pressure to bear to drive schemes through Congress merely because they want them and not entirely because they should have them. Might it not be well to draft a bill on the Regional Reserve Bank lines, taking care of all the details discussed last Thursday, and put on the advocates of the Aldrich bill the burden of showing that a central superstructure should be imposed, requiring them to suggest a superstructure that shall not possess the evils of bank monopoly and the dangers of centralized power? We may ourselves have in readiness such a "capstone" as I understood you to suggest, having the wholesome powers of a central supervisory control.

If I might have a further brief talk with you some day at your convenience before we begin hearings, I think matters would be decidedly facilitated. I know how busy you are and I dislike to take up any part of your time; but I likewise know what a powerful factor you must be in the solution of this problem if we are to have any currency legislation at all.

I think all Virginia was delighted at the home-coming event at Staunton yesterday and I hope the strangers in our midst were not too much wearied with the recital of Virginia's greatness. It seemed to some of us, if I may be permitted to say it, that the one present object lesson might have sufficed. Mr. McCoombs' reference to John Allen's darkey[2] had an immediate application,[3] which I am sure Mr. McCoombs did not intend, but which was, nevertheless, a little smarting.

Yours very truly,   Carter Glass.

TLS (WP, DLC).

1 Glass and H. Parker Willis conferred for two hours with Wilson in his home in Princeton on December 26. Wilson was in bed with a severe cold. The discussion centered around a draft of a banking and currency reform bill which Willis had drawn up for Glass's subcommittee. This draft bill called for a decentralized, privately controlled reserve system with an unspecified number of local reserve banks, each having full reserve banking powers. Wilson agreed with most of the provisions of the draft but doubted that Willis's plan to give the Comptroller of the Currency general supervision of the reserve system would provide sufficient co-ordination and control. Willis suggested, as he later recalled, "that a very marked degree of centralization would be obtained by uniting the banks in the several proposed [reserve] districts under a consolidated type of organization subject to general federal oversight." Wilson apparently seized upon this vague hint. "That such a general central organ of the proposed banking system should be assigned very broad and inclusive powers was the decided view of the President-elect." Willis felt that the conversation indicated clearly that Wilson "was desirous of effecting a substantial degree of centralization, although heartily maintaining the concept of local self-control. . . . While not specific in his conception of the kind of centralized control which should be developed, or, as he expressed it in the Princeton interview, the 'capstone to be placed upon the structure,' it appeared probable that he would favor an organization designed to control and supervise and that he felt no partiality to the idea of a central bank of some kind. He recognized the fact that such an organization was politically impossible even if economically desirable, and that what was to be sought was the provision of those central banking powers which were unmistakably desirable and the elimination of those central banking powers which had caused danger in the past." Henry Parker Willis, *The Federal Reserve System: Legislation, Organization and Operation* (New York, 1923), pp. 141-42, 146. See also Carter Glass, *An Adventure in Constructive Finance* (Garden City, N. Y., 1927), pp. 81-84. See also C. Glass to H. P. Willis, Dec. 29, 1912, and H. P. Willis to C. Glass, Dec. 31, 1912.

2 See the campaign speech in Salem, N. J., printed at Oct. 25, 1910, and n. 3 thereto, Vol. 21.

3 An allusion to his bitter campaign against Claude A. Swanson for the Democratic senatorial nomination in 1911.

Carter Glass to Henry Parker Willis

Dear Doctor Willis: Lynchburg, Va., December 29, 1912.

I am just back from the Wilson celebration at Staunton and am literally worn to a frazzle. I had hoped that I might get, perhaps, an hour with Mr. Wilson on currency matters; but it was plain to be seen that every moment of his time was taken up with parade and reception. I have been thinking much over our interview at Princeton and find some trouble in sifting anything out of it. It is clear to me that Mr. Wilson has been written to and talked to by those who are seeking to mask the Aldrich plan and give us dangerous centralization; but we shall have to keep quiet on this point for the present.

I think it would be well if you can immediately redraft those sections of our bill which we have most discussed. I am engaged for another banquet in Roanoke tomorrow night and cannot in the compass of a letter say to you what I would like to say; but I think it extremely important for us to get together at the earliest possible moment in order to go over the bill by sections. We should make the alterations that you and I have talked over and should so alter certain sections of the bill as to meet the tentative views expressed by the President-elect—that is if you understand what they are. You will recall that he would take away from the individual banks the right of issue; but was disposed to compromise on my suggestion to lodge the right of issue with the divisional reserve bank instead of centralizing it at Washington. As I recall he also took kindly to the suggestion that there should be no inducement for the country banks to keep money on deposit in New York beyond their actual needs for exchange purposes and that, therefore, it would be well not to permit payment of interest by banks on bank deposits. Then there is the matter of divisional reserve bank organization. I mean the method of appointing directors and the character of men who are to direct. We shall have to hit upon some distinction between "bankers" and "business men," perhaps defining the former as men whose "chief business" is that of banking.

I did not get the impression that Mr. Wilson at this time is opposed to the guarantee of deposits. I have no doubt, however, that great pressure will be brought to bear to put him against that feature of the bill; but I am disposed to insist. Very likely you will recall my remark that, speaking for myself, I would cheerfully go with the President-elect for some body of central *supervisory* control, if such a body can be constituted and divested of the practical attributes of a central bank. In my judgment this is the point of danger. This is where the bombardment will be directed. If we can devise a superstructure or, to use Mr. Wilson's phrase, "a capstone," for the plan we have as it shall be revised, it would be well to be prepared for that emergency.

I would like the best in the world to get another hour or two with Mr. Wilson. I am a little afraid that the embarrassment of being between the fire of two learned professors somewhat confused me on Thursday; but I have some very definite ideas, not only on the currency itself, but on the practical situation at Washington and on this line I would like a further discussion with President-elect. I shall write to him immediately and suggest this.

Yours very truly,   [Carter Glass]

Suppose you wire me here, on receipt of this, how soon you can meet me in Wash.

CCL (C. Glass Papers, ViU).

From William Jennings Bryan

My Dear Gov,   Miami, Florida Dec. 30 [1912]

Do not take time to answer my letters, except when you want to communicate something to me but I feel I ought to report on a number of letters just rec'd. I have a number of letters urging Burke for Sec of the Interior. I need not quote from them. We have gone over the subject & you know my opinion. Have quite a number also recommending Folk for Atty Gen.[,] Campbell & Cone Johnson of Texas are commended—both are excellent men.

Osborne of Wyoming & Adams[1] of Colo are being urged for Interior dept—both good men. I gave you my opinion of Osborn when you were at my house. He is one of the best men I know of for any position. Norris[2] of Mont & King of Oregon[3] are also candidates for Sec of Interior—both are competent & progressive[.] Wood of Oregon[4] is also a good man but information rec'd leads me to fear that Teal of Oregon[5] is questionable. If you think of him in connection with the office I suggest that you scrutinize his endorsements. I remember that you question the propriety of selecting a man from the Mountain States—and there is force in the objection, & it probably applies to Oregon & Washington where the timber & water power questions are as acute as in the Mountain States. Ballinger came from Washington & Senator Mitchell[6] who was implicated in the land frauds represented Oregon. Two new men have been brought to my attention, viz. Creamer Tres of O. for Sec of Treasury[7] & Prof. Waters of Kas[8] for Sec of Agriculture. If you find it necessary to consider any new names for the position of Sec of Treas. Creamer is worth considering. He is a progressive & an excellent man. He has made a success of his present position, Treasurer of one of the great States. In mentioning him I must not be understood as offering any objection to McAdoo for I share your confidence in him and appreciate your desire to recognize his valuable services during the campaign. I am very favorably impressed with the endorsements of Waters. He fits the requirements as you set them forth & may be the very man you are looking for.

I sympathize with you in your effort to select a cabinet that will combine the maximum of capacity for service with a sufficient amount of reputation to win popular approval. In writing you about men I am treating you as I would want you to treat me. I want all the light I can get and I then decide for myself & I expect you to feel as free to reject my suggestions—if your judgment leads you in another direction—as you would an anonymous suggestion.

Am having a good deal of outdoor life here and am enjoying it immensely. Mrs. Bryan joins me in wishing you and your family a Happy New Year.   Yours truly   W. J. Bryan

Every one praises Brandeis for Atty Gen. but I would regard Hoke Smith as the ideal man for that place if he could accept.

ALS (WP, DLC).
    [1] John E. Osborne, former Governor of Wyoming; Alva Adams, former Governor of Colorado. For the latter's political career, see B. B. Lindsey to WW, April 24, 1911, n. 2, Vol. 22.
    [2] Edwin Lee Norris, Governor of Montana, 1908-1913.
    [3] William Rufus King, lawyer of Portland; associate justice of the Supreme Court of Oregon, 1908-1911.
    [4] Perhaps Charles Erskine Scott Wood, former army officer, lawyer, and author of Portland, Oregon.
    [5] Joseph Nathan Teal, lawyer of Portland. He belonged to various conservation groups but also served as counsel for the West Coast Lumber Manufacturers Association.
    [6] John Hipple Mitchell, Republican senator from Oregon, 1873-79, 1885-97, 1901-1905. Just prior to his death in 1905, Mitchell had been convicted in a federal district court on a charge of having received fees for expediting the land claims of clients before the United States Land Commissioner.
    [7] David Staley Creamer, Treasurer of Ohio since 1908.
    [8] Henry Jackson Waters, president of Kansas State Agricultural College (now Kansas State University), Manhattan.

From Cleveland Hoadley Dodge

My dear Woodrow   New York. Dec. 30th 1912

Hearty congratulations on your beautiful speech last Saturday, which will be an inspiration to the whole country.

I sincerely hope the trip didn't do you any harm & that your cold is better.

By the papers, you have apparently selected your man to be your secretary. In fact they name three or four men as having been appointed. Probably you have made your decision, but if perchance you have not, I want to merely suggest the name of Andie Imbrie. I have no idea whether he would fill the bill, but he has some admirable qualifications

I can imagine your thoughts as the New Year comes in, & can only wish you & yours a very happy & blessed time in the coming months.

If you ever get over the present rush, I hope I may be able to see you   Ever faithfully & affly yr's   C. H. Dodge

ALS (WP, DLC).

From Henry St. George Tucker

My dear Gov'r,   Lexington Va. Dec 30th, 1912

I enclose you a clipping from the Times-Dispatch of Richmond on your speech at the Staunton banquet.[1] It has produced a profound impression, & while criticism abounds *all* agree you spoke the truth—in this the incident is likened unto the Harvey-Watterson episode.

It is my deliberate judgment that nothing you have said or done since your nomination has so stirred the enthusiasm of your real friends in the State as this speech.

Most of the crowd who opposed you at Norfolk[2] and Baltimore are today only waiting the opportunity to oppose your plans of reform. Fear will drive them to your open support, but obstacles will secretly be interposed to thwart their full success. Your friends endorse the speech without reserve, and I am again thankful that you have been permitted to stand in a position commended by all of your friends and condemned by none save those who have pretended to be such.

In a short speech at the Hotel in Staunton Friday night I opened with these words "I am glad to speak to the people of Staunton, who did not need the action of the Baltimore Convention to make them advocates of Woodrow Wilson."

You have put renewed life into us. Keep it up!

Sincly yrs.   H. S. G. Tucker

ALS (WP, DLC).
    [1] The clipping is missing. There were several reports of Wilson's speech in the Richmond *Times-Dispatch*, Dec. 29, 1912. However, the clipping sent by Tucker probably was one of two editorials, "Wilson and Virginia's Bill of Rights," and "Trust the People," which appeared in the issue of December 30, 1912. Both commented favorably on Wilson's speech and explicitly approved Wilson's pointed remarks about Virginia's conservative political leaders.
    [2] That is, the Democratic state convention which met at Norfolk on May 23, 1912.

From Josephus Daniels

Dear Governor: Raleigh, North Carolina Dec. 30th, 1912.

Your speech at Staunton came as an invigorating tonic and made the people "sit up and take notice" as did your Haman reference at the Southern Society banquet. I cannot tell you how much those two utterances cheered me and all others who have "enlisted for the war" and not for a short period.

Do not take the trouble to answer. You have graver problems, with more complexities, than any man of our generation. You have my sympathy and I have the faith that you will be given the wisdom to solve them for the common weal.

With New Year greetings to all the Wilson family from all the Daniels family, I am,

Sincerely your friend,   Josephus Daniels

ALS (WP, DLC).

To Thomas Bell Love

Personal.

My dear Mr. Love: [Trenton, N. J.] December 31, 1912.

I value very highly your letter of December twenty-seventh. It is so entirely frank and to the point and you may be sure that it will enter into my thought as furnishing some of the considerations which I must steadily hold in view.

Cordially and sincerely yours,   Woodrow Wilson

TLS (photostat in the T. B. Love Papers, Dallas Hist. Soc.).

To William Jennings Bryan

My dear Mr. Bryan: [Trenton, N. J.] December 31, 1912.

I value very highly your letter of Christmas Day. Everything that you say adds something valuable to my thought and furnishes me further means of forming a judgment.

Your suggestion about Mr. Gonzales of South Carolina particularly interests me and is of special significance in its setting. Of course there would be many instances in which it might be unwise to send as our representatives, natives of the country to which they were accredited, but in Gonzales' case the idea strikes me most favorably. Have you any means of knowing whether it would be acceptable to him or not, I wonder.

In haste,   Cordially yours,   Woodrow Wilson

TLS (W. J. Bryan Papers, DLC).

From William Jennings Bryan

My Dear Gov.   Miami, Florida Dec 31 [1912]

The editorial on "The Blight of Seniority"[1] was written before I saw you & it never occurred to me that I would be accused of speaking for you. If you think best I will write a brief editorial stating that it was written before I saw you and that I alone am responsible for it. If you wire "I advise course suggested" I will understand it & wire editorial for next weeks issue.[2] And this raises a question as to my running the Commoner while in office. I fear that everything I say will by those who are unfriendly be assumed to represent your views. Do you think that is likely to embarrass either of us?

It has occurred to me that *one month* of Chautauqua work each summer would be sufficient to supplement my income & that I might reduce criticism to a minimum by providing that there should be *no admission charge for my lecture*. I think the advantage which the Chautauqua would derive from sale of *season tickets* would be sufficient to justify a reasonable compensation for me. What do you think?[3]

The Menace had an editorial stating that you were considering our mutual friend McGraw for Post Master Gen.[4] As a result I have rec'd about twenty protests. I hope, however, that you will not allow these protests to prevent the appointment of a Catholic to some position in the Cabinet. A new friend suggests Ex-Atty Gen Jackson of N. Y.[5] for Atty Gen. He is a good man & made an excellent record. Lieut Gov Glynn of N. Y. is also a good man.

Yours truly   W. J. Bryan

I see Nixon of N. Y.[6] is mentioned for Navy. He is a very intelligent fellow & takes a deep interest in naval affairs. Think he would follow your view on battleships.

Nathan Strauss is a man you can use. He is the strongest of the Strauss brothers.

ALS (WC, NjP).

  [1] An enclosed clipping, "The Blight of Seniority," *The Commoner*, XII (Dec. 27, 1912), in which Bryan argued that the progressive Democrats in the Senate and House of Representatives should ignore the rule of seniority in making committee assignments.

  [2] Wilson never responded to this question.

  [3] See WW to W. J. Bryan, Jan. 16, 1913, Vol. 27.

  [4] *The Menace* was an anti-Catholic weekly magazine published in Aurora, Missouri. The subject of its attack was John Thomas McGraw, lawyer and businessman of Grafton, West Va., who had been a member of the Democratic National Committee since 1896.

  [5] William Schuyler Jackson, lawyer of Buffalo, Attorney-General of New York, 1907-1909.

  [6] Lewis Nixon, designer of naval ships and submarines; proprietor of ship-building and gunpowder manufacturing companies in New Jersey. He resided in New York and was active in Tammany Hall.

From Moorfield Storey

My dear Governor Wilson: Boston 31st December 1912

I hope you will permit me to say that nothing has given me greater pleasure for a good many years than the declaration in regard to Philippine independence which you made at Staunton. I am satisfied that nothing will gratify the people of the United

States more than to feel that they are relieved from the charge of the Islands, because deep in their consciences they know that our retention of them is inconsistent with all the principles on which our government rests. They have never taken any intelligent interest in the Islands, and I trust your administration will have the glory of putting an end to a very discreditable chapter in our history.

I hope, too, that this will be done soon so that the experiment may have the chance of succeeding under a friendly administration. Hoping that your administration may be in every respect successful, and thoroughly appreciating the difficulties which confront you, I am   Sincerely yours,   Moorfield Storey

TLS (WP, DLC).

Henry Parker Willis to Carter Glass

Dear Mr. Glass: New York December 31, 1912.

I received your letter of December 29th, this morning and read it with a great deal of interest. I agree with you in everything you say regarding the interview but I think that the outcome was rather more important than you seem to feel at present in regard to its showing up of Mr. Wilson's ideas. I felt as if I had learned a good deal about his views as to the practical side of the problem. Certainly I trust that what I had to say did not interfere too much with your own development of argument and ideas on the various topics dealt with though I feared from your letter it might have done so. I hope too that you will have a further interview with him at which you will lay stress on the conditions in Congress. I think that that side of the matter was too little emphasized. . . .

It is undoubtedly true that the great difficulty in getting in getting [sic] any unanimous agreement will be found in connection with the establishment of a general central mechanism, such as Governor Wilson referred to as being the "capstone" of the whole proposition. Evidently the problem will be in the last analysis whether this mechanism should be simply a mechanism of "control" or "oversight" or whether it shall be an actual means of doing business, with a capital and other accessories necessary for that end. Insofar as it possesses those it will to the same degree approximate to a central bank which is what the platform took ground against. I will try to work up the redraft of the bill in such a way as to make clear what I have in mind on this point.   Sincerely yours,   H. Parker Willis

TLS (C. Glass Papers, ViU).

INDEX

NOTE ON THE INDEX

THE alphabetically arranged analytical table of contents at the front of the volume eliminates duplication, in both contents and index, of references to certain documents, such as letters. Letters are listed in the contents alphabetically by name, and chronologically within each name by page. The subject matter of all letters is, of course, indexed. The Editorial Notes and Wilson's writings are listed in the contents chronologically by page. In addition, the subject matter of both categories is indexed. The index covers all references to books and articles mentioned in text or notes. Footnotes are indexed. Page references to footnotes which place a comma between the page number and "n" cite both text and footnote, thus: "624,n3." On the other hand, absence of the comma indicates reference to the footnote only, thus: "55n2"—the page number denoting where the footnote appears.

We have ceased the practice of indicating first and fullest identification of persons and subjects in earlier volumes by index references accompanied by asterisks. Volume 13, the cumulative index-contents volume is already in print. Volume 26, which will cover Volumes 14-25, will appear in the near future.

The index supplies the fullest known form of names and, for the Wilson and Axson families, relationships as far down as cousins. Persons referred to by nicknames or shortened forms of names can be identified by reference to entries for these forms of the names.

All entries consisting of page numbers only and which refer to concepts, issues, and opinions (such as democracy, the tariff, the money trust, leadership, and labor problems), are references to Wilson speeches and writings. Page references that follow the symbol △ in such entries refer to the opinions and comments of others who are identified.

INDEX